W9-BID-483

1959 C. Wright Mills's *The Sociological Imagination* published

1960 John F. Kennedy and Richard Nixon meet in the Great Debates

Television in 90 percent of all U.S. homes

Joseph Klapper's *Effects of Mass Communication* published

1961 Key's *Public Opinion and American Democracy* published

Kennedy makes nation's first live TV presidential press conference

Schramm team's *Television in the Lives of Our Children* published

1962 Festinger's cognitive dissonance article appears
Sidney Kraus's *Great Debates* published

Air Force commissions Paul Baran to develop a national computer network 1963 JFK assassinated

Albert Bandura's aggressive modeling experiments first appear

Networks begin one-half-hour newscasts

1964 McLuhan's *Understanding Media* published

1965 Color comes to all three commercial TV networks

Comsat satellite launched

1966 Mendelsohn's *Mass Entertainment* published

Berger and Luckmann's *The Social Construction of Reality* published

1967 Merton's *On Theoretical Sociology* published

1969 Blumer coins "symbolic interaction"

ARPANET, forerunner to Internet, goes online

1971 Bandura's *Psychological Modeling* published

1972 *Surgeon General's Report on Television and Social Behavior* released

McCombs and Shaw introduce "agenda-setting"

Gerbner's Violence Profile initiated

FCC requires cable companies to provide "local access"

Ray Tomlinson develops e-mail

1973 Watergate Hearings broadcast live

1974 Blumler and Katz's *The Uses of Mass Communication* published

Noelle-Neumann introduces "spiral of silence"

Goffman pioneers frame analysis

Home use of VCR introduced

Term "Internet" coined

1975 ASNE's *Statement of Principles* replaces *Canons*

Bill Gates and Paul Allen develop operating system for personal computers

1977 Steve Jobs and Stephen Wozniak perfect Apple II

1978 Digital audio and video recording adopted as media industry standard

1981 IBM introduces the PC

Petty and Cacioppo's Elaboration Likelihood Model introduced

1983 *Journal of Communication* devotes entire issue to "Ferment in the Field"

CD introduced

1985 Meyrowitz's *No Sense of Place* published

1990 Signorielli and Morgan's *Cultivation Analysis* published

1991 Gulf War explodes, CNN emerges as important news source

1992 ACT disbands, says work is complete

1992 World Wide Web released

1993 Ten years after "Ferment," *Journal of Communication* tries again with special issue, "The Future of the Field"

1996 Telecommunications Act passes, relaxes broadcast ownership rules, deregulates cable television, mandates television content ratings

1998 *Journal of Communication* devotes entire issue to media literacy

MP3 introduced

2000 Name change of *"Critical Studies in Mass Communication"* to *"Critical Studies in Media Communication"*

2001 Terrorist attacks on New York City and Washington, D.C.

2003 FCC institutes new, relaxed media ownership rules

U.S. invasion of Iraq

Social networking websites appear

Bloggers' Code of Ethics formalized

2004 *Journalism & Mass Communication Quarterly* focuses edition on media framing

American Behavioral Scientist devotes two entire issues to media literacy

Facebook launched

2005 YouTube launched

News Corp (Rupert Murdoch) buys MySpace

2006 Google buys YouTube

Twitter launched

2007 *Journal of Communication* publishes
      special issue on framing, agenda-setting,
      and priming
2008 *Journal of Communication* publishes special
      issue on the "intersection" of different mass
      communication research methods and
      theoretical approaches
2009 Potter's *Arguing for a General Framework for
      Mass Media Scholarship* published

Internet overtakes newspapers as a source of
news for Americans

American Society of Newspaper Editors
becomes American Society of News Editors

Radio and Television News Directors
Association becomes Radio Television
Digital News Association
Social networking use exceeds e-mail

From the Wadsworth Series in Mass Communication and Journalism

General Mass Communication

Biagi, *Media/Impact: An Introduction to Mass Media*, Tenth Edition

Hilmes, *Connections: A Broadcast History Reader*

Hilmes, *Only Connect: A Cultural History of Broadcasting in the United States*, Third Edition

Lester, *Visual Communication: Images with Messages*, Fifth Edition

Overbeck, *Major Principles of Media Law*, 2011 Edition

Straubhaar/LaRose, *Media Now: Understanding Media, Culture, and Technology*, Seventh Edition

Zelezny, *Cases in Communications Law*, Sixth Edition

Zelezny, *Communications Law: Liberties, Restraints, and the Modern Media*, Sixth Edition

Journalism

Bowles/Borden, *Creative Editing*, Sixth Edition

Davis/Davis, *Think Like an Editor: 50 Strategies for the Print and Digital World*

Hilliard, *Writing for Television, Radio, and New Media*, Tenth Edition

Kessler/McDonald, *When Words Collide: A Media Writer's Guide to Grammar and Style*, Eighth Edition

Rich, *Writing and Reporting News: A Coaching Method*, Sixth Edition

Public Relations and Advertising

Diggs-Brown, *Strategic Public Relations: Audience Focused Approach*

Diggs-Brown, *The PR Styleguide: Formats for Public Relations Practice*, Second Edition

Drewniany/Jewler, *Creative Strategy in Advertising*, Tenth Edition

Hendrix, *Public Relations Cases*, Eighth Edition

Newsom/Haynes, *Public Relations Writing: Form and Style*, Ninth Edition

Newsom/Turk/Kruckeberg, *This is PR: The Realities of Public Relations*, Tenth Edition

Research and Theory

Baran and Davis, *Mass Communication Theory: Foundations, Ferment, and Future*, Sixth Edition

Sparks, *Media Effects Research: A Basic Overview*, Third Edition

Wimmer and Dominick, *Mass Media Research: An Introduction*, Ninth Edition

MASS COMMUNICATION THEORY

Foundations, Ferment, and Future

SIXTH EDITION

Stanley J. Baran, Ph.D.
Bryant University

Dennis K. Davis, Ph.D.
Pennsylvania State University

WADSWORTH
CENGAGE Learning

Australia • Brazil • Japan • Korea • Mexico • Singapore • Spain • United Kingdom • United States

Mass Communication Theory: Foundations, Ferment, and Future, Sixth Edition
Stanley J. Baran and Dennis K. Davis

Senior Publisher: Lyn Uhl

Publisher: Michael Rosenberg

Development Editor: Erin Pass

Assistant Editor: Jillian D'Urso

Media Editor: Jessica Badiner

Marketing Director: Jason Sakos

Marketing Coordinator: Gurpreet Saran

Marketing Communications Manager:
Caitlin Green

Content Project Management: PreMediaGlobal

Art Director: Marissa Falco

Print Buyer: Justin Palmeiro

Rights Acquisitions Specialist (text and image):
Amanda Groszko

Production Service: PreMediaGlobal

Cover Designer: Wing Ngan

Cover Image: John Lund/Getty Images

Compositor: PreMediaGlobal

For product information and technology assistance, contact us at
Cengage Learning Customer & Sales Support, 1-800-354-9706

For permission to use material from this text or product, submit all requests online at **www.cengage.com/permissions**.
Further permissions questions can be emailed to
permissionrequest@cengage.com.

Library of Congress Control Number: 2010933368

ISBN-13: 978-0-495-89887-0

ISBN-10: 0-495-89887-2

Wadsworth
20 Channel Center Street
Boston, MA 02210
USA

Cengage Learning is a leading provider of customized learning solutions with office locations around the globe, including Singapore, the United Kingdom, Australia, Mexico, Brazil and Japan. Locate your local office at **international.cengage.com/region**

Cengage Learning products are represented in Canada by Nelson Education, Ltd.

For your course and learning solutions, visit **www.cengage.com**.

Purchase any of our products at your local college store or at our preferred online store **www.cengagebrain.com**.

Instructors: Please visit **login.cengage.com** and log in to access instructor-specific resources.

Printed in the United States of America
2 3 4 5 6 7 14 13 12 11

CONTENTS

PREFACE

We wrote the first and second editions of this textbook at a prosperous time in the life of our nation, when U.S. media industries were undergoing rapid change. American corporations were spreading around the world. Dot-com companies were thriving in a "New Economy" many thought likely to expand for decades. New media technology was evolving so rapidly and new media applications were proliferating so fast that a new scale of "Internet time" was created to measure change. "Brick and mortar" companies were disdained in favor of virtual enterprises.

Change was also going on in media theory and research. Theory was in ferment as new perspectives challenged long-standing assumptions. Researchers struggled with questions flowing from the changes in media. They debated how best to understand the role of new media and chart their place among the well-established mass media. Considerable research focused on mass media entertainment and its effects. Researchers asked whether new media-based entertainment would displace established mass media. Would the Internet replace television or would the tube absorb the Internet? Would people pay the extra price to get HDTV? Did the protection of children from online smut require new laws? What would happen to face-to-face communication in the wake of the e-mail onslaught? Virtual democracy? MP3? Smartphones and augmented reality?

On September 11, 2001, everything changed. As we wrote the third edition to this textbook, the Western world was reeling from the terrorist attacks on the World Trade Center in New York and on the Pentagon in Washington, DC. A new type of war was declared, a war not against an identifiable nation, but against a tactic, terrorism. Americans were told to make important sacrifices and to be vigilant, but at the same time to carry on our daily lives as though September 11 had never happened. When we prepared the fourth edition, our country had just embarked on what was—and would become even more so—a controversial war.

Many if not all of the reasons that sent us to combat, unexamined and unchallenged by much of the media we count on to help us govern ourselves, proved to be false. Where was the Fourth Estate "when it might have made a difference?" (Massing, 2004, p. 1). Growing awareness of the media industries' powers and responsibilities led to significant criticism of their performance in the run-up to war and its coverage, and more surprising, an unprecedented public outcry against media concentration. The American people, writes media critic Todd Gitlin, "rub their eyes and marvel that a nation possessed of such an enormous industry ostensibly specializing in the gathering and distribution of facts could yet remain so befogged" (2004a, p. 58). But befogged we remained, as the media, our political leaders, and those in the financial industries failed to heed—or even notice—the coming economic crash that would damage so badly our lives, homes, savings, and jobs.

As authors, we now face a serious challenge as we produce this, the sixth edition. When it comes to media theories, what is still relevant and what is unimportant? How can and should we understand the role media now play in the world that has been so radically altered? What has happened to trust in media? In our system of self-governance and our ability to know ourselves, our neighbors, and our world? In previous editions we argued, "The price to be paid for our failure to understand the role of media is dear." We pointed to controversies over the effects of media violence and the banning of rap music lyrics. We worried about growing dissatisfaction with modern election campaigns and the role in our democracy of a press increasingly focused on the "bottom line." These questions remain important and will doubtlessly arise again on the media research agenda. But for a time these questions have been overshadowed by more pressing issues: an obvious one, the war in the Middle East. Where were democratic debate and public discourse in the run-up to this costly conflict? Where were the media when it counted, or in the words of Michael Massing in the *New York Review of Books*, "Now they tell us." But consider that five years after the start of what was supposed to be a "cake walk" and three years after President Bush himself told the public that there was no link between Iraq and September 11, "as many as four in 10 Americans [41 percent] continued to believe that Saddam Hussein's regime was directly involved in financing, planning, or carrying out the terrorist attacks on that horrible day" (Braiker, 2007). "Where were and are the media?" is an important question for those interested in mass communication theory, but so is "Where were and are the people?"

This textbook takes a historical approach to presenting media theory. In previous editions, we argued that the value of this framework resides in its ability to reveal how social theory generally—and media theory specifically—develops as an ongoing effort to address pressing technological, social, and political problems. Often the most important eras for media theory development have been those of crisis and social turmoil. These are the times when the most important questions about media are asked and the search for their answers is most desperate. For half a century after the 1940s, we relied on media theories forged in the cauldron of economic depression and worldwide warfare. But by the 1990s, the concerns of earlier eras had faded. In our first two editions, we asked whether an era of dramatic technological change might give rise to new media theories for a world whose problems were different from those of the 1940s. Did we need new media theories to fit a stable and orderly world with rising economic prosperity and startling but beneficent technological change?

After 9/11 we were confronted by the challenges of a world in which many old questions about the role of media suddenly had new urgency. As you read this edition, you will find that we devote considerable attention to propaganda. In the 1930s and 1940s, the most important questions concerning media centered on propaganda. Could media propaganda induce widespread conversions from one political ideology to another? Was systematic censorship of media essential to the preservation of democracy as we faced the totalitarian threats of fascism and communism? Was propaganda inherently bad, or should it have been used to promote democracy at a time when its deficiencies were so evident and the fruits of totalitarianism so alluring to masses of people around the world? After September 11, and then again after tens of thousands of deaths in Iraq and our failure to find the weapons that were the stated reason for the conflict that killed them (Carter, 2004), similar questions were again being asked and answered in the highest circles of the American government, in the offices of media organizations, in colleges and universities, and in people's homes. They were asked again in the wake of the country's "surprise" economic crash, and again as the interminable, often ugly health care reform debate dragged on for the first two years of the Obama presidency, a presidency resulting from what some called the "first YouTube election," raising even another series of questions. An understanding of media theory will provide crucial insights as we work to come to grips with a new kind of public discourse, a new kind of America, a new kind of world.

A UNIQUE APPROACH

One unique feature of this book is the balanced, comprehensive introduction to the two major bodies of theory currently dominating the field: the social/behavioral theories and the cultural/critical theories. We need to know the strengths and the limitations of these two bodies of theory. We need to know how they developed in the past, how they are developing in the present, and what new conceptions they might produce, because not only do these schools of thought represent the mass communication theory of today, but they also promise to dominate our understanding of mass communication for some time to come.

Many American texts emphasize social/behavioral theories and either ignore or denigrate cultural/critical theories. As critical/cultural theories have gained in popularity in the United States, there have been more textbooks written that explain these theories, but they often ignore or disdain social/behavioral theories. Instructors and students who want to cover all types of media theories are forced to use two or more textbooks and then need to sort out the various criticisms these books offer of competing ideas. To solve this problem (and we hope advance understanding of all mass communication theory), we systematically explain the legitimate differences existing between researchers who use the different theories. We also consider possibilities for accommodation or collaboration. This edition considers these possibilities in greater depth and detail. It is becoming increasingly clear how these bodies of theory can complement each other and provide a much broader and more useful basis for thinking about and conducting research on media.

THE USE OF HISTORY

In this book, we assume that it is important for those who study mass communication theory to have a strong grounding in the historical development of media theory. Therefore, in the pages that follow, we trace the history of theory in a clear, straightforward manner. We include discussions of historical events and people we hope students will find inherently interesting, especially if instructors use widely available DVDs, video downloads, and other materials to illustrate them (such as political propaganda, the *War of the Worlds* broadcast, newsreels from the World War II era and the early days of television, and so on). More and more historical audiovisual material is readily available via the Internet, so instructors can ask students to assist them in illustrating key leaders and events.

Readers familiar with previous editions of this textbook will find that we've made some significant changes in the way that we present the unfolding of media theory. For example, one theme of this book ever since its first edition is that theory is inevitably a product of its time. You will see that this edition is replete with examples of media's performance during our ongoing "war on terror" and their own ongoing institutional upheaval, but you will also see that many individual conceptions of mass communication theory themselves have been reinvigorated, challenged, reconsidered, or otherwise altered.

NEW TO THIS EDITION

As has been the case in each of the past editions, we have updated all statistics and examples. But as in the past, we have made a number of more significant changes. To be specific:

Chapter 5: In the discussion of normative theory, we look at the pressures of falling audiences and revenues on the media industries, especially as they attempt to perform their public service function. We debate the merits of public subsidy of journalism in a section that asks if we should worry about saving newspapers or saving journalism.

Chapter 6: This chapter reflects new insights into early mass communication research provided by media research historians. Our look at the rise of the limited effects perspective is augmented by an examination of more current thinking that suggests a return to viewing media as having limited effects.

Chapter 7: We have enriched our discussion of social cognitive theory with the addition of two relatively recent ideas, Albert Bandura's social prompting and Leonard Berkowitz's cognitive-neoassociationistic perspective. This chapter's discussion of effects on children also takes into account the latest media consumption data released by the Kaiser Family Foundation in their periodic Generation M studies.

Chapter 9: We have made a major addition with an examination of the elaboration likelihood model (ELM). Mass communication researchers of late have made meaningful use of ELM—long considered an interpersonal communication theory—especially as it pertains to information processing in the Internet age. Specifically, because ELM assumes different levels and types of processing (and therefore effects) when individuals use different routes to process information (central or peripheral), pull media (new media) may produce greater or more lasting effects than push media (traditional media) because their use is personally motivated.

Chapter 10: We have added a discussion of the use of meta-analyses in developing mass communication theory as well as expansion of two existing sections. The first, social marketing theory, is experiencing renewed interest in its application to health communication issues. The second, knowledge gap theory, has reemerged in the age of the Internet because of its implications for the digital divide. We discuss this in terms of the Obama Administration's proposal to bring high speed Internet to the entire country and the FCC's parallel plan for a "digital literacy corps" to ensure that all Americans can access the technology.

Chapter 11: We reluctantly deleted our discussion of social semiotic theory, as the promise it once held for the integration of mass and interpersonal communication theory has gone unfulfilled. We replaced it with an examination of the development of personal identity in the Facebook era and recent thinking on cultivation theory as new media possibly challenge television's cultural dominance.

Chapter 12: We elaborated our discussion of the trends in theory development and the three primary challenges facing media researchers: new media, globalization, and research on the human organism. As new media rise in importance, media theory is evolving to replace mass communication theory.

THE USE OF TOPICS FOR CRITICAL THINKING

It is important, too, that students realize that researchers develop theories to address important questions about the role of media—enduring questions that will again become important as new media continue to be introduced and as we deal with a world reordered by September 11, the ongoing war on terrorism, and systemic economic distress. We must be aware of how the radical changes in media that took place in the past are related to the changes taking place now.

We attempt this engagement with mass communication theory in several ways. Each chapter includes a section entitled *Critical Thinking Questions*. Its aim, as the title suggests, is to encourage students to think critically, even skeptically, about how that chapter's theories have been applied in the past or how they are being applied today. Each chapter also includes at least two *Thinking about Theory* boxes. These pedagogical devices are also designed to encourage critical thinking. Some discuss how a theorist addressed an issue and tried to resolve it. Still others highlight and criticize important, issue-related examples of the application of media theory. Students are asked to relate material in these boxes to contemporary controversies, events, and theories. A few examples are Chapter 3's *Murrow versus McCarthy*, Chapter 4's *Engineering of Consent: WMD and the War in Iraq*, Chapter 8's *Media Coverage of Work and Workers*, and Chapter 9's *Semiotic Disobedience*. We hope that they will find these useful in developing their own thinking about these issues. We believe that mass communication theory, if it is to have any meaning for students, must be used by them.

We have also sprinkled the chapters with *Instant Access* boxes, presenting the advantages and disadvantages of the major theories we discuss. The advantages are those offered by the theories' proponents; the disadvantages represent the views of their critics. These presentations are at best sketchy or partial, and although they should give a pretty good idea of the theories, the picture needs to be completed with a full reading of the chapters and a great deal of reflection on the theories they present. All chapters also provide marginal definitions of important terms, and chapter summaries; and finally, at the end of the text there is an extensive bibliography and a thorough index.

THE BIG PICTURE

This textbook provides a comprehensive, historically based, authoritative introduction to mass communication theory. We have provided clearly written examples, graphics, and other materials to illustrate key theories. We trace the emergence of two main schools of mass communication theory—social/behavioral and critical/cultural. Then we discuss how theories developed by each of these schools contribute to our understanding of the use of media by audiences, the role of media in society, and finally the links between media and culture. The book ends with a brief chapter that summarizes challenges facing the field and anticipates how media theory may develop to meet these challenges.

We offer many examples of social/behavioral and critical/cultural theory and an in-depth discussion of their strengths and limitations. We emphasize that media theories are human creations typically intended to address specific problems or issues. We believe that it is easier to learn theories when they are examined with contextual information about the motives of theorists and the problems and issues they addressed.

In the next few years, as mass media industries continue to experience rapid change and as we continue to come to terms with the post–September 11/war on terrorism "new world order" and Internet-dominated, "YouTube" democratic discourse, understanding media theory will become even more necessary and universal. We've argued in this edition that many of the old questions about the role of media in culture, in society, and in people's lives have resurfaced with renewed relevance. This book traces how researchers and theorists have addressed these questions in the past, and we provide insights into how they might do so in the future.

THE SUPPORTING PHILOSOPHY OF THIS BOOK

The philosophy of this book is relatively straightforward: Though today's media technologies might be new, their impact on daily life might not be so different from that of past influences. Changes in media have always posed challenges but have also created opportunities. We can use media to improve the quality of our lives, or we can permit our lives to be seriously disrupted. As a society, we can use media wisely or foolishly. To make these choices, we need theories—theories explaining the role of media for us as individuals and guiding the development of media industries for our society at large. This book should help us develop our understanding of theory so we can make better use of media and play a bigger role in the development of new media industries.

ACKNOWLEDGMENTS

In preparing this sixth edition, we have had the assistance of many people. Most important, we have drawn on the scholarly work of several generations of social and cultural theorists. Their ideas have inspired and guided contemporary work. It's an exciting time to be a communication scholar!

We work within a research community that, although it may be in ferment, is also both vibrant and supportive. In these pages, we acknowledge and explain the contributions that our many colleagues across the United States and around the world have made to mass communication theory. We regret the inevitable errors and omissions, and we take responsibility for them. We are also grateful to our reviewers:

Benjamin Bates, University of Tennessee, Knoxville
Glen Cummins, Texas Tech University
Rachel Kovacs, College of Staten Island (CUNY)
Carol Lomicky, University of Nebraska, Kearney

These reviewers helped us avoid some errors and omissions, but they bear no responsibility for those that remain. We also wish to thank our Wadsworth/Cengage friends, whose encouragement and advice sustained us. Their task was made less difficult than it might otherwise have been by our first Wadsworth editor, Becky Hayden, and Chris Clerkin, the editor for the first edition of this text. These accomplished professionals taught us how to avoid many of the sins usually committed by novice authors. The editor who has worked with us the longest, Holly Allen, is as sharp as her predecessors, and she became quite adept at using her gentle hand with what had become two veteran textbook authors. Our new editorial team, Michael Rosenberg, Megan Garvey, and Erin Pass, continued the competence and professionalism to which we have become accustomed. We are proud of this, our sixth edition and their first.

We must also thank our families. The Davis children—Jennifer, Kerry, Andy, Mike—are now scattered across the Midwest in Norman, Lincoln, Nashville, and Chicago, so they have been less involved with (or impacted by) the day-to-day development of this edition. Nonetheless, they often assisted with insights drawn from the academic fields in which they themselves have become expert: history, philosophy, Asian studies, marketing, and computer science. In Wakefield, the Baran kids—Jordan and Matt Dowd—remained close to the book-writing process, so they suffered more of the authors' detachment and absences as this edition unfolded. They did so with charm and love.

It would be impossible to overstate the value of our wives' support. Nancy Davis continues to provide a sympathetic audience for efforts to think through media theory and brainstorm ways to apply it. Susan Baran, an expert in media literacy in her own right, has a remarkable ability to find the practical in the most theoretical. This is why more than a few of the ideas and examples in these pages found their refinement in her sharp mind. She keeps her husband grounded as a thinker and author while she lifts him as a man and father.

Finally, this book is the product of a collaboration that has gone on for nearly forty years. We started our professional careers at Cleveland State University in 1973 in a communication department headed by Sidney Kraus. Sid inspired us, along with most other junior faculty, to become active, productive researchers. Today, a disproportionate number of active communication scholars have direct or indirect links to the Cleveland State program. Sid demonstrates the many ways that a single person can have a powerful impact on a discipline. Through his scholarship, his mentorship, and his friendship he has left a truly indelible mark.

S.J.B. & D.K.D

INTRODUCTION TO MASS COMMUNICATION THEORY

UNDERSTANDING AND EVALUATING MASS COMMUNICATION THEORY

The matter before the court in the June 2009 hearing was the legality of the Barack Obama administration's efforts to keep secret notes from an FBI interview with former Vice President Dick Cheney surrounding his involvement, several years earlier, in the outing of an undercover CIA operative. The stakes were high—accountability in our government's highest elected officials—and U.S. District Judge Emmet Sullivan was confused. Why would a Democratic president, elected in part on his promise of greater transparency in government, defend secrets from the previous Republican administration that he had so vigorously campaigned against as improper? Justice Department attorney Jeffrey Smith offered the court an explanation: "I don't want a future vice president to say, 'I'm not going to cooperate with you because I don't want to be fodder for *The Daily Show*.'" In other words, elected officials might not cooperate with criminal investigations for fear of ridicule from late-night comics. Judge Sullivan was unmoved, demanding "more precise reasons for keeping the information confidential" (Pickler, 2009).

Fear of late-night comics? Could the likes of *The Daily Show* and *The Colbert Report*, two satirical news programs on cable channel Comedy Central, be so influential as to become a point of argument in an important federal court case? Maybe. Network news anchor Brian Williams confesses that *The Daily Show* has become "indispensible" in shaping how "real" news operations conduct their business. "On occasion," he wrote, "when we've been on the cusp of doing something completely inane on *NBC Nightly News*, I will gently suggest to my colleagues that we simply courier the tape over to Jon [Stewart's] office, to spare *The Daily Show* interns the time and trouble of logging our broadcasts that night. That usually gets us to rethink the inane segment we were planning on airing" (2009). The public pays attention to these satirical news programs as well. A March 2009 Rasmussen poll reported that "nearly one-third of Americans under 40 say they get more of their news from Jon Stewart, Stephen Colbert and other late night comedy shows than they do from traditional sources of news" (Winship, 2009). A similar study, an April 2007 examination of Americans' knowledge of national public affairs conducted by the Pew Research Center for the People and the Press, discovered that the "best-informed media consumers" were frequent newspaper readers and regular viewers of these very same programs.

Are you surprised that a federal attorney in an important court case would attribute so much significance to something as trivial as television comedy? Are you surprised at the apparent informational value of what are supposed to be fake news programs? Why would viewers of faux TV news shows know more about current affairs than those of "legitimate" television news programs? Media critic Eric Alterman wrote, "It's a sad—almost terrifying—comment on the state of the American media that we have come to rely on these two funnymen to tell us the truth about our country in the same way we relied on [Edward R.] Murrow in the '50s and Walter Cronkite in the '60s" (2009b, p. 10). Do you agree, or does journalist Thomas Mucha's view better resonate with you? He wrote of fake news, "Intelligence and humor, when mixed with a little ground truth, can add depth to very serious matters" (2009). And whether you fear or welcome this new role of comedy news, the question of why it has come to a position of influence remains. Television writer Lizz Winstead explained what motivated her to create *The Daily Show*: "The media were the watchdog for … the government and corporate America, and when the media were in bed, or were lazy or in bed with their advertisers, comics naturally started to fill the role of the watchdog of the watchdog…. We just started asking the questions that journalists weren't asking anymore … asking questions that our audience wanted to hear" (2009). But was her audience really asking questions that were going unanswered, or did it tune in simply to be entertained and inadvertently became better informed? After all, aren't young people notoriously politically uninvolved?

Your answers to these questions are naturally based on *your* ideas or assumptions about the relationships between people, their media use, their knowledge of the news, and their interest in public affairs. You no doubt take into consideration factors such as what was going on in the world at the time of the two surveys and differences in expectations of the media in light of people's ages, consumption habits, and other individual differences. You might also have wondered if the relationship between news source and knowledge can be looked at in the reverse—that is, watching comedy news shows might not make people better informed; instead, better-informed individuals just might prefer to watch satirical news programs specifically because satirical content is more fun to watch if people already know more.

The Rasmussen and Pew researchers had their ideas or assumptions, as did critic Alterman, journalist Mucha, attorney Smith, and *Daily Show* creator Winstead; so do you. These ideas and assumptions can—and often do—become the bases for something more formal, more systematic: theories. That formality, that systematic understanding, comes from the social sciences. When these social scientific theories involve relationships between media and the people and societies that use them, they are theories of mass communication.

OVERVIEW

In this chapter, we will discuss just what separates an idea or an assumption from a theory. We will examine the field of social science and the theories it spawns—specifically mass communication theories. We'll look at some of the difficulties faced by those who attempt to systematically study human behavior and the particular problems encountered when the issue is human behavior *and* the mass media. We'll see, too, that when the issue is mass communication, the definition of *social science* can be quite elusive. We'll define *theory* and offer several classifications of communication theory and mass communication theory. Most important, we will try to convince you that the difficulties that seem to surround the development and study of mass communication theory aren't really difficulties at all: rather they are challenges that make the study of mass communication theory interesting and exciting. As John D. Barrow wrote, "A world that [is] simple enough to be fully known would be too simple to contain conscious observers who might know it" (1998, p. 3).

DEFINING AND REDEFINING MASS COMMUNICATION

In recent decades, the number and variety of mass communication theories have steadily increased. Media theory has emerged as a more or less independent body of thought in both the social science and humanistic literatures. This book is intended as a guide to this diverse and sometimes contradictory thinking. You will find ideas developed by scholars in every area of the social sciences, from history and anthropology to sociology and psychology. Ideas have also been drawn from the humanities, especially from philosophy and literary analysis. The resulting ferment of ideas is both challenging and heuristic. These theories provide the raw materials for constructing even more useful and powerful theoretical perspectives.

grand theory
Theory designed to describe and explain all aspects of a given phenomenon

If you are looking for a concise, definitive definition of theory, you won't find it in this book. We have avoided narrow definitions of theory in favor of an inclusive approach that finds value in most systematic, scholarly efforts to make sense of media and their role in society. We have included recent theories that some contemporary researchers consider unscientific. Some of the theories reviewed are **grand**; they try to explain entire media systems and their role in society. Others are very small and provide narrower insight into specific uses or effects of media. Our selection of theories for inclusion in this book is based partly on their enduring historical importance and partly on their potential to contribute to future scholarship. This process is necessarily subjective and is based on our own understanding of mass communication. Our consideration of contemporary perspectives is focused on those that illustrate enduring or innovative conceptualizations. But before we embark on that consideration, we need to offer definitions of some important concepts.

mass communication
When a source, typically an organization, employs a technology as a medium to communicate with a large audience

When an organization employs a technology as a medium to communicate with a large audience, **mass communication** is said to have occurred. The professionals at the *New York Times* (an organization) use printing presses and the newspaper (technology and medium) to reach their readers (a large audience). The writers, producers, filmmakers, and other professionals at the Cartoon Network use various audio and video technologies, satellites, cable television, and home receivers to communicate with their audience. Warner Brothers places ads in magazines to tell readers what movies it is releasing.

But as you no doubt know—and as you'll be reminded constantly throughout this text—the mass communication environment is changing quite radically. When you receive a piece of direct-mail advertising addressed to you by name, and in which your name is used throughout, you are an audience of one—not the large audience envisioned in traditional notions of mass communication. When you sit at your computer and send an e-mail to twenty thousand people who have signed on to a **Listserv** dedicated to a particular subject, you are obviously communicating with a large audience, but you are not an organization in the sense of a newspaper, cable television network, or movie studio. The availability of lightweight, portable, inexpensive video equipment, combined with the development of easy-to-use Internet video sites like YouTube, makes it possible for an "everyday" person like you to be a television writer and producer, reaching audiences numbering in the tens of millions.

Although most theories we will study in this text were developed before our modern communications revolution, they are not useless or outmoded. But we must remember that much has changed in how people use technologies to communicate. One useful way to do this is to think of **mediated communication** as existing on a continuum that stretches from **interpersonal communication** at one end to traditional forms of mass communication at the other. Where different media fall along this continuum depends on the amount of control and involvement people have in the communication process. The telephone, for example (the phone as traditionally understood—not the one you might own that has Internet access, GPS, and some 500 other "killer apps"), sits at one end. It is obviously a communication technology, but one that is most typical of interpersonal communication: At most, a very few people can be involved in communicating at any given time, and they have a great deal of involvement with and control over that communication. The conversation is theirs, and they determine its content. A big-budget Hollywood movie or a network telecast of the Super Bowl sits at the opposite pole. Viewers have limited control over the communication that occurs. Certainly, people can apply idiosyncratic interpretations to the content before them, and they can choose to direct however much attention they wish to the screen. They can choose to actively seek meaning from media content, or they can choose to passively decode it. But their control and involvement cannot directly alter the content of the messages being transmitted. Message content is centrally controlled by media organizations.

As you'll see when we examine the more contemporary mass communication theories, new communication technologies are rapidly filling in the middle of the continuum between the telephone and television. Suddenly, media consumers have the power to alter message content if they are willing to invest the time and have the necessary skill and resources. Audiences can be *active* in ways that are hard to anticipate, and the consequences of this activity may not be understood for decades to come. The instant popularity of downloading music from the Internet demonstrates that a generation of young adults is willing to invest the time, acquire the skills, and purchase the technology necessary to take greater control over the music they consume. We have seen this process play out even more recently, and possibly

Listserv
Software employed to manage online mailing lists, bulletin boards, or discussion groups that cover a variety of subjects

mediated communication
Communication between a few or many people that employs a technology as a medium

interpersonal communication
Communication between two or a few people, typically face-to-face

even more dramatically, with the overnight success of video and social networking websites like YouTube and Facebook, and we'll surely see it repeated again and again as we actively engage the technologies that allow us to create and control media content that is important to us. As this happens, there will be profound consequences for our personal lives, the media industries, and the larger social world. As communication theorists Steven Chaffee and Miriam Metzger explain, "Contemporary media allow for a greater quantity of information transmission and retrieval, place more control over both content creation and selection in the hands of their users, and do so with less cost to the average consumer" (2001, p. 369). Technology writer Dan Gilmor (2004) explained the situation more succinctly when he wrote that the world is now populated by "people formerly known as the audience."

SCIENCE AND HUMAN BEHAVIOR

Ours is a society that generally respects and believes its scientists. Science is one of the fundamental reasons why we enjoy our admirable standard of living and have a growing understanding of the world around us. But not all scientists are revered equally. British astronomer and philosopher John D. Barrow opened his 1998 book, *Impossibility: The Limits of Science and the Science of Limits,* with this observation on the value of science and its practitioners:

> Bookshelves are stuffed with volumes that expound the successes of the mind and the silicon chip. We expect science to tell us what can be done and what is to be done. Governments look to scientists to improve the quality of life and safeguard us from earlier "improvements." Futurologists see no limit to human inquiry, while social scientists see no end to the raft of problems it spawns. (p. 1)

The physical *scientists* and engineers are the dreamers, the fixers, the guardians. They have sent us photos of stars aborning, detailed the inner workings of the atom, and invented the microwave oven, the World Wide Web, and cell phones that take and send video. *Social scientists* are the naysayers, the Grinches of the world. They tell us that television corrupts our morals, political campaigns render us too cynical to participate meaningfully in our democracy, and parents rely too heavily on television to babysit their kids. Or, as columnist David Brooks reminds us, "A survey of the social science of the past century shows it to be, by and large, an insanely pessimistic field" (2002, p. 22). We tend to readily accept most of the good findings of Barrow's *scientists.* The universe is continually expanding? Of course. The existence of quarks? Naturally. At the same time, we tend to be more suspicious of the findings of the *social scientists.* Playing with Barbies destroys little girls' self-esteem? I don't think so! Videogames teach violence? That's so Twentieth Century! Texting kills spelling and grammar? OMG! U r wrng. LOL!

social scientists
Scientists who examine relationships among phenomena in the human or social world

Why does our society seem to have greater difficulty accepting the theories and findings of **social scientists**, those who apply logic and observation—that is, science—to the understanding of the social world, rather than the physical world? Why do we have more trust in the people who wield telescopes and microscopes to probe the breadth of the universe and the depth of human cells but skepticism about the tools used by social observers to probe the breadth of culture or the depth of human experience?

causality
When a given factor influences another, even by way of an intervening variable

causal relationship
When the alterations in a particular variable under specific conditions always produce the same effect in another variable

scientific method
A search for truth through accurate observation and interpretation of fact

hypothesis
A testable prediction about some event

At the center of our society's occasional reluctance to accept the theories of the social scientists is the *logic of* **causality**. We readily understand this logic. You've no doubt had it explained to you during a high school physics or chemistry class, so we'll use a simple example from those classes: boiling water. If we (or our representatives, the scientists) can manipulate an independent variable (heat) and produce the same effect (boiling at 100 degrees centigrade) under the same conditions (sea level) every time, then a **causal relationship** has been established. Heating water at sea level to 100 degrees will cause water to boil. No matter how many times you heat beakers of water at sea level, they will all boil at 100 degrees. Lower the heat; the water does not boil. Heat it at the top of Mount Everest; it boils at lower temperatures. Go back to sea level (or alter the atmospheric pressure in a laboratory test); it boils at 100 degrees. This is repeated observation under controlled conditions. We even have a name for this, the **scientific method**, and there are many definitions for it. Here is a small sample:

1. "A means whereby insight into an undiscovered truth is sought by (1) identifying the problem that defines the goal of the quest, (2) gathering data with the hope of resolving the problem, (3) positing a **hypothesis** both as a logical means of locating the data and as an aid to resolving the problem, and (4) empirically testing the hypothesis by processing and interpreting the data to see whether the interpretation of them will resolve the question that initiated the research" (Leedy, 1997, pp. 94–95).
2. "A set of interrelated constructs (concepts), definitions, and propositions that present a systematic view of phenomena by specifying relations among variables, with the purpose of explaining and predicting phenomena" (Kerlinger, 1986, p. 9).
3. "A method … by which our beliefs may be determined by nothing human, but by some external permanency—by something upon which our thinking has no effect…. The method must be such that the ultimate conclusion of every man [*sic*] shall be the same. Such is the method of science. Its fundamental hypothesis … is this: There are real things whose characters are entirely independent of our opinions about them" (Peirce, 1955, p. 18).

Throughout the last century and into this one, some social researchers have tried to apply the scientific method to the study of human behavior and society. As you'll soon see, an Austrian immigrant to the United States, Paul Lazarsfeld, was an important advocate of applying social research methods to the study of mass media. But although the essential logic of the scientific method is quite simple, its application in the social (rather than physical) world can be more complicated.

Take, for example, the much-discussed issue of press coverage of political campaigns and its impact on voter turnout. We know that more media attention is paid to elections than ever before. Today, television permits continual eyewitness coverage of candidate activity. Mobile vans trail candidates and beam stories off satellites so that local television stations can air their own coverage. The Internet and Web offer instant access to candidates, their ideas, and those of their opponents. Twitter lets us track their every move in real time. Yet, despite advances in media technology and innovations in campaign coverage, voter participation in the United States remains low. Not since 1968 has turnout in a presidential election exceeded

60 percent. Even in the 2008 race between Barack Obama and John McCain, considered "the most technologically innovative, entrepreneurially driven campaign in American political history," only 56.8 percent of registered voters cast ballots (Dickinson, 2009; U.S. Election Project, 2009). Should we assume that media campaign coverage suppresses potential voter turnout? This is an assertion that some mass communication observers might be quick to make. But would they be right? How could or should we verify whether this assertion is valid?

As we shall see, the pioneers of mass communication research faced this situation during the 1930s. There were precious few scientific studies of, but many bold assertions about, the bad effects of mass media. A small number of social scientists began to argue that these claims should not be accepted before making **empirical** observations that could either support them or permit them to be rejected. While these early researchers often shared the widely held view that media were powerful, they believed that the scientific method might be used to harness this power to avoid negative effects like juvenile delinquency and produce positive effects such as promoting Americans' trust in their own democratic political system while subverting the appeal of totalitarian propaganda. In this way, scientific research would allow media to be a force for good in shaping the social world.

empirical
Capable of being verified or disproved by observation

These researchers faced many problems, however, in applying the scientific method to the study of mass communication. How can there be repeated observations? No two audiences, never mind any two individuals, who see political coverage are the same. No two elections are the same. Even if a scientist conducted the same experiment on the same people repeatedly (showing them, for example, the same excerpts of coverage and then asking them if and how they might vote), these people would now be different each additional time because they would have had a new set of experiences (participation in the study).

How can there be control over conditions that might influence observed effects? Who can control what people watch, read, or listen to, or to whom they talk, not to mention what they have learned about voting and civic responsibility in their school, family, and church? One solution is to put them in a laboratory and limit what they watch and learn. But people don't grow up in laboratories or watch television with the types of strangers they meet in a laboratory experiment. They don't consume media messages hooked to galvanic skin response devices or scanned by machines that track their eye movements. And unlike atoms under study, people can and sometimes do change their behaviors as a result of the social scientists' findings, which further confounds claims of causality. And there is another problem. Powerful media effects rarely happen as a result of exposure to a few messages in a short amount of time. Effects take place slowly, over long periods of time. At any moment, nothing may seem to be happening.

This implementation of the scientific method is difficult for those studying the social world for four reasons:

1. **Most of the significant and interesting forms of human behavior are quite difficult to measure.** We can easily measure the temperature at which water boils. With ingenious and complex technology, we can even measure the weight of an atom or the speed at which the universe is expanding. But how do we measure something like civic duty? Should we count the incidence of voting? Maybe a person's decision not to vote is her personal expression of that duty. Try something a

little easier, like measuring aggression in a television violence study. Can aggression be measured by counting how many times a child hits a rubber doll? Is gossiping about a neighbor an aggressive act? How do we measure an attitude (a predisposition to do something rather than an observable action)? What is three pounds of tendency to hold conservative political views or sixteen point seven millimeters of patriotism?

2. **Human behavior is exceedingly complex.** Human behavior does not easily lend itself to causal description. It is easy to identify a single factor that causes water to boil. But it has proved impossible to isolate single factors that serve as the exclusive cause of important actions of human behavior. Human behavior may simply be too complex to allow scientists to ever fully untangle the different factors that combine to cause observable actions. We can easily control the heat and atmospheric pressure in our boiling experiment. We can control the elements in a chemistry experiment with relative ease. But if we want to develop a theory of the influence of mediated communication on political campaigns, how do we control which forms of media people choose to use? How do we control the amount of attention they pay to specific types of news? How do we measure how well or poorly they comprehend what they consume? How do we take into account factors that influenced people long before we started our research? For example, how do we measure the type and amount of political socialization produced by parents, schools, or peers? All these things (not to mention countless others) will influence the relationship between people's use of media and their behavior in an election. How can we be sure what *caused* what? Voting might have declined even more precipitously without media coverage. Remember, the very same factors that lead one person to vote might lead another to stay home.

3. **Humans have goals and are self-reflexive.** We do not always behave in response to something that has happened; very often we act in response to something we hope or expect will happen. Moreover, we constantly revise our goals and make highly subjective determinations about their potential for success or failure. Water boils *after* the application of heat. It doesn't think about boiling. It doesn't begin to experience boiling and then decide that it doesn't like the experience. We think about our actions and inactions; we reflect on our values, beliefs, and attitudes. Water doesn't develop attitudes against boiling that lead it to misperceive the amount of heat it is experiencing. It stops boiling when the heat is removed. It doesn't think about stopping or have trouble making up its mind. It doesn't have friends who tell it that boiling is fun and should be continued even when there is insufficient heat. But people do think about their actions, and they frequently make these actions contingent on their expectations that something will happen. "Humans are not like billiard balls propelled solely by forces external to them," explained cognitive psychologist Albert Bandura. "Billiard balls cannot change the shape of the table, the size of the pockets, or intervene in the paths they take, or even decide whether to play the game at all. In contrast, humans not only think, but, individually and collectively, shape the form those external forces take and even determine whether or not they come into play. Murray Gell-Mann, the physicist Nobelist, underscored the influential role of the personal determinants when he remarked, 'Imagine how hard physics would be if particles could think'" (2008, pp. 95–96).

4. **The simple notion of causality is sometimes troubling when it is applied to ourselves.** We have no trouble accepting that heat causes water to boil at 100 degrees centigrade at sea level; we relish such causal statements in the physical world. We want to know how things work, what makes things happen. As much as we might like to be thrilled by horror movies or science fiction films in which physical laws are continually violated, we trust the operation of these laws in our daily lives. But we often resent causal statements when they are applied to ourselves. We can't see the expanding universe or the breakup of the water molecule at the boiling point, so we are willing to accept the next best thing, the word of an objective expert, that is, a scientist. But we can see ourselves watching cable news and not voting and going to a movie and choosing a brand-name pair of slacks and learning about people from lands we've never visited. Why do we need experts telling us about ourselves or explaining to us why we do things? We're not so easily influenced by media, we say. But ironically, most of us are convinced that other people are much more likely to be influenced by media (the **third-person effect**). So although we don't need to be protected from media influence, *others* might; they're not as smart as we are (Grier and Brumbaugh, 2007). We are our own men and women—independent, freethinking individuals. We weren't affected by those McDonald's ads; we simply bought that Big Mac, fries, and a large Coke because, darn it, we deserved a break today. And after all, we did need to eat something and the McDonald's did happen to be right on the way back to the dorm.

third-person effect
The idea that "media affect others, but not me"

DEFINING THEORY

theory
Any organized set of concepts, explanations, and principles of some aspect of human experience

Scientists, physical or social (however narrowly or broadly defined), deal in **theory**. "Theories are stories about how and why events occur.... Scientific theories begin with the assumption that the universe, including the social universe created by acting human beings, reveals certain basic and fundamental properties and processes that explain the ebb and flow of events in specific processes" (Turner, 1998, p. 1). Theory has numerous other definitions. John Bowers and John Courtright offered a traditional scientific definition: "Theories ... are sets of statements asserting relationships among classes of variables" (1984, p. 13). So did Charles Berger: "A theory consists of a set of interrelated propositions that stipulate relationships among theoretical constructs and an account of the mechanism or mechanisms that explain the relationships stipulated in the propositions" (2005, p. 417). Kenneth Bailey's conception of theory accepts a wider array of ways to understand the social world: "Explanations and predictions of social phenomena ... relating the subject of interest... to some other phenomena" (1982, p. 39).

Our definition, though, will be drawn from a synthesis of two even more generous views of theory. Assuming that there are a number of different ways to understand how communication functions in our complex world, Stephen Littlejohn and Karen Foss defined theory as "any organized set of concepts, explanations, and principles of some aspect of human experience" (2008, p. 14). Emory Griffin also takes this broader view, writing that a theory is an idea "that explains an event or behavior. It brings clarity to an otherwise jumbled situation; it draws order out of chaos.... [It] synthesizes the data, focuses our attention on what's crucial, and helps us ignore that which makes little difference" (1994, p. 34). These latter two writers are acknowledging an important reality of communication and mass communication theories: There are a lot of them, the questions they produce are testable to varying degrees, they are situationally based, and they sometimes seem contradictory and chaotic. As communication theorist Katherine Miller explained, "Different schools of thought will define *theory* in different ways depending on the needs of the theorist and on beliefs about the social world and the nature of knowledge" (2005, pp. 22–23). Scholars have identified four major categories of communication theory—(1) postpositivism, (2) hermeneutic theory, (3) critical theory, and (4) normative theory—and although they "share a commitment to an increased understanding of social and communicative life and a value for high-quality scholarship" (Miller, 2005, p. 32), they differ in

ontology
The nature of reality, what is knowable

- Their goals
- Their view of the nature of reality, what is knowable—their **ontology**
- Their view of how knowledge is created and expanded—their **epistemology**
- Their view of the proper role of values in research and theory building—their **axiology**

epistemology
How knowledge is created and expanded

axiology
The proper role of values in research and theory building

These differences not only define the different types of theory, but they also help make it obvious why the definition of *social science* in mass communication theory is necessarily flexible.

POSTPOSITIVIST THEORY

When communication researchers first wanted to systematically study the social world, they turned to the physical sciences for their model. Those in the physical sciences (physics, chemistry, astronomy, and so on) believed in *positivism,* the idea that knowledge could be gained only through empirical, observable, measurable phenomena examined through the scientific method. But as we saw earlier in this chapter, people are not beakers of water. As a result, social scientists committed to the scientific method practice **postpositivist theory**. This theory is based on empirical observation guided by the scientific method, but it recognizes that humans and human behavior are not as constant as elements of the physical world.

postpositivist theory
Theory based on empirical observation guided by the scientific method

The goals of postpositivist theory are explanation, prediction, and control (and in this you can see the connection between this kind of social science and the physical sciences). For example, researchers who want to explain the operation of political advertising, predict which commercials will be most effective, and control the voting behavior of targeted citizens would, of necessity, rely on postpositivist theory. Its ontology accepts that the world, even the social world, exists apart from our perceptions of it; human behavior is sufficiently predictable to be studied systematically. (Postpositivists do, however, believe that the social world does have more variation than the physical world; for example, the names we give to things define them and our reaction to them—hence the *post* of postpositivism). Its epistemology argues that knowledge is advanced through the systematic, logical search for regularities and causal relationships employing the scientific method. Advances come when there is **intersubjective agreement** among scientists studying a given phenomenon. That is, postpositivists find confidence "in the community of social researchers," not "in any individual social scientist" (Schutt, 2009, p. 89). It is this

intersubjective agreement
When members of a research community independently arrive at similar conclusions about a given social phenomenon

cautious reliance on the scientific method that defines postpositivism's axiology—the objectivity inherent in the application of the scientific method keeps researchers' and theorists' values out of the search for knowledge (as much as is possible). Postpositivist communication theory, then, is theory developed through a system of inquiry that resembles as much as possible the rules and practices of what we traditionally understand as science.

HERMENEUTIC THEORY

hermeneutic theory
The study of understanding, especially by interpreting action and text

But many communication theorists do not want to explain, predict, and control social behavior. Their goal is to *understand* how and why that behavior occurs in the social world. This **hermeneutic theory** is the study of understanding, especially through the systematic interpretation of actions or texts. Hermeneutics originally began as the study or interpretation of the Bible and other sacred works. As it evolved over the last two centuries, it maintained its commitment to the examination of "objectifications of the mind" (Burrell and Morgan, 1979, p. 236), or what Miller calls "social creations" (2005, p. 52). Just as the Bible was the "objectification" of early Christian culture, and those who wanted to understand that culture would study that text, most modern applications of hermeneutics are likewise focused on understanding the culture of the users of a specific text.

social hermeneutics
Theory seeking to understand how those in an observed social situation interpret their own lot in that situation

There are different forms of hermeneutic theory. For example, **social hermeneutics** has as its goal the understanding of how those in an observed social situation interpret their own lot in that situation. As ethnographer Michael Moerman explained, social hermeneutic theory tries to understand how events "in the alien world make sense to the aliens, how their way of life coheres and has meaning and value for the people who live it" (1992, p. 23). Another branch of hermeneutics looks for hidden or deep meaning in people's interpretation of different symbol systems—for example, in media texts. As you might have guessed from these descriptions, hermeneutic theory is sometimes referred to as *interpretive theory*. Another important idea embedded in these descriptions is that any **text**, any product of social interaction—a movie, the president's State of the Union Address, a series of Twitter tweets, a conversation between a soap opera hero and heroine—can be a source of understanding.

text
Any product of social interaction that serves as a source of understanding

The ontology of hermeneutic theory says that there is no truly "real," measurable social reality. Instead, "people construct an image of reality based on their own preferences and prejudices and their interactions with others, and this is as true of scientists as it is of everyone else in the social world" (Schutt, 2009, p. 92). As such, hermeneutic theory's epistemology, how knowledge is advanced, relies on the subjective interaction between the observer (the researcher or theorist) and his or her community. Put another way, knowledge is local; that is, it is specific to the interaction of the knower and the known. Naturally, then, the axiology of hermeneutic theory embraces, rather than limits, the influence of researcher and theorist values. Personal and professional values, according to Katherine Miller, are a "lens through which social phenomena are observed" (2005, p. 58). A researcher interested in understanding teens' interpretations of social networking websites like Facebook, or one who is curious about meaning-making that occurs in the exchange of information among teen fans of an online simulation game, would rely on hermeneutic theory.

CRITICAL THEORY

critical theory
Theory seeking emancipation and change in a dominant social order

structure
In critical theory, the social world's rules, norms, and beliefs

agency
In critical theory, how humans behave and interact within the structure

dialectic
In critical theory, the ongoing struggle between agency and structure

There are still other scholars who do not want explanation, prediction, and control of the social world. Nor do they seek understanding of the social world as the ultimate goal for their work. They start from the assumption that some aspects of the social world are deeply flawed and in need of transformation. Their aim is to gain knowledge of that social world so they can change it. This goal is inherently political because it challenges existing ways of organizing the social world and the people and institutions that exercise power in it. **Critical theory** is openly political (therefore its axiology is aggressively value-laden). It assumes that by reorganizing society, we can give priority to the most important human values. Critical theorists study inequality and oppression. Their theories do more than observe, describe, or interpret; they criticize. Critical theories view "media as sites of (and weapons in) struggles over social, economic, symbolic, and political power (as well as struggles over control of, and access to, the media themselves)" (Meyrowitz, 2008, p. 642). Critical theory's epistemology argues that knowledge is advanced only when it serves to free people and communities from the influence of those more powerful than themselves. Its ontology, however, is a bit more complex.

According to critical theory, what is real, what is knowable, in the social world is the product of the interaction between **structure** (the social world's rules, norms, and beliefs) and **agency** (how humans behave and interact in that world). Reality, then, to critical theorists, is constantly being shaped and reshaped by the **dialectic** (the ongoing struggle or debate) between the two. When elites control the struggle, they define reality (in other words, their control of the structure defines people's realities). When people are emancipated, *they* define reality through their behaviors and interactions (agency). Researchers and theorists interested in the decline (and restoration) of the power of the labor movement in industrialized nations or those interested in limiting the contribution of children's advertising to the nation's growing consumerism would rely on critical theory. Some critical theorists are quite troubled by what they view as the uncontrolled exercise of capitalist corporate power around the world. They see media as an essential tool employed by corporate elites to constrain how people view their social world and to limit their agency in it.

NORMATIVE THEORY

normative media theory
Theory explaining how a media system should operate in order to conform to or realize a set of ideal social values

Social theorists see postpositivist and hermeneutic theory as *representational*. That is, they are articulations—word pictures—of some other realities (for postpositivists, those representations are generalizable across similar realities, and for interpretive theorists, these representations are local and specific). Critical theory is *nonrepresentational*. Its goal is to *change* existing realities.

There is another type of theory, however. It may be applied to any form of communication but is most often applied to *mass* communication. Its aim is neither the representation nor the reformation of reality. Instead, its goal is to set an ideal standard against which the operation of a given media system can be judged. A **normative media theory** explains how a media system *should* operate in order to conform to or realize a set of ideal social values. As such, its ontology argues that what is known is situational (or, like interpretive theory, local). In other words, what is real or knowable about a media system is real or knowable only

As we've seen, different communication theorists deal differently with the role of values in the construction of their ideas. Inasmuch as they model their research on that of those who study the physical world, postpositivists would ideally like to eliminate values from their inquiry. But they know they can't, so objectivity becomes their regulatory ideal; that is, they rely on the scientific method to reduce the impact of values on their work as much as possible. They also distinguish between two types of values in their work. Postpositivists cherish **epistemic values**—they value high standards in the conduct of research and development of theory. But they also confront **nonepistemic values**—the place of emotion, morals, and ethics in research and theory development. There is little debate about the former among postpositivists—who wouldn't want high standards of performance? But what about emotions, morals, and ethics? Why, for example, would researchers want to study media violence? Certainly they believe a relationship exists between media consumption and human behavior on some level. But what if an individual theorist strongly believes in the eradication of all violence on children's television because of her own son's problems with bullies at school? How hard should she work to ignore her personal feelings in her research and interpretation of her findings? Should she examine some other aspect of mass communication to ensure greater objectivity? But why should anybody have to study something that he or she has no feeling about?

Interpretive theorists, even though they more readily accept the role of values in their work than do postpositivists, also wrestle with the proper application of those values. Accepting the impossibility of separating values from research and theory development, interpretive theorists identify two ends of a continuum. Those who wish to minimize the impact of their personal values on their work **bracket** their values; that is, they recognize them, set them aside by figuratively putting them in brackets, and then do

their work. At the other end of the continuum are those who openly celebrate their values and consciously inject them into their work. In truth, most interpretive researchers and theorists fall somewhere in the middle. If you were really thinking about theory, though, you would have asked, "But if an interpretive theorist openly celebrates his or her values and injects them into the research or theory development, hasn't she moved into critical theory?" And you would be correct, because it is hard to conceive of someone willing to inject personal values into social research and theory who did not want, at the very least, to advance those values. And in advancing those values, the status quo would be altered—hence, critical theory.

Critical and normative theorists, in their open embrace of values, face fewer questions about objectivity than do other theorists. But they, like all social researchers and theorists, must employ high epistemic values. Critical theorists advocate change; normative theorists advocate media striving to meet a social system's stated ideals of operation. These open articulations of nonepistemic values, however, do not excuse sloppy data gathering or improper data analysis.

What should be clear is that all involved in the serious study of human life must maintain the highest standards of inquiry *within the conventions* of their research and theory development communities. Given that, which axiology do you find most compatible with your way of thinking about human behavior? Should you someday become a mass communication researcher or theorist, which set of values do you think would prove most valuable in guiding your efforts?

epistemic values High standards in the conduct of research and theory development
nonepistemic values The place of emotion, morals, and ethics in research and theory development
bracket In interpretive theory, setting values aside

for the specific social system in which that system exists. Its epistemology, how knowledge is developed and advanced, is based in *comparative analysis*—we can only judge (and therefore understand) the worth of a given media system in comparison to the ideal espoused by the particular social system in which it operates.

Finally, normative theory's axiology is, by definition, value-laden. Study of a media system or parts of a media system is undertaken in the explicit belief that there is an ideal mode of operation based in the values of the social system. Theorists interested in the press's role in a democracy would most likely employ normative theory, as would those examining the operation of the media in an Islamic republic or an authoritarian state. Problems arise if media systems based on one normative theory are evaluated according to the norms or ideals of another normative theory. Chapter 6 is devoted in its entirety to normative theory. You can more deeply investigate the role of values in the four broad categories of theory we've discussed when reading the box entitled "True Values: A Deeper Look at Axiology."

EVALUATING THEORY

French philosopher André Gide wrote, "No theory is good unless it permits, not rest, but the greatest work. No theory is good except on condition that one uses it to go on beyond" (quoted in Andrews, Biggs, and Seidel, 1996, p. 66). In other words, good theory pushes, advances, improves the social world. There are some specific ways, however, to judge the value of the many theories we will study in this book.

When evaluating postpositivist theory, we need to ask these questions:

1. How well does it explain the event, behavior, or relationship of interest?
2. How well does it predict future events, behaviors, or relationships?
3. How testable is it? In other words, is it specific enough in its assertions that it can be systematically supported or rejected based on empirical observation?
4. How parsimonious is it? In other words, is it the simplest explanation possible of the phenomenon in question? Some call this *elegance*. Keep in mind that communication theories generally tend to lack parsimony. In fact, one of the reasons many social scientists avoid the study of communication is that communication phenomena are hard to explain parsimoniously.
5. How practical or useful is it? If the goals of postpositivist theory are explanation, prediction, and control, how much assistance toward these ends is provided by the theory?

When evaluating hermeneutic theory, we need to ask these questions:

1. How much new or fresh insight into the event, behavior, or relationship of interest does it offer? In other words, how much does it advance our understanding?
2. How well does it clarify the values inherent in the interpretation, not only those embedded in the phenomenon of interest, but those of the researcher or theorist?
3. How much support does it generate among members of the scholarly community also investigating the phenomenon of interest?
4. How much aesthetic appeal does it have? In other words, does it enthuse or inspire its adherents?

When evaluating critical theory, we need to ask the same questions we do of hermeneutic theory, but we must add a fifth:

5. How useful is the critique of the status quo? In other words, does it provide enough understanding of elite power so that power can be effectively challenged? Does the theory enable individuals to oppose elite definitions of the social world?

When evaluating normative theory, we need to ask the following questions:

1. How stable and definitive are the ideal standards of operation against which the media system (or its parts) under study will be measured?
2. What, and how powerful, are the economic, social, cultural, and political realities surrounding the actual operation of a system (or its parts) that must be considered in evaluating that performance?
3. How much support does it generate among members of the scholarly community also investigating a specific media system (or its parts)?

FLEXIBLE SOCIAL SCIENCE

Now that you've been introduced to the four broad categories of social scientific theory, you might have guessed another reason that those who study the social world often don't get the respect accorded their physical science colleagues. Sociologist Kenneth Bailey wrote, "To this day you will find within social science both those who think of themselves as scientists in the strictest sense of the word and those with a more subjective approach to the study of society, who see themselves more as humanists than as scientists" (1982, p. 5). In other words, and as you've just seen, not all who call themselves social scientists adhere to the same standards for conducting research or accepting evidence. But complicating matters even more is the fact that social science researchers and theorists often blend (or mix and match) categories as they do their work (Benoit and Holbert, 2008). To some observers, especially committed postpositivists, this seems unsystematic. It also generates disagreement among social scientists, not about the issue under examination, say the influence of video violence on children's behavior, but about the appropriateness of the methods used, the value of the evidence obtained, or the influence of values on the work (that is, debates over ontology, epistemology, and axiology).

MASS COMMUNICATION THEORY

"The scholarship about the mass media has grown so large and become so fragmented," argues W. James Potter, "that it is very difficult for scholars to understand, much less appreciate, the incredible array of great ideas and findings that have been produced" (2009, p. xiv). You'll see these "great ideas and findings" throughout this text and discover how in their harmony and dissonance they have shaped the discipline's thinking. For now, though, let's take this example, the impact of video violence, and see how different social scientists might approach it.

Do you believe that watching televised or videogame violence can cause kids to act more aggressively? Surely this must be an easier thing to demonstrate than the existence of an ever-expanding universe. This link has been theorized ever since the first silent-movie hero slugged the first silent-movie villain. What is the most useful way to study the complex relationship between this specific form of media content and those who consume it? Maybe we could put two groups of children, some of whom had seen a violent cartoon and some who had not, in a room and count the number of times each engaged in some form of violent play. Maybe we could examine the disciplinary records of two schools, one where children had ready access to television at home and one where there was no television allowed. Maybe we could take a three-month position as a teacher's aide in a preschool and record the interaction between the children, television, and one another. Perhaps we could interview heavy and light television viewers and frequent and infrequent game players. Maybe the best way is to ignore what is going on with specific individuals and classrooms and focus our research on how television programs and videogames present violence: Who metes it out? Who is on the receiving end? Is it successful? How graphic or unrealistic is it? Maybe the question is about money—it's obvious that violent content improves television ratings and violent videogames attract teenage boys, the group that spends the most on games. This economic incentive motivates broadcasters and game designers to continue to make this material available despite decades of evidence of its harmful effects on individuals and society. Maybe the most useful way to understand the role of violent media content in the culture is to craft a detailed, logical argument based on observation of a season's worth of prime-time television programming and a deep analysis of the top-ten bestselling games.

Every one of these solutions—regardless of how perfectly (or imperfectly) it adheres to traditional notions of social science or how neatly it fits into one of the four categories of social science theory—is offered either because of existing theory or because the answers it produces can be used to add to or develop theory. And every one of these solutions—and countless more that could have been offered—is designed to help people, us, produce a more livable, humane world. In this way, they are all social scientific.

Now it should be clear that mass communication theory is really mass communication *theories,* each more or less relevant to a given medium, audience, time, condition, and theorist. But this shouldn't be viewed as a problem. Mass communication theory can be personalized; it is ever-evolving; it is dynamic. What we hope to do in the following pages is to provide you with the basics: the traditions that have given us what we now view as classic theories of mass communication, some idea of the contexts in which they were developed and in which they flourished (if they did), the knowledge to decide for yourself what does and does not make sense, and some definite clues about where mass communication theory stands today.

Some three decades ago, Englishman Jeremy Tunstall, a keen observer of American media and American media theory, foretold the route we will travel: "'Communication' itself carries many problems. Either the 'mass media' or 'communication' would cover a dozen disciplines and raise a thousand problems. When we put the two together, the problems are confounded. Even if the field is narrowed to 'mass media,' it gets split into many separate media, many separate disciplines, many separate stages in the flow, and quickly you have several hundred subfields"—in other words, a lot of theories (1983, pp. 92–93). In fact, W. James Potter identified "more than 150 theories"—some new, some vintage—used actively in published mass communication research in the five years from 2004 to 2009 (Potter, 2009, p. 14).

SUMMARY

As we move ever more deeply into the ever-evolving communication revolution, we need an understanding of mass communication theory to guide our actions and decisions. This understanding recognizes that all social theory is a human construction and that it is dynamic, always changing as society, technology, and people change. This dynamism can be readily seen in the transformation of our understanding of the process of mass communication itself. New communication technologies have changed traditional notions of the mass audience, the mass communicator, and the relationships between the two. To understand this change, we rely on social science and its theories.

Social science is often controversial because it suggests causal relationships between things in the environment and people's attitudes, values, and behaviors. In the physical sciences, these relationships are often easily visible and measurable. In the study of human behavior, however, they rarely are. Human behavior is quite difficult to quantify, often very complex, and often goal-oriented. Social science and human behavior make a problematic fit. The situation is even further complicated because social science itself is somewhat variable—it is many different things to many different people.

Nonetheless, the systematic inquiry into mass communication relies on theories—any organized

---

THINKING *about* **THEORY** **WHAT'S YOUR QUESTION? WHAT'S YOUR APPROACH?**

Social networking site Facebook hit the Internet in 2003. Five years later it had 100 million users; by mid-2010 it had half-a-billion members networking in 40 languages (Kang, 2010). Half the teenagers using Facebook check in at least once a day, but the greatest growth in members has been among adults aged 35 to 54. These grown-ups spend nearly four hours a day on Facebook, more than any other age group (Orenstein, 2009). What questions do these few facts raise for you?

One obvious question is, "Who are these social networkers?" Does the growth in the number of "older" social networkers surprise you? Why or why not? What about the amount of time they spend networking? What about networkers' gender? Does that play a factor? Where do they access these sites? Why would middle-aged people be such heavy users of a new technology almost ritualistically identified with the young and hip? Another obvious question is, "Why do people use social networking sites?" The Pew Internet & American Life Project (Lenhart, 2009) reported that 91 percent say they use them to stay in touch with friends they regularly see; 82 percent to stay in touch with friends they rarely see; and 49 percent to make new friends (naturally, people could give more than one answer).

Now what questions arise for you? Are there gender differences in why and how people use these sites? Are there age differences?

But what about a different kind of question, maybe a bit bigger in scope? How do these net-maintained or net-originated friendships differ from more traditionally maintained and originated friendships (that is, face-to-face)? Are the kinds of conversations that take place between net-friends different from those that up-close-and-personal friends engage in? How much "truth" happens in online friendships? How is meaning made when friends can't see facial expressions like smiles or hear voice inflection?

Maybe it isn't enough to describe these users by age and gender; maybe a more interesting question concerns what's going on in their lives. For example, can lonely or depressed people find comfort or relief in social networking sites? There is research linking the amount of time spent online to loneliness, depression, and alienation from friends and family (Engelberg and Sjöberg, 2004). Are social networking sites a symptom or a cure? After all, there is solid evidence that instant messaging has a "direct positive effect" on young people's friendships (Valkenburg and Peter, 2009, p. 79). Might not the same thing be said of social networking sites?

(Continued)

THINKING *about* **THEORY**   WHAT'S YOUR QUESTION? WHAT'S YOUR APPROACH? (CONTINUED)

And those marketers! What happens to social networking on the Internet when the sites where this activity occurs become increasingly commercialized? There have been several instances where fake "friends" have been created specifically to push a company's new product or to trash a competitor, and Facebook has suffered three major user revolts over its commercialization of members' chats (O'Brien, 2010). What happens when trust is lost?

Every major national politician is "making friends" on these sites (Williams, 2007). How might these sites differ from "real" friends' sites? Will candidates' sites attract more young people to politics? How might candidates tailor their messages on different issues for these sites? Test yourself—how many more interesting questions can you develop?

Now, what's your approach? What is the best way to answer the question or questions you find most interesting? As a postpositivist, for example, can you devise an experiment comparing the level of trust between friends who meet online and those who meet in person? Using hermeneutics, you could

examine the kinds of exchanges (texts) that occur between social networking friends. But maybe you want to take a critical look at the intrusion of advertising on the content of these sites. Or from a normative perspective, you might want to assess how politicians' use of social networking sites changes traditional notions of the role of the media in electoral politics. But wait. What if you want to understand the kinds of exchanges that occur between social networking friends, but you want to compare different age groups, or people at different stages of their relationship? Haven't you blended postpositivism and hermeneutics? And how can you assess the impact of advertising on the content of these sites unless you are familiar on a fairly deep level with commercial content as a text?

So, what's your question? Or should we ask, what are your *questions*? What's your approach? Or should we ask, what are your *approaches*? And what about your own interests and values? Are you a member of a social networking site? Does that experience shape your thinking? How could it not?

set of concepts, explanations, and principles of some aspect of human experience. The explanatory power of mass communication theory, however, is constantly challenged by the presence of many media, their many facets and characteristics, their constant change, an always-developing audience, and the ever-evolving nature of the societies that use them. Still, social theorists have identified four general categories of communication theory. Two are representational, postpositivist theory (theory based on empirical observation guided by the scientific method) and hermeneutic theory (the study of understanding, especially by interpreting actions and texts). A third, critical theory, seeks emancipation and change in a dominant social order.

While these types of theory have a commitment to an increased understanding of the social world,

they differ in their goals, their ontology (the nature of reality, what is knowable), their epistemology (how knowledge is created and expanded), and their axiology (the proper role of values in research and theory building). As such, postpositivist theory is traditionally social scientific; hermeneutic theory is based on interpretation of texts (and the product of any social interaction can serve as a text); and critical theory, in seeking change, studies the struggle—the dialectic—between a society's structure (its rules, norms, and beliefs) and its agency (how people interact in the face of that structure). Finally, there is a fourth type of mass communication theory, one that is neither representational nor seeking change: normative theory—theory designed to judge the operation of a given media system against a specific social system's norms or ideals.

Critical Thinking Questions

1. How well informed are you about public affairs? Where do you get most of your information about the world around you? Do you talk about current affairs with the people around you? How often do you reflect on the relationship between keeping up with the issues of the day and your responsibilities as a citizen, or is this just something that politicians and professors talk about? Can you craft a theory of why you do not pay more attention to the news than you already do?

2. Can you think of any social science "findings" that you reject? What are they? On what grounds do you base your skepticism? Can you separate your personal experience with the issue from your judgment of the social scientific evidence?

3. Social scientists may have differences of opinion about the role of values in research and theory (axiology), but what about you? Where do you stand on the proper place of values in the conduct of social science? Should social scientists engage in research and theory development to advance ideas and issues they think are important? Why or why not?

Key Terms

grand theory

mass communication

Listserv

mediated communication

interpersonal communication

social scientists

causality

causal relationship

scientific method

hypothesis

empirical

third-person effect

theory

ontology

epistemology

axiology

postpositivist theory

hermeneutic theory

intersubjective agreement

social hermeneutics

text

epistemic values

nonepistemic values

bracket

critical theory

structure

agency

dialectic

normative media theory

2 | FOUR ERAS OF MASS COMMUNICATION THEORY

convergence
The erasure of
distinctions
among media

Technophiles have been hailing **convergence,** the erasure of distinctions among media, ever since the introduction of the personal computer in the late 1970s and early 1980s. Microsoft cofounder Bill Gates heralded its full arrival in 2004 at the annual Consumer Electronics Show. Convergence, he told his listeners,

> doesn't happen until you have everything in a digital form that the consumer can easily use on all the different devices. So, if we look at the three types of media of greatest importance—we look at photos, we look at music and we look at video—the move toward giving people digital flexibility on them is pretty incredible on every one of them. It's been discussed for a long, long time. And now, it's really happening. (quoted in Cooper, 2004, p. 1)

In fact, it's happening today in ways that Gates might not have anticipated those many long years ago (in Internet time). We now receive clear, full-motion video on cell phones—that is, when we're not using them to surf the Web or locate, via global positioning, the nearest pizza shop. The technology allowing people to retransmit the content received on their home televisions to their laptop computer or cell phone no matter where they are is available, easy to use, and relatively inexpensive. As wireless Internet networks (**Wi-Fi**) have improved and become more widespread, full-motion live video, movies-on-demand, and television-on-demand have joined already-existing anyplace-anytime reception of voice, e-mail, web pages, music downloads, written and data texts, interactive video games, and still photos. So, while you use your cell phone to watch a video download of *Superbad,* are you on the phone, on the Internet, watching television, or viewing a film? What becomes of the distinction between newspapers, magazines, radio, and television when all can be accessed anywhere, anytime on a single handheld device and when each medium can combine graphics, video, printed text, sound, music, and interactivity to satisfy your entertainment and information needs?

Wi-Fi
Wireless Internet
networks

We are in the midst of a revolution in communication technology that many scholars believe is transforming social orders and cultures around the world. Each new technological device expands the possible uses of the existing technologies. New technologies combine to create media systems spanning great distances but also serve a broad range of highly specific purposes. In retrospect, we now regard the first centuries of mass communication as dominated by expensive, clumsy technologies that provided a limited array of services to gigantic audiences. Large corporations located in the largest cities established and controlled highly centralized media systems. People accommodated their needs to what the older media technologies could provide. For many of us, the term *mass media* still is synonymous with these "big media." And now, although we are caught up in a communications revolution, much of our attention is still riveted on the media dinosaurs. We may dismissively refer to "older" media as the MSM (mainstream media), but we are only beginning to understand the potential of the "new," alternative media to serve needs we didn't know we had. If this were not so, the Internet and World Wide Web would be neither as explosively popular nor as constantly controversial as they are.

For many of us, the immediate consequences of this revolution seem quite pleasant and benign. The new media have greatly expanded our options for entertainment and information content. Instead of choosing from a handful of movies at local theaters or on three network television stations, we can select from tens of thousands of titles available on cable channels, satellites, videotapes, DVDs, and Internet downloads. We can exchange CDs in their digital file form on the Internet to create massive home music libraries. At any given moment, we can tune to several different newscasts on television, radio, and the net. Using personal computers, or even our cell phones, we can access remote databases and scan endless reams of information on diverse, specialized topics. Rather than the handful of local radio stations available on our dials, we can hear ten thousand stations on the Web. We can use the Internet's interactive capabilities to experiment with and create new identities. An array of print media is available—many edited to suit the tastes of relatively small audiences. The old marketplace of ideas has become a gigantic 24/7 supermarket. If you want it, you can get it somewhere. And if you want it but can't get it, you can create it yourself, as the Internet and digital technologies have turned us all into potential content producers.

In this textbook, we examine how communication scholars have conceptualized the role of media during this and the last two centuries. Our purpose is to provide you with a broad and historically grounded perspective on what media can do *for* you and *to* you. As digital media converge, you will have new opportunities to make media serve your purposes, but there may also come powerful new ways for media to invade your privacy and shape your views of the social world. We review some of the best (and worst) thinking concerning the role and potential of media. We ask that you join us in looking back to the origins of media and the early efforts to understand their influence and role. We will trace the challenges posed by ever-changing media technology and the rise of various media industries, focusing on the theories that were developed to make sense of them. Finally, we will conclude with a review of current theory and assist you in developing a personally relevant perspective on media.

Keep in mind, though, that this is not a book about new media technology, although we will often use examples of new technology to illustrate our points and to demonstrate the relevance of various theories. Our purpose is to help you place new communication technology into historical and theoretical perspective. The challenges we face today as a society and as individuals are similar in many ways to those people faced during the previous communication revolutions, such as the era of the penny press or the Golden Age of Radio. We can learn much from examining how researchers have tried to understand media technology and anticipate its consequences for society. We can try to avoid repeating their mistakes and can build on their ideas that have proved useful. The theories of past generations can assist us as we face the challenges of today's new media.

This book is structured more or less chronologically. This organizational scheme represents, in part, our support of Everett Rogers, James Dearing, and Donne Bergman's belief that

> the most common means of investigating intellectual histories is the historical method, which seeks to understand paradigmatic change by identifying key instances of personal and impersonal influence, which are then interpreted as determining the parameters and directions of a particular field of study. A social scientific understanding of such histories, while acknowledging the importance of key instances of intellectual influence, must seek to identify patterns that represent influence over time. (1993, p. 69)

Our chronological structuring also reflects our view that most social theories, including media theory, are never completely innovative and are always the products of the particular era in which they are constructed. As geologist and zoologist Stephen Jay Gould writes of science in general, those who deal with theories "can work only within their social and psychological contexts. Such an assertion does not debase the institution of science, but rather enriches our view of the greatest dialectic in human history: the transformation of society by scientific progress, which can only arise within a matrix set, constrained, and facilitated by society" (Gould, 2000, p. 31). Communication scholar Gary Gumpert makes the same argument, specifically for his "splendid, splintered discipline." It is important, he wrote, "to know that we are not alone, but connected to what was before, what may be, and what is next to come" (2007, p. 170). In other words, as historian Joan Jacobs Brumberg explained to those who traffic in social theory, "Science in and of itself has some culture embedded in it. How could it be otherwise?" (quoted in Belkin, 2000, p. 43).

Present-day theories are mostly updated versions of old ideas, even when they provide seemingly radical revisions or sophisticated syntheses of earlier notions. To understand contemporary theories, it's important to understand the theories on which they are based. This does not mean, however, that mass communication theory developed or unfolded in an orderly, chronologically stable way, with new, improved ideas supplanting older, disproved notions. Theories about media and violence, for example, have been around as long as there have been media (Ball-Rokeach, 2001; Wartella and Reeves, 1985). Concerns about harmful media effects were voiced in this country as early as 1900 and were strongly articulated in the 1930s and again in the 1950s. The 1960s were the heyday of mass communication scholars' theoretical attention to the problem of media and subsequent viewer, listener, or reader aggression. They were also the heyday of the argument that media aren't the problem, poor parenting is. A seemingly definitive government-funded series of studies, the *Surgeon General's Report by the Scientific Advisory Committee on Television and Social Behavior*, published in 1972, did little to settle scholarly and public debate. So the Telecommunications Act of 1996 required that manufacturers of television sets install an electronic violence-screening device, the V-chip (which very few parents use); Congress has held hearings on the effects, if any, of media violence every year since; and in 2009 the FCC began consideration of rules requiring a single, standardized ratings system to "warn parents of programming on television, video games, and wireless telephones that could be inappropriate for children" (Shields, 2009).

This book is also based on the assumption that all social theory is a *human construction—an active effort by communities of scholars to make sense of their social world.* Scholarly communities differ in what they want to accomplish with the theories they create, as we saw in Chapter 1. From one decade to the next, there are important qualitative shifts in theory construction as new groups of scholars emerge with new objectives and new ways of organizing older ideas. For example, during times of social turmoil or external threat, scholarly communities often become allied with powerful elites and work to preserve the status quo. At other times, scholarly communities critical of the existing social order spring up and work to reform or transform it. Still other communities have long-term humanistic goals that include liberal education and cultural enlightenment.

Not only are there many mass communication theories constructed for many different ends, but they, like the world they attempt to explain, understand, or change, are ever evolving. So, not only are these theories human constructions; they are *dynamic.* Mass communication scholars Jennings Bryant and Donna Miron dramatically explained:

> Like volatile stormy weather, at some level changes in mass communication theory and research occur almost too rapidly and unpredictably for even the best-intentioned reporters to chronicle and explain accurately.... For example, (a) all of the media of mass communication are undergoing dramatic changes in form, content, and substance ... which are explained only partially by the notion of convergence; (b) newer forms of interactive media, such as the Internet, are altering the traditional mass communication model from that of communication of one-to-many to communication of many-to-many ...; (c) media ownership patterns are shifting dramatically and sometimes ruthlessly in ways that tend to disregard the entertainment, informational, educational, political, and social needs of consumers and that potentially cause major problems for their host societies ...; (d) the viewing patterns and habits of audiences worldwide are changing so rapidly as to be almost mercurial (e.g., consider the transition from children's bedrooms to children's media rooms) ...; (e) the very nature of the primary unit in which most media consumption takes place—the family—is undergoing remarkable changes in its own right that markedly affect our uses of media and their impacts on our psychological and cultural well-being.... Moreover, (f) even in stable, more traditional home environments, with most of today's youth "Growing up Wired," ... interactive media are "Redefining Life at Home." (2004, pp. 662–663)

OVERVIEW

Bryant and Miron are certainly correct about what is happening in mass communication theory today. But the rapid and remarkable change they describe has *always* existed in mass communication. For example, the changes wrought by today's

"Internet Revolution" are quite similar to those people experienced during the "Wireless (Radio) Revolution," or the "Television Revolution," or the "Cable Revolution." The great "democratizing power" envisioned for the Internet and World Wide Web is very much like that predicted with the emergence of inexpensive urban newspapers in the 1800s, radio in the early 1900s, sound motion pictures in the 1920s, and television and cable television in the middle decades of the last century. Today's evolving definitions of family are no more dramatic than those our culture faced at the end of the Second World War or during the "Youth Revolution" of the 1960s. How true today is Bryant and Miron's 2004 assertion that "most media consumption" takes place with "the family"?

Therefore, to best understand not only the many mass communication theories but also the storm of change they constantly undergo, we need to understand the different approaches that individual communities of scholars take to make sense of their social worlds during the times they find themselves in. In later chapters we will review how scholars struggled to assess how and why media have effects at certain times and not others—why some people are strongly affected by certain media content while others aren't. Early thinking about media was often quite simplistic; media were sometimes regarded as information machines—mere conveyor belts that could be trusted to transfer information and ideas from one person to another. At other times media were feared as possessing seemingly magical powers, able to suddenly transform the religious and political beliefs of entire nations—to turn Godfearing freedom lovers into atheistic Communists. As we will see, media are neither of these things. Their role in our lives and our society is much more complicated and becoming more so as new media technologies proliferate.

FOUR ERAS OF MEDIA THEORY

Media theory has undergone important transformations over the past two centuries. We have identified four distinct eras in the development of mass communication theories, beginning with the origin of media theory in the nineteenth century and ending with the emergence of an array of contemporary perspectives. As we explore each of these eras, we will describe the various types of mass communication theories that were constructed, consider their objectives, and illustrate both their strengths and their limitations. We will point out the purposes these theories served and the reasons why they were replaced or ignored by later scholars. In some cases, theories were rejected when they couldn't be validated by scientific research or supported by logical arguments. Empirical evidence contradicted their key notions, or they proved difficult to explain or defend. Occasionally, proponents gave up trying to find evidence to support them or they became irrelevant as media or society changed.

We will tell the story of mass communication theory development. It will help you better understand how past theories evolved and why current theories are considered important. Although many of the older theories have been rejected as unscientific or otherwise useless and no longer guide our thinking, they remain important as milestones (Lowery and DeFleur, 1995), and some continue to enjoy contemporary acceptance by segments of the public and some media practitioners. Most important, though, is that knowledge of earlier perspectives enables you to appreciate present-day theories.

In each era, the emergence of important conflicting perspectives can best be seen as the accomplishment of a research community working within the constraints imposed by its own values, preexisting ideas, and research standards. Each research community was also constrained by competing theories, limited financial resources, externally imposed political restrictions, and values held in the larger society. Although isolated theorists can produce innovative conceptualizations, research communities recognize, develop, and then popularize these notions. We will consider how such communities have grown and functioned as we describe the theories they fostered or rejected.

THE ERA OF MASS SOCIETY AND MASS CULTURE

Our description of the eras of mass communication theory begins with a review of some of the earliest thinking about media. These ideas were initially developed in the latter half of the nineteenth century, at a time when rapid development of large factories in urban areas was drawing more and more people from rural areas to cities. At the same time, ever more powerful printing presses allowed the creation of newspapers that could be sold at declining prices to rapidly growing populations of readers. Although some theorists were optimistic about the future that would be created by industrialization, urban expansion, and the rise of print media, many were extremely pessimistic (Brantlinger, 1983). They blamed industrialization for disrupting peaceful, rural communities and forcing people to live in urban areas merely to serve as a convenient workforce in large factories, mines, or bureaucracies. These theorists were fearful of cities because of their crime, cultural diversity, and unstable political systems. For these social thinkers, mass media symbolized everything that was wrong with nineteenth-century urban life. They singled out media for virulent criticism and accused them of pandering to lower-class tastes, fomenting political unrest, and subverting important cultural norms. Most theorists were educated **elites** who feared what they couldn't understand. The old social order was crumbling, and so were its culture and politics. Were media responsible for this, or did they simply accelerate or aggravate these changes?

elites
People occupying elevated or privileged positions in a social system

mass society theory
Perspective on Western, industrial society that attributes an influential but often negative role to media

The dominant perspective on media and society that emerged during this period has come to be referred to as **mass society theory**. It is an inherently contradictory theory rooted in nostalgia for a "golden age" of rural community life that never existed, and it anticipates a nightmare future where we all lose our individuality and become servants to the machines. Some version of mass society theory seems to recur in every generation as we try to reassess where we are and where we are going as individuals and as a nation wedded to technology as the means of improving the quality of our lives. Each new version of mass society theory has its criticisms of contemporary media. It is surprising that the Internet has not yet become the focus of a new version of mass society theory. These criticisms do exist, but they have not become popular in the way that complaints about television, radio, movies, newspapers, even comic books, came to dominate public discourse in previous eras. Perhaps this is a sign that mass society notions have ceased to be relevant. Or more likely, the Internet is still relatively new and its threats to social order are still too ambiguous to be taken seriously by elites.

Thus, mass society theory can be regarded as a collection of conflicting notions developed to make sense of what was happening as industrialization allowed big cities to spring up and expand. Mass society notions came from both ends of the political spectrum. Some were developed by people who wanted to maintain the old political order, and others were created by revolutionaries who wanted to impose radical changes. But these ideological foes often shared at least one assumption—mass media were troublesome if not downright dangerous. In general, mass society ideas held strong appeal for any social elite whose power was threatened by change. Media industries, such as the **penny press** in the 1830s or **yellow journalism** in the 1890s, were easy targets for elites' criticisms. They catered to readers in the working and other lower social classes using simple, often sensational content. These industries were easily attacked as symptomatic of a sick society—a society needing to either return to traditional, fundamental values or be forced to adopt a set of totally new values fostered by media. Many intense political conflicts strongly affected thinking about the mass media, and these conflicts shaped the development of mass society theory.

An essential argument of mass society theory is that media subvert and disrupt the existing social order. But media are also seen as a potential solution to the chaos they engender. They can serve as a powerful tool that can be used to either restore the old order or institute a new one. But who should be trusted to use this tool? Should established authorities be trusted to control media—to produce or censor media content? Should media be freely operated by private entrepreneurs whose primary goal is to make money? Should radical, revolutionary groups be given control over media so they can pursue their dreams of creating an ideal social order? At the end of the nineteenth century and the beginning of the twentieth century, fierce debate erupted over these questions. This conflict often pitted traditional elites, whose power was based on an agrarian society, against urban elites, whose power was increasingly based on industrialization and urbanization.

Among these elites, the most powerful were those who controlled the factories and other forms of industrialization. They have come to be referred to as **capitalists**, because their power was based on the profits they generated and then reinvested. In time, these urban elites gained enormous influence over social change. They strongly favored all forms of technological development, including mass media. In their view, technology was inherently good because it facilitated control over the physical environment, expanded human productivity, and generated new forms of material wealth. They argued that technology would bring an end to social problems and lead to the development of an ideal social world. Newspapers would create an informed electorate that would choose the best political leaders; the telegraph would bind together diverse, contentious communities into a strong and stable union; and the telephone would improve the efficiency of business so that everyone would benefit. But in the short term, industrialization brought with it enormous problems—exploitation of workers, pollution, and social unrest. Chapters 3, 4, and 5 trace the thinking about media of this era.

Today, the fallacies of both the critics and advocates of technology are readily apparent. Mass society notions greatly exaggerated the ability of media to quickly undermine social order, just as media advocates exaggerated their ability to create an ideal social order. These ideas failed to consider that media's power ultimately

penny press Newspapers that sold for one penny and earned profits through the sale of increased numbers of readers to advertisers

yellow journalism Newspaper reporting catering to working and other lower social class audiences using simple, often sensational content

capitalists Economic elites whose power was based on the profits they generated and then reinvested

resides in the freely chosen uses that audiences make of it. All mass society thinkers were unduly paternalistic and elitist in their views of average people and the ability of media to have powerful effects on them. Those who feared media exaggerated their power to manipulate the masses and the likelihood they would bring inevitable social and cultural ruin. Technology advocates were also misguided and failed to acknowledge the many unnecessary, damaging consequences that resulted from applying technology without adequately anticipating its impact.

A SCIENTIFIC PERSPECTIVE ON MASS COMMUNICATION LEADS TO THE EMERGENCE OF THE LIMITED-EFFECTS PERSPECTIVE

Mass society notions were especially dominant among social theorists beginning in the mid-1800s and lasting until the 1950s. Since then these ideas have enjoyed intermittent popularity whenever new technology has posed a threat to the status quo. In 2005, for example, conservative religious leaders attacked cable television's cartoon *SpongeBob SquarePants* for promoting "the homosexual agenda" (Olbermann, 2005), and in 2007 film critic Michael Medved accused *Happy Feet,* the digital animation film about penguins, of containing "a bizarre anti-religious bias," an "endorsement of gay identity," and a "propagandist theme" of condemnation of the human race, support for environmentalism, and exaltation of the United Nations (quoted in Hightower, 2007, p. 3).

During the 1930s, world events seemed to continually confirm the truth of mass society ideas. In Europe, reactionary and revolutionary political movements used media in their struggles for political power. German Nazis improved on World War I propaganda techniques and ruthlessly exploited new media technology like motion pictures and radio to consolidate their power. Viewed from America, the Nazis seemed to have found powerful new ways to manipulate public attitudes and beliefs. All across Europe, totalitarian leaders like Hitler, Stalin, and Mussolini rose to political power and were able to exercise seemingly total control over vast populations. The best explanation for these sudden changes seemed to be propaganda delivered by newspapers, radio, and movies. Most European nations replaced private ownership of media, especially broadcast media, with direct government control. The explicit purpose of these efforts was to maximize the usefulness of media in the service of society. But the outcome in most cases was to place enormous power in the hands of ruthless leaders who were convinced that they personally embodied what was best for all their citizens.

In the late 1930s and early 1940s, mass society notions began to be empirically investigated by Paul Lazarsfeld, who would eventually overturn some of its basic assumptions. Trained in psychological measurement, Lazarsfeld fled the Nazis and came to the United States on a Ford Foundation fellowship (Lazarsfeld, 1969). For the emerging field of mass communication research, he proved to be a seminal thinker and researcher. Like many of his academic colleagues, Lazarsfeld was interested in exploring the potential of newly developed social science methods, such as surveys and field experiments, to understand and solve social problems. He combined academic training with a high level of entrepreneurial skill. Within a few years after arriving in the United States, he had established a very active and successful social research center, the Bureau for Applied Social Research at Columbia University.

Lazarsfeld provides a classic example of a transitional figure in theory development—someone well grounded in past theory but also innovative enough to consider other concepts and methods for evaluating new ideas. Though quite familiar with and very sympathetic to mass society notions (Lazarsfeld, 1941), Lazarsfeld was committed to the use of empirical social research methods in order to establish the validity of theory. He argued that it wasn't enough to merely speculate about the influence of media on society. Instead, he advocated the conduct of carefully designed, elaborate surveys and even field experiments in which he would be able to observe media influence and measure its magnitude. It was not enough to assume that political propaganda is powerful—hard evidence was needed to prove the existence of such effects (Lazarsfeld, Berelson, and Gaudet, 1944). Lazarsfeld's most famous research efforts, the "American Voter Studies," actually began as an attempt to document the media's power during election campaigns, yet they eventually raised more questions about the influence of media than they answered. As we shall see, this is a common outcome of empirical social research when it is used to assess the role of media.

By the mid-1950s, Lazarsfeld's work and that of other empirical media researchers had generated an enormous amount of data (by precomputer standards). Interpretation of these data led Lazarsfeld and his colleagues to conclude that media were not nearly as powerful as had been feared or hoped. Instead, these researchers found that people had numerous ways of resisting media influence, and their attitudes were shaped by many competing factors, such as family, friends, and religious community. Rather than serving as a disruptive social force, media more often seemed to reinforce existing social trends and strengthen rather than threaten the status quo. They found little evidence to support the worst fears of mass society theorists. Though Lazarsfeld and others never labeled this theory, it is now referred to as **limited-effects theory**.

Today, as you'll see in Chapters 6 and 7, the limited-effects theory encompasses numerous smaller media theories. This set of theories views media as playing a limited, somewhat minimal role in the lives of individuals and the larger society. They are still widely used in guiding research, even though their shortcomings are recognized. They are especially useful in explaining the short-term influence of routine media usage by various types of audiences. Several of these theories are referred to as **administrative theories** because they are used to guide practical decisions for various organizations. For example, these theories can guide research by television advertisers as they develop and evaluate campaign strategies to boost sales. And as you might imagine, the research generated by administrative theories is called **administrative research**. You can get a better idea of exactly what *administrative* as used here means in the box entitled "Administrative versus Critical Research: The Example of Prescription Drug Advertising."

Throughout the 1950s, limited-effects notions about media continued to gain acceptance within academia. These notions dominated the new field of mass communication research as it was developing in the 1950s and 1960s. Several important clashes occurred between their adherents and those who supported mass society ideas (Bauer and Bauer, 1960). This is hardly surprising, since the rise of

limited-effects theory
View of media as reinforcing existing social trends and strengthening rather than threatening the status quo

administrative theories
Media theories used to guide practical decisions for various organizations

administrative research
Research that examines audiences to interpret consumer attitudes and behaviors; the use of empirical research to guide practical administrative decisions

Communism across Eastern Europe seemed to provide ample evidence that media could be used as powerful tools to meld more and more masses of individuals into an ever more powerful totalitarian state. How could the United States expect to win the Cold War unless it could somehow find a way to use mass media to confront and overcome the Soviets?

THINKING *about* **THEORY**   ADMINISTRATIVE VERSUS CRITICAL RESEARCH: THE EXAMPLE OF PRESCRIPTION DRUG ADVERTISING

Paul Lazarsfeld may well be one of social science's seminal thinkers, and his work did much to cement the limited-effects perspective in American mass communication theory, but seven decades ago he warned that overreliance on administrative research was dangerously short-sighted. He drew a distinction between administrative research—focused on mass communication's immediate, observable influence—and what he called **critical research**—asking important questions about what kind of culture results from our media use. In 1941, well before media like the Internet, cell phones that let you play interactive videogames with people on another continent, and 24-hour cable news networks, he wrote:

> Today we live in an environment where skyscrapers shoot up and elevateds [commuter trains] disappear overnight; where news comes like shock every few hours; where continually new news programs keep us from ever finding out details of previous news; and where nature is something we drive past in our cars, perceiving a few quickly changing flashes which turn the majesty of a mountain range into the impression of a motion picture. Might it not be that we do not build up experiences the way it was possible decades ago? (1941, p. 12)

You'll see elsewhere in this chapter (somewhat briefly) and in subsequent chapters (in greater detail) that despite the demands of the limited-effects perspective and its reliance on administrative research, many mass communication researchers eventually answered Lazarsfeld's call. We can see this conflict between administrative and critical research in the contemporary controversy surrounding direct-to-consumer advertising (DTCA) of prescription drugs. Market researchers, for example, conduct administrative research based on administrative theory to discover better and more

efficient ways to match products and consumers. Of course, there is nothing wrong with that. But what Lazarsfeld did consider wrong, and what he warned his colleagues in the research community against, was stopping there, thinking that there weren't other, equally if not more important questions to which they could turn their attention and skill.

The United States and New Zealand are the only nations in the world that permit DTCA. That alone, argue its critics, is enough to generate at least one obvious critical question: What is it about American culture that makes permissible here a practice that all but one of the remainder of the world's countries forbids? Nonetheless, significant amounts of administrative research have been conducted on DTCA ever since it was made legal in the early 1980s. Researchers studied how to best present important technical and medical information in a short television or radio commercial or on a magazine or newspaper page. How did doctors feel about dealing with better-informed patients? Were patients indeed better informed? Industry research indicated that consumers, as they became more aware of the existence of and options available to them for troublesome medical conditions, made better patients. DTCA-informed patients can "detect medical problems, seek treatments, and ask physicians questions" that they, the harried physicians, might not offer them on their own initiatives (Richardson and Luchsinger, 2005, p. 102). A six-year study of public reaction to DTCA by *Prevention and Men's Health* magazines (2003) showed that one-third of consumers talked to their doctors about ailments and treatments as a result of DTCA, with 29 million people doing so for the first time during that span. Consumers did not "demand" the advertised drugs, but rather they used the DTCA-provided information as the basis of inquiry and conversation. Another study, conducted by the Food and Drug

(Continued)

Administration's Division of Drug Marketing, Advertising, and Communication, surveyed doctors. Although a majority of physicians still preferred to be the sole source of drug information for their patients, 37 percent said that DTCA had a "somewhat positive" effect on their patients and practices, 3 percent said a "very positive" effect, 28 percent said no effect, and 27 percent said a "somewhat negative" effect (in Thomaselli, 2003).

But, argue many medical and mass communication researchers, there are important *critical* questions about this $5 billion-a-year-practice that deserve attention. One might be, "What happens to a society that routinely *medicalizes aspects of ordinary life?*" For example, excess weight, thinning hair, heartburn, and diminished sex drive, all natural aspects of aging, are now "diseases" treatable by well-advertised prescription drugs. Counseling researcher Lawrence Rubin has labeled this phenomenon *commodifying mental illness,* when the ailments to be alleviated are the "very common problems of shyness, sadness, nervousness, malaise, and even suspicion" because the "boundaries between discomforts of daily living and psychiatric symptomatology" are blurred "to the point that both can be equally and efficiently remedied through mass-marketed products" (Rubin, 2004, pp. 369–370).

Another set of critical questions revolves around the issue of what kind of health system is produced when DTCA is allowed to operate. Critics contend that it distorts—even perverts—the entire health care system by obfuscating the definition of *disease* itself. As medical technology writer Thomas Goetz explained, for patients, "disease puts a name to an affliction"; for doctors, "disease identifies why people are sick and suggests a course of treatment"; for medical researchers, "disease fixes an area of investigation, a mystery to be studied in the hopes of finding a cause or, perhaps, a cure"; for the pharmaceutical industry, disease is "a business model. Disease offers an opportunity to develop and market drugs that help people get better and, along the way, help companies make money" (2006, pp. 152–155).

DTCA further disrupts health care, say critics, because it frees our society from the need to find political solutions to ongoing health problems. "Where individualized solutions become prevalent, societal, population-based interventions tend to fall away, and the result is worsening health inequalities," wrote physician Iona Heath. Further disrupting the effective maintenance of public health, she argues, is the fact that

> population-based intervention favours the poor because such interventions are applied universally and the poor are the most at-risk; individually based interventions favour the rich because they are more likely to make use of what is offered.... The huge amount of money that can be made from preventative technologies has diminished the economic importance of treatment technologies.... This has meant a shift of attention from the sick to the well and from the poor to the rich. (2006, p. e146)

In other words, there is little need for school or government intervention in America's worsening childhood obesity problem because kids can simply take a pill for "metabolic syndrome," what we used to call "being overweight." As for other "ailments" treatable by heavily advertised prescription drugs, rest and diet can often alleviate many of the problems associated with RLS (restless leg syndrome), PMDD (premenstrual dysphoric disorder), FSD (female sexual dysfunction), acid reflux disease, and erectile dysfunction. Alterations in school curricula to stress interpersonal communication and public speaking skills can often reduce the number of sufferers of SAD (social anxiety disorder) and GAD (generalized anxiety disorder).

Were you aware of the kinds of administrative and critical questions that are being asked about DTCA? Which set of questions do you think has received more research attention? Do administrative research questions tend to dominate because they are more manageable, more likely to be answered by traditional postpositivist research, more likely to find financial support, less threatening to the status quo? Can you think of other reasons? What do we as a people lose when critical questions are not asked and therefore are not investigated?

critical research Asking important questions about what kind of culture results from our media use

In 1960, several classic studies of media effects (Campbell et al., 1960; Deutschmann and Danielson 1960; Klapper, 1960) provided apparently definitive support for the limited-effects notions. By 1961, V. O. Key had published *Public Opinion and American Democracy*, a theoretical and methodological tour de force integrating limited-effects notions with social and political theory to create a perspective that is now known as **elite pluralism**. This theory views democratic society as made up of interlocking pluralistic groups led by opinion leaders who rely on media for information about politics and the social world. These leaders are well informed by media even though their followers are mostly apathetic and ignorant.

elite pluralism
Theory viewing society as composed of interlocking pluralistic groups led by opinion leaders who rely on media for information about politics and the social world

In the 1950s and 1960s, advocates of mass society notions came under increasing attack from limited-effects theorists as "unscientific" or "irrational" because they questioned "hard scientific findings." Mass society notions were further discredited within academia because they became associated with the anti-Communist **Red Scare** promoted by Senator Joseph McCarthy in the early 1950s. McCarthy and his allies focused considerable attention on purging alleged Communists from the media. These purges were justified using mass society arguments—average people needed to be protected from media manipulation. Limited-effects theorists argued that average people were well protected from media influence by opinion leaders who could be trusted to filter out Communist propaganda before it reached these ordinary Americans.

Red Scare
Period in U.S. history, late 1950s to early 1960s, in which basic freedoms were threatened by searches for "Reds," or communists, in media and government

By the mid-1960s, the debate between mass society and limited-effects advocates appeared to be over—at least within the mass communication research community. The body of empirical research findings continued to grow, and almost all were consistent with the latter view. Little or no empirical research supported mass society thinking. This was not surprising, because most empirical researchers trained at this time were warned against its fallacies. For example, in the 1960s, a time of growing concern about violence in the United States and the dissolution of respect for authority, researchers and theorists from psychology, rather than mass communication, were most active and prominent in examining television's contribution to these societal ills (we will examine their efforts in Chapter 8). Many communication scientists stopped looking for powerful media effects and concentrated instead on documenting minimal, limited effects. Some of the original media researchers had become convinced that media research would never produce any important new findings and returned to work in political science or sociology.

In a controversial essay, Bernard Berelson (1959), who worked closely with Paul Lazarsfeld, declared the field of communication research to be dead. There simply was nothing left to study when it came to the mass media. Berelson argued that it was time to move on to more important work. Ironically, he wrote his essay just before the field of media research underwent explosive growth. Throughout the late 1960s and the 1970s, students flooded into university journalism schools and communication departments. As these grew, so did their faculty. As the number of faculty members increased, so did the volume of research. But was there anything left to study? Were there any important research questions that weren't already answered? Were there any important findings left to uncover? In fact, many American social science researchers believed there were. Challenge came to limited-effects theory from several fronts, primarily from psychologists and sociologists interested in media's large-scale societal influence.

FERMENT IN THE FIELD: COMPETING CULTURAL PERSPECTIVES CHALLENGE LIMITED-EFFECTS THEORY

reductionism
Reducing complex communication processes and social phenomena to little more than narrow propositions generated from small-scale investigations

neo-Marxism
Social theory asserting that media enable dominant social elites to maintain their power

British cultural studies
Perspective focusing on mass media and their role in promoting a hegemonic worldview and a dominant culture among various subgroups in a society

deterministic assumptions
Assumptions that media have powerful, direct effects

Despite these pockets of domestic resistance, most mass communication researchers in the United States still found limited-effects notions and the empirical research findings on which they were based persuasive. But challenge also came from researchers in other parts of the world who were less convinced, as you'll see in Chapter 9. Mass society notions continued to flourish in Europe, where both left-wing and right-wing concerns about the power of media were deeply rooted in World War II experiences with propaganda. Europeans were also skeptical about the power of postpositivist, quantitative social research methods to verify and develop social theory (they saw this approach to research as reductionist—reducing complex communication processes and social phenomena to little more than narrow propositions generated from small-scale investigations). This **reductionism** was widely viewed as a distinctly American fetish. Some European academics were resentful of the influence enjoyed by Americans after World War II. They argued that American empiricism was both simplistic and intellectually sterile. Although some European academics welcomed and championed American notions about media effects, others strongly resisted them and argued for maintaining approaches considered less constrained or more traditionally European.

One group of European social theorists who vehemently resisted postwar U.S. influence was the **neo-Marxists** (Hall, 1982). These left-wing social theorists argued that media enable dominant social elites to create and maintain their power. Media provide the elite with a convenient, subtle, yet highly effective means of promoting worldviews favorable to their interests. Mass media can be viewed, they contended, as a public arena in which cultural battles are fought and a dominant, or hegemonic, culture is forged and promoted. Elites dominate these struggles because they start with important advantages. Opposition is marginalized, and the status quo is presented as the only logical, rational way of structuring society. Values favored by elites are subtlety woven into and promoted by the narratives of popular programs—even children's cartoons. Within neo-Marxist theory, efforts to examine media institutions and interpret media content came to have high priority.

During the 1960s, some neo-Marxists in Britain developed a school of social theory widely referred to as **British cultural studies**. It focused heavily on mass media and their role in promoting a hegemonic worldview and a dominant culture among various subgroups in the society. Researchers studied how members of those groups used media and assessed how this use could lead people to develop ideas that supported dominant elites. This research eventually produced an important breakthrough. As they conducted postpositivist-oriented, empirical audience research, social scientists at Birmingham University discovered that people often resisted the hegemonic ideas and propagated alternative interpretations of the social world (Mosco and Herman, 1981). Although British cultural studies began with **deterministic assumptions** about the influence of media (that is, the media have powerful, direct effects), their work came to focus on audience reception studies that revived important questions about the potential power of media in certain types of situations and the ability of active audience members to resist media influence—questions that 1960s American media scholars ignored because they were skeptical about the power of media and assumed that audiences were passive.

And as we discussed in Chapter 1, while the blending of two broad categories of theory, in this case critical and postpositivist, could indeed produce useful ideas, it also left many researchers and theorists unsatisfied.

cultural criticism
Collection of perspectives concerned with the conflict of interests in society and the ways communication perpetuates domination of one group over another

During the 1970s, questions about the possibility of powerful media effects were again raised in U.S. universities. Initially, these questions were advanced by scholars in the humanities who were ignorant of the limited-effects perspective and skeptical about the usefulness of the scientific method for social research. Their arguments were routinely ignored and marginalized by social scientists because they were unsupported by "scientific evidence." Some of these scholars were attracted to European-style cultural criticism. Others attempted to create an "authentic" American school of cultural studies—though they drew heavily on Canadian scholars like Harold Innis and Marshall McLuhan (Carey, 1977). This **cultural criticism**, although initially greeted with considerable skepticism by "mainstream" effects researchers, gradually established itself as a credible and valuable alternative to limited-effects notions.

EMERGENCE OF MEANING-MAKING PERSPECTIVES ON MEDIA

Limited-effects notions have undergone important transformations, partially because of pressures from cultural studies, but also because of the emergence of new communication technologies that have forced a rethinking of traditional assumptions about how people use (and are used by) media. We are in the early stages, then, of what may well become the fourth era of mass communication theory. These new perspectives are transforming how we think about media effects.

framing theory
Assertion that people use expectations of the social world to make sense of that social world

For example, **framing theory** and the **media literacy** movement offer compelling and cogent arguments concerning the way mass communication influences individuals and plays an important role in the social world. We are again living in an era when we are challenged by the rise of powerful new media that clearly are altering how most of us live our lives and relate to others. And we have developed new research strategies and methods that provide us with better measures of media influence and that have already identified a number of contexts in which media can have powerful effects (for example, Iyengar and Kinder, 1986; Wartella, 1997).

media literacy
The ability to access, analyze, evaluate, and communicate media messages

At the heart of these new perspectives are notions about an *active audience that uses media content to create meaningful experiences*. These perspectives acknowledge that important media effects can occur over longer periods and often are a direct consequence of viewer or reader intent. People can make media serve certain purposes, such as using media to learn information, manage moods, and seek excitement. When we use media in these ways, we are intentionally working to induce meaningful experiences. The various "meaning-making perspectives" assert that when people use media to make meaning—when they are able to intentionally induce desired experiences—there often are significant results, some intended and others unintended. So when young adults download billions of songs from the net in order to alter or sustain a mood, there will be consequences. Some of these consequences are intended, but sometimes the results are unanticipated and unwanted.

Have you ever sought thrills from a horror movie and then been troubled afterward by disturbing visual images? Factors that intrude into and disrupt this making of meaning can have unpredictable consequences. These meaning-making perspectives imply that future research should focus on people's successes or failures in their efforts to make meaning using media, and on intended and unintended consequences. These consequences should be considered both from the point of view of individuals and from the point of view of society. You can read about one view of meaning-making theory in the box entitled "Semiotic Democracy."

THINKING *about* THEORY — SEMIOTIC DEMOCRACY

Interviewed just before the April 2007 broadcast of his documentary on the media's performance in the run-up to the 2003 invasion of Iraq, journalist and social critic Bill Moyers was asked what gave him hope that the American media system might better operate in the service of democracy and its people. His reply was simple: "What encourages me is the Internet. Freedom begins the moment you realize someone else has been writing your story and it's time you took the pen from his hand and started writing it yourself" ("Bill Moyers," 2007).

Twenty years earlier, British media theorist John Fiske suggested that mass communication theorists take a more culturally centered view of a different medium, television. He wrote:

> The pleasures of television are best understood not in terms of a homogeneous psychological model, but rather in those of a heterogeneous, sociocultural one. In many ways play is a more productive concept than pleasure because it asserts its activity, its creativity. Play is active pleasure: it pushes rules to the limits and explores the consequences of breaking them; centralized pleasure is more conformist. Television may well produce both sorts of pleasure, but its typical one is the playful pleasure that derives from, and enacts, that source of all power for the subordinate, the power to be different. Television's playfulness is a sign of its **semiotic democracy**, by which I mean its delegation of production of meanings and pleasures to its viewers. (1987, pp. 235–236)

The freedom to make one's own meaning (Fiske's semiotic democracy) and the availability of technology to investigate, recreate, and disseminate that meaning (Moyers' writing one's own story) are powerful pieces of evidence that we now reside firmly in the era of the meaning-making perspective of mass communication theory. Even *Time* acknowledged this reality when it named "YOU" (meaning "US") person of the year for 2007. "If the Web's first coming was all about grafting old businesses onto a new medium (pet food! On the Internet!), Web 2.0 is all about empowering individual consumers. It's not enough just to find that obscure old movie; now you can make your own film, distribute it worldwide, and find out what people think almost instantly," wrote the magazine's Jeff Howe. In today's mass communication environment, "You make it…. You name it…. You work on it…. You find it" (Howe, 2007, p. 60).

Contemporary mass communication theorists now confront a mass media system that operates in a social world where individuals and audiences can create and disseminate their own content and relish making their own meaning. This means researchers and theorists must explain, understand, or control a mass communication process in which individuals and audiences can produce their own effects—big or small, immediate or long-term, sometimes wanted, sometimes unintended.

There'll be much more to say about this in Chapter 11, but for now you should consider these questions. Can you see a link between media literacy and semiotic democracy (freedom to make personally relevant meaning)? Do either Fiske or Moyers give too much credit to people? That is, do we really enjoy making our own meaning from media content? Will we really use the Internet to write our own stories? Do you find any significance in the fact that Howe used the phrase "empowering individual *consumers*" rather than "empowering individual *citizens*"? What is it? Can you find hints of neo-Marxist theory in Fiske's comments? (Hint: Who constitutes his "subordinate"?) If so, can you explain how he and Moyers are making an essentially similar point about modern mass media and their audiences?

semiotic democracy Individuals' freedom to make their own meaning from media content

The limited-effects perspective was unable to understand or make predictions about media's role in cultural change. By flatly rejecting the possibility that media can play an important role in such change, theorists were unable to make sense of striking instances when the power of media appeared to be obvious. For example, limited-effects theorists were forced to deny that media could have played a significant role in the civil rights, anti–Vietnam War, women's, and 1960s counterculture movements. More recently, they cannot account for the media's role in such high-profile public debates as the rush to war in the wake of the 9/11 attacks and the Obama administration's campaign to reform the American healthcare system. These theorists are equally at a loss to explain the social transformations that are linked to the rise of the Internet. One possible cause of the limited-effects perspective's failure to account for these obvious examples of large-scale media influence rests in the idea of **levels of analysis.**

levels of analysis
The focus of a researcher's attention, ranging from individuals to social systems

Social research problems can be studied at a number of levels, from the **macroscopic** "down" to the **microscopic**. Researchers, for example, can study media impact on cultures, societies, or nations; organizations or groups; small groups; and individuals. It should be possible to approach the issue of media effects at any of these levels and discover comparable results. But the limited-effects researchers tend to focus their attention on the microscopic level, especially on individuals, from whom they can easily and efficiently collect data. When they have difficulty consistently demonstrating effects at the micro level, they tend to dismiss the possibility of effects at the cultural, or macroscopic, level.

macroscopic theory
Attempts to explain effects at the cultural or societal level

For example, the limited-effects perspective denies that advertising imagery can lead to significant cultural changes. Instead, it argues that advertising merely reinforces existing social trends. At best (or worst), advertisers or politicians merely take advantage of these trends to serve their purposes. Thus, political candidates might be successful in seizing on patriotism and racial backlash to promote their campaigns in much the same way that product advertisers exploit what they think are attitude trends among the baby boom generation or soccer moms. But who would deny the significant cultural changes of running political campaigns in this manner? Surely political leaders' appeals to our baser tendencies must have some effect on our democracy and our culture? Can you speak kindly of the quality of discourse exhibited in today's politics?

microscopic theory
Attempts to explain effects at the personal or individual level

The limited-effects/reinforcement arguments might have been valid, but in their early forms they were unnecessarily limited in scope. Today's meaning-making theorists have developed reinforcement notions into a broader theory that identifies important new categories of media influence. These argue that at any point in time there are many conflicting or opposing social trends. Some will be easier to reinforce using the marketing techniques available to advertisers. Potentially useful trends can be undermined as public attention is drawn toward opposing ones. From among the trends that can be easily reinforced by existing marketing techniques, advertisers and political consultants are free to base their promotional communication on those that are likely to best serve their short-term self-interests rather than the long-term public good.

Thus, many potentially constructive social trends may fail to develop because existing techniques can't easily reinforce them or because opposing trends are reinforced by advertisers seeking immediate profits (or candidates seeking immediate votes). The very same Saturday morning cartoons promoting the sale of sugared cereals could instead just as effectively encourage child viewers to consume healthier food. The very same political spot that sets race against race might just as effectively raise important issues of diversity and community. Or to return to this chapter's opening, the very same wireless Internet that can encourage the creation of new and important intellectual, cultural, and social communities unfettered by time and geography, the same technology that can provide us with virtually unlimited control over our mediated communication, can be overwhelmed by more advertising, greater commercialization, and increasing sponsor control.

For example, here, from the trade group Cellular Telecommunications and Internet Association (CTIA), is a common view of our new digital media environment: "Early adopters of the Internet were driven by a desire to capture, build, and share knowledge. It was all about capturing and sharing information." This situation has evolved for the better, proclaims the CTIA, now that we are constantly connected: "In a mobile environment, it is not about research. It is about instant gratification" (CTIA, 2004). The CTIA offered as an example of this instant gratification discount coupons sent directly to your cell phone as you walk by a store. Time and money saved as your phone alerts you to nearby bargains; what a great idea! But do you like the idea of advertisers (or the government) knowing precisely where you are every minute of the day? And just what does it mean to you as a person, to us as a people, when the Internet fully evolves from that old-fashioned medium for capturing and sharing knowledge into a new, more modern means of instant gratification? We hope that you can add dozens more questions to these two. If you do, they will be based in your experience, raised by your expectations, framed by your values. And this is exactly how questions about mass communication have always been raised and answered. This is exactly how mass communication theory has always been developed and advanced.

ONGOING DEBATE OVER ISSUES

The popularity of cultural studies and the rise of meaning-making notions have intensified disagreement over media effects. What are the consequences of routine exposure to violent images and sexual behavior in videogames? How much do television commercials for fast food and blockbuster movie tie-ins for candy and corn chips contribute to our country's epidemic of obesity? Does media coverage of important issues such as war and the economy contribute to or diminish public understanding and democratic discourse? Is there a relationship between kids' media use and poor school performance? Between consumption levels and negative health outcomes? Do sexy television shows contribute to rising rates of teen pregnancy? Does public corruption grow when town and city newspapers are forced to cut staff or close altogether? How much responsibility must teen and fashion magazines take for young girls' dissatisfaction with their physical selves? Did online music piracy kill the record industry, or did listeners tire of record companies' overreliance on formulaic music and overpriced CDs? How much freedom of the press is too much—and who gets to decide?

Even though these and a thousand similar debates can stimulate increased research and the development of better theories, they can also generate more heat than light. We must better understand why it has been so hard to come to a clear understanding of media influence and why it has been so easy to promote fallacious ideas about media.

The closing chapters of this book look at several emerging perspectives on media and how they translate into contemporary research efforts. We encourage you to use these theories to develop your own positions on the issues and to defend your views against alternate arguments. The theories in this book will remain abstract ideas until you incorporate them into your own views about media and their importance in your life. Ultimately, you are responsible for making media work for you and for guarding against negative consequences.

In the first decades of the twenty-first century, we are entering a period in history not unlike that at the close of the nineteenth—an era in which an array of innovative media technologies is being shaped into powerful new media institutions. Have we learned enough from the past to face this challenging and uncertain future? Will we merely watch as media entrepreneurs shape new media institutions to fill gaps created by the collapse of existing institutions? Or will we be part of an effort to shape new institutions that better serve our own needs and the long-term needs of the communities in which we live? We invite you to address these questions as you read this book, and we will pose them again as a final challenge.

SUMMARY

Mass communication theory, in fact all theory, is a human construction, an active effort by communities of scholars to make sense of their social world. Scholarly communities differ in what they want to accomplish with the theories they build and champion. And because mass communication theory is built during specific social and political times and in specific technological and media contexts, it is also dynamic; that is, mass communication theories are ever changing.

As such, our contemporary understanding of mass communication theory is the product of four eras of development. The era of mass society theory is characterized by overinflated fears of media's influence on "average" people and overly optimistic views of their ability to bring about social good. Powerful social and cultural elites, who saw the traditional social order that

was serving them so well undermined by popular media content, were the primary advocates of the former view. Urban elites—the new capitalists whose power was increasingly based on industrialization and urbanization—viewed technology, including the mass media, as facilitating control over the physical environment, expanding human productivity, and generating new forms of material wealth. Both ignored the fact that mass communication's power resides in the uses that people make of it.

In the second era of mass communication theory, the development of a scientific perspective on mass communication led to the emergence of the limited-effects perspective. To serve commercial clients and help defend the country from the threat of propaganda, communication researchers turned to administrative research and theory to guide their investigation of media's influence. This shift to empirical research discredited naive mass society theories as "unscientific." They were replaced with limited-effects theories that argued that because people could resist media's power and were influenced by competing factors such as friends and family, mass communication most often served to reinforce existing social trends and strengthen rather than threaten the status quo. Elite pluralism is an example of a limited-effects theory. It says that democratic society is made up of interlocking pluralistic groups led by opinion leaders who rely on media for information about politics and the social world. These opinion leaders are well informed, even though their followers are apathetic and ignorant. As a result, democracy works well.

But the idea that media could indeed have large-scale cultural influence was not dead. In this third era, mass communication theory turned toward critical and cultural studies, driven primarily by the cultural theorists of Europe who held to neo-Marxist assumptions about the wielding of power by economic and media elites. British cultural studies, focusing on mass media's role in promoting a hegemonic worldview and a dominant culture, is an example of the critical cultural theories spawned during this era.

We are in the fourth era of mass communication theory, the emergence of meaning-making perspectives. This era recognizes that mass communication can indeed be powerful, or somewhat powerful, or not powerful at all, because active audience members can (and often do) use media content to create meaningful experiences for themselves. Framing theory, asserting that people use expectations of the social world to make sense of that world, and the media literacy movement, calling for improvement in people's ability to access, analyze, evaluate, and communicate media messages, are two examples of recent meaning-making theory.

This process of mass communication theory's development has not been orderly, as you'll see, nor have all issues been settled. One continuing source of disagreement among media researchers resides in the matter of levels of analysis, where researchers focus their attention in the search for effects. Those who operate at the microscopic level search for effects on individuals. Those who work at the macroscopic level expect media's influence to manifest itself on larger social and cultural levels.

Critical Thinking Questions

1. How has convergence changed the way you interact with or use mass media? Can you identify "effects" that have occurred because of that use? Do you typically media multitask, that is, consume two or more media at the same time? If so, how do you think this influences the presence or absence of possible effects? Can you offer any possible negative effects to balance any positive effects that might have occurred from any of your media use?

2. Do you accept that mass communication significantly influences our society and culture? How do you reconcile your answer with Paul Lazarsfeld's call for increased attention to what he labeled *critical research*? Once you reach the end of this text, revisit this question to see if your thinking has changed.

3. How skilled are you at making meaning from media content? How media literate do you think you are? Do you often make meaning from content that is markedly different from that of your friends? If so, why do you suppose this happens?

Key Terms

Convergence

Wi-Fi

elites

mass society theory

penny press

yellow journalism

capitalists

limited-effects theory

administrative theories

administrative research

critical research

elite pluralism

Red Scare

reductionism

neo-Marxists

British cultural studies

deterministic assumptions

cultural criticism

framing theory

media literacy

semiotic democracy

levels of analysis

macroscopic theory

microscopic theory

THE ERA OF MASS SOCIETY AND MASS CULTURE

1833	Benjamin Day's *New York Sun* ushers in penny press
1836	Charles Babbage develops plans for a mechanical computer in England
1844	Samuel Morse invents telegraph
1876	Alexander Graham Bell invents telephone
1877	Thomas Edison demonstrates phonograph
1894	America's first movie (kinetoscope) house opens
1895	Louis and Auguste Lumière introduce single-screen motion picture exhibit William Randolph Hearst and Joseph Pulitzer embark on yellow journalism
1896	Hearst sends infamous telegram to reporter in Cuba Press services founded
1912	Radio Act of 1912 signed into law
1915	Pulitzer endows prize that bears his name
1920	KDKA goes on the air
1922	Walter Lippmann's *Public Opinion* published First commercial announcement broadcast on radio
1924	The American Society of Newspaper Editors' *Canons of Journalism* adopted
1926	NBC begins network broadcasting Talking pictures introduced
1927	Radio Act of 1927 creates the Federal Radio Commission
1928	Payne Fund's *Movies, Delinquency, and Crime* published
1929	Communications Act passes, creates the Federal Communications Commission

1938	*War of the Worlds* broadcast
1939	First public broadcast of television
1940	World War II erupts in Europe Paperback book introduced in the United States Paul Lazarsfeld's voter studies begin in Erie County, Ohio
1941	United States enters World War II British develop first binary computer
1942	Carl Hovland conducts first war propaganda research British develop Colossus, the first electronic digital computer, to break German war code
1945	World War II ends Gordon Allport and Leo Postman's rumor study published
1946	John Mauchly and John Atanasoff introduce ENIAC, the first "full-service" electronic digital computer
1947	Hutchins Commission issues report on press freedom The Hollywood Ten called before the House Un-American Activities Committee

THE RISE OF MEDIA INDUSTRIES AND MASS SOCIETY THEORY

CHAPTER 3

Singer Janet Jackson's "wardrobe malfunction" during the halftime show of the 2004 Super Bowl football game reinflamed the endless debate about media's corrupting influence on society. Jackson's three-quarters-of-a-second of exposed breast produced congressional hearings on indecency in broadcasting and Kansas Republican senator Sam Brownback's claim that the pop star's momentarily bared breast "gave ammunition to terrorists in the 'cultural war' being waged in Iraq" (Eggerton, 2004, p. 1). The Federal Communication Commission's subsequent crackdown on offensive content, including even "fleeting expletives" (offhand, live comments caught on air), was eventually upheld in a 5 to 4 2009 Supreme Court decision highlighted by Justice Antonin Scalia's written dismay over "foul-mouthed glitteratae from Hollywood" and the "coarsening of public entertainment" (Savage, 2009, p. A4).

Peek-a-boo half-time singers and cursing celebrities were not the only media effects controversies of the first decade of the new century. Among other things, the American Psychological Association issued a national report documenting and condemning the "increasing commercialization of childhood" (Kunkel et al., 2004); the scientific journal *Pediatrics* published one report tying teens' consumption of online and other media violence to subsequent "seriously violent behavior" (Ybarra et al., 2008) and another linking exposure to sexual content on television to teen pregnancy (Chandra et al., 2008); the journal *Archives of Pediatrics & Adolescent Medicine* presented evidence of lagging language development in children as a result of infant television viewing (Bryner, 2009); *Circulation: Journal of the American Heart Association* published research demonstrating that every daily hour spent watching television was linked to an 18 percent greater risk of dying from heart disease, an 11 percent greater risk from all causes of death, and a 9 percent greater risk of death from cancer (Dunstan et al., 2010); boycotts were called against the Campbell Soup Company because its ad in the gay magazine *The Advocate* gave "approval to the entire homosexual agenda" (Edwards, 2009); and boycotts were also called against the NBC television network because of its coverage of the 2008 Athens Olympic Games, which showed actors in bodysuits depicting "indecent" Greek classical nude statues (Epps, 2008).

A televised fraction-of-a-second glimpse of a woman's breast corrupts the culture and gives aid to those killing American soldiers in the Middle East? An occasional broadcast swear word produces a coarsened culture? Advertising can recruit children to the cause of materialism, condemning them to living childhood as little consumers-in-training? Watching television and going online creates violent kids, gets teens pregnant, stunts language acquisition, and increases the risk of death? Magazine ads lead to homosexuality, and televised Olympic Opening Ceremonies are offensive? Some say yes; some say no.

For more than a century now, the role of media has been debated. Conservatives lament the decline of values sped by a liberal media elite. Liberals fear the power of a media system more in tune with the conservative values of its owners than of its audiences. The school boards and city councils of hundreds of towns have debated installing filtering software on school and library computers, pitting advocates of free expression against proponents of child protection. Journalistic organizations willingly ceded much of their freedom to cover and report news of the war on terrorism to the military with little public outcry. Controversial rappers are celebrated on television while their music is banned on scores of radio stations because it is considered racist and misogynistic. Think-tanks on the political right and left ponder the contribution of talk radio to increases in ethnic and racial intolerance. A blue-ribbon panel recommends that the networks be forbidden from predicting the winners in political elections because those announcements keep people away from the polls. Media industries promise their sponsors significant impact for their advertising dollars but claim their fare has little or no influence when challenged on issues of violence, gender stereotyping, and drugs. Every company, government agency, and nonprofit group of any size maintains or retains a public relations operation. Why would anyone bother if media have little or no impact? Why would the **First Amendment** to our Constitution, our "First Freedom," protect the expression of media industries if they have no influence? Why do we grant media outlets and their personnel special protection if their contributions to our society are so insignificant?

First Amendment
Guarantees freedom of speech, press, assembly, and religion

OVERVIEW

Clearly, a lot is at stake when we debate the role of media. Controversy over media influence can have far-reaching consequences for society and for media institutions. In this chapter, we will trace the rise and fall of *mass society theory,* a perspective on society that emerged at the end of the nineteenth century and was influential through the first half of the twentieth century. As we explained in Chapter 2, mass society theory is an all-encompassing perspective on Western industrial society that attributes an influential but largely negative role to media. It views media as having the power to profoundly shape our perceptions of the social world and to manipulate our actions, often without our conscious awareness. This theory assumes that media influence must be controlled. The strategies for control, however, are as varied as the theorists who offer them.

As we review the rise of mass society theory, we will highlight central assumptions and arguments, many of which have failed the test of time or of scientific study.

Some issues first raised by mass society theorists still deserve attention. We will return to these arguments in later chapters and see how contemporary media critics have used them.

The debate over media that we trace in this chapter is one aspect of what some scholars have termed a **culture war**. This "war" is actually a society-wide debate concerning the cultural foundations of the broader social order in which we all live. The participants in this debate are drawn from all segments of society. Media entrepreneurs are key players in this debate, because they have an important stake in it. Production and distribution of some forms of content, such as violent or sexually explicit material, can earn large profits for these entrepreneurs. This content is controversial because it challenges and threatens to subvert the cultural norms and values of some groups in the larger society. So when entrepreneurs choose to produce and widely distribute content, their actions are opposed by the leaders of groups whose norms and values are challenged. All sides claim the moral high ground in this struggle over culture. Media entrepreneurs use a variety of arguments to defend their actions: We live in a free society where citizens should be able to have access to whatever fare they want; media are only assisting people so they can exercise this freedom. Media defenders also argue that there is no clear evidence that controversial content is harmful even if it is offensive. Finally, they embrace the freedom granted in the First Amendment to the Constitution. They remind their critics that this freedom is fundamental to democracy.

Critics answer these arguments by defending the norms and values they see as under attack. They argue that their groups will be harmed by distribution of immoral content. They charge that when press freedom is abused, when what they consider higher values are threatened, then media must be censored. But, just who determines which values are higher and who determines when they have been threatened so severely that censorship is necessary?

culture war
Struggle to define the cultural foundation of the broader social order in which we live

THE BEGINNINGS

In 1896, William Randolph Hearst, a prominent newspaper publisher, sent an illustrator to Cuba to cover the possible outbreak of war against Spain. Historian Frank Luther Mott (1941, pp. 527–537) reported that the artist, upon his arrival, sent this telegram:

> HEARST, JOURNAL, NEW YORK
> EVERYTHING IS QUIET. THERE IS NO TROUBLE HERE. THERE
>   WILL BE NO WAR. WISH TO RETURN.

The publisher's reply was quick and to the point:

> PLEASE REMAIN. YOU FURNISH THE PICTURES AND I'LL
>   FURNISH THE WAR. HEARST.

At the time, Hearst was publisher of one of the largest newspapers in New York City as well as head of a chain of papers stretching as far west as San Francisco. He was a leader in the dominant medium of his era—the mass newspaper. Every city on the U.S. East Coast had several large, highly competitive papers, as did major cities across the continent. Competition, unfortunately, encouraged irresponsibility. Most urban newspapers resembled today's weekly supermarket scandal sheets like the *National Enquirer*.

Although there is new scholarship (Campbell, 2010) questioning whether Hearst actually did send an illustrator to Havana to make up war stories that would sell papers, his irresponsibility, apocryphal or otherwise, triggered harsh critical response. The first mass media theories developed as a reaction against such practices—in other words, against the excesses of a rapidly maturing, highly competitive media industry.

This was a turbulent era in world history, one characterized by enormous social change. Industrialization and urbanization were reshaping both Europe and the United States. Most of this change was made possible by the invention and then rapid dissemination of new forms of technology. But technological change occurred with little consideration for its environmental, social, or psychological impact.

As with every instance of rapid social change, new social elites emerged, challenging the power of existing elites. In the late 1800s, increasing social control was wielded by a handful of industrial entrepreneurs—men who created vast monopolies based on factories, railroads, and the exploitation of natural resources. These men were respected and feared. Some were denounced as robber barons because they used questionable business practices to amass large fortunes. The social change they wrought could be rationalized as progress, but a high price was paid: workers were brutalized, vast urban slums were created, and huge tracts of wilderness were ravaged.

Media were among the many technologies that shaped and were shaped by this modern era. An industrial social order had great need for the fast and efficient distribution of information. The advantages of new media like the telegraph and telephone were soon recognized, and each new communication technology was quickly adopted—first by businesses and then by the public. During the 1860s, the telegraph was to the Civil War what twenty-four-hour cable news networks like CNN were to the war in Iraq: It helped fuel and then satisfy widespread public interest in fast-breaking news coverage of the conflict. By the time the Civil War ended, the telegraph had spawned a number of **wire services**—the first electronically based media networks—supplying news to affiliated papers spread across the nation.

wire services
News organizations that provide content to subscribing media outlets

In the mid- and late nineteenth century, large urban populations' growing demand for cheap media content drove the development of several new media: the penny press, the nickel magazine, and the dime novel. High-speed printing presses and Linotype machines made it practical to mass-produce the printed word at very low cost. Urban newspapers boomed all along the East Coast and in major trading centers across the United States. Newspaper circulation wars broke out in many large cities and led to the development of *yellow journalism,* a form of journalism that seriously challenged the norms and values of most readers.

Intense competition swept aside many small-circulation and more specialized print media. By increasing accessibility through lower prices, however, the new mass newspapers were able to serve people who had never before had easy access to print. Many papers succeeded because they attracted large numbers of readers in urban slums: first-generation immigrants, barely literate in English, who wanted their piece of the American dream. But these readers were not attracted by lengthy treatises on important events of the day. They bought papers to read comic strips, follow sports, and read largely fictitious accounts of trivial happenings.

THE RISE OF YELLOW JOURNALISM

At the beginning of the twentieth century, every industry had its barons, and the most notorious—if not the greatest—of the press lords was Hearst. Hearst specialized in buying up failing newspapers and transforming them into profitable enterprises. He demonstrated that the news business could be as profitable as railroads, steel, or oil. One secret to his success was devising better strategies for luring low-income readers. His newspapers combined a low-selling price with innovative new forms of content that included lots of pictures, serialized stories, and comic strips. Some experts even say that yellow journalism got its name from one of the first comic strips: "The Yellow Kid."

Like most yellow journalists, Hearst had little respect for reporting accuracy. His papers routinely overdramatized even the most mundane events. With other New York newspaper publishers, Hearst was blamed for initiating, through inflammatory coverage, the Spanish–American War in 1898, goading Congress into declaring war over an unexplained explosion on the battleship *Maine*. Hearst's telegram to his illustrator (real or not) embodies much of what was wrong with yellow journalism. Reporters typically gathered only sketchy details about events and turned them over to editors who wrote exaggerated and largely fictitious accounts. Not surprisingly, during this period the public status of reporters was among the lowest for any profession or trade. By contrast, the printers who operated high-speed presses enjoyed greater respect as skilled technicians.

CYCLES OF MASS MEDIA DEVELOPMENT AND DECLINE

The rise of mass media in the 1900s followed a pattern of industrial development that has been duplicated following every subsequent "revolution" in media technology. Whenever important new media technologies appear, they destabilize existing media industries, forcing large-scale and often very rapid restructuring. Large corporations based on old technologies go into precipitous decline while a handful of the upstart companies reaps enormous profits. We are witnessing another repetition of this cycle with the rise of Microsoft, Google, YouTube, Facebook, and Twitter, just a few of the new media giants challenging older media companies whose income is derived from television, radio, and newspapers. To survive, older media corporations are forced into cutthroat competition with each other and with the companies that use new technology to deliver content to audiences. Sometimes they succeed in preventing rapid decline, but more often they fail.

functional displacement
When the functions of an existing medium are replaced by a newer technology, the older medium finds new functions

This process is called **functional displacement**. For example, over the past two decades we have witnessed the steady erosion of network television viewership brought about by the growing popularity of cable and satellite television, DVDs, and the Internet. At the same time, we are seeing the rise of new video content providers, scores of cable channels and online news and entertainment outlets such as CNN, MSNBC, FOX News, Atom.com, Funny or Die, Salon, Huffington Post, The Onion, and the iStore. The movie industry has experienced a strong resurgence fueled by profits from DVDs, on-demand movies, and suburban theater revenues. Functional displacement theory argues that if network television is to survive amid all this change, it must find functions that it can serve better than any of the newer media. Most corporations controlling network television have already diversified their holdings and purchased companies that operate the new media. For example, whereas there was once NBC Television, there is now NBC Universal Television Studios, NBC Universal Television Distribution, the NBC Television Network, 27 local television stations, NBC Digital Media, cable channels MSNBC (produced in conjunction with Microsoft), Bravo, Mun2TV, Trio, USA, and SyFy, all-news cable channel CNBC, Spanish-language television network Telemundo and its 14 stations, World Wide Web sites for each of these holdings, partial ownership of Internet video site Hulu, cable and satellite companies in Europe and Asia, and theme parks used to promote NBC television programs. In 2010, these entities became part of Comcast, the nation's largest cable company and biggest provider of broadband Internet into American homes. CBS, through its parent company, Viacom, and ABC, through its parent, Disney, are also linked to a long list of other media enterprises.

The success of new media often brings a strong critical reaction—especially when media adopt questionable competitive strategies to produce content or attract consumers. During the era of the penny press, mass newspapers quickly displaced small-circulation, specialized papers, and many did so using highly suspect formulas for creating content. These strategies became even more questionable as competition increased for the attention of readers. Compared to yellow journalism, current-day "trash TV" programs like *Cops, Real Housewives of New Jersey,* and *Jersey Shore* are as tame as fluffy puppies. But yellow journalists justified their practices by arguing that "everyone else is doing it" and "the public likes it or else they wouldn't buy it—we're only giving the people what they want."

New media industries often do specialize in giving people what they want—even if the long-term consequences might be negative. We see this in the current controversies over online indecency and hate speech. Unlike the "established" older media, new media lack the ties to other traditional social institutions that encourage or compel social responsibility. As each of the new media technologies developed, and as industries grew up around them to ensure stable supplies of attractive (if questionable) content, these technologies and industries necessarily displaced earlier industries and forms of communication. Often social roles and relationships were seriously disrupted as people adjusted to new media and their content. Most of these problems were seemingly impossible to anticipate. For example, during the 1950s, one of the first serious sociological studies of television's impact on American life found little evidence of disruption. The study noted that one of the most important changes brought about by television was that people spent less time playing cards with extended family members or friends. On the other hand, nuclear families actually spent more time together—mesmerized in front of the ghostly shadows on tiny television screens. They spent less time talking with neighbors and friends. Research by Wilbur Schramm, Jack Lyle, and Edwin Parker (1961) reported optimistically that towns with television actually had higher levels of library use and lower comic book sales than those with only radio. Given widespread public distrust of comic books in the 1950s, these findings implied that television could be a positive force. We see this pattern mirrored today—those who argue that the Internet will eventually produce a return to greater participatory democracy counter critics of controversial online content. Some critics of the Internet worry that it will encourage social isolation, whereas proponents celebrate the power of instant messaging and social networking websites to keep people connected.

As media industries mature, they often become more socially responsible—more willing to censor or limit distribution of controversial content and more concerned about serving long-term public needs rather than pandering to short-term popular passions. Cynics say that responsibility is achieved only when it will enhance rather than impede profit making; that is, responsibility is possible only when cutthroat competition gives way to **oligopoly**—a handful of surviving companies stop competing and agree to carve up the market and the profits. In this situation, companies can turn their attention to public relations and eliminate the most offensive content production practices (and, incidentally, ward off formal regulation).

oligopoly
The concentration of increasing numbers of media businesses in the hands of a few large companies

During the 1920s, two of the most powerful yellow journalists did just that, reforming so much that they succeeded in making their names synonymous with public service rather than bad journalism. The Pulitzer Prize and the work of the Hearst Foundation are widely (and properly) credited with advancing the professionalization of journalism and raising the ethical standards of the industry. Also during this decade, the American Society of Newspaper Editors was formed and pledged to "tell the truth about the news" in its famous *Canons of Journalism* (Schramm, 1960, pp. 623–625). An irresponsible new media industry had transformed itself and come of age. Again, we see this process in effect today. Most of the major Internet content providers willingly submit their sites to evaluation and coding tied to popular and freely distributed content-rating software, touting their commitment to meeting public concerns over privacy and decency. After YouTube was purchased by Google, presumably becoming less "guerilla" and more legitimate, it began to more systematically monitor content posted to its website and has greatly increased the amount of content that it removes or to which it restricts access.

The history of mass media in the United States has been one of ebb and flow between periods dominated by mature, socially responsible media industries and competitive eras characterized by innovative and sometimes irresponsible practices. About the time that competition among mass newspapers was finally brought under control, publishers faced challenges from powerful new entertainment media—records, movies, and radio.

As these newer industries grew, they also experienced periods of intense competition that tested or crossed moral and ethical boundaries. Censorship of the movie industry was hotly debated throughout the 1930s. Government control of radio was widely and frequently advocated. In time, each industry matured and carved out a particular niche in the overall market for media content. Each developed codes of ethics and procedures for applying these codes. In almost every case, these new industries faced serious threats of government regulation and censorship. In response, they chose to engage in self-regulation and self-censorship rather than accept external controls. Of course, their self-imposed propriety was much less restrictive than proposed government regulations, and the penalties for violation were less serious. The rapid spread of television in the 1950s brought another major restructuring of media. Today, yet another set of powerful communication technologies is transforming media. Personal computers and smart cell phones deliver ever-increasing amounts of information anywhere we happen to be via the Internet and World Wide Web. In less than a decade, these media have proven to be fundamental, even existential, threats to the survival of newspapers, broadcast media, and the recording industry.

To meet the challenge of the Web, for example, the recording industry initially followed a strategy that had failed many times in the past. It attacked the new media and their users, prosecuting for copyright violation people who downloaded and shared music from the Internet, bringing lawsuits against Internet service providers and music-sharing services to force them to stop users from sharing music, and imbedding its music with **digital rights management** code, rendering it impossible to be copied for personal use or shared even if legally purchased (and therefore encouraging even more illegal music downloading). Newspapers brought similar litigation against radio stations in the 1920s, when it was common practice for broadcasters to read newspaper stories on the air. The Hollywood studios futilely spent twenty years and millions of dollars using an array of legal strategies to fight the rise of television. In the same way (and with the same results), television went to court to stop cable television's development, cable went to court to stop the growth of direct satellite systems, Hollywood and the television industry went to court to stop the spread of videocassette technology ("The VCR is to the American film producer and the American public as the Boston Strangler is to the woman home alone," an industry executive told Congress in 1982; quoted in Barmann, 2004, p. E8), the recording industry went to court to limit the availability of digital audiotape, and all the traditional media are now in court fighting the diffusion of digital video recording systems such as TiVo. Functional displacement may be slowed, but past history indicates that it can't be stopped by lawsuits.

The most powerful forces influencing restructuring in American media industries are technological change, content innovation, and consumer demand. None of these operates independently. During eras of rapid change such as we are now experiencing, innovations in media technology force (or permit) rapid alterations in both the form and type of media content we receive. Our demand for this content is also changing. Old media-use habits break down and new habits form as emerging media provide new choices in content. Some of us rent more and more DVDs, but others prefer cable television offerings or video downloaded on home computers. Many of us get our news from television and radio, but growing numbers of us go online for our information about the doings of the world. Our use of the Google search engine has made *Google* a verb (as in "to Google someone") and has created a multibillion-dollar enterprise.

digital rights management
Electronic protection of digitally distributed media content

MASS SOCIETY CRITICS AND THE DEBATE OVER MEDIA

With every change in the media industries, media critics have emerged to pose questions about unethical practices and to voice concern about long-term negative consequences. These critics raise important and appropriate issues. During the early stages of development or restructuring, media industries are especially susceptible to complaint. Although this criticism is often warranted, we must recognize that many of the critics are not neutral observers having only the best interest of the public in mind. Most critics are not objective scientists or dispassionate humanists relying on systematic observation or well-developed theory for their positions. Rather, their criticisms are to some extent rooted in their own self-interests.

You can evaluate the criticism that accompanied the diffusion of media we now find commonplace in the box entitled "Fearful Reactions to New Media."

Even when individual critics are selfless, they are increasingly likely to be paid by special interests for their work. Often their ideas or their research would go unnoticed without promotion by special interests. For example, when television began to compete with newspapers, the latter were filled with stories reporting the complaints of television critics and researchers. During the 1970s, much of the research critical of children's television would have gone unnoticed by the general public had it not been for the promotional work of Action for Children's Television, a grassroots activist organization heavily reliant on grants from the Markle, Ford, and Carnegie Foundations.

THINKING *about* THEORY — FEARFUL REACTIONS TO NEW MEDIA

The introduction of each new mass medium of the twentieth century was greeted with derision, skepticism, fear, and sometimes silliness. Here is a collection of the thinking of the times that welcomed movies, talkies, radio, and television. Can you find examples of mass society theory's most obvious characteristics—the conceit that the elite way is the right way and condescension toward others?

Once you have read through these examples, go online or to the library and find similar dire predictions about the Internet and the Web. No doubt you've already read or heard concerns about Internet addiction, loss of parental authority, child pornography, online gambling, poor writing skills and "mall speak" from instant messenging, the loss of community, reduced attention spans, violent and offensive online gaming, privacy invasion, and identity theft. Can you identify other concerns associated with the coming of the new communication technologies?

Movies and Talkies

When you first reflect that in New York City alone, on a Sunday, 500,000 people go to moving picture shows, a majority of them perhaps children, and that in the poorer quarters of town every teacher testifies that the children now save their pennies for picture shows instead of candy, you cannot dismiss canned drama with a shrug of contempt. It is a big factor in the lives of the masses, to be reckoned with, if possible to be made better, if used for good ends. Eighty

percent of present day theatrical audiences in this country are canned drama audiences. Ten million people attended professional baseball games in America in 1908. Four million people attend moving pictures theaters, it is said, every day. $50,000,000 are invested in the industry. Chicago has over 300 theaters, New York 300, St. Louis 205, Philadelphia 186, even conservative Boston boasts more than 30. Almost 190 miles of film are unrolled on the screens of America's canned drama theaters every day in the year. Here is an industry to be controlled, an influence to be reckoned with.

Source: *American Magazine*, September, 1909, p. 498.

And if the speech recorded in the dialogue (of talking pictures) is vulgar or ugly, its potentialities for lowering the speech standard of the country are almost incalculable. The fact that it is likely to be heard by the less discriminating portion of the public operates to increase its evil effects; for among the regular attendants at moving picture theaters there are to be found large groups from among our foreign-born population, to whom it is really vitally important that they hear only the best speech.

Source: *Commonweal*, April 10, 1929, p. 653.

Radio

In general one criterion must be kept in mind: the radio should do what the teacher cannot do;

(Continued)

THINKING about THEORY | FEARFUL REACTIONS TO NEW MEDIA (CONTINUED)

it ought not to do what the teacher can do better. However radio may develop, I cannot conceive of the time when a good teacher will not continue to be the most important object in any classroom.

Source: *Education*, December, 1936, p. 217.

Is radio to become a chief arm of education? Will the classroom be abolished, and the child of the future stuffed with facts as he sits at home or even as he walks about the streets with his portable receiving set in his pocket?

Source: *Century*, June, 1924, p. 149.

Television

Seeing constant brutality, viciousness and unsocial acts results in hardness, intense selfishness, even in mercilessness, proportionate to the amount of exposure and its play on the native temperament of the child. Some cease to show resentment to insults, to indignities, and even

cruelty toward helpless old people, to women and other children.

Source: *New Republic*, November 1, 1954, p. 12.

Here, in concept at least, was the most magnificent of all forms of communication. Here was the supreme triumph of invention, the dream of the ages—something that could bring directly into the home a moving image fused with sound-reproducing action, language, and thought without the loss of measurable time. Here was the magic eye that could bring the wonders of entertainment, information and education into the living room. Here was a tool for the making of a more enlightened democracy than the world had ever seen. Yet out of the wizardry of the television tube has come such an assault against the human mind, such a mobilized attack on the imagination, such an invasion against good taste as no other communications medium has known, not excepting the motion picture or radio itself.

Source: *Saturday Review*, December 24, 1949, p. 20.

Changes in media industries typically increase the pressure on other social institutions to change. Instability in the way we routinely communicate has unsettling consequences for all other institutions. Typically, the leaders of these institutions resent external pressures and are reluctant to change their way of doing things. In our society, critics have interpreted the rise of the media industries as threatening every other social institution, including political, religious, business, military, and educational institutions. The constant calls for overhauling political campaign financing are only one example. Social critics even accuse media of profoundly altering families—the most basic social institution of all.

It's hardly surprising, then, that leaders of these social institutions, and the special interest groups they sponsor, have raised a constant stream of concern about the power and harmful impact of media. As new media develop, critics fight to prevent their growth or to control their structure. For example, the development of television and later cable television were frozen for several years while the Federal Communications Commission listened to the arguments of industry critics. Although it is unfair to place all this criticism into a single category, many of the views expressed are consistent with mass society theory. This venerable theory has a long and checkered history. Mass society theory is actually many different theories sharing some common assumptions about the role of media and society.

ASSUMPTIONS OF MASS SOCIETY THEORY

Mass society theory first appeared late in the nineteenth century as various traditional social elites struggled to make sense of the disruptive consequences of modernization. Some (that is, the landed aristocracy, small-town shopkeepers, schoolteachers, the clergy, upper-class politicians) lost power or were overwhelmed in their efforts to deal with social problems. For them, the mass media were symbolic of all that was wrong with modern society. Mass newspapers of the yellow journalism era were viewed as gigantic, monopolistic enterprises employing unethical practices to pander to semiliterate mass audiences. Leaders in education and religion resented media's power to attract readers using content they considered highly objectionable, vulgar, even sinful (Brantlinger, 1983).

The rise of the mass press after 1840 posed a direct threat to the political and business establishment. Political newspapers were swept aside by the penny press in the 1840s and 1850s and then buried by the yellow journalism of the 1880s and 1890s. The political ambitions of the leading yellow journalist, Hearst, posed a very real threat to established politicians and businessmen. Hearst was a populist of his own devising—a man likely to pursue whatever cause would increase his personal popularity and power, even at the expense of the professional politicians around him. Hearst papers joined with other mass newspapers and magazines in producing sensational news stories that savagely attacked opponents in business and government. These accounts had strong reader appeal and came to be more feared by their targets than today's *60 Minutes* crew.

Envy, discontent, and outright fear were often at the roots of mass society thinking. These emotions undergirded the development of a theory that is both radically conservative and potentially revolutionary. It fears the emergence of a new type of social order—a mass society—that would fundamentally and tragically transform the social world. To prevent this, technological change generally and changes in media specifically must be controlled or even reversed. A conservative effort must be made to restore an idealized, older social order, or revolutionary action must be taken so that technology and media are brought under elite control and used to forge a new and better social order.

Mass society theory makes several basic assumptions about individuals, the role of media, and the nature of social change. Here we list these assumptions and then discuss each in some detail:

1. The media are a powerful force within society that can subvert essential norms and values and thus undermine the social order. To deal with this threat media must be brought under elite control.
2. Media are able to directly influence the minds of average people, transforming their views of the social world.
3. Once people's thinking is transformed by media, all sorts of bad long-term consequences are likely to result—not only bringing ruin to individual lives but also creating social problems on a vast scale.
4. Average people are vulnerable to media because in mass society they are cut off and isolated from traditional social institutions that previously protected them from manipulation.

5. The social chaos initiated by media will likely be resolved by establishment of a totalitarian social order.

6. Mass media inevitably debase higher forms of culture, bringing about a general decline in civilization.

The first assumption is that the media subvert essential norms and values and threaten the social order. Thus, elite control of media is necessary. Opponents of the new media have consistently proposed turning control of them over to elites who will preserve or transform the social order. In Europe, this argument won out during the 1920s, and broadcast media were placed under the control of government agencies. These efforts had disastrous consequences when Hitler narrowly won election in Germany. His Nazi party quickly turned radio into an effective propaganda tool that helped consolidate his power. In the United States, many schemes were proposed in the 1920s that would have turned control of broadcasting over to churches, schools, or government agencies. Ultimately, a compromise was reached and a free-enterprise broadcasting industry was created under the more-or-less watchful eye of a government agency—the Federal Radio Commission, which later evolved into the Federal Communications Commission. Until World War II, the compromise involved allowing nonprofit and government agencies to produce a large amount of programming that was broadcast by the radio networks during prime listening hours.

But why are the media so dangerous to society? What makes them threatening? How are they able to subvert traditional norms and values? A second assumption is that media have the power to reach out and directly influence the minds of average people so that their thinking is transformed (Davis, 1976). This is also known as the **direct-effects assumption** and has been hotly debated since the 1940s. James Carey offered this accurate articulation of mass society theory's view of the influence of mass communication: "The media collectively, but in particularly the newer, illiterate media of radio and film, possessed extraordinary power to shape the beliefs and conduct of ordinary men and women" (1996, p. 22). Although each version of mass society theory has its own notion about the type of direct influence different media may have, all versions stress how dangerous this influence can be and the extreme vulnerability of average people to immediate media-induced changes. Average citizens are thought to be helpless before the manipulative power of media content. For several generations now, critics have envisioned innocent audiences of teenagers succumbing to gangster movies or rock-and-roll or rap or videogames, gullible farmers converted to Fascism or Communism by radio propagandists, naive grade-school children victimized by comic books or the Teletubbies, unsuspecting adults transformed magically into couch potatoes by the power of *Survivor* and *Lost,* mentally impaired elderly folks handing over their last dime to televised insurance hucksters or greedy televangelists, and hate-filled misfits fueling social discord with racist online treatises.

Although it is not hard to locate isolated examples that illustrate every one of these conditions, it is misleading to regard any one of them as widespread. When empirical researchers tried to measure the pervasiveness of effects like these in the 1940s and 1950s, they were surprised to discover how difficult it was to develop conclusive evidence. People simply were not as vulnerable to direct manipulation

direct-effects assumption

The media, in and of themselves, can produce direct effects

as mass society critics wanted to assume. Often empirical researchers found that other factors block direct media influence or severely limit it.

The third assumption is that once media transform people's thinking, all sorts of bad long-term consequences result—not only bringing ruin to individual lives but also creating social problems on a vast scale (Marcuse, 1941). Over the years, virtually every major social problem we have confronted has been linked in some way to media—from prostitution and delinquency to urban violence and drug usage to the "defeat" in Vietnam and our loss of national pride. Tramps in the gutter have had their work ethic destroyed by reading trashy novels. Teenage delinquents have seen too many gangster movies. Disaffected housewives watched too many soap operas, teenage girls hate their bodies because of beauty magazines, and drug addicts have taken too seriously the underlying message in most advertising: the good life is achieved through consumption of a product, not by hard work. There is some truth in these criticisms, but they are also misleading. Media are only one of the many technologies that have shaped and continue to shape modern life. For these criticisms to be constructive, they must go beyond sweeping assertions. In later chapters we will discuss how it is possible to construct more useful theories addressing these problems by identifying the many factors related to media use and media influence. Unfortunately, most early mass society theory failed to do this, and many present-day critics repeat this error.

Mass society theory's fourth assumption is that average people are vulnerable to media because they have been cut off and isolated from traditional social institutions that previously protected them from manipulation (Kreiling, 1984). The early mass society theorists idealized the past and had romantic visions of what life must have been like in medieval villages in Europe. Older social orders were thought to have nurtured and protected people within communities whose culture gave meaning to their lives. Although these views have some validity (most social orders have some redeeming qualities), they neglect to consider the severe limitations of traditional premodern social orders. Most premodern social orders limited individual development and creativity for most community members. People were routinely compelled to do the jobs their parents and grandparents had done. People learned specific social roles based on the accident of being born in a certain place at a certain time. The freedom to develop ourselves in ways that we find meaningful was unknown. Folk communities were essentially closed systems in which traditional culture structured social life from generation to generation. Even now, for example, we hear people speak longingly of the traditional values of pretelevision America. But small-town America of the 1930s, 1940s, and 1950s afforded few opportunities to minorities, confined most women to homemaker roles, limited access to higher education to a small elite, and imposed a host of other conditions that we now view as unacceptable, if not unimaginable.

Yet the claims that mass society theorists make about the vulnerability to manipulation of isolated individuals are compelling. These arguments have been restated in endless variations with every revolution in media technology. They assert that when people are stripped of the protective cocoon provided by the traditional community, they necessarily turn to media for the guidance and reassurance previously provided by their communities. Thus when people leave sheltered rural communities and enter big cities, media can suddenly provide communication that replaces messages from social institutions that have been left behind. Media can become the trusted and valued sources of messages about politics, entertainment, religion, education, and on and on. Thus, in the urban slums of nineteenth-century America, as in twenty-first-century suburbia, news media compete to be our friendly neighbors: "It's like hearing it from a friend." Scholars who have studied the penny press and yellow journalism have argued that part of their success was based on informal accounts of trivial events that effectively substituted for (functionally replaced) small-town gossip (McIntyre, 1975).

If you are skeptical about these mass society arguments, you might consider your personal situation. Or you can look at your peers. In our social order, young adults are expected to leave the sheltering influence of their families and communities. Unlike tradition-bound social orders, we expect that young adults can and should seek new places where they can "find themselves" and develop new views of the social world. They typically leave their homes and go away to college or to places where they might find work. They are allowed or even expected to develop personal identities that are independent of their families. When individuals face these types of changes in their lives, they usually deal with them through various forms of communication. How have you dealt with these changes? What about your peers? Did you anticipate college life by reading about it, seeing movies, talking about it with siblings or friends in college? Since starting college, have you used social networking websites to stay in touch with high school friends or to assist you in communicating with a network of college friends? Are you using media to explore how to develop your personal identity—to assess what you find meaningful and valuable? What sorts of personal identities are encouraged by social networking websites that give prominence to partying or sports?

The disintegration of traditional communities has unquestionably provided many opportunities for media entrepreneurs. For example, storytelling was an important form of entertainment in many folk communities. As these communities declined, a market opened up for different forms of mediated entertainment such as movies, television, and videos. Should mass media be blamed for luring people away from folk communities by offering more powerful forms of entertainment? Or were media simply providing people with attractive content at a time when folk communities had lost their ability to control their members? Trends toward social isolation continue. Today, millions of American children grow up in single-parent households where the parent often feels forced to rely on television as a convenient, low-cost babysitter. We can be nostalgic about two-parent households, but it is more useful to work to understand and deal with the reality of what happens when children grow up with the tube as their most constant companion.

It is also useful to recognize that the influence of media can fluctuate sharply in relatively short periods. Certain media can indeed play more important roles during times of social instability or national crisis. But this doesn't mean that they are routinely or consistently dominant in comparison with other institutions or organizations.

The fifth assumption is that the social chaos initiated by media will be resolved by establishment of a totalitarian social order (Davis, 1976). This assumption was developed during the 1930s and reached its peak of popularity in the United States during the Red Scare of the 1950s. Mass society is envisioned as an inherently chaotic, highly unstable form of social order that will inevitably collapse and then be replaced by totalitarianism. Mass society, with its teeming hordes of isolated individuals, must give way to an even worse form of society—highly regimented, centrally controlled, totalitarian society. Thus, to the extent that media promote the rise of mass society, they increase the likelihood of totalitarianism.

From 1930 to 1960, mass society theorists outlined a classic scenario for the degeneration of mass society into totalitarianism. This scenario describes rather accurately, for example, the rise of Adolf Hitler in Germany. In times of rapid and chaotic social change, demagogues arise who promise average people that important social problems can be solved by joining extremist political movements. These demagogues very effectively use media to manipulate average people and attract their support. As their movements gain strength, they place heavy political pressure on the traditional elites. Compromises place increasing power in the hands of demagogues. This power is exercised irresponsibly—political opposition is suppressed and democratic political institutions are undermined. Gradually, power is consolidated in the hands of the most ruthless demagogue, and this person establishes a totalitarian state.

Fear of totalitarianism is a modern fear—a fear that people who value individualism and democracy are most likely to experience. For such people, totalitarianism is a nightmare society—one in which everything they value most has low priority. Government severely limits and monitors most forms of communication. Expression of individualism is minimized. Novelist George Orwell constructed an enduring vision of this nightmare world in 1948. His novel *1984* effectively articulates the view of media inherent in mass society theory. In Orwell's world, Big Brother watches all citizens through an eye on the top of their televisions. Televised propaganda is used to foment hatred against external enemies and promote love of Big Brother. The hero of the novel, Winston Smith, works at a job in which he literally rewrites history. He disposes of old newspaper stories, photographs, and other documents deemed inconsistent with current propaganda. All records of dissidents and "traitors" are wiped out. Government engages in doublespeak—language whose meaning is so corrupted that it has become useless as a medium of expression. "Peace" means "war." "Freedom" means "enslavement." "Justice" means "inequity" and "prejudice." Anyone who deviates from the dictates of the regime is "re-educated," that is, imprisoned. Orwell describes the struggles and ultimate conversion of Winston Smith. At the conclusion of the novel, proof of Smith's loyalty is demonstrated by his spontaneous emotional response to Big Brother on the telescreen. Smith's individuality and critical ability have been destroyed.

Throughout the twentieth century, fear of the spread of totalitarianism grew in most democracies. For many, it symbolized everything that was loathsome and evil, but others saw it as the "wave of the future." Totalitarians dismissed democracy as impossible because average people could never effectively govern themselves—they were too apathetic and ignorant to do that. Cultivation of individuality led to inefficiency, jealousy, and conflict. Democracies were perceived as inherently weak, unable to resist the inevitable rise of charismatic, strong, determined leaders. Across Europe, in Latin America, and in Asia, fledgling democracies faltered and collapsed as the economic Great Depression deepened. Fascism in Germany and Communism in Russia provided examples of what could be accomplished by totalitarian rule. The United States was not immune. Radical political movements arose, and their influence spread rapidly. In several states, right-wing extremists were elected to political office. Pro-Fascist groups held gigantic public rallies to demonstrate their support for Hitler. The supremacist and anti-Semitic writings of automaker Henry Ford were translated and published in Nazi Germany. Radio propagandists like Father Coughlin achieved notoriety and acceptance. Radicals fought for control of labor unions. The thousand-year Reich envisioned by Hitler seemed a more realistic outcome than the survival of democracy in modern nation-states.

Why was totalitarianism so successful? Why was it sweeping the world just as the new mass media of radio and movies were becoming increasingly prominent? Was there a connection? Were radio and movies to blame? Many mass society theorists believed they were. Without these media, they thought, dictators couldn't have gained popularity or consolidated their power. They argued that the broadcast media were ideally suited for directly persuading average people and welding vast numbers of them into regimented, cohesive societies. Movies communicated powerful images that instilled the positive and negative associations desired by dictators.

What these critics failed to note is that when the Nazis or Communists were most successful, average people had strong reasons for *wanting* to believe the promises about jobs and personal security made by the extremists. Personal freedom has little value when you are starving and a wheelbarrow full of money won't buy a loaf of bread. The success of Nazi or Communist propaganda was also dependent on silencing critics and shutting down media that provided competing viewpoints.

One of the profound ironies of the efforts to oppose the rise of totalitarianism is that these efforts often threatened to produce the very form of government they were intended to prevent. In the United States, an important example of this is Joseph McCarthy, an obscure Republican senator from Wisconsin who came to national prominence in the 1950s by claiming to oppose the spread of Communism inside the U.S. government. Just how far should we go in the defense of democracy? Are there times when we have to indefinitely suspend basic democratic principles in order to "save" it? McCarthy argued that Communists were so close to gaining control in the United States that it was necessary to purge many people from government and the media. He claimed that if the rules of democracy were followed, these evil people would escape discovery and bring down our political system. McCarthy claimed to have a long list of names of Communists; he dramatically displayed it to reporters and newsreel cameras. Journalists cooperated by publishing his charges in front-page stories under banner headlines.

Media criticism of McCarthy was muted. Many journalists feared being labeled Communists if they opposed him. Indeed, McCarthy followers were very successful in getting media practitioners fired from their jobs. Blacklists were circulated, and threats were made against media organizations that hired those named on them. Edward R. Murrow, the most prominent broadcast journalist of the 1950s, is credited with stopping McCarthy's rise with news investigations questioning his tactics and the substance of his charges. Should media be blamed for causing McCarthy's rise—or credited with stopping him? Read the box entitled "Murrow versus McCarthy" before you answer this question.

Totalitarianism was the biggest fear aroused by mass society theorists, but they also focused attention on a more subtle form of societal corruption—mass culture. The sixth and final assumption of mass society theory, then, is that mass media inevitably debase higher forms of culture, bringing about a general decline in

Enlightenment
Eighteenth-century European social and philosophical movement stressing rational thought and progress through science

civilization (Davis, 1976). To understand this criticism, you must understand the perspective held by Western cultural and educational elites during the past two centuries. In the decades following the **Enlightenment** (an eighteenth-century European social and philosophical movement stressing rational thought and progress through science), these elites saw themselves as responsible for nurturing and promulgating a higher form of culture, high culture, not only within their own societies but also around the world. In retrospect, their perspective suffers from some serious limitations. The literary canon, one of the tools used to promote high culture, consisted mostly of works written by white, male, Western, Anglo-Saxon, and Protestant authors. Too often, elites believed that the "white man's burden" was to bring civilization and high culture to uncivilized parts of the world—even if this meant suppressing indigenous cultures and annihilating the people who practiced them. As we saw in 1992, the five-hundredth anniversary of Christopher Columbus's arrival on the American continent, this event is no longer universally hailed as a giant step in the march of civilization. People from all walks of life were openly questioning his and other explorers' brutality toward and destruction of indigenous peoples and their functioning cultures.

THINKING *about* THEORY   MURROW VERSUS MCCARTHY

The face-off between Tail-Gunner Joe, as Senator McCarthy was called, and legendary newsman Edward R. Murrow has become the stuff of journalistic legend as well as American history itself. It is also the subject of a highly acclaimed movie, *Good Night, and Good Luck*. The televised 1954 conflict and the 2005 film both highlight aspects of mass society theory—as it existed then and as it is articulated today.

In true mass society theory fashion, the senator played on people's postwar insecurities. The Soviets had "The Bomb," Communism was taking hold around the world, and not only were the Pinkos opposed to Capitalism, they didn't even believe in God. But American society was anxious because of much more than the Red Threat. The years immediately after World War II saw dramatic upheaval in "traditional" America. Women were entering the workforce. Racial minorities demanded civil rights. People were abandoning the countryside and moving to the cities. Young folks were shouting for independence. And as was the case during Durkheim and Tönnies's time, new technologies were being introduced amid all this social change, in this case new communication technologies like network television, spectacular cinemascope movies (as well as gritty low-budget independent films),

and FM radio (introducing black music to white teens). McCarthy had little trouble convincing a scared public that the media needed to be rid of subversives and brought under stricter control. After all, traditional American values were under assault!

But Murrow's counter to McCarthy was another traditional American value: freedom. He told his *See It Now* audience (at the time and in the movie), "We must not confuse dissent with disloyalty. We cannot defend freedom abroad by deserting it at home." As history and the movie demonstrate, however, Murrow's bosses, although committed to freedom and eventually in full support of Murrow, were extremely frightened. Like other media outlets of the time, they understood that the people were worried, that many shared the senator's fears. To challenge him too strongly risked alienating viewers and advertisers. "The terror is right here in this room," observed Murrow to his producer, Fred Friendly, as he and his team were assembling materials for the McCarthy broadcast. McCarthy had created in America what film critic David Denby called "a noxious atmosphere of intimidation" (2005, p. 95). Even the president, Dwight Eisenhower, who privately loathed McCarthy and his tactics, would not speak out against him.

(Continued)

THINKING *about* THEORY   MURROW VERSUS MCCARTHY (CONTINUED)

Many moviegoers and film critics, however, saw *Good Night, and Good Luck* not as a historical drama detailing a time in America when mass society beliefs were in full sway and their political champion was brought low by a courageous journalist (although that is what happened). Instead, they saw it as commentary on very modern concerns that concentration of media ownership into fewer and fewer corporate hands was rendering media once again inordinately powerful, not because people in 2005 were any more or less fearful than they were in 1954, but because media professionals were. Ty Burr of the *Boston Globe* called the movie "a puzzle: a hermetically sealed period piece so intensely relevant to our current state of affairs that it takes your breath away" (2005, p. E13). *USA Today's* Mike Clark labeled it "the best movie ever about the in-bred tension between news-folk and their advertisers" (2005, p. 4E). The *New Yorker's* Denby wrote, "There is little gravy in attacking Joe McCarthy in 2005." He added that *Good Night, and Good Luck's* real "intention appears to be to deliver a blow to the patella of a conglomerate-controlled press corps" (2005, p. 95).

But it was Murrow himself who spoke most prophetically (according to today's critics of media concentration) about our current media system. The film ends with a speech Murrow delivered at a broadcasters' dinner in 1958. He said of his industry's future:

We are currently wealthy, fat, comfortable, and complacent. We have currently a built-in allergy to unpleasant or disturbing information. Our mass media reflect this. But unless we get up off our fat surpluses and recognize that television in the main is being used to distract, delude, amuse, and insulate us, then television and those who finance it, those who look at it, and those who work at it, may see a totally different picture too late. (In Burr, 2005, p. E13)

Evidence of mass society theory thinking is fairly obvious in Senator McCarthy's attacks on media. The times were right, both socially and technologically. But what of the more modern fears over concentration? In 1954 Murrow's network was frightened by McCarthy, afraid of losing viewers, advertisers, and as a result, revenues. Network executives did the right thing nonetheless. Are things different now? Will highly concentrated, profit-driven media companies stand up for what's right, even if it costs them money? More than a few observers, including the three reviewers cited here, read *Good Night, and Good Luck*, which was written and directed by Hollywood's George Clooney, a vocal war critic, as a powerful parable of journalism's failure to serve the American public in the run-up to the invasion of Iraq. Do you think the media did its job before the invasion? Why or why not? Can you find parallels between postwar America in the 1950s and post-9/11 America? If you think journalists failed to serve the public well, why do you think this happened? Would an Edward R. Murrow have made a difference?

For defenders of high culture, mass media represented an insidious, corrosive force in society—one that threatened their influence by popularizing ideas and activities they considered trivial or demeaning. Rather than glorify gangsters (as movies did in the 1930s), why not praise great educators or religious leaders? Why pander to popular taste—why not seek to raise it to higher levels? Why give people what they want instead of giving them what they need? Why trivialize great art by turning it into cartoons (as Disney did in the 1930s)? Mass society theorists raised these questions—and had long and overly abstract answers for them.

In Europe, these concerns were used to justified government supervision of media through direct control or through indirect means such as public corporations like the British Broadcasting Corporation (BBC). As such, an important model of public service media developed that rivaled the American model of privately operated media. European governments assumed responsibility for using media to advance high culture and provide a broad array of other public service content. Broadcasts of symphony concerts and Shakespearean drama were intended to enlighten the masses. Media were supposed to give people what they needed rather than what they wanted. This earned the BBC the nickname "Auntie Beebe."

This debate over mass versus high culture is now becoming a worldwide debate about the corrupting influence of American media content as it reaches every corner of the globe. The people of many nations find troubling the norms and values inherent in U.S. content. American media entrepreneurs advocate opening worldwide media markets to the inflow of inexpensive American-produced entertainment. Why should poor and developing nations waste resources producing domestic media fare when U.S. content is easily and readily accessible? Educated elites in those nations worry about the power of this content to undermine their national cultures. What Americans see as content extolling the freedom to pursue the American Dream, these elites see as propaganda for the irresponsible American pursuit of selfish and materialistic goals. But the United States makes no pretense of being a civilizing force in the world—or does it? We don't claim to have a political agenda when we produce and distribute movies or use satellites to distribute television programs. And after all, it's only entertainment, isn't it?

EARLY EXAMPLES OF MASS SOCIETY THEORY

Now we'll summarize a few of the early examples of mass society theory. This set of theories is by no means complete. Rather, these perspectives combine ideas developed by others and represent how people in a given culture at a particular point in time thought about their social world. The examples we describe and discuss were influential at the time they were written and provided important reference points for later theorists. It is important to remember, too, that even where not specifically mentioned, the emerging mass media were clearly implicated in most examples.

In subsequent chapters, we will deal with the development of later theories that grew out of mass society theory. These continued to gain popularity until late in the 1950s. By 1965, however, mass society theory, in its classic formulation, was collapsing—inherent flaws had become obvious even to adamant supporters. Fear of totalitarianism had ebbed (at least within academia), and if mass culture was going to cause the end of civilization, it was already too late (at least in the United States).

In the last chapters of this book, we will consider important new theories that articulate innovative thinking about popular culture—including ideas about the influence of U.S.-style mass entertainment in other nations. These inevitably draw on older notions about mass society and mass culture, but most reject the simplistic assumptions and criticisms of earlier eras. These newer theories no longer accept elite high culture as the standard against which all others must be measured. Totalitarianism is no longer feared as inevitable, but censorship of media by authoritarian regimes is widespread. Current criticism tends to focus on the inherent biases of media when it comes to developing new forms of culture. Media are no longer seen as corrupting and degrading high culture. Rather, they are viewed as limiting or disrupting cultural development. Media don't subvert culture, but they do play a major and sometimes counterproductive role in cultural change. Fear of totalitarianism has been replaced worldwide by growing disillusionment with consumerism and its power to undermine cultural and national identities.

Should current theories of popular culture be labeled as mass society theories? Or should we officially declare mass society theory dead? Although some contemporary theorists clearly continue to draw on mass society notions, most are aware of their limitations. Our preference here is to limit use of the term *mass society theory* to formulations that (a) were developed before 1970 and (b) fail to account for the findings of media effects research.

GEMEINSCHAFT AND GESELLSCHAFT

gemeinschaft
In Tönnies's conception, traditional folk cultures

gesellschaft
In Tönnies's conception, modern industrial society

Among the originators of mass society notions was a German sociologist, Ferdinand Tönnies. Tönnies sought to explain the critical difference between earlier forms of social organization and European society as it existed in the late nineteenth century. He proposed a simple dichotomy—**gemeinschaft**, or folk community, and **gesellschaft**, or modern industrial society. In folk communities, people were bound together by strong ties of family, by tradition, and by rigid social roles—basic social institutions were very powerful. Gemeinschaft "consisted of a dense network of personal relationships based heavily on kinship and the direct, face-to-face contact that occurs in a small, closed village. Norms were largely unwritten, and individuals were bound to one another in a web of mutual interdependence that touched all aspects of life" (Fukuyama, 1999, p. 57). In addition, "a collective has the character of a gemeinschaft insofar as its members think of the group as a gift of nature created by a supernatural will" (Martindale, 1960, p. 83). Although folk communities had important strengths as well as serious limitations, Tönnies emphasized the former. He argued that most people yearn for the order and meaning provided by folk communities. They often find life in modern societies troublesome and meaningless. As far as mass society theorists were concerned, not only did the emerging mass media disrupt kinship and direct face-to-face contact, but they certainly were not gifts of nature.

In gesellschaft, people are bound together by relatively weak social institutions based on rational choices rather than tradition. Gesellschaft represents "the framework of laws and other formal regulations that characterized large, urban industrial societies. Social relationships were more formalized and impersonal; individuals did not depend on one another for support... and were therefore much less morally obligated to one another" (Fukuyama, 1999, pp. 57–58). Naturally, it was the established elites (the traditional wielders of power and the most vocal champions of mass society theory) who stood to lose the most influence in the move from gemeinschaft to gesellschaft, as "average" people came to depend less on their influence and more on formalized and more objectively applied rules and laws. For example, when you take a job, you sign a formal contract based on your personal decision. You don't sign it because you are bound by family tradition to work for a certain employer. You make a more or less rational choice. You agree to perform a particular job in return for a salary. The contract lasts as long as you and your employer meet its conditions. If you fail to show up for work often enough, you'll be fired. If your employer goes broke and can't pay you, you'll stop working for him or her.

The marriage vow is another example of how important social institutions have been affected by the transition to modernity. In folk communities, these vows were defined as lifelong commitments that ended only with the death of spouses. Marriage partners were chosen by the heads of families using criteria determined by tradition and family needs. Marriage served as a means of linking networks of extended families in ways that strengthened the overall community. It was about assuming necessary obligations so the community would be sustained. If you violated marriage vows, you were likely to be ostracized by everyone in the community. In these social orders, families endured crises and people found ways of surviving within them.

In modern societies, the marriage contract is often treated as just another formal arrangement based on personal decision—much like signing an employment agreement. If the "pay" isn't good enough, or if there is a better offer, why not tear up the contract and move on? What community will be harmed by this action? Who will impose sanctions? Today, marriage contracts are often violated, and though offenders can endure many negative consequences, they are not condemned by the society at large. For example, a divorced man, Ronald Reagan, became president of the United States with almost no mention of that fact; Bill Clinton enjoyed the highest public approval ratings of his presidency at the height of the adultery scandal that led to his impeachment. A 2007 national poll revealed that only 39 percent of America's registered voters would be less likely to vote for a candidate because he or she had committed adultery. The remainder said marital infidelity made no difference when judging a person's worth for elective office (Luo, 2007). As it was, three of the top contenders for the Republican spot on the 2008 presidential ballot—Rudy Giuliani, John McCain, and Newt Gingrich, each presenting himself to voters as a holder of traditional, conservative values—together had had eight marriages.

Over the years, media have been continually accused of breaking down folk communities (gemeinschaft) and encouraging the development of amoral, weak social institutions (gesellschaft). The late Reverend Jerry Falwell, founder of the Moral Majority, and fellow televangelist Pat Robertson reflected this view in 2001 when they charged that the September 11 terrorist attacks on the World Trade Center and the Pentagon were the products, not of Islamic radicalism, but of the "American cultural elite's" systematic subversion of traditional family and social values (Adbusters, 2002). Popular television shows prominently feature unwed couples living together, homosexual unions, and unwed mothers bearing children. Do these programs merely reflect social changes, or are they somehow responsible for them? As we'll see throughout this text, there is no simple answer to this question.

MECHANICAL AND ORGANIC SOLIDARITY

French sociologist Émile Durkheim offered a theory with the same dichotomy as that of Tönnies but with a fundamentally different interpretation of modern social orders. Durkheim compared folk communities to machines in which people were little more than cogs. These machines were very ordered and durable, but people were forced by a collective consensus to perform traditional social roles. Think for a moment about all the family names used today that are derived from professions: Farmer, Taylor, Hunter, Goldsmith, Forester, Toepfer and Shumacher (German for Potter and Shoemaker), Barbiere and Panetta (Italian for Barber and Baker). Your name was, literally, what you were: John the Smith. Or consider the many family names that end in "son" or "sen." People were identified by their father's name: Peterson is Peter's son. People were bound by this consensus to one another like the parts of a great engine—**mechanical solidarity**.

mechanical solidarity
In Durkheim's conception, folk cultures bound by consensus and traditional social roles

Durkheim compared modern social orders to animals rather than to machines. As they grow, animals undergo profound changes in their physical form. They begin life as babies and progress through several developmental stages on their way to adulthood and old age. The bodies of animals are made up of many different kinds of cells—skin, bone, blood—and these cells serve very different purposes. Similarly, modern social orders can undergo profound changes, and therefore the people in them can grow and change along with the society at large. In Durkheim's theory, people are like the specialized cells of a body rather than like the cogs of a machine. People perform specialized tasks and depend on the overall health of the body for their personal survival. Unlike machines, animals are subject to diseases and physical threats. But they are capable of using mental processes to anticipate threats and cope with them. Durkheim used the term **organic solidarity** to refer to the social ties that bind modern social orders together.

organic solidarity
In Durkheim's conception, modern social orders bound by culturally negotiated social ties

Social orders with organic solidarity are characterized by specialization, division of labor, and interdependence (Martindale, 1960, p. 87). Be warned, though, it is easy to confuse Durkheim's labeling of mechanical and organic solidarity, because we naturally associate machines with modernity. Remember that he uses the metaphor of the machine to refer to folk cultures—not modern society.

Durkheim's praise for organic solidarity has been echoed in the many theories that have extolled the virtues of new media and new technology. Proponents of new media usually argue that communication technology will permit the formation of important new social bonds. Keep in mind the frequent allusions to an Internet-fueled "electronic democracy" in which the people can communicate directly with their leaders. There will be "electronic town halls" where the people will be able to decide what they want government to do for them. In the 2008 presidential campaign, electronic democracy took on a new form when all of the major Democratic and Republican candidates used Facebook and YouTube to aggressively and systematically promote their candidacies (Williams, 2007). And during the contentious 2009 health care reform debate, it was only the bravest legislators who did not maintain a continuous Twitter feed to their constituents. Proponents of new media assume that these new mediated relationships will be an improvement over older forms of representative democracy. What do you think? Have you gained useful insights about the candidates from Facebook or YouTube? Are you a better-informed citizen?

It would be a mistake to view Durkheim as a naive optimist concerning the rise of modern society. His most enduring book, *Suicide* (1951), documented rising suicide rates in those countries where traditional religious and social institutions had lost their preeminence. In these nations, Durkheim argued, people experienced high levels of anomie, or normlessness. In his later work, Durkheim showed

INSTANT ACCESS

Mass Society Theory

Strengths	Weaknesses
1. Speculates about important effects	1. Is unscientific
2. Highlights important structural changes and conflicts in modern cultures	2. Is unsystematic
3. Draws attention to issues of media ownership and ethics	3. Is promulgated by elites interested in preserving power
	4. Underestimates intelligence and competence of "average people"
	5. Underestimates personal, societal, and cultural barriers to direct media influence

growing concern for the declining strength of common morality (Ritzer, 1983, p. 99). People were no longer bound by traditional values, but were free to follow their personal passions and needs. Durkheim believed that these problems were best viewed as social pathologies that could be diagnosed and cured by a social physician—in other words, a sociologist like himself (Ritzer, 1983, p. 110). Unlike conservatives who demanded a return to old social orders or radicals who called for revolution, Durkheim believed that scientifically chosen reforms would solve the problems inherent in modernity.

MASS SOCIETY THEORY IN CONTEMPORARY TIMES

Although mass society theory has very little support among contemporary mass communication researchers and theorists, its basic assumptions of a corrupting media and helpless audiences have never completely disappeared. Attacks on the pervasive dysfunctional power of media have persisted and will persist as long as dominant elites find their power challenged by media and as long as privately owned media find it profitable to produce and distribute content that challenges widely practiced social norms and values. Two contemporary writers provide clear articulations of mass society theory as it is now expressed. In addition to modernizing mass society notions, they amply demonstrate mass society theory's many limitations (for example, distrust of "average people" and the presumption that the authors' values are the "right values"). Michael Medved in *Hollywood vs. America: Popular Culture and the War on Traditional Values* (1992) argues precisely what the title implies: American culture has declined because "the gatekeeper/cleric has wandered away and the carnival barker/programmer has taken his place" (p. 3). You may remember Medved from Chapter 2 as the film critic who uncovered the homosexual agenda, environmentalism, disdain for the human race, and support for the United Nations in the 2007 animated movie *Happy Feet*. In *Saving Childhood: Protecting Our Children from the National Assault on Innocence,* he warned that "nihilistic messages that frighten and corrupt now come at our children from so many directions at once that childhood innocence barely stands a chance" (Medved and Medved, 1998, p. 3).

But mass society theory's most influential contemporary champion may well be British social critic, philosopher, and intellectual Roger Scruton. In *An Intelligent Person's Guide to Modern Culture* (2000), he makes clear mass society's elitism and support of elite culture:

> This book presents a theory of modern culture, and a defense of culture in its higher and more critical form. It is impossible to give a convincing defense of high culture to a person who has none. I shall therefore assume that you, the reader, are both intelligent and cultivated. You don't have to be familiar with the entire canon of Western literature, the full range of musical and artistic masterpieces or the critical reflections which all these things have prompted. Who is? But it would be useful to have read *Les fleurs du mal* by Baudelaire and T. S. Eliot's *Waste Land*. I shall also presume some familiarity with Mozart, Wagner, Manet, Poussin, Tennyson, Schoenberg, George Herbert, Goethe, Marx, and Nietzsche. (p. x)

Scruton also weighs in on the decline of traditional values: "Something new seems to be at work in the contemporary world—a process that is eating away the very heart of social life, not merely by putting salesmanship in place of moral virtue, but by putting everything—virtue included—on sale" (p. 55).

On popular culture:

> Pop culture is ... an attempt to provide easy-going forms of social cohesion, without the costly rites of passage that bring moral and emotional knowledge. It is a culture which has demoted the aesthetic object, and elevated the advert in its place; it has replaced imagination by fantasy and feeling by kitsch; and it has destroyed the old forms of music and dancing, so as to replace them with a repetitious noise, whose invariant harmonic and rhythmic textures sound all about us, replacing the dialect of the tribe with the grammarless murmur of the species, and drowning out the unconfident stutterings of the fathers as they trudge away towards extinction. (p. 121)

And on the failings of higher education:

> The gap between the culture acquired spontaneously by the young, and that which ... should be imparted in the university, is so cavernously wide that the teacher is apt to look ridiculous, as he perches on his theatrical pinnacle and beckons the youth across to it. Indeed, it is easier to make the passage the other way, to join your young audience in the enchanted field of popular entertainment, and turn your intellectual guns on the stately ruin across the chasm. (pp. 121–122)

Beyond the ongoing concern of those who see "traditional values" and average people jeopardized by new communication technologies, two other factors have given new, albeit weak, life to current rearticulations of mass society theory. The first is the phenomenally rapid diffusion of the Internet and the World Wide Web; the second is changes in the way media companies are structured and operated.

New forms of media, in this case the Internet and Web, mean new forms of communication, which mean the development of new relationships and the creation of new centers of power and influence. You'll recognize this as a near mirror image of the situation that faced our society during the nineteenth and into the early twentieth century, the incubation period of mass society theory. Today, in many parts of the world, advances in media technology facilitate the formation of multinational alliances and trade relationships that challenge existing elites. Everywhere older social institutions are questioned and new social roles pioneered. Traditional forms of communication are abandoned, and new messages and the media that carry them are embraced. We can see this conflict between the "old" and "new" in a debate that continue to roil the Internet and the academy, the disappearance of *reading*.

Technology writer Nicholas Carr ignited the controversy with his article entitled "Is Google Making Us Stupid?" In it he argued, "It is clear that users are not reading online in the traditional sense; indeed there are signs that new forms of 'reading' are emerging as users 'power browse' horizontally through titles, contents pages, and abstracts going for quick wins. It almost seems that they go online to avoid reading in the traditional sense" (2008b, p. 57). Insisting that "deep reading… is indistinguishable from deep thinking" (p. 62), he admitted that online reading promotes efficiency, immediacy, and interaction, but "our ability to interpret text, to make the rich mental connections that form when we read deeply and without distraction, remains largely disengaged" (p. 58).

Technology writer Christine Rosen agreed, taking a more macro-level view: "Enthusiasts and self-appointed experts assure us that this new digital literacy represents an advance for mankind; the book is evolving, progressing, improving, they argue, and every improvement demands an uneasy period of adjustment," she wrote. "Sophisticated forms of collaborative 'information foraging' will replace solitary deep reading; the connected screen will replace the disconnected book. What is 'reading' anyway, they ask, in a multimedia world like ours? We are increasingly distractible, impatient, and convenience-obsessed—and the paper book just can't keep up. Shouldn't we simply acknowledge that we are becoming people of the screen, not people of the book?" (2008, p. 20).

Acclaimed novelist John Updike also spoke of cultural-level change: "Tastes have coarsened. People read less; they're less comfortable with the written word. They're less comfortable with novels. They don't have a backward frame of reference that would enable them to appreciate things like irony and allusions. It's sad…. And who's to blame? Well, everything's to blame. Movies are to blame…. Television is to blame…. Now we have these cultural developments on the Internet, and online, and the computer offering itself as a cultural tool, as a tool of distributing not just information but arts—and who knows what inroads will be made into the world of the book" (Famed, 2009).

In response, educational psychologist Rand J. Spiro offered a more "modern" view of reading. Young readers, he said, "aren't as troubled as some of us older folks are by reading that doesn't go in a line. That's a good thing because the world doesn't go in a line, and the world isn't organized into separate compartments or chapters…. It takes a long time to read a 400-page book. In a tenth of the time the Internet allows a reader to cover a lot more of the topic from different points of view" (in Rich, 2008, p. 14). Language and literacy scholar Donna Alvermann added, "Kids are using sound and images so they have a world of ideas to put together that aren't necessarily language oriented. Books aren't out of the picture, but they're only one way of experiencing information in the world today" (in Rich, 2008, p. 15).

concentration
Ownership of
different and
numerous media
companies con-
centrated in fewer
and fewer hands

The second factor in contemporary rearticulations of mass society theory involves **concentration** of ownership of different media companies in fewer and fewer hands. We've already seen that media industries, when facing challenges from new technologies, undergo rapid restructuring. This is one of the reasons behind today's dazzling number and scope of media industry mergers. In the last several years alone, AT&T and British Telecommunications entered into a $10 billion merger to ensure their survival in the competitive telephone, cellular communication, cable television, and Internet markets. With the same goals in mind, Westinghouse bought CBS, Disney bought Capital Cities/ABC and Marvel Entertainment, and Time Warner bought Turner Broadcasting. Seagram bought Polygram Music. AT&T took over cable company TCI, bought another, Media One, and entered partnerships with two more, Time Warner and Comcast. Comcast then took over all of AT&T's cable holdings and as we saw earlier, NBC Universal and its myriad media holdings, producing a single entity, the world's largest television company delivering "one out of every five television hours" into American homes (Kang, 2009). News Corporation bought a major stake in DirectTV and all the media holdings of the Wall Street Journal companies. Dominant search engine Google bought dominant video-sharing site YouTube in 2006, dominant Internet advertising company DoubleClick in 2007, and dominant cell phone banner ad company AdMob in 2009; software giant Microsoft acquired search engine Yahoo, "the world's most visited homepage," in a 2009 takeover worth $44.6 billion. Each of these deals produced giant communication companies with holdings across many different forms of media reaching unimaginably large audiences across the globe. According to journalist and media critic Ben Bagdikian (2004), the number of corporations controlling most of the country's newspapers, magazines, radio and television stations, book publishers, and movie studios has shrunk from fifty, when he wrote the first edition of his classic *The Media Monopoly,* to five today. He has this to say about the concentration of ownership of media industries:

> Left to their own devices, a small number of the most powerful firms have taken control of most of their countries' printed and broadcast news and entertainment. They have their own style of control, not by official edict or state terror, but by uniform economic and political goals. They have their own way of narrowing political and cultural diversity, not by promulgating official dogma, but by quietly emphasizing ideas and information congenial to their profits and political preferences. Although they are not their countries' official political authorities, they have a disproportionate private influence over the political authorities and over public policy. (Bagdikian, 1992, pp. 239–240)

Bagdikian, a strong proponent of media freedom, is no mass society theorist. But his concern is shared by many who hold mass society views of an ever-powerful media system wielding unassailable power over helpless people.

SUMMARY

Criticism of media and new media technology is not a new phenomenon. For more than a century now, new media industries have inspired harsh criticism from a variety of sources. Media entrepreneurs have countered criticisms from traditional elites and from media scholars. Although some concerns about media have faded, many remain. Critics still argue that the quality of much mass entertainment content has been lowered to satisfy audiences' basest tastes and passions. Early news media attracted—and today's supermarket tabloids still attract—huge audiences by printing speculative, overdramatized, and gossipy stories. Through much of the last two centuries, criticism of media took the form of mass society theory. Tönnies and Durkheim helped frame a debate over the fundamental nature of modernity that has not ended. For mass society theorists and media apologists, media were symbolic of modernity—representing either the worst or the best of modern life.

Early mass society theorists argued that media are highly problematic forces that have the power to directly reach and transform the thinking of individuals so that the quality of their lives is impaired and serious social problems are created. Through media influence, people are atomized, cut off from the civilizing influences of other people or high culture. In these early theories, totalitarianism inevitably results as ruthless, power-hungry dictators seize control of media to promote their ideology.

Initially, mass society theory gained wide acceptance—especially among traditional social elites threatened by the rise of media industries. In time, however, people questioned its unqualified assertions about the media's power to directly influence individuals. Mass society notions enjoyed

longer acceptance in Europe, where commitments to traditional ways of life and high culture have been stronger and where distrust of average people and mass democracy runs deeper.

For the past sixty years, U.S. postpositivist media researchers have been skeptical of the power of media to have direct effects. In subsequent chapters, we will show how their skepticism was grounded in empirical observation. In study after study, researchers found it difficult to demonstrate that media could directly and routinely influence what people thought or did. But we will also consider the limitations of this research and why it fostered an inadequate understanding of media's role in society.

The debate about the role of media in modern life has not ended. Though many U.S. scholars were satisfied with the answers supplied by empirical research, European theorists were not. Many old questions about the power of media have recently been revived, especially because of the emergence of the Internet and the recent spate of giant communication industry mergers. The rising tide of hate speech and pornography on the Internet has renewed other concerns. Cogent new theories argue that media do play an important role in the development and maintenance of culture. The revival of this debate, as we'll see in later chapters, has reinvigorated media theory and research.

Critical Thinking Questions

1. Have you read *1984* or seen either *Citizen Kane* (a fictionalized account of the life of William Randolph Hearst) or *Good Night, and Good Luck*? If so, can you identify elements of mass society thinking (or challenges to it) in these movies?

2. Think about your first few months in college. Relate your experience to the kinds of social upheaval society faced in the transformation from gemeinschaft to gesellschaft and from mechanical to organic solidarity. Can you make an argument for the proposition that media become particularly attractive, useful, or powerful during

these traumatic times? Can you argue that longing for past securities may have changed how you looked at the world around you?

3. Roger Scruton wants to tell us what it means to be an intelligent person. He assumes that he can do this only if we already have a basic understanding of the great works. "It would be useful to have read *Les fleurs du mal* by Baudelaire and T. S. Eliot's *Waste Land*," he wrote; "I shall also presume some familiarity with Mozart, Wagner, Manet, Poussin, Tennyson, Schoenberg, George Herbert, Goethe, Marx, and Nietzsche." How many

of these masters and masterworks are you familiar with? If you don't know many of them, does that make you an unintelligent person? Can you make an argument for different definitions of intelligence? What would you say to Scruton about his definition of an intelligent person should you run in to him on campus?

Key Terms

First Amendment

culture war

wire services

functional displacement

oligopoly

digital rights management

direct-effects assumption

Enlightenment

gemeinschaft

gesellschaft

mechanical solidarity

organic solidarity

concentration

THE RISE OF MEDIA THEORY IN THE AGE OF PROPAGANDA

Imagine that you have gone back in time to the beginning of the twentieth century. You live in a large metropolitan area along the East Coast of the United States, and you are a second- or third-generation American. You are a white, middle-class, Anglo-Saxon, Protestant. Your city is growing rapidly, with new neighborhoods springing up daily to house waves of immigrants from poorer nations in Eastern Europe and the Far East. These people speak strange languages and practice strange cultures. Many claim to be Christians, but they don't behave like any Christians you've ever met. Most keep to themselves in ghetto neighborhoods in which there are many social problems.

Most disturbing of all, these people seem to have no sense of what it means to live in a free and democratic nation. They are governed by political bosses who turn them out to vote for what you perceive to be corrupt party-machine candidates. If you pay attention to gossip (or read the right books or magazines), you hear about groups like the Mafia or Cosa Nostra. You also hear (or read in your newspaper) that various extremist political groups are active in these ghettos, spreading all sorts of discontent among these ignorant, irresponsible aliens. Many of these nefarious groups are playing upon the newcomers' loyalties to foreign nations. What would you do about this situation?

Well, you might adopt a Conservative approach and start an America-for-Americans movement to remove these foreigners from the sacred soil of your homeland. If you are of a more liberal bent, you might be reluctant to send these immigrants back to where they came from (even though they do represent a threat to your way of life). As a forward-thinking person, you may want to convert these people away from their obviously misguided beliefs about government. You are aware that greedy employers are exploiting these people with sixteen-hour workdays and child labor, but you believe that's why they should join mainstream political parties and work within the system. Perhaps, you figure, if they would only abstain from alcohol and adopt more rational forms of religion that might help them see their problems more clearly. This was how the political movement known as Progressivism tried to help immigrants in the late 1800s, but, unfortunately, most of these recent arrivals don't seem to respond well to efforts designed to help them. They reject both Conservative and Progressive efforts to reform them. Resistance grows ever more determined and is accompanied by violence on both sides. Labor unions are organized to oppose the power of monopoly capitalists. Strikes become increasingly common and violent. Now what do you do? You could become a prohibitionist and successfully ban the sale of liquor. But this only creates a market for bootleggers, strengthening rather than reducing the power of organized crime. Political party bosses flourish. How will these newcomers ever become true Americans and be absorbed into the American melting pot?

Now imagine that you are one of those aliens. How do you cope with life in the world's greatest democracy? You turn to your family and the friends of your family. Your cousin is a member of the political machine. He promises a patronage job—if you vote for his boss. You fight exploitation by joining labor unions that promise to correct bad working conditions. Above all, you practice the culture you grew up with, and you stay within the confines of the ghetto where that culture is practiced. You resent prohibition and see nothing wrong with occasionally consuming alcohol. You listen to family members and local political bosses who can do things for you and can be trusted to keep their promises.

Throughout the nineteenth century, the United States was a nation of many cultures. At any given point in time, people in different racial and ethnic groups were exploited and feared. Some of these groups escaped the ghettos, and their children were absorbed into the amorphous American middle class. Others were less successful. Some members of dominant cultural groups attempted to assist these minority groups, but their efforts were only partially successful. Too often, their work was actually self-serving—not selfless. They sought to protect their way of life from the threats posed by these other cultures and lifestyles. This led them to adopt solutions that sometimes made problems worse. Put yourself back there in time. Take whichever role you choose. How comfortable would you be? What would you do? How would you feel about the changes around you?

OVERVIEW

muckraker
Crusading journalist, typically challenging the powerful on behalf of those less so

propaganda
No-holds-barred use of communication to propagate specific beliefs and expectations

This situation was an ideal breeding ground for violent social conflict. The battle was waged in the streets and through the ever-expanding mass media. Yellow journalists and **muckrakers** fought wars of words in the media; battle lines were drawn between defenders of immigrant groups and representatives of existing elites, and the coverage was not confined to polite newspaper editorials or human-interest feature stories. It was a fight for the heart and soul of the nation (Altschull, 1990; Brownell, 1983). Nor was the struggle unique to the United States. In Europe, conflict across social-class lines was even more intense and deadly. These clashes led to the development of extremist political groups that demanded an end to democracy and the establishment of totalitarian states.

In the United States, advocates on all sides were convinced of the Truth and Justice of their causes. Their way was the American way, the Right way, the only True way. They were opposed by the forces of Evil and Chaos. These advocates appealed to the strongest emotions—hate and fear. Mass-mediated **propaganda** spread throughout America, across Europe, and around the world. Everywhere it deeply affected politics and culture.

In this chapter, we will discuss how political propaganda was used and then survey some of the theories developed to understand and control it. With the normative theories discussed in the next chapter, these were the first true media theories. Mass society theory saw media as only one of many disruptive forces. However, in propaganda theories, media became the focus of attention. Propaganda theorists specifically analyzed media content and speculated about its influence. They wanted to understand and explain the ability of messages to persuade and convert thousands or even millions of individuals to extreme viewpoints.

Propaganda commanded the attention of early media theorists because it threatened to undermine the very foundation of the U.S. political system and of democratic governments everywhere. By the late 1930s, many, if not most, American leaders were convinced that democracy wouldn't survive if extremist political propaganda was allowed to be freely distributed. But censorship of propaganda meant imposing significant limitations on that essential principle of Western democracy, communication freedom. This posed a terrible dilemma. Strict censorship might also undermine democracy. In this chapter we will trace how propaganda theorists attempted to address and resolve this dilemma.

At first, some experts were optimistic that the American public could be educated to resist propaganda. After all, propaganda violates the most basic rules of fair democratic political communication. Propaganda freely uses lies and deception to persuade. If people could be taught to critically evaluate propaganda messages, they could learn how to reject them as unfair and false. These experts believed that public education could save democracy. Nevertheless, optimism about the power of public education faded as both Nazism and Communism spread from Europe to America during the 1930s. More and more Americans, especially first-generation immigrants from Europe, turned away from mainstream politicians and instead chose to listen to leaders who espoused totalitarian ideals and visions of social justice and jobs. Social movements sprang up based on propaganda imported more or less directly from Europe. In the United States, rallies were held to celebrate Adolf Hitler or Joseph Stalin and to denigrate inferior races and Wall Street bosses.

white propaganda
Intentional suppression of potentially harmful information and ideas, combined with deliberate promotion of positive information or ideas to distract attention from problematic events

Propaganda experts became convinced that even if public education were a practical means of resisting propaganda, it would simply take too long. It might also teach people to resist all forms of propaganda at a time when some powerful elites saw as necessary the use of propaganda of their own making to promote democracy. Time was running out as the Depression deepened. It appeared likely that a Nazi or Communist leader would seize power before public education had a chance to succeed. So propaganda theorists abandoned idealism in favor of strategies they regarded as realistic and scientific. Propaganda must be resisted by whatever means possible. Even though the threat of propaganda was great, there might be a silver lining to this cloud. If we could find a way to harness the power of propaganda to promote good and just ideals, then we would not only survive its threat but have a tool to help build a better social order. This was the promise of what came to be called **white propaganda**—a strategy that used propaganda techniques to fight "bad" propaganda and promote objectives that elites considered good. After World War II ended, these white propaganda techniques provided a basis for the development of strategic (promotional) communication methods that are widely used today in advertising and public relations. In fact, propaganda theory is experiencing a resurgence of interest precisely for this reason: the techniques used in these modern promotional efforts appear to many observers to be even more effective in the contemporary world of corporate media ownership (Laitinen and Rakos, 1997).

THE ORIGIN OF PROPAGANDA

Propaganda was not an American invention. The term originated with the Roman Catholic Congregatio de Propaganda Fide (Committee for the Propagation of the Faith), an order of the church established by a papal bull in 1622. The Propaganda Fide was originally founded in an effort to suppress the Protestant Reformation. Throughout the first half of the twentieth century, the meaning of *propaganda* was debated. Was propaganda necessarily bad or was it a good form of communication that could be corrupted? Many forms of communication seek to persuade people—were all of them propaganda? Gradually, the term *propaganda* came to refer to a certain type of communication strategy. It involves the no-holds-barred use of communication to propagate specific beliefs and expectations. The ultimate goal of propagandists is to change the way people act and to leave them believing that those actions are voluntary, that the newly adopted behaviors—and the opinions underlying them—are their own (Pratkanis and Aronson, 1992, p. 9). To accomplish this, though, propagandists must first change the way people conceive of themselves and their social world. A variety of communication techniques is used to guide and transform those beliefs. During the 1930s, the new media of radio and movies provided propagandists with powerful new tools.

Fritz Hippler, head of Nazi Germany's film propaganda division, said that the secret to effective propaganda is to (a) simplify a complex issue and (b) repeat that simplification over and over again (*World War II*, 1982). J. Michael Sproule (1994) argues that effective propaganda is covert: it "persuades people without seeming to do so" (p. 3); features "the massive orchestration of communication" (p. 4); and emphasizes "tricky language designed to discourage reflective thought" (p. 5). The propagandist believes that the end justifies the means. Therefore, it is not only right but necessary that half-truths and even outright lies be used to convince people to abandon ideas that are "wrong" and to adopt those favored by the propagandist. Propagandists also rely on **disinformation** to discredit their opposition. They spread false information about opposition groups and their objectives. Often the source of this false information is concealed so that it can't be traced to the propagandist.

As U.S. theorists studied propaganda, they came to differentiate black, white, and gray propaganda, but definitions of these types of propaganda varied (Snowball, 1999; Becker, 1949). **Black propaganda** was usually defined as involving deliberate and strategic transmission of lies—its use was well illustrated by the Nazis. According to Howard Becker, a sociologist who worked as an Office of Strategic Services propagandist during World War II, black propaganda always misrepresented the source of the message so that it appeared to come from an "inside," trustworthy source with whom its target had a close relationship. Deliberately propagated rumors or gossip would fit this definition. White propaganda

disinformation
False information spread about the opposition to discredit it

black propaganda
Deliberate and strategic transmission of lies

was, as we have seen, usually defined as involving intentional suppression of contradictory information and ideas, combined with deliberate promotion of highly consistent information or ideas that support the objectives of the propagandist. Sometimes white propaganda was used to draw attention away from problematic events or to provide interpretations of events that were useful for the propagandist. Becker asserts that to be white propaganda, it must be openly identified as coming from an "outside" source—one that doesn't have a close relationship to the target of the propaganda.

gray propaganda
Transmission of information or ideas that might or might not be false. No effort is made to determine their validity

Gray propaganda involved transmission of information or ideas that might or might not be false. The propagandist simply made no effort to determine their validity and actually avoided doing so—especially if dissemination of the content would serve his or her interest. Becker argues that the truth or falsity of propaganda is often hard to establish, so it isn't practical to use veracity as a criterion for differentiating types of propaganda. He asserts that during World War II, the Office of War Information was restricted to transmitting white propaganda (intended for American and friendly overseas audiences), whereas the Office of Strategic Services could transmit only black propaganda (aimed at unfriendly foreign audiences). The work of these two agencies was loosely coordinated by Psychological Warfare, an armed services organization. Today we find the attribution of labels like "black" and "white" to the concepts of bad and good propaganda offensive. But remember one of this book's constant themes: These ideas are products of their times.

Propagandists then and now live in an either/or, good/evil world. American propagandists in the 1930s had two clear alternatives. On one side were truth, justice, and freedom—in short, the American way—and on the other side were falsehood, evil, and slavery—totalitarianism. Of course, Communist and Nazi propagandists had their own versions of truth, justice, and freedom. For them the American vision of Utopia was at best naive and at worst likely to lead to racial pollution and cultural degradation. The Nazis used propaganda to cultivate extreme fear and hatred of minority groups. In *Mein Kampf* (1933), Hitler traced the problems of post–World War I Germany to the Jewish people and other ethnic or racial minorities. Unlike the American elites, he saw no reason to bother converting or deporting these groups—they were Evil Incarnate and therefore should be exterminated. Nazi propaganda films, of which director Hippler's hate-filled *The Eternal Jew* is a noted example, used powerful negative imagery to equate Jews with rats and to associate mental illness with grotesque physical deformity, whereas positive images were associated with blond, blue-eyed people.

Thus, for the totalitarian propagandist, mass media were a very practical means of mass manipulation—an effective mechanism for controlling large populations. If people came to share the views of the propagandist, they were said to be converted: they abandoned old views and took on those promoted by propaganda. Once consensus was created, elites could then take the actions that it permitted or dictated. They could carry out the "will of the people," who have become, in the words of journalism and social critic Todd Gitlin, "cognoscenti of their own bamboozlement" (1991).

Propagandists typically held elitist and paternalistic views about their audiences. They believed that people needed to be converted for their "own good"—not just to serve the interest of the propagandist. Propagandists often blamed the people for the necessity of engaging in lies and manipulation. They thought people so irrational, so illiterate, or so inattentive that it was necessary to coerce, seduce, or trick them into learning bits of misinformation. The propagandists' argument was simple: If only people were more rational or intelligent, we could just sit down and explain things to them, person to person. But most aren't—especially the ones who need the most help. Most people are children when it comes to important affairs like politics. How can we expect them to listen to reason? It's just not possible. In the post–World War II United States, for example, this became known as the **engineering of consent**, a term coined by "the father of modern public relations," Edward L. Bernays. Sproule quotes Bernays as wanting to expand freedom of press and speech to include the government's "freedom to persuade.... Only by mastering the techniques of communication can leadership be exercised fruitfully in the vast complex that is modern democracy," because in a democracy, results "do not just happen" (Sproule, 1997, p. 213).

engineering of consent
Official use of communication campaigns to reach "good" ends

The propagandist also uses similar reasoning for suppressing opposition messages: Average people are just too gullible. They will be taken in by the lies and tricks of others. If opponents are allowed to freely communicate their messages, a standoff will result in which no one wins. Propagandists are convinced of the validity of their cause, so they must stop opponents from blocking their actions. You can test your thinking about the engineering of consent in the box entitled "Engineering Consent: WMD and the War in Iraq."

THINKING *about* THEORY — ENGINEERING CONSENT: WMD AND THE WAR IN IRAQ

A nation divided over the wisdom of the 2003 invasion of Iraq found itself even more torn when, after months of war and the loss of tens of thousands of lives, the main justifications for the invasion and occupation—Iraq's possession of weapons of mass destruction (WMD)—proved to be false (Powers, 2003). Had the United States been victimized by poor or inadequate intelligence, or had our leaders intentionally overestimated the threat in order to lead us into a conflict they sought for other reasons (Suskind, 2004; Clarke, 2004; Bamford, 2004)? The debate raged in homes, at work, on editorial pages, and in several congressional hearings. Typically, those who favored the invasion blamed poor intelligence; those who opposed it saw something a bit less benign at work—the no-holds-barred use of communication to propagate the belief that our country was at risk from a madman who possessed WMD and the expectation that he would use them against us—in other words, propaganda.

The tone of the debate shifted, however, when in May 2003 Deputy Secretary of Defense Paul

Wolfowitz, one of the war's architects and primary advocates, told an interviewer for *Vanity Fair* that "from the outset, contrary to so many claims from the White House, Iraq's supposed cache of WMD had never been the most important casus belli. It was simply one of several reasons. 'For bureaucratic reasons we settled on one issue, weapons of mass destruction, because it was the one reason everyone could agree on'" (Black, 2003, p. 1A).

To the war's opponents, many of whom doubted the existence of Iraqi WMD all along, this admission was vindication of their opposition to the conflict. It too closely mirrored Nazi Germany's second-in-command Hermann Goering's recipe for marshaling public support for conflict:

It is always a simple matter to drag people along whether it is a democracy, or a fascist dictatorship, or a parliament, or a communist dictatorship. Voice or no voice, the people can always be brought to the bidding of the leaders. This is easy. All you have to do is tell them they are being

(Continued)

THINKING *about* THEORY	ENGINEERING CONSENT: WMD AND THE WAR IN IRAQ (CONTINUED)

attacked, and denounce the pacifists for lack of patriotism and exposing the country to danger. It works the same in every country. (In Crowther, 2004, p. 12)

But to many of the war's supporters this was betrayal. They had believed their government, and their government had misled them. Michael Getler, ombudsman for the *Washington Post* (an early supporter of the invasion), explained, "Almost everything we were told [by the administration] before the war, other than Saddam Hussein is bad, has turned out…. not to be the case: the weapons of mass destruction, the imagery of nuclear mushroom clouds, the links between al-Qaida and Saddam, the welcome, the resistance, the costs, the number of troops needed" (quoted in Rich, 2004, p. 12). More dramatically, *Vanity Fair* editor Graydon Carter concurred: "All the manufactured justifications for going to war crumbled on a bloody bone pile of deception and dissolution" (2004, p. 62).

Still other war supporters argued that the manufactured justifications really didn't matter. The war was a good thing—it removed a madman from power, freed the Iraqi people, and would bring democracy to the Middle East. In other words, they accepted Edward Bernays's idea of the need for the government to engineer consent—the "freedom to persuade … because in a democracy, results 'do not just happen'" (quoted in Sproule, 1997, p. 213). They accepted Lasswell's fatalism, that in our modern society "it is no longer possible to fuse the waywardness of individuals in the furnace of the war dance…. A new flame must burn out the canker of dissent and temper the steel of bellicose enthusiasm. The name of this new

hammer and anvil of social solidarity is propaganda" (Lasswell, 1927a, pp. 220–221). Six years after the invasion, former British Prime Minister Tony Blair admitted that this was the Allies' goal all along. He told the BBC that Saddam Hussein's presence in the Middle East was enough of a threat to justify the war, but "obviously you would have had to use and deploy different arguments about the nature of the threat" (in Ritchie, 2009).

What do you think? Do you believe that the government has the right (or obligation) to engineer your consent, because "in a democracy, results don't just happen?" Do you agree with Goering, that use of the "we're being threatened" master symbol works the same in all countries? Do you think that it is appropriate for our leaders to propagandize us into the "furnace of the war dance" and actively suppress "the canker of dissent"? In a democracy, can dissent ever be a "canker"? Or do you agree with Canadian scholar Stanley Cunningham, who argues that government propaganda is always a "disservice" to democracy because

it plays upon perplexity; it cultivates confusion; it poses as information and knowledge; it generates belief systems and tenacious convictions; it prefers credibility and belief states to knowledge; it supplies ersatz assurances and certainties; it skews perceptions; it systematically disregards superior epistemic values such as truth, understanding and knowledge; it discourages reasoning and a healthy respect for rigor, evidence, and procedural safeguards; it promotes the easy acceptance of unexamined belief and supine ignorance. (2000, p. 6)

PROPAGANDA COMES TO THE UNITED STATES

Americans first began to give serious consideration to the power of propaganda in the years following World War I. The war had demonstrated that modern propaganda techniques could be used with startling effectiveness to assemble massive armies and to maintain civilian morale through long years of warfare. Never before had so many people been mobilized to fight a war. Never before had so many died with so little to show for it over such a long period of time and under such harsh conditions. Earlier wars had been quickly settled by decisive battles. But in this war, massive armies confronted each other along a front that extended for hundreds of miles. From their trenches they bombarded each other and launched occasional attacks that ended in futility.

Harold Lasswell, a political scientist who developed several early theories of media, expressed considerable respect for the propaganda efforts marshaled in the cause of the First World War. He wrote:

> When all allowances have been made and all extravagant estimates pared to the bone, the fact remains that propaganda is one of the most powerful instrumentalities in the modern world. . . . In the Great Society [modern industrial society] it is no longer possible to fuse the waywardness of individuals in the furnace of the war dance; a newer and subtler instrument must weld thousands and even millions of human beings into one amalgamated mass of hate and will and hope. A new flame must burn out the canker of dissent and temper the steel of bellicose enthusiasm. The name of this new hammer and anvil of social solidarity is propaganda. (1927a, pp. 220–221)

Many social researchers in the 1920s and 1930s shared these views. Propaganda was an essential tool that had to be used to effectively manage modern social orders, especially when they are in deadly competition with other nations that rely on propaganda to mobilize their masses.

After World War I, the propaganda battle continued, and inevitably it spread beyond Europe, as nations sought to spread their influence and new political movements attracted members. During the 1920s, radio and movies provided powerful new media for propaganda messages. Hitler's rise to power in Germany was accompanied by consolidation of his control over all forms of media—beginning with radio and the film industry and ending with newspapers. In the United States, the battle lines in the propaganda war were quickly drawn. On one side were the elites dominating major social institutions and organizations, including the major political parties, businesses, schools, and universities. On the other side was a broad range of social movements and small extremist political groups. Many were local variants of Fascist, Socialist, or Communist groups that in Europe were much larger and more significant. From the point of view of the old-line elites, these groups were highly suspect. Foreign subversion was a growing fear. The elites believed the influence of these movements and groups had to be curbed before they ruined *our* way of life.

Extremist propagandists, whether foreign-based or domestically grown, found it increasingly easy to reach and persuade audiences during the 1930s. Only a part of this success, however, can be directly attributed to the rise of the powerful new media. In the United States, large newspapers, movies, and radio were controlled mainly by the existing elites. Extremists were often forced to rely on older media like pamphlets, handbills, and political rallies. When the social conditions were right and people were receptive to propaganda messages, however, even older, smaller media could be quite effective. And conditions were right. Remember the discussion of gemeinschaft and gesellschaft from the previous chapter. Mass society theorists and the elites they supported believed that "average people" were particularly open to demagogic propaganda because those "unfortunates" lived in a rapidly industrializing world characterized by psychological and cultural isolation and the loss of the security once sustained by traditional, binding, and informal social rules and obligations. As the economic depression deepened in the 1930s, many people no longer had jobs to provide an income to support their families and their relationships with others.

American elites therefore watched with increasing horror as extremist political groups consolidated their power in Europe and proceeded to establish totalitarian governments wielding enormous control over vast populations. How could they remain complacent when madmen like Hitler's propaganda chief, Joseph Goebbels, could openly espouse such antidemocratic ideas as "It would not be impossible to prove with sufficient repetition and psychological understanding of the people concerned that a square is in fact a circle. What after all are a square and a circle? They are mere words and words can be molded until they clothe ideas in disguise" (quoted in Thomson, 1977, p. 111) and "In politics power prevails, not moral claims of justice" (quoted in Herzstein, 1978, p. 69)? Fear grew that Fascist or Communist groups could and would come to power in the United States. In several American universities, researchers began to systematically study both foreign and domestic propaganda—searching for clues to what made it effective. Support for this research came from a variety of government agencies and private foundations, most notably military intelligence agencies and the Rockefeller Foundation (Gary, 1996).

We will review the propaganda theories of three of the most prolific, imaginative, and complex thinkers of their time: Harold Lasswell, Walter Lippmann, and John Dewey. Given the number of books these men wrote, it is impossible to provide a complete presentation of their work. Instead, we will highlight some of their most influential and widely publicized ideas. In nearly every case, these men later refined or even rejected some of these ideas. Our objective in presenting their theories is to show how thinking about media evolved during a very critical period in world history—not to demean these individuals or to denigrate their work.

Most of the propaganda theories that developed during the 1930s were strongly influenced by two theories: behaviorism and Freudianism. Some combined both. Before presenting the ideas of the major propaganda theorists, we will first look at the two theories that often guided their thinking.

BEHAVIORISM

behaviorism
The notion that all human action is a conditioned response to external environmental stimuli

John B. Watson, an animal experimentalist who argued that all human action is merely a conditioned response to external environmental stimuli, first popularized stimulus-response psychology. Watson's theory became known as **behaviorism** in recognition of its narrow focus on isolated human behaviors. Behaviorists rejected psychology's widely held assumption that higher mental processes (that is, conscious thought or reflection) ordinarily control human action. In contrast to such "mentalist" views, behaviorists argued that the only purpose served by consciousness was to rationalize behaviors *after* they are triggered by external stimuli. Behaviorists attempted to purge all mentalist terms from their theories and to deal strictly with observable variables—environmental stimuli on the one hand and behaviors on the other. By studying the associations that existed between specific stimuli and specific behaviors, behaviorists hoped to discover previously unknown causes for action. One of the central notions in behaviorism was the idea of conditioning. Behaviorists argued that most human behavior is the result of conditioning by the external environment. We are conditioned to act in certain ways by positive and negative stimuli—we act to gain rewards or avoid punishments.

magic bullet theory
Idea that propaganda is powerful enough to penetrate most people's defenses and condition them to act in ways that are useful to the propagandist

Early mass communication theorists, who saw the media as providing external stimuli that triggered immediate responses, frequently used behaviorist notions. For example, these ideas could be applied to the analysis of the Nazi propaganda films described earlier. The powerful, ugly images presented of Jews or the mentally ill were expected to trigger negative responses in their German audiences. Repeated exposure to these images would condition them to have a negative response whenever they see or think about Jews. These behaviorist notions were used by some theorists to develop what has come to be known as **magic bullet theory,** the idea that propaganda can be powerful enough to penetrate most people's defenses and condition them to act in ways useful to the propagandist. As we shall see, most propaganda theorists rejected such ideas as too simplistic. There was more to propaganda than conditioning.

FREUDIANISM

Freudianism
Freud's notion that human behavior is the product of the conflict between an individual's Id, Ego, and Superego

Freudianism, on the other hand, was very different from behaviorism, though Sigmund Freud shared Watson's skepticism concerning people's ability to exercise effective conscious or rational control over their actions. Freud spent considerable time counseling middle-class women who suffered from hysteria. During hysterical fits, seemingly ordinary individuals would suddenly "break down" and display uncontrolled and highly emotional behavior. It was not uncommon for quiet and passive women to "break down" in public places. They would scream, have fits of crying, or become violent. Often these outbursts occurred at times when the likelihood of embarrassment and trouble for themselves and others was at its highest. What could be causing this irrational behavior?

Ego
In Freudianism, the rational mind

Id
In Freudianism, the egocentric pleasure-seeking part of the mind

Superego
In Freudianism, the internalized set of cultural rules

To explain hysteria, Freud reasoned that the self that guides action must be fragmented into conflicting parts. Normally one part, the rational mind, or **Ego,** is in control, but sometimes other parts become dominant. Freud speculated that human action is often the product of another, darker side of the self—the **Id.** This is the egocentric pleasure-seeking part of ourselves that the Ego must struggle to keep under control. The Ego relies on an internalized set of cultural rules (the **Superego**) for guidance. Caught between the primitive Id and the overly restrictive Superego, the Ego fights a losing battle. When the Ego loses control to the Id, hysteria or worse results. When the Superego becomes dominant and the Id is completely suppressed, people turn into unemotional, depressed social automatons who simply do what others demand.

Propaganda theorists used Freudian notions to develop very pessimistic interpretations of media influence. For example, propaganda would be most effective if it could appeal directly to the Id and short-circuit or bypass the Ego. Alternatively, if through effective propaganda efforts the cultural rules (the Superego) moved the self in the direction of the Id, people's darker impulses would become normal—a strategy that some propaganda theorists believe was skillfully used by the Nazis.

Behaviorism and Freudianism were combined to create propaganda theories that viewed the average individual as incapable of rational self-control. These theories saw people as highly vulnerable to media manipulation using propaganda; media stimuli and the Id could trigger actions that the Ego and the Superego were powerless to stop. Afterward, the Ego merely rationalizes actions that it couldn't control and experiences guilt about them. Accordingly, media could have instantaneous society-wide influence on even the most educated, thoughtful people.

HAROLD LASSWELL'S PROPAGANDA THEORY

Lasswell's theory of propaganda blended ideas borrowed from behaviorism and Freudianism into a particularly pessimistic vision of media and their role in forging modern social orders. Lasswell was one of the first political scientists to recognize the usefulness of various psychological theories and to demonstrate how they could be applied to understanding politics. The power of propaganda was not so much the result of the substance or appeal of specific messages but, rather, the result of the vulnerable state of mind of average people. This state of mind can be assessed using psychological theories. Lasswell argued that economic depression and escalating political conflict had induced widespread psychosis, and this made most people susceptible to even crude forms of propaganda. When average people are confronted daily by powerful threats to their personal lives, they turn to propaganda for reassurance and a way to overcome the threat.

In Lasswell's view, democracy has a fatal flaw. It seeks to locate truth and make decisions through openly conducted debates about issues. But if these debates escalate into verbal or even physical conflict between advocates for different ideas, then widespread psychosis will result. Spectators to these conflicts will be traumatized by them. According to Floyd Matson (1964, pp. 90–93), Lasswell concluded that even relatively benign forms of political conflict were inherently pathological. When conflict escalates to the level it did in Germany during the Depression, an entire nation could become psychologically unbalanced and vulnerable to manipulation. Lasswell argued that the solution was for social researchers to find ways to "obviate conflict." This necessitates controlling those forms of political communication that lead to conflict. In Lasswell's view, even routine forms of political debate could escalate into conflicts threatening the social order. Matson stated, "In short, according to Lasswell's psychopathology of politics, the presumption in any individual case must be that political action is maladjustive, political participation is irrational, and political expression is irrelevant" (1964, p. 91). But how do you maintain a democratic social order if any form of political debate or demonstration is problematic? Lasswell had an answer to this question: replace public discourse with democratic propaganda.

Lasswell rejected simplistic behaviorist notions about propaganda effects. Here is how he described the task of the propagandist in a 1927 article:

> The strategy of propaganda, which has been phrased in cultural terms, can readily be described in the language of stimulus-response. Translated into this vocabulary, which is especially intelligible to some, the propagandist may be said to be concerned with the multiplication of those stimuli which are best calculated to evoke the desired responses, and with the nullification of those stimuli which are likely to instigate the undesired responses. Putting the same thing into terms of social suggestion, the problem of the propagandist is to multiply all the suggestions favorable to the attitudes which he wishes to produce and strengthen, and to restrict all suggestions which are unfavorable to them. (1927b, p. 620)

In other words, a few well-targeted messages couldn't bring down a democratic social order. He argued that propaganda was more than merely using media to lie to people in order to gain temporary control over them. People need to be slowly prepared to accept radically different ideas and actions. Communicators need a well-developed, long-term campaign strategy ("multiplication of those stimuli") in which new ideas and images are carefully introduced and then cultivated. Symbols must be created, and people must be gradually taught to associate specific emotions such as love or hate with these symbols. If these cultivation strategies are successful, they create what Lasswell referred to as **master (or collective) symbols** (Lasswell, 1934). Master symbols are associated with strong emotions and possess the power to stimulate beneficial large-scale mass action if they are used wisely. In contrast to behaviorist notions, Lasswell's theory envisioned a long and quite sophisticated conditioning process. Exposure to one or two extremist messages would not likely have significant effects. And propaganda messages can be delivered through many different media, not just radio or newspapers. Lasswell wrote:

> The form in which the significant symbols are embodied to reach the public may be spoken, written, pictorial, or musical, and the number of stimulus carriers is infinite. If the propagandist identifies himself imaginatively with the life of his subjects in a particular situation, he is able to explore several channels of approach. Consider, for a moment, the people who ride the street cars. They may be reached by placards posted inside the car, by posters on the billboards along the track, by newspapers which they read, by conversations which they overhear, by leaflets which are openly or surreptitiously slipped into their hands, by street demonstrations at halting places, and no doubt by other means. Of these possible occasions there are no end. (1927b, p. 631)

Lasswell argued that successful social movements gain power by propagating master symbols over a period of months and years using a variety of media. For example, the emotions we experience when we see the American flag or hear the national anthem are not the result of a single previous exposure. Rather, we have observed the flag and heard the anthem in countless past situations in which a limited range of emotions were induced and experienced. The flag and the anthem have acquired emotional meaning because of all these previous experiences. When we see the flag on television with the anthem in the background, some of these emotions may be aroused and reinforced. Once established, such master symbols can be used in many different types of propaganda. In the case of the flag, it is used continually during political campaigns as a means of suggesting that political candidates are patriotic and can be trusted to defend the nation.

Lasswell believed that past propagation of most master symbols had been more or less haphazard. For every successful propagandist, there were hundreds who failed. Although he respected the cunning way that the Nazis used propaganda, he was not convinced that they really understood what they were doing. He respected Joseph Goebbels, the chief Nazi propagandist, because he had a Ph.D., but he regarded Hitler as a mad genius who relied on intuition to guide his use of propaganda. When it came to using media, Hitler was an evil artist but not a scientist. Lasswell proposed combating Hitler with a new science of propaganda. Power to control delivery of propaganda through the mass media would be placed in the hands of a new elite, a **scientific technocracy** who would pledge to use its

master (or collective) symbols
Symbols that are associated with strong emotions and possess the power to stimulate large-scale mass action

scientific technocracy
An educated social science–based elite charged with protecting vulnerable average people from harmful propaganda

knowledge for good rather than evil—to save democracy rather than destroy it. Lasswell and his colleagues developed a term to refer to this strategy for using propaganda. They called it the "science of democracy" (Smith, 1941). But could a democratic social order be forged by propaganda? Wouldn't essential principles of democracy be sacrificed? Is democracy possible without public discourse?

In a world where rational political debate is impossible because average people are prisoners of their own conditioning and psychoses (remember behaviorism and Freudianism) and therefore subject to manipulation by propagandists, Lasswell argued, the only hope for us as a nation rested with social scientists who could harness the power of propaganda for Good rather than Evil. It is not surprising, then, that many of the early media researchers took their task very seriously. They believed that nothing less than the fate of the world lay in their hands.

Lasswell's propaganda-for-good was adopted by the Office of War Information as its basic strategy during World War II. In the Cold War that followed that global hot war, using agencies such as the Voice of America, the United States Information Agency, the Office of International Information and Educational Exchange, and the State Department, it served as the foundation for numerous official efforts to counter Communism and spread democracy (Sproule, 1997, pp. 213–215). Not all of Lasswell's contemporaries, however, were taken by his call for elite control of media. Floyd Matson, a severe critic of Lasswell's theory, complained that Lasswell's "contemplative analysis of 'skill politics and skill revolution' has disclosed to Lasswell that in our own time the most potent of all skills is that of propaganda, of symbolic manipulation and myth-making—and hence that the dominant elite must be the one which possesses or can capture this skill" (Matson, 1964, p. 87).

WALTER LIPPMANN'S THEORY OF PUBLIC OPINION FORMATION

Throughout the 1930s, many other members of the social elite, especially those at major universities, shared Lasswell's vision of a benevolent social science–led technocracy. They believed that physical science and social science held the keys to fighting totalitarianism and preserving democracy. As such, Lasswell's work commanded the attention of leading academics and opinion leaders, including one of the most powerful opinion makers of the time—Walter Lippmann, a nationally syndicated columnist for the *New York Times*.

Lippmann shared Lasswell's skepticism about the ability of average people to make sense of their social world and to make rational decisions about their actions. In *Public Opinion* (1922), he pointed out the discrepancies that necessarily exist between "the world outside and the pictures in our heads." Because these discrepancies were inevitable, Lippmann doubted that average people could govern themselves as classic democratic theory assumed they could. The world of the 1930s was an especially complex place, and the political forces were very dangerous. People simply couldn't learn enough from media to help them understand it all. Even if journalists took their responsibility seriously, they couldn't overcome the psychological and social barriers that prevented average people from developing useful pictures in their heads. Political essayist Eric Alterman quoted and summarized Lippmann's position:

> Writing in the early twenties, Lippmann famously compared the average citizen to a deaf spectator sitting in the back row. He does not know what is happening, why it is happening, what ought to happen. "He lives in a world he cannot see, does not understand and is unable to direct." Journalism, with its weakness for sensationalism, made things worse. Governance was better left to a "specialized class of men" with inside information. No one expects a steel-worker to understand physics, so why should he be expected to understand politics? (2008, p. 10)

These ideas raised serious questions about the viability of democracy and the role of a free press in it. What do you do in a democracy if you can't trust the people to cast informed votes? What good is a free press if it is impossible to effectively transmit enough of the most vital forms of information to the public? What can you do if people are so traumatized by dealing with everyday problems that they have no time to think about global issues? The fact that Lippmann made his living working as a newspaper columnist lent credibility to his pessimism. In advancing these arguments, he directly contradicted the Libertarian assumptions (free speech and free press; see Chapter 5) that were the intellectual foundation of the U.S. media system.

Like Lasswell, Lippmann believed that propaganda posed such a severe challenge that drastic changes in our political system were required. The public was vulnerable to propaganda, so some mechanism or agency was needed to protect them from it. A benign but enormously potent form of media control was necessary. Self-censorship by media probably wouldn't be sufficient. Lippmann shared Lasswell's conclusion that the best solution to these problems was to place control of information gathering and distribution in the hands of a benevolent technocracy—a scientific elite—who could be trusted to use scientific methods to sort fact from fiction and make good decisions about who should receive various messages. To accomplish this, Lippmann proposed the establishment of a quasi-governmental intelligence bureau that would carefully evaluate information and supply it to other elites for decision making. This bureau could also determine which information should be transmitted through the mass media and which information people were better off not knowing.

REACTION AGAINST EARLY PROPAGANDA THEORY

Lasswell and Lippmann's propaganda theories seemed to carry the weight of real-world proof—the globe had been engulfed by a devastating world war, The War to End All Wars in fact, yet global turmoil continued to rage. These conflicts were infused with sophisticated and apparently successful propaganda. Yet there was opposition. One prominent critic of propaganda theory was philosopher John Dewey. In a series of lectures (Dewey, 1927), he outlined his objections to Lippmann's views. Throughout his long career, Dewey was a tireless and prolific defender of public education as the most effective means of defending democracy against totalitarianism. He refused to accept the need for a technocracy that would use scientific methods to protect people from themselves. Rather, he argued that people could learn to defend themselves if they were only taught the correct defenses. He asserted that even rudimentary public education could enable people to resist propaganda methods. Dewey "took violent issue" with Lippmann's "trust in the beneficence of elites." "'A class of experts,' Dewey argued, 'is inevitably too removed from common interests as to become a class of private interests and private knowledge.'... He saw democracy as less about information than conversation. The media's job, in Dewey's conception, was 'to interest the public in the public interest'" (Alterman, 2008, p. 10).

Dewey's critics saw him as an idealist who talked a lot about reforming education without actually doing much himself to implement concrete reforms (Altschull, 1990, p. 230). Dewey did no better when it came to reforming the media. He argued that newspapers needed to do more than simply serve as bulletin boards for information about current happenings. He issued a challenge to journalists to do more to stimulate public interest in politics and world affairs—to motivate people to actively seek out information and then talk about it with others. Newspapers should serve as vehicles for public education and debate. They should focus more on ideas and philosophy and less on descriptions of isolated actions. They should teach critical thinking skills and structure public discussion of important issues. His efforts to found such a publication never got very far, however.

Pragmatism
School of philosophical theory emphasizing the practical function of knowledge as an instrument for adapting to reality and controlling it

Dewey based his arguments on **Pragmatism**, a school of philosophical theory emphasizing the practical function of knowledge as an instrument for adapting to reality and controlling it. We'll take a closer look at this theory in Chapter 11. James Carey (1989, pp. 83–84) contends that Dewey's ideas have continuing value. He argues that Dewey anticipated many of the concerns now being raised by cultural studies theories. And as you'll also read in Chapter 11, Dewey's belief that educating people to think critically about media content and how they use it is at the heart of the media literacy movement and current concerns about public education and public discourse.

In one very important respect, Dewey's ideas about the relationship between communities and media were quite innovative. Lasswell and Lippmann saw media as external agencies, as conveyor belts delivering quantities of information to isolated audience members. In Chapter 7 we will consider Lasswell's classic linear model of mass communication: *who says what to whom through what medium with what effect.* Dewey believed models like this were far too simplistic. They ignored the fact that effective media must be well integrated into the communities they serve; media are at the center of the complex network of relationships that define a community. Media should be understood not as external agents but as servants that facilitate public discussion and debate, as guardians and facilitators of the public forum in which democratic politics are conducted.

Dewey believed that communities, not isolated individuals, use communication (and the media of communication) to create and maintain the culture that bonds and sustains them. When media assume the role of external agents and work to manipulate the "pictures in people's heads," they lose their power to serve as credible facilitators and guardians of public debate; they become just another competitor for our attention. The potentially productive interdependence between the community and media is disrupted, and the public forum itself is likely to be destroyed. This argument concerning the disconnection of media from communities is now of considerable interest (see Chapters 10 and 11) and foreshadows contemporary debate over the proper role of media in communities.

INSTANT ACCESS

Propaganda Theory

Strengths

1. Is first systematic theory of mass communication
2. Focuses attention on why media might have powerful effects
3. Identifies personal, social, and cultural factors that can enhance media's power to have effects
4. Focuses attention on the use of campaigns to cultivate symbols

Weaknesses

1. Underestimates abilities of average people to evaluate messages
2. Ignores personal, social, and cultural factors that limit media effects
3. Overestimates the speed and range of media effects

THE INSTITUTE FOR PROPAGANDA ANALYSIS

Should the power of propaganda be used for democratic ends (the Lasswell/Lippmann view), or because propaganda, by its very existence, was antidemocratic, was education the best way to deal with it (the Dewey view)? The disagreement over the proper place of propaganda in a democracy was no theoretical exercise. Social scientists believed the fate of the country, the world in fact, rested on its outcome.

In 1937, the threat of external propaganda was so great that a group of social scientists, journalists, and educators founded the Institute for Propaganda Analysis with the goal of orchestrating a nationwide educational effort to combat its effects. During the four years of its existence, the institute was quite productive, generating numerous pamphlets, books, and articles explaining how propaganda works (read more about propaganda techniques in the box entitled "Applying the Seven Propaganda Techniques"). The institute was successful in developing an antipropaganda curriculum adopted by high schools and adult education programs across the country. It was so successful that it came under attack for undermining the effectiveness of propaganda techniques seen as essential to defending democracy.

In 1941, an opponent and a defender of the institute's educational efforts faced off in the pages of *Public Opinion Quarterly,* a journal that devoted considerable attention to propaganda during the 1930s and 1940s. Bruce L. Smith questioned the value of propaganda analysis, that is, education, because he believed it fostered cynicism that could actually lead most students toward authoritarian views. At the time he wrote this article, he headed the U.S. Justice Department's efforts to censor propaganda and arrest foreign agents who engaged in it. He argued:

> Students at first become tremendously interested in the sportive side of launching an attack on "propaganda devices." . . . After this first excitement, they tend to become morally indignant, at least in most cases, about the sheer quantity of fraud and misleading utterance to which they have been exposed all their lives, especially in paid advertising and in political speeches. At this point they have a tendency to espouse some program or other of violent censorship and even suppression of those who issue

"antisocial" propaganda. They demand a Board of Public Opinion Censors, with wide and confiscatory powers. At this level of opposition to free speech many of them remain, even if it is pointed out to them that censorship of anyone who claims to support democracy is in no way compatible with the traditions and program of the American people. (Smith, 1941, p. 251)

THINKING *about* THEORY — APPLYING THE SEVEN PROPAGANDA TECHNIQUES

The Institute of Propaganda Analysis had at its core the goal of identifying common propaganda techniques and teaching average people about them so they could defend themselves against the propagandist's work. The institute regularly sent out information fliers and published books to teach people how to think, rather than what to think.

It identified seven propaganda "tricks of the trade":

1. **Name-calling:** By using negative labels and bad names, propagandists create distrust toward their subjects. Name-calling is a substitute for arguing an idea's merits.
2. **Glittering generalities:** Typically in the guise of slogans or simple catchphrases, propagandists use vague, sweeping statements without offering supporting evidence.
3. **Transfer:** Propagandists claim the approval of some one or thing as theirs, hoping that the public's support for that "authority" will transfer to them.
4. **Testimonial:** Propagandists use respected people to endorse their ideas, hoping that stamp-of-approval will move the public closer to their goals.
5. **Plain folks:** The propagandist is always "just a regular guy or gal, just like you or me," or "just one of you," or "just a simple working stiff." The public can trust this humble soul because his or her ideas are "of the people."
6. **Bandwagon:** Propagandists claim widespread support, appealing to people's desire to be on the winning side. They offer no evidence or even lie about the level of support they claim their idea enjoys.
7. **Card-stacking:** Propagandists make the best case possible for their side and the worst case possible for any alternatives; they "stack the cards" against the public reaching an informed decision.

Your turn. Take these seven techniques and apply them to a controversial contemporary issue that interests you (e.g., gun control, reproductive choice, health care reform, media deregulation, immigration reform). Take a position in the debate and analyze the appeals of the side with which you disagree (that's propaganda, of course). Then subject your side's appeals to the same analysis. What do you find? Or you can choose an identifiable public personality who speaks strongly or regularly on public issues (a politician or media personality, for example). Apply the same steps.

A trio of mass communication researchers at Indiana University did just this. Mike Conway, Maria Elizabeth Grabe, and Kevin Grieves (2007) used the Institute of Propaganda Analysis's seven techniques to analyze 115 episodes (six months' worth) of "Talking Points Memo," the editorial portion of the television program *The O'Reilly Factor*. You can see the research itself at http://journalism.indiana.edu/papers/oreilly.html. These researchers chose the Fox Cable News show for their study for three reasons. First, host Bill O'Reilly labels his program the "No Spin Zone," and they wanted to test that assertion. Second, a 2005 Annenberg Public Policy Center survey found that 40 percent of American adults consider O'Reilly a journalist (compared, for example, to 30 percent who see Bob Woodward of the *Washington Post* and Watergate fame as a journalist). They thought it interesting that a "journalist" might utilize propaganda techniques. Third, O'Reilly is one of the most powerful voices in the media today, so he was worthy of study.

In brief, the researchers discovered that O'Reilly employed six of the seven tricks of the trade nearly thirteen times in each minute of his editorials. For example, he calls some person or group a bad name every 6.8 seconds. Watch an episode or two of this program to see if this analysis makes sense to you. Can you argue that one person's propaganda is another's truth? Compare the Indiana University results to the results of your own study. What conclusions can you draw about the seven techniques? About using them to search for the presence of propaganda?

Smith was cynical in his assessment of the ability of ordinary students to learn how to deal with propaganda on a day-to-day basis. Only a few could be expected to be "far-sighted" and able to develop the "intellectual vitality" to "undertake the lifelong burden of preserving free speech." His argument was that the burden would prove to be so heavy that those who carried it would demand censorship rather than education as the solution to combating propaganda. Smith saw the American social order as inherently, and properly, elitist—a democracy of the *few* because the *many* had little ability to participate effectively. Average people must necessarily be governed by a paternalistic elite. But if education wouldn't work, then what was the alternative? According to Smith (1941, p. 252), "The teacher, therefore, needs to look ahead. To be sure, democracy demands that we constantly and vigorously practice propaganda analysis (education). But we must also look beyond it to the establishment of a 'science of democracy,' of which propaganda analysis is but one indispensable part."

But what was the "science of democracy" and how would it be superior to propaganda analysis's educational approach? Smith explained:

> Students frightened by their recent discovery of the gullibility and irrationality of the great mass of mankind cannot be expected to retain much faith in the value of social control by democratic discussion. To preserve and develop this faith, it is necessary to encourage them to analyze and appraise the potency of such common mechanisms of wishful thinking as regression, rationalization, repression, projection, sadism, and masochism. It is not necessary, however, to clutter up their vocabularies with a great number of terms like these in order to put over the essential points. What is needed is a concise, structuralized picture of individual human motives, comparable with the structuralized picture of society already drawn. (Smith, 1941, p. 258)

What Smith was proposing was a form of "democratic propaganda" that could be used to combat the cynicism generated by propaganda analysis. Students who suddenly realized just how gullible they and others were and how systematically they were being manipulated had to be reassured that there were elite experts who understood this phenomenon and had developed concepts to deal with it. But since these concepts were too hard and too complicated to explain, they needed to be simplified into a "concise, structuralized picture" that didn't "clutter up the vocabularies with a great number of terms." In other words, they needed to be subjected to "good" propaganda; in Bernays's terms, they needed to have their consent engineered.

Clyde Miller, an education professor at Columbia University and secretary for the Institute for Propaganda Analysis, found Smith's call for good or democratic propaganda unpersuasive:

> In propaganda analysis the Institute has been emphasizing an objective, scientific approach to controversial issues and, as an integral part of that approach, has been trying to build—to use Mr. Smith's phrase—"a vigorous faith in the values and ultimate triumph of democratic practice." Mr. Smith states that many teachers have been making early attempts to build "propaganda resistance" among their students. True. It is not propaganda resistance, however valuable as that may be at times in dealing with antidemocratic propagandas, which is stressed in the educational program of the Institute for Propaganda Analysis; it is understanding of why and how propaganda works— how it relates to our fears and hopes, our hates and loves, our mental and emotional

conditioning, our basic needs. . . . As Secretary of the Institute for Propaganda Analysis, I can assure Mr. Smith that I have not heard of any students demanding authoritarianism as a means of dealing with propaganda, but I do know for a fact that the educational program has caused many thousands of teachers and students to have a surer faith in the present and ultimate values of the scientific method and democratic practices. (Miller, 1941, pp. 657–659)

Miller also defended the effectiveness of the Institute's efforts to combat Fascism, racism, and class hatred. He shared many of Smith's views about why propaganda is effective, but he remained convinced that propaganda could best be defeated by teaching students to understand how propaganda works—not by using democratic propaganda to oppose bad or undemocratic propaganda:

In the task of combating the unscientific theories of racism, which Hitler and Goebbels have utilized so effectively to create class hatreds, the Institute may be doing its best work. No student, once he has gone through the recommended educational program of the Institute, is likely to succumb to propaganda causing him to hate Jews as Jews and Negroes as Negroes. This approach does immunize students against propagandas inciting to hatred based on racial and religious differences. The process of scientific analysis in combination with a faith which holds fast to the values of democracy is the most powerful instrument for combating the wave of Ku Klux Klanism that is developing rapidly as a result of war tensions. (Miller, 1941, p. 664)

Who won this debate? Did Miller manage to persuade other elites that education was the best strategy for dealing with propaganda, or did Smith's views win out? About the time that Miller's article appeared, the Institute for Propaganda Analysis published a newsletter entitled "We Say Au Revoir." It announced that it had been persuaded that for the good of the war effort, it should cease all activities. You will read much about these "democratic propaganda" campaigns such as the *Why We Fight* films in later chapters. And even when World War II ended and other wars—the Korean and the Cold—began, the Institute for Propaganda Analysis never reopened, and John Dewey's calls for education were similarly marginalized. The task of defending democracy was handed over to Lasswell and his colleagues. The "science of democracy" ushered in an era of propaganda-for-good, or democratic propaganda.

MODERN PROPAGANDA THEORY

Consider the Hippler and Sproule characterizations of propaganda from earlier in this chapter: simplify a complex issue and repeat that simplification; use covert, massively orchestrated communication; and use tricky language to discourage reflective thought. Some contemporary critical theorists argue that propaganda conforming to these rules is alive and well today and that it is practiced with a stealth, sophistication, and effectiveness unparalleled in history. They point to a number of "natural beliefs" that have been so well propagandized that meaningful public discourse about them has become difficult if not impossible. Political discourse and advertising are frequent areas of modern propaganda study, and the central argument of this modern propaganda theory is that powerful elites so thoroughly control the mass media and their content that they have little trouble imposing their Truth on the culture.

Close your eyes and think *welfare*. Did you envision large corporations accepting government handouts, special tax breaks for businesses, companies building ships and planes that the military does not want? Or did you picture a single mother, a woman of color, cheating the taxpayers so she can stay home and watch *Jerry Springer?* This narrowing of public discourse and debate is examined in works such as historian Herb Schiller's *Culture, Inc.: The Corporate Takeover of Public Expression* (1989); communication theorist Robert McChesney's *Corporate Media and the Threat to Democracy* (1997) and *The Problem of the Media* (2004); mass communication researchers Kathleen Hall Jamieson and Paul Waldman's *The Press Effect* (2003); and linguist Noam Chomsky's *American Power and the New Mandarins* (1969), *Deterring Democracy* (1991), and with Edward S. Herman, *Manufacturing Consent* (Herman and Chomsky, 1988). All offer a common perspective. In Jamieson and Waldman's words, it is, "'Facts' can be difficult to discern and relate to the public, particularly in a context in which the news is driven by politicians and other interested parties who selectively offer some pieces of information while suppressing others" (xiii).

Take one such "interested party," advertisers and their advertising, as an example. Different ads may tout one product over another, but all presume the logic and rightness of consumption and capitalism. Our need for "more stuff" is rarely questioned: the connection between wealth/consumption and success/acceptance is never challenged; and concern about damage to the environment caused by, first, the manufacture of products and second, their disposal, is excluded from the debate. The point is not that consumption and capitalism are innately bad, but that as in all successful propaganda efforts, the alternatives are rarely considered. When alternatives *are* considered, those who raise them are viewed as out of the mainstream or peculiar. By extension, this failure to consider alternatives benefits those same economic elites most responsible for limiting that consideration and reflection. Sproule has written thoughtfully and persuasively on advertising as propaganda in *Channels of Propaganda* (1994) and *Propaganda and Democracy: The American Experience of Media and Mass Persuasion* (1997).

This current reconsideration of propaganda theory comes primarily from critical theorists and, as a result, its orientation tends to be from the political Left (Chapter 2). For example, economist and media analyst Edward S. Herman identified five *filters* that ensure the "multi-leveled capability of powerful business and government entities and collectives (for example, the Business Roundtable; U.S. Chamber of Commerce; industry lobbies and front groups) to exert power over the flow of information" (1996, p. 117). These filters enable powerful business and government elites "to mobilize an elite consensus, to give the appearance of democratic consent, and to create enough confusion, misunderstanding, and apathy in the general population to allow elite programs to go forward" (p. 118). The first two of Herman's elite-supporting filters are *ownership* and *advertising,* which "have made bottom line considerations more controlling. . . . The professional autonomy of journalists has been reduced" (p. 124). The next two are *sourcing* and *flack,* increasingly effective because "a reduction in the resources devoted to journalism means that those who subsidize the media by providing sources for copy gain greater leverage" (p. 125). Here he is specifically speaking of the power of corporate and government public relations. Finally, the fifth filter motivating media toward propagandists' support of the status quo is the media's "belief in the 'miracle of the market.' There is now an almost religious faith in the market, at least among the elite, so that regardless of the evidence, markets are assumed benevolent and non-market mechanisms are suspect" (p. 125). These themes, as you will see in Chapters 8 and 11, accurately mirror many of the core assumptions of critical cultural theory.

Behaviorists Richard Laitinen and Richard Rakos (1997) offer another critical view of contemporary propaganda. They argue that modern propaganda—in their definition, "the control of behavior by media manipulation" (p. 237)—is facilitated by three factors: an audience "that is enmeshed and engulfed in a harried lifestyle, less well-informed, and less politically involved, . . . the use of sophisticated polling and survey procedures, whose results are used by the propagandists to increase their influence, . . . [and] the incorporation of media companies into megaconglomerates" (pp. 238–239). These factors combine to put untold influence in the hands of powerful business and governmental elites without the public's awareness. Laitinen and Rakos wrote:

> In contemporary democracies, the absence of oppressive government control of information is typically considered a fundamental characteristic of a "free society." However, the lack of aversive control does not mean that information is "free" of controlling functions. On the contrary, current mechanisms of influence, through direct economic and indirect political contingencies, pose an even greater threat to behavioral diversity than do historically tyrannical forms. Information today is more systematic, continuous, consistent, unobtrusive, and ultimately powerful. (1997, p. 237)

There is also renewed interest in propaganda theory from the political Right. This conservative interest in propaganda takes the form of a critique of liberal media bias (see, for example, Coulter, 2002, 2006; Goldberg, 2002, 2003, 2009; Morris and McGann, 2008). Other than surveys indicating that a majority of journalists vote Democratic, there is little serious scholarship behind this assertion. In fact, what research there is tends to negate the liberal media bias thesis, as the large majority of media outlet managers and owners tend to vote Republican, the majority of the country's syndicated newspaper columnists write with a conservative bent, and the majority of "newsmakers" on network and cable public affairs talk shows are politically right-of-center (Alterman, 2003). McChesney commented:

> The fundamental error in the conservative notion of the "liberal" media [is] it posits that editors and journalists have almost complete control over what goes into news. . . . In conservative "analysis," the institutional factors of corporate ownership, profit-motivation, and advertising support have no effect on media content. . . . The notion that journalism can regularly produce a product that violates the fundamental interests of media owners and advertisers and do so with impunity simply has no evidence behind it. (1997, p. 60)

LIBERTARIANISM REBORN

By the end of the 1930s, pessimism about the future of democracy was widespread. Most members of the old-line elites were convinced that totalitarianism couldn't be stopped. They pointed to theories like those of Lasswell and Lippmann as proof that average people could not be trusted. The only hope for the future lay with technocracy and science.

In the next chapter, we will trace the development of theories that arose in opposition to these technocratic views. Advocates of these emerging ideas didn't base their views of media on social science; rather, they wanted to revive older notions of democracy and media. If modern democracy was being threatened, then maybe the threat was the result of having strayed too far from old values and ideals. Perhaps these could be restored and modern social institutions could somehow be purified and renewed. Theorists sought to make the **Libertarianism** of the Founding Fathers once again relevant to democracy. In doing so, they created views of media that are still widely held.

Libertarianism
A normative theory that sees people as good and rational and able to judge good ideas from bad

SUMMARY

The first half of the twentieth century was a highly traumatic period in which the basic principles of democracy were tested. The power of mass media was demonstrated by totalitarian propagandists who used media to convert millions to their ideas. Though Nazi and Communist propagandists wielded media with apparent effectiveness, the basis for their power over mass audiences was not well understood. Early theorists combined Freudianism and behaviorism to argue that propaganda messages were like magic bullets easily and instantly penetrating even the strongest defenses. No one was safe from their power to convert. Later theorists like Harold Lasswell held that propaganda typically influenced people in slow and subtle ways. It created new master symbols that could be used to induce new forms of thought and action. Both magic bullet and Lasswell's theories assumed that media could operate as external agents and be used as tools to manipulate essentially passive mass audiences. Also believing in the propaganda power of mass media was columnist Walter Lippmann, whose skepticism at the self-governance abilities of average people and distrust of lazy media professionals brought him to the conclusion that the inevitably incomplete and inaccurate "pictures in people's heads" posed a threat to democracy.

There was disagreement among propaganda theorists on how to deal with its threat to "our way of life." Advocates of a "science of democracy" thought the best way to protect average people from bad (antidemocratic) propaganda was to use good (democratic) propaganda. A scientific technocracy could be developed to ensure the dissemination of good propaganda. Others, despite their fear of propaganda, believed that propaganda analysis, like that undertaken at the Institute for Propaganda Analysis, was the only truly democratic way to deal with propaganda. That is, rather than use "good" propaganda, teach average people how propaganda operates so they can defend themselves against it. John Dewey's solution to propaganda's threat relied on traditional notions of democracy. Because people were in fact good and rational, the counter to propaganda was not control of media by a technocratic elite, but more education of the public.

Contemporary propaganda theory, centered in critical theory, argues that public discourse is shaped and limited by powerful elites to serve their own ends. Advertising's underlying theme that consumption and capitalism are beneficial is another area of interest to propaganda theorists.

Critical Thinking Questions

1. This chapter spent a good deal of time on the debate over the proper role of propaganda in a democracy. Where do you stand? Should those who "know better" use powerful propaganda techniques for the public good, or is propaganda inherently antidemocratic? Reread the box concerning engineering of consent and the invasion of Iraq. Can you identify those who take the Lasswell/Lippmann view and those who might favor Dewey and the Institute of Propaganda Analysis's perspective?

2. Founding Father Benjamin Franklin said that Americans who would exchange a bit of freedom in order to secure a bit of security deserve neither freedom nor security. What does he mean by this? Can you relate this sentiment to the debate over the role of propaganda in a democracy? Where would Franklin have stood on the issue?

3. Can the traditional news media ever be truly "liberal," given their corporate ownership? Doesn't the now widely accepted view that the media failed the country in the run-up to the invasion of Iraq prove that they are anything but liberal? Why or why not? What about the media's failure to detect the looming financial crisis that nearly brought down the global economy? Wouldn't a media with an anti-corporate bias—that is, a liberal media—been more vigilant?

Key Terms

muckraker	gray propaganda	Ego	scientific technocracy
propaganda	engineering of consent	Superego	Pragmatism
white propaganda	behaviorism	Id	Libertarianism
disinformation	magic bullet theory	master (or collective) symbols	
black propaganda	Freudianism		

5 | NORMATIVE THEORIES OF MASS COMMUNICATION

At around half past nine on the morning of April 16, 2007, a deranged young man gunned down two students in a dormitory at Virginia Tech University. He would later that day use his automatic weapons to kill thirty more people on that idyllic campus. Between the two attacks, however, the shooter took the time to mail a package to NBC News. Arriving at the broadcast network's New York headquarters at eleven in the morning two days later, the parcel included a twenty-five-minute self-made videotape and forty-three photographs. Accompanying these visuals, all featuring the angry, gun- and knife-wielding murderer, was a twenty-three-page manifesto. The network debated what to do with this material. By six o'clock that night, the regularly scheduled start of its evening national news program, NBC's news professionals had made their decision. That night's coverage of the rampage included two minutes of video, seven photographs, and thirty-seven sentences from the written screed. "We hit the brake pedal," said NBC News president Steve Capus. Brian Williams, anchor of the NBC *Nightly News,* admitted that his own family could not watch the repeatedly shown images. But he added, "However uncomfortable it is, it proves this was journalism. This was news and a material advance in the story." Not only was it "journalism," offered Capus, but in showing restraint in the airing of the images, writings, and video of the murder, NBC practiced "good journalism" (NBC President, 2007). The airing was proper, said NBC's Capus, "The news-value question is long gone. Every journalist is united on this" (in Gizbert, 2007).

Not every journalist. The Canadian Broadcasting Corporation (CBC) did not air any of the NBC footage. CBC news chief Tony Burman explained:

> [NBC's] handling of these tapes was a mistake. As I watched last night, sickened as I'm sure most viewers were, I imagined what kind of impact this broadcast would have on similarly deranged people. In horrific but real ways, this is their 15 seconds of fame. I had this awful and sad feeling that there were parents watching these excerpts on NBC who were unaware that they will lose their children in some future copycat killing triggered by these broadcasts. (in Gizbert, 2007)

Media critic Todd Gitlin was likewise saddened by NBC's coverage. He wrote that killers like the Virginia Tech gunman are "endlessly bitter men" who "turn themselves into walking arsenals." Gitlin continued:

> They turn themselves into broadcasters as well. These killers are in the communication business. They will send messages to prove that they are not, after all, tiny. They claim recognition as giants, virulent in their potency. They are going to force the whole world to suffer their purported greatness. And the means toward this end are double: The killers are going to kill whomever they please, and they are going to make the rest of the world know it.
>
> Having left behind a record of depravity, the killer is then going to exit. He will vanish into an eternity of fame. As his markers, he will leave corpses behind. He will be unforgettable—not only a killer, but a great killer. And in a world saturated with media, a great killer must also be a famous killer. Notoriety is immortality. So to complete his glorious task, he turns to his accomplices—the media.... The broadcasters do not share the killer's purpose, exactly, but they serve it. (Gitlin, 2007)

How did the broadcasters "serve" the killer's purpose? On the day of the shooting, both CBS and NBC News sent their best-known personalities, their prime-time anchors, to the campus for "live reporting," guaranteeing increased viewership. To heighten the drama, all news networks—broadcast and cable—repeatedly used on-screen graphics declaring the senseless murders a "massacre" and a "bloodbath." "This story didn't need any sensationalism," said ABC News senior vice president Paul Slavin, "but people are always looking for that extra rating point" (in Grossman, 2007, p. 15).

How would you balance "that extra rating point" against the very real possibility of a copycat killer? After all, the Virginia Tech gunman gave credit in the video he mailed to NBC to the Columbine High School killers as his "comrades in rejection."

Modern media-saturated society is rife with conflicts such as this. They may appear to be less dramatic, but given the central role our media system plays in the conduct of our lives and the maintenance of our democracy, their resolution is no less significant. Here is a recent sampling. The Kaiser Family Foundation issued a report entitled *Food for Thought: Television Food Advertising to Children in the United States,* identifying snack and fast-food advertising as a major contributor to childhood obesity and calling for restrictions on this type of marketing (Kaiser, 2007). Pediatricians, teachers, parents, and politicians quickly took up the cause, but better parental supervision would obviate the need for government intrusion, said marketers.

A battle also erupted between journalists calling for investigations into the mistreatment of detainees during the "War on Terror" and those who thought it unwise. The *Atlantic's* Andrew Sullivan insisted that as the voice of the people, the media had an obligation to investigate the "pre-eminent moral question in American politics," the "question of torture—and the United States' embrace of inhumanity as a core American value" (2009). *Salon's* Glenn Greenwald commented on what he saw as the media's failure: "It should be emphasized that yet again, it is not the Congress or the establishment media which is uncovering these abuses and forcing disclosure of government misconduct. Rather, it is the ACLU [and] other human rights organizations that has had to fill the void left by those failed institutions" (2009b). But syndicated columnist Peggy Noonan countered, telling ABC News, "Some things in life need to be mysterious. Sometimes you need to just keep walking" (in Alterman, 2009a, p. 10), and Chuck Todd, Chief White House Correspondent and political director for NBC News, called investigations into the torture and death of hundreds of detainees little more than "cable catnip" (in Kapur, 2009). There was even controversy over many outlets' refusal to use the word *torture* when describing methods used by American interrogators that when used by foreign countries they readily labeled as such (Drum, 2009).

In 2009, Congress and the public demanded to know why the media had missed the looming financial crisis that devastated the world economy. Many accused the media, enthralled by powerful CEOs and their companies' advertising dollars, of abetting the disaster (Starkman, 2009). Financial reporters countered, "No one knew; they lied to us; we're only as good as our sources" (Mitchell, 2009, p. 16).

The *New York Times* kept secret for eight months the abduction in Afghanistan of its reporter David Rohde, enlisting forty other news organizations in the news blackout. After Rohde escaped, "a major debate ignited in and out of the journalism community about how responsible the coordinated secret had been. Was sitting on a story for so long mainly because a colleague was involved a breach of journalistic ethics" (Strupp, 2009, p. 6)?

Here's another controversial issue. The Associated Press distributed a horrifying photograph of a Marine in Afghanistan, badly wounded and dying. Several papers ran the image; Americans must see the real cost of war, they reasoned. They were attacked as unpatriotic. Just as many outlets refused to use the photograph, agreeing with Defense Secretary Robert Gates that publishing the image was disrespectful and compassionless (McMichael, 2009). They were attacked as Pentagon apologists.

Two more examples: The *Washington Post* announced "salons" where, for a fee, "stakeholders" in the critical topics of the day could engage in "news-driven and off-the-record conversation" with its reporters (Wasserman, 2009), and a Columbia, South Carolina, newspaper, *The State*, revealed that it had been holding e-mail messages sent between Governor Mark Sanford and his Argentinean lover for six months before the adulterous affair was ultimately revealed (Arango and Stelter, 2009).

Despite seemingly well-reasoned journalistic explanations for each of these actions, each was met with fierce challenge. These controversies are not easily resolved, and perhaps they should not be. Each houses the conflict between our basic belief in freedom of press and expression and our desire to build a humane, meaningful society in which all people can live safely and with dignity.

As we saw in Chapter 3, this conflict is not new, nor is the question of whose values should prevail in its resolution. This is precisely why we value our First Freedom: it protects (or should protect) the resolving debate. As we saw in Chapter 4, in the first half of the twentieth century many people inside and outside the media industries were so mistrustful of the people and the press that curtailment of our freedom of press and expression had significant support among many elites. Who could blame them?

OVERVIEW

During the era of yellow journalism, most media professionals cared very little for the niceties of accuracy, objectivity, and public sensitivies. But in the first decades of the twentieth century, a crusade began among some media industry people and various social elites to clean up the media and make them more respectable and credible. The watchword of this crusade was *professionalism,* and its goal was elimination of shoddy and irresponsible content.

Some sort of theory was needed to guide this task of media reform. The goal of this theory would be to answer questions such as these:

- Should media do something more than merely distribute whatever content will earn them the greatest profits in the shortest time?
- Are there some essential public services that media should provide even if no immediate profits can be earned?
- Should media become involved in identifying and solving social problems?
- Is it necessary or advisable that media serve as watchdogs and protect consumers against business fraud and corrupt bureaucrats?
- What should we expect media to do for us in times of crisis?

These broad questions about the role of media are linked to issues concerning the day-to-day operation of media. How should media management and production jobs be structured? What moral and ethical standards should guide media professionals? Do they have any obligation beyond personal and professional self-interest? Exactly what constitutes being a journalist? Are there any circumstances when it is appropriate or even necessary to invade people's privacy or risk ruining their reputations? If someone threatens to commit suicide in front of a television camera, what should a reporter do—get it on tape or try to stop it? Should a newspaper print a story about unethical business practices even if the company involved is one of its biggest advertisers? Should television networks broadcast a highly rated program even if it routinely contains high levels of violence?

Answers to questions like these are found in normative theory—a type of theory that describes an ideal way for a media system to be structured and operated. Normative theories are different from most of the theories we will study in this book. They don't describe things as they are, nor do they provide scientific explanations or predictions. Instead, they describe the way things *should be* if some ideal values or principles are to be realized. Normative theories come from many sources. Sometimes media practitioners themselves develop them. Sometimes social critics or academics do. Most normative theories develop over time and contain elements drawn from previous theories. This is especially true of the normative theory that currently guides mass media in the United States: It is a synthesis of ideas developed over the past three centuries.

This chapter examines a variety of normative theories of media, including some that are questionable or even objectionable. We proceed from earlier forms of normative theory to more recent examples. Our attention is on the normative theory that is predominantly used to guide and legitimize most media operation in the United States: social responsibility theory. For a long time the debate about normative theory was muted in the United States. Social responsibility theory seemingly provided such an ideal standard for media that further debate was considered unnecessary. But the past thirty years have seen unprecedented growth and consolidation of control in the media industries, and as a result, gigantic conglomerates—conceivably more committed to the bottom line than to social responsibility—dominate the production and distribution of media content. In addition, the Internet has greatly expanded the number and variety of "media outlets," all with varying commitments to traditional standards of social responsibility.

In this chapter, we will assess why social responsibility theory has had enduring appeal for American media practitioners. We contrast it with theories popular in other parts of the world. Then we speculate about its future, as its assumptions are regularly challenged by an ever-evolving media landscape and new relationships between content creators and providers and their audiences. As new industries based on new media technologies emerge, will social responsibility theory continue to guide them or will alternatives develop? Social responsibility theory is suited to a particular era of national development and to specific types of media. As the media industries change, this guiding theory might very well have to be substantially revised or replaced.

Take a few minutes now, before you read the remainder of this chapter, to think about your views concerning the role of media for yourself, your community, your state, your nation, and your world. What are the most important things that media should and shouldn't do? What standards of behavior should media practitioners follow as they perform these tasks? Just what makes someone a "journalist"? Is it permissible to do beneficial things but use questionable or unethical practices? For example, should reporters deliberately lie or engage in burglary to expose corrupt business practices? What about using a hidden camera to catch a corrupt politician taking a bribe? What about the high percentage of entertainment programming on television? Should there be less entertainment and more content that informs and educates? Should reporters unquestioningly accept and pass on official government statements about controversial matters? Should radio stations broadcast rap music containing lyrics that many listeners consider ugly and demeaning? If you were at NBC News when the parcel arrived from the Virginia Tech shooter, what would you have done with the materials? Would you have added other variables, beyond ratings and the possibility of a copycat, to your decision-making equation? Might you have considered the public's right to know? The feelings of the victims' families? The obligation of journalism to encourage public discourse, in this case of gun control or mental health care in the United States? Knowingly or not, your decisions would be based in normative theory.

radical Libertarianism The absolute belief in Libertarianism's faith in a good and rational public and totally unregulated media

THE ORIGIN OF NORMATIVE THEORIES OF MEDIA

First Amendment absolutists Those who believe in the strictest sense that media should be completely unregulated

Since the beginning of the last century, the role of mass media in American society, as we've already seen, has been hotly debated. Sharply conflicting views have been expressed. At one extreme are people who argue for **radical Libertarian** ideals. They believe that there should be no laws governing media operations. They are **First Amendment absolutists,** who take the notion of "free press" quite literally to mean that all forms of media must be totally unregulated. These people accept as gospel that the First Amendment dictate—"Congress shall make no law …

abridging the freedom of speech or of the press"—means exactly what it says. As Supreme Court Justice Hugo Black succinctly stated, "No law means no law."

At the other extreme are people who believe in direct regulation of media, most often by a government agency or commission. These include advocates of **technocratic control,** people like Harold Lasswell and Walter Lippmann. They argue that media practitioners can't be trusted to communicate responsibly or to use media effectively to serve vital public needs—especially during times of war or social upheaval. Some sort of oversight or control is necessary to ensure that important public needs are satisfied. In some cases, this may mean providing provocative information; in others, withholding such information.

technocratic control
Direct regulation of media, most often by government agency or commission

As we saw in Chapter 4, advocates of control based their arguments on propaganda theories. The threat posed by propaganda was so great that they believed information gathering and transmission had to be placed under the control of wise people—technocrats who could be trusted to act in the public interest. These technocrats would be highly trained and have professional values and skills that guaranteed that media content would serve socially valuable purposes—for example, stopping the spread of terrorism or informing people about natural disasters or a disease like AIDS.

Other proponents of regulation based their views on mass society theory (Chapter 3). They were troubled by the power of media content to undermine high culture with trivial forms of entertainment. Their complaints often centered on the way that sex and violence were presented by media. These regulation proponents also objected to the trivialization of what they consider important moral values.

Thus, both propaganda and mass society theories can be used to lobby for media regulation. Both perspectives view media as powerful, subversive forces that must be brought under the control of wise people, those who can be trusted to act in the public interest. But who should be trusted to censor media? Social scientists? Religious leaders? The military? The police? Congress? The Federal Communications Commission? Although many powerful people believed in the necessity of controlling media, they couldn't reach consensus about who should do it. Media practitioners were able to negotiate compromises by pointing out the dangers of regulation and by offering to engage in self-regulation—to become more socially responsible.

social responsibility theory
A normative theory that substitutes media industry and public responsibility for total media freedom on the one hand and for external control on the other

Advocates of regulation were opposed by people who favored various forms of Libertarianism. Eventually, social responsibility theory emerged from this debate. It represents a compromise between views favoring government control of media and those favoring total press freedom. This didn't satisfy everyone, but it did have broad appeal, especially within the media industries. Even today, most mainstream media practitioners use some variant of **social responsibility theory** to justify their actions. To fully understand social responsibility theory, we must review the ideas and events that led to its development.

THE ORIGIN OF LIBERTARIAN THOUGHT

Modern Libertarian thought can be traced back to sixteenth-century Europe—an era when feudal aristocracies exercised arbitrary power over the lives of most people. This era was also rocked by major social upheaval. International trade and urbanization undermined the power of these rural aristocracies and several social and political movements sprang up, most notably the Protestant Reformation that demanded greater freedom for individuals over their own lives and thoughts (Altschull, 1990).

authoritarian theory

A normative theory that places all forms of communication under the control of a governing elite or authorities

Libertarian theory arose in opposition to **authoritarian theory**—an idea that placed all forms of communication under the control of a governing elite or authorities (Siebert, Peterson, and Schramm, 1956). Authorities justified their control as a means to protect and preserve a divinely ordained social order. In most countries, this control rested in the hands of a king, who in turn granted royal charters or licenses to media practitioners. These practitioners could be jailed for violating their charters, and charters or licenses could be revoked. Censorship of all types, therefore, was easily possible. Authoritarian control tended to be exercised in arbitrary, erratic ways. Sometimes considerable freedom might exist to publicize minority viewpoints and culture, as long as authorities didn't perceive a direct threat to their power. Unlike totalitarianism, authoritarian theory doesn't prioritize cultivation of a homogeneous national culture. It only requires acquiescence to a governing elite.

In rebelling against authoritarian theory, early Libertarians argued that if individuals could be freed from the arbitrary limits on communication imposed by church and state, they would "naturally" follow the dictates of their conscience, seek truth, engage in public debate, and ultimately create a better life for themselves and others (McQuail, 1987; Siebert, Peterson, and Schramm, 1956). Libertarians blamed authorities for preserving unnatural, arbitrary social orders. They believed strongly in the power of unrestricted public debate and discussion to create more natural ways of structuring society. Many early Libertarians were Protestants rebelling against church restrictions on their freedom to communicate. They believed that without these restrictions, individuals could follow their conscience, communicate accordingly, and ultimately come to a knowledge of the Truth.

self-righting principle

Milton's idea that in a fair debate, good and truthful arguments will win out over lies and deceit

In *Areopagitica*, a powerful Libertarian tract published in 1644, John Milton asserted that in a fair debate, good and truthful arguments will always win out over lies and deceit. It followed that if this were true, a new and better social order could be forged using public debate. This idea came to be referred to as Milton's **self-righting principle**, and it continues to be widely cited by contemporary media professionals as a rationale for preserving media freedom (Altschull, 1990). It is a fundamental principle within social responsibility theory. Unfortunately, most early Libertarians had a rather unrealistic view of how long it would take to find the "truth" and establish an ideal social order. This ideal order was not necessarily a democracy, and it might not always permit communication freedom. Milton, for example, came to argue that the "truth" had been found by Oliver Cromwell, and its validity had been demonstrated by his battlefield victories. Because he was convinced that Cromwell had created the ideal social order, Milton was willing to serve as the chief censor in Cromwell's regime. He expressed few regrets about limiting what Catholic leaders could communicate (Altschull, 1990). As far as Milton was concerned, Catholic ideas had been demonstrated to be false and therefore should be censored so right-thinking people wouldn't be confused by them.

When it became clear during the eighteenth century that definitive forms of "truth" couldn't be quickly or easily established, some Libertarians became discouraged. Occasionally they drifted back and forth between Libertarian and authoritarian views. Even Thomas Jefferson, author of the Declaration of

Independence, wavered in his commitment to press freedom and his faith in the self-righting principle. Jefferson, who famously affirmed Milton's self-righting principle in a letter to a friend—"Were it left to me to decide whether we should have a government without newspapers or newspapers without government, I should not hesitate to prefer the latter" (quoted in Altschull, 1990, p. 117)—voiced deep frustration with scurrilous newspaper criticism during the second term of his presidency. Nevertheless, he placed Libertarian ideals at the heart of the United States' long-term experiment with democratic self-government. The revolution of the American Colonies against Britain was legitimized by those ideals. As Jefferson himself wrote in 1779, "That truth is great and will prevail if left to herself, that she is the proper and sufficient antagonist to error, and has nothing to fear from the conflict, unless by human interposition disarmed of her natural weapons, free argument and debate" (in Packer, 2006b, p. 59).

John Keane (1991) identified three fundamental concepts underpinning the Founders' belief in press freedom:

1. Theology: media should serve as a forum allowing people to deduce between good and evil.
2. Individual rights: press freedom is the strongest, if not the only, guarantee of liberty from political elites.
3. Attainment of truth: falsehoods must be countered; ideas must be challenged and tested or they will become dogma.

Bill of Rights
The first ten amendments to the U.S. Constitution

As such, the newly formed United States was one of the first nations to explicitly adopt Libertarian principles, as it did in the Declaration of Independence and the **Bill of Rights.** The latter asserts that all individuals have natural rights that no government, community, or group can unduly infringe upon or take away. Various forms of communication freedom—speech, press, and assembly—are listed as among the most important of these rights. The ability to express dissent, to band together with others to resist laws that people find to be wrong, to print or broadcast ideas, opinions, and beliefs—these rights are proclaimed as central to democratic self-government. You can test your own commitment to freedom of expression in the box entitled "A Stirring Defense of Free Expression."

Despite the priority given to communication freedom, however, it is important to recognize that many restrictions—accepted by media practitioners and media consumers alike—have been placed on communication. Libel laws protect against the publication of information that will damage reputations. Judges can issue gag orders to stop the publication of information they think will interfere with a defendant's right to a fair trial. Other laws and regulations protect against false advertising, child pornography, and offensive language. The limits to communication freedom are constantly renegotiated.

In some eras, the balance shifts toward expanding communication freedom, but at other times, most notably in times of war, freedom is curtailed. In the wake of the September 11, 2001, terrorist attacks, for example, Congress passed legislation known as the Patriot Act that imposed a variety of restrictions on Americans' communication freedom. And whenever new media technologies are invented, it is necessary to decide how they should be regulated. The debate over communication freedom never ends, as we see today in the ongoing and heated debates over

Concurring with the majority in the 1927 Supreme Court decision in *Whitney v. California,* Justice Louis Brandeis penned this stunning defense for freedom of expression:

> Those who won our independence believed that the final end of the State was to make men free to develop their faculties; and that in its government the deliberative forces should prevail over the arbitrary. They valued liberty both as an end and as a means. They believed liberty to be the secret of happiness and courage to be the secret of liberty. They believed that freedom to think as you will and speak as you think are means indispensable to the discovery and spread of political truth; that without free speech and assembly discussion would be futile; that with them, discussion affords ordinarily adequate protection against the dissemination of noxious doctrine; that the greatest menace to freedom is an inert people; that public discussion is a political duty; and that this should be a fundamental principle of the American government. They recognized the risks to which all human institutions are subject. But they knew that order cannot be secured merely through fear of punishment for its infraction; that it is hazardous to discourage thought, hope, and imagination; that fear breeds repression; that repression breeds hate; that hate menaces stable government; that the path of safety lies in the opportunity to discuss freely supposed grievances and proposed remedies; and that the fitting remedy for evil counsels is good ones.

> Believing in the power of reason as applied through public discussion, they eschewed silence coerced by law—the argument of force in its worst form. Recognizing the occasional tyrannies of governing majorities, they amended the Constitution so that free speech and assembly should be guaranteed. (Gillmor and Barron, 1974, pp. 21–22)

Of course you see and support the wisdom of Justice Brandeis's powerful enunciation of our First Freedom. But the world was a much different place in 1927. In the wake of the terrorist attacks on the United States on September 11, 2001, many people questioned if freedom of speech, press, assembly, in fact, "freedom to think as you will and speak as you think" were luxuries we could still afford. Attorney General John Ashcroft told reporters that media professionals who question his decisions and tactics in defending the country against further attack "aid terrorists" and "give ammunition to America's enemies" (quoted in Naureckas, 2002, p. 2). When the late-night talk show *Politically Incorrect* was dropped by several ABC stations and eventually canceled by the network because of host Bill Maher's comments critical of U.S. military action, White House press secretary Ari Fleischer told journalists that those events "are reminders to all Americans that they need to watch what they say, watch what they do" (quoted in Hart and Ackerman, 2002, p. 6). Dissent equals aid to terrorists? Americans watching what they say, what they do? Can you reconcile these comments with the impassioned arguments of Justice Brandeis?

Internet music and video file-sharing, offensive media content (remember the Janet Jackson wardrobe malfunction from Chapter 3), press access to military activities in times of armed conflict, and the right of domestic Islamic groups to engage in activities that others worry may threaten national security.

Why is it necessary to place limits on communication freedom? The most common reason for limiting communication freedom is a conflict over basic rights. The Bill of Rights guarantees citizens many different rights in addition to communication freedom. But where do the rights guaranteed to you end and those of another person begin? Do you have the right to shout "Fire!" in a crowded movie theater if there is no fire? The U.S. Supreme Court has ruled that you don't. If you did, many other people would be hurt—don't they have a right to be protected against your irresponsible behavior? Similar questions arise when groups attempt to stir up hatred and resentment against racial or ethnic minorities. Does a group opposing abortion have the right to place the names, addresses, and photographs of doctors who perform the procedure on its website, calling them murderers, all in the format of a wanted poster, complete with "reward"? Does it have the right to publish the names, ages, and school addresses of those doctors' children? Does a member of the Ku Klux Klan have the right to tell lies about African Americans or gays? Shouldn't such irresponsible forms of communication be controlled? Over the years, the U.S. Congress, state legislatures, and even many municipalities have addressed these types of questions. They have written laws to restrict communication freedom so that other, seemingly equally important rights might be guaranteed. Courts have upheld many of these laws, and others have been struck down because they deemed communication freedom more important.

THE MARKETPLACE OF IDEAS: A NEW FORM OF RADICAL LIBERTARIANISM

marketplace of ideas
In Libertarianism, the notion that all ideas should be put before the public, and the public will choose the best from that "marketplace"

laissez-faire doctrine
The idea that government shall allow business to operate freely and without official intrusion

Though Libertarian thought in the United States dates from the country's founding, it has undergone many transformations. An important variant emerged in the 1800s during the penny press and yellow journalism eras. Throughout this period, public confidence in both business and government was shaken by recurring economic depressions, widespread corruption, and injustice. As we noted in Chapter 3, large companies led by robber barons—most notably in the oil, railroad, and steel industries—created nationwide monopolies to charge unfair prices and reap enormous profits. Workers were paid low salaries and forced to labor under difficult or hazardous conditions. Public respect for newspapers also ebbed as publishers pursued profits and created news to sell papers. They ignored or suppressed news about the robber barons. Several social movements, especially the Progressive (liberal) and Populist (champion of average folks) movements sprang up to call for new laws and greater government regulation (Brownell, 1983; Altschull, 1990). Congress enacted antitrust legislation to break up the big monopolies.

Libertarians feared that these laws and regulations would go too far. Wanting to rekindle public support for Libertarian ideals, media practitioners developed a cogent response to Progressive and Populist criticisms. They argued that media should be regarded as a *self-regulating* **marketplace of ideas**. This theory is a variation of a fundamental principle of capitalism—the notion of a self-regulating market. In classical capitalist theory as formulated by Adam Smith, there is little need for the government to regulate markets. An open and competitive marketplace should regulate itself. If a product is in high demand, prices will "naturally" rise as consumers compete to buy it. This encourages other manufacturers to produce the product. Once demand is met by increased manufacturing, the price falls. If one manufacturer charges too much for a product, competitors will cut their prices to attract buyers. No government interference is necessary to protect consumers or to force manufacturers to meet consumer needs. Another term used to refer to these ideas is the **laissez-faire doctrine**.

According to the marketplace-of-ideas theory, the laissez-faire doctrine should be applied to mass media; that is, if ideas are "traded" freely among people, the correct or best ideas should prevail. The *ideas* compete, and the best will be "bought." They will earn profits that will encourage others to compete and market similar good ideas. Bad ideas will have no buyers and thus there will be no incentive to produce and market them. But there are some difficulties in applying this logic to our large contemporary media. Media content is far less tangible than other consumer products. The meaning of individual messages can vary tremendously from one person to the next. Just what is being traded when news stories or television dramas are "bought" and "sold"? When we buy a newspaper, we don't buy individual stories; we buy packages of them bundled with features like comics and horoscopes. We can choose to ignore anything in the package that we find offensive. But there is no direct connection between our purchase of the paper and the fact that we may or may not find some useful ideas in it. When we watch television, we don't pay a fee to the networks. Yet buying and selling are clearly involved with network programs. Advertisers buy time on these shows and then use the programs as vehicles for their messages. When they buy time, they buy access to the audience for the show; they do not necessarily buy the rightness or correctness of the program's ideas. Sponsors pay more to advertise on programs with large or demographically attractive audiences, not for programs with better ideas in them. Clearly, the media marketplace is a bit more complicated than the marketplace for refrigerators or toothpaste, as you can investigate in the box entitled "Which Model of the Marketplace?"

In the American media system, the marketplace of ideas was supposed to work like this: Someone comes up with a good idea and then transmits it through some form of mass communication. If other people like it, they buy the message. When people buy the message, they pay for its production and distribution costs. Once these costs are covered, the message producer earns a profit. If people don't like the message, they don't buy it, and the producer goes broke trying to produce and distribute it. If people are wise message consumers, the producers of the best and most useful messages will become rich and develop large media enterprises, and the producers of bad messages will fail. Useless media will go out of business. If the purveyors of good ideas succeed, these ideas should become more easily available at lower cost. Producers will compete to supply them. Similarly, the cost of bad ideas should rise and access to them should diminish. Eventually, truth should win out in the marketplace of ideas, just as it should triumph in the public forum envisioned by the early Libertarians. According to marketplace-of-ideas theory, the self-righting principle should apply to mass media content as well as to public debate.

The marketplace of ideas is self-regulating, so there is no need for a government agency to censor messages. Audiences won't buy bad messages, and therefore irresponsible producers will go out of business. But what if advertiser support permits bad messages to be distributed for free? Will people be less discriminating if they don't have to pay directly to receive these messages? What if the bad messages are distributed as part of a large bundle of messages (e.g., a newspaper or television news program; a package of cable television channels)? If you want the good messages, you also pay to subsidize the bad messages. What is bad for you might be

THINKING *about* THEORY | WHICH MODEL OF THE MARKETPLACE?

The marketplace-of-ideas theory sees the operation of the mass media system as analogous to that of the self-regulating product market. Take this example and judge for yourself the goodness-of-fit.

What do these models imply about the quality of candy in the United States? What do they say about the quality of television?

Product Producer	Product	Consumer
Model 1 A product producer	produces a product as efficiently and inexpensively as possible	for its consumers, who wield the ultimate power: to buy or not to buy.
Model 2 Hershey's	produces candy efficiently and inexpensively on a production line	for people like us. If we buy the candy, Hershey's continues to make similar candy in a similar way.
Model 3 NBC	produces people using programs (their production line)	for advertisers. If they buy NBC's product, NBC continues to produce similar audiences in similar ways.

INSTANT ACCESS

Marketplace-of-Ideas Theory

Strengths

1. Limits government control
2. Allows "natural" fluctuations in tastes, ideals, and discourse
3. Puts trust in the audience
4. Assumes "good" content will ultimately prevail

Weaknesses

1. Mistakenly equates media content with more tangible consumer products
2. Puts too much trust in profit-motivated media operators
3. Ignores the fact that content that is intentionally "bought" is often accompanied by other, sometimes unwanted content
4. Has an overly optimistic view of audiences' media consumption skills
5. Mistakenly assumes audience—not advertiser—is consumer
6. Definition of "good" is not universal (for example, what is "good" for the majority might be bad for a minority)

good for someone else. You might not like horoscopes or soap operas, but you have friends who do.

Just how useful is the marketplace-of-ideas theory? After all, government regulation of the consumer marketplace is now generally accepted as necessary. Few people question the need for consumer protection laws or laws regulating unfair business practices. The consumer marketplace benefited from regulation, so why not regulate the marketplace of ideas? Since 1930, media critics have asked this question more and more frequently, and the recent rampant concentration of media companies and rapid diffusion of digital technologies have added new urgency to the call for government intervention.

Even so, marketplace-of-ideas theory enjoys significant support within the media industries. That support resides in the "duality" inherent in the marketplace-of-ideas philosophy, one that "has allowed widely divergent interpretations of the metaphor to develop" (Napoli, 1999, p. 151). Media policy researcher Philip Napoli identified two interpretations of the marketplace of ideas. He wrote:

> Economic theory-based interpretations of the marketplace of ideas emphasize efficiency, consumer satisfaction, and competition. Whereas democratic theory-based interpretations emphasize citizen knowledge, informed decision making, and effective self-government. Within discussions of the marketplace-of-ideas metaphor, economic theory-based interpretations typically have been associated with arguments against government regulation of the communications industry, whereas democratic theory-based interpretations typically have been associated with calls for such regulation. (Napoli, 1999, pp. 151–152)

Media practitioners are satisfied with this distinction because, as numerous researchers have demonstrated (e.g., Lavey, 1993; Simon, Atwater, and Alexander, 1988), government—especially agencies such as the Federal Communications Commission and the Federal Trade Commission, which regulates advertising—"historically has devoted much greater empirical attention to the economic effects of its policies than to the social and political effects" (Napoli, 1999, p. 165).

GOVERNMENT REGULATION OF MEDIA

During the 1920s and 1930s, a new normative theory of mass communication began to emerge that rejected both radical Libertarianism and technocratic control. One source of this theory was congressional hearings over government regulation of radio. In 1927, these debates led to the establishment of the Federal Radio Commission, which was the forerunner of the Federal Communications Commission. As the debates raged, some people—especially Progressive and Populist politicians—argued that the excesses of yellow journalism proved that self-regulation wasn't enough. Overdramatized and fictitious news was so profitable that publishers and broadcasters couldn't resist producing it. Without some sort of regulation, radio was not likely to serve the public interest as well as it should. Even so, Progressives were cautious about turning control of radio over to government technocrats. A compromise solution was needed.

By the 1920s, the American public had come to accept government regulation of public utilities as a means of ending wasteful competition while preserving private enterprise. Before government regulation of power and telephone companies, cities were blanketed with competing networks of wires. Anyone who wanted to talk to people on other networks had to buy phones from all the competing companies. The cost of building entirely independent networks increased the cost of phone service and electricity. The solution to these problems was to allow one company to have a monopoly on supplying these needed services. In return for the grant of that monopoly, the company accepted government regulation of prices and services. In this way, public utilities were created with government commissions to oversee their operation. Could a government commission be used to regulate radio as a public utility? The answer was yes. In fact, Secretary of Commerce (later President) Herbert Hoover himself was moved to remark that this was one of the few instances in history where the country—industry and public alike—was unanimous in its desire for more regulation (Barnouw, 1966).

In the debate over the establishment of the Federal Radio Commission (FRC), Secretary Hoover championed one especially important philosophy—the airwaves belong to the people. If airwaves are public property like other national resources (national forests, for example), then privately operated stations can never own them. Instead, they must be licensed from the people and used in the public interest. If license holders violate the public trust, their licenses can be revoked. The FRC was created to act on behalf of the public. But some historians claim that the "compromise solution" between Populist demands for freedom and technocrats' calls for control produced a somewhat limited definition of the "public interest." In fact, they argue, the intent of the legislation creating the FRC, the Radio Act of 1927, was *not* to encourage an open forum for public debate because such a free-wheeling discussion was considered a threat to the very "public interest, convenience, and necessity" that Congress wanted broadcasters to serve. Congress specifically designed the 1927 act to "deny the public access to the ideas of their enemies, such as unions, socialists, communists, evolutionists, improper thinkers, non-Christians, and immigrants.... Broadcasters could have free speech as long as they served the public interest by denying access to speakers who did not serve the public interest as they [Congress] defined it" (Goodman, 2001).

Nonetheless, the relative success of the FRC encouraged efforts to regulate other media industries. Government censorship of movies was widely advocated, especially by religious groups. Over time, the movie industry adopted various forms of self-censorship in an effort to avoid government regulation. As the threat of propaganda grew, even regulation of newspapers was seriously considered. In 1942, for example, the Hutchins Commission on Freedom of the Press was established to weigh the merits of and necessity for newspaper regulation (we'll say more about this later).

PROFESSIONALIZATION OF JOURNALISM

As pressure for government regulation of media mounted in the 1920s, industry leaders responded with efforts to professionalize. As noted in Chapter 3, Joseph Pulitzer and William Randolph Hearst established professional awards. Leaders in the newspaper industry lobbied for and occasionally subsidized the establishment of professional schools to train media practitioners. Rather than cede control of media to a government agency, media managers went on record with pledges to serve public needs. In 1923, the American Society of Newspaper Editors (ASNE) adopted a set of professional standards entitled *The Canons of Journalism* (which were replaced in 1975 by the *ASNE Statement of Principles*). Since then, virtually every association of media practitioners has adopted similar standards. In doing so, these associations are emulating professionals in fields like law and medicine. These standards typically commit media practitioners to serving the public as effectively as possible.

Industry codes of ethics began to formalize another important conception about the role of media—that of a watchdog guarding the welfare of the public. Muckraking journalists first articulated this role around the turn of the twentieth century. This idea assumes that media should continually scan the social world and alert the public to problems. Initially, yellow journalists greeted this view of media with skepticism. Would investigations of corruption sell more newspapers than sensational news about trivial events? The answer was yes. Muckraking investigations of corruption proved so popular that newspapers specializing in them came to dominate the markets in some large cities. The Scripps Howard newspaper chain adopted the lighthouse as its symbol and chose the phrase "Give light and the people will find their own way" as its motto. Gradually, the watchdog role was widely accepted as a necessary and appropriate one for news media.

Fourth Estate
Media as an independent social institution that ensures that other institutions serve the public

In some ambitious formulations of this role, the media are envisioned as independent watchdogs, a social institution, the **Fourth Estate** of government, charged with making certain that all other institutions—the three branches of government, business, religion, education, and family—serve the public. In the words of social critic and veteran journalist Bill Moyers (2001, p. 13), properly functioning media are needed "to keep our leaders honest and to arm the powerless with the information they need to protect themselves against the tyranny of the powerful, whether that tyranny is political or commercial." This perspective assumes that once people are informed about wrongdoing, incompetence, or inefficiency, they will take action against it. But there has always been concern that the watchdog might be subverted by the powerful, becoming a lapdog. Or the watchdog could become irresponsible and vicious. Criticisms of government or business could be exaggerated to sell newspapers. Both these concerns are evident in James Curran's call for a rethinking of the "traditional public watchdog definition of the media, in the context of an expanding broadcasting system." He wrote:

> While the watchdog role of the media is important, it is perhaps quixotic to argue that it should be paramount. This conventional view derives from a period when the "media" were highly politicized and adversarial. Most modern media are now given over mainly to entertainment. Coverage of public affairs accounts for only a small part of even news media content, and only a proportion of this takes the form of critical scrutiny of government.... The traditional approach appears time-worn in another way. It defines the watchdog role of the media as applying only to the state. This antiquated formulation derives from a period when the state was unrepresentative, corrupt and potentially despotic, and free speech and a free press were viewed as a defense against absolutism.... [Yet] as a consequence of the take-over boom of the last three decades, a large number of media enterprises are now tied to core sectors of finance and industrial capital. (1991, p. 86)

So what type of watchdog coverage should we expect from media when most are owned by the very corporations they could be expected to criticize? And how likely is it that these media will criticize governments having the power to make decisions that affect their profits? Is it still reasonable to expect our profit-oriented press to comfort the afflicted and afflict the comfortable?

LIMITATIONS OF PROFESSIONALIZATION

In joining the trend toward professionalization, media practitioners, like doctors and lawyers before them, pledged to uphold standards of professional practice. They promised to weed out irresponsible people and give recognition to those who excel. Those who violated standards would be censured. In extreme cases, they could be barred from professional practice. And as an alternative to direct government regulation, media professionalization worked rather well. Certain limitations, however, lead to recurring problems:

1. Professionals in every field, including journalism, have been reluctant to identify and censure colleagues who violate professional standards. To do so is often seen as admitting that embarrassing problems exist. Public trust in all media professionals might be shaken if too many people are barred from practice. Professional societies tend to operate as closed groups in which members are protected against outside threats and criticism. Attacks from outsiders are routinely dismissed as unwarranted, even when evidence against a practitioner mounts. Often action is taken only in extreme cases, when it cannot be avoided. Even then, news media either avoid covering the case or provide brief and superficial coverage.

This problem is amply demonstrated by *New York Times* reporter Judith Miller and her reporting on weapons of mass destruction (WMD) in the run-up to the 2003 invasion of Iraq (Okrent, 2004). Well after her own newspaper's disavowal of her "flawed journalism" once Coalition forces failed to turn up the WMD her sources had assured her were in fact there, several of Miller's one-time colleagues admitted that they were suspicious of much of her work on the issue, but they remained quiet because of Miller's close ties with the paper's senior editors. But one *Times* writer, Craig Pyes, who had teamed with Miller for a series on the terrorist group al Qaeda, did attempt to alert the paper's editors to his concerns, asking that his byline not appear on one article. "I'm not willing to work further on this project with Judy Miller," he wrote; "I do not trust her work, her judgment, or her conduct. She is an advocate, and her actions threaten the integrity of the enterprise, and of everyone who works with her. She has turned in a draft of a story ... that is little more than dictation from government sources over several days, filled with unproven assertions and factual inaccuracies" (in Kurtz, 2005). Because Miller was a Pulitzer Prize–winning journalist with contacts high in the administration, the *Times* ignored this warning, continuing to run her "well-sourced" stories on its front page. Miller was "allowed to resign" only after she and her paper could no longer withstand the scrutiny and criticism that followed her role, however insignificant, in the illegal outing of undercover CIA agent Valerie Plame in 2005.

2. Professional standards can be overly abstract and ambiguous. They can be difficult to implement and enforce. Mission statements and broad codes of ethics are notoriously vague. The Radio-Television News Directors Association's Code of Ethics and Professional Conduct (2000), for example, instructs its members to "pursue truth aggressively and present the news accurately, in context, and completely as possible." But news directors must make choices concerning allocation of resources. Increasingly, the news we see consists of corporate and government public relations **video news releases** (VNRs). In fact, almost every American local television news operation makes use of these outsider-provided public

video news release
Report produced by an outside organization, typically a public relations firm, that is distributed free of charge to television stations

relations pieces, and one recent study of seventy-seven stations discovered that not a single one disclosed the source of the VNR (Farsetta, 2006). How do editors decide when to stop airing VNRs and start engaging in independent digging and reporting? There might be no reason to doubt the truth of a VNR unless a reporter takes the time to conduct an independent investigation.

But what if an independent journalistic investigation leads a large advertiser to cancel its account with the station? Why risk producing stories that might prove embarrassing to someone or some organization? In the news business, telling the truth can sometimes be difficult and expensive. Professional standards are vague, so nothing forces journalists to endanger relationships with friendly sources or their profit margins. And in fact, it is a poorly kept broadcast industry secret that many stations maintain printed lists of people and issues that are untouchable—they may not be covered—"for fear of alienating an advertiser" (Potter, 2001, p. 68).

3. **In contrast with medicine and law, media professionalization doesn't include standards for professional training and licensing.** Other professions mandate that practitioners receive long and closely monitored professional training. For example, doctors and lawyers undergo from four to ten years of specialized training in addition to completing four years of college. But media practitioners are unwilling to set requirements for professional training and have strongly resisted efforts to license journalists. They argue that these requirements would inevitably be used by government to control the press. If the press is to remain free from control, it must be free to hire anyone—no matter how untrained or unqualified. Anyone should be able to claim the title of journalist, start a newspaper, and exercise his or her rights to free press. No government agency should be able to step in and shut down a paper just because some of its reporters or editors are unlicensed.

bloggers
Writers who maintain blogs, regularly updated online journals of news and opinion

Since journalists refuse to set specific requirements for practicing their craft, they are now having difficulty differentiating what they do from what **bloggers** do. Internet bloggers can (and do) easily argue that they are engaging in another form of journalism—citizen journalism. Most make no pretence about doing original newsgathering. They depend on journalists to do that. They spend their time monitoring news coverage from a broad range of sources. They follow discussions and rumors about news events on the Internet. Bloggers "add value" to the news by reflecting on and raising questions about it. Much of what they write is highly speculative and reflects their values. They make no effort to be objective or even-handed in their treatment of news. Is what they do journalism? Does it serve to inform the public? Later in this chapter we will discuss recent efforts to establish a code of ethics for bloggers. Will this make them journalists? Similar issues arise concerning comedy shows that focus on news, such as *The Daily Show with Jon Stewart*. Is Stewart a journalist? Why not? Earlier we noted that viewers of his program are better informed about politics than the viewers of most news programs produced by "real" journalists. He conducts nightly interviews with newsmakers, often with directness rare even for "real" journalists. So what does it mean to be a "journalist"?

Arguments against specialized training and licensing of media practitioners fail to consider how these standards are enforced in other professions. Licensing has not brought doctors and lawyers directly under government control. Even when government agencies issue licenses, professional associations effectively control the standards used to determine who will get a license.

4. In contrast with other professions, media practitioners tend to have less independent control over their work. Media practitioners don't work as autonomous practitioners and therefore have difficulty assuming personal responsibility for their work. They tend to work in big, hierarchically structured bureaucracies. Individual reporters, editors, producers, and directors have only a limited ability to control what they do. Reporters are given assignments by editors, advertising designers work for account executives, and television anchors and camera operators follow the instructions of news directors. Editors, account managers, and directors are all responsible to higher management. In these large bureaucracies, it is difficult to assign responsibility. Those at lower levels can claim that they are only "following orders," whereas people at higher levels can simply disavow any knowledge of what was going on below them. Earlier we discussed the example provided by Judith Miller and her problematic news writing about Iraq prior to the start of the war. Miller's editors claimed ignorance of her actions. Her colleagues suspected what she was doing but chose to ignore it. So is Miller fully responsible for misleading coverage, or do her colleagues and supervisors share blame?

5. In the media industries, violation of professional standards rarely has immediate, directly observable consequences. Thus it is hard for critics to cite violations or to identify the harm that has been done. When doctors fail, people die. When lawyers fail, people go to jail unnecessarily. The results of unethical or incompetent media practice are harder to see. "The media blew both of the major catastrophes of our time," wrote Greg Mitchell, editor-in-chief of *Editor & Publisher*, "I speak, of course, of the Iraq war and the financial meltdown." The outcome of "missing stories of this enormity" naturally had "consequences that will echo … for decades," but at the time of the initial failed reporting there was little way to know that would be the case (2009, p. 16).

Cable news network MSNBC offers one example. Two of its personalities, Phil Donohue and Ashleigh Banfield, were the only journalists to lose their jobs over their coverage of the Iraq war: Donohue for inviting war skeptics onto his talk show and Banfield for criticizing the lack of depth of war coverage (Cohen, 2008; Greenwald, 2008). MSNBC's morning news show host Joe Scarborough, however, remained in his anchor's chair despite war commentary that proved not only to be wrong but critical of reporting that would, in fact, turn out to be accurate. Scarborough editorialized soon after the invasion, "I doubt that the journalists at the *New York Times* and NPR or at ABC or at CNN are going to ever admit just how wrong their negative pronouncements [on the war] were" (in "The Final Word," 2006).

Sometimes, unethical conduct might even do some good. The classic case of Janet Cooke is instructive. Cooke, a reporter for the *Washington Post*, wrote a series of news stories about ghetto children that was nominated for a Pulitzer Prize in 1980 (Altschull, 1990, pp. 361–364). Later these stories were found to be based on fabricated interviews. Cooke took personal details and comments from several people and then wove them together to create a fictitious interviewee. The resulting stories had great dramatic impact, educating readers about the reality of drugs in the inner city and spurring official action to clean up particularly troublesome areas. Nevertheless, her reports violated professional standards of truth and accuracy. Cooke was fired, and the Pulitzer Prize was returned. The *Post* expressed profound embarrassment, and its legendary editor, Ben Bradlee, called it the worst failure of his long career.

SOCIAL RESPONSIBILITY THEORY OF THE PRESS: A POSTWAR COMPROMISE

Despite moves toward professionalization and self-regulation, pressure for greater government regulation of media mounted throughout World War II and continued during the anti-Communist agitation that followed. In response, Henry Luce, CEO of Time Inc., provided funding for an independent commission to make recommendations concerning the role of the press. The Hutchins Commission on Freedom of the Press was established in 1942 and released a major report of its findings in 1947 (Davis, 1990; McIntyre, 1987). Its members consisted of leaders from many areas of society, including academics, politicians, and heads of social groups.

Commission members were sharply divided between those who held strongly Libertarian views and those who thought some form of press regulation was necessary. Those who favored regulation were fearful that the "marketplace of ideas" was much too vulnerable to subversion by antidemocratic forces. Several of these proponents of regulation were guided by notions about public communication developed by social researchers at the University of Chicago—the **Chicago School.** The Chicago School envisioned modern cities as "Great Communities" composed of hundreds of small social groups—everything from neighborhood social organizations to citywide associations. For these Great Communities to develop, all the constituent groups had to work together and contribute. These were referred to as **pluralistic groups** in recognition of their cultural and racial diversity (Davis, 1990).

The Chicago School opposed marketplace-of-ideas notions and argued that unregulated mass media inevitably served the interests and tastes of large or socially dominant groups. Small, weak, pluralistic groups would be either neglected or denigrated. (Recall the "compromise" that produced the Radio Act of 1927 discussed earlier.) This perspective also held that ruthless elites could use media as a means of gaining personal political power. These demagogues could manipulate media to transmit propaganda to fuel hatred and fear among a majority and unite them against minorities. Hitler's use of media to arouse hatred of the Jews served as a prime example.

To prevent this tyranny by the majority and to mandate support for pluralistic groups, some commission members favored creation of a public agency—a press council—made up of people much like themselves and having the power to prevent publication of hate propaganda. In the view of these Hutchins Commission members, this "new and independent agency [would] appraise and report annually upon the performance of the press." It would base that appraisal on its comparison of "the accomplishments of the press with the aspirations which the people have for it" (in Bates, 2001). This agency might, for example, have required that newspapers devote a certain portion of their coverage to minority groups. Or it might

Chicago School Social researchers at the University of Chicago in the 1940s who envisioned modern cities as "Great Communities" made up of hundreds of interrelated small groups

pluralistic groups In a Great Community, the various segments defined by specific unifying characteristics

have required that these groups be given regular columns in which they could publish whatever they wanted.

Commission members recognized that such regulations might impose additional costs on newspapers. If this happened, government subsidies might cover these expenses. By serving pluralistic groups, media would strengthen them and enable them to contribute to the Great Community. This fostering of pluralism and restraint on propaganda was seen as essential to preventing the spread of totalitarianism in the United States.

Although the majority of the Hutchins Commission members had some sympathy for Chicago School ideas, they opposed any direct form of press regulation (Davis 1990; McIntyre, 1987). This meant they faced a serious dilemma. On the one hand, they recognized that the marketplace of ideas was not self-regulating and that the media were doing less than they could to provide services to minority groups. However, they feared that any form of press regulation would open the door to official control of media—the very thing they were trying to prevent.

The situation seemed dire at the time. Without some form of regulation, a ruthless and cunning demagogue might be able to use hate propaganda to gain power in the United States. However, establishing a national press council might put too much control in the hands of existing elites, and they might abuse it. Ultimately, the Hutchins Commission members decided to place their faith in media practitioners, calling on them to redouble their efforts to serve the public.

> [They] endorsed professional responsibility ... [as] a way of reconciling market flaws with the traditional conception of the democratic role of the media. [The Hutchins Commission's report] asserted journalists' commitment to higher goals—neutrality, detachment, a commitment to truth. It involved the adoption of certain procedures for verifying facts, drawing on different sources, presenting rival interpretations. In this way, the pluralism of opinion and information, once secured through the clash of adversaries in the free market, could be recreated through the "internal pluralism" of monopolistic media. Market pressures to sensationalize and trivialize the presentation of news could be offset by a commitment to inform. (Curran, 1991, p. 98)

The synthesis of ideas put forward in the Hutchins Commission report has become known as the *Social Responsibility Theory of the Press* (Siebert, Peterson, and Schramm, 1956). It emphasized the need for an independent press that scrutinizes other social institutions and provides objective, accurate news reports. The most innovative feature of social responsibility theory was its call for media to be responsible for fostering productive and creative "Great Communities." It said that media should do this by prioritizing cultural pluralism—by becoming the voice of all the people—not just elite groups or groups that had dominated national, regional, or local culture in the past.

In some respects, social responsibility theory is a radical statement. Instead of demanding that media be free to print or transmit whatever their owners want, social responsibility theory imposes a burden on media practitioners. As the commission argued, "The press is not free if those who operate it behave as though their position conferred on them the privilege of being deaf to ideas which the processes of free speech have brought to public attention" (quoted in Bates, 2001).

Social responsibility theory appealed to the idealism of individual media practitioners and tried to unite them in the service of cultural pluralism—even when this might reduce their profits or antagonize existing social elites. Social responsibility theory challenged media professionals' ingenuity to develop new ways of serving their communities. It encouraged them to see themselves as front-line participants in the battle to preserve democracy in a world drifting inexorably toward totalitarianism. By helping pluralistic groups, media were building a wall to protect democracy from external and internal foes. Denis McQuail (1987) summarized the basic principles of social responsibility theory as follows:

- Media should accept and fulfill certain obligations to society.
- These obligations are mainly to be met by setting high or professional standards of informativeness, truth, accuracy, objectivity, and balance.
- In accepting and applying these obligations, media should be self-regulating within the framework of law and established institutions.
- The media should avoid whatever might lead to crime, violence, or civil disorder or give offense to minority groups.
- The media as a whole should be pluralist and reflect the diversity of their society, giving access to various points of view and to rights of reply.
- Society and the public have a right to expect high standards of performance, and intervention can be justified to secure the, or a, public good.
- Journalists and media professionals should be accountable to society as well as to employers and the market.

THE COLD WAR TESTS SOCIAL RESPONSIBILITY THEORY

The first major test of social responsibility theory occurred during the 1950s with the rise of anti-Communist sentiments at the time of the Cold War. Mainland China fell to the Communists in 1949. Almost simultaneously, most of Eastern Europe was coming under Communist control in a series of staged popular uprisings and coups. Spies who stole important secrets from the United States aided Soviet development of nuclear weapons. World War II had stopped one form of totalitarianism but had unleashed another that appeared to be even stronger and more deadly. A generation of American politicians, including Richard Nixon and John F. Kennedy, gained national prominence by aggressively opposing the spread of Soviet Communism.

Joseph McCarthy led the vanguard opposing Communism, as discussed in Chapter 3. Though McCarthy presented himself as a crusader for democracy, he soon exhibited all the traits of the classic demagogue. He successfully used propaganda techniques to draw national attention to himself and to stimulate widespread public hatred and suspicion of people or minorities whom he linked, most often inaccurately, to Communism. McCarthy charged that many in both government and the media were Communist agents or sympathizers, and he drew strong support from anti-Communist groups across the nation. The House Un-American Activities Committee (HUAC) launched congressional investigations of media practitioners.

Media executives responded to pressure from anti-Communist groups and from Congress by blacklisting many people who were accused, even in the absence of evidence, of Communist leanings. Prominent practitioners were barred from working in the media. Ultimately, there was little evidence of any widespread conspiracy to subvert democracy in the United States. Though there were Soviet agents at work in the United States, their numbers and effectiveness were never as great as the anti-Communist groups asserted.

This Red Scare episode illustrates how difficult it can be for journalists to adhere to social responsibility theory in crisis situations. Most reporters initially hailed McCarthy as someone taking a heroic stand against the Red Menace. His dramatic pronouncements provided ideal material for big headlines and popular front-page news stories. As long as McCarthy confined his witch-hunt to Reds in federal bureaucracies, many journalists printed his charges without criticism. When he began to look for "Pinkos" and Communist sympathizers in the media, many began to have misgivings. But by then his popularity was so great that it was risky for them to oppose him, so most cowered. Months of congressional hearings passed before significant media criticism of McCarthy appeared. Many credit Edward R. Murrow with taking the initiative to produce a television news documentary that finally exposed McCarthy's propaganda tactics to public scrutiny.

How should media have reacted if they took social responsibility theory seriously? Should they have made a greater effort earlier to investigate the truth of McCarthy's frequent and dramatic allegations? They would have risked charges that they were pro-Communist or the unwitting dupes of the Communists. By waiting, they risked the possibility that McCarthy would seize political power and use it to suppress all forms of dissent, including media criticism. Without a journalist of Murrow's stature to confront McCarthy, the United States might have turned toward McCarthy's brand of Fascism.

USING SOCIAL RESPONSIBILITY THEORY TO GUIDE PROFESSIONAL PRACTICE

The ideals of social responsibility theory have proved quite durable, even if their full implications are rarely understood by working journalists. In fact, many scholars argue, "social responsibility doctrine has always been relegated to the fringes of journalism education and the newsroom. More than sixty years after the Hutchins Commission report, news personnel generally remain hostile to its focus on the public good and on broad-based reporting about significant events of the day" (Christians, Ferre, and Fackler, 1993, p. 38). Furthermore, in the competing "ethos of news as business [and] that of news as socially responsible institution" (Lind and Rockier, 2001, p. 119), social responsibility often comes in second. In our current era of large media corporations, "Friends of the 'liberty of the press' must recognize that *communication markets restrict freedom of communication* by generating barriers to entry, monopoly and restrictions upon choice, and by shifting the prevailing definition of information from that of a public good to that of a privately appropriated commodity" (Keane, 1991, pp. 88–89, emphasis in original).

So, if social responsibility theory is to remain a viable normative theory, greater effort might be needed to implement it. Compared with the vast amount of research conducted on media effects, relatively little work has examined whether existing news production practices actually serve societal goals as intended. For example, one primary goal is communicating accurate information about important events to average people. The findings of research on this goal are mixed. Evidence indicates that people don't learn much from news reports and what they do learn is quickly forgotten (Graber, 1987). People become easily confused by stories that are poorly structured or use dramatic but irrelevant pictures. Findings from this research have had little or no impact on the practice of journalism. These findings have been largely ignored or misinterpreted by media practitioners (Davis and Robinson, 1989).

In the 1970s and 1980s, sociologists published a series of studies that raised important questions about the value of routine news production practices (Bennett, 1988; Epstein, 1973; Fishman, 1980; Gans, 1979; Glasgow University Media Group, 1976, 1980; Tuchman, 1978). Most of this research has been ignored or dismissed by journalists as biased, irrelevant, and misguided. It deserves a more careful reading. Gaye Tuchman, for example, presents a well-developed argument concerning the role played by media in the discovery and cultivation of social movements. She conceptualizes news production practices as "strategic rituals" and believes that these practices appear to satisfy the requirements imposed by social responsibility norms but fall far short of achieving their purpose. For example, journalists ritualistically construct "balanced" stories in which they contrast opposing views. However, these rites might actually undermine rather than advance pluralism. She maintains that "balanced stories" about minority groups frequently contain statements from social or political leaders that subtly or blatantly denigrate groups and their ideas. The emotionally charged opinions of little-known group leaders are contrasted with reasoned pronouncements from well-known credible officials. Reporters make little effort to create a context for new groups' broader goals or culture. Instead, their reports tend to focus on dramatic events staged by isolated group members.

Tuchman cites early news coverage of the women's movement in the 1960s and early 1970s to illustrate her criticisms. The movement achieved national prominence with a protest outside the 1968 Miss America pageant in Atlantic City, at which bras were purportedly burned. Feminists threw *Playboy* magazines, high-heeled shoes, and girdles—"items they felt were symbolic of women's oppression"—into a "Freedom Trash Can," but they burned no bras (Levy, 2009, p. 78). Yet news reports unfairly labeled the women's movement an extremist group akin to the "radicals" who were burning draft cards (hence the burning bras). Instead of assisting the movement and enabling it to contribute to the larger society, these stories and those that followed hindered it. They frustrated rather than advanced pluralism. Journalist Daniel Schorr (1992) offered a personal recollection from the civil rights movement that perfectly demonstrates Tuchman's ideas:

> I found [in the mid-1960s] that I was more likely to get on the CBS *Evening News* with a black militant talking the language of "Burn, baby, burn!" ... [Then], in early

February 1968, the Rev. Martin Luther King, Jr. came to Washington.... I came to his news conference with a CBS camera crew prepared to do what TV reporters do—get the most threatening sound bite I could to ensure a place on the evening news lineup. I succeeded in eliciting from him phrases on the possibility of "disruptive protests" directed at the Johnson Administration and Congress.

As I waited for my camera crew to pack up, I noticed that King remained seated behind a table in an almost empty room, looking depressed. Approaching him, I asked why he seemed so morose.

"Because of you," he said, "and because of your colleagues in television. You try to provoke me to threaten violence and, if I don't, then you will put on television those who do. And by putting them on television, you will elect them our leaders. And if there is violence, will you think about your part in bringing it about?" (p. 5C)

IS THERE STILL A ROLE FOR SOCIAL RESPONSIBILITY THEORY?

Although U.S. media have developed many professional practices in an effort to conform to the ideals of social responsibility theory, the long-term objective—the creation of "Great Communities"—has never seemed more elusive. Our cities have undergone decades of urban renewal, yet slums remain, and in some cities they continue to spread. There have been national "wars" to combat poverty, crime, pollution, disease (from polio to cancer to AIDS), and drugs, but the quality of life for many Americans has not improved. Ethnic and racial subcultures are still widely misunderstood. Minority group members continue to be discriminated against and harassed. It is estimated that there are 12 million illegal immigrants in the United States whose work is critical to the economy but whom most Americans distrust and would deport if possible. There is evidence that hate groups are increasing in size and that their propaganda is effectively reaching larger audiences. Politicians still find it possible to win elections by stirring up public fear of various minorities.

Does this mean that social responsibility theory is wrong? Has it been poorly implemented? What responsibility can or should media practitioners assume on behalf of the Great Communities they serve? More important, how should this responsibility be exercised? With helicopters circling over riot scenes? With inflammatory coverage of hate groups? With boring coverage of the routine work of neighborhood associations? With sensational coverage of political candidates when they demean and stereotype minorities? With endless listing of bad news about crime and disease? Was there merit in the Chicago School arguments concerning coverage of pluralistic groups? If so, what forms might that coverage take? Should group members be allowed some direct control of what is printed about them in newspapers or broadcast on television?

local origination (or mandatory access) rule
Rule requiring local cable television companies to carry community-based access channels

Our society's experience with local access channels on cable television suggests that it is not easy to use media to support pluralistic groups. In 1972, the Federal Communications Commission for the first time required local cable companies to provide local access channels in an effort to serve pluralistic groups, and although these **local origination (or mandatory access) rules** have been altered, suspended, and otherwise tinkered with during the last forty years, they have generally failed

INSTANT ACCESS

Libertarianism

Strengths

1. Values media freedom
2. Is consistent with U.S. media traditions
3. Values individuals
4. Precludes government control of media

Weaknesses

1. Is overly optimistic about media's willingness to meet responsibilities
2. Is overly optimistic about individuals' ethics and rationality
3. Ignores need for reasonable control of media
4. Ignores dilemmas posed by conflicting freedoms (for example, free press versus personal privacy)

to serve their intended purpose. Very few people watch the access channels, and few groups use them.

low power FM radio (LPFM) Community-based, noncommercial stations broadcasting over small areas, typically 3 to 7 miles

Many observers believe that social responsibility theory will be given new strength by emerging technologies that allow communities greater power to disseminate information. The FCC licenses **low power FM radio** stations (**LPFM**), community-based, noncommercial stations broadcasting over small areas, typically 3 to 7 miles. The more than 825 stations currently on-air are operated by community groups, labor unions, churches, and other nonprofit groups usually absent from the airwaves. Cable television, though never approaching the reempowering-the-public revolution predicted for it in the 1960s, has at least made literally hundreds of channels available, many of which are dedicated to ethnic and specific-interest communities. Now, with the near total diffusion of the Internet and World Wide Web, audience size and ability to make a profit have become unimportant concerns for literally millions of "voices." The website for a tribe of Native Americans, for example, sits electronically side-by-side with those of the most powerful media organizations. What many theorists fear, however, is that this wealth of voices—each speaking to its own community—will **Balkanize** the larger U.S. culture. That is, rather than all Americans reading and viewing conscientiously produced content about all the Great Communities that make the United States as wonderfully diverse and pluralistic as it is, communities will talk only to people residing within their borders. The values, wants, needs, and ideas of others will be ignored.

Balkanize Dividing a country, culture, or society into antagonistic subgroups

They see the passing of the mass market national magazine in the face of television's 1950s assault on its ad revenues and audiences as the first step in the demise of their hope for Great Communities. Whereas the entire nation once read the *Saturday Evening Post*, individual-taste publics now read *Ski, Wired, Mondo 2000, Model Airplane Builder, Ebony,* and *Organic Farmer.* When cable began to provide scores of alternatives to the big three commercial television networks, they expressed the same fears. In the early 1970s, ABC, NBC, and CBS commanded more than 90 percent of the viewing audience. Today, they draw fewer than 60 percent. The Internet has exacerbated this trend, prompting journalist Bree Nordenson to argue that "shared public knowledge is receding, as is the likelihood

INSTANT ACCESS

Social Responsibility Theory

Strengths

1. Values media responsibility
2. Values audience responsibility
3. Limits government intrusion in media operation
4. Allows reasonable government control of media
5. Values diversity and pluralism
6. Aids the "powerless"
7. Appeals to the best instincts of media practitioners and audiences
8. Is consistent with U.S. legal tradition

Weaknesses

1. Is overly optimistic about media's willingness to meet responsibility
2. Is overly optimistic about individual responsibility
3. Underestimates power of profit motivation and competition
4. Legitimizes status quo

that we come in contact with beliefs that contradict our own. Personalized home pages, newsfeeds, and e-mail alerts, as well as special-interest publications lead us to create what sociologist Todd Gitlin disparagingly referred to as 'my news, my world.' Serendipitous news—accidently encountered information—is far less frequent in a world of TiVo and online customization tools" (2008, p. 37). William Gibson, author of *Neuromancer* and guru to the cybergeneration, predicts that there will indeed be Great Communities, but they will be communities built around brands—Planet Nike and the World of Pepsi—rather than around common values and aspirations (Trench, 1990).

Since the report of the Hutchins Commission on Press Freedom in 1947, and despite these profound changes in the nature of the American media system, there has been relatively little effort to develop a more contemporary normative theory of media in the United States. Social responsibility theory emerged at a time of world crisis, when democracy itself was clearly threatened. Will the end of the Cold War and increasing globalization and consolidation of media industries bring forth or require a new normative theory? How must this theory be rethought and restructured to reflect the new media environment where anyone can be a publisher? It is useful to examine some alternative normative theories practiced in other parts of the world. We will do this after a discussion of the Internet community's efforts to produce a theory of social responsibility for its members.

THE PUBLIC INTEREST IN THE INTERNET ERA

More than 196 million Americans use the Internet; computers sit in more than 80 percent of their homes and 92 percent of these have Internet access. In a typical month, more than 70 million individuals, or 36 percent of all U.S. net users, will visit a newspaper website, spending 2.7 billion minutes on 3.5 billion page views

(Sass, 2009a; "Home Internet," 2009). Internet news sites MSNBC, Yahoo News, CNN, and AOL News each attract more unique monthly visitors than the 18 million of the top newspaper site, the *New York Times* ("Nielsen: Newspapers," 2009).

There are, however, millions of other "news" sites, blogs—regularly updated online journals, many offering news and commentary as well as links to related or supporting information on the Web. Search engine Technorati has indexed more than 130 million blogs worldwide, 1.5 million of which are updated at least weekly ("State of," 2008). While the vast majority may quickly go dormant, and many are no doubt personal diaries, family gathering sites, and other idiosyncratic outlets, many more are "citizen publishers," "stand-alone journalists," and "networks of dedicated amateurs" who do meaningful journalism (Stepp, 2006, p. 62). "Freedom of the press now belongs not just to those who own printing presses," wrote journalism scholar Ann Cooper, "but also to those who use cell phones, video cameras, blogging software, and other technology to deliver news and views to the world" (2008, p. 45). But are these newly empowered citizens actually *journalists*? Perhaps, as one angry news source labeled them to investigative reporter Jane Mayer, they are merely "Cheeto-eating people in the basement working in their underwear" (2009, p. 50).

Despite continued denigration, primarily from traditional journalism elites, blogs have assumed a growing news gathering and dissemination function in our society as well as a central role in our democracy's public discourse. They have become mainstream. Bloggers are routinely granted official access to major news events such as Presidential press conferences and Supreme Court hearings; bloggers have a professional association, the Online News Association (at *www.cyberjourn alist.net*), and a code of ethics; online journalists are eligible for Pulitzer Prizes; and in 2009, in order to include online journalists among their members, both the Radio and Television News Directors Association (RTNDA) and the American Society of Newspaper Editors (ASNE) changed names. The RTNDA became the RTDNA—the Radio Television Digital News Association—and the ASNE dropped "paper" from its name to become the American Society of News Editors. As such, blogs are forcing a major reconsideration not only of the practice of journalism, but of social responsibility and the public interest.

Here's an example. One day, on NBC's *Meet the Press,* the *New York Times's* Tom Friedman told the television audience, "The Internet is an open sewer of untreated, unfiltered information, left, right, center, up, down.... And I always felt, you know, when modems first came out, when that was how we got connected to the Internet, that every modem sold in America should actually come with a warning from the surgeon general that would have said, 'judgment not included,' OK? That you have to upload the old-fashioned way." *Salon* blogger Glenn Greenwald responded that it was the many failures of the "old-fashioned way" that paved the road for bloggers' new roles. It was "traditional" journalism, he wrote, that produced the news "that Saddam Hussein had purchased aluminum tubes that were used to build nuclear weapons ... dismissed European objections to the invasion as 'not Serious'; demonized war opposition as coming from 'knee-jerk liberals and pacifists'; justified the war with the demented desire to make Iraqis 'Suck On This' [Friedman's own words]; ... called for France to be removed from the U.N.

Security Council; ... uncritically repeated what they were told by the U.S. military to disseminate myths about Jessica Lynch's heroic firefight and Pat Tillman's tragic death at the hands of Taliban monsters ... [and] spent a week screaming to the country that government tests showed Saddam was likely responsible for the anthrax attacks" (Greenwald, 2009a). *Columbia Journalism Review* managing editor Brent Cunningham added that "traditional" journalism failed not only in the run-up to the war in Iraq, but as the groundwork for the global financial meltdown was being laid during the "1990s, when investment regulation was quietly dismantled (Glass-Steagall), NAFTA was enshrined without a thorough public airing of probable consequences, the World Trade Organization protests were treated as street theater, and first the Internet wizards and then Wall Street's titans were elevated to the altar of infallibility" (2009, p. 32).

Most American media outlets allow—even encourage—their writers to maintain blogs to better engage readers. The *New York Times*, for example, has more than sixty news and opinion blogs on its Website. The *Washington Post* supports media reporter Howard Kurtz's blogging on mass communication issues among its more than eighty *Post*-affiliated blogs. The *New Yorker* magazine gives prominent blog space to political essayist Hendrik Hertzberg. The *Atlantic* is home to one of the country's most influential bloggers, Andrew Sullivan. The *L.A. Times's* Hector Tobar blogs about Latin America. Almost every local newspaper and broadcaster offers online readers at least a few—if not many—blogs, either from its existing personnel or from topic-specific experts. Some of this work echoes the parent company's content; much provides additional, even alternative view material. But these establishment media blogs generally operate under the same standards of practice and professionalism as do their parent outlets. The question of service in the public interest on the Internet, then, is really about the operation of independent news and commentary blogs—that is, citizen journalists.

Some of the best-known and most influential blogs are *Moveon.org, The Huffington Post, The Daily Kos, Crooks and Liars,* and *Salon's* Glenn Greenwald (more or less on the political Left) and *Wizbang, Little Green Footballs,* and *BuzzMachine* (more or less on the political Right). Many blogs are general interest and others are issue specific. *Altercation* and *Truthdig,* for example, focus on media performance commentary, and *247wallst.com* and *Footnoted.org* deal with the economy. *Democracy Arsenal* offers sophisticated analyses of national security debates and issues. All invite comment, dissent, addition, and correction as well as links to related sites and data. Beyond responding to individual postings, most blogs give readers their own opportunity to blog: *Crooks & Liars* provides "Open Thread," *Talking Points Memo* has TPMCafe, and *Salon* hosts Open *Salon,* Table Talk, and The Well.

enterprise reporting
Original reporting, typically initiated by a specific media outlet

One oft-cited criticism of blogs is that they do not practice "real" journalism; they rely on the efforts of established news-gathering organizations. Most do not have the time and money to do original **enterprise reporting**—investigatory stories initiated by a specific media outlet. Significant resources are necessary, explains *Mother Jones* co-editor Clara Jeffery, "to be able to send people down rabbit holes without guarantee of the story" (in Dumenco, 2009). It was an "old line" media outlet, the *Washington Post,* not bloggers, for example, that dedicated hundreds of

THINKING about THEORY   SAVING NEWSPAPERS OR SAVING JOURNALISM?

In Fall, 2009, Carolyn Maloney of New York announced that her House of Representatives Joint Economic Committee would undertake hearings "to examine the treacherous economic landscape newspapers face" with these words: "It is no secret that the newspaper industry has fallen on hard times which have only been exacerbated by the painful economic woes our country is still working its way out of. Digital media, bloggers, news aggregators, and citizen journalists all on the Internet have forever altered the speed at which news and ideas are disseminated. And while there are many out there chronicling what ails our country's newspapers, community dailies continue to shut down their presses, and not nearly enough is being done to find ways to preserve these institutions" (Maloney, 2009). In the Senate, the Commerce Committee's communication subcommittee proposed the Newspaper Revitalization Act which would grant newspapers nonprofit status similar to that enjoyed by churches, hospitals, and schools. Newspapers' ad and subscription revenue would be tax-exempt and donations to these publications would be tax-deductible. Papers, however, would be forbidden from endorsing political candidates. President Obama said he was "open" to such legislation, and several states were already working on other ways to save newspapers. Washington, for example, reduced its business tax on printers and publishers by 40 percent, and Connecticut offered papers a combination of tax breaks, training funds, and financing opportunities (O'Brien, 2009).

These efforts were based on the view that journalism, because it is essential to the functioning of democracy and the maintenance of our way of life, is a *public good*, something our "society needs and people want but market forces are now incapable of generating in sufficient quality or quantity" (Nichols and McChesney, 2010, p. 13). However, the U.S. public was not inclined to bail newspapers out. In fact, two-thirds of Americans believe news stories are often inaccurate and three-quarters think they're biased (Smillie, 2009); newspapers have registered the steepest decline in customer satisfaction of any industry in the fifteen years of the annual American Customer Satisfaction Index (Fine, 2009).

Beyond dissatisfaction with the performance of the newspaper industry, justified or not, there was also opposition to government support for the medium based on the belief that there should be separation of newspapers and government lest papers bend to the needs and interests of their official benefactors. But, argue supporters of government subsidy, we already expect newspapers to resist bending to the needs and interests of their benefactors (advertisers), and our nation already has a two-century-long history of subsidizing newspapers in particular, through postal subsidies and the federal tax code (Pérez-Peña, 2010), and journalism in general, such as the Corporation for Public Broadcasting, spectrum space for broadcasters, and the underwriting of journalism higher education. Moreover, they contend, public subsidy has not damaged Britain's BBC, arguably the most respected journalistic enterprise on the globe.

Still, if there was little interest in "saving newspapers," surely, in a great democracy such as ours, there is interest in "saving the news." "What is really threatened by the decline of newspapers and the related rise of online media is reporting—on-the-ground reporting by trained journalists who know the subject, have developed sources on all sides, strive for objectivity, and are working with editors who check their facts, steer them in the right direction, and are a further check against unwarranted assumptions, sloppy thinking and reporting, and conscious or unconscious bias," argued *Salon's* Gary Kamiya (2009).

Technologist Clay Shirky was even more direct: "So who covers all that news if some significant fraction of the currently employed newspaper people lose their jobs? I don't know. Nobody knows. We're collectively living through 1500 [after the invention of the printing press], when it's easier to see what's broken than what will replace it." He continued, "Society doesn't need newspapers. What we need is journalism.... When we shift our attention from 'save newspapers' to 'save society', the imperative changes from 'preserve the current institutions' to 'do whatever works'" (2009).

One solution that might work is "to do what other mature democracies have long done: fully fund our public media with tax dollars" argued former PBS

(Continued)

station president William Baker. Making the public-good argument, he likened "efforts to solve the news crisis [to] a national infrastructure project.... We don't leave it up to private nonprofits to maintain our roads and bridges, outfit the Army, or provide public transportation." He might have added universal public education, the police, and the fire department to his list of public goods. But cognizant of minimal public support for the Newspaper Revitalization Act (51 percent of the public was opposed; Rasmussen, 2009), Baker predicted that "calling in the resources of the central government to bear on any national problem is sure to be obscured by the fog of ideological and partisan distractions" producing "hysterical, clamoring opposition to 'socialized media' or 'government takeover of the news'" (2009, p. 22).

Perhaps private nonprofits might save journalism. Between 2005 and 2009, more than 180 American foundations gave nearly $128 million to news and information projects, half of that amount going specifically for investigative journalism (Lewis, 2009). The Knight and the Sandler Foundations, for example, underwrite Spot.us, a website that invites journalists to pitch stories to people who then contribute small amounts of money to those they deem worthy, a practice known as **community-funded (or crowd-funded) journalism**. These foundations also fund ProPublica, a nonprofit investigative reporting group that partners with for-profit news outlets to do stories those media might not otherwise cover. In 2009 it teamed with CBS to report on the spending of federal stimulus money and with the *New York Times* on coverage of the American reconstruction effort in Iraq. The Knight Foundation, through its New Voices program administered by the Institute for Interactive Journalism at American University, also provides grants to aid the launch of local news organizations. Backyard News, serving six Harrisburg, Pennsylvania suburbs, and GrossePointToday.com in Michigan are two examples. The Center for Independent Media and its national portal, the *Washington Independent*, support a number of state-based political news

websites, including the *Colorado Independent* and the *Minnesota Independent*.

Scores of other local, nonprofit journalism sites, using a variety of funding schemes and employing varying mixes of professional and citizen journalists, also operate. Among the more successful are MinnPost.com, NewJerseyNewsroom.com, and Pressforthepeople.com. So extensive has the collection of nonprofit news organizations become (an exhaustive list is available at *www.hks.harvard.edu/hauser/engage/artsculturemedia/nonprofit-news-organizations/index.html*) that twenty of the biggest met in July, 2009 to issue the "Pocantico Declaration." Named after the conference center on the Rockefeller estate outside New York City where they gathered, it announced, "We have hereby established, for the first time ever, an Investigative News Network of nonprofit news publishers throughout the United States of America." Among its assumptions was that the number of "member organizations—and thus the subject range, sheer volume, and potential public impact of available content—will increase substantially over the ensuing months" and "the network will inevitably become international" (Lewis, 2009, p. 17).

It is too early to tell which financial model or models will "save journalism," but something must. Watching layoffs decimate his profession, former *New York Times* reporter Chris Hedges wrote, "A democracy survives when its citizens have access to trustworthy and impartial sources of information, when it can discern lies from truth. Take this away and a democracy dies. The fusion of news and entertainment, the rise of a class of celebrity journalists on television who define reporting by their access to the famous and the powerful, the retreat by many readers into the ideological ghettos of the Internet, and the ruthless drive by corporations to destroy the traditional news business are leaving us deaf, dumb and blind" (2008).

community-funded (or crowdfunded) journalism Journalists propose projects online to people who then contribute to those they deem worthy

thousands of dollars and countless hours to the investigation and reporting of the substandard care received by wounded veterans at Walter Reed Army Medical Center in 2007. Few can match the two years, $400,000, and army of reporters, editors, and staff that the *New York Times* dedicated to its account of doctors euthanizing elderly patients in a New Orleans hospital during the worst days of the Hurricane Katrina disaster (Jeffery, 2009).

But even this is changing. Many blogs do indeed engage in original journalism and many maintain paid, professional staffs. For example, journalists at *Thuthout.org* belong to The Newspaper Guild/Communications Workers of America. *The Huffington Post*, among its paid reporters and editors, employs a ten-reporter investigation team that produces stories that once run on its own blog are available and free to any other media outlet. *Talking Points Memo*, the blog that broke the story of the illegal firing of U.S. attorneys, ultimately leading to the resignation of Attorney General Alberto Gonzales (McLeary, 2007), has professional reporters in its TPMuckrakers unit. Watchdog sites like *The Smoking Gun* and *Fact-Check* undertake tasks once considered essential to good journalism—wading through government and corporate reports and documents, filing Freedom of Information lawsuits to force the publication of materials governments want kept hidden, and measuring government and corporate statements against objective reality—that in the face of declining profits and increased concentration of ownership are disappearing from traditional media outlets (Chapter 4).

The question facing blogs and their social responsibility, then, is really no longer whether they practice journalism. It is whether or not they can remain independent of the pressures that seem to limit more traditional outlets. "Blogging has entered the mainstream, which—as with every new medium in history—looks to its pioneers suspiciously like death," argued technology blogger Nick Carr (2008a). Not death, but constant reinvigoration, responded *Atlantic Monthly's* Andrew Sullivan. Blogging, he wrote, "is generating a new and quintessentially postmodern idiom that's enabling writers to express themselves in ways that have never been seen or understood before. Its truths are provisional, and its ethos collective and messy. Yet the interaction it enables between writer and reader is unprecedented, visceral, and sometimes brutal. And make no mistake: it heralds a golden era for journalism" (2008, p. 106). You can read more about several controversial efforts to support Web-based news gathering and revitalize traditional news organizations' commitment to news in the box entitled "Saving Newspapers or Saving Journalism?"

OTHER NORMATIVE THEORIES

Denis McQuail (1987) cites other normative theories of media developed in other parts of the world. Each assigns a particular social role to media. **Developmental media theory** advocates media support for an existing political regime and its efforts to bring about national economic development. Several developing South American countries—Honduras and Brazil, for example—exemplify developmental media theory. By supporting government development efforts, media aid

developmental media theory A normative theory calling for government and media to work in partnership to ensure that media assist in the planned beneficial development of the country

democratic-participant theory A normative theory advocating media support for cultural pluralism at a grassroots level

Western concept A normative theory combining aspects of Libertarianism and social responsibility theory

development concept A normative theory describing systems in which government and media work in concert to ensure that the media aid the planned, beneficial development of a given nation

revolutionary concept A normative theory describing a system in which media are used in the service of revolution

society at large. This theory argues that until a nation is well established and its economic development well under way, media must be supportive rather than critical of government. Journalists must not pick apart government efforts to promote development but, rather, assist government in implementing its policies. U.S. journalists have been critical of this view. They believe that it is an updated version of authoritarian theory and that media should never surrender the power to criticize government policies, even if voicing those criticisms risks causing them to fail.

Democratic-participant theory advocates media support for cultural pluralism at a grassroots level. Media are to be used to stimulate and empower pluralistic groups. Unlike social responsibility theory, which assumes that mass media can perform this function, democratic-participant theory calls for development of innovative "small" media that can be directly controlled by group members. If they cannot afford such media, then the government should provide them subsidies so they can do so. Government should identify and fund existing small media and establish training programs to teach group members how to operate small media. Most Scandinavian countries practice some form of democratic-participant theory.

William Hachten (1992) provided a different perspective on normative theories used by various countries and political systems. He identified five "concepts": (1) Western, (2) development, (3) revolutionary, (4) authoritarian, and (5) communism. The **Western concept,** exemplified by the United States, Great Britain, and most other well-developed industrial nations, combines aspects of Libertarianism and social responsibility theory. It recognizes that there are no completely free media systems and that even in the most profit-oriented media systems, there exists not only a public expectation of service and responsibility, but an official expectation as well, one backed by "significant communication related activities of government"—in other words, regulation (Stevenson, 1994, p. 109).

The **development concept** describes systems in which government and media work in concert to ensure that media aid the planned, beneficial development of a given nation. This concept is exemplified by the media systems of most developing nations in Africa, Asia, the former Eastern bloc of Europe, and Latin America. Media and government officials work together to produce content that meets specific cultural and societal needs—for example, disease eradication and the dissemination of new farming techniques. There is more government involvement in the operation of the media than there is in the Western concept, but little overt official censorship and control.

The **revolutionary concept** describes a system in which media are used in the service of revolution. No country officially embraces this concept, but that does not mean that the people and media practitioners cannot use a nation's communication technologies to upset the government. The goals of media in the revolutionary concept are to end government monopoly over information, building an opposition to the existing government, destroying the legitimacy of an existing government, and bringing down that government (Stevenson, 1994). The revolutionary concept was in clear evidence in the Polish democracy movement— Solidarity—and its adroit manipulation of that country's media system in its 1989 overthrow of its Communist regime and in the banding together of most of the big media outlets in Yugoslavia in opposition to its undemocratic leader Slobodan Milosevic.

More recently, Iran's "Green Revolution" demonstrates how the Internet is forcing a reconsideration of the revolutionary concept just as it has led to new thinking on social responsibility theory. The tools of revolutionary media had long been opposition pamphlets and newspapers, loud-speaker trucks, clandestine radio and television broadcasts from inside and outside a country's borders, and even guerilla takeover of government-controlled media. These methods are usually thwarted by arrests, military crackdowns, and electronic blocking of broadcast signals. So when Iranian citizens from all walks of life took to the streets in the Summer of 2009 to protest what they saw as the illegitimate re-election of President Mahmoud Ahmadinejad, the government, after expelling or placing under house arrest all foreign journalists, shuttered opposition papers like *Yas-e-No*, blocked Farsi-language satellite transmissions from dissident immigrants working out of Los Angeles at AFN Farsi-Net, and used its own state-run radio and television stations to first ignore the protests and then blame them on outside Western agitators hostile to Iran (Johnson, 2009).

Rather than stop the insurrection, these moves pushed the protesters to make even greater and more effective use of the Internet, especially Twitter and You-Tube. Using cell phones to direct people to Twitter (#IranElection), thousands of dissidents were instantly mobilized into hundreds of daily demonstrations and nightly roof-top protests, shouting "Allahu Akbar" (God is Great) in defiance of the government. Hours of often violent and bloody cell phone video made their way onto YouTube and then to media outlets across the globe. Kelly Golnoush Niknejad's *Tehran Bureau* (*www.tehranbureau.com*) offered a stream of Twitter feeds, videos, e-mail reports, and other messages "from the front" in original English or English translation meant for all readers inside and outside Iran but especially for use by traditional global media outlets. The Iranian immigrant, a graduate of Columbia University's journalism school, produced this outlet of revolutionary voices from her living room in Newton, Massachusetts (Smith, 2009).

When the government began airing the trials of jailed dissidents, the opposition turned to YouTube to broadcast contrasting images of the prisoners before their arrests with those showing the effects of the torture that produced their false confessions. "And so a spectacle that was meant to produce compliance and terror has instead stoked fury and derision," wrote reporter Laura Secor, "The regime has lost control of the political discussion within Iran, which is focusing on the abuse of prisoners rather than on the perfidy of foreigners or the futility of resistance" (2009, p. 26). And if there is one norm that all revolutionary media hope to upset, it is authority's control over political discussion.

Because there are now only three remaining communist countries (North Korea, China, and Cuba), the **authoritarian** and **communism concepts** are typically discussed as one. Both advocate the complete domination of media by the government for the purpose of forcing those media to serve, in the case of the authoritarian system, the government's desires, and in the case of the communism concept, the Communist Party's.

Recently, however, some scholars have been arguing for a less category-based, more flexible approach to normative theory. Chengju Huang, for example, argued for a **transitional media approach** to evaluating specific media systems, because

authoritarian concept
A normative theory advocating the complete domination of media by a government for the purpose of forcing those media to serve the government

communism concept
A normative theory advocating the complete domination of media by a Communist government for the purpose of forcing those media to serve the Communist Party

transitional
media approach
A less category-
based, more flex-
ible approach to
evaluating media
systems than tra-
ditional norma-
tive theory

"the post–Cold War era in the information age is witnessing an accelerated social and media transition across the world." As such, media researchers "confront more mixed social and media systems than the standard ones described by various normative models" (2003, p. 456). This approach would be *nonnormative,* making media system "change and adaptation its primary orientation." It would accept change and adaptation as *a historical process occurring through both revolution and evolution.*" And it would be *culturally open-minded,* maintaining "that media transition in various societies may take different paths in different political, cultural, and socioeconomic contexts, and therefore may lead to different and often complex media systems" (pp. 455–456). Naturally, it is the changing world political environment, advances in communication technologies (especially "borderless" technologies such as satellite and the Internet), and rapid globalization encouraging this call for a more flexible approach to evaluating a given media system against that society's hypothetical ideal (the basis for normative theory).

SUMMARY

During the 1940s, social responsibility theory emerged as the predominant normative theory of media practice in the United States. It represented a compromise between radical Libertarian views and calls for technocratic control. Social responsibility theory put control of media content in the hands of media practitioners, who were expected to act in the public interest. No means existed, however, to compel them to serve the public. They were free to decide what services were needed and to monitor the effectiveness of those services.

Since its articulation by the Hutchins Commission, most media practitioners have at least been introduced to the basic ideals of social responsibility theory. As such, when they are questioned about their work, most provide explanations based on social responsibility notions. In addition, many different news production practices have been developed in an effort to implement these ideas. Still, there seems to be little enthusiasm among many media professionals for social responsibility theory's focus on the public good and on broad-based reporting about significant events. In addition, as the conflict between social responsibility and profitability continues to grow in our increasingly concentrated and commercialized media, responsibility becomes less central to the mission of many media organizations.

Media critics such as Gaye Tuchman (1978) and W. Lance Bennett (1988) have charged that media coverage of minority groups and social movements actually impedes or subverts group activities. They argue that ritualistic balancing of news combined with overdramatized coverage has popularized false impressions of groups or reinforced negative stereotypes. Groups get little real assistance from media. Most media services are aimed at demographic segments favored by advertisers—not at those groups in greatest need of help. Media have chronicled the decay of cities but have done little to create "Great Communities." Their target audiences are generally in the affluent suburbs, not the inner-city ghettos. The harshest critics of social responsibility theory argue that this ideology simply legitimizes and rationalizes the status quo (Altschull, 1990). We will consider these criticisms more fully in Chapter 10.

Despite little revamping or reexamination, social responsibility theory remains the normative theory guiding most media operation in the United States today. But recent changes in media technology and world politics make it reasonable to reassess social responsibility theory's usefulness as currently applied. New media such as niche cable channels and LPFM are available to ethnic or other minority groups at low cost, and the Internet has made it possible for even the smallest groups to enter their voices into the marketplace of ideas. But some critics see the rise of many such small groups as a Balkanization of the larger U.S. culture. Before we can judge the validity of this worry, however, the normative theory on which our media system is grounded must be reformulated, especially given technological and economic changes reshaping the media. This will require a critical reexamination of social responsibility theory and careful consideration of alternatives.

Alternative normative theories, however, already exist, although they may not be a good fit for our political and social system. Developmental media theory advocates media support for an existing political regime in its efforts to foster national economic development. Democratic-participant theory advocates media support for grassroots cultural pluralism. Hachten offered five concepts: (1) Western, combining Libertarian and social responsibility ideals; (2) development, something akin to developmental media theory; (3) revolutionary, in which the people and media professionals use mass media to challenge an existing regime; and (4) authoritarian and (5) communism, in which media serve the dictates of those in power. Recently, however, there have been calls for a less category-based and more flexible approach to normative theories, a transitional media approach to evaluating a given society's media system.

Critical Thinking Questions

1. Do you read news blogs? If so, which ones? Which engage primarily in commentary and which do original reporting? Do you trust these online news sites more or less than you do more traditional media outlets? Why or why not? Do you agree with Nick Carr that blogs have lost their fire, or are you with Andrew Sullivan in thinking that their unique writer-reader relationship creates something so different from what was once considered reporting that they will usher in "a golden era for journalism"? Defend your answer.

2. Libertarianism is based on the self-righting principle—if all the information is available, good ideas will survive and bad ideas will die. But this also assumes that the "debate" between the ideas is fair. Do you think fairness can be achieved in contemporary mass media? Libertarianism also assumes that people are good and rational, that they can tell good ideas from bad ideas. Do you think this highly of your fellow citizens? Why or why not?

3. Social responsibility theory assumes a press that balances profit and service under the watch of an interested public. Many critics, as you've read, believe the media have favored profit over service as the public has remained disinterested. But if journalism becomes the product of a primarily non-profit or philanthropic system, how might social responsibility theory have to be reconfigured? What will it mean if profit is no longer essential? What additional demands, if any, will this place on the public?

Key Terms

social responsibility theory

radical Libertarian

First Amendment absolutists

technocratic control

authoritarian theory

self-righting principle

Bill of Rights

marketplace of ideas

laissez-faire doctrine

Fourth Estate

video news releases

bloggers

Chicago School

pluralistic groups

local origination (or mandatory access) rule

low power FM radio (LPFM)

Balkanize

enterprise reporting

developmental media theory

democratic-participant theory

Western concept

development concept

revolutionary concept

transitional media approach

community-funded (or crowdfunded) journalism

FROM LIMITED-EFFECTS TO CRITICAL CULTURAL THEORIES: FERMENT IN THE FIELD

1455	Johann Gutenberg invents printing press
1644	Milton's *Aeropagetica* published
1690	*Publick Occurrences*, first newspaper in America
1704	First newspaper ad appears
1741	First magazines appear in the Colonies
1790	Bill of Rights and First Amendment adopted
1833	Benjamin Day's *New York Sun* ushers in penny press
1836	Charles Babbage develops plans for a mechanical computer in England
1844	Samuel Morse invents telegraph
1876	Alexander Graham Bell invents telephone
1877	Thomas Edison demonstrates phonograph
1894	America's first movie (kinetoscope) house opens
1895	Louis and Auguste Lumière introduce single-screen motion picture exhibit William Randolph Hearst and Joseph Pulitzer embark on yellow journalism
1896	Hearst sends infamous telegram to reporter in Cuba Press services founded
1912	Radio Act of 1912 passed

1915	Pulitzer endows prize that bears his name
1920	KDKA goes on the air
1922	Walter Lippmann's *Public Opinion* published First commercial announcement broadcast on radio
1924	The American Society of Newspaper Editors' *Canons of Journalism* adopted
1926	NBC begins network broadcasting Talking pictures introduced
1927	Radio Act of 1927 creates the Federal Radio Commission
1933	Payne Fund's *Movies, Delinquency, and Crime* published
1934	Communications Act passes, creates the Federal Communications Commission
1938	*War of the Worlds* broadcast
1939	First public broadcast of television World War II erupts in Europe Paperback book introduced in the United States
1940	Paul Lazarsfeld's voter studies begin in Erie County, Ohio
1941	United States enters World War II British develop first binary computer
1942	Carl Hovland conducts first war propaganda research British develop Colossus, the first electronic digital computer, to break German war code
1945	World War II ends Gordon Allport and Leo Postman's rumor study published
1946	John Mauchly and John Atanasoff introduce ENIAC, the first "full-service" electronic digital computer
1947	Hutchins Commission issues report on press freedom The Hollywood Ten called before the House Un-American Activities Committee
1948	Norbert Wiener's *Cybernetics* published Cable television invented
1949	George Orwell's *1984* published Carl Hovland, Arthur Lumsdaine, and Fred Sheffield's *Experiments in Mass Communication* published
1951	Harold Innis's *The Bias of Communication* published Edward R. Murrow's *See It Now* premieres UNIVAC becomes the first successful commercial computer
1953	Carl Hovland, Irving Janis, and Harold Kelley's *Communication and Persuasion* published
1954	Murrow challenges McCarthy on television
1955	Paul Lazarsfeld and Elihu Katz's *Personal Influence* published

1957	C. Wright Mills's *Power Elite* published Soviet Union launches *Sputnik*, Earth's first human-constructed satellite Leon Festinger's *Cognitive Dissonance* published
1958	Television quiz show scandal erupts
1959	C. Wright Mills's *The Sociological Imagination* published
1960	John F. Kennedy and Richard Nixon meet in the Great Debates Television in 90 percent of all U.S. homes Joseph Klapper's *Effects of Mass Communication* published
1961	V. O. Key's *Public Opinion and American Democracy* published Kennedy makes nation's first live TV presidential press conference Schramm team's *Television in the Lives of Our Children* published
1962	Festinger's cognitive dissonance article appears Sidney Kraus's *Great Debates* published Air Force commissions Paul Baran to develop a national computer network
1963	JFK assassinated Albert Bandura's aggressive modeling experiments first appear Networks begin one-half-hour newscasts

THE RISE OF LIMITED-EFFECTS THEORY

Two wars—one imaginary, one real—helped move mass communication theory away from notions of powerful and subversive mass media to a more moderate and benign view. What was to become the discipline's long adherence to limited-effects thinking began on a peaceful evening in late October, 1938. On that night, many Americans were listening to a ballroom dance music program on the CBS radio network when the show was interrupted by a series of news bulletins. Early announcements told of strange astronomical observations and sightings of lights in the sky. The reports grew steadily more ominous. An alien spaceship had landed and was attacking the military forces that surrounded it. Transmissions from the scene ended suddenly, followed by an appeal from the Secretary of the Interior for calm in the face of the alien threat. In cities across the nation, Americans reacted with alarm.

In that year, the medium of radio was still new, but it had become enormously popular. Expansive national networks had been established only a few years earlier. Listeners were starting to rely on the new medium for news, which was free and easily accessible and provided compelling on-the-spot reports of fast-breaking situations. In a very troubled era, with many unusual and threatening events, such as impending war in Europe, people listened to radio for the latest reports of threatening news. Orson Welles, a young radio program producer, conceived a radio theater program in which simulated news bulletins would be used to play a Halloween joke on the entire nation. Borrowing freely from a novel by H. G. Wells entitled *War of the Worlds,* Welles and scriptwriter Howard Koch created a radio drama in which listeners heard a series of compelling eyewitness reports of an alien invasion. Afraid that the program might be too dull, Koch embellished the script with allusions and authentic detail (Lowery and DeFleur, 1995).

The last half of the program recounted the aftermath of the invasion. News bulletins gave way to a monologue from the sole human survivor, telling of the aliens' ultimate defeat by earthly bacteria. Because this portion of the program was clearly fantasy, Welles saw no need to provide announcements of the program's fictitious nature. For many listeners, it was too late anyway. As soon as they heard the early bulletins, they fled their homes and aroused their neighbors.

Many observers saw the invasion-from-Mars panic as definitive proof of mass society theory. If a single radio program could induce such widespread panic, obviously concerted propaganda campaigns could do much worse. The American masses were clearly at the mercy of any demagogue who could gain control of the airwaves. Eventually some bully would seize the opportunity and take power, as Adolf Hitler had done in Germany. A demagogue would use propaganda to win a close election, and once he gained sufficient control, he would crush political opposition.

At Princeton University, a group of social researchers set out to determine why the Welles broadcast had been so influential (Cantril, Gaudet, and Herzog, 1940). Their research found that many people acted too hastily after hearing only the first fragmentary reports of the invasion. They trusted without question the simulated news bulletins, especially the eyewitness reports and interviews with phony experts with official-sounding but fictitious titles. The people who were most upset by the program didn't stay glued to their radios waiting for updates. In that era, before portable and car radios had become commonplace, these people lost touch with the program once they left their homes. Word of mouth spread news of the ersatz invasion through entire neighborhoods. Often people who heard about the invasion from others didn't think to turn on their radios to check out the news for themselves. They trusted their neighbors and acted. Even though the researchers found considerable evidence of panic, they also found that most people were not taken in by Welles's practical joke. Most people had enough critical ability that they easily checked the validity of the broadcast, so they had little trouble disconfirming news of the invasion. Only listeners who tuned in late and for just a few minutes were likely to be upset. The researchers concluded that these people had one or more psychological traits that made them especially susceptible to media influence: emotional insecurity, phobic personality, lack of self-confidence, and fatalism.

OVERVIEW

The *War of the Worlds* researchers, led by Hadley Cantril, were part of a vanguard of social scientists who transformed our view of how media influence society. Within twenty years of Welles's broadcast, the way many scholars looked at mass media had been radically altered. They no longer feared media as potential instruments of political oppression and manipulation, but instead portrayed mass communication as a relatively benign force with much potential for social good. Researchers gradually came to see media's power over the public as limited—so limited that no government regulations were deemed necessary to prevent manipulation. They viewed the public itself as resistant to persuasion and extremist manipulation. The belief grew that most people were influenced by other people rather than by the media; opinion leaders in every community and at every level of society were responsible for guiding and stabilizing public views on everything from politics to fashion and shopping. Only a very small minority of people had psychological traits that made them vulnerable to direct manipulation by media. Media were conceptualized as relatively powerless in shaping public opinion in the face of more potent intervening variables like people's individual differences and their group memberships. This new view of media arose and persisted even after the new medium of television transformed and dominated the media landscape.

How and why did such a radical transformation in media theory take place in such a relatively short period of time? In this chapter, we trace the rise of what became the dominant perspective in U.S. media research for several decades. We describe the work of researchers led by Paul Lazarsfeld, Cantril's colleague at Princeton University. Lazarsfeld later moved to Columbia University, where he pioneered the use of sophisticated surveys to measure media influence on how people thought and acted. These surveys seemed to provide definitive evidence that media rarely had a powerful direct influence on individuals. The effects that did occur were quite limited in scope—affecting only a few people or influencing less important thoughts or actions. Later research showed similar findings and led to development of a perspective on media that was referred to as the **limited-effects perspective.**

limited-effects perspective
The guiding idea that media have minimal or limited effects

We also review experimental studies of the persuasive power of media, focusing on the work of Carl Hovland. Like Lazarsfeld, Hovland was a methodological innovator who introduced new standards for evaluating media influence. He too found that media lacked the power to instantly convert average people away from strongly held beliefs. Even in laboratory situations where the potential for media influence was exaggerated, he could demonstrate only modest effects. Hovland and his team identified many factors that appeared to limit media influence.

Finally, we consider how proponents of limited effects were able to establish this perspective as the dominant way of looking at media. Data from an impressive array of elaborate empirical studies were assembled into an important series of classic reports (e.g., Bauer and Bauer, 1960; Campbell et al., 1960; DeFleur and Larsen, 1958; Katz and Lazarsfeld, 1955; Klapper, 1960). These reports seemed to provide definitive evidence of limited effects.

As we trace the rise of the limited-effects perspective and the development of middle-range theories of mass communication, it is important to note the parallels to our own times (as well as the important differences). As there was for the theorists in the 1930s and 1940s, there is seemingly obvious evidence all around us of the power of media to alter our experience of the social world. In the first seven days following the massive 2010 earthquake in Haiti, for example, dramatic reporting from the scene moved tens of thousands of Americans to pick up their cell phones and donate by text message $22 million to the Red Cross relief effort (Heath, 2010). How can this be explained if media are not capable of having powerful effects? But it is not only in times of crisis that we turn to media as a means of making sense of what is going on and trying to anticipate what might happen in the future. The more we depend on media to do this, the more we effectively place our faith in them to guide us, and the more likely it is that they will influence our lives. To what extent should media be held responsible for altering our views of the social world? To what extent should we be held responsible if we choose to trust the media to provide useful information? It is important to recognize that this apparent power of the media is not inherent in the technology itself or even in the specific media content being transmitted. The power lies in ourselves—in the way we choose to allow media to affect our lives. This is the essential insight that comes out of the limited-effects perspective—an insight that continues to have relevance as we seek to assess the role of media today.

As you read this chapter, you will be introduced to a perspective on the role of media in society that differs profoundly from the mass society and propaganda perspectives discussed in earlier chapters. Concern about the power and role of propaganda in society fades away and is replaced by interest in the processes that determine whether or not mass communication will have specific effects on certain types of individuals. Does this mean that propaganda disappeared after World War II? Was the postwar world suddenly free from messages designed to serve special interests? The Cold War was at its peak in the 1950s. Widespread fear of Communism was combined with fear of nuclear war. Americans were constantly being reminded to build shelters and be prepared for the bombs likely to fall at any time. School children watched government-issued films that urged them to "duck and cover" under their desks during nuclear bomb attacks.

Some contemporary researchers have begun to question Cold War propaganda efforts and the role played by communications researchers in planning and studying them. Timothy Glander (2000), for example, has argued that the rise of mass communication research during the Cold War was the result of a collaboration among media researchers who became colleagues during World War II and then supported each other in later years. These people effectively channeled government and foundation funding toward favored mass communication research. In Glander's view, these researchers consciously abandoned any interest in systematic public education such as Dewey had advocated in the 1930s. Funding that might have been used to educate the public about the Cold War instead went toward funding effects research that Glander argues was intended to find ways to manipulate the public in the service of elite objectives. Campaigns were launched to denigrate the Soviet Union and Communism and to promote preparations for nuclear war. Other scholars (Park and Pooley, 2008) who have examined the development of mass communication research in the United States during that period confirm most of Glander's assertions. They provide evidence that the focus on media effects was consistent with ideological biases prevalent in the United States at the time. As we will see in Chapter 8, American researchers in the 1950s and 1960s saw European theory as heavily biased by neo-Marxist theory but considered their own work to be objective because it was grounded in empirical research. We'll have more to say about these assertions in later chapters.

THE DEVELOPMENT OF LIMITED-EFFECTS THEORY

The people who developed limited-effects theory during the 1940s and 1950s were primarily methodologists—not theorists. In this chapter we focus attention on two such men, Paul Lazarsfeld and Carl Hovland. There were a number of others who worked with them and were influenced by them. Hovland's wartime colleagues included Irving Janis, Arthur Lumsdaine, Nathan Macoby, and Fred Sheffield. Lazarsfeld worked with Hadley Cantril, Bernard Berelson, Hazel Gaudet, and Harold Mendelsohn. Both Hovland and Lazarsfeld were convinced that we could best assess the influence of media by employing objective empirical methods to measure it. They argued that new research methods such as experiments and surveys made it possible to directly observe and draw objective conclusions about the effects of media. These conclusions would guide the construction of more useful theory that was grounded in systematic observation, not wild speculation.

Both Lazarsfeld and Hovland were trained in the empirical research methods that had been developed in psychology. In addition, Lazarsfeld spent time as a social statistician in Austria and was trained in survey research methods. Working independently, they demonstrated how their research techniques could be adapted to the study of media effects. Both were successful in convincing others of the usefulness and validity of their approach. With ongoing backing from the Rockefeller Foundation, Lazarsfeld secured government and private funding that enabled him to conduct expensive large-scale studies at Columbia University of media influence. After conducting propaganda experiments during World War II—the real war mentioned at the start of this chapter—Hovland established a research center at Yale, where hundreds of persuasion experiments were conducted for more than a decade. Both Columbia and Yale became very influential research centers, attracting and educating some of the most prominent social researchers of the time.

Neither Lazarsfeld nor Hovland set out to overturn the way mass communication was understood. They had broader objectives. During the war years, they were drawn into media studies as part of the larger effort to understand the power of propaganda and the threat it posed. Government agencies looked to them for advice concerning how to mobilize Americans to fight the Germans and the Japanese. Unlike many colleagues, who automatically assumed that media were quite powerful, Lazarsfeld and Hovland were determined to conduct empirical research that might reveal how media influence worked. They hoped that if media's power could be better understood, it might be controlled and used toward good ends.

Lazarsfeld and Hovland were part of a new generation of empirical social researchers who argued that scientific methods provided the essential means to understand the social world and to control media's power over society. These researchers sought to remake their academic disciplines: to convert sociology, psychology, political science, and even history into true social sciences. They cited the tremendous accomplishments made in the physical sciences. Fields like physics and chemistry vividly demonstrated the ability of science to understand and control the physical world. Some of the most striking examples could be found in new military technology: amazing aircraft, highly destructive bombs, and unstoppable tanks. These weapons could be used for either good or evil, to defend democracy or bolster totalitarianism. Like Harold Lasswell (Chapter 4), these would-be social scientists believed that if democracy were to survive, it would have to produce the best scientists, and these people would have to do a better job of harnessing technology to advance that political ideology.

As the new social scientists conducted their research, they found that media were not as powerful as mass society or propaganda theory had suggested. Media influence over public opinion or attitudes often proved hard to locate. Media influence was typically less important than that of factors such as social status or education. Those media effects that were found seemed to be isolated and were sometimes contradictory. Despite the weak findings—study after study provided growing insight into the limited power of media—funding for additional research was easy to secure. Much of this support was provided by a government anxious to maintain its control in a fearful nation under siege from Communist ideology and nuclear weapons that render today's threats from stateless Islamic radicals pale by comparison (Pooley, 2008).

During the 1950s, as the limited-effects perspective began to take shape, new social research centers modeled after those at Yale and Columbia opened across the United States. One of the early leaders in the field, Wilbur Schramm, was personally responsible for establishing communication research centers at the University of Illinois, Stanford University, and the University of Hawaii. By 1960, many of the "classic studies" of limited effects had been published and become required reading for the first generation of doctoral students in the newly created field of mass communication research. This new perspective dominated during the 1960s; it remained quite strong through the 1970s, and its influence echoes even today.

Did the creators of the limited-effects perspective believe that the power of media was limited? Recently, historians have argued that the same researchers who published limited-effects findings were also accepting large government contracts to design and test propaganda, which they obviously thought to be effective (Park and Pooley, 2008). During the Cold War much of this propaganda was targeted at Third World populations also targeted by the Communists. These researchers were also accepting contracts to improve the effectiveness of domestic Civil Defense propaganda.

As we discuss the early research, we will illustrate the factors that combined to make development of the perspective possible. We list these factors here, and we will refer to them in later sections.

1. **The refinement and broad acceptance of empirical social research methods was an essential factor in the emergence of the limited-effects perspective.** Throughout this period, empirical research methods were effectively promoted as an ideal means of measuring, describing, and ultimately explaining social phenomena. A generation of empirical social scientists working in several academic disciplines declared them to be the only "scientific" way of dealing with social phenomena. They dismissed other approaches as overly speculative, unsystematic, or too subjective (see the discussion of postpositivism in Chapter 1). Because so few people at the time understood the limitations of empirical research methods, they often uncritically accepted the findings and conclusions derived from them. When these outcomes conflicted with past theories, the older theories were questioned and rejected, often on the basis of a handful of inconclusive findings.

2. **Empirical social researchers successfully branded people who advocated mass society and propaganda notions as "unscientific."** They accused mass society theory advocates of being fuzzy-minded humanists, doomsayers, political ideologues, or biased against media. Also, mass society and propaganda notions lost some of their broad appeal as the threat of propaganda seemed to fade in the late 1950s and 1960s. Within social science departments, study of propaganda was abandoned in favor of public opinion research.

3. **Social researchers exploited the commercial potential of the new research methods and gained the support of private industry.** One of the first articles Lazarsfeld wrote after arriving in the United States was about the use of survey research methods as a tool for advertisers (Kornhauser and Lazarsfeld, 1935).

Researchers promoted surveys and experiments as a means of probing media audiences and interpreting consumer attitudes and behaviors. Most of Hovland's persuasion studies had more or less direct application to advertising and marketing. As we saw in Chapter 2, Lazarsfeld coined the term *administrative research* to refer to these applications. He persuasively argued for the use of empirical research to guide administrative decision making.

4. **The development of empirical social research was strongly backed by various private and government foundations, most notably the Rockefeller Foundation and the National Science Foundation.** This support was crucial, particularly in the early stages, because large-scale empirical research required much more funding than previous forms of social research had required. Without support from the Rockefeller Foundation, Lazarsfeld might never have come to the United States or have been able to develop and demonstrate the validity of his approach. Without the government funding provided during the Cold War, large mass communication research centers might never have been established at major universities. The generation of empirical researchers trained in these centers might never have come to dominate the field during the 1970s and 1980s.

5. **As empirical research demonstrated its usefulness, media companies began to sponsor and eventually conduct their own empirical research on media.** In time, both CBS and NBC formed their own social research departments and employed many outside researchers as consultants. Two of the most influential early media researchers were Frank Stanton and Joseph Klapper—the former collaborated with Lazarsfeld on numerous research projects in the 1940s, and the latter was Lazarsfeld's student. Both Stanton and Klapper rose to become executives at CBS. As media corporations grew larger and earned sizable profits, they could afford to fund empirical research—especially when that research helped to justify the status quo and block moves to regulate their operations. Media funding and support were vital to the development of commercial audience ratings services such as Nielsen and Arbitron. These companies pioneered the use of survey research methods to measure the size of audiences and guide administrative decision making in areas such as advertising and marketing.

   Media support was also crucial to the growth of various national polling services, such as Gallup, Harris, and Roper. Media coverage of polls and ratings data helped establish their credibility in the face of widespread commonsense criticism. During the 1940s and 1950s, most people were skeptical about the usefulness of data gathered from small samples. They wondered, for example, how pollsters could survey just 300 or 1200 people and draw conclusions about an entire city or nation. To answer these questions, media reported that opinion polls and ratings were valid because they were based on "scientific" samples. Often, there was little explanation of what the term *scientific* meant in this context.

6. **Empirical social researchers successfully established their approach within the various social research disciplines—political science, history, social psychology, sociology, and economics.** These disciplines, in turn, shaped the development of communication research. During the 1960s and 1970s, several communication areas—for example, advertising and journalism—rapidly

expanded to meet growing student interest in studying communication and preparing for careers in related industries. As these areas developed, empirical social researchers from the more established social sciences provided leadership. Social science theories and research methods borrowed from the more established disciplines assumed an important—often dominant—role in structuring research conducted in university journalism, advertising, speech communication, and broadcasting departments. Empirical research became widely accepted as the most scientific way to study communication, even though it proved difficult to find conclusive evidence of media influence. Communication researchers working in hundreds of small academic departments spread across the United States relied on better-funded colleagues at major universities to lead the field.

THE TWO-STEP FLOW OF INFORMATION AND INFLUENCE

Lazarsfeld was not a theorist, yet by promoting empirical research, he did more than any of his peers to transform social theory generally and media theory specifically. Lazarsfeld believed theory must be strongly grounded in empirical facts. He was concerned that macroscopic social theories, including the various mass society and propaganda theories, were too speculative. He preferred a highly **inductive** approach to theory construction—that is, research should begin with empirical observation of important phenomena, not with armchair speculation. After the facts are gathered, they are sifted, and the most important pieces of information are selected. This information is used to construct empirical generalizations—assertions about the relationships between variables. Then researchers can gather more data to see whether these generalizations are valid.

inductive
An approach to theory construction that sees research beginning with empirical observation rather than speculation

This research approach is cautious and inherently conservative. It avoids sweeping generalizations that go beyond empirical observations and demands that theory construction be "disciplined" by data collection and analysis (observation leads to research … and more research … and more research leads to theory development). Theory, therefore, is never too far removed from the data on which it is based. The research process proceeds slowly—building step-by-step on one data-collection effort after another. You'll recognize this from Chapter 1 as the epistemology of postpositivism. Eventually, researchers will find and test a large number of empirical generalizations.

middle-range theory
A theory composed of empirical generalizations based on empirical fact

Theory is gradually created by combining generalizations to build what Robert Merton (1967) referred to as **middle-range theory** (see Chapter 7 for a fuller discussion). Unlike earlier forms of grand social theory—mass society theory or the propaganda theories, for example—middle-range theory comprises empirical generalizations that are solidly based on empirical facts. At the time, most social researchers thought that this was how theories were developed in the physical sciences. By emulating physical scientists, social scientists hoped they would be just as successful in controlling the phenomena that interested them. If so, the scientific methods that produced nuclear bombs might also eliminate poverty, war, and racism.

During the presidential election campaign of 1940, pitting incumbent Franklin Delano Roosevelt against Republican Wendell Willkie, Lazarsfeld had his first major opportunity to test the validity of his approach. He designed and carried out what was, at the time, the most elaborate mass communication field experiment ever conducted. Lazarsfeld assembled a large research team in May 1940 and sent it to Erie County, Ohio—a relatively remote region surrounding and including the town of Sandusky, west of Cleveland along the shores of Lake Erie. The total population of the county was 43,000, and it was chosen because it was considered to be an average American locality. Though Sandusky residents tended to vote Democratic, the surrounding rural area was strongly Republican. By the time the research team left in November, it had personally interviewed more than 3,000 people in their homes. Six hundred were selected to be in a panel that was interviewed seven times—once every month from May until November. The researchers estimated that an interviewer visited one out of every three of the county's households (Lazarsfeld, Berelson, and Gaudet, 1944).

In his data analysis, Lazarsfeld focused attention on changes in voting decisions. As people were interviewed each month, their choice of candidates was compared with the previous month's choice. During the six months, several types of changes were possible. Lazarsfeld created a label for each. *Early deciders* chose a candidate in May and never changed during the entire campaign. *Waverers* chose one candidate, then were undecided or switched to another candidate, but in the end they voted for their first choice. *Converts* chose one candidate but then voted for his opponent—they had been converted from one political ideology to another. *Crystallizers* had not chosen a candidate in May but made a choice by November. Their choice was predictable, based on their political party affiliation, their social status, and whether they lived on a farm or in the city. Lazarsfeld reasoned that for these people, mass media simply served as a means of helping them sort out a choice that was to some extent predetermined by their social situation.

Lazarsfeld used a very long and detailed questionnaire dealing extensively with exposure to specific mass media content, such as candidate speeches on radio. This focus was not surprising given his considerable background and interest in radio research. If propaganda was as powerful as propaganda theories predicted, his research should have allowed him to pinpoint media influence. If these notions

INSTANT ACCESS

Two-Step Flow Theory

Strengths

1. Focuses attention on the environment in which effects can and can't occur
2. Stresses importance of opinion leaders in formation of public opinion
3. Is based on inductive rather than deductive reasoning
4. Effectively challenges simplistic notions of direct effects

Weaknesses

1. Is limited to its time (1940s) and media environment (no television)
2. Uses reported behavior (voting) as only test of media effects
3. Downplays reinforcement as an important media effect
4. Uses survey methods that underestimate media impact
5. Later research demonstrates a multistep flow of influence

were valid, he reasoned that he should have found that most voters were either converts or waverers. He should have observed people switching back and forth between candidates as they consumed the candidates' latest media messages. Those who showed the most change should have been the heaviest users of media.

But Lazarsfeld's results directly contradicted notions based on propaganda theory. Fifty-three percent of the voters were early deciders. They chose one candidate in May and never changed. Twenty-eight percent were crystallizers—they eventually made a choice consistent with their position in society and stayed with it. Fifteen percent were waverers, and only eight percent were converts. Lazarsfeld could find little evidence that media played an important role in influencing the crystallizers, the waverers, or the converts. Media use by those in the latter two categories was lower than average, and very few of them reported being specifically influenced by media messages. Instead, these voters were much more likely to say that they had been influenced by other people. Many were politically apathetic. They failed to make clear-cut voting decisions because they had such low interest. Often they decided to vote as the people closest to them voted—not as radio speeches or newspaper editorials told them to vote.

Lazarsfeld concluded that the most important influence of mass media was to reinforce a vote choice that had already been made. Media simply gave people more reasons for choosing a candidate whom they (and the people around them) already favored. For some voters—the crystallizers, for example—media helped activate existing party loyalties and reminded them how people like themselves were going to vote. Republicans who had never heard of Willkie were able to at least learn his name and a few reasons why he would make a good president. On the other hand, Lazarsfeld found very little evidence that media converted people. Instead, the converts were often people with divided loyalties; as Lazarsfeld described this situation, they were "cross-pressured." They had group ties or social status that pulled them in opposing directions. Willkie was Catholic, so religion pulled some people toward him and pushed others away. Most Republican voters were rural Protestants; to vote for Willkie, they had to ignore his religion. The same was true of urban Catholic Democrats; they had to ignore religion to vote for Roosevelt.

By 1944, Lazarsfeld seemed quite convinced that media were unimportant during election campaigns. In a coauthored article summarizing his views on the prediction of political behavior in U.S. elections, he makes no reference to any form of mass communication (Lazarsfeld and Franzen, 1945). Changes in vote decisions are attributed to social and psychological variables, not exposure to media.

But if media weren't directly influencing voting decisions, what was their role? As Lazarsfeld worked with his data, he began to formulate an empirical generalization that ultimately had enormous importance for media theory. He noticed that some of the hard-core early deciders were also the heaviest users of media. They even made a point of seeking out and listening to opposition speeches. On the other hand, the people who made the least use of media were most likely to report that they relied on others for help in making a voting decision. Lazarsfeld reasoned that the "heavy user/early deciders" might be the same people whose advice was being sought by more apathetic voters. These "heavy user/early deciders" might be sophisticated media users who held well-developed political views and used media wisely and critically. They might be capable of listening to and evaluating opposition speeches. Rather than be converted themselves, they might actually gain information that would help them advise others so that they would be more resistant to conversion. Thus, these heavy users might act as **gatekeepers**—screening information and only passing on items that would help others share their views. Lazarsfeld chose the term **opinion leader** to refer to these individuals. He labeled those who turned to opinion leaders for advice as **opinion followers.**

Lazarsfeld designed subsequent research to directly investigate the empirical generalizations emerging from the 1940 research. He refused to speculate about the attributes of opinion leaders or their role—he wanted empirical facts (Summers, 2006b). In 1945 he sent a research team to Decatur, Illinois, to interview more than 800 women about how they made decisions about fashion, product brands, movies, and politics. Decatur, a city in the heartland of America, was widely viewed as representative of most small- to medium-sized cities. His researchers used a "snowball" sampling technique, contacting an initial sample of women. During the interviews, they asked these women if they had influenced or been influenced by other people in their thinking about international, national, or community affairs or news events. The researchers then followed up, conducting interviews with those who had been identified as influential. In this way Lazarsfeld tried to empirically locate women who served as opinion leaders. Their nomination by themselves or others was taken as factual evidence of their opinion-leader status.

More than ten years passed before the Decatur research was published. During some of this time, the field director of the project, C. Wright Mills, was tasked with writing the research report. In 1947, with the report more than sixteen months overdue, "Mills was living in a cabin in the Sierra Nevada Mountains. He wrote to Lazarsfeld to say that he had decided, once and for all, that the tables and figures made no sense.... He was going to set aside the tabulation machinery and he was going to write the goddamned book then and there" (Pooley, 2006, p. 31). To Lazarsfeld this was scientifically unacceptable, so he fired Mills. Several years later, Lazarsfeld turned to one of his graduate students, Elihu Katz, and together they used the Decatur data as the basis for their 1955 *Personal Influence*. It formally advanced **two-step flow theory**—a middle-range theory that influenced communication research for more than two decades. But what if Mills had published the book he planned to write? How would he have used the data? Would his views have had an impact on media research? Later in this chapter we will discuss Mills and explain how his work directly challenged Lazarsfeld's research methods and approach to theory construction. In many ways, Mills's thinking presaged the challenges to postpositivist research that were to gain prominence in the 1980s.

Katz and Lazarsfeld provided a very positive depiction of American society and assigned a restricted and benign role to media. They reported that opinion leaders existed at all levels of society and that the flow of their influence tended to be horizontal rather than vertical. Opinion leaders influenced people like themselves rather than those above or below them in the social order. Opinion leaders differed from followers in many of their personal attributes—they were more gregarious, used media more, were more socially active—but they often shared the same social status.

Pooley (2006) argues that *Personal Influence* did more than introduce an innovative way of understanding why the power of media is limited. In its first fifteen

---

gatekeepers
In two-step flow, people who screen media messages and pass on those messages and help others share their views

opinion leaders
In two-step flow, those who pass on information to opinion followers

opinion followers
In two-step flow, those who receive information from opinion leaders

two-step flow theory
The idea that messages pass from the media, through opinion leaders, to opinion followers

pages, *Personal Influence* offered a summary of the history of propaganda research that provided boilerplate language that would be used in media theory textbooks and literature reviews written over the next five decades. These few pages dismissed pre–World War II theory and research as naïve and overly speculative, erroneously grounded in the myth of media power. They promoted empirical research as providing more accurate findings that encouraged useful skepticism of media's power.

LIMITATIONS IN THE LAZARSFELD APPROACH

The Lazarsfeld research approach has several important limitations that its defenders have been slow to recognize. Although these limitations don't invalidate specific findings, they do force us to be very careful in their interpretation. We'll examine several specific limitations, but a closer look at the Decatur research provides a useful introduction.

When the Decatur research was undertaken, men dominated American politics; why did Lazarsfeld choose to study political communication among housewives? Was there a theoretical or methodological reason for this focus? And why study leadership in fashion, movies, and marketing? Why not focus on more serious issues facing the nation during World War II, such as rationing or Fascist ideology? The answer is that the company that paid for the research, MacFadden Publications, was not interested in men or in serious social issues. It was interested in how women make fashion, movie, and marketing decisions, because as a publisher of magazines aimed primarily at lower- and middle-class women, MacFadden was losing advertising. Prevailing thought among advertisers at the time was that high-society women served as "taste leaders" for all other women. As such, there was little reason for them to buy space in MacFadden's downscale publications. Lazarsfeld's opinion-leadership findings disproved that assumption, indicating the necessity of advertising to opinion leaders at all levels of society. But in designing research to serve the interests of MacFadden, did Lazarsfeld make too many compromises? In hindsight, we now see that some administrative, limited-effects research of the time suffered this "deficiency." Now, the specific limitations:

1. **Surveys can't measure how people actually use media on a day-to-day basis.** Surveys can only record how people *report* their use of media. As our experience with surveys has grown, we have identified some common biases in reports of media use. For example, more-educated people tend to underestimate media influence on their decisions, whereas less-educated people might overestimate it. Estimates of influence tend to be strongly linked to people's perceptions of various media. For example, because television is widely viewed by educated people as a less socially acceptable medium (that is, the boob tube), they are less willing to admit to using it and being influenced by it.

2. **Surveys are a very expensive and cumbersome way to study people's use of specific media content, such as their reading of certain news stories or their viewing of specific television programs.** Since Lazarsfeld's early work, most research has dealt with overall patterns of media use rather than use of specific content. Critics charge that this means that media content is being ignored. The impact of powerful individual messages isn't routinely assessed, only the

amount of use routinely made of a given medium. We can learn a great deal from studying patterns of media use. There are important research questions, however, that can be addressed only if use and influence of specific content is studied.

3. **The research design and data analysis procedures Lazarsfeld developed are inherently conservative in assessing the media's power.** Media influence is gauged by the amount of change media cause in an effect variable (e.g., voting decision) after statistically controlling a set of social and demographic variables. Under these conditions, media are rarely found to be strong predictors of effects. Overall patterns of media use tend to be strongly associated with social and demographic variables like age, sex, social status, and education. When these variables are statistically controlled, there is little impact (variance) left for media-use patterns to explain. Does this mean that media use really isn't very powerful? Or is such a conclusion a methodological artifact—something that appears to be true only because a research method leads to biased or incomplete observations?

4. **Subsequent research on the two-step flow has produced highly contradictory findings.** Most theorists who still find this conceptualization useful talk about multistep flows. These flows have been found to differ greatly according to the type of information being transmitted and the social conditions that exist at a particular time (Rogers, 1983). Although information flow from media to audiences has general patterns, these patterns are subject to constant change. Powerful messages could radically alter patterns of flow.

5. **Surveys can be useful for studying changes over time, but they are a relatively crude technique.** In 1940, Lazarsfeld interviewed people once a month. Considerable change could occur during a thirty-day period that isn't measured. People tend to selectively remember and report what they think they should be doing rather than what they actually do. They could very well misreport listening or reading that took place days earlier. If surveys are taken more often and at closer intervals, they can become intrusive. But the primary reason these surveys aren't conducted frequently is that they are too expensive.

6. **Surveys omit many potentially important variables by focusing only on what can be easily or reliably measured using existing techniques.** Too often, these variables—for example, how a person was raised—are dismissed as unimportant or unduly speculative. Because they are hard or impossible to measure, their very existence can be questioned. This greatly limits theory construction because entire categories of variables are necessarily eliminated.

7. **The period during which Lazarsfeld conducted his research made it unlikely that he would observe the effects that he tried to measure.** The primary effect that he looked for in his voting research was whether people changed their decisions about whom to vote for in 1940. It's not surprising that very few people altered their voting preferences during the summer and fall of 1940, as Nazi troops invaded much of Western Europe. For example, if a national election had been held in the immediate aftermath of American troops' apparent easy victory in Iraq in spring 2003 instead of in the fall of 2007—as U.S. casualties mounted, Iraq was torn by sectarian fighting, and most members of the "coalition of the willing" had withdrawn their forces—it's likely that the overwhelmingly high

approval ratings for President Bush would have translated into a landslide election victory for his Republican Party. In this hypothetical spring election, would the failure of a Democrat challenge to the Republicans have been convincing evidence of the weakness of media during all political campaigns?

LIMITED-EFFECTS THEORY

indirect-effects theory
When media do seem to have an effect, that effect is "filtered" through other parts of the society, for example, through friends or social groups

limited-effects theory
The theory that media have minimal or limited effects because those effects are mitigated by a variety of mediating or intervening variables

Two popular labels for the perspective on media that developed out of Lazarsfeld's work are **indirect-effects theory** and **limited-effects theory.** They call attention to key generalizations about the role of media in society. Here are some of the most important generalizations emerging from the limited-effects research work conducted between 1945 and 1960.

1. **Media rarely influence individuals directly.** Research findings consistently indicated that most people are sheltered from direct media manipulation by their family, friends, coworkers, and social groups. People tend to ignore political media content, and their attitudes are not easily changed by what they read, hear, or see. If they encounter new ideas or information, they turn to others for advice and critical interpretation. This generalization and the findings on which it is based contradict mass society and propaganda theory notions that view people as isolated and highly vulnerable to direct manipulation.

2. **There is a two-step flow of media influence.** This generalization asserts that media will be influential only if the opinion leaders who guide others are influenced first. Because these opinion leaders are sophisticated, critical media users, they are not easily manipulated by media content. They act as effective gatekeepers and form a barrier to media influence. Opinion followers constantly turn to opinion leaders for guidance and reassurance.

3. **By the time most people become adults, they have developed strongly held group commitments such as political party and religious affiliations. These affiliations provide an effective barrier against media influence.** Media use tends to be consistent with these commitments. For example, voters with Republican affiliations subscribe to Republican magazines and listen mostly to Republican politicians on radio.

4. **When media effects do occur, they are modest and isolated.** Research consistently showed that media-induced changes in attitudes or actions were rare. When such changes did occur, they could be explained by unusual circumstances. Individuals who changed were found to have been cut off from the normal influence of other people, or their long-term group commitments were undermined by crisis.

FROM PROPAGANDA RESEARCH TO ATTITUDE-CHANGE THEORIES

Although persuasion and attitude change have been speculated about almost since the beginning of recorded history, systematic study of these phenomena began only in the twentieth century, and World War II provided the "laboratory" for the development of a cohesive body of thought on attitude change and, by obvious extension, media and attitude change. As we saw in Chapter 4, the United States entered that conflict convinced it was as much a propaganda battle as it was a shooting war. The Nazis had demonstrated the power of the Big Lie. America needed to be able to mount an effective counteroffensive. Before the United States could confront the Japanese and the Germans on the battlefield, however, it had to change people's opinions on the home front. During the 1930s, there were powerful isolationist and pacifist sentiments in the country. These movements were so strong that in the election of 1940, Roosevelt promised to keep the United States out of the war, even though the Nazis were quickly conquering much of Western Europe. Aid to Britain was handled secretly. Until the bombing of Pearl Harbor, American and Japanese diplomats were engaged in peace negotiations.

Thus the war provided three important motivations for people interested in what would come to be known as attitude-change research. First, the success of the Nazi propaganda efforts in Europe challenged the democratic and very American notion of the people's wisdom. It seemed quite likely that powerful bad ideas could overwhelm inadequately defended good ideas. Strategies were needed to counter Nazi propaganda and defend American values. Early in the war, for example, Carl J. Friedrich (1943), a consultant to the Office of War Information, outlined the military's ongoing research strategy: detect psychological barriers to persuasion and assess how effectively a given set of messages could overcome those barriers.

A second war-provided research motivation was actually more imperative. Large numbers of men and women from all parts of the country and from all sorts of backgrounds had been rapidly recruited, trained, and tossed together in the armed forces. The military needed to determine what these soldiers were thinking and to find a way to intellectually and emotionally bind them—Yankee and Southerner, Easterner and Westerner, city boy and country girl—to the cause.

The third motivation was simple convenience: Whereas the military saw soldiers in training, psychologists saw research subjects—well-tracked research subjects. The availability of many people about whom large amounts of background information had already been collected proved significant because it helped define the research direction of what we now call attitude-change theory. Major General Frederick Osborn, director of the army's Information and Education Division, enthused, "Never before had modern methods of social science been employed on so large a scale, by such competent technicians. [The data collection's] value to the social scientist may be as great as its value to the military for whom the original research was done" (Stouffer et al., 1949, p. vii). Equally important to those social scientists was that this groundbreaking research set the tenor for their work for the next two decades. By the time the war ended, concern about propaganda and propaganda effects had given way to concern about mass communication and mass media effects. The study of attitude change was an important focus in this research.

CARL HOVLAND AND THE EXPERIMENTAL SECTION

The army's Information and Education Division had a research branch. Inside the research branch was the Experimental Section, headed by psychologist Hovland. Its primary mission "was to make experimental evaluations of the effectiveness of various programs of the Information and Education Division" (Hovland, Lumsdaine, and Sheffield, 1949, p. v). At first, the Experimental Section focused on documentary films and the war department's orientation movie series, *Why We Fight*, produced by Hollywood director Frank Capra. But because of the military's increasing use of media, the Experimental Section also studied "other media ... quite diverse in character" (p. vi). As the researchers themselves wrote, "The diversity of topics covered by the research of the Experimental Section made it unfeasible to publish a single cohesive account of all the studies. However, it did appear possible to integrate the group of studies on the effects of motion pictures, film strips, and radio programs into a systematic treatment concerning the effectiveness of mass communication media" (p. vii). The researchers called their account *Experiments in Mass Communication,* and it bore the mark of group leader Hovland.

controlled variation
Systematic isolation and manipulation of elements in an experiment

With his background in behaviorism and learning theory, Hovland's strength was in identifying elements in media content that might influence attitudes and devising straightforward experiments employing **controlled variation** to assess the strength of these elements. Hovland took some piece of stimulus material (a film, for example) and systematically isolated and varied its potentially important elements independently and in combination to assess their effects.

To meet the military's immediate needs, the Experimental Section began with evaluation research, simply testing whether the *Why We Fight* film series met its indoctrinational goals. Prevailing notions about the power of propaganda implied that the researchers would find dramatic shifts in attitude as a result of viewing the films. According to mass society or propaganda theory, every soldier, no matter what his or her background or personality, should have been easily manipulated by the messages in the films. Military training should have induced an ideal form of mass society experience. Individual soldiers were torn from their families, jobs, and social groups. They were isolated individuals, supposedly highly vulnerable to propaganda.

Nevertheless, Hovland's group found that the military's propaganda wasn't as powerful as had been assumed. The researchers discovered that although the movies were successful in increasing knowledge about the subjects in the films, they were not highly effective in influencing attitudes and motivations (their primary function). Even the most effective films primarily strengthened (reinforced) existing attitudes. Conversions were rare. Typically, only the attitudes specifically targeted by the films showed any change. More global attitudes, such as optimism or pessimism about the war, were resistant to change.

The fact that the films produced little attitude change and that what change did occur was influenced by people's individual differences directly contradicted mass society theory and its assumption that media could radically change even strongly held beliefs and attitudes. If isolated soldiers being hurriedly prepared for battle were resistant to the most sophisticated propaganda available, were average people likely to be more susceptible? As with Lazarsfeld's research, these empirical facts contradicted the prevailing theoretical perspective and implied that it would be necessary to develop new conceptualizations.

A second outcome of the initial evaluation work was important in determining the direction of future attitude-change theory. In examining one of the three films in the series, the fifty-minute *The Battle of Britain,* Hovland and his colleagues found that, although initially more effective in imparting factual information than in changing attitudes about the British, as time passed, factual knowledge decreased but attitudes toward the British actually became more positive. Time, the researchers discovered, was a key variable in attitude change. Possibly propaganda effects were not as instantaneous as mass society theory or behaviorist notions suggested. Hovland's group formulated various explanations for these slow shifts in attitude. But with no precise way to scientifically answer the question of why the passage of time produced increased attitude change in the direction of the original media stimulus, Hovland and his research team developed a new type of research design—controlled variation experiments—"to obtain findings having a greater degree of generalizability. The method used is that of systematically varying certain specified factors while other factors are controlled. This makes it possible to determine the effectiveness of the particular factors varied" (Hovland, Lumsdame, and Sheffield, 1949, p. 179).

One of the most important variables the researchers examined was the presentation of one or two sides of a persuasive argument. Using two versions of a radio program, they presented a one-sided argument (that the war would be a long one) and a two-sided argument (the war would be long, but the alternative view that the war would be short was also addressed). Of course, those who heard either version showed more attitude change than those who had heard no broadcast, but there was no difference in attitude change between the groups who had listened to the two versions. Hovland had anticipated this. Accordingly, he had assessed the participants' initial points of view, and here he did find attitude change. What he demonstrated was that one-sided messages were more effective with people already in favor of the message; two-sided presentations were more effective with those holding divergent perspectives. In addition, Hovland looked at educational level and discovered that the two-sided presentation was more effective with those people who had more schooling.

Thus, this group of psychologists determined that attitude change was a very complex phenomenon and that attributes of the messages themselves can and often did interact with attributes of the people receiving them. An enormous number of significant research questions suddenly could be posed. What happens, for example, when two-sided presentations are directed toward people who are initially predisposed against a position but have low levels of education? Such questions fueled several decades of persuasion research and challenged two generations of researchers.

THE COMMUNICATION RESEARCH PROGRAM

The concept of attitude change was so complex that Hovland proposed and conducted a systematic program of research that occupied him and his colleagues in the postwar years. He established the Communication Research Program at Yale University, which was funded by the Rockefeller Foundation. Its work centered on many of the variables Hovland considered central to attitude change. He and his colleagues systematically explored the power of both communicator and message attributes to cause changes in attitudes, and they examined how audience attributes mediated these effects (made effects more or less likely).

This work produced scores of scientific articles and a number of significant books on attitude and attitude change, but the most seminal was the 1953 *Communication and Persuasion*. Although a close reading of the original work is the best way to grasp the full extent of its findings, a general overview of this important research offers some indication of the complexity of persuasion and attitude change.

Examining the communicator, Hovland and his group studied the power of source credibility, which they divided into trustworthiness and expertness. As you might expect, they found that high-credibility communicators produced increased amounts of attitude change; low-credibility communicators produced less attitude change.

Looking at the content of the communication, Hovland and his group examined two general aspects of content: the nature of the appeal itself and its organization. Focusing specifically on fear-arousing appeals, the Yale group tested the logical assumption that stronger, fear-arousing presentations will lead to greater attitude change. This relationship was found to be true to some extent, but variables such as the vividness of the threat's description and the audience's state of alarm, evaluation of the communicator, and already-held knowledge about the subject either mitigated or heightened attitude change.

The Hovland group's look at the organization of the arguments was a bit more straightforward. Should a communicator explicitly state an argument's conclusions or leave them implicit? In general, the explicit statement of the argument's conclusion is more effective, but not invariably. The trustworthiness of the communicator, the intelligence level of the audience, the nature of the issue at hand and its importance to the audience, and the initial level of agreement between audience and communicator all altered the persuasive power of a message.

Regardless of how well a persuasive message is crafted, not all people are influenced by it to the same degree, so the Yale group assessed how audience attributes could mediate effects. Inquiry centered on the personal importance of the audience's group memberships and individual personality differences among people that might increase or reduce their susceptibility to persuasion.

Testing the power of what they called "counternorm communications," Hovland and his cohorts demonstrated that the more highly people value their membership in a group, the more closely their attitudes will conform to those of the group and, therefore, the more resistant they will be to changes in those attitudes. If you attend a Big Ten university and closely follow your school's sports teams, it isn't very likely that anyone will be able to persuade you that the Atlantic Coast Conference fields superior athletes. If you attend that same Big Ten university but care little about its sports programs, you might be a more likely target for opinion change, particularly if your team loses to an Atlantic Coast Conference team in a dramatic fashion.

The question of individual differences in susceptibility to persuasion is not about a person's willingness to be persuaded on a given issue. In persuasion research, *individual differences* refers to those personality attributes or factors that render someone generally susceptible to influence. Intelligence is a good example. It is easy to assume that those who are more intelligent would be less susceptible to persuasive arguments, but this isn't the case. These people are more likely to be persuaded if the message they receive is from a credible source and based on solid logical arguments. Self-esteem, aggressiveness, and social withdrawal were several of the other individual characteristics the Yale group tested. But, as with intelligence, each failed to produce the straightforward, unambiguous relationship that might have seemed warranted based on commonsense expectations. Why? None of a person's personality characteristics operates apart from his or her evaluation of the communicator, judgments of the message, or understanding of the social reward or punishment that might accompany acceptance or rejection of a given attitude. As we'll see, these research findings and the perspective on attitude change they fostered were to color our understanding of media effects for decades.

MASS COMMUNICATION RESEARCH AND THE FOCUS ON MEDIA EFFECTS

From the 1950s to the 1990s, persuasion research provided a dominant strategy for conducting inquiry on media. This represented an important shift away from concerns about the role of propaganda in society and toward a focus on what happens when people are exposed to various forms of media content. Following the models provided by the early persuasion studies as well as those of Lazarsfeld's group, empirical media research focused heavily on the study of media effects. Melvin DeFleur (1970, p. 118) wrote: "The all-consuming question that has dominated research and the development of contemporary theory in the study of the mass media can be summed up in simple terms—namely, 'what has been their effect?' That is, how have the media influenced us as individuals in terms of persuading us?"

The study of media effects was obviously a worthwhile focus for research, but should it have been the dominant focus? In their pursuit of insights into media effects processes, researchers were turning their attention away from larger questions about the role of media in society. Despite Lazarsfeld's warning, they were focused on administrative rather than critical issues. Some researchers defended this emphasis on effects by arguing that larger questions can't be answered by empirical research. Others maintained that they could address these larger questions only after they had a thorough understanding of the basic processes underlying media effects. The pursuit of this understanding has occupied many mass communication researchers over the past eighty years. Effects research articles still fill the pages of most of the major academic journals devoted to mass communication research. The rise of new forms of media has sparked a new round of research to see if these media have effects that are different from legacy media.

Although the individual findings of effects research were enormously varied and even contradictory, two interrelated sets of empirical generalizations emerged: (1) The influence of mass media is rarely direct, because it is almost always mediated by *individual differences;* and (2) the influence of mass media is rarely direct, because it is almost always mediated by *group membership or relationships.* These sets of generalizations emerged out of both survey and experimental research. They identify two factors that normally can serve as effective barriers to media influence, but they can also increase the likelihood of influence. Both sets of generalizations are consistent with the limited-effects perspective and thus serve to buttress it. Study after study confirmed their existence and expanded our understanding of how they operate. Over time, these sets of generalizations gave rise to middle-range theories of media effects, which are as follows:

individual differences Individuals' different psychological make-ups that cause media influence to vary from person to person

1. **Individual differences** theory argues that because people vary greatly in their psychological makeup and because they have different perceptions of things, media influence differs from person to person. More specifically,

social categories
The idea that members of given groups or aggregates will respond to media stimuli in more or less uniform ways

"media messages contain particular stimulus attributes that have differential interaction with personality characteristics of members of the audience" (DeFleur, 1970, p. 122).

2. **Social categories** theory "assumes that there are broad collectives, aggregates, or social categories in urban-industrial societies whose behavior in the face of a given set of stimuli is more or less uniform" (DeFleur, 1970, pp. 122–123). In addition, people with similar backgrounds (e.g., age, gender, income level, religious affiliation) will have similar patterns of media exposure and similar reactions to that exposure.

THE SELECTIVE PROCESSES

cognitive consistency
The idea that people consciously and unconsciously work to preserve their existing views

One central tenet of attitude-change theory that was adopted (in one way or another or under one name or another) by influential mass communication theorists from Lazarsfeld to Klapper to DeFleur is the idea of **cognitive consistency**. We noted earlier that Lazarsfeld found that people seemed to seek out media messages consistent with the values and beliefs of those around them. This finding implied that people tried to preserve their existing views by avoiding messages that challenged them. As persuasion research proceeded, researchers sought more direct evidence. Cognitive consistency is "a tendency (on the part of individuals) to maintain, or to return to, a state of cognitive balance, and ... this tendency toward equilibrium determines ... the kind of persuasive communication to which the individual may be receptive" (Rosnow and Robinson, 1967, p. 299). These same authors wrote: "Although the consistency hypothesis is fundamental in numerous theoretical formulations, ... of all the consistency-type formulations, it is Leon Festinger's theory of **cognitive dissonance** which has been the object of greatest interest and controversy" (1967, pp. 299–300).

cognitive dissonance
Information that is inconsistent with a person's already-held attitudes creates psychological discomfort, or dissonance

Festinger explained that the bedrock premise of dissonance theory is that information that is not consistent with a person's already-held values and beliefs will create a psychological discomfort (dissonance) that must be relieved; people generally work to keep their knowledge of themselves and their knowledge of the world somewhat consistent (Festinger, 1957). Later, and more specifically, Festinger wrote, "If a person knows various things that are not psychologically consistent with one another, he will, in a variety of ways, try to make them more consistent" (1962, p. 93). Collectively, these "ways" have become known as the **selective processes**. Some psychologists consider these to be defense mechanisms we routinely use to protect ourselves (and our egos) from information that would threaten us. Others argue that they are merely routinized procedures for coping with the enormous quantity of sensory information constantly bombarding us. Either way, the selective processes function as complex and highly sophisticated filtering mechanisms screening out useless sensory data while quickly identifying and highlighting the most useful patterns in this data.

selective processes
Exposure (attention), retention, and perception; psychological processes designed to reduce dissonance

In arguing that "the [mass] communication itself appears to be no sufficient cause of the effect," Klapper (1960, pp. 18–19) offered his conclusion that "reinforcement is or may be abetted by predispositions and the related processes of selective exposure, selective perception and selective retention." His explanation of how these selective processes protect media content consumers from media's impact neatly echoes Festinger's own presentation. Klapper wrote:

> By and large, people tend to expose themselves to those mass communications that are in accord with their existing attitudes and interests. Consciously or unconsciously, they avoid communications of opposite hue. In the event of their being nevertheless exposed to unsympathetic material, they often seem not to perceive it, or to recast and interpret it to fit their existing views, or to forget it more readily than they forget sympathetic material. (1960, p. 19)

Attitude-change researchers studied three forms of selectivity: (1) exposure, (2) retention, and (3) perception. Keep in mind that these notions have since been widely criticized and should be interpreted very carefully. We will point out some of the major limitations as we discuss each.

selective exposure
The idea that people tend to expose themselves to messages that are consistent with their preexisting attitudes and beliefs

Selective exposure is people's tendency to expose themselves to or attend to media messages they feel are in accord with their already-held attitudes and interests and the parallel tendency to avoid those that might create dissonance. Democrats will watch their party's national convention on television but go bowling when the GOP gala is aired. Paul Lazarsfeld, Bernard Berelson, and Hazel Gaudet, in their Erie County voter study, discovered that "about two-thirds of the constant partisans (Republicans and Democrats) managed to see and hear more of their own side's propaganda than the opposition's…. But—and this is important—the more strongly partisan the person, the more likely he is to insulate himself from contrary points of view" (1944, p. 89).

In retrospect, we now realize that during the 1940s people commonly had media-use patterns strongly linked to their social status and group affiliation. Newspapers had definite party connections. Most were Republican. Thus, Republicans read newspapers with a strongly Republican bias, and Democrats either read Democratic newspapers or learned how to systematically screen out pro-Republican content. Radio stations tried to avoid most forms of political content but occasionally carried major political speeches. These weren't hard to avoid if you knew you didn't like the politics of the speaker. Labor unions were very influential during this era and structured the way their members used media.

selective retention
The idea that people tend to remember best and longest those messages that are most meaningful to them

Selective retention is the process by which people tend to remember best and longest information consistent with their preexisting attitudes and interests. Name all the classes in which you've earned the grade of A. Name all the classes in which you've earned a C. The As have it, no doubt. But often you remember disturbing or threatening information. Name the last class you almost failed. Have you managed to forget it and the instructor, or are they etched among the things you wish you could forget? If selective retention always operated to protect us from what we don't want to remember, we would never have any difficulty forgetting our problems. Although some people seem able to do this with ease, others tend to dwell on disturbing information. Contemporary thinking on selective retention ties that retention to the level of importance the recalled phenomenon holds for individuals.

selective perception
The idea that people will alter the meaning of messages so they become consistent with preexisting attitudes and beliefs

Keeping in mind that these processes are not discrete (you cannot retain that to which you have not been exposed), **selective perception** is the mental or psychological recasting of a message so that its meaning is in line with a person's beliefs and attitudes. Gordon Allport and Leo Postman's now-classic 1945 study of rumor is among the first and best examples of selective perception research. The two psychologists showed a picture of a fight aboard a train to some people. The combatants were a Caucasian male grasping a razor and an unarmed African American male. Those who saw the scene were then asked to describe it to another person, who in turn passed it on. In 1945 America, white people recounting the story of the picture inevitably became confused, saying the blade was in the hands of the black man, not the white man. Allport and Postman concluded, "What was outer becomes inner; what was objective becomes subjective" (1945, p. 81).

The attitude researchers who documented the operation of selective processes were good scientists. But their findings were based on people's use of a very different set of media and very different forms of media content than we know today. In the 1940s and 1950s, movies were primarily an entertainment medium; radio disseminated significant amounts of news, but typically as brief, highly descriptive reports that expressed no partisan opinion; newspapers were the dominant news medium; and television did not exist. Television moved all the media away from dissemination of information toward the presentation of images and symbols. Many contemporary movies sacrifice story line and character development for exciting and interesting visuals; your favorite radio station probably presents minimal news, if any; newspaper stories are getting shorter and shorter, the graphics more colorful and interesting, and more than a few papers across the country regularly present pictures snapped from a television screen in their pages. It's not surprising that we process information very differently today than our grandparents did in the 1940s.

Let's transport the valuable Allport and Postman experiment to our times to explain why the selective processes categorized by the attitude researchers and quickly appropriated by mass communication theorists might be less useful now in understanding media influence than they were in Allport and Postman's time.

If a speaker were to appear on television and present the argument, complete with charts and "facts," that a particular ethnic group or race of people was inherently dangerous, prone to violent crime, and otherwise inferior to most other folks, the selective processes should theoretically kick in. Sure, some racists would tune in and love the show. But most people would not watch. Those who might happen to catch it would no doubt selectively perceive the speaker as stupid, sick, beneath contempt. Three weeks later, this individual would be a vague, if not nonexistent, memory.

INSTANT ACCESS

Attitude-Change Theory

Strengths

1. Pays deep attention to process in which messages can and can't have effects
2. Provides insight into influence of individual differences and group affiliations in shaping media influence
3. Attention to selective processes helps clarify how individuals process information

Weaknesses

1. Experimental manipulation of variables overestimates their power and underestimates media's
2. Focuses on information in media messages, not on more contemporary symbolic media
3. Uses attitude change as only measure of effects, ignoring reinforcement and more subtle forms of media influence

But what if television news—because covering violent crime is easier, less expensive, and less threatening to the continued flow of advertising dollars than covering white-collar crime, and because violent crime, especially that committed downtown near the studio, provides better pictures than a scandal in the banking industry—were to present inner-city violence to the exclusion of most other crime? What if entertainment programmers, because of time, format, and other pressures (Gerbner, 1990), continually portrayed their villains as, say, dark, mysterious, different? Do the selective processes still kick in? When the ubiquitous mass media that we routinely rely on repeatedly provide homogeneous and biased messages, where will we get the dissonant information that activates our defenses and enables us to hold onto views that are inconsistent with what we are being told? Does this situation exist in the United States today? Do most mainstream media routinely provide inherently biased messages? We will return to these and similar questions in later chapters.

Today, more than sixty years after the Allport and Postman study, would the knife still find its way from the white man's hand into the black man's? Have the civil rights movement and television programming like *The Cosby Show* and *That's So Raven* made a difference? Or does routine news coverage of violent crime continue to fuel our apprehensions and therefore our biases? Later chapters that deal with theories that view mass communication as more symbolically, rather than informationally, powerful will address these questions. For now, though, you can explore the issue with help from the box entitled "Drug Users: Allport and Postman Revisited."

LIMITATIONS OF THE EXPERIMENTAL PERSUASION RESEARCH

Like the research approach developed by Lazarsfeld, the Yale approach had important limitations. Here we list and compare them with those described for the Lazarsfeld research.

1. **Experiments were conducted in laboratories or other artificial settings to control extraneous variables and manipulate independent variables.** But it was often difficult to relate these results to real-life situations. Researchers made many serious errors in trying to generalize from laboratory results. Also, most experiments take place over relatively short time periods. Effects that don't take place immediately remain unidentified. Hovland found long-term effects only because the military trainees he was studying were readily accessible for a longer period. Most researchers don't have this luxury. Some are forced to study "captive" but atypical populations like students or prisoners.

2. **Experiments have the opposite problems from surveys when researchers study the immediate effects of specific media messages.** As noted earlier, it is cumbersome if not impossible to study effects of specific messages using surveys. By contrast, experiments are ideally suited to studying the immediate effects of specific media content on small or homogeneous groups of people. Experiments aren't, however, suited to studying the cumulative influence of patterns of overall media use within large heterogeneous populations.

   This limitation of experimental research has produced serious biases in its accumulated findings. Because the study and comparison of an individual medium's influence was difficult, research often failed to distinguish results based on messages delivered through a mass medium (like film) from those generated in research dependent on messages presented by speakers (e.g., an adult speaking about the value of woodcrafts to a group of Boy Scouts) or by printed expressions of opinion. As a result, the persuasion research directed attention away from the power of the media themselves and focused attention on message content. As late as 1972, for example, social psychologist Alan Elms wrote, "The medium itself may indeed be the principal message in certain artistic productions or entertainments; it is seldom so in communication designed (with any sort of competence) to be persuasive" (p. 184). But if serious lectures exhorting young American soldiers to trust the Brits could have done the job, why did the army commission the movie *Battle of Britain*? Clearly, the medium can largely be the message when we are considering persuasion. Not until much later was this proposition seriously considered.

THINKING *about* THEORY   DRUG USERS: ALLPORT AND POSTMAN REVISITED

In October, 1990 expectant father Charles Stuart frantically phoned Boston 911: "My wife's been shot. I've been shot." The tape of his call was played on local and national media. A news crew riding with the emergency responders caught the gruesome scene on film: the 30-year-old pregnant woman, dead, her head smashed by the assailant's bullet. Fortunately, Stuart could describe the animal who had committed this atrocity—a raspy-voiced black man, dressed in a jogging suit, brandishing a snub-nosed .38. Police swept through predominantly black neighborhoods and soon the perp was collared. Except it was all a lie. Three months later, about to be exposed by his brother, Stuart jumped to his death from a bridge. He had killed his wife and shot himself to collect insurance money and set up a new life with his mistress. But America learned. Never again.

Until October, 1994, when a frantic caller dialed Union, South Carolina, 911 pleading, "There's a lady who came to our door. Some guy jumped into her car with her two kids in it, and he took off." But at least the lady, Susan Smith, could ID the animal who had abducted her three-year-old and fourteen-month-old children: black, in his twenties, wearing jeans, plaid shirt, and a knit cap. Susan went on national television, appearing on NBC's *The Today Show*, to tearfully appeal for their safe return. As she played videotapes of her young sons the country cried with her. But it was all a lie. She had strapped her children into their safety seats and ran her car into a lake, drowning them. She wanted to set up a new life with her lover and she thought the kids would get in the way. But America learned. Never again.

Until May, 2009, when Bonnie Sweeten made a frantic 911 call to Philadelphia police. She and her nine-year-old daughter had been abducted in broad daylight by two black men and tossed into the back of their dark-colored Cadillac. Anthony Rakoczy, dad to the little girl and Ms. Sweeten's ex-husband, went on national television, appearing on NBC's *The Today Show*, to tearfully appeal for their safe return. But this, too, was a lie. Ms. Sweeten had stolen $700,000 from her employer to maintain a lavish lifestyle and was looking for a way out.

Of course, what these three inept criminals were counting on was our culture's inclination to "put the razor" in the black man's hands—that is, to attribute violence and crime to African Americans, just as Allport and Postman had demonstrated more than half a century before. But there is other, real-world evidence that what the two psychologists discovered long ago has yet to disappear. Our country's uneven record of arresting and incarcerating users of illegal drugs exemplifies the operation of selective perception.

(Continued)

THINKING *about* THEORY   DRUG USERS: ALLPORT AND POSTMAN REVISITED (CONTINUED)

Test yourself by answering this question. What percentage of all regular users of illegal drugs in this country is black: 72 percent, 61 percent, or 13 percent? The introduction to this essay may have clued you to choose a lower percentage, but are you surprised to know that of all Americans who regularly use illegal drugs, 78 percent are white, 9 percent are Latino, and 13 percent are African American? These percentages match roughly the proportion that each group occupies in the population as a whole (Glasser, 2006). This is what we should expect, unless our selective perception places the razor where it might not otherwise be.

But there is an even nastier by-product of this phenomenon. Even though African Americans represent only 13 percent of the country's illegal drug users, they represent 37 percent of all drug-related arrests and 53 percent of all convictions for illegal drug use; adult African Americans were arrested on drug charges at rates that were 2.8 to 5.5 times as high as those of white adults in every year from 1980 through 2007 (Glasser, 2006; Human Rights Watch, 2009). Once convicted, 33 percent of white illegal drug users are sentenced to prison, while 51 percent of convicted black defendants are sent to jail (Durose and Langan, 2001). If our justice system were truly color-blind, however, African Americans would represent 13 percent of all drug arrests, 13 percent of all drug-related convictions, and 13 percent of all the people in prison for drugs. But they aren't. "Jim Crow may be dead, but the drug war has never been color-blind," argues Human Rights Watch's Jamie Fellner. "Although whites and blacks use and sell drugs, the heavy hand of the law is more likely to fall on black shoulders" (Human Rights Watch, 2009).

But how can this be? Do police, prosecutors, judges, and juries selectively perceive drugs (the razor) as a "black" problem? *Chicago Tribune* columnist Salim Muwakkil cited research from the Justice Policy Group that "found that media coverage of crime exaggerates its scope and unduly connects it to youth and race.... A disproportionate number of perpetrators on the news are people of color, especially African-Americans, [so much so] that the term 'young black males' was synonymous with the word 'criminal'" (2003).

This perception of African Americans, especially young black males, damages not only them. It diminishes all Americans. Human Rights Watch (2000) explained:

> The racially disproportionate nature of the war on drugs is not just devastating to black Americans. It contradicts faith in the principles of justice and equal protection of the laws that should be the bedrock of any constitutional democracy; it exposes and deepens the racial fault lines that continue to weaken the country and belies its promise as a land of equal opportunity; and it undermines faith among all races in the fairness and efficacy of the criminal justice system.

Would Allport and Postman be surprised that the "reality" of illegal drug use that many Americans perceive is so out of tune with objective reality? Are you? Would they predict that drugs, like the razor, would pass from the white hands to the black? Would you?

Here's another test for you. In the stories that opened this box, did you consider Stuart, Smith, and Sweeten's race? They were all white, but did you assume this was the case? Why or why not? Can you explain these phenomena in terms of dissonance reduction and the selective processes?

3. **Like the Lazarsfeld approach, the Hovland work is also inherently cautious in assessing media influence, but for very different reasons.** Lazarsfeld insisted on comparing the power of media with that of other social and demographic variables. These other variables were usually stronger. In an experiment, other variables aren't statistically controlled as is done in analyzing survey data; control is exercised by excluding variables from the laboratory and by randomly assigning research participants to treatment and control groups. In controlling for extraneous variables, however, the researchers often eliminated

factors that we now know to be crucial in reinforcing or magnifying media influence. For example, we now know that conversations with other people during or immediately after viewing television programs are likely to strengthen a broad range of media effects. A researcher who eliminates conversation from the laboratory will systematically underestimate the power of media when personal conversations are otherwise likely.

4. **Like surveys, experiments are a very crude technique for examining the influence of media over time.** Conceivably, a researcher could set up an experimental group and bring it back to a laboratory after weeks or months. This ongoing experimentation could easily affect or bias the results. Imagine yourself as a participant, required to come in to a laboratory every few days over a period of several months so that you can watch films in which women are violently attacked, raped, or murdered. What do you suppose your long-term reaction to these movies would be? Would it be the same as if you were a fan of these movies and regularly sought them out? Research like this has found that male subjects become desensitized to violence against women (e.g., Jo and Berkowitz, 1994, p. 46). They show a greater likelihood to blame rape victims rather than the rapists for causing this crime. What does this research demonstrate? That a persistent researcher can turn an average male into an insensitive animal if he or she can just get him to sit through enough scenes of torture and mayhem? Or does it demonstrate that college students attending biweekly violence film fests will eventually get bored and stop being aroused by every violent episode? Would you as a male participant be more likely to blame real-life rape victims, or are you simply more likely to blame the victims that you see on videotapes in the laboratory? Long-term effects of generic forms of media content have been quite hard to establish and have fueled legitimate debates among some of the most skilled researchers.

5. **As with surveys, there are many variables that experiments cannot explore.** For example, some real-life conditions are far too complex to be simulated in laboratories. In other cases, it would be unethical or even illegal to manipulate certain independent variables. For example, the September 11, 2001 terrorist attacks on New York and Washington triggered profound changes in the U.S. media system and its messages, demonstrating the raw power of media when powerful images are combined with consistent narratives dominated by elite voices and ideas. The events of that day transformed American thinking in ways that could never have been predicted and that certainly could never be duplicated in any laboratory or field experiment.

CONTEMPORARY SELECTIVE EXPOSURE: THE RETURN OF MINIMAL EFFECTS

Beyond these specific limitations of the persuasion research, there is another factor that has shaped thinking about the selectivity/limited-effects link, specifically the issue of audience members' ability to engage in selective exposure. From the 1950s until 2000, research consistently documented low levels of selective exposure to political information in mainstream media.

As media evolved over the decades that followed the early effects research, newspapers became much less partisan. And until recently, other traditional print and broadcast media tended to produce news accounts that avoided or carefully balanced the presentation of politically sensitive content. Naturally, this made it harder for people to select media sources based on preexisting beliefs and to screen out partisan ideas. But the rise of outlets such as cable television's Fox News, which has eighteen Republican viewers for every one Democrat, and MSNBC, which has six Democrats for every one Republican (Auletta, 2010, p. 47), and the popularity of talk radio (overwhelmingly conservative) have heralded a new era of partisan media, one echoed in other media. As newspapers and news magazines continue to lose readership, partisan websites and blogs gain audience and influence. As these partisan media sources multiply, selectivity patterns may be reemerging.

This contemporary mass communication reality led two prominent political communication scholars to declare that we are entering a new era of minimal media effects in which media largely reinforce existing political views and inoculate partisan audiences against influence by opposing media, a classic limited-effects argument. Consider, wrote W. Lance Bennett and Shanto Iyengar,

> the famous earlier era of "minimal effects" that emerged from studies done in the 1940s and early 1950s.... The underlying context for this scholarship consisted of a premass communication media system and relatively dense membership in a group-based society networked through political parties, churches, unions, and service organizations.... At this time, scholars concluded that media messages were filtered through social preference processes.... Indeed, with the continued detachment of individuals from the group-based society, and increased capacity of consumers to choose from a multitude of media channels (many of which enable user-produced content), the effects picture may be changing again. As receivers exercise greater choice over both the content of messages and media sources, effects become increasingly difficult to produce or measure in the aggregate. (2008, pp. 707–708)

As you can imagine, given this text's premise that mass communication theory is dynamic, a function of the times and the technology and people who interact in them, we will return to this and similar arguments throughout later chapters.

INFORMATION-FLOW THEORY

During the 1950s, social scientists conducted many surveys and field experiments to assess the flow of information from media to mass audiences. Among them were studies of how quickly people found out about individual news stories (Funkhouser and McCombs, 1971). The overall objective of this work was to assess the effectiveness of media in transmitting information to mass audiences. The research was patterned after persuasion research, but instead of measuring shifts in attitudes, it investigated if information was learned. Survey research rather than controlled experiments was used to gather data. This work drew on methods pioneered by both Lazarsfeld and Hovland. It was based on the empirical generalizations growing out of their work, and it yielded similar empirical generalizations.

Information-flow research addressed questions thought to be quite important. Many researchers believed that if our democracy was to survive the challenges of the Cold War, it was critical that Americans be well informed about a variety of issues. For example, Americans needed to know what to do in the event of a nuclear attack. They also needed to know what their leaders were doing to deal with threats from abroad. Classic theories of democracy assume that the public must be well informed so that people can make good political decisions. As such, the flow of information from elites to the public was essential if the United States was to counter the Communist threat.

Persuasion research had identified numerous barriers to persuasion. News-flow research focused on determining whether similar barriers impeded the flow of information from media to typical audience members. It gathered generalizations derived from laboratory-based attitude-change research and assessed their usefulness in understanding real-world situations and problems. Some of the barriers investigated included level of education, amount of media use for news, interest in news, and talking about news with others. The researchers differentiated between "hard" and "soft" news. Hard news typically included news about politics, science, world events, and community organizations. Soft news included sports coverage, gossip about popular entertainers, and human-interest stories about average people.

News-flow research found that most U.S. citizens learned very little about hard news because they were poorly educated, made little use of media for hard news, had low interest in it, and didn't talk to other people about it (Davis, 1990). Except for major news events such as President Eisenhower's heart attack or the assassination of President John F. Kennedy, most people didn't know or care much about national news events. Soft news generally was more likely to be learned than hard news, but even the flow of soft news was not what might have been hoped. The most important factor accelerating or reinforcing the flow of news was the degree to which people talked about individual news items with others. News of the Kennedy assassination reached most people very rapidly because people interrupted their daily routine to tell others about it (Greenberg and Parker, 1965). Think back to how you first heard about the events of 9/11. Did you hear or see a media report or did someone else talk to you about them? Without talk, learning about most hard news events rarely reached more than 10 to 20 percent of the population and was forgotten by those people within a few days or weeks.

Studies of the flow of civil defense information identified similar barriers. In most cases, members of the public were even less interested in mundane civil defense information than they were in politics. In a series of field experiments (DeFleur and Larsen, 1958), researchers dropped hundreds of thousands of leaflets on small isolated towns in the state of Washington. They signaled their view of the importance of their research by titling it "Project Revere"—like Paul Revere, they were seeking ways to inform the nation about an impending attack. DeFleur and Larsen wanted to determine how effective leaflets would be in warning people about incoming Soviet bombers. For example, one set of leaflets announced that a civil defense test was being conducted. Every person who found a leaflet was instructed to tell someone else about it and then drop the leaflet in a mailbox.

The researchers were disappointed that relatively few folks read or returned the leaflets. Children were the most likely to take them seriously. To get the most useful effect, eight leaflets had to be dropped for every resident in town. Speculating that people were ignoring the leaflets because they only warned of a hypothetical attack, and threatening people with a real attack was considered too problematic,

INSTANT ACCESS

Information-Flow Theory

Strengths

1. Examines process of mass communication in real world
2. Provides theoretical basis for successful public information campaigns
3. Identifies barriers to information flow
4. Helps the understanding of information flow during crises

Weaknesses

1. Is simplistic, linear, and source-dominated
2. Assumes ignorant, apathetic populace
3. Fails to consider utility or value of information for receivers
4. Is too accepting of status quo

---

information-flow theory
Theory of how information moves from media to audiences to have specific intended effects (now known as information or innovation diffusion theory)

source-dominated theory
Theory that examines the communication process from the point of view of some elite message source

the researchers designed another field experiment in which people were supposed to tell their neighbors about a slogan for a new brand of coffee. Survey teams visited homes in a small town and told people that they could earn a free pound of coffee by teaching their neighbors the coffee slogan. The survey team promised to return the following week, and if they found that neighbors knew the slogan, then both families would receive free coffee. The experiment produced mixed results. On the one hand, almost every neighboring family had heard about the coffee slogan and tried to reproduce it. Unfortunately, many gave the wrong slogan. The researchers reported interesting distortions of the original slogan; many people had shortened it, confused it with similar slogans, or recited garbled phrases containing a few key words. The research confirmed the importance of motivating people to pass on information, but it suggested that even a free gift was insufficient to guarantee the accurate flow of information. If word of mouth was crucial to the flow of information, the possibility of distortion and misunderstanding was high. Even if media deliver accurate information, the news that reaches most people might be wrong.

The most important limitation of **information-flow theory** is that it is a simplistic, linear, **source-dominated theory**. Information originates with authoritative or elite sources (the established media or the government, for example) and then flows outward to "ignorant" individuals. It assumes that barriers to the flow of information can be identified and overcome, but little effort is typically made to consider whether the information has any value or use for average audience members. Audience reactions to messages are ignored unless they form a barrier to that flow. Then those barriers must be studied only so they can be overcome. Like most limited-effects theories, information-flow theory assumes that the status quo is acceptable. Elites and authorities are justified in trying to disseminate certain forms of information, and average people will be better off if they receive and learn it. Barriers are assumed to be bad and, where possible, must be eliminated. Information-flow theory is also an example of a middle-range theory. It serves to summarize a large number of empirical generalizations into a more or less coherent explanation of when and why media information will be attended to and what sorts of learning will result.

JOSEPH KLAPPER'S PHENOMENISTIC THEORY

In 1960, Joseph Klapper finally published a manuscript originally developed in 1949 as he completed requirements for a Ph.D. at Columbia University and worked as a researcher for CBS. *The Effects of Mass Communication* was a compilation and integration of all significant media effects findings produced through the mid-1950s and was intended for both scholars and informed members of the public. Klapper was concerned that average people exaggerated the power of media. Though informed academics (i.e., empirical researchers) had rejected mass society theory, too many people still believed that media had tremendous power. He wanted to calm their fears by showing how constrained media actually were in their ability to influence people.

phenomenistic theory
Theory that media are rarely the sole cause of effects and are relatively powerless when compared with other social factors

Klapper introduced an excellent example of a middle-range theory of media that he called **phenomenistic theory.** It states that media rarely have any direct effects and are relatively powerless when compared to other social and psychological factors such as social status, group membership, strongly held attitudes, education, and so forth. According to Klapper:

1. Mass communication ordinarily does not serve as a necessary and sufficient cause of audience effects but, rather, functions among and through a nexus of mediating factors and influences.
2. These mediating factors are such that they typically render mass communication as a contributory agent, but not the sole cause, in the process of reinforcing existing conditions. (1960, p. 8)

These generalizations about media were not very original, but Klapper expressed them forcefully and cited hundreds of findings to support them. His book came to be viewed as the definitive statement on media effects—especially by postpositive researchers and those outside the media research community.

reinforcement theory
More common name for phenomenistic theory, stressing the theory's view that media's most common effect is reinforcement

Klapper's theory is often referred to now as **reinforcement theory** because its key assertion is that the primary influence of media is to reinforce (not change) existing attitudes and behaviors. Instead of disrupting society and creating unexpected social change, media generally serve as agents of the status quo, giving people more reasons to go on believing and acting as they already do. Klapper argued that there simply are too many barriers to media influence for dramatic change to occur except under very unusual circumstances.

Even today, some fifty years after its introduction, reinforcement theory is still raised by those unconvinced of media's power. Yet with benefit of hindsight, we can easily see its drawbacks. When published in 1960, Klapper's conclusions relied heavily on studies (from Lazarsfeld, Hovland, and their contemporaries) of a media environment that did not include the mass medium of television and the restructured newspaper, radio, and film industries that arose in response to television. Certainly Klapper's work did not envision a world of Internet and digital media. Much of the research he cited examined the selective processes, but with the coming of television, media were becoming more symbolically than informationally oriented, producing potentially erroneous conclusions. In addition, the United States that existed after World War II looked little like the one that existed before. As we'll see in later chapters, Klapper's "nexus of mediating variables"—that is, church, family, and school—began to lose their powerful positions in people's socialization (and therefore in limiting media effects).

Finally, Klapper might have erred in equating reinforcement with no effects. Even if it were true that the most media can do is reinforce existing attitudes and beliefs, this is hardly the same as saying they have no effect. You'll see in Chapter 8, as you did in the Chapter 4 discussion of contemporary propaganda theory, that many contemporary critical scholars see this as media's most negative influence. The box entitled "Joseph Klapper's Phenomenistic Theory" presents Klapper's own explanation of his theory and asks you to assess it in light of some recent momentous events.

THINKING *about* **THEORY**   JOSEPH KLAPPER'S PHENOMENISTIC THEORY

Joseph Klapper's own summary of his reinforcement, or phenomenistic, theory makes it clear that his ideas are very much at home in the limited-effects perspective. The following is drawn directly from his landmark work, *The Effects of Mass Communication,* published in 1960 (p. 8).

Theoretical Statements

1. Mass communication ordinarily does not serve as a necessary and sufficient cause of audience effects but, rather, functions among and through a nexus of mediating factors and influences.
2. These mediating factors are such that they typically render mass communication a contributing agent, but not the sole cause, in a process of reinforcing the existing conditions.
3. On those occasions that mass communication does function to cause change, one of two conditions is likely to exist:

    a. The mediating factors will be found to be inoperative and the effect of the media will be found to be direct.
    b. The mediating factors, which normally favor reinforcement, will be found to be themselves impelling toward change.

4. There are certain residual situations in which mass communication seems to produce direct effects, or directly and of itself to serve certain psychophysical functions.
5. The efficacy of mass communication, either as a contributory agent or as an agent of direct effect, is affected by various aspects of the media and

communications themselves or of the communication situation.

Your Turn

Can you find hints in Klapper's overview of his theory's links to the dominant perspective of its time? Can you identify his subtle explanation of why advertising seems to work, an important point to make for a fine scientist who was also chief researcher for broadcast network CBS? After reading his summary of phenomenistic theory, can you explain why it remains, even today, the clearest and most used articulation of media's limited effects? Based on point number 3 in Klapper's summary, can you develop an explanation for the power of media during times of war, for example in the Middle East? Are the factors that normally mediate the power of media "inoperative"? Or are these factors "themselves impelling toward change"? List some of the factors that normally mediate the power of media. These would include things like personal relationships with friends and family, relationships with opinion leaders, contacts with teachers and classmates, or contacts with church members or religious leaders. Klapper would likely label the power demonstrated by media during war and occupation as an anomaly—an exception to the rule that media power is constantly checked by "a nexus of mediating factors and influences." Do you agree? How would he (and you) explain the precipitous drop in support for the conflict in Iraq after broadcast and publication of the horrific images of detainee abuse at Abu Ghraib prison (Time/CNN, 2004), if not a media effect? Would you argue that media have somehow become more powerful since Klapper developed his theory in the 1940s? If so, how?

ELITE PLURALISM

elite pluralism
Theory viewing
society as com-
posed of inter-
locking pluralistic
groups led by
opinion leaders
who rely on
media for infor-
mation about
politics and the
social world

All the preceding efforts at theory construction were limited in scope compared
with the development of **elite pluralism**. This idea was spawned partly as an effort
to make sense of the voter research initiated by Lazarsfeld. In their report on the
1948 election campaign (Berelson, Lazarsfeld, and McPhee, 1954), Lazarsfeld and
his colleagues noted important inconsistencies between their empirical observation
of typical voters and the assumptions that classical democratic theory made about
those same people. If the Lazarsfeld data were right, classical democratic theory
must be wrong. If so, what did this mean for the long-term survival of our social
and political order? Was our political system a facade for a benign ruling class?
Could a democratic political system continue to flourish if most citizens were politically apathetic and ignorant?

In characteristic fashion, the Lazarsfeld group offered a guardedly optimistic
assessment. They asserted that classical democratic theory should be replaced with
an up-to-date perspective based on empirical findings. Classical democratic theory
assumed that everyone must be well informed and politically active. But their new
perspective was based on empirical data showing that average people didn't know
or care very much about politics. They were more likely to base their voting decisions on personal influence than on reasoned consideration of the various candidates. People voted as their friends, family, and coworkers told them to vote, not
as a political theorist would have liked them to vote.

The Lazarsfeld group argued that voter apathy and ignorance weren't necessarily a problem *for the political system as a whole.* A system in which most people
voted based on long-standing political commitments or alliances would be a stable
system, even if these commitments were based on prejudice and were held in place
by emotional bonds to family and friends. The Lazarsfeld group believed that the
important factor was not the quality of voting decisions but rather their stability—
we are better off if our political system changes very slowly over time as a result of
gradual conversions. We don't want sudden changes that could occur if everyone
made rational informed decisions using information from media. For example,
there would be tragic consequences if many people based their vote decisions on
bad or biased information from media. Nor could our political system handle the

INSTANT ACCESS

Phenomenistic Theory

Strengths

1. Combines impressive amount of research into a convincing theory
2. Highlights role of mediating variables in the mass communication process
3. Persuasively refutes lingering mass society and propaganda notions

Weaknesses

1. Overstates influence of mediating factors
2. Is too accepting of status quo
3. Downplays reinforcement as an important media effect
4. Is too specific to its time (pre-1960s) and media environment (no television)

high levels of political activism that would occur if everyone took a strong interest in politics.

These arguments reject Libertarian theory (Chapter 5). If voters don't need to be informed, or if informing them might actually lead to political disorder, then there is no need for media to deliver information. Research findings demonstrated that uncensored and independent media typically failed to diffuse political information to most people. If so, what political role should media be expected to play? To reinforce the status quo except in times of crisis? Was there really a need for media to serve as a public forum as Libertarian theory had assumed? Or as Dewey had advocated, to systematically educate the people so they could be critical thinkers as well as informed voters? If so, how should this forum operate and what resources would be necessary to make it work effectively? Limited-effects research findings were quite pessimistic concerning the effectiveness of such a forum. They implied that such a public forum would serve little purpose except for the handful of people who were already well informed about and engaged in politics. These conclusions directed researchers away from the study of mass media and the formation of media policy and toward political parties, political socialization, and the institutions of government such as legislatures, political executives such as the president, and the legal system. These topics soon dominated the research agenda in political science.

The political perspective implicit in these arguments became known as elite pluralism. During the 1960s, elite pluralism strongly challenged traditional forms of democratic theory and was widely debated in political science. Elite pluralism claimed to be scientific because, unlike classical democratic theory, it was based on empirical data. V. O. Key provided one of its best formulations in *Public Opinion and American Democracy* (1961). Like Lazarsfeld, Key was optimistic in the face of apparently discouraging voter data. His book emphasized the strength and enduring value of the American political system, even if it fell short of being a classical democracy.

In some respects, elite pluralism is as contradictory as the two terms that make up its label. *Elite* implies a political system in which power is ultimately in the hands of a small group of influential persons, a political elite. *Pluralism* refers to cultural, social, and political diversity. It implies a political system in which many diverse groups have equal status and representation. Can there be a political system that is based on both—a system in which power is centralized in the hands of the few but in which the rights and status of all minority groups are recognized and advanced? Not only did V. O. Key argue that it is possible to combine these two principles, he also cited study after study that he interpreted as demonstrating that our political system already accomplished this.

Like the other examples of limited-effects theory, elite pluralism assumes that media have little ability to directly influence people. Thus media alone can't fundamentally alter politics. It rejects Libertarian notions and argues that media, in the name of stability, should reinforce political party loyalties and assist parties to develop and maintain large voter coalitions. Media shouldn't be expected to lead public opinion but, rather, should reinforce it. If change is to occur, it must come from the pluralistic groups and be negotiated and enacted by the leaders of these groups.

INSTANT ACCESS

Elite Pluralism

Strengths

1. Explains a stable U.S. social and political system
2. Is based on wealth of empirical data
3. Is a well-developed and cogent theory

Weaknesses

1. Legitimizes an undemocratic view of U.S. politics
2. Goes well beyond empirical evidence for conclusions
3. Is too accepting of the status quo
4. Paints a negative picture of average people and their media use

It is important to recognize that in constructing his perspective on American society, Key, like most limited-effects researchers, went far beyond the narrow insights provided by his research. Although the ideas he advanced were consistent with the data available to him, other conclusions were equally reasonable. But when Key wrote his book, this was not well understood. His ideas gained widespread acceptance as a definitive interpretation of the data, and his talents as a writer also lent force to his theory.

C. WRIGHT MILLS AND *THE POWER ELITE*

Opposition to elite pluralism came from across the political spectrum. The debate in many ways foreshadowed the ferment over all forms of limited-effects theory that arose in the 1970s and 1980s. Most classical democratic theorists were offended by and disdainful of elite pluralism. They argued that if the present political system was not a true democracy, efforts should be made to move the system in that direction, however difficult. Either we should recapture the essence of democracy as envisioned by the Founders, or we should take steps to break the power of existing elites. To opponents, elite pluralism was a rationalization of the status quo providing no direction for future development.

In an era when respect for normative and grand social theories was declining, however, it was hard for classical democratic theorists to defend their views against a "scientific" theory like elite pluralism. During the Cold War, with the American political system seemingly locked in mortal combat with a ruthless totalitarian foe, it's not surprising that people would find elite pluralism attractive. After all, it suggested that the American political system was stable and resilient, even if not perfect. Maintaining this system didn't require radical change, just some tinkering to make sure that various pluralistic groups were routinely co-opted into the system and that political elites were bound by informal rules stopping them from engaging in demagoguery.

The opposition to elite pluralism from the political left was spearheaded by C. Wright Mills, a Harvard sociologist and, as mentioned earlier, the man who served as field director for Lazarsfeld's Decatur research project. Mills was well aware of the limitations of theories based on empirical research. He wrote a book (1959) in which he castigated Lazarsfeld for engaging in what Mills termed "abstracted empiricism." He rejected the argument that elite pluralism was more scientific than other forms of political theory. Because of his knowledge of survey research, he was deeply skeptical of the data marshaled in its support. He argued that in American society, political power was not decentralized across a broad range of pluralistic groups. Instead, he believed that power was centralized in a small group of military-industrial-complex leaders, whom he called the power elite (1957). This elite group was not at all representative of pluralistic groups. It was isolated from them and typically acted against their interests. "The 'awesome means of power' enthroned upon these monopolies of production, administration, and violence included the power to prevent issues and ideas from reaching Congress in the first place," Mills argued. Mills believed that "most Americans still believed the ebb and flow of public opinion guided political affairs" (Summers, 2006a, p. 39). Instead, Mills urged, "But now we must recognize this description as a set of images out of a fairy tale.... They are not adequate even as an approximate model of how the American system of power works" (in Summers, 2006a, p. 39).

For a brief period in the early 1960s, the followers of Mills and Key were arrayed against each other. In this conflict, Key and his allies had many crucial advantages. Their research had larger and more secure funding from government agencies and private foundations. As such, elite pluralists successfully defended their claim of being more scientific. Ultimately, Mills brought his own perspective into question in the United States by backing Fidel Castro's revolution in Cuba. Then, in 1962, he was killed in a tragic motorcycle accident. Criticism of elite pluralism was soon muted as the nation focused its attention on Communist threats in Vietnam.

In *The Power Elite* and other books, Mills raised many disturbing questions about American politics. If elite pluralism was operating so effectively, why were so many minority groups receiving so little help? Why did average people feel so powerless and apathetic? Why did people choose to remain ignorant about politics? Why did the same people serve over and over again as leaders of supposedly independent social institutions? Why were the interests of the few so often pursued at the expense of average people? Why did political parties and other social institutions make no determined efforts to educate people about their interests or to mobilize them to take actions that might serve those interests? Why did mass media tend to merely reinforce the status quo rather than inspire people to take action against race- and social-class-based discrimination? Mills proved prophetic, because these same issues surfaced a decade later as part of a broad-based challenge to American social science and the American political system; these form the focus of Chapter 8.

A SUMMARY OF LIMITED-EFFECTS GENERALIZATIONS

The several views of media's impact described in this chapter can be assembled into a broader, middle-range theory of limited effects. This perspective of the media's power and influence is made up of several interrelated generalizations, and it has numerous limitations, which we have already discussed. We'll consider some of these limitations at greater length in the next chapter. But for now, these limited-effects generalizations are as follows:

1. **The role of mass media in society is limited; media primarily reinforce existing social trends and only rarely initiate social change.** The media will cause change only if the many barriers to their influence are broken down by highly unusual circumstances such as a terrorist attack or war. The empirical mass communication research discussed in this chapter supports this assumption. Study after study found little evidence of strong media influence. Even evidence of reinforcement was often lacking.

2. **Mass media's role in the lives of individuals is limited, and although this role tends to be positive, it can occasionally be dysfunctional for some types of people.** Media provide a convenient and inexpensive source of entertainment and information. But neither use has much long-term or important impact on the daily life of most people. Almost all information is either ignored or quickly forgotten. Entertainment mainly provides a temporary distraction from work, allowing people to relax and enjoy themselves so that they can go back to work refreshed. People who are adversely affected by media tend to have severe personality or social adjustment problems; they would be deeply troubled even if media weren't available. We'll have more to say about this in the next chapter.

3. **The role of mass media in the U.S. political and social system is overwhelmingly positive.** Although not democratic in the classic sense, the U.S. system is nevertheless a viable and humane system that respects and nurtures cultural pluralism while preserving social order. Media play an important though somewhat minor role in supporting this system through their reinforcement of the status quo.

DRAWBACKS OF THE LIMITED-EFFECTS PERSPECTIVE

We've discussed many of the limitations of the limited-effects perspective in this chapter, but here they are briefly listed, accompanied by some new concerns.

1. **Both survey and experimental research have serious methodological limitations not adequately recognized or acknowledged.** Empirical researchers were anxious to popularize their approach and sometimes made exaggerated claims for it. Naive people outside the empirical research community made false assumptions about the power and usefulness of this type of research. When empirical researchers were directly challenged in the late 1960s, they were slow to acknowledge the limitations of their work and reacted defensively.

2. **The methodological limitations of early empirical social research led to findings that systematically underestimated the influence of mass media for society and for individuals.** Researchers like Lazarsfeld and Hovland were inherently cautious. They didn't want to infer the existence of effects that might not be there—**spurious effects.** The researchers developed methods designed to guard against this, but they risked overlooking or dismissing evidence that could have been interpreted as an argument for significant media effects. In their conclusions, they often failed to emphasize that they might be overlooking many types of media effects because they had no way of measuring them.

spurious effects
A finding in a research study of a phenomenon that exists only in that study; a research artifact

3. **Early empirical social research centered on whether media had immediate, powerful, direct effects; other types of influence were ignored.** This focus was justified for two reasons. First, the mass society perspective and propaganda theories, which had been dominant, asserted that such effects existed and should be easy to observe. These perspectives needed to be evaluated, and the early limited-effects research did so. Second, the early research methods were best suited to studying immediate, direct effects—if researchers couldn't "see" an effect, it didn't exist. Only later, as we'll see in subsequent chapters, did researchers develop techniques that permitted other types of influence to be empirically assessed.

CONTRIBUTIONS OF THE LIMITED-EFFECTS PERSPECTIVE

1. **The limited-effects perspective effectively supplanted mass society theory and the propaganda theories as the dominant perspective on media.** This had both useful and problematic consequences. On the one hand, the limited-effects perspective reduced unjustified fears about massive uncontrollable media effects. This benefited media practitioners. Most important, it helped ease pressures for direct government censorship of media and permitted media practitioners to implement useful forms of self-regulation. On the other hand, it served to discourage attempts to systematically educate the public and foster critical thinking about the mass media. It dismissed such attempts as naive and impractical. Resources that might have been devoted to public education were diverted to mass communication research, where they were used to continue development of limited-effects theory.

2. **The perspective prioritized empirical observation and downgraded more speculative forms of theory construction.** It demonstrated the practicality and utility of empirical research and inspired development of a broad range of innovative methods for data collection as well as new techniques for data analysis. These empirical techniques have proved to be powerful and useful for specific purposes. If the perspective had not become dominant, scientists might not have devoted the time and resources necessary to develop these techniques.

3. **Although the limited-effects perspective ultimately turned many established social scientists away from media study, it provided a useful framework for research conducted in universities and colleges during the 1950s and 1960s.** In hindsight, we see that the perspective was, to some extent at least, a self-fulfilling prophecy. It asserted that media had no socially important effects. This belief was based on research findings provided by crude data collection and analysis methods. These methods can now be interpreted as having grossly underestimated the influence of media by focusing too much attention on effects on individuals while ignoring other aspects of media's role. Unfortunately, by the time more sophisticated research techniques were developed, most social researchers in the established disciplines of sociology, psychology, and political science had stopped looking for important media effects. During the 1960s and 1970s, the work of mass communication researchers was viewed with considerable skepticism outside their field. What was there that we didn't already know about the role of media? Quite a lot, as we shall see.

THE HOVLAND-LAZARSFELD LEGACY

The wealth of empirically based knowledge generated by persuasion and information-flow research and—possibly more important—the often conflicting, inconclusive, and situationally specific research questions they inspired have occupied many communication researchers for decades. Together with the survey research findings produced by Lazarsfeld, this work challenged and ultimately undermined mass society theory and notions about the power of propaganda. Gerry Miller and Michael Burgoon acknowledged the powerful initial influence of this research when they commented regarding the Hovland work, "The classic volumes of the 'Yale Group' ... were accorded a seminal status comparable to that conferred on the *Book of Genesis* by devoted followers of the Judeo-Christian religious faith" (1978, p. 29). Similar remarks could have been made about the landmark study of information flow conducted by DeFleur and Larsen.

This body of work deserves recognition but not reverence. For its time, it was thorough, sophisticated, and groundbreaking—but it did not yield a definitive explanation of the role or power of media. With Lazarsfeld's research, Hovland's work spawned literally thousands of research efforts on and dozens of intellectual refinements of the process of mass communication. But now, more than half a century later, we have only begun to put this work into perspective and understand its limitations as well as its considerable merits. The beam cast by this research is narrow; it fails to provide us with a broad understanding of media as it often highlights trivial properties. Thus its contribution to our overall understanding of the role of mass media in the society at large was to some extent misleading. To the extent that we relied upon limited-effects notions about media power, we made crucial errors in understanding media.

SUMMARY

The 1938 *War of the Worlds* broadcast ushered in the limited-effects perspective. Development of this perspective was led by Paul Lazarsfeld and Carl Hovland and benefited from the refinement of empirical research methods, the failure of the mass society and propaganda thinkers to offer empirical evidence for their views, the commercial nature of the new research methods and their support by both government and business, and the spread of these methods to a wide variety of academic disciplines.

Lazarsfeld championed the inductive approach to theory construction and employed it in his 1940 voter studies and other research to develop the idea of a two-step flow of media influence. With other research of the time, this helped develop the outlines of the limited-effects perspective: Media rarely have direct effects; media

influence travels from media, through opinion leaders, to opinion followers; group commitments protect people from media influence; and when effects do occur, they are modest and isolated.

Hovland and other psychologists offered support for this limited-effects view. Using controlled variation, they demonstrated that numerous individual differences and group affiliations limited media's power to change attitudes. This led logically to the development of dissonance theory, the idea that people work consciously and unconsciously to limit the influence of messages running counter to their preexisting attitudes and beliefs. This dissonance reduction operated through selectivity in exposure (attention), retention, and perception.

The work of Lazarsfeld and Hovland inspired other limited-effects thinking. Information-flow theory studied media's effectiveness in transmitting information to mass audiences. Klapper's phenomenistic, or reinforcement, theory provided a powerful argument for media as reinforcers of the status quo, unable to have powerful effects. Elite pluralism, forcefully argued by Key and forcefully challenged by Mills, also offered a benign perspective on media influence: As most people were not interested or intelligent enough to use media to form meaningful political attitudes, this ineffectiveness of media actually served the U.S. social system by giving it its stability. As long as those who were more involved in or better at political discourse could get the information they needed, all Americans would be served.

Together, these middle-range theories came to define the limited-effects perspective and shared these assumptions: Empirical research can be used to generate useful theory; the role of media in society is limited; sometimes media can be dysfunctional for some types of individuals; and the U.S. social and political system is stable and fair. But the limited-effects perspective has its drawbacks: Both surveys and experiments have serious methodological limitations; these limitations consistently produced research findings that underestimated media's influence; and "effects" were defined as only those that were immediate and observable, ignoring other, possibly more important effects.

Critical Thinking Questions

1. Are you typically an opinion leader or an opinion follower? Are there specific topics on which you are one or the other? Identify an issue (movies, music, sports, fashion, domestic politics) on which you can identify another whose opinion you usually seek. How well does that person fit the description of opinion leaders embodied in two-step flow? Has membership in a social networking site such as Facebook or Twitter altered your role as an opinion leader or follower or that of any of your friends? How?

2. Klapper's phenomenistic theory argues that media's greatest power rests in their ability to reinforce existing attitudes and values. At the time, this was evidence that media had limited effects—they were limited to reinforcement. But more contemporary thinking (as you'll read in later chapters) sees reinforcement as anything but a limited effect. Can you anticipate some of the arguments in support of this view?

3. Does the recent trend toward partisan media outlets herald a new era of minimal media effects? If so, what are the consequences? Are we becoming a nation in which we no longer share common media but rely increasingly on media tailored to appeal to people who think and act like ourselves? What about your own media use? What is your opinion of media outlets such as *The Daily Show* or Fox News or MSNBC that cater to specific audiences?

Key Terms

limited-effects perspective	two-step flow theory	cognitive dissonance	source-dominated theory
inductive	indirect-effects theory	selective processes	phenomenistic theory
middle-range theory	limited-effects theory	selective exposure	reinforcement theory
gatekeepers	controlled variation	selective retention	elite pluralism
opinion leaders	individual differences	selective perception	spurious effects
opinion followers	social categories	information-flow theory	
	cognitive consistency		

7 | MOVING BEYOND LIMITED EFFECTS: FOCUS ON FUNCTIONALISM AND CHILDREN

In the 1950s and 1960s the United States stood as the undisputed economic, social, and technological leader of the world. Fascist totalitarianism had been defeated in a long and brutal world war, and although much of Europe and Asia still smoldered as their nations worked to rebuild from that carnage, the U.S. economy roared, homes and suburbs were built, college enrollment soared, and new television networks and interstate highways linked Americans in nationwide optimism.

Despite this progress, the country's social fabric was beginning to unravel. A wide variety of domestic social ills, from racial discrimination to juvenile delinquency, suggested that all was not well. Abroad, the United States was threatened by the spread of Communism in Third World nations. Obviously, the American system worked—there was much that was good. And yet at times the system seemed not to be working as well as people expected and hoped.

Again and again critics emerged who blamed many of the problems on media. Media fomented racial unrest, they said; media encouraged young people to challenge adult authority. The media were an easy and logical target for criticism as the country searched for answers to the era's dramatic social change. After all, the end of the 1950s and the early 1960s saw the development and commercial application of the computer; television in almost every home in the country; and the emergence of FM radio as a medium in its own right, youth-oriented and distinct from the AM radio favored by parents. The invention of the transistor allowed radios to become portable, allowing teens to enjoy rock 'n' roll anywhere, especially away from those judgmental adults. But if media could contribute to society's ills, surely they could contribute to society's health.

OVERVIEW

In this chapter, we examine changes in post–World War II American society that forced a reconsideration of the prevailing thought on mass communication theory.

These changes—in American society and in mass communication theory—were significant. American technological know-how had helped win World War II, and in the 1950s it provided many citizens with a comfortable and independent lifestyle. At the heart of this success were increasingly complex large-scale social, economic, and technological systems. Surely factors such as new communication technologies, efficient superhighways, universally available home ownership and higher education, the population's migration to the suburbs, an exploding advertising industry, women entering the workforce in ever larger numbers, expanded leisure time, the rise of the youth culture with its new music and social styles, the geographic displacement of millions of GIs as they were ushered out of the military, the increased voice and visibility of racial minorities, and the Cold War with its threat of imminent global destruction (to name only a few) worked—or functioned—together to produce the America that offered so much that was good and so much that was troubling.

Mass communication theories needed to be developed to explain media's role in the operation of our society, but they could not stray too far from the dominant thinking of the time that media had, at most, limited effects. As such, **functionalism** "became dominant in American [social] theory in the 1950s and 1960s. The cornerstone of functionalist theory is the metaphor of the living organism, whose parts and organs, grouped and organized into a system, function to keep its essential processes going. Similarly, members of a society can be thought of as cells and its institutions as organs whose functioning ... preserves the cohesive whole and maintains the system's homeostasis" (Bryant and Miron, 2004, p. 677). Through functionalism, mass communication's obvious influence on the social world could be explained and understood, and at the same time that effect could be seen as "limited" by other parts of the system.

But some researchers thought that functionalism could also be applied to the study of mass communication itself and not just to the social system it helped support. The resulting **communication systems theory** offered hope to those who were beginning to reject limited-effects notions. They argued that a communication systems theory could allow us to conceptualize the role of media in the society at large and assess the usefulness of the powerful new communications technologies. Perhaps media's power could be better assessed at the macroscopic level—that is, by understanding its *larger* role in the social system.

During this same period of great social upheaval, psychologists, unfettered by communication researchers' adherence to the limited-effects perspective, thought they could explain some of the turmoil in microscopic—that is, individual—terms. Psychologists turned their attention to how people, especially children, learned from the mass media, especially television. What would eventually become known as **social cognitive theory** and its early focus on children moved communication theorists even further from a focus on limited or minimal media effects. They directed much of their attention toward increases in the amount of real-world violence and the possible contribution of the new medium of television to that rise. "The media" was one of the factors eventually blamed for causing or aggravating violent actions.

Social scientists developed several different perspectives on the effects of television violence, including catharsis, social learning, social cognitive theory, aggressive

functionalism
Theoretical approach that conceives of social systems as living organisms whose various parts work, or function, together to maintain essential processes

communication systems theory
Theory that examines the mass communication process as composed of interrelated parts that work together to meet some goal

social cognitive theory
Theory of learning through interaction with the environment that involves reciprocal causation of behavior, personal factors, and environmental events

cues, and priming effects. Whereas the latter four perspectives see media as a possible factor in increasing the likelihood of actual violence, catharsis argues just the opposite. We will study these approaches as well as the context of mediated violence—that is, how violence and aggression are presented in the media. We will also examine differing understandings of how children interact with the media, specifically the active theory of television viewing and the developmental perspective. What is important to remember throughout your reading of this chapter, however, is that together, functionalism's macroscopic approach and social cognitive theory's microscopic orientation would reshape mass communication theory.

THEORIES OF THE MIDDLE RANGE AND THE FUNCTIONAL ANALYSIS APPROACH

One of the most influential social theorists of the 1940s and 1950s was Robert Merton, a sociologist who, when at Columbia University, collaborated with Paul Lazarsfeld. Merton was trained as a social theorist but was intrigued by Lazarsfeld's empirical research. Lazarsfeld rarely relied on social theory to plan his research. He used his surveys to investigate things that intrigued him, such as his fascination with opinion leaders. His surveys generated hundreds of findings. But how should these findings be interpreted? Could they be used to construct theory? Was there a strategy that could be used to integrate findings so that the social structures underlying them might be revealed? In the preceding chapter we noted that when C. Wright Mills wanted to deal with the opinion leader findings, he wanted to "throw out the tabulation machinery" and write a book that presumably would be grounded in his qualitative assessment of what he had observed in Decatur. His work would likely have been less concerned with opinion leaders and more concerned with the Power Elite. Lazarsfeld quickly rejected this solution and fired Mills. But if Mills's approach wasn't acceptable, what was?

The questions posed by Lazarsfeld's findings were not unique. As funding and respect for empirical research grew, findings increased exponentially. In an era before computers revolutionized data analysis, results were generated in rooms filled with boxes of questionnaires and people punching numbers into tabulation machines. When results from several hundred questionnaires had to be compiled, it could take weeks to produce a set of cross-tabulation tables or to calculate a small set of correlation coefficients. And once the results were obtained, how could they be interpreted? Most empirical research wasn't based on theory. At best, researchers conceptualized attributes that could be measured using questionnaire items. Research could show that some attributes were related to other attributes, but it couldn't explain how or why these relationships existed. What was needed was a way to inductively develop theory based on these findings. Merton offered a solution.

In 1949 Merton wrote *Social Theory and Social Structure,* a book that established his reputation as a sociologist and earned him the gratitude of the first generation of empirical social scientists. He continued to develop his ideas and eventually published *On Theoretical Sociology* (1967). For more than two decades, Merton tutored a host of thoughtful and reflective empirical researchers. He gave them a perspective from which to plan and then interpret their work. He taught them a practical way of combining induction with deduction.

Merton's solution to the dilemma posed by the rising tide of research findings was development of "theories of the middle range." Unlike grand social theories (e.g., mass society theory) that attempt to explain a broad range of social action, middle-range theories were designed to explain only limited domains or ranges of action that had been or could be explored using empirical research. These theories could be created by carefully interpreting empirical findings. According to Merton,

> Some sociologists still write as though they expect, here and now, formulation of the general sociological theory broad enough to encompass the vast ranges of precisely observed details of social behavior, organization, and change and fruitful enough to direct the attention of research workers to a flow of problems for empirical research. This I take to be a premature and apocalyptic belief. We are not ready. Not enough preparatory work has been done. (1967, p. 45)

Merton (1967, p. 68) described middle-range theory as follows:

1. Middle-range theories consist of limited sets of assumptions from which specific hypotheses are logically derived and confirmed by empirical investigation.
2. These theories do not remain separate but are consolidated into wider networks of theory.
3. These theories are sufficiently abstract to deal with differing spheres of social behavior and social structure, so that they transcend sheer description or empirical generalization.
4. This type of theory cuts across the distinction between micro-sociological problems.
5. The middle-range orientation involves the specification of ignorance. Rather than pretend to knowledge where it is in fact absent, this orientation expressly recognizes what must still be learned to lay the foundation for still more knowledge.

Middle-range theory provided a useful rationale for what most empirical researchers, including media scientists, were already doing. Many were determined to ignore what they considered unnecessary theoretical baggage and focus on developing and applying empirical research methods. They believed that the future of social science lay in producing and collating empirical generalizations. Following the examples set by Paul Lazarsfeld and Carl Hovland, researchers conducted endless surveys and experiments, gathering data to support or reject individual generalizations and constantly discovering new research questions requiring yet more empirical research. Merton argued that all this research work would eventually be brought together to first create an array of middle-range theories, and then to construct a comprehensive theory having the power and scope of theories in the physical sciences. Moreover, when it was finally constructed, this theory would be far superior to earlier forms of social theory that were not empirically grounded.

Thus middle-range theory provided an ideal rationale and justification for small-scale, limited-effects studies. It implied that eventually all these individual-effects studies would add up, permitting the construction of a broad perspective on the role of media. Yet middle-range theory had important shortcomings that were not immediately apparent. Countless empirical generalizations were studied, but the effort to combine them into broader theories proved more difficult than had been expected. In this and later chapters we will consider numerous interesting and useful middle-range theories, but when broader theories were developed based on these middle-range notions, they had crucial limitations. The first few generations of empirical researchers had little success at integrating their empirical generalizations into broader theories. But that may be changing. During the last decade, media researchers have begun a serious effort to integrate findings into broader theories (Potter, 2009). We'll take a careful look at this trend, first in Chapter 9 and then in Chapter 12.

In *Social Theory and Social Structure* (1949), Merton proposed what he called a "paradigm for functional analysis" outlining how an inductive strategy centered on the study of social artifacts (such as the use of mass media) could eventually lead to the construction of theories that explained the "functions" of these items. Merton derived his perspective on functional analysis from carefully examining research in anthropology and sociology. Functionalism, as we've seen, assumes that a society can be usefully viewed as a "system in balance." That is, the society consists of complex sets of interrelated activities, each of which supports the others. Every form of social activity is assumed to play some part in maintaining the system as a whole. By studying the functions of various parts of such systems, a theory of the larger system might be developed. This would be a middle-range theory, because it would integrate research findings from the studies that examined the different parts of the system.

manifest functions Intended and observed consequences of media use

latent functions Unintended and less easily observed consequences of media use

classic four functions of the media Surveillance, correlation, transmission of the social heritage, and entertainment

One feature of functional analysis that appealed to Merton and his followers was its apparent *value-neutrality*. Older forms of social theory had characterized various parts of society as either "good" or "evil" in some ultimate sense. For example, mass society theory saw media as essentially disruptive and subversive, a negative force that somehow had to be brought under control. Functionalists rejected such thinking and instead argued that empirical research should investigate both the functions and dysfunctions of media. In that way a systematic appraisal could be made of media's overall impact by weighing useful outcomes of media use against negative outcomes. Functionalists argued that social science had no basis and no need for making value judgments about media. Rather, empirical investigation was necessary to determine whether specific media perform certain functions for the society. Merton also distinguished **manifest functions**—those consequences that are intended and readily observed—and **latent functions**—those unintended and less easily observed.

Functional analysis was widely adopted as a rationale for many mass communication studies during the late 1950s and 1960s. Researchers tried to determine whether specific media or forms of media content were functional or dysfunctional. They investigated manifest and latent functions of media. In his classic 1959 book, *Mass Communication: A Sociological Perspective*, Charles Wright identified what have become known as the **classic four functions of the media.** He wrote: "Harold Lasswell, a political scientist who has done pioneering research in mass communications, once noted three activities of communication specialists: (1) surveillance of the environment, (2) correlation of the parts of society in responding to the environment, and (3) transmission of the social heritage from one generation to the next" (Wright, 1959, p. 16). To these, he added a fourth: entertainment. In as much as any one of these functions could have positive or negative influence, and because each carried manifest as well as latent functions, it's clear that functional analysis could give rise to very complicated assessments of the role of media.

For example, various forms of media content can be functional or dysfunctional for society as a whole, for specific individuals, for various subgroups in the society, and for the culture. Media advertising for fast-food chains might be functional for their corporations and stockholders and for the economy as a whole, but dysfunctional for the growing number of obese children enticed by their music and images (Kunkel et al., 2004). As obesity-related health problems increase, insurance costs could spiral, a dysfunction for working parents, but functional for those selling weight-reduction programs and fitness camps to exasperated parents. Thus the functions for society can be offset by the dysfunctions for individuals or for specific groups of individuals.

Lance Holbert, Kelly Garrett, and Laurel Gleason offer a contemporary example. We can judge the self-selected, echo-chamber media consumption facilitated by cable television, talk radio, and the Internet as a dysfunction because it fosters antagonism toward the political system. This view assumes that "trust and confidence" in the political system are "unqualified goods." But, they argue, "Trust and confidence are *not* unqualified goods; they must be earned or warranted" (2010, p. 29). Loss of trust may be a dysfunction for individuals as they lose confidence in a system designed to support them (a micro-level assessment), but may ultimately be a beneficial function because it will force the system to improve (a macro-level assessment).

This thinking leads to one of functionalism's primary problems—it rarely permits definitive conclusions to be drawn about the overall functions or dysfunctions of media. For example, one of the first media effects to be studied in some depth using functional analysis was the **narcotizing dysfunction,** the idea that as news about an issue inundates people, they become apathetic to it, substituting knowing about that issue for action on it (Lazarsfeld and Merton, 1948). The narcotizing dysfunction was used to explain why extensive, often dramatic coverage of 1950 congressional hearings concerning organized crime didn't lead to widespread public demands for government action. Although the heavily reported hearings went on

narcotizing dysfunction
Theory that as news about an issue inundates people, they become apathetic to it, substituting knowing about that issue for action on it

INSTANT ACCESS

Functionalism

Strengths

1. Positions media and their influence in larger social system
2. Offers balanced view of media's role in society
3. Is based on and guides empirical research

Weaknesses

1. Is overly accepting of status quo
2. Asserts that dysfunctions are "balanced" by functions
3. Asserts that negative latent functions are "balanced" by positive manifest functions
4. Rarely permits definitive conclusions about media's role in society

for fifteen months, were conducted in fourteen cities, and featured more than eight hundred witnesses, researchers found that average Americans thought that nothing could be done to combat organized crime. These findings were disturbing because they suggested that even when media are effective at surveying the environment and calling attention to societal problems (a manifest function), the public may react by doing nothing. Instead of activating people to demand solutions to problems, media coverage might "narcotize" them so that they become apathetic and decide that they are powerless to do anything (a latent dysfunction). But what would account for this narcotizing effect? Researchers argued that members of the public will be narcotized when they are exposed day after day to dramatic negative news coverage dwelling on the threats posed by a problem and emphasizing the difficulty of dealing with it. This research was one of the first studies to suggest that media can fail to perform an important function even when practitioners do what their profession defines as the socially responsible thing to do.

In general, functional analysis tends to produce conclusions that largely legitimize or rationalize the status quo. A classic example of how functional analysis leads to status quo conclusions is found in the work of Harold Mendelsohn (1966). He was concerned that people widely misunderstood the influence of television, the powerful new medium of his era. He blamed elite critics of media (mostly mass society theorists) for fostering misconceptions about television's entertainment function. He charged that these critics were protecting their own self-interests and ignoring empirical research findings, dismissing most criticisms as prejudiced speculation inconsistent with empirical data.

According to Mendelsohn, mass society critics were paternalistic and elitist. They were upset because television entertainment attracted people away from the boring forms of education, politics, or religion that they themselves wanted to promote. Mendelsohn argued that people needed the relaxation and harmless escapism that television offered. If this entertainment weren't available, people would find other releases from the tensions of daily life. Television simply served these needs more easily, powerfully, and efficiently than alternatives.

Instead of condemning television, Mendelsohn argued that critics should acknowledge that it performs its function very well and at extremely low cost. He was concerned that critics had greatly exaggerated the importance and long-term consequences of television entertainment, and he asserted that it had a limited and ultimately quite minor social role. Television entertainment did not disrupt or debase high culture; it merely gave average people a more attractive alternative to high-brow entertainment like operas and symphony concerts. It did not distract people from important activities like religion, politics, or family life; rather, it helped them relax so that they could later engage in these activities with renewed interest and energy.

mass entertainment theory
Theory asserting that television and other mass media, because they relax or otherwise entertain average people, perform a vital social function

Mendelsohn cited numerous psychological studies to support his **mass entertainment theory.** He admitted that a small number of people might suffer because they became addicted to television entertainment. These same people, however, would most likely have become addicted to something else if television weren't available. Chronic couch potatoes might otherwise become lounge lizards or fans of romance novels. Mendelsohn viewed addiction to television as rather benign compared to other alternatives: It didn't hurt other people and viewing might even be slightly educational.

INSTANT ACCESS

Mass Entertainment Theory

Strengths	Weaknesses
1. Stresses media's prosocial influence	1. Is too accepting of the status quo
2. Provides cogent explanation for why people seek entertainment from media	2. Paints negative picture of average people and their use of media

Functionalist arguments continue to hold sway in many contemporary effects debates. Here, for example, is developmental economist Charles Kenny (2009) wondering about the impact of the world's more than one billion television households and the average of four hours a day consumed by each individual living in them. "So," he asks, "will the rapid, planetwide proliferation of television sets and digital and satellite channels, to corners of the world where the Internet is yet unheard of, be the cause of global decay [as] critics fear?" His near-perfect, "yes, but" functionalist answer: "A world of couch potatoes in front of digital sets will have its downsides—fewer bowling clubs, more Wii bowling. It may or may not be a world of greater obesity.... But it could also be a world more equal for women, healthier, better governed, more united in response to global tragedy, and more likely to vote for local versions of *American Idol* than shoot at people" (p. 68). You can assess the power of functionalism in the current debate over American youngsters' over-emersion in media in the box entitled "Generation M2: Are the Kids Alright?"

Mass entertainment theory and the narcotizing dysfunction provide excellent examples of how functional analysis and its findings can legitimize the status quo. Harmful effects are balanced by a number of positive effects. Who can judge whether the harm being done is great enough to warrant making changes? Congress? The courts? The public? When the evidence is mixed, the best course of action would appear to be inaction, especially in a democratic system that seems to have functioned quite well in the two and a half centuries since the Founders penned the First Amendment.

Functionalism allows researchers and theorists to easily avoid drawing controversial conclusions by simply noting that dysfunctions are balanced by functions. After all, we wouldn't want media to avoid publishing news about organized crime just because some people will be narcotized. Sure, a few folks may abuse mass entertainment, but the benefits of such wonderful diversions surely outweigh this small problem. There is a conservative logic inherent in these arguments. It says that if the social world isn't literally falling apart with riots in the streets and people jumping off rooftops, things must be "in balance." Dysfunctions of media must certainly be balanced by other functions. If society is in balance, we can deduce that the overall influence of factors such as media must be either positive or only slightly negative. Obviously negative effects are offset by positive effects. If we eliminate the negative effects, we might also eliminate the positive effects balancing them. Are we willing to pay that price?

THINKING *about* THEORY — GENERATION M2: ARE THE KIDS ALRIGHT?

Allowing for media multitasking—that is consuming multiple messages at one time—eight- to eighteen-year-old Americans spend ten hours and forty-five minutes a day using media, a two-and-a-quarter-hour rise from just five years earlier (Rideout, Foehr, and Roberts, 2010). Not only is this more time than adults spend at work, it's every day, not the five days of a typical work week. All this plugged-in time can't possibly be good, argue countless critics. In fact, the research from which these data are drawn discovered that "youth who spend more time with media report lower grades and lower levels of personal contentment." Its authors, however, properly warn, "This study cannot establish whether there is a cause and effect relationship … and if there are such relationships, they could well run in both directions simultaneously" (p. 4). As you might guess, this is a perfect situation for a functionalist defense of these record amounts of media consumption.

Less personal contentment? Maybe, but "Internet use in general and use of social networking services such as Facebook in particular are associated with more diverse social networks" (Hampton et al., 2009). There's even good science that says instant messaging improves the quality of kids' friendships (Valkenburg and Peter, 2009).

Lower grades? Possibly, but new media are teaching young people a newer, better way of learning and accessing information. "Kids are using sound and images so they have a world of ideas to put together that aren't necessarily language oriented," argues one literacy expert. "In a tenth of the time [it takes to read a book]," writes another, "the Internet allows a reader to cover a lot more of the topic from different points of view" (both in Rich, 2008). An hour and thirteen minutes a day with videogames? Games are fine; they improve manual dexterity! And the iPhone alone has more than 1,800 games and applications dedicated to a healthy lifestyle, and what about all those keeping fit games on Wii and cancer awareness games from Games for Good outfits like HopeLab (Chiang, 2010)? Four and a half hours a day of television? Economist Kenny has already responded to that.

As you can see, functionalism seems reasonable. All technology is a double-edged sword. Remember, for example, our discussion from Chapter 5 about saving journalism. The same technology that makes more news available to readers than ever before, the Internet, also makes it more difficult for news organizations to afford quality news gathering. Therefore, the question remains, what does functionalism add to our understanding of media effects? Does it broaden our knowledge or offer convenient justifications for inaction? Where do you stand?

Researchers were content to simply point to the existence of such balanced effects and conclude that there was little that could or should be done about them. Remember, this was an era when the goal of researchers was to be objective observers of the social world, reporting dispassionately on what they found and leaving it to others to decide whether anything should be done about their findings. Not surprisingly, most findings were ignored by media—especially the findings suggesting that media bear some responsibility for social problems.

Functional analysis, middle-range theory, and the limited-effects perspective made a good fit. If media influence was modest, media couldn't be too dysfunctional. Findings from limited-effects research could be combined to create a middle-range theory. For example, in their classic and influential 1961 book, *Television in the Lives of Our Children,* Wilbur Schramm, Jack Lyle, and Edwin Parker found that although viewing certain forms of violent television content encouraged *some* children to be aggressive, this was more than offset by *most* children, who showed little or no influence. And there were important positive functions.

Children read fewer violent comic books. Some might even learn how to anticipate and cope with aggressive peers. Thus, Schramm, Lyle, and Parker concluded that as far as the social system as a whole was concerned, violent television content makes little difference despite being dysfunctional for a few children (those "damned" by their "bad" parents to be manipulated by television violence).

Although it doesn't claim to do so, their book can be interpreted as presenting a reassuring, empirically grounded, middle-range theory that explains the role of television for children. By contrast, and as you'll see in the second half of this chapter, at precisely the same time Schramm, Lyle, and Parker were explaining television's impact in such balanced terms, researchers from the field of psychology, bound by neither functionalism nor the limited-effects perspective, were making significant and persuasive arguments about the harmful effects of mediated violence.

SYSTEMS THEORIES OF COMMUNICATION PROCESSES

Other communication researchers were not so sanguine about media's "balancing" of effects. Systems engineers alerted them to the possibility of developing holistic explanations for societal, or macro-level, effects. Those engineers were concerned with designing and analyzing increasingly complex mechanical and electrical systems. They had achieved great successes during World War II and had laid the basis for many of the spectacular postwar technological breakthroughs in broadcasting and computers. It is no surprise, then, that their approach would be attractive to researchers interested in studying the most complex system of all: society.

system
Any set of interrelated parts that can influence and control one another through communication and feedback loops

A **system** *consists of a set of parts that are interlinked so that changes in one part induce changes in other parts.* System parts can be directly linked through mechanical connections, or they can be indirectly linked by communication technology. Because all parts are linked, the entire system can change as a result of alterations in only one element. Systems can be *goal-directed* if they are designed to accomplish a long-term objective. Some systems are capable of *monitoring the environment and altering their operations in response to environmental changes.*

During World War II, electronics engineers began to develop systems that were programmed to pursue goals, monitor the environment, and adjust actions to achieve those goals. One example occurs when a guided missile is able to make midcourse adjustments by monitoring internal and external changes. Engineers were concerned with designing systems in which communication links functioned efficiently and transmitted information accurately. Communication was a means to an end. If a communication link didn't work properly, then the solution was obvious: Communication technology had to be improved so the desired levels of effectiveness and accuracy were achieved. Thus, in designing and engineering systems of this type, communication problems could be solved by technological change.

Could communication problems in the society be solved in the same way? Could improving the accuracy, reliability, and range of communication solve societal problems? Would a nation bound together by networks of telephone cables be less troubled by regional disputes? Would a world bound together by satellite-based communication be less troubled by war? During the 1950s and 1960s, there was increasing optimism that important societal-level communication problems might also be solved by improving the accuracy of message transmissions.

THE RISE OF SYSTEMS THEORIES

cybernetics
The study of regulation and control in complex systems

After the successes achieved by systems engineers during World War II, social theorists became intrigued by systems notions as a way of conceptualizing both macroscopic and microscopic phenomena. Some decided that the idea of systems offered a means of constructing useful models of various social processes, including communication. Rather than merely adding more variables, these models altered how relationships between variables were understood. In developing these models, theorists drew on a variety of sources. But most 1960s social systems theorists acknowledged that the greatest and most recent impetus toward the development of systems theories came from an engineering subfield known as **cybernetics**, the study of regulation and control in complex machines. Cybernetics investigates how communication links between the various parts of a machine enable it to perform very complex tasks and adjust to changes taking place in its external environment.

Cybernetics emerged as an important new field during World War II, partly because of its use for designing sophisticated weapons (Wiener, 1954, 1961). It proved especially useful for communications engineering—the design of powerful new communication systems for military applications, such as radar and guided missiles. Communications engineers had abandoned simple linear models of the communication process by the 1940s. They conceptualized a circular but evolving communication process in which messages come back from receivers to influence sources that in turn alter their messages. They referred to these circular processes as **feedback loops**. In these systems, ongoing mutual adjustment is possible, ultimately leading to the achievement of a long-term objective or function.

feedback loops
Ongoing mutual adjustments in systems

communication systems
Systems that function primarily to facilitate communication

Complex machines rely on feedback loops as a means of making ongoing adjustments to changes caused by the environment. Feedback loops enable sources to monitor the influence of their messages on receivers. But just as important, receivers can in turn influence sources. If the effects are not what was expected or desired, a source can keep altering a message until the desired feedback is obtained. As World War II progressed, machines were built that used ever more powerful forms of communication technology, such as radar and television cameras, to monitor the environment. These provided sophisticated means of detecting subtle changes so that a weapons system could achieve its objective. We refer to these as **communication systems** if their function is primarily to facilitate communication. By this definition, a guided missile is not a communication system; it is a weapons system that contains a communication subsystem.

MODELING SYSTEMS

model
Any representation of a system, whether in words or diagrams

The term *system* is used in communication engineering and cybernetics to refer to any set of interrelated parts that can influence and control one another through communication and feedback loops. Any representation of a system, whether in words or diagrams, is a **model.** In systems with many interrelated parts, a change in one part affects the others because all are interconnected through channels.

Interdependence and self-regulation are key attributes of such systems. Each part can have a specialized role or function, but all must interrelate in an organized manner for the overall system to operate properly and regulate itself so that goals are achieved. Systems can be relatively simple or quite complex. They can display a high or low level of internal organization. They can operate in a static fashion, or they can evolve and undergo profound change over time. They can operate in isolation or be interconnected with a series of other machines to form an even larger system.

goal-oriented
Characteristic of a system that serves a specific overall or long-term purpose

Another key attribute of systems is that they are **goal-oriented**. That is, they constantly seek to serve a specific overall or long-term purpose. We usually associate goals with thinking and planning. But, of course, machines can't think. Their goal-orientation is built in, hardwired, or otherwise programmed. Once a machine is started, it will seek its goal even if the goal is mistaken or can't be achieved. Like the robots in a science fiction movie, machines carry out their mission even if doing so makes no sense.

Although complex systems can be hard to describe and understand, the basic principles of a self-regulating system can be illustrated by looking at the way the furnace in your home operates. That device is part of a self-regulating system that uses a simple feedback loop to adjust to the external environment. The furnace communicates with a thermostat monitoring the environment, signaling it when it needs to turn on or off. As long as the temperature in your home remains within a desired range, the furnace remains inactive. When the thermostat detects a temperature below the desired range, it sends an electronic message telling the furnace to turn on. The furnace communicates with the thermostat by heating the air in your home. The thermostat monitors the air temperature, and when that reaches the desired level, the thermostat sends another message telling the furnace to turn off. In this simple system, the furnace and the thermostat work together to keep the temperature in balance. Communication in the form of a simple feedback loop linking the furnace and the thermostat enables the system to operate effectively.

APPLYING SYSTEMS MODELS TO HUMAN COMMUNICATION

Even simple systems models can be used to represent some forms of human communication. You and a friend can be seen as forming a system in which your friend plays the role of "thermostat." By maintaining communication with your friend, you find out whether your actions are appropriate or inappropriate. Are these the right clothes to wear now? Should you go to a dance or join friends for a movie? During your conversation, you might not be trying to affect your friend but rather want your friend to guide you. You want your friend's feedback so you can adjust your actions.

This example also illustrates key limitations of systems models when they are used to represent human communication—the easiest models to create tend to be too simple and too static. Unless you and your friend have a very unusual relationship, you will play many other kinds of roles and communicate with each other across a very broad range of topics. If the only function your friend serves for you is that of a thermostat, you probably need to reexamine your relationship. Assuming that you do have a more complex relationship with your friend, you could probably spend weeks trying to map out a systems model to represent the intricacies of your interrelationship. By the time you finished, you would discover that significant changes have occurred and the model is no longer accurate. Unlike mechanical parts linked by simple forms of communication, both you and your friend can easily alter your roles, your communication links, and the content and purposes of your messages. In other words, you regularly and routinely transform the system that links you to others. New feedback loops spring up while old ones vanish. New purposes develop and old purposes are forgotten.

ADOPTION OF SYSTEMS MODELS BY MASS COMMUNICATION THEORISTS

transmissional model

The view of mass media as mere senders or transmitters of information

Like other social scientists, mass communication researchers were drawn to systems models. They came to see moderately complex systems models as an ideal means of representing communication processes—a big advance over simplistic linear communication process models common before 1960. Gradually, systems models replaced the **transmissional model** implicit in most of the early effects research. Harold Lasswell (1949) provided a cogent, succinct version of this model when he described the communication process as *who says what to whom through what medium with what effect.* This transmissional model assumes that a message source dominates the communication process and that its primary outcome is some sort of effect on receivers—usually one intended by the source. Influence moves or flows in a straight line from source to receivers. The possibility that the message receivers might also influence the source is ignored. Attention is focused on whether a source brings about intended effects and whether unintended negative effects occur. Mutual or reciprocal influence is not considered.

Communication theorists proposed new models of communication processes with feedback loops in which receivers could influence sources and mutual influence was possible. The potential for modeling mutual influence was especially attractive for theorists who wanted to understand interpersonal communication. Most conversations involve mutual influence. Participants send out messages, obtain feedback, and then adjust their actions. In everyday life, people are

INSTANT ACCESS

Systems Theory

Strengths

1. Can be conceptualized as either micro- or macro-level theory
2. Represents communication as a process
3. Can be used to model a limitless variety of communication processes
4. Moves mass communication theory beyond simple linear-effects notions

Weaknesses

1. Has difficulty assessing causal relationships
2. Is often too simplistic to represent complex communication patterns
3. Is perceived by some as overly mechanistic and dehumanizing
4. Focuses attention on observable structures, ignoring the substance of communication
5. Is unparsimonious

constantly adjusting to one another. The overall social environment can be understood as something created by ongoing negotiation between actors.

The usefulness of systems models for representing mass communication processes was less obvious, although Bruce Westley and Malcolm MacLean (1957) offered one widely accepted effort, as you can see in the box entitled "The Westley-MacLean Model of the Communication Process." With most traditional forms of mass media, there are few if any *direct* communication links from receivers to sources. Message sources can be unaware of the impact of their messages or find out what that impact was only after days or weeks have elapsed. During the 1960s, however, refinement of media ratings systems and improved, more scientific public opinion polls allowed the establishment of indirect communication links between message sources and receivers. Ratings and opinion poll results provided message producers with feedback about audience reaction to their messages. For television ratings this feedback was quite crude—either people watch a show or they don't. If they don't, producers change the message without much understanding of what people want. If ratings are high, then they provide more of the same—until people get so tired of the same programming that they finally tune to something else. With opinion polls, the feedback can provide a bit more information to message sources, but not much. Politicians, for example, are constantly experimenting with messages in an effort to alter voter opinions and produce favorable evaluations of themselves.

THINKING *about* THEORY   THE WESTLEY-MACLEAN MODEL OF THE COMMUNICATION PROCESS

The Westley-MacLean model of the communication process is a well regarded representation of mass communication as a system.

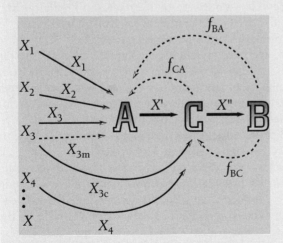

The messages (X″) that C, a mass communication channel, transmits to B, a member of the audience,

represent its selections both from messages (X′) it receives from a number of possible A's, *purposive communicators* in the environment such as advertisers, programmers, and government agencies that have something to transmit, and its selections and abstractions from entities and events in its own sensory field (X_{3c}, X_4), which may not be messages in the purposive communicators' field. Feedback moves not only from B to A (f_{BA}) and from B to C (f_{BC}) but also from C to A (f_{CA}). Clearly, in a mass communication system, a large number of Cs receive a large number of messages from a large number of As while they themselves, the Cs, are surveying a large environment and transmitting to a vastly larger number of Bs, who simultaneously receive from a large number of other Cs.

How well do you think this model represents the complex process of communication? Can you use it to clarify your understanding of the process of mass communication? Why or why not?

FUNCTIONALISM'S UNFULFILLED PROMISE

Although they did indeed help advance mass communication theory beyond a focus on specific limited-effects and middle-range theory, functionalism and systems theory suffered much criticism and are not among the central schools of thought in contemporary thinking about media. However, as we will explain later in this book, they have influenced the development of some important theories. These approaches to theory have not been more influential because scholars who construct interpretive and postpositivist theories see them as having serious limitations.

Humanistic scholars who develop interpretive theories tend to reject the mechanistic or biological analogies inherent in functionalism and systems models. They are fundamentally opposed to the use of functional analysis and systems models because they perceive them to be dehumanizing and overly simplistic. They argue that systems models are often nothing more than elaborate metaphors—sets of descriptive analogies. They are dissatisfied with the ability of functional analysis and systems models to adequately represent complex human or societal interrelationships. After all, people aren't parts of machines. The relationships in a family aren't like the mechanism in an old-fashioned pocket watch. Even complex mechanical systems are simple when compared with the human relationships that are found within a family. Humanists are fearful that in applying functional or mechanistic analogies we demean or trivialize human existence and experience.

Social scientists who develop postpositivist theories argue that research must stay focused on development of causal explanations and predictions. They reject complicated systems models because they don't permit the assessment of causality. In our earlier heating system model, which is the causal agent and which agent is being affected? Does the furnace cause the thermostat to act? Yes. Does the thermostat cause the furnace to act? Yes. So which is dominant in this relationship? Which controls the other? In this model, neither agent is clearly "causal." Each causes the other to change. Thus, in even this very simple process involving feedback, causality can be hard to assess. If we measure the furnace and the thermostat at only one point in time, we are likely to get a completely mistaken impression of their relationship. When these processes become more complicated with more agents and more feedback loops, we need a schematic diagram to sort out the flow of influence. The effort to assign causality soon becomes a meaningless exercise. For example, given the complexity of the systems we create when we interact with other people, it becomes literally impossible to sort out causality—except for the simplest and most narrowly defined systems or parts of systems.

Should we be concerned about the difficulty of assigning causality in systems models? Is assignment of causality necessary to have a truly scientific theory? Or should we be satisfied if our theories are useful for other purposes? If we could simulate a set of interrelationships that provides insight into people playing certain roles in a particular situation over a limited time span, is that enough? Do we need to be able to say that the person playing role X has .23 causal dominance over the person playing role Y, whereas the person in role Y has .35 dominance over person X? Just how precise must our understanding of these interrelationships be for the simulation to be of value? Just how precise can we afford to make our simulations, given the time and research effort necessary?

Researchers who assert the importance of assigning causality are concerned that if researchers lower their concern for causality, they will create and use systems models based on little more than informed speculation. Although sophisticated systems models might allow them to construct fascinating computer simulations, will they serve any practical purpose? How can the utility of these models be evaluated if causality is not used as an explanatory standard? It might appear that a model fits a particular set of relationships and gives insight into interconnections between particular parts, but how can they be sure? How can they choose between two competing models that seem to represent a particular set of relationships equally well? These critics are deeply skeptical of the value of constructing models that contain complex interconnections between agents. Critics view systems models as unparsimonious—containing too many unnecessary variables and overly complex interrelationships.

Finally, as we have already noted here, functionalism and systems theory have a third limitation that many find troublesome: they have a bias toward the status quo. Because they tend to concentrate attention on observable structures (e.g., the functioning parts of the organism or machine), functionalism and systems theory often lead to the assumption that the primary function or role of these structures is to maintain and serve the overall system.

FOCUS ON CHILDREN AND VIOLENCE

On August 6, 1945, the United States dropped an atom bomb on Hiroshima, effectively ending World War II. That four-year global conflict forced cataclysmic changes in the nation's economic, industrial, demographic, familial, and technological character, the impact of which would be felt most powerfully in the 1960s.

The mass medium that transformed that decade had an inauspicious introduction as a novelty at the 1939 World's Fair in New York. Its tiny picture, poor sound quality, and high cost led some to doubt its future as a popular medium. How could it compete with movies? Would people really want to sit at home and watch ghostly black-and-white images on a small screen when they could walk a few blocks to see powerful Technicolor images on a gigantic screen? During the next three years, a small number of experimental television stations began broadcasting a limited number and variety of programs to a minuscule audience. When the United States entered the war, television's already limited diffusion to the public halted, as the technologies and materials needed to improve and produce the medium went to the war effort. Technological research, however, did not stop. Therefore, when the war ended and materials were once again available for the manufacture of consumer goods, a technologically mature new medium was immediately available. Anticipating not only this, but also dramatic changes in American society that would benefit the new medium, the national commercial radio networks were ready to move their hit shows and big stars to television.

This technological advance occurred simultaneously with profound alterations in U.S. society. The war changed the country from a primarily rural society boasting an agriculturally based economy into a largely urban nation dependent on an industrially based economy. After the war, more people worked regularly scheduled jobs (rather than the sunrise-to-sunset workday of farmers), and they had more leisure. More people had regular incomes (rather than the seasonal, put-the-money-back-into-the-land farmer's existence), and they had more money to spend on that leisure. Because the manufacturing capabilities developed for the war were still in existence, the economy had the ability to mass-produce items on which that money could be spent. Because more consumer goods were competing in the marketplace, there was a greater need to advertise, which provided the economic base for the new television medium. Because non-Caucasian Americans had fought in the war and worked in the country's factories, they began to demand their rightful share of the American dream. Because women entered the workforce while the men were off to battle, it was more common and acceptable to have both parents working outside the home. Because people had moved away from their small towns and family roots, the traditional community anchors— church and school—began to lose their dominance in the social development of children who were present in the 1960s—in their teenage years—in inordinately large numbers because of the baby boom that occurred soon after war's end.

This new social landscape took shape at precisely the same time that the new mass medium arrived. As in all periods of significant societal change, there were serious social problems. The rapid rise in the number of teenagers brought sharp increases in delinquency and crime. The schools were blamed for not doing their job of educating children to be responsible citizens. Crime waves swept one city after another. Race riots broke out in several urban areas, including Watts, Detroit, and Newark. Successive social movements captured the attention of the nation, especially the civil rights and the anti–Vietnam War movements. Some movements like the Black Panthers and the Weathermen became notorious for their willingness to use violence to pursue their objectives. Political instability reached new heights with the assassinations of President John F. Kennedy, Martin Luther King Jr., and Robert Kennedy. Young people were behaving strangely. Many were listening more to new, unfamiliar music and less to their increasingly "old-fashioned, irrelevant" parents. Social scientists discovered the existence of a "generation gap" between conservative middle-class parents and their increasingly liberal, even radical children.

Media's role in all these changes was hotly debated. Although social researchers and media practitioners typically argued from the limited-effects perspective, a new generation of observers charged that media were harming children and disrupting their lives. Evidence mounted that families, schools, and churches had become less important to children. As Urie Bronfenbrenner (1970) said, the backyards were growing smaller and the school yards growing bigger. In other words, young people were more and more being socialized away from parents' and teachers' influence. Bronfenbrenner's research demonstrated that, whereas parents and church had been the primary socializing agents for prewar American adolescents, by the mid-1960s, media and peers shared top billing in the performance of that crucial function.

It is no surprise, then, that the media, particularly television, became the target of increasing criticism and the object of intense scientific inquiry, especially where harmful effects were presumed. But these renewed efforts to probe the negative influence of mass media occurred when the limited-effects perspective was cementing its dominance among academics. An intense and continuing debate erupted between social researchers who had confidence in that perspective and those skeptical of its conclusions despite the consistency of its empirical findings. Strong advocates of limited-effects notions were accused of being paid lackeys of the media industries, and overzealous critics of television were accused of failing to take a scientific approach, of oversimplifying complex problems and ignoring alternative causes.

The argument about the media's role in fomenting social instability and instigating violence reached a peak in the late 1960s. After disruptive riots in the Los Angeles suburb of Watts and in the cities of Cleveland, Newark, and Detroit, President Lyndon Johnson established two national commissions, the Kerner Commission in 1967 and the National Commission on the Causes and Prevention of Violence in 1968. They offered some serious criticisms of media and recommended a variety of changes in both news reporting and entertainment content. Writing in the preface to the 1968 commission's staff report, *Violence and the Media,* editor Paul Briand asked, "If, as the media claim, no objective correlation exists between media portrayals of violence and violent behavior—if, in other words, the one has no impact upon the other—then how can the media claim an impact in product selection and consumption, as they obviously affect the viewers' commercial attitudes and behavior? Can they do one and not the other?" (Baker and Ball, 1969, vii). This question reflected growing public and elite skepticism concerning limited-effects assertions.

The federal government itself tried to locate new answers to this problem by establishing the Surgeon General's Scientific Advisory Committee on Television and Social Behavior in 1969. Its purpose was to commission a broad range of research on television effects that might determine whether television could be an important influence on children's behavior.

What did this collection of scientists conclude after two years and a million dollars of study? The surgeon general, Jesse L. Steinfeld, reported to a U.S. Senate subcommittee:

> While the ... report is carefully phrased and qualified in language acceptable to social scientists, it is clear to me that the causal relationship between televised violence and antisocial behavior is sufficient to warrant appropriate and immediate remedial action. The data on social phenomena such as television and violence and/or aggressive behavior will never be clear enough for all social scientists to agree on the formulation of a succinct statement of causality. But there comes a time when the data are sufficient to justify action. That time has come. (U.S. Congress, 1972, p. 26)

Nevertheless, this report did little to end the controversy over television's effects. Industry officials and lobbyists worked hard to block development and implementation of new Federal Communications Commission regulations for children's programming. They cited inconclusive research and restated limited-effects arguments. The primary opposition to the industry was Action for Children's Television (ACT)—a Boston-based group that grew rapidly during the 1970s in response to increasing public fears about television effects. Eventually the industry agreed to a self-imposed family viewing hour in which violent content was ostensibly minimized, and at the time, all three networks tightened their programming standards and worked closely with program producers to limit gratuitous violence.

TELEVISION VIOLENCE THEORIES

The most important outcome of the violence research was the gradual development of a set of theories that summarized findings and offered increasingly useful insight into the media's role in the lives of children. Taken together, they offered strong support for the link between television viewing and aggression. Two decades ago, after reviewing years of relevant research on the question, Aletha Huston and her colleagues wrote:

> The accumulated research clearly demonstrates a correlation between viewing violence and aggressive behavior—that is, heavy viewers behave more aggressively than light viewers.... Both experimental and longitudinal studies support the hypothesis that viewing violence is causally associated with aggression.... Field [naturalistic] experiments with preschool children and adolescents found heightened aggression among viewers assigned to watch violent television or film under some conditions. (1992, pp. 54–55)

Still, debate and disagreement persist.

CATHARSIS

catharsis
Also called *sublimation*; the idea that viewing mediated aggression sates, or reduces, people's natural aggressive drives

The findings from the surgeon general's report on one aspect of the television violence debate, **catharsis**, were quite clear and did generate significant agreement. Testified CBS's Joseph Klapper, "I myself am unaware of any, shall we say, hard evidence that seeing violence on television or any other medium acts in a cathartic or sublimated manner. There have been some studies to that effect; they are grossly, greatly outweighed by studies as to the opposite effect" (U.S. Congress, 1972, p. 60). Yet catharsis (sometimes called sublimation)—the idea that viewing violence is sufficient to purge or at least satisfy a person's aggressive drive and therefore reduce the likelihood of aggressive behavior—has lived a long if not thoroughly respectable life in mass communication theory.

Common sense and your own media consumption offer some evidence of the weakness of the catharsis hypothesis. When you watch couples engaged in physical affection on the screen, does it reduce your sexual drive? Do media presentations of families devouring devilish chocolate cakes purge you of your hunger drive? If viewing mediated sexual behavior does not reduce the sex drive and viewing media presentations of people dining does not reduce our hunger, why should we assume that seeing mediated violence can satisfy an aggressive drive? Moreover, think back to when you attended movies like *Avatar* or the *Transporter* and *Grindhouse* films. Did you walk out of the theater a tranquil, placid person? Probably not.

Yet it isn't difficult to see why the proposition seemed so attractive. For one thing, the philosopher Aristotle originally discussed catharsis in his *Poetics* to explain audience reaction to Greek tragedy. Even though he never wrote of the "purging" of an innate aggressive drive, but rather about audiences "purging" their own emotions of pity and fear because in a tragic play they saw misfortune befalling others (Gadamer, 1995), catharsis developed a conventional wisdom-based validity. For another, catharsis suggested that television violence had social utility—that is, it was functional, providing young people with a harmless outlet for their pent-up aggression and hostility. In television's early days, many people were anxious to rationalize their use of this attractive new medium.

There was even early scientific evidence suggesting that catharsis was indeed at work. Seymour Feshbach (1961) demonstrated what he said was catharsis by insulting college-age men with "a number of unwarranted and extremely critical remarks" in an experimental setting and then having them watch either filmed aggression (a brutal prize fight) or a neutral film (on the spread of rumors). The men were then asked to evaluate the experiment and the insulting experimenter. Those who had seen the prize fight were less aggressive in their attitudes than those who had seen the other film.

But, as F. Scott Andison wrote in 1977 after reviewing twenty years' worth of scientific evidence, "We can conclude on the basis of the present data cumulation that television, as it is shown today, probably does stimulate a higher amount of aggression in individuals within society. Therefore, it seems reasonable to tentatively accept the 'TV violence as a stimulant to aggression' theory and to reject the ... 'cathartic' theories" (p. 323). Or as James D. Halloran (1964/65), then director of Britain's Center for Mass Communication Research at the University of Leicester, more directly put it, catharsis is a "phony argument."

But Feshbach *did* demonstrate a reduction in aggression after viewing, and he obtained similar results in a 1971 study (Feshbach and Singer) conducted with funding from NBC. The research was undertaken in a group home for preadolescent boys. For six weeks, half of the boys were restricted to watching television programs with little or no violence while the other half was allowed to watch violent content. A variety of behavioral measures indicated that the boys viewing the violent programs were less aggressive. These results may not have been caused by catharsis, however. The boys who were placed in the nonviolent programming group may have been frustrated because they were not allowed to watch some of their favorite shows. Heightened frustration might account for their increased aggressiveness.

What social scientists would eventually learn, however, is that certain presentations of mediated violence and aggression *can reduce* the likelihood of subsequent viewer aggression. But catharsis is not the reason. Rather, viewers *learn* that violence might not be appropriate in a given situation. Think about the first Feshbach study (1961). Maybe those who had seen the brutal boxing match, who had seen unnecessary pain inflicted on another human, simply said to themselves, "Aggression is not a good thing." Their aggressive drive might not have been purged, but they might have simply *learned* that such treatment of another human is inappropriate. In other words, their inclination toward aggression (remember, they had been insulted) was inhibited by the information in the media presentation. This leads us to the theory that is generally accepted as most useful in understanding the influence of media violence on individuals—social cognitive theory.

SOCIAL LEARNING

Humans learn from observation. There has been some question, however, about how much and what kinds of behaviors people learn from the media. This debate has been fueled, in part, by a definitional problem. No one questions whether

imitation
The direct reproduction of observed behavior

people can imitate what they see in the media. **Imitation** is the direct mechanical reproduction of behavior. After watching Spike TV's *Ultimate Fighting Championship*, twenty-three Connecticut teens engage in a backyard slugfest/tournament that results in their arrest. Or two teenagers set fire to a New York subway tollbooth, killing its attendant, after seeing the movie *Money Train*. Both are true stories. Both demonstrate imitation. The problem for mass communication theorists, however, is that these obvious examples of media influence, dramatic as they may be, are relatively rare. Moreover, such gross examples of media influence lend substance to the argument that negative effects occur only in those "predisposed" to aggression—in other words, those crazy to begin with.

identification
A special form of imitation that springs from wanting to be and trying to be like an observed model relative to some broader characteristics or qualities

Identification, on the other hand, is "a particular form of imitation in which copying a model, generalized beyond specific acts, springs from wanting to be and trying to be like the model with respect to some broader quality" (White, 1972, p. 252). Although only one or a very few people might have *imitated* the behaviors seen in our *Ultimate Fighting Championship* and *Money Train* examples, how many others *identified* with their characters? How many others might choose different forms of violence against someone they might encounter? How many others identified with the characters' mode of problem solving, although they might never express it exactly as did our mediated aggressors? Imitation from media is clearly more dramatic and observable than is identification. But identification with media models might be the more lasting and significant of the media's effects. (For a detailed discussion of this distinction and its importance to media theory, see Baran and Meyer, 1974.)

The first serious look at learning through observation was offered by psychologists Neal Miller and John Dollard (1941). They argued that imitative learning occurred when observers were motivated to learn, when the cues or elements of the behaviors to be learned were present, when observers performed the given behaviors, and when observers were positively reinforced for imitating those behaviors. In other words, people could imitate behaviors they saw; those behaviors would be reinforced and therefore learned.

Instead of presenting a means of understanding how people learn from models (including media models), however, Miller and Dollard were simply describing an efficient form of traditional stimulus-response learning. They assumed that individuals behaved in certain ways and then shaped their behavior according to the reinforcement they actually received. The researchers saw imitation as replacing random trial-and-error behaviors. Imitation simply made it easier for an individual to choose a behavior to be reinforced. That actual reinforcement, they argued, ensured learning. But this insistence on the operation of reinforcement limited their theory's application for understanding how people learn from the mass media. Its inability to account for people's apparent skill at learning new responses through observation rather than actually receiving reinforcement limited its applicability to media theory.

social learning
Encompasses both imitation and identification to explain how people learn through observation of others in their environments

Two decades later, Miller and Dollard's ideas about what they called **social learning** and imitation were sufficiently developed, however, to become valuable tools in understanding media effects. Whereas Miller and Dollard saw social learning as an efficient form of stimulus-response learning (the model provided information that helped the observer make the correct response to be reinforced), contemporary social cognitive theory (as social learning theory is now known) argues that observers can acquire symbolic representations of the behavior, and these "pictures in their heads" provide them with information on which to base their own subsequent behavior. Media characters (models) can influence behavior simply by being depicted on the screen. The audience member need not be reinforced or rewarded for exhibiting the modeled behavior.

SOCIAL COGNITION FROM MASS MEDIA

operant learning theory
Asserts that learning occurs only through the making and subsequent reinforcement of behavior

Operant (or traditional) learning theory as developed by the early behaviorists (see Chapter 4) asserts that people learn new behaviors when they are presented with stimuli (something in their environment), make a response to those stimuli, and have those responses reinforced either positively (rewarded) or negatively (punished). In this way, new behaviors are learned, or added to people's **behavioral repertoire**—the individual's available behaviors in a given circumstance.

behavioral repertoire
The learned responses available to an individual in a given situation

Two things are clear, however. First, this is an inefficient form of learning. We all know, for example, how to deal with fire. If each of us had to learn our fire-related behavior individually, we would have overcrowded hospitals. According to operant learning theory, each of us, when presented with that stimulus (fire), would render a chance response (put our hand in it), and be burned. To ensure that we would not be scorched in the future, we would add avoidance of fire to our behavioral repertoire. Because that initial burned hand "increases the probability of a given behavior over time" (in our case, avoiding flames), the stimulus (the burned hand) is a **negative reinforcer** (Zimbardo and Weber, 1997, p. 215). This process is very inefficient. Instead we observe, in a variety of settings (mass-mediated and otherwise), the operation of that stimulus-response-reinforcement chain, and we in turn add avoidance to the store of behaviors that we can use when confronted in everyday life by the stimulus. In essence, then, we have substituted a representation—a picture in our head—of an experience for an actual (and, in this case, painful) experience.

negative reinforcer
A particular stimulus whose removal, reduction, or prevention increases the probability of a given behavior over time

A second obvious point is that we do not learn in only this operant manner. We have all experienced learning through observation, even when we have not seen the stimulus-response-reinforcement chain—that is, when there has been no reinforcement, either to us or to the person in the representation. Observation of a behavior is sufficient for people to learn that behavior. Even people who have never shot an arrow from a bow, for example, know how it's done. **Modeling** from the mass media, then, is an efficient way to learn a wide range of behaviors and solutions to problems that we would otherwise learn slowly or not at all, or pay too high a price to learn in the actual environment.

modeling
The acquisition of behaviors through observation

This learning from observation of the environment, or social cognition, is the basis of social cognitive theory. According to Albert Bandura, "Social cognitive theory explains psychosocial functioning in terms of triadic reciprocal causation. In this model of reciprocal determinism, behavior; cognitive, biological, and other personal factors; and environmental events all operate as interacting determinants that influence each other bidirectionally" (1994, p. 61). In other words, things they experience in their environments (e.g., mass media) can affect people's behaviors, and that effect is influenced by various personal factors specific to those people and their situations.

This social cognition through the use of media representations operates in one or more of three ways (see Bandura, 1971, 1994, for excellent extended discussions):

observational learning
When the observation of a behavior is sufficient to learn that behavior

inhibitory effects
The effects of seeing a model punished for a behavior, thus reducing the likelihood that the observer will engage in that behavior

disinhibitory effects
The effects of seeing a model rewarded for a prohibited or threatening behavior, thus increasing the likelihood that the observer will engage in that behavior

vicarious reinforcement
Reinforcement that is observed rather than directly experienced

reinforcement contingencies
The value, positive or negative, associated with a given reinforcer

1. **Observational learning.** Consumers of representations can acquire new patterns of behavior by simply watching these representations. We all know how to shoot a gun, although many of us have never actually performed or been reinforced for that act. Many of us probably even think that we can rob a convenience store. We've seen it done.

2. **Inhibitory effects.** Seeing a model in a representation punished for exhibiting a certain behavior decreases the likelihood that the observers will make that response. It is as if the viewers themselves are actually punished. We see the villain brought low for evil deeds, or in *A Christmas Story* we observe Flick, challenged by Schwartz's triple-dog-dare, with his tongue painfully stuck to the frozen flag pole as the bell rings and his friends scurry away. Our likelihood of responding to various real-world stimuli in similar ways is reduced. Experimental studies using film and video of people being punished for various behaviors have shown that these representations can inhibit in observers such things as aggression, exploratory behavior, and antisocial interaction with peers.

3. **Disinhibitory effects.** A media representation that depicts reward for a threatening or prohibited behavior is often sufficient to increase the likelihood that the consumer of the representation will make that response. A young man sees Johnny Knoxville and his *Jackass* crew set themselves afire, apparently suffering no ill effects. His likelihood of responding to various real-world stimuli in similar ways is increased. Experimental studies using film and television representations of various threatening and prohibited encounters have successfully reduced fear of dentists, dogs, and snakes and increased aggression by reducing viewers' inhibitions regarding such action.

Vicarious reinforcement is central to social cognition through the mass media. Although observational learning can occur in the absence of any reinforcement, vicarious or real, whether observers *actually engage in* that learned behavior is a function of the **reinforcement contingencies** (positive or negative) they associate with it. For example, when we see a television character rewarded or punished for some action, it is as if we ourselves have actually been rewarded or punished. This vicarious reinforcement tells us where to place the observationally learned behavior in our *behavioral hierarchy*—the likelihood that we will choose a given behavior. When presented with certain stimuli in our environment, we will be likely to choose a highly placed behavior for demonstration. One that promises punishment will be given a lower place in that hierarchy. We do not actually have to experience those rewards and sanctions; we have experienced them vicariously through the use of media representations.

Clearly, there are times when we ignore possible negative consequences and perform a behavior that we associate with punishment or restraints, such as running into a burning house. In these cases, sufficient incentive is present in the actual environment (saving a child from the flames, for example) to move that behavior up the

INSTANT ACCESS

Social Cognitive Theory

Strengths

1. Demonstrates causal link between media and behavior
2. Applies across several viewer and viewing situations
3. Has strong explanatory power (e.g., rejects catharsis, stresses importance of environmental and content cues)

Weaknesses

1. Laboratory demonstration raises question of generalizability
2. Experimental demonstration might overestimate media power
3. Has difficulty explaining long-term effects of media consumption
4. Underestimates people's active use of media messages
5. Focuses too narrowly on individual rather than on cultural effects

social prompting
Demonstration of previously learned behavior when it is observed as socially acceptable or without restraints

hierarchy to a point where we choose it from among a number of alternatives. Bandura calls this **social prompting** of previously learned behaviors. This effect is "distinguished from observational learning and disinhibition because no new behavior has been acquired, and disinhibitory processes are not involved because the elicited behavior is socially acceptable and not encumbered by restraints" (2009, p. 108).

Bandura (1965) conducted what is now considered a classic experiment in modeling aggressive behavior from television, one having direct bearing on several aspects of the media effects debate. He showed nursery school children a television program in which a character, Rocky, was either rewarded for aggression (given candy and a soft drink and called a "strong champion") or punished for those same behaviors (reprimanded, called a "bully," and spanked with a rolled-up magazine). Those who saw aggression rewarded showed more aggressive activity in a "free play" period (disinhibition), and those who saw it punished displayed less (inhibition). You can almost hear those people who believe that media have no effects on viewer aggression crowing, "See, the bad guy is punished, so media portrayals of violence actually reduce subsequent aggression."

aggressive cues
Information contained in media portrayals of violence that suggests (or cues) the appropriateness of aggression against specific victims

But Bandura went one step further. He offered those in the inhibited group "sticker-pictures" for each of Rocky's aggressive acts they could demonstrate. Boys and girls alike could produce the "forbidden" behaviors. The environment offered them sufficient reward to demonstrate those observationally learned but previously inhibited behaviors. The response to the "TV violence apologists," then, is simple: The bad guy is usually "out-aggressed" by the good guy, who is rewarded for his or her more proficient display of aggression, and besides, that might not matter because the behaviors are observationally learned and can appear later when the conditions in the viewer's world call them (or similar ones) forward.

AGGRESSIVE CUES

One direct outgrowth of social cognitive theory focuses on the **aggressive cues** inherent in media portrayals of violence. People who see mediated violence are believed to show higher levels of subsequent aggression. The question involves when and against whom do they aggress. The answer is that media portrayals of violence are almost always in some dramatic context, and that context provides information, or *cues,* telling viewers when and against whom violence is acceptable.

Leonard Berkowitz (1965) produced a representative piece of research in which male college students were shown a film of a brutal boxing scene (the closing sequence of the movie *The Champion).* To some, it was presented in the context of a story that said the loser deserved his beating—that is, the violence against him was justified. In a second version of the narrative, the defeated boxer was victimized—that is, the violence against him was unjustified.

The students were then given an opportunity to "grade" another student's design of "an original and imaginative floor plan for a house." Unbeknownst to them, all the participants were given the same floor plan from that other student (who was actually Berkowitz's accomplice). In half the cases, that accomplice introduced himself as a "college boxer," and in the other half as a "speech major." A "new form of grading" was to be used, grading by electrical shock: one shock was very good; ten was very bad. Of course, the accomplice was not actually zapped; the shocks administered by the participants were read by a metering device as the accomplice feigned a response. Any differences in shocking the accomplice would be the result of differences in what participants had seen on the screen. To confuse matters even more, half the participants were insulted (angered) by the experimenter before they began.

priming effects
The idea that presentations in the media heighten the likelihood that people will develop similar thoughts about those things in the real world

cognitive-neoassociationistic perspective
Frequent viewing of violent media portrayals primes particular constructs, making them more likely to be used in behavioral decisions

What happened? The "college boxer" was shocked more than the speech major; the angered subjects gave more shocks regardless of whom they were shocking; and those who had seen the justified version of the film also gave more shocks. Berkowitz's conclusions? First, viewers' *psychological state* can lead them to respond to cues in programs that meet the needs of that state. Second, viewers who see justified violence not only learn the behavior but also learn that it can be a good or useful problem-solving device (disinhibition). Third, cues associated with a victim, in this case a boxer, can disinhibit viewers toward aggression against similar people in the real world. Berkowitz said, "The findings show that the film context can affect the observer's inhibitions against aggression and that the people encountered soon afterwards vary in the extent to which they can evoke aggressive responses from the observer" (p. 368). In a later study (Berkowitz and Geen, 1966), Berkowitz produced similar results simply by having the real-world target of the viewers' aggression share little more than the same first name (Kirk) as the character in the film.

This idea of aggressive cues is supported by contemporary thinking on **priming effects,** which "maintains that the presentation of a certain stimulus having a particular meaning 'primes' other semantically related concepts, thus heightening the likelihood that thoughts with much the same meaning as the presentation stimulus will come to mind" (Jo and Berkowitz, 1994, p. 46). Berkowitz labeled this the **cognitive-neoassociationistic perspective,** explaining "that frequent viewing of violent media portrayals primes particular constructs (e.g., aggression, hostility) and thus makes these constructs more likely to be used in behavioral decisions as well as judgments about others" (Shrum, 2009, p. 56).

In December 2003, a collection of the country's most prominent media effects researchers presented a major overview of the current state of thought on the influence of media violence on youth (Anderson et al., 2003). Published in the journal *Psychological Science in the Public Interest,* it attempted to do three things: (1) assess current thinking on the media-violence link in the wake of new interactive media such as video games and the Internet; (2) counter the "intransigent assertions made by a number of vocal critics" and "various interest groups" that the media-violence link does not exist; and (3) respond to "recent news reports [that] imply the scientific evidence is weaker" than it really is (p. 82). In other words, the researchers wanted to set the record straight. In fact, their report was to have been part of a Surgeon General's report on youth violence in 2000 but was omitted from that government study after "editors sought heavy revisions," presumably because of its critical stance on the issue (Patterson, 2004, p. A4).

The researchers focused on five specific questions, listed here and accompanied by their conclusions. Can you find hints of social cognitive theory? Aggressive cues? Priming effects? Do you accept these findings? Why or why not? Do you fall prey to the third-person effect (Chapter 1)? Try to remember your reactions to these issues when you read later chapters dealing with the most current understandings of media influence. Revisit your thinking to see if you develop a new or different view of the media-violence link.

1. **What does research say about the relation—both short-term and long-term—between media violence and violent behavior?** The researchers offered five general observations:
    a. Media violence has a modest direct effect on serious forms of violent behavior.
    b. There is documented research evidence of the impact of media violence on aggression (including violence).
    c. The research base (scientific methods, samples of people, media genres) for these first two assertions is large and

diverse, and the results are consistent.
    d. For many people, the negative effects of heavy childhood exposure to mediated violence extend well into adulthood, even in the absence of continued consumption of violent fare.
    e. Even people who are not highly aggressive are negatively affected by exposure to violent media, both in the short-term and over longer periods of time (Anderson et al., 2003, p. 104).

2. **How does media violence produce its effects on violent behavior?** "Media violence produces short-term increases in aggression by activating (priming) aggressive thoughts, increasing physiological arousal, and triggering an automatic tendency to imitate observed behaviors (especially among children). Media violence produces long-term increases in aggression and violence by creating long-lasting (and automatically accessible) aggressive scripts and interpretational schemas, and aggression-supporting beliefs and attitudes about appropriate social behavior" (p. 104).

3. **What characteristics of media violence are most influential, and who is most susceptible to such influences?** The causal relationship between media violence and behavior is influenced by: (a) viewer characteristics such as age, aggressiveness, perceptions of the realism of the content, and identification with aggressive characters; (b) viewers' social environment, that is, parents and family; and (c) aspects of the content itself, for example, perpetrator characteristics, realism of portrayal, justification of the violence, and the depiction of its consequences.

4. **How widespread and accessible is violence in the media?** The researchers identify "the abundant presence of electronic media" in our homes and the "extensive presence of violence" across those media. They document the "expansion of opportunities for children's exposure to media violence at home through the proliferation of new media, including video games, music videos, and the Internet." They also suggest that

(continued)

the interactivity of much of the new media may lead to even more powerful effects than those produced by traditional television (p. 104).

5. **How can individuals and society counteract the influence of media violence?** The scientific literature identifies several means of intervention. The most effective, obviously, is reduced exposure to violent content. There is some, but less, evidence of the effectiveness of counter-attitudinal interventions (structured lessons negating themes presented in media portrayals), parental interventions (adults watching and talking with young viewers), and increased media literacy (p. 105).

Aggressive cues, priming effects, and the cognitive-neoassociationistic perspective form the basis of some of the most interesting and controversial media violence research now being conducted. As the link between media violence and viewer aggression came to be generally accepted, attention turned to the issue of violence against a specific target—women. In terms of aggressive cues, media portrayals cue viewers to consider women likely or appropriate targets of violence. In terms of priming effects and the cognitive-neoassociationistic perspective, media presentations of women as victims of violence heighten the likelihood that viewers, when confronted by real-life women, will have similar thoughts (constructs) about them; heavy viewing of such content primes those constructs, increasing the likelihood they will be employed.

Richard Frost and John Stauffer wrote, "But even though members of an audience for a violent film or television program may not be moved to actual behavioral imitation, do they not experience different levels of emotional arousal? ... Could arousal also be influenced by the type of violence being portrayed, such as violence against women as opposed to men?" (1987, p. 29). Two studies (Peterson and Pfost, 1989; Johnson, Jackson, and Gatto, 1995) demonstrated that rock music and rap videos featuring aggression against women could indeed lead, in the Peterson and Pfost work, to negative evaluations of women and, in the Johnson, Jackson, and Gatto work, to greater acceptance of violence toward women and heightened intention to use violence to resolve conflicts with females.

THE CONTEXT OF MEDIATED VIOLENCE

contextual variables

The information (or context) surrounding the presentation of mediated violence

Writing in 1994, Bandura summed the accumulated knowledge of social cognitive theory to conclude that television viewers "acquire lasting attitudes, emotional reactions, and behavioral proclivities towards persons, places, or things that have been associated with modeled emotional experiences" (p. 75). What is it about specific presentations of media violence that encourages this acquisition through modeling? W. James Potter (1997) identified seven important **contextual variables**:

1. **Reward/punishment.** Rewarded aggression is more frequently modeled; punished aggression is less frequently modeled. We know these to be disinhibitory and inhibitory effects, respectively.

2. **Consequences.** Mediated violence accompanied by portrayals of negative or harmful consequences produces less modeling. Again, this shows inhibitory effects at work.

3. **Motive.** Motivated media aggression produces greater levels of modeling, and unjustified media violence results in less viewer aggression. Viewers are cued to the appropriateness (or inappropriateness) of using aggression.

4. **Realism.** Especially with boys, realistic media violence tends to produce more real-world aggression. As Potter explained, "Realistic [media] perpetrators are more likely to reduce inhibitions because their behaviors are more applicable to real life situations than are unrealistic perpetrators such as cartoon or fantasy characters" (p. 234).

5. **Humor.** Because it reduces the seriousness of the behavior, humorously presented media violence leads to the greater probability that viewers will behave aggressively in real life.

6. **Identification with media characters.** The more viewers identify with media characters (e.g., with those they consider like themselves or attractive), the more likely it is that they will model the behaviors demonstrated by those characters.

7. **Arousal.** Potter explained: "Emotional appeals can serve to increase the dramatic nature of the narrative, and this can increase attention, ... positive dispositions toward the characters using violence, ... and higher levels of arousal." This dramatically induced arousal and emotional attachment to violent characters, according to Potter, are "likely to result in aggressive behavior" (p. 235)

ACTIVE THEORY OF TELEVISION VIEWING

active theory
View of television consumption that assumes viewer comprehension causes attention and, therefore, effects or no effects

viewing schema
Interpretational skills that aid people in understanding media content conventions

The operation of these contextual variables underscores the idea that media consumers do indeed bring something to the viewing situation. That is, they make judgments about what it is they are seeing as they consume: for example, is this violence justified? What are the consequences of engaging in that behavior? Presenting "a theory of visual attention to television which has as its central premise the cognitively active nature of television viewing," Daniel Anderson and Elizabeth Lorch (1983, pp. 27–28), as well as several other researchers (e.g., Bryant and Anderson, 1983; Singer and Singer, 1983) challenged the idea that "television viewing is fundamentally reactive and passive."

This **active theory** of television viewing sees viewers in general—and in the violence debate, particularly children—as actively and consciously working to understand television content. The researchers argue that by the age of two and a half, children have sufficiently developed **viewing schema** that allow them to comprehend specific television content conventions. "Beyond two and a half years," they wrote, "visual attention to television increases throughout the preschool years ... and may level off during the school-age years.... We suggest this increase reflects cognitive development, increased world knowledge, and an understanding of the cinematic codes and format structures of television" (Anderson and Lorch, 1983, p. 13).

Those who argue for this active theory of viewing claim that social cognitive theorists generally subscribe "to the proposition that the child is an active, cognitive, and social being [but] television is seen as providing such an exceptionally powerful influence that the child becomes reactive in its presence" (Anderson and Lorch, 1983, p. 5). This pessimistic view of children's viewing and cognitive abilities, they claim, inevitably leads social cognition advocates to overestimate the power of the medium and underestimate the influence that individual viewers have in determining effects. Put another way, "reactive theory" assumes that attention causes comprehension and, therefore, effects. The active theory of television viewing assumes that comprehension causes attention and, therefore, effects (or no effects).

active-audience theories
Theories that focus on assessing what people do with media; audience-centered theories

As we will see in later chapters (especially Chapter 9), this debate over the ability of individual television viewers to resist the influence of powerful content has emerged as a central theme in contemporary media theory. One of the most important sets of media theories is referred to as **active-audience theories**. These theories, which argue that average audience members routinely resist the influence of media content and make it serve their own purposes, are opposed by other perspectives questioning people's ability to resist the influence of messages systematically structured to convey certain meanings. Both types of theories are increasingly supported by growing bodies of empirical evidence. It's quite possible that both are valid, even if they seem to offer contradictory views of the relative power of media over audiences.

THE DEVELOPMENTAL PERSPECTIVE

developmental perspective
The view of learning from media that specifies different intellectual and communication stages in a child's life that influence the nature of media interaction and impact

But obviously not all viewers, especially children, are active viewers, and not all are equally active. This understanding has led to support for the **developmental perspective**, one that assumes that children undergo "extensive and varied cognitive growth between birth and adulthood … that is extremely rich, complex, and multifaceted" (Flavell, 1992, p. 998). As such, this perspective also assumes that an important aspect of people's power to deal with television is their ability to comprehend it at different stages in their intellectual development. Logically, older children will "read" television differently than will younger children. As Ellen Wartella wrote, this developmental perspective "seeks to describe and explain the nature of the communicative differences between four-year-olds, six-year-olds, ten-year-olds, etc., and adults" (1979, p. 7).

Leslie Regan Shade, Nikki Porter, and Wendy Sanchez (2005) made the same argument for the Internet, demonstrating developmental differences in children's ability to understand its true nature, with preteens unable to comprehend that Internet content does not reside "inside" the computer itself. Similarly, Yan found "significant age differences … in technical [the physical reality of computer networks] and social [the personal consequences of Internet use] understandings of the Internet across age groups 9–17" (2009, p. 112).

This notion of developmental stages in children's communicative abilities is drawn from developmental psychology, especially the work of Jean Piaget, who argued that children, as they move from infancy through adolescence, undergo qualitative changes in the level of cognitive and intellectual abilities available to them.

Although it might be easy to assume that older children's processing of television's messages is more developed and therefore somehow better at insulating them from television effects, this was neither the conclusion of developmental research, nor was it the goal. Wartella said, "While questions of children's modeling of televised behavior have been the major focus of experimental and survey research," the developmental perspective asks "new questions and [deals with] different sorts of communication issues regarding children's learning from television and use of television" (1979, pp. 8–9). Much of this research actually focused on differences in attention and comprehension at different stages of development to better tailor educational programming to specific groups of children.

VIDEO GAMES REIGNITE INTEREST IN MEDIA VIOLENCE

The link between television and viewer aggression is accepted by all but the most ardent media defenders. As a result, most recent research attention has focused on violence in video games. Indeed, significant research supports the causal link between violent video games and subsequent player aggression. This work is uniform in its assessment. "Violent videogame play was positively related to aggressive behavior and delinquency" (Anderson and Dill, 2000, p. 772); "Videogame violence [is] positively correlated with trait hostility" (Gentile et al., 2004, p. 18); video game exposure is "related to increases in aggressive behavior … aggressive affect … aggressive cognitions (i.e., aggressive thoughts, beliefs, and attitudes) … and physiological arousal" (Anderson et al., 2003, p. 92).

Mounting research evidence aside, four factors drive this scholarly attention as well as public concern. First is the amount of video game play that children engage in. A nationwide Kaiser Family Foundation study revealed that nearly 9 in 10 young people have a game console at home, and half have a game device in their bedroom (Rideout, Foehr, and Roberts, 2010). Second is the "presence" of video games in high-profile school shootings such as those that occurred in 1999 at Columbine High School in Colorado and in 1998 in Jonesboro, Arkansas. Third is video games' interactivity; that is, *players* are much more involved in the on-screen activity than are television *viewers*. They are participants in the violence, not mere observers. This active involvement in the on-screen violence is problematic because, as social cognitive theory argues, "rehearsal" of observed behaviors greatly increases the amount of modeling (Bandura, 1994), and as Potter (1997) argues, identification and realism increase modeling. What could be more real than aggression in which players themselves participate? With whom could they identify more closely than themselves as they play? Fourth is the sheer brutality of bestselling games such as the *Grand Theft Auto* series in which players control violent, criminal characters or first-person shooter games such as the popular *Call of Duty* games in which players, from their personal point-of-view, employ a variety of weapons in virtual warfare.

A 2010 review of the existing video game effects literature led Craig Anderson and his colleagues to conclude that "debates can and should finally move beyond the simple question of whether violent video game play is a causal risk factor for aggressive behavior; the scientific literature has effectively and clearly shown the answer to be 'yes.' Instead, we believe the public policy debate should move to questions concerning how best to deal with this risk factor.... It is true that as a player you are 'not just moving your hand on a joystick' but are indeed interacting 'with the game psychologically and emotionally.' It is not surprising that when the game involves rehearsing aggressive and violent thoughts and actions, such deep game involvement results in antisocial effects on the player" (Anderson et al., 2010, p. 171).

In sum, "research on violent television and film, videogames, and music reveals unequivocal evidence that media violence increases the likelihood of aggressive and violent behavior in both immediate and long-term contexts" (Anderson et al., 2003, p. 81). This research leads to the accepted contemporary view that "children have many influences operating on them, but the media stand out as the best resource for surveying and understanding the larger social environment, its threats, and its opportunities" (Ball-Rokeach, 2001, p. 16). According to Brandon Centerwall in the *Journal of the American Medical Association,* "Manifestly, every violent act is the result of an array of forces coming together—poverty, crime, alcohol and drug abuse, stress—of which childhood exposure to television is just one. Nevertheless, the epidemiological evidence indicates that if, hypothetically, television technology had never been developed, there would today be 10,000 fewer homicides each year in the United States, 70,000 fewer rapes, and 700,000 fewer injurious assaults" (quoted in Vander Neut, 1999, p. 40). You can assess for yourself the current state of thinking on media violence by reading the box entitled "Setting the Record Straight on Media Violence."

MEDIA AND CHILDREN'S SOCIALIZATION

Mass communication researchers' focus on children extends beyond social cognition and aggression. The issue of media's contribution to children's socialization has attracted significant attention, especially in the areas of understanding of gender (or sex) roles, advertising's effects, and the loss of (or changing the meaning of) childhood.

Quite obviously, children grow up in a mass-mediated world. Today's typical eight- to eighteen-year-old spends daily four hours, twenty-nine minutes with television; two and a half hours listening to music; one and a half hours on the computer; one hour thirteen minutes with videogames; and half an hour with print. In fact, "use of every type of media has increased over the past 10 years, with the exception of reading" (Rideout, Foehr, and Roberts, 2010, p. 2). As such, media become an **early window**. That is, they allow children to see the world well before they are capable of competently interacting with it. Or, as Joshua Meyrowitz (1985, p. 238) explained speaking specifically of television, it "escorts children across the globe even before they have permission to cross the street." What happens to children's social development when television treats them as "mini-adults"? Children's books, for example, are the only types of books that children are capable of reading, and their themes are geared to children's interests and experiences. Yet, as Meyrowitz argues, because all television is "educational television," there's no such thing as "children's television."

early window
The idea that media allow children to see the world before they have the skill to successfully act in it

[Television] allows the very young child to be "present" at adult interactions. Television removes barriers that once divided people of different ages and reading abilities into different social situations. The widespread use of television is equivalent to a broad social decision to allow young children to be present at wars and funerals, courtships and seductions, criminal plots and cocktail parties. Young children may not fully understand the issues of sex, death, crime, and money that are presented to them on television. Or, put differently, they may understand these issues only in childlike ways. Yet television nevertheless exposes them to many topics and behaviors that adults have spent several centuries trying to keep hidden from children. Television thrusts children into a complex adult world, and it provides the impetus for children to ask the meanings of actions and words they would not yet have heard or read about without television. (1985, p. 242)

One thing that children do learn about from the early window is gender (or sex) roles. George Comstock (1991, p. 175) reviewed decades of research on children's sex role socialization and concluded that a "modest but positive association" exists between television exposure and the holding of traditional notions of gender and sex roles. He also acknowledged that those who consume nontraditional portrayals of gender can and do develop similarly nontraditional perceptions of sex roles. Moreover, not only can media portrayals socialize children by encouraging certain expectations of themselves, these portrayals can encourage expectations of others. Comstock wrote: "Portrayals in television and other media of highly attractive persons may encourage dissatisfaction [with] or lowered evaluations of the attractiveness of those of the pertinent sex in real life" (1991, p. 176). Levina Clark and Manka Tiggemann (2007, p. 84) used this line of thinking to examine young girls' satisfaction with their own attractiveness. Searching for the sources of nine- to twelve-year-old girls' "body dissatisfaction," they demonstrated that "increased exposure to appearance media (both television and magazines) and taking part in peer appearance conversations were related to body dissatisfaction and dieting behaviors."

Advertising's impact on children's socialization has been studied from several different angles. Research indicates that although children as young as seven can tell the difference between commercials and other televised content, they might not understand the commercials' selling intent and that much advertising, especially premium advertising (ads that promise a gift or toy with purchase), can cause conflict between parents and children. In addition, the failure of many products to live up to the expectations created for them by children's advertising can lead to frustration and even cynicism (Kunkel et al., 2004). The most recent application of this line of inquiry has centered on the advertising to kids of junk food and sugared snacks (Institute of Medicine, 2006; Committee on Communications, 2006), linking it to epidemic levels of obesity in American children (Hellmich, 2004). Lending emphasis to these investigations is the ban on all such advertising to children under sixteen years old instituted in Great Britain at the end of 2006 (Hall, 2006) and its ubiquity in the United States. According to the Kaiser Family Foundation (2007, p. 3), American children aged two to seven see more than 4,400 food ads a year on television alone; those aged eight to twelve annually view more than 7,600; thirteen- to seventeen-year-olds watch more than 6,000. Half of all advertising time on children's television is devoted to food, and 34 percent of those are for candy and snacks, 28 percent are for cereal, and 10 percent are for fast food (Kaiser, 2007, p. 3).

Research and theory on administrative issues such as the effects of food advertising on children's diets, the link between media violence and aggression, and media use and learning of gender roles have led logically to larger, critical research and theory on childhood itself, or more specifically, on the redefinition or loss of childhood. Sociologist Neil Postman's argument for "the disappearance of childhood" rests in large part on the idea of the early window. He wrote: "Unlike infancy, childhood is a social artifact, not a biological category," one that is "difficult to sustain and, in fact, irrelevant," because ubiquitous connection to the media robs youngsters of "the charm, malleability, innocence, and curiosity" of childhood, leaving them "degraded and then transmogrified into the lesser features of pseudo-adulthood" (1994, pp. xi–xii).

Cultural theorists Shirley Steinberg and Joe Kincheloe take a similar approach when describing *kinderculture*, "the information explosion so characteristic of our contemporary era [that] has played a central role in undermining traditional notions of childhood." They concluded: "Those who have shaped, directed, and used the information technology of the late twentieth century have played an exaggerated role in the reformulation of childhood" (1997, p. 1). Psychologist Susan Linn calls the cultural product of the disappearance of childhood the "adultification of children," in which their "physical, psychological, social, emotional, and spiritual development are all threatened when their value as consumers trumps their value as people" (2004, p. 10). Social critic Benjamin Barber has called for a truly civil society that

> acknowledges the true delights of childhood, and helps children be children again by preserving them from the burdens of an exploitative and violent adult world. It refuses to "empower them" by taking away their dollies and blocks and toy wagons in which to haul them and replacing them with cell phones and videogames and credit cards with which to pay for them. It refuses to "free" them from parents and other gatekeepers in order to turn them over to market-mad pied pipers who lead them over a commercial precipice down into the mall. Children should play not pay, act not watch, learn not shop. Where capitalism can, it should help protect the boundaries of childhood and preserve the guardianship of parents and citizens; otherwise it should get out of the way. Not everything needs to earn a profit, not everyone needs to be a shopper—not all the time. (2007, p. 338)

The work of these last few scholars—Postman, Steinberg and Kincheloe, Linn, and Barber—is not only firmly planted in the critical (rather than administrative) research tradition, but with its critique of the large-scale social and cultural influence of capitalism and the market-driven media system that supports it, it also resides firmly in *other* approaches to mass communication theory that question limited-effects assumptions. But you'll have to wait until the next chapter to read about these ideas.

SUMMARY

New media are always blamed for societal troubles that happen to occur at the time of their introduction. Yet most limited-effects research examining media effects on young people concluded that media influence was, if not inconsequential, at least tempered by traditional forces like church, family, and school. In the 1960s, however, the mass diffusion of a new powerful medium, television, the clear presence of significant social upheaval, and a weakening of those traditional forces' influence over young people gave rise to several penetrating looks at the (macro-level) role of mass communication in the functioning of the American social system as well as the (micro-level) influence of media on viewer aggression.

The rise of functionalism, middle-range, and systems theories in the 1950s and 1960s encouraged theorists to move beyond simplistic, fragmented, linear models of mass communication. At a time when limited-effects notions dominated, functionalism's value-neutrality was attractive to researchers and theorists studying media's influence, especially as functional analyses accepted the presence of latent as well as manifest functions. The strategy of developing middle-range theory offered hope of moving beyond the empirical generalizations produced by run-of-the-mill effects research. These generalizations could be "added up" to create broader theories of media. Ultimately, functionalism's promise to more meaningfully alter the direction of mass communication theory was weakened by its inability to draw definitive conclusions about effects and by what many saw as its status quo orientation, as exemplified by research on the narcotizing dysfunction and mass entertainment theory.

Some mass communication researchers looked to a concept related to functionalism developed by communications engineers, systems, which evolved from cybernetics, the study of the regulation and control of complex machines. Systems consist of sets of parts interlinked so changes in one part induce changes in other parts. Systems theory allows the creation of models demonstrating the interdependence, self-regulation, and goal-orientation of systems. The application of systems theories to mass communication raised many important questions that forced reconsideration of the limited-effects perspective.

Reconsideration of limited-effects thinking about media also came from people interested in the influence of mediated violence on subsequent viewer aggression. Television and children were the focus of this inquiry. Defense of the media (and the limited-effects perspective) came from proponents of catharsis, the idea that viewing violence substitutes for the actual demonstration of aggression by the viewer. But this theory was ultimately discredited as social cognitive theory became widely accepted.

Social cognitive theory proved to be a useful way of understanding how people learn behaviors from television. By differentiating between imitation and identification and identifying several different modeling processes, such as observational learning, inhibitory and disinhibitory effects, and vicarious reinforcement, it helped explain how individuals learn from the media. Even as these ideas have been applied to "new" media such as video games, they have left many questions unanswered, especially as these insights were extrapolated from micro-level analyses (where they were initially formulated) to more macro-level explanations of effects.

Research regarding aggressive cues and priming effects attempted to add some specificity to social cognitive theory, as did the developmental perspective. Another advance was the consideration of different contextual variables, aspects of the presentation of violence in the media content itself, in determining the amount of learning from viewing. Still another was a reconception of the young audience—the active theory of television viewing—that, although not dismissing media effects, did suggest that young viewers have more influence over their interaction with media than social cognitive theory seemed to imply.

The demonstration of significant media effects on individuals naturally led to the critical study of larger, macro-level effects, especially in the realm of mass communication and the socialization of children. Early notions of media as an early window on the world have recently been updated and expanded into important work on the redefinition, or even the loss, of childhood itself.

Critical Thinking Questions

1. Are you convinced of the causal link between mediated violence and subsequent viewer aggression? Why or why not? Was your view altered by the information presented in this chapter? Why or why not? If you are convinced that the link *does not exist*, explain why all the scientists referenced here are so wrong.

2. Are you a video game player? If so, what is your reaction to the research presented in this chapter? If you think it does not apply to you, why is that? What about your friends? Is it possible you are engaging in the third-person effect we discussed in Chapter 1? Do you draw a distinction between different kinds of games or game play when you consider the issue of effects?

3. Do you think childhood has been redefined in contemporary times? Talk about this with your parents. Ask them if they think their childhoods were similar to the one you lived. If they see differences, ask them why they think those differences exist. How much attention do they pay to mass media issues? How much attention do you?

Key Terms

functionalism

communication systems theory

social cognitive theory

manifest functions

latent functions

classic four functions of the media

narcotizing dysfunction

mass entertainment theory

system

cybernetics

feedback loops

communication systems

model

goal-oriented

transmissional model

catharsis

imitation

identification

social learning

operant (or traditional) learning theory

behavioral repertoire

negative reinforcer

modeling

observational learning

inhibitory effects

disinhibitory effects

vicarious reinforcement

reinforcement contingencies

social prompting

aggressive cues

priming effects

cognitive-neoassociationistic perspective

contextual variables

active theory

viewing schema

active-audience theories

developmental perspective

early window

THE EMERGENCE OF CRITICAL AND CULTURAL THEORIES OF MASS COMMUNICATION

Moviegoers in the late 1950s and early 1960s could see the same type of Hollywood spectacular they had become familiar with before World War II. *The Ten Commandments* (1956), *Ben-Hur* (1959), *El Cid* (1961), *Spartacus* (1960), and *Cleopatra* (1963) were gigantic productions filled with color and grandeur. But a different kind of movie was appearing on theater screens with increasing frequency. In the United States, these were called message movies, and they depicted an America that was not universally fair and democratic, a jarring message for the world's mightiest power. Hadn't the United States and its allies just made the world safe for democracy?

The Men (1950) focused on the difficult lot of injured GIs returning home. *Blackboard Jungle* and *Rebel Without a Cause,* both released in 1955, provided stark, pessimistic views of the alienation of youth. *Twelve Angry Men* (1957), *Imitation of Life* (1959), and *To Kill a Mockingbird* (1962) challenged prejudice and racism in the "Land of the Free." *The Pawnbroker* (1964) examined the clash of class and culture in urban America. In Great Britain, message movies became the basis of a powerful cinematic movement, the British New Wave. *Room at the Top* (1959), *The Entertainer* (1960), *A Taste of Honey* (1961), *The L-Shaped Room* (1962), and *The Loneliness of the Long Distance Runner* (1962)—dark, brooding films—"emphasized the poverty of the worker, the squalor of working-class life, the difficulty of keeping a home and keeping one's self-respect at the same time, [and] the social assumptions that sentence a person with no education and a working-class dialect to a lifetime of bare survival.... In the midst of this gray world, the directors focus on a common man reacting to his surroundings—bitter, brutal, angry, tough" (Mast and Kawin, 1996, p. 412).

Anger might have run deeper in England than in the United States, but these films reflected a disillusionment and frustration common to both countries. Soldiers—especially minorities and working-class people—and women who had served their countries well during the war wanted to know why they were denied the full benefits of their countries' wealth and freedoms. Their curiosity turned to resentment because they were unwilling to return to the way things had been before the war. This social unrest manifested itself in both England and the United States in many profound ways—for example, the rise of the civil rights and feminist movements in the United States and the erosion of Great Britain's rigid class structures. The unrest also shaped mass communication theory.

OVERVIEW

Alternatives to the limited-effects perspective can be found in theories other than those we considered in the last chapter. During the 1950s and 1960s, interest in cultural theories of mass communication began to develop and take hold—first in Europe, then in Canada and other British Commonwealth nations, and finally in the United States. As we noted in previous chapters, the limited-effects perspective makes several questionable assumptions and has important limitations. It focuses on whether media content can have an immediate and direct effect on individuals' specific thoughts and actions. Researchers typically look for evidence of these effects using traditional postpositivist approaches, primarily highly structured experiments or surveys. But it is possible to study mass communication in other ways, that is, through cultural studies and critical theory approaches. "The space for these newer models grew," explained researcher Joshua Meyrowitz, "as it became clearer that the stimulus-response concept (even when refined through studies of individual and group differences in response to messages and even when explored in terms of the modulating influence of the opinions of influential peers) did not sufficiently account for the complexity of interactions with media" (2008, p. 642). Instead of focusing on specific effects on individuals, theory can focus on changes in culture, on how shared understandings and social norms change. Instead of trying to locate hundreds of small effects and add them all up, researchers can ask whether the development of mass media has profound implications for the way people create, share, learn, and apply culture.

In this chapter, we will trace the emergence of theories directly addressing questions about the way media might produce profound changes in social life through their subtle influence on the myriad of social practices that form the foundation of everyday life. These new perspectives argued that media might have the power to intrude into and alter how we make sense of ourselves and our social world. Media could alter how we view ourselves, our relationship to others, even the image that we have of our body. Social institutions, including political, economic, and educational institutions, might be disrupted and transformed as media institutions play an increasingly central role in contemporary societies. These theories are quite diverse and offer very different answers to questions about the role of media in social life. In all these theories, the concept of **culture** is central. Media affect society because they affect how culture is created, learned, shared, and applied. Cultural theories offer a broad range of interesting ideas about how media can affect culture and provide many different views concerning the long-term consequences of the cultural changes affected by media. The theories introduced in this chapter, therefore, proved to be quite useful for raising questions about the role of media for individuals and for society.

culture
The learned behavior of members of a given social group

CHANGING TIMES

Children begin watching television attentively by the age of three. Before most children start school or form close relationships with peers, they have learned the names of countless television characters and are fans of particular programs. By the first day of elementary school, they are already watching nearly three hours a day. By eight years old, they are watching four full hours. By the time they finish high school, average teenagers will have spent more time in front of their television sets than they will have been engaged in any other activity except sleep; this means more time with television than in school. Most children also spend more time with their television sets than they do communicating with their friends or family. If other forms of media like radio, MP3 players, movies, video games, magazines, the Internet, and newspapers are considered, the contrast between time spent with media and time with the "actual" world and "real" people becomes even more striking. As the authors of the Kaiser Family Foundation's study of "Generation M^2" (for "media") argued, "As anyone who knows a teen or a tween can attest, media are among the most powerful forces in young people's lives today. Eight- to eighteen-year-olds spend more time with media than in any other activity besides (maybe) sleeping—an average of more than 7½ hours a day, seven days a week. The TV shows they watch, video games they play, songs they listen to, books they read, and websites they visit are an enormous part of their lives, offering a constant stream of messages about families, peers, relationships, gender roles, sex, violence, food, values, clothes, and an abundance of other topics too long to list. (Rideout, Foehr, and Roberts, 2010, p. 2). Increasingly, children and young adults live in a mediated world where face-to-face communication with others is supplemented by and interwoven with a broad range of mediated communication, from instant- and text-messaging to e-mail to television to movies to interactive video games.

Modern mass media dominate everyday communication. From the time children learn to talk, they are mesmerized by the sounds and moving images of *Sesame Street*. Fully 25 percent of American children under two years old have a television set in their bedroom (Hopkinson, 2003). During the teen years, media supply vital information on peer group culture and—most important—the opposite sex. In middle age, as people rear families, they turn to television for convenient entertainment and to magazines and the Internet for tips on raising teenagers. In old age, as physical mobility declines, people turn to television for companionship and advice. Today, not only do 54 percent of all American homes have three or more television sets, but they house more sets (2.86) than human beings (2.5; "More Than," 2009).

Media have become a primary means by which most of us experience or learn about many aspects of the world around us. Even when we don't learn about these things directly from media, we learn about them from other people who get their ideas of the world from media. With the advent of mass media, many forms of folk culture fell into sharp decline. Everyday communication was fundamentally altered. Storytelling and music making ceased to be important for extended families. Instead, nuclear families gathered in front of an enthralling electronic storyteller. Informal social groups dedicated to cultural enrichment disappeared, as did vaudeville and band concerts. It is no coincidence that our culture's respect for older people and the wisdom they hold has declined in the age of media. If respected theorists like Joshua Meyrowitz (1985) and Robert McChesney (2004) are correct, we're losing touch with locally based cultures and are moving into a media-based global cultural environment. If new media researchers like Himanshu Tyagi (Facebook Generation, 2008) and Scott Caplan (2005) are correct, young adults who have inadequate social skills and difficulty with face-to-face communication will turn to e-mail and instant messaging as more comfortable ways of developing or maintaining social relations.

Mass society theory (see Chapter 3) greeted similar types of social change with alarm. It viewed mediated culture as inferior to elite culture. As mass culture spread, theorists feared it would undermine the social order and bring chaos. People's lives would be disrupted. The sudden rise of totalitarian social orders in the 1930s seemed to fulfill these prophecies. In Fascist and Communist nations alike, media were used to propagate new and highly questionable forms of totalitarian culture. But were media ultimately responsible for the creation and promotion of these forms of government? Was the linkage between the new media and their messages so great that the drift into totalitarianism was inevitable? Or could media promote individualism and democracy as easily as they did collectivism and dictatorship? We have struggled with these questions throughout a century of mass communication theory.

During the 1960s and 1970s, as the overt threat of a totalitarian takeover of the United States and the world declined, mass society theory lost its relevancy. By 1960, most mass communication researchers in the United States adopted the limited-effects perspective, which asserts that media rarely produce significant, widespread long-term changes in people's thoughts and actions. Limited-effects researchers no longer assumed that mediated mass culture was inherently antidemocratic. American media had become highly effective promoters of capitalism, individualism, and free enterprise. Today some critics argue that newer media technologies, such as iPods, the Internet, and video-enabled cell phones, are "personal media" that are inherently biased toward individualism and market economies rather than toward collectivism and state control. So the role of media in culture seems to be settled—doesn't it? After all, we've won the Cold War. Shouldn't we conclude that media are benign? Can't we safely ignore the warnings in books like *1984* and *Brave New World*?

cultural studies
Focus on use of media to create forms of culture that structure everyday life

THE CULTURAL TURN IN MEDIA RESEARCH

hegemonic culture
Culture imposed from above or outside that serves the interests of those in dominant social positions

The various cultural theories of media can be identified in several ways. In this chapter, we use a dichotomy widely employed by cultural theorists to differentiate their scholarship (Garnham, 1995): *Microscopic interpretive theories* focus on how individuals and social groups use media to create and foster forms of culture that structure everyday life. These theories are usually referred to as **cultural studies** theory. *Macroscopic structural theories* focus on how media institutions are structured within capitalist economies. These theories focus attention on the way social elites operate media to earn profits and exercise influence in society. They argue that elites sometimes use media to propagate **hegemonic culture** as a means of maintaining their dominant position in the social order. But they also contend that media are used to create and market seemingly apolitical cultural commodities that serve

political economy theories

Focus on social elites' use of economic power to exploit media institutions

to earn profits for those elites. This set of theories is called **political economy theory** because they place priority on understanding how economic power provides a basis for ideological and political power. Some researchers speculate about how alternate forms of culture and innovative media uses are systematically suppressed. These theories directly challenge the status quo by exposing elite manipulation of media and criticizing both hegemonic culture and cultural commodities.

MACROSCOPIC VERSUS MICROSCOPIC THEORIES

Cultural studies theories are less concerned with the long-term consequences of media for the social order and more concerned with looking at how media affect our individual lives. These theories, as we've seen throughout this book, are micro-level, or *microscopic*, because they deemphasize larger issues about the social order in favor of questions involving the everyday life of average people. Political economy theories, by contrast, are *macroscopic* cultural theories. They are less concerned with developing detailed explanations of how individuals are influenced by media and more interested with how the social order as a whole is affected. Ideally, these theories ought to be complementary. Individual-level explanations of what media do to people (or what people do with media) should link to societal-level theories. Yet, until recently, macroscopic and microscopic cultural theories developed in relative isolation. Theorists were separated by differences in geography, politics, and research objectives. But that may be changing, as we'll see in Chapter 11.

Microscopic cultural studies researchers prefer to interpret what is going on in the world immediately around them. Many of them find the social world an endlessly fascinating place. They are intrigued by the mundane, the seemingly trivial, the routine. They view our experience of everyday life and of reality itself as an artificial social construction that we somehow maintain with only occasional minor breakdowns. They want to know what happens when mass media are incorporated into the routines of daily life and play an essential role in shaping our experience of the social world—are there serious disruptions or do media enhance daily experience? Could media be causing problems that are somehow being compensated for or concealed? If so, how does this happen? Will there eventually be a breakdown—are we being systematically desensitized and trained to be aggressive? Or is everyday life being transformed in useful ways—are we somehow becoming kinder and gentler?

Macroscopic researchers are troubled by the narrow focus of microscopic theory. So what if some people experience everyday life in certain ways? Why be concerned about whether everyday life culture is enhanced by media? These researchers demand answers to larger questions. They view media as industries that turn culture into a commodity and sell it for a profit. They want to assess the overall consequences to the social order when these industries become a major part of national economies. In what ways do media affect how politics is conducted, how the national economy operates, how vital social services are delivered? Macroscopic researchers want to know if media are intruding into or disrupting important, large-scale social processes. For example, have media disrupted the conduct of national politics and therefore increased the likelihood that inferior politicians will be elected? Macroscopic researchers believe that such large-scale questions can't be answered if you focus on what individuals are doing with media.

CRITICAL THEORY

critical theories
critical theories
Theories openly
espousing certain
values and using
these values to
evaluate and crit-
icize the status
quo, providing
alternate ways of
interpreting the
social role of mass
media

Some cultural studies and political economy theories are also referred to as **critical theories** because their axiology openly espouses specific values and uses them to evaluate and criticize the status quo. Those who develop critical theories seek social change that will implement their values (Chapter 1). Political economy theories are inherently critical, but many cultural studies theories are not. A critical theory raises questions about the way things are and provides alternate ways of interpreting the social role of mass media. For example, some critical theorists argue that media in general sustain the status quo—even, perhaps especially, when it is under stress or breaking down. Critical theory often provides complex explanations for media's tendency to consistently do so. For example, some critical theorists identify constraints on media practitioners that limit their ability to challenge established authority. They charge that few incentives exist that encourage media professionals to overcome those constraints and that media practitioners consistently fail to even acknowledge them.

Critical theory often analyzes specific social institutions, probing the extent to which valued objectives are sought and achieved. Mass media and the mass culture they promote have become a focus for critical theory. Critical researchers link mass media and mass culture to a variety of social problems. Even when they do not see mass media as the source of specific problems, they criticize media for aggravating or preventing problems from being identified or addressed and solved. For example, a theorist might argue that content production practices of media practitioners either cause or perpetuate specific problems. A common theme in critical theories of media is that content production is so constrained that it inevitably reinforces the status quo and undermines useful efforts to effect constructive social change.

Consider, for example, the last time you read news reports about members of an American social movement strongly challenging the status quo. How were their actions described? How were movement members and their leaders portrayed? Why did the mainstream American media portray college students protesting against the Communist Chinese government in Tiananmen Square as "heroes of democracy" bravely "standing up to tyranny" and those marching in protests against the 2003 invasion of Iraq as "the usual protesters" and "serial protesters" whose "rallies delight Iraq" (Krugman, 2003, p. 288)?

Stories about social movements usually imply problems with the status quo. Movements typically arise because they identify social problems that aren't addressed, and they make demands for social change. Media professionals are caught in the middle of the confrontation. Movement leaders demand coverage of their complaints, and they stage demonstrations designed to draw public attention to their concerns. Elites want to minimize coverage or to exercise "spin control" so coverage favors their positions. How do journalists handle this? How should they handle it? Existing research indicates that this coverage almost always denigrates movements and supports elites (Gitlin, 1980; Goodman, 2004; McChesney, 2004; FAIR, 2005). Coverage focuses on the deviant actions or appearance of some movement members and ignores the way movements define problems and propose solutions for them.

INSTANT ACCESS

Critical Theory

Strengths

1. Is politically based, action-oriented
2. Uses theory and research to plan change in the real world
3. Asks big, important questions about media control and ownership

Weaknesses

1. Is too political; call to action is too subjective
2. Typically lacks scientific verification; based on subjective observation
3. When subjected to scientific verification, often employs innovative but controversial research methods

COMPARING CULTURAL THEORIES WITH THOSE BASED ON EMPIRICAL RESEARCH

It is useful to keep in mind both the strengths and the limitations of the theories introduced in this chapter. Many of the theorists whose ideas we discuss believe that media play a central role in modern social orders or our daily lives. Rather than presenting us with the types of empirical evidence favored by postpositivists, they ask us to accept their view of media influence using logic, argument, and our own powers of observation. Some describe compelling examples to illustrate their arguments. Others offer empirical evidence for their belief in powerful media, but they use innovative research methods, and so their work is challenged and questioned by postpositivist researchers. During the 1970s and 1980s, supporters of the limited-effects perspective were especially troubled by the rise of cultural theories. They were quick to question the evidence offered by cultural theorists. They saw cultural theories as new variations of mass society theory—a theory they felt they had quite effectively debunked in the 1950s and 1960s. Limited-effects researchers believed that cultural theories were too speculative and the empirical research generated from these theories was too loosely structured.

Cultural studies and political economy theorists employ a broad range of research methods and theory-generation strategies, including some that are unsystematic and selective. As a result, critics believe that personal biases and interests inevitably motivate culture researchers and affect the outcome of their work. But, argue cultural theory's defenders, this is acceptable as long as researchers openly acknowledge those biases or interests.

qualitative methods

Research methods that highlight essential differences (distinctive qualities) in phenomena

In contrast with the quantitative empirical research methods described in previous chapters, the techniques used by many critical or cultural researchers are often **qualitative methods;** that is, they highlight essential differences (distinctive qualities) in phenomena. Epistemologically, the creation and advancement of knowledge tends to be accomplished through discourse (debate and discussion) involving proponents of contrasting or opposing theoretical positions. Theory is advanced through the formation of schools of thought in which there is consensus about the validity of a specific body of theory. Often rival schools of theory emerge to challenge existing theories while developing and defending their own. Proof of a theory's power often rests in its ability to attract adherents and be defended against attacks from opponents.

Not surprisingly, researchers who adopt a postpositivist approach find cultural theories hard to accept. They are skeptical of theories evaluated more through discourse than through empirical research. Postpositivist media researchers place far less stress on theory development or criticism. Their research methods are used to generate theory and to *test* theory rather than as a means of making qualitative differentiations. They argue that if empirical research is conducted according to prevailing standards, findings can be readily accepted throughout the research community. If other researchers doubt the validity of specific findings, they can replicate (duplicate) the research and then report conflicting findings. But in truth, these conflicting reports are quite rare and provoke considerable controversy when they are published. Though there is verbal debate between those who espouse conflicting empirically based theories, these disagreements rarely appear in print. When they do, both sides present empirical findings to support their positions. Arguments often center on methodological disputes about the reliability and validity of research findings rather than the strength of the theoretical propositions—researchers disagree about whether appropriate methods were used, question the application of specific methods, or argue that the data were improperly analyzed. Much less attention is given to the structure and consistency of theoretical propositions. When theory is developed, it takes the form of middle-range theory—theory that summarizes sets of empirical generalizations and doesn't make strong assertions or assumptions about the role of media.

THE RISE OF CULTURAL THEORIES IN EUROPE

grand social theories
Highly ambitious, macroscopic, speculative theories that attempt to understand and predict important trends in culture and society

Despite its popularity in American social science, the limited-effects perspective was never widely accepted by social researchers in Europe. European social research has instead continued to be characterized by what U.S. observers regard as **grand social theories**—highly ambitious, macroscopic, speculative theories that attempt to understand and predict important trends in culture and society. Mass society theory was a nineteenth-century example of a European-style grand social theory. It illustrated both the strengths and the limitations of this type of theory. Dissatisfied with these limitations, American social researchers, especially those trained in the Columbia School of empirical social research, chose to construct more modest middle-range theories.

In Europe, the development of grand social theory remained a central concern in the social sciences and humanities after World War II. Mass society theory gave way to a succession of alternate schools of thought. Some were limited to specific nations or specific academic disciplines or even certain universities. Others achieved widespread interest and acceptance. Most were not theories of media—they were theories of society offering observations about media and their place in society or the lives of individuals. Some of the most widely accepted were based on the writings of Karl Marx. **Marxist theory** influenced even the theories created in reaction against it. Marx's ideas formed a foundation or touchstone for much post–World War II European social theory. Cold War politics made them quite controversial in the United States. Theories developed in France or Germany were often not translated into English until several years after they became popular in Europe. Even theories developed in Britain were treated with skepticism and suspicion in the United States.

In the 1970s and 1980s, at the very time that Marxism itself was being rejected as a practical guide for politics and economics all across Europe, grand social

Marxist theory
Theory arguing that the hierarchical class system is at the root of all social problems and must be ended by a revolution of the proletariat

theories based in part on Marxist thought were gaining increasing acceptance (Grossberg and Nelson, 1988). We briefly summarize key arguments in the Marxist perspective and pay particular attention to ideas about media. Then we present some more recent theories based on these ideas.

MARXIST THEORY

Karl Marx developed his theory in the latter part of the nineteenth century, during one of Europe's most volatile periods of social change. In some respects, his is yet another version of mass society theory—but with several very important alterations and additions. Marx was familiar with the grand social theories of his era. He was a student of the most prominent German Idealist philosopher, Georg Wilhelm Friedrich Hegel. Early in his career, Marx drew on Hegel's ideas, but later he constructed his own in opposition to them. From Hegel he derived insights into the human construction of the social world and of human reason itself. But while Hegel attributed social change to a metaphysical force, a "World Spirit," Marx eventually adopted a materialist position—human beings shape the world using the technology and physical resources available to them. It is the availability of and control over technology and resources that limit and determine what people can achieve.

Like some mass society theorists, Marx identified the myriad problems associated with industrialization and urbanization as the consequence of actions taken by powerful elites. Industrialization and urbanization were not inherently bad. Problems resulted when unethical capitalists attempted to maximize personal profits by exploiting workers. On the basis of a similar analysis, conservative mass society theorists demanded restoration of traditional social orders, but Marx was a Utopian, calling for the creation of an entirely new social order in which all social class distinctions would be abolished. The workers should rise against capitalists and demand an end to exploitation. They should band together to seize the means of production (i.e., labor, factories, and land) so they might construct an egalitarian democratic social order—Communism. In Marx's theory, media are one of many modern technologies that must be controlled and used to advance Communism.

base (or substructure) of society
In Marxist theory, the means of production

superstructure
In Marxist theory, a society's culture

ideology
In Marxist theory, ideas present in a culture that mislead average people and encourage them to act against their own interests

Marx argued that the hierarchical class system was at the root of all social problems and must be ended by a revolution of the workers, or proletariat. He believed that elites dominated society primarily through their direct control over the means of production, the **base (or substructure) of society**. But elites also maintained themselves in power through their control over culture, or the **superstructure** of society. Marx saw culture as something elites freely manipulated to mislead average people and encourage them to act against their own interests. He used the term **ideology** to refer to these forms of culture. Ideology fostered a "false consciousness" in the minds of average people so they came to support elite interests rather than their own. Marx believed an ideology operated much like a drug. Those who are under its influence fail to see how they are being exploited—it blinds them or it distracts them. In the worst cases, they are so deceived that they actually undermine their own interests and do things that increase the power of elites while making their own lives even worse.

Marx concluded that the only realistic hope for social change was a revolution in which the masses seized control of the base—the means of production. Control

> ## INSTANT ACCESS
>
> ### Cultural Studies Theory
>
> **Strengths**
>
> 1. Provides focus on how individuals develop their understanding of the social world
> 2. Asks big, important questions about the role of media
> 3. Respects content consumption abilities of audience members
>
> **Weaknesses**
>
> 1. Has little explanatory power at the macroscopic level
> 2. Focuses too narrowly on individual compared with societal effects
> 3. Typically lacks scientific verification; is based on subjective observation
> 4. When subjected to scientific verification, often employs nontraditional (controversial) research methods

over the superstructure—over ideology—would naturally follow. He saw little possibility that reforms in the superstructure could lead to social evolution, or if they could, the resulting transformation would be very slow in coming. These views stemmed in part from his rejection of German Idealist philosophy. Ideologies could be endlessly debated, and existing elites always had ways of making sure their ideas were dominant. Revolution was the quickest and most certain way to bring about necessary change. Elites would never willingly surrender power; it must be taken from them. Little purpose would be served by making minor changes in ideology without first dominating the means of production.

NEO-MARXISM

Most British cultural studies discussed in this and the next chapter are called *neo-Marxist theories* because they deviate from classic Marxist theory in at least one important respect—they focus concern on the superstructure issues of ideology and culture rather than on the base. The importance that neo-Marxists attach to the superstructure has created a fundamental division within Marxist studies. Many neo-Marxists assume that useful change can be achieved through ideological battles—through discourse in the public arena—rather than by violent revolution. Some neo-Marxists have developed critiques of culture that demand radical transformations in the superstructure, whereas others argue that modest reforms can lead to useful changes. Tensions have arisen among Marxist scholars over the value of the work undertaken by the various schools of neo-Marxist theory. Nonetheless, since the end of the Cold War, neo-Marxist positions have achieved great popularity and broad acceptance in the social sciences.

TEXTUAL ANALYSIS AND LITERARY CRITICISM

Modern European cultural studies have a second, very different source—a tradition of humanist criticism of religious and literary texts based in hermeneutics (Chapter 1).

Humanists have specialized in analyzing written texts since the Renaissance. One common objective was to identify those texts having greatest cultural value and interpreting them so their worth would be appreciated and understood by others. These humanists saw texts as a civilizing force in society (Bloom, 1987), and hermeneutics was seen as a scholarly tool that could be used to enhance this force. Humanist scholars ranged from religious humanists, who focused on the Bible or the writings of great theologians, to secular humanists working to identify and preserve what came to be known as the "literary canon"—a body of the great literature. The literary canon was part of what was referred to as **high culture,** a set of cultural artifacts including music, art, literature, and poetry that humanists judged to have the highest value. By identifying and explaining these important texts, humanists attempted to make them more accessible to more people. Their long-term goal was to preserve and gradually raise the level of culture—to enable even more people to become humane and civilized. In this way it would be possible to advance civilization in Europe and its colonies.

high culture
Set of cultural artifacts including music, art, literature, and poetry that humanists judge to have the highest value

Over the years, many different methods for analyzing written texts have emerged from hermeneutic theory. They are now being applied to many other forms of culture, including media content. They share a common purpose: to criticize old and new cultural practices so those most deserving of attention can be identified and explicated and the less deserving can be dismissed. This task can be compared with that of movie critics who tell us which films are good or bad and assist us in appreciating or avoiding them. But movie critics are typically not committed to promoting higher cultural values; most only want to explain which movies we are likely to find entertaining.

Contemporary critical theory includes both neo-Marxist and hermeneutic approaches. Hybrid theories combine both. Before examining these, we will look at some of the historically important schools of critical theory that have produced work that is still influential.

THE FRANKFURT SCHOOL

One early prominent school of neo-Marxist theory developed during the 1920s and 1930s at the University of Frankfurt and became known as the **Frankfurt School.** Two of the most prominent individuals associated with the school were Max Horkheimer, its longtime head, and Theodor Adorno, a prolific and cogent theorist. In contrast with some later forms of neo-Marxism, the Frankfurt School combined Marxist critical theory with hermeneutic theory. Most Frankfurt School theorists were trained in humanistic disciplines but adopted Marxist theories as a basis for analyzing culture and society. Frankfurt School writings identified and promoted various forms of high culture such as symphony music, great literature, and art. Like most secular humanists, members of the Frankfurt School viewed high culture as having its own integrity and inherent value and thought that it should not be used by elites to enhance their personal power. Oskar Negt (1978, p. 62) has argued that Frankfurt School writing can best be understood from a political position that "takes a stand for people's needs, interests, and strivings toward autonomy and which also conscientiously undertakes practical steps toward making these things a reality today."

Frankfurt School
Group of neo-Marxist scholars who worked together in the 1930s at the University of Frankfurt

culture industries
Mass media that turn high culture and folk culture into commodities sold for profit

The Frankfurt School celebrated high culture while denigrating mass culture (Arato and Gebhardt, 1978). In one of their later and most influential books, Adorno and Horkheimer (1972) criticized mass media as **culture industries**—industries that turned high culture and folk culture into commodities sold for profit. The goal of that commodification was "to deceive and mislead ... [having] only one real function: to reproduce incessantly the values of capitalist culture" (O'Brien and Szeman, 2004, p. 105). Here is how Adorno and Horkheimer themselves expressed this view:

> Under monopoly all mass culture is identical, and the lines of its artificial framework begin to show through. The people at the top are no longer so interested in concealing monopoly: as its violence becomes more open, so its power grows. Movies and radio need no longer pretend to be art. The truth that they are just business is made into an ideology in order to justify the rubbish they deliberately produce. They call themselves industries; and when their directors' incomes are published, any doubt about the social utility of the finished products is removed. (1972, p. 121)

Many of the specific criticisms of mass culture offered by Frankfurt School theorists were not that different from those of conservative humanistic scholars. But humanist critics tended to focus on specific media content, whereas Horkheimer and Adorno began to raise questions about the larger industries producing the content.

The Frankfurt School had a direct impact on American social research because the rise of the Nazis forced its Jewish members into exile. Horkheimer, for one, took up residency at the New School for Social Research in New York City. During this period of exile, Frankfurt School theorists remained productive. They devoted considerable effort, for example, to the critical analysis of Nazi culture and the way it undermined and perverted high culture. In their view, Nazism was grounded on a phony, artificially constructed folk culture cynically created and manipulated by Hitler and his propagandists. This hodgepodge of folk culture integrated many bits and pieces of culture borrowed from various Germanic peoples. But Nazism did appeal to a people humiliated by war and deeply troubled by a devastating economic depression. It helped them envision the Germany they longed to see—a unified, proud nation with a long history of achievement and a glorious future. As they rose to power, the Nazis replaced high culture with their pseudo–folk culture and discredited important forms of high culture, especially those created by Jews.

DEVELOPMENT OF NEO-MARXIST THEORY IN BRITAIN

During the 1960s and 1970s, two important schools of neo-Marxist theory emerged in Great Britain: British cultural studies and political economy theory. British cultural studies combines neo-Marxist theory with ideas and research methods derived from diverse sources, including literary criticism, linguistics, anthropology, and history (Hall, 1980a). It attempted to trace historic elite domination over culture, to criticize the social consequences of this domination, and to demonstrate how it continues to be exercised over specific minority groups and subcultures. British cultural studies criticizes and contrasts elite notions of culture, including high culture, with popular everyday forms practiced by minorities and other subcultures. It challenges the superiority of all forms of elite culture, including high culture, and compares it with useful, meaningful forms of popular culture. Hermeneutic attention is shifted from the study of elite cultural artifacts to the study of minority group "lived culture" and the way that media are used by groups to enhance their lives.

Graham Murdock (1989b) traced the rise of British cultural studies during the 1950s and 1960s. Most of its important theorists came from the lower social classes that were the focus of the movies discussed at the beginning of this chapter. The British cultural studies critique of high culture and ideology was an explicit rejection of what its proponents saw as alien forms of culture imposed on minorities. They defended indigenous forms of popular culture as legitimate expressions of minority groups. Raymond Williams was a dominant early theorist and a literary scholar who achieved notoriety with his reappraisals of cultural development in England. Williams pieced together a highly original perspective of how culture develops based on ideas taken from many sources, including literary theories, linguistics, and neo-Marxist writing. He questioned the importance of high culture and took seriously the role of folk culture. Not surprisingly, his ideas were viewed with suspicion and skepticism by many of his colleagues at Cambridge University. Throughout most of his career, he labored in relative obscurity at his own university while achieving a growing reputation among left-wing intellectuals at other academic institutions and in the media.

Toward the end of the 1960s and into the 1970s, Williams (1967, 1974) turned his attention to mass media. Although media weren't the primary focus of his work, he developed an innovative, pessimistic perspective of mass media's role in modern society. His ideas inspired a generation of young British cultural studies scholars, first at the Centre for Contemporary Cultural Studies at the University of Birmingham and then at other universities across England and Europe. Williams was more broadly concerned with issues of cultural change and development, as well as elite domination of culture. Committed to certain basic humanistic values, including cultural pluralism and egalitarianism, he argued that mass media posed a threat to worthwhile cultural development. In contrast with most humanists of his time, Williams rejected the literary canon as a standard, and with it, traditional notions of high culture. But he was equally reluctant to embrace and celebrate folk culture—especially when it was repackaged as popular mass media content. If there were to be genuine progress, he felt, it would have to come through significant reform of social institutions.

The first important school of cultural studies theorists was formed at the University of Birmingham during the 1960s and was led first by Richard Hoggart and then by Stuart Hall. Hall (1982) was especially influential in directing several analyses of mass media that directly challenged limited-effects notions and introduced innovative alternatives. Building on ideas developed by Jurgen Habermas (1971, 1989) and Williams, Hall (1981b) understood ideology to be "those images, concepts, and premises which provide frameworks through which we represent, interpret, understand, and make sense of some aspect of social existence" (p. 31). As such, he argued that mass media in liberal democracies can best be understood as a **pluralistic public forum** in which various forces struggle to shape popular notions about social existence. In this forum, new concepts of social reality are negotiated and new boundary lines between various social worlds are drawn. Unlike traditional neo-Marxists, however, Hall did not argue that elites can maintain complete control over this forum. In his view, elites don't need total control to advance their

pluralistic public forum

In critical theory, the idea that media may provide a place where the power of dominant elites can be challenged

INSTANT ACCESS

British Cultural Studies

Strengths

1. Asserts value of popular culture
2. Empowers "common" people
3. Empowers minorities and values their culture
4. Stresses cultural pluralism and egalitarianism

Weaknesses

1. Is too political; call to action is too subjective
2. Typically lacks scientific verification; is based on subjective observation
3. When subjected to scientific verification, often employs innovative but controversial research methods

interests. The culture expressed in this forum is not a mere superficial reflection of the superstructure but is instead a dynamic creation of opposing groups. To Hall (1981a, p. 228), popular culture "is the ground on which the transformations are worked." Elites, however, *do* retain many advantages in the struggle to define social reality. Counterelite groups must work hard to overcome them. Hall acknowledged that heavy-handed efforts by elites to promote their ideology can fail, and well-planned efforts to promote alternative perspectives can succeed even against great odds. Nevertheless, the advantages enjoyed by elites enable them to retain a long-term hold on power.

A key strength *and* limitation of some British cultural studies theorists is their direct involvement in various radical social movements. In keeping with their commitment to critical theory, they not only study movements but also enlist in and even lead them. Some cultural studies advocates argue that a person cannot be a good social theorist unless he or she is personally committed to bringing about change (O'Connor, 1989). Cultural studies theorists have been active in a broad range of British social movements, including feminism, youth movements, racial and ethnic minority movements, and British Labour party factions. But active involvement can make objective analysis of movements and movement culture difficult. These cultural studies theorists usually don't worry about this because their axiology rejects the possibility of objectivity anyway and dismisses its utility for social research. Their intention is to do research that aids the goals of movements rather than conduct work that serves the traditional aims of scholarship or science.

British cultural studies has addressed many questions, producing a variety of research on popular media content and the use that specific social groups make of it. Does this content exploit and mislead individuals or does it enable them to construct meaningful identities and experiences? Can people take ambiguous content and interpret it in new ways that fundamentally alter its purpose for them? Can useful social change be achieved through cultural reform rather than through social revolution?

In the United States, British cultural studies is influencing research by scholars in many fields, particularly the work of feminists (Long, 1989) and those who study popular culture (Grossberg, 1989). They see it as providing an innovative way of studying media audiences that has many advantages over approaches grounded in limited-effects theory. We will examine some of the most important recent work in Chapter 10.

INSTANT ACCESS

Political Economy Theory

Strengths

1. Focuses on how media are structured and controlled
2. Offers empirical investigation of media finances
3. Seeks link between media content production and media finances

Weaknesses

1. Has little explanatory power at microscopic level
2. Is not concerned with scientific verification; is based on subjective analysis of finances

POLITICAL ECONOMY THEORY

Political economy theorists study elite control of economic institutions, such as banks and stock markets, and then try to show how this control affects many other social institutions, including the mass media (Murdock, 1989a). In certain respects, political economists accept the classic Marxist assumption that the base dominates the superstructure. They investigate the means of production by looking at economic institutions, expecting to find that these institutions shape media to suit their interests and purposes. For example, Herb Schiller, "one of the most widely recognized and influential political economists of communication" (Gerbner, 2001, p. 187), wrote for decades that "corporate influence pervades nearly every aspect of society. From simple things, like our daily diet and the clothes we wear, to matters of larger scale, like the way we communicate with each other" (Schiller, 2000, p. 101).

Political economists have examined how economic constraints limit or bias the forms of mass culture produced and distributed through the media. We've already seen Frankfurt School theorists express similar concerns. Political economists are not interested in investigating how mass culture influences specific groups or subcultures. They focus on how the processes of content production and distribution are constrained. Why do some forms of culture dominate prime-time television schedules whereas other forms are absent? Does audience taste alone explain those differences or can other, less obvious reasons be linked to the interests of economic institutions?

During the past four decades, compared to cultural studies theorists, political economy theorists have worked in relative obscurity. Although political economy theories gained respect in Europe and Canada, they were largely ignored in the United States. Later in this chapter we'll consider the work of Harold Innis, a Canadian economist who pioneered political economy research in Canada. Even though American communication theorists were intrigued by cultural studies theory, few found the views of political economists interesting or persuasive until quite recently, as we'll see in Chapter 11.

Although the two schools of neo-Marxist theory—British cultural studies and political economy theory—appear to be complementary, there has been considerable rivalry between them (Murdock, 1989b). Some genuine theoretical differences separate the two, but they also differ in their research methods and the academic disciplines in which they are based. With their macroscopic focus on economic institutions and their assumption that economic dominance leads to or perpetuates cultural dominance, political economists were slow to acknowledge that cultural changes can affect economic institutions. Nor do political economists recognize the diversity of popular culture or the variety of ways in which people make sense of cultural content. Murdock suggested that the two schools should cooperate rather than compete. For this to happen, however, researchers on both sides would have to give up some of their assumptions and recognize that the superstructure and the base—culture and the media industries—can influence each other. Both types of research are necessary to produce a complete assessment of the role of media.

In Chapter 11, we examine some recent proposals for creating integrated perspectives. One of the most interesting and powerful of these proposals builds on the notions of media as culture industries first proposed by Horkheimer and Adorno. It assesses the ways in which the production and distribution of cultural commodities have profoundly disrupted modern social orders (Enzensberger, 1974; Hay, 1989; Jhally, 1987).

THE DEBATE BETWEEN CULTURAL STUDIES AND POLITICAL ECONOMY THEORISTS

Despite their shared concerns and assumptions, key differences have led to serious debates between these two major schools of cultural theory. Cultural studies theorists tend to ignore the larger social and political context in which media operate. They focus instead on how individuals and groups consume popular culture content. Their research has led them to become increasingly skeptical about the power of elites to promote hegemonic forms of culture. Instead, they have found that average people often resist interpreting media content in ways that would serve elite interests (see the discussion of oppositional decoding in Chapter 9). Some cultural studies theorists have been less interested in making or influencing social policy, and their research often doesn't provide a clear basis for criticizing the status quo. Political economy theorists accuse some cultural studies researchers of abandoning the historical mission of critical theory in favor of an uncritical celebration of popular culture. Political economy adherents argue that it is important for theorists to actively work for social change. You can get some idea of why they think this is important by reading the box entitled "Media Coverage of Work and Workers."

Political economy theorists have remained centrally concerned with the larger social order and elites' ownership of media. They have criticized the growing privatization of European media, the decline of public service media institutions in Europe, and the increasing privatization and centralization of media ownership around the world. They take pride in remaining true to the mission of critical theory by remaining politically active and seeking to shape social policy. They have formed social movements and serve as leaders in others. Above all, political economy theorists are critical—they have an explicit set of values providing a basis for their evaluation of the status quo.

Think *organized labor*. What comes to mind? More than likely strikes (probably rowdy if not violent) and cigar-chomping, burly bosses. Critical theorists, especially political economy theorists, would tell you that these perceptions of labor—work and workers—are a product not only of the American media system, but of a national economy that devalues its poorest workers. "You could argue, without any shortage of compassion," wrote sociologist Barbara Ehrenreich, "that 'Low-Wage Worker Loses Job, Home' is nobody's idea of news." But at a time when the official national unemployment rate had reached double-digits and "blue-collar unemployment is increasing three times as fast as white-collar unemployment" stories such as the *Washington Post's* "Squeaking by on $300,000" and "World's Wealthy Pay a Price in Crisis" seem coldly out of place (Ehrenreich, 2009, p. WK 10; Hart, 2009a, p. 5).

The working poor are invisible in our media system, argue political economists, but all labor, especially organized labor, fares badly as well. What can we expect, they argue, from a system whose celebrity journalists consider $250,000 to be "middle-class" although only 2.0 percent of all U.S. households earn that much (Gross, 2010)? More specifically, they offer media coverage of the 2009 "Miracle on the Hudson" (Langewiesche, 2009) as an example of how working people and their contribution to the nation's well-being are ignored.

That January, Capt. Sully Sullenberger guided his crippled US Airways jetliner to a safe splashdown on the frigid Hudson River minutes after it had taken off from La Guardia Airport. In full view of hundreds of amateur and professional video cameras, "what might have been a catastrophe was averted not only by the pilot's quick thinking and deft maneuvers, but by the nearness of rescue boats" ("All Survive," 2009, p. A1). But were all 155 on-board lives saved by a *miracle* or by the skill of the workers on the plane and boats? Media reports failed to identify the heroes as "labor" or "union people," but on the blog *Firedoglake* we learned that Captain Sullenberger was the former safety chairman for the Airline Pilots Association, his onboard personnel were members of the Association of Flight Attendants, the air traffic controllers who guided him to his dramatic landing were members of the National Air Traffic Controllers Association, the

rescue boats' crews were members of the Seafarers International Union, and the wet-suited divers dropped from helicopters were members of the Patrolmen's Benevolent Association, the Uniformed Firefighters Association, and the Uniformed Fire Officers Association (the same professionals who performed so courageously on September 11, 2001 when the Twin Towers were destroyed; Wheeler, 2009).

Is this much ado about nothing (What does it matter if these folks happened to belong to a union?) or do you agree with David Swanson (2005) of the International Labor Communications Association, who said, "News reports that pay any respect to the interests of working people or to organized labor are virtually non-existent on broadcast television, national cable television, and radio…. Labor news does not exist in the national media that provide most people with their understanding of public affairs. And it exists in the most marginalized, distorted, and silenced way in the corporate print medium"? Media critic Norman Solomon (2006) agrees, writing, "Just about every paper has a 'Business' section where the focus is on CEOs, company managers, profit reports and big-time investors. But a lot more readers are working people—and a daily 'Labor' section would be a welcome addition to the newsprint mix." So does the *Chronicle of Higher Education's* David Glenn, who demands of his fellow journalists, "Maybe a few more of us should abandon our profiles of the most recent YouTube star or today's other vaudeville descendants and make our way to the next textile strike in North Carolina or Pakistan or China" (2007, p. 50).

Mass communication researcher Christopher Martin (2004) collected empirical evidence for Swanson's observations, as did press critic Peter Hart (2005). Hart and his colleagues demonstrated that in one nineteen-month span of Sunday morning network television news shows featuring 364 different guests, only two were representatives of organized labor. Martin examined labor coverage in the three major television networks, *USA Today,* and the *New York Times,* examining their reporting of several high-profile labor strikes in the 1990s, including work stoppages by flight attendants at American Airlines, delivery people at UPS, assembly line workers at a

(Continued)

Michigan GM plant, and the 1994 baseball strike. He discovered that these outlets invariably based their presentations of labor disputes on five "key assumptions":

1. The consumer is always right; reports stress how strikes affect consumers while ignoring workplace issues and conditions leading to the action.
2. The public doesn't need to know about the "process of production," that is, how the workers do their jobs and how that fits into the overall functioning of their organizations.
3. Business leaders are the true heroes of the American economy (they keep costs down; they settle strikes).
4. The workplace is and should be a meritocracy (so why should all workers get a raise or better benefits?).
5. Collective action by workers distorts the market—we all pay more because workers want more.

These assumptions, according to Martin, produce coverage that is inevitably biased against workers because it sets them apart from and in opposition to those in the audience (who, of course, are themselves likely to be workers).

Similarly, Mark Harmon's (2001) examination of labor coverage demonstrated that in disputes between labor and management, network television news tells us that labor makes "demands" while management makes "offers"; it details workers' compensation while ignoring executive pay; and company, not union, logos typically appear onscreen over anchors' shoulders. More recently, David Madland (2008) studied coverage of four economic issues—employment, minimum wage, trade, and credit card debt—in the five highest circulation American newspapers, the three major broadcast networks, and the three top cable news networks. He found that across all four issues, representatives of business were quoted or cited nearly two and a half times as frequently as workers or their union representatives. In coverage of the minimum wage and trade, the views of businesses were quoted more than one and a half times as frequently as those of workers. And in coverage of employment, businesses were quoted or cited more than six times as frequently as workers.

Outcomes such as these are inevitable, argue political economists, because American journalism "is founded on a couple of very bad ideas: It's a bad idea to have journalism mainly carried out by large corporations whose chief interest in news is how to make the maximum amount of money from it. And it's a bad idea to have as these corporations' main or sole source of revenue advertising from other large corporations" (Naureckas, 2009, p. 5). "You don't need to be a rocket scientist or a social scientist," explained syndicated columnist Norman Solomon, "to grasp that multibillion-dollar companies are not going to own, or advertise with, media firms that challenge the power of multibillion-dollar companies" (2009, p. 16).

The relationship between the economic interests of media companies and the corporations they rely and report on, argue political economists, misshapes not only journalism, but the presentation of work and workers in entertainment fare as well, where labor is either invisible or represented by blue collar workers who are physically threatening, lacking in self-control, inarticulate, irrational, unattractive, and overweight—think televised truck drivers and construction workers (Sumser, 1996). When we do see workers on television, "today, the young dudes working ho-hum retail jobs on NBC's *Chuck* and CW's *Reaper* are distracted from the daily grind by their secret identities and truly fantastic adventures," writes *Variety's* Cynthia Littleton. "Who wants to become involved with characters fretting about losing their homes when there's fresh dirt on Britney," she asks, and then answers, "With viewers having so many more entertainment options, major network shows need a high concept hook that is easily marketed as something different" (2008, p. 1). She quotes veteran comedy writer Ken Levine: "If you came in to pitch *Cheers* today, I think the networks would say, 'There's not a lot of sizzle there. It's just people in a bar.'... If the networks said, 'We're looking for blue-collar comedies,' [television would have] blue-collar comedies again" (in Littleton, 2008, p. 81).

Will the commercial television networks ask for programming about work and workers any time soon? Of course not, answer critical theorists; they are immersed in and enriched by a political economy that benefits from the devaluation of work and workers. Your turn. What do you think?

CULTURAL STUDIES: TRANSMISSIONAL VERSUS RITUAL PERSPECTIVES

James Carey was a leading American proponent of cultural studies, writing and speaking prolifically for the past three decades. At a time when U.S. media researchers viewed most cultural studies work with suspicion and skepticism, Carey, in a series of seminal essays (1989), drew on the work of British and Canadian scholars to defend cultural studies and contrast it with the limited-effects perspective. One essential difference he found is that limited-effects theories focus on the transmission of accurate information from a dominant source to passive receivers, whereas cultural studies is concerned with the everyday rituals we rely on to structure and interpret our experiences. Carey argued that the limited-effects view is tied to the **transmissional perspective**—the idea that mass communication is the "process of transmitting messages at a distance for the purpose of control. The archetypal case ... then is persuasion, attitude change, behavior modification, socialization through the transmission of information, influence, or conditioning" (Newcomb and Hirsch, 1983, p. 46). In the transmissional perspective, car commercials attempt to persuade us to buy a certain make of automobile, and political campaign messages are simply that: campaign messages designed to cause us to vote one way or another. They might or might not be effective in causing us to act as they intend.

transmissional perspective
View of mass communication as merely the process of transmitting messages from a distance for the purpose of control

ritual perspective
View of mass communication as the representation of shared belief where reality is produced, maintained, repaired, and transformed

The **ritual perspective,** on the other hand, views mass communication as "not directed toward the extension of messages in space but the maintenance of society in time; not the act of imparting information but the representation of shared beliefs" (Newcomb and Hirsch, 1983, p. 46). Carey (1975a, p. 177) believed, in other words, that "communication is a symbolic process whereby reality is produced, maintained, repaired, and transformed." According to Carey, a car commercial sells more than transportation. It is, depending on its actual content, possibly reaffirming the American sense of independence ("Chevy, the American Revolution!"), reinforcing cultural notions of male and female attractiveness (we don't see many homely actors in these ads), or extolling the personal value of consumption, regardless of the product itself ("Be the first on your block to have one"). Similarly, political campaign messages often say much more about our political system and us as a people than they say about the candidates featured in them.

Carey traced the origin of the ritual view to hermeneutic literary criticism. Scholars who study great literary works have long argued that these texts have far-reaching, long-lasting, and powerful effects on society. A classic example is the impact that Shakespeare has had on Western culture. By reshaping or transforming culture, these works indirectly influence even those who have never read or even heard of them. Literary scholars argue that contemporary cultures are analyzed and defined through their arts, including those arts that depend on media technology. These scholars have not been interested in finding evidence of direct media effects on individuals. They are more concerned with macroscopic questions of cultural evolution—the culture defining itself for itself. Thus ritual perspective theorists presume a grand-scale interaction between the culture, the media used to convey that culture, and the individual media content consumers of that culture.

During the 1970s and 1980s, some communication theorists began to move away from more transmissionally oriented questions like "What effects do media have on society or on individuals?" and "How do people use the media?" toward broader examinations of how cultures become organized, how people negotiate common meaning and are bound by it, and how media systems interact with the culture to affect the way culture develops. This, as we'll see in Chapter 11, allowed cultural theories to become home for a variety of people who presumed the operation of powerful mass media—for example, advertising and market researchers, neo-Marxist media critics, and even sophisticated social researchers. The primary focus was no longer on whether media have certain effects on individuals, but rather on the kind of people we are, we have become, or we are becoming in our mass-mediated world.

RESEARCH ON POPULAR CULTURE IN THE UNITED STATES

During the 1960s and 1970s, some American literary scholars began to focus their research on popular culture. By 1967, this group had grown large enough to have its own division (Popular Literature Section) within the Modern Language Association of America and to establish its own academic journal, *The Journal of Popular Culture*. These scholars were influenced by British cultural studies and by Canadian media scholar Marshall McLuhan. They adapted a variety of theories and research methods, including hermeneutics and historical methods, to study various forms of popular culture. Unlike British critical theorists, most have no links to social movements. They focus much of their attention on television and, now, the Internet as the premier media of the electronic era. Many express optimism about the future and the positive role of electronic media, rather than subscribing to the pessimistic vision of Williams.

Some of the best examples of popular culture research have been provided by Horace Newcomb in *TV: The Most Popular Art* (1974) and in his much-respected anthology, *Television: The Critical View*, which has had several updated editions (2007). These books summarize useful insights produced by researchers in popular culture, emphasizing that popular media content generally, and television programming specifically, are much more complex than they appear on the surface. Multiple levels of meaning are often present, and the content itself is frequently ambiguous.

Sophisticated content producers recognize that if they put many different or ambiguous meanings into their content, they will have a better chance of appealing to different audiences. If these audiences are large and loyal, the programs will have high ratings. Though Newcomb wrote long before the advent of *24, Big Bang Theory,* and *The Simpsons,* and cable television series such as *South Park, Curb Your Enthusiasm, Dexter,* and *Weeds,* these programs illustrate his argument. They make an art of layering one level of meaning on top of another so that fans can watch the same episode over and over to probe its meaning.

multiple points of access
Idea that some people make interpretations at one level of meaning, whereas others make their interpretations at others

A second insight well articulated by Newcomb is that audience interpretations of content are likely to be quite diverse. The fact that some people make interpretations at one level of meaning, whereas others make their interpretations at other levels, is referred to as **multiple points of access**. Some interpretations will be highly idiosyncratic, and some will be very conventional. Sometimes groups of fans will develop a common interpretation, and sometimes individuals are content to find their own meaning without sharing it. This is similar to John Fiske's concept of semiotic democracy (Chapter 2), and we'll revisit it in Chapter 9's discussion of reception studies.

One researcher whose work combines the popular culture approach with neo-Marxist theory is Larry Grossberg (1983, 1989). His take on popular culture "signals [the] belief in an emerging change in the discursive formations of contemporary intellectual life, a change that cuts across the humanities and the social sciences. It suggests that the proper horizon for interpretive activity, whatever its object and whatever its disciplinary base, is the entire field of cultural practices, all of which give meaning, texture, and structure to human life" (Grossberg and Nelson, 1988, p. 1). Although his synthesis has proved controversial (O'Connor, 1989), it gained wide attention. Part of its popularity stems from Grossberg's application of contemporary European theories to the study of popular culture. More recently, he has moved more toward neo-Marxist theory and has coedited two large anthologies of research, *Marxism and the Interpretation of Culture* (Nelson and Grossberg, 1988) and *Cultural Studies* (Grossberg, Nelson, and Treichler, 1992).

The serious study of popular culture poses a direct challenge to mass society theory, the limited-effects perspective, and notions of high culture for several reasons. In asserting the power of audiences to make meaning, popular culture researchers grant a respect to *average* people that is absent from mass society and limited-effects thinking. In treating popular culture as culturally important and worthy of study, they challenge high culture's bedrock assumption of the inherent quality of high-culture artifacts like symphonies and opera. In suggesting that individual audience members use media content to create personally relevant meaning, they open the possibility of media effects that are consumer-generated or -allowed. In short, in arguing the crucial cultural role played by the interaction of people and media texts, researchers studying popular culture lend support to all the cultural theories.

MARSHALL MCLUHAN: THE MEDIUM IS THE MESSAGE AND THE MASSAGE

During the 1960s, a Canadian literary scholar, Marshall McLuhan, gained worldwide prominence as someone who had a profound understanding of electronic media and their impact on both culture and society. McLuhan was highly trained in literary criticism but also read widely in communication theory and history. Although his writings contain few citations to Marx (McLuhan actually castigated Marx for ignoring communication), he based much of his understanding of media's historical role on the work of Harold Innis, a Canadian political economist. Still, in his theory, McLuhan synthesized many other diverse ideas. We place him at the end of this chapter because his most influential writing was done in the 1960s, when cultural studies emerged as a serious challenge to limited-effects perspectives on media. But his work anticipates the development of the culture-centered theories that are the focus of Chapter 11 and so can be read as a preface to much of what is covered in that chapter.

With James Carey, whom many consider the founder of American cultural studies and who shared McLuhan's respect for Innis, McLuhan did much to inspire and legitimize macroscopic theories of media, culture, and society in North America. He wrote at a time when the limited-effects perspective had reached the peak of its popularity among academics in the United States, a time when most American communication researchers regarded macroscopic theory with suspicion, if not outright hostility. In the humanities, it was a time when the high-culture canon still consisted largely of "classic" work (European novels, symphonies, serious theater) produced by, white, Anglo-Saxon males, now dead. McLuhan's focus on the cultural role of popular media quickly posed a challenge both to limited-effects notions and to the canon.

McLuhan and his ideas are again in vogue. It is no small irony that McLuhan, hailed (or denigrated) in the 1960s as the "High Priest of Popcult," the "Metaphysician of Media," and the "Oracle of the Electronic Age," to this day is listed as "Patron Saint" on the masthead of *Wired* magazine, the "Bible of Cyberspace." McLuhan, featured on the March 3, 1967, cover of *Newsweek,* graced the cover of the January 1996 *Wired,* twenty-nine years later.

McLuhan's "theory" is actually a collection of lots of intriguing ideas bound together by some common assumptions. The most central of these, "All media, from the phonetic alphabet to the computer, are extensions of man [sic] that cause deep and lasting changes in him and transforms his environment" (1962, p. 13), argued that *changes in communication technology inevitably produce profound changes in both culture and social order.*

technological determinist
A person who believes that all social, political, economic, and cultural change is inevitably based on the development and diffusion of technology

Even though McLuhan drew on critical cultural theories such as political economy theory to develop his perspective, his work was rejected by political economists because it failed to provide a basis on which to produce positive social change. McLuhan had no links to any political or social movements. He seemed ready to accept whatever changes were dictated by and inherent in communications technology. Because he argued that technology inevitably causes specific changes in how people think, in how society is structured, and in the forms of culture that are created, McLuhan was a **technological determinist.**

HAROLD INNIS: THE BIAS OF COMMUNICATION

Harold Innis was one of the first scholars to systematically speculate at length about the possible linkages between communication media and the various forms of social structure found at certain points in history. In *Empire and Communication* (1950) and *The Bias of Communication* (1951), he argued that the early empires of Egypt, Greece, and Rome were based on elite control of the written word. He contrasted these empires with earlier social orders dependent on the spoken word. Innis maintained that before elite discovery of the written word, dialogue was the dominant mode of public discourse and political authority was much more diffuse. Gradually, the written word became the dominant mode of elite communication, and its power was magnified enormously by the invention of new writing materials (specifically paper) that made writing portable yet enduring. With paper and pen, small centrally located elites were able to gain control over and govern vast regions. Thus new communication media made it possible to create empires.

Innis argued that written word-based empires expanded to the limits imposed by communication technology. Thus expansion did not depend as much on the skills of military generals as it did on the communication media used to disseminate orders from the capital city. Similarly, the structure of later social orders also depended on the media technology available at a certain point in time. For example, the telephone and telegraph permitted even more effective control over larger geographic areas. Everett Rogers paraphrased Innis: "The changing technology of communication acted to reduce the cost and increase the speed and distance of communication, and thus to extend the geographic size of empires" (2000, p. 126). As such, the introduction of new media technology gradually gave centralized elites increased power over space and time.

bias of communication
Innis's idea that communication technology makes centralization of power inevitable

Innis traced the way Canadian elites used various technologies, including the railroad and telegraph, to extend their control across the continent. As a political economist, he harbored a deep suspicion of centralized power and believed that newer forms of communication technology would make even greater centralization inevitable. He referred to this as the inherent **bias of communication**. Because of this bias, the people and the resources of outlying regions that he called *the periphery* are inevitably exploited to serve the interests of elites at *the center.*

MCLUHAN: UNDERSTANDING MEDIA

Although he borrowed freely from Innis, McLuhan didn't dwell on issues of exploitation or centralized control. His views on the cultural consequences of capitalist-dominated media were much more optimistic than those of the Frankfurt School. He was fascinated by the implications of Innis's arguments concerning the transformative power of media technology. He didn't fear the ways this power might be exercised by elites. If the technology itself determines how it can be used, then there is nothing to fear from elites. If media could be used to create empires, what else could they do? Was it possible that media could transform our sensory experiences as well as our social order? After all, the acts of reading a book and viewing a movie or television program employ different sensory organs. During the 1960s, we were clearly moving from an era grounded in print technology to one based on electronic media. McLuhan asked an important question: "If communication technology plays such a critical role in the emergence of new social orders and new forms of culture, what are the implications of abandoning print media in favor of electronic media?"

the medium is the message
McLuhan's idea that new forms of media transform our experience of ourselves and our society, and this influence is ultimately more important than the content of specific messages

McLuhan explained his vision of the implications of the spread of electronic media using catchy, and what proved to be lasting, phrases. He proclaimed that **the medium is the message** *(and the massage).* In other words, new forms of media transform (massage) our experience of ourselves and our society, and this influence is ultimately more important than the content that is transmitted in its specific messages—technology determines experience.

global village
McLuhan's conception of a new form of social organization emerging as instantaneous electronic media tie the entire world into one great social, political, and cultural system

He used the term **global village** to refer to the new form of social organization that would inevitably emerge as instantaneous electronic media tied the entire world into one great social, political, and cultural system. Unlike Innis, McLuhan didn't bother to concern himself with questions about control over this village or whether village members would be exploited. To McLuhan, these questions didn't matter. He was more concerned with microscopic issues, with the impact of media on our senses and where this influence might lead.

the extensions of man
McLuhan's idea that media literally extend sight, hearing, and touch through time and space

McLuhan proclaimed, as we've seen, media to be **the extensions of man** *[sic]* and argued that media quite literally extend sight, hearing, and touch through time and space. Electronic media would open up new vistas for average people and enable us to be everywhere instantaneously. But was this an egalitarian and democratic vision? What would ordinary people do when their senses were extended in this way? Would they succumb to information overload? Would they be stimulated to greater participation in politics? Would they flee into the virtual worlds opened to them by their extended senses? In his writing and interviews, McLuhan tossed out cryptic and frequently contradictory ideas that addressed such questions. Occasionally, his ideas were profound and prophetic. More often, they were arcane, mundane, or just confusing.

Though he was often a cryptic prophet, McLuhan's observations concerning the global village and the role of electronic media in it are seen by many as anticipating the most recent developments in electronic media—this is precisely why the editors of *Wired* made McLuhan their patron saint. At a time when satellite communication was just being developed, he seemed to foretell the rise of twenty-four-hour cable news networks and their ability to seemingly make us eyewitnesses to history as it's made on the battlefield or at the barricade. At a time when mainframe computers filled entire floors of office buildings, he envisioned a time when personal computers would be everywhere and the Internet would give everyone instant access to immense stores of information. But as one media critic (Meyrowitz, 1985) noted, to be everywhere is to be nowhere—to have no sense of place. To have access to information is not the same thing as being able to effectively select and use information. The global village isn't situated in space or time. Is it possible to adjust to living in such an amorphous, ambiguous social structure? Or will the global village merely be a facade used by cynical elites to exploit people? These questions go far beyond the paeans to electronic media that can be found throughout *Understanding Media*.

McLuhan's ideas achieved enormous public popularity. He became one of the first pop culture gurus of the 1960s. His pronouncements on the Nixon/Kennedy presidential race propelled him to national prominence. (Nixon was too "hot" for the "cool" medium of television; Kennedy was appropriately "cool.") McLuhan's ideas received serious attention but then fell into disfavor. Why the rise and sudden fall?

Initially, McLuhan's work fit the spirit of the early 1960s—"The Age of Camelot." In sharp contrast with political economists like Innis or neo-Marxist thinkers like those of the Frankfurt School, he was unabashedly optimistic about the profound but ultimately positive changes in our personal experience, social structure, and culture that new media technology would make possible. Unlike limited-effects theorists, he didn't dismiss media as unimportant. McLuhan was the darling of the media industries—their prophet with honor. For a brief period, he commanded huge fees as a consultant and seminar leader for large companies. His ideas were used to rationalize rapid expansion of electronic media with little concern for their negative consequences. They were corrupted to become broadcast industry gospel: So what if children spend most of their free time in front of television sets and become functionally illiterate? Reading is doomed anyway—why prolong its demise? Eventually, we will all live in a global village where literacy is as unnecessary as it was in preliterate tribal villages. Why worry about the negative consequences of television when it is obviously so much better than the old media it is replacing? Just think of the limitations that print media impose. Linear, logical thinking is far too restrictive. If the triumph of electronic media is inevitable, why not get on with it? No need for government regulation of media. The ideal form of media can be

---

THINKING *about* **THEORY**   **WAS MCLUHAN REALLY AN OPTIMIST?**

McLuhan's writing could be pretty dense at times. But even his critics have had to admit that he was indeed way ahead of his time in anticipating much of the technology we now take for granted. Read what he had to say in *Understanding Media* (1964) about the relationship between the earth's growing population and how its inhabitants might coexist:

> The stepping-up of speed from the mechanical to the instant electric form reverses explosion into implosion. In our present electric age the imploding or contracting energies of our world now clash with the old expansionist and traditional patterns of organization. Until recently our institutions and arrangements, social, political, and economic, had shared a one-way pattern. We still think of it as "explosive," or expansive; and though it no longer obtains, we still talk about the population explosion and the explosion in learning. In fact, it is not the increase of numbers in the world that creates our concern with population. Rather, it is the fact that everybody in the world has to live in the utmost proximity created by our electric involvement in one another's lives. (p. 36)

It's safe to say that by "the utmost proximity created by our electric involvement in one another's lives," McLuhan is invoking the global village, where "proximity" would be enforced and maintained by instantaneous electronic media. But is he saying that this is necessarily a good thing? Remember, many of McLuhan's critics charged that he was overly optimistic about technology's influence. What do you make of "our concern" with population? To be "concerned" about something doesn't imply great optimism.

Technology optimist and McLuhan devotee Joseph C. R. Licklider relied on McLuhan's ideas when writing his seminal 1960 essay called *Man-Computer Symbiosis*. In it he predicted an America composed of citizens linked by "home computer consoles" and "informed about, and interested in, and involved in the process of government…. The political process would essentially be a giant teleconference, and a campaign would be a months-long series of communications among candidates, propagandists, commentators, political action groups, and voters. The key is the self-motivating exhilaration that accompanies truly effective interaction with information through a good console and a good network to a good computer" (quoted in Hafner and Lyon, 1996, p. 34). It was Licklider's, and therefore by extension McLuhan's, writing that encouraged scores of engineers and scientists to move toward the development of the Internet at a time when big, powerful mainframe computers were only just becoming available. McLuhan's and Licklider's optimism was rewarded.

Or was it? Are you an optimist or a pessimist about large numbers of people in close, electronic proximity? What has been your experience with the Internet, in general, and social networking websites like Facebook and Twitter in particular? Have these sites changed the social world of college students for better or worse? Has the Internet transformed the political process into a big, robust conversation, or has the screaming match only become more global and more unwieldy?

McLuhan himself might argue that he never was as optimistic about the "neighborliness" of the global village as his critics liked to assert. Speaking of our electronically imposed proximity, he said, "There is more diversity, less conformity under a single roof in any family than there is with the thousands of families in the same city. The more you create village conditions, the more discontinuity and division and diversity. The global village absolutely insures maximal disagreement on all points" (McLuhan and Stearn, 1967, p. 279).

expected to evolve naturally, no matter what we try to do. No need to worry about media conglomerates. No need to complain about television violence. No need to resist racist or sexist media content. Adopt McLuhan's long-term global perspective. Think big. Think nonlinearly. Just wait for the future to happen. But was McLuhan *really* an optimist about the electronic future? You can judge for yourself by reading the box entitled "Was McLuhan Really an Optimist?"

But even as McLuhan's work became more accepted within the media industries, it aroused increasing criticism within academia. Perhaps the most devastating criticism was offered by other literary critics, who found his ideas too diverse and inconsistent. They were astounded by his notion that literacy was obsolete and found his praise of nonlinear thinking nonsensical or even dangerous. These critics thought nonlinear thinking was just an excuse for logically inconsistent, random thoughts. They called McLuhan's books brainstorms masquerading as scholarship. McLuhan answered by charging that these critics were too pedantic, too concerned with logic and linear thinking. They were too dependent on literacy and print media to be objective about them. They were the elitist defenders of the high-culture canon. Their jobs depended on the survival of literacy. He recommended that they work hard to free their minds from arbitrary limitations. Not surprisingly, few were willing to do so.

Post-positivist media researchers were also uniformly critical of McLuhan, but for different reasons. Although a few tried to design research to study some of his notions, most found his assumptions about the power of media to be absurd. They were indoctrinated in the limited-effects perspective and skeptical about the possibility that media could transform people's experience. Even if this was possible, how could research be designed to systematically study things as amorphous as "people's experience of the social world" or the "global village"? When early small-scale empirical studies failed to support McLuhan's assertions, their suspicions were confirmed. McLuhan was just another grand theorist whose ideas were overly speculative and empirically unverifiable.

McLuhan fared even less well with most critical cultural theorists. Although many of them respected Innis, they found McLuhan's thinking to be a perversion

INSTANT ACCESS

McLuhanism

Strengths

1. Is comprehensive
2. Is macro-level
3. Resonates with general public
4. Elevates cultural value of popular media content
5. Enjoys longevity as a result of introduction of new electronic media

Weaknesses

1. Is empirically unverifiable
2. Is overly optimistic about technology's influence
3. Ignores too many important effects issues
4. Calls for nonlinear thinking, the value of which is questioned
5. Is overly apologetic of electronic media

of Innis's basic ideas. Rather than attempt reform of the superstructure or lead a revolution to take control of the base, McLuhan seemed to be content to wait for technology to lead us forward into the global village. Our fate is in the hands of media technology, and we are constrained to go wherever it leads, he implied. Political economists saw this as a self-fulfilling prophecy, encouraging and sanctioning the development of potentially dangerous new forms of electronic media. These might well lead us to a painful future—a nightmare global village in which we are constantly watched and coerced by remote elites. As long as existing elites remained in power, political economists saw little hope for positive change. They condemned McLuhan for diverting attention from more important work and perverting the radical notions found in Innis's writing. Some political economists even saw McLuhan's ideas as a form of disinformation, deliberately designed to confuse the public so neo-Marxist work would be ignored or misinterpreted.

Despite these criticisms of McLuhan's work, much in it merits attention. Everett Rogers (2000) has argued that McLuhan's perspective deserves more attention by mass communication scholars, especially those interested in studying new media. Some young scholars find it an exciting starting point for their own thinking (Wolf, 1996). This is possible because McLuhan's work is so eclectic and open-ended.

SUMMARY

Over the past four decades, cultural studies and political economy theory have emerged as important alternative perspectives on the role of media in society. These approaches have their intellectual roots in Marxist theory, but they have incorporated and been influenced by other perspectives, including literary criticism. Theorists argue that mass media often support the status quo and interfere with the efforts of social movements to bring about useful social change. But they also argue that ordinary people can resist media influence and that media might provide a pluralistic public forum in which the power of dominant elites can be effectively challenged.

Many forms of theory and research examined in this book are based on postpositivist approaches in which values are excluded as irrelevant to the work at hand. Some cultural theory, however, is critical theory. It is more or less explicitly based on a set of specific social values. Critical theorists use these values to critique existing social institutions and social practices. They also criticize institutions and practices that

undermine or marginalize important values. They offer alternatives to these institutions and practices and develop theory to guide useful social change.

Unlike earlier schools of Marxist theory, or even early neo-Marxist Frankfurt School theory, recent neo-Marxist cultural theorists reject the view that mass media are totally under the control of well-organized dominant elites who cynically manipulate media content in their own interest. Instead, they view media as a pluralistic public forum in which many people and groups can participate. However, they do recognize that elites enjoy many advantages in the forum because most media content, they believe, implicitly or explicitly supports the status quo. Also, critical theorists reject simplistic notions of powerful and negative audience effects like those found in mass society theory. Even when media content explicitly supports the status quo, audiences can reinterpret or reject this content.

The ritual perspective of mass communication as articulated by James Carey sees the media as central to the representation of shared beliefs. This contrasts with the transmissional perspective that views media as mere senders of information, usually for the purpose of control. As dissatisfaction with the limited-effects perspective grew in the 1970s and 1980s, more and more communication theorists, even those with a post-positivist orientation, began to move toward this ritual perspective.

Current research on media has begun to converge on a common set of themes and issues. These are shared by many qualitative and quantitative researchers (see Chapter 11). Cultural studies and political economy theory have played an important role in identifying these themes and prioritizing these issues. Despite questions about the value of these approaches, they have proved heuristic. Cultural theorists make bold assertions and explicitly incorporate values into their work. They provide a useful challenge to mainstream media theory, as do popular culture researchers who grant much power to audiences and cultural value to such popular texts as television series and popular music. Although controversial at the time, the ideas of Marshall McLuhan—many of which were based on the much-respected work of Harold Innis—underlie, at least implicitly, much contemporary critical and cultural theory.

Critical Thinking Questions

1. Critical theory, by definition, questions and challenges the status quo in hopes of changing it. But is this a proper role for any social scientific theory? After all, the status quo seems to be working for most of us; it certainly is for those who engage in critical theory. They probably have nice jobs at comfortable universities or think tanks. Can you reconcile fundamental assumptions about the value of your social system with efforts to change it?

2. Does your hometown or state capital have a sponsored symphony, theater, or dance troupe, for example, the Boston Opera House, the New York Philharmonic, or the Houston Ballet? Why do municipal or state governments offer financial support to elite arts organizations such as these? Shouldn't the market decide? If these operations cannot survive on their own, why should taxpayers underwrite them? After all, does your city or state underwrite hip-hop or jazz clubs, rock 'n' roll or R & B venues? What would someone from the Frankfort School say about this state of affairs? Someone from political economy theory?

3. What kind of car do you want, ideally, once you leave school? Why? What realities do you attribute to what is, in effect, little more than a sophisticated piece of steel, plastic, and glass? Where did these realities originate? How free are you to develop your own personally meaningful reality of the car you drive? And does it matter that you might not be as independent or idiosyncratic as you think? If you think cars are important primarily to men, why would this be the case? Does it suggest that the "reality" of cars is indeed constructed? If not, wouldn't men and women share the same reality? If the question asked you to consider style and fashion instead of cars, would your answers be the same?

Key Terms

culture

cultural studies

hegemonic culture

critical theories

qualitative methods

grand social
theories

Marxist theory

base (or substructure)
of society

superstructure

ideology

high culture

Frankfurt School

culture industries

pluralistic public
forum

transmissional
perspective

ritual perspective

multiple points of
access

technological determinist

bias of communication

the medium is the
message

global village

the extensions of man

Contemporary Mass Communication Theory: From Active-Audience to Meaning-Making Theories

1964	McLuhan's *Understanding Media* published
1965	Color comes to all three commercial TV networks
	Comsat satellite launched
1966	Mendelsohn's *Mass Entertainment* published
	Berger and Luckmann's *The Social Construction of Reality* published
1967	Merton's *On Theoretical Sociology* published
1969	Blumer coins "symbolic interaction"
	ARPANET, forerunner to Internet, goes online
1971	Bandura's *Psychological Modeling* published
1972	*Surgeon General's Report on Television and Social Behavior* released
	McCombs and Shaw introduce "agenda-setting"
	Gerbner's Violence Profile initiated
	FCC requires cable companies to provide "local access"
	Ray Tomlinson develops e-mail
1973	Watergate Hearings broadcast live
1974	Blumler and Katz's *The Uses of Mass Communication* published

	Noelle-Neumann introduces "spiral of silence"
	Goffman pioneers frame analysis
	Home use of VCR introduced
	Term "Internet" coined
1975	ASNE's *Statement of Principles* replaces *Canons*
	Bill Gates and Paul Allen develop operating system for personal computers
1977	Steve Jobs and Stephen Wozniak perfect Apple II
1978	Digital audio and video recording adopted as media industry standard
1981	IBM introduces the PC
	Petty and Cacioppo's Elaboration Likelihood Model introduced
1983	*Journal of Communication* devotes entire issue to "Ferment in the Field"
	CD introduced
1985	Meyrowitz's *No Sense of Place* published
1990	Signorielli and Morgan's *Cultivation Analysis* published
1991	Gulf War explodes, CNN emerges as important news source
1992	ACT disbands, says work is complete
	World Wide Web released
1993	Ten years after "Ferment," *Journal of Communication* tries again with special issue, "The Future of the Field"
1996	Telecommunications Act passes, relaxes broadcast ownership rules, deregulates cable television, mandates television content ratings
1998	*Journal of Communication* devotes entire issue to media literacy
	MP3 introduced
2000	Name change of *"Critical Studies in Mass Communication"* to *"Critical Studies in Media Communication"*
2001	Terrorist attacks on New York City and Washington, D.C.
2003	FCC institutes new, relaxed media ownership rules
	U.S. invasion of Iraq
	Social networking websites appear
	Bloggers' Code of Ethics formalized
2004	*Journalism & Mass Communication Quarterly* focuses edition on media framing
	American Behavioral Scientist devotes two entire issues to media literacy
	Facebook launched
2005	YouTube launched

	News Corp (Rupert Murdoch) buys MySpace
2006	Google buys YouTube
	Twitter launched
2007	*Journal of Communication* publishes special issue on framing, agenda-setting, and priming
2008	*Journal of Communication* publishes special issue on the "intersection" of different mass communication research methods and theoretical approaches
2009	Potter's *Arguing for a General Framework for Mass Media Scholarship* published
	Internet overtakes newspapers as a source of news for Americans
	American Society of Newspaper Editors becomes American Society of News Editors
	Radio and Television News Directors Association becomes Radio Television Digital News Association
	Social networking use exceeds e-mail

Audience Theories: Uses, Reception, and Effects

Consider the ways we use media during a typical day. For most of us, that use is a routine activity that takes up a considerable amount of our free time and requires little planning. With the development of new media and with new technology applied to old media, we can surround ourselves with powerful forms of entertainment and information wherever we go. In the past, we could carry print media with us, but now we can enjoy rich audiovisual media wherever and whenever we choose. If there are empty spaces in our daily routines, we can easily fill them with media content. We can check Facebook or we can send a text message. But why do we use media the way we do? What are we seeking from media, and are we getting what we want? Do media easily satisfy us, or do we constantly change our uses in search of something more? Has the increasing availability of new media enabled us to make changes so that media might better serve us? Or are we merely getting more of the same delivered to us in more attractive audiovisual packages?

During the past five years, the sharing of digital media content on the Internet has risen exponentially. Initially, this growth was driven by Internet music services (legal and otherwise) such as Mog, iTunes, RealPlayer, Kazaa, and Morpheus. But now the Internet is used to share movies, television programs, photos, ebooks; anything that can be digitized can be shared. Millions of college students trade tens of millions of digital files over the net every day.

This sharing of digital content is revolutionizing how we use media. Once we have downloaded and stored content, we can access it any time we want using an ever-increasing array of devices. Sales of devices for storing and playing digital files are rising exponentially. What is going on? Why are so many people becoming so active in their use of media that they are willing to buy expensive new forms of technology and learn somewhat complicated media-use skills? If we are collecting, organizing, and playing digital files, how satisfied are we with what we are doing? Do we enjoy experimenting with the technology? Do we compete with friends to download more files? Do we now have easy access to unusual, highly specialized music we can't get from a local music store (if there still is one)? Do we appreciate the ability to create highly personalized collections of movies or television shows? Do we rely solely on the pay-services, those that are completely legal, or do we wander to the legally questionable peer-to-peer options like BitTorrent and The Pirate Bay?

The digital file-sharing phenomenon provides a dramatic example of how the availability of a new media technology can bring about widespread changes in what people do with media. In turn, these changes can have a powerful impact on the media industries, on technology manufacturers, and on ourselves and the people around us. Even if we don't change our uses of media, we can be affected if others change theirs.

It's important to remember that our personal uses of media are never unique to ourselves—thousands and often millions of other people engage in the same activities—often at the same time. As we have seen in previous chapters, this widespread simultaneous use of media has long been of interest to media researchers. Media audience research dates from the beginning of the twentieth century. Early researchers focused mostly on describing audiences, however, and on determining whether media had direct effects on people. By the 1960s, this research had ceased to produce new insights. Over the last thirty years, however, researchers have turned their attention to new questions and developed new theories of media that have produced a new understanding of why people use specific media and the meaning that use has for them.

This simple idea—that people put specific media and specific media content to specific use in the hopes of having some specific need or set of needs gratified—forms the basis of some of the theories discussed in this chapter. Unlike many of the perspectives we've examined already, these **active-audience theories** do not attempt to understand what the media do to people but, rather, focus on assessing what people do with media. For this reason, they are referred to as audience-centered rather than source-dominated theories. Most are micro-level theories concerned with understanding how and why individuals use media rather than more macro-level perspectives. They have been developed by both empirical and critical or cultural studies researchers.

Much of the postpositivist research we reviewed in previous chapters was "effects research," which assumed that media do things to people, often without their consent or desire. This research typically focused on negative effects—the bad things that happen to people because they use media. Effects were caused by a variety of content, from political propaganda to dramatized presentations of sex and violence. Later in this chapter we will look at how this type of effects research has evolved beyond the classic limited-effects findings considered in Chapter 6. But first we consider a very different type of media effects—positive effects we consciously or routinely seek every time we turn to media for some particular purpose.

Study of these effects was slow to develop. Mass society theory and the response to it focused researchers' attention on the unintended negative consequences of media. Audience members were seen as passively responding to whatever content media companies made available to them. There were some early critics of this viewpoint. For example, John Dewey (1927) argued that educated people could make good use of media. To him, propaganda was a problem that should be solved through public education rather than censorship; if people could be taught to make better use of

active-audience theories

Theories that focus on assessing what people do with media; audience-centered theories

media content, they wouldn't need to be sheltered from it (Chapter 4). Despite these arguments, empirical research remained focused on locating evidence of how average people were manipulated by media. Similarly, early political economy and cultural studies research assumed that mass audiences were easily manipulated by elites. Media content served to promote false consciousness that led people to act against their interests.

Eventually, effects research found that people weren't as vulnerable to propaganda as had been predicted by mass society theory. People were protected from manipulation by opinion leaders and their own well-formed, intensely held attitudes. But even this seemingly optimistic conclusion was associated with a pessimistic view of the average person. Researchers concluded that if the barriers protecting people were broken down, individuals could be easily manipulated. They were slow to develop the perspective that average people can be responsible media consumers who use media for their own worthwhile purposes—an active audience.

The theories covered in this chapter are similar to those in the next. The major difference between them resides in their attention to and concern about the larger social order in which media operate. Those in this chapter for the most part ignore the larger social order and concentrate on understanding how audiences routinely use media and are affected by this use. They ask, "Why do people seek information from media or how do they cope with the flow of information from media?" They don't ask, "Should people be seeking information from media or what are the consequences for society when people learn or fail to learn from media each day?" This doesn't mean the findings generated by the theories covered in this chapter don't have larger implications or can't be used to answer questions about the social order.

OVERVIEW

During the 1970s and 1980s, empirical and cultural studies researchers became increasingly focused on media audiences. Their goal was to gain a more useful understanding of what people were doing with media in their daily lives. Television viewing was escalating during the 1960s and 1970s, but very little research was undertaken to examine what people were doing when they watched. Were viewers primarily passive consumers of entertainment, or was television viewing serving more important purposes? Were people couch potatoes or serious viewers? As this research developed, new and less pessimistic conceptualizations of audiences were formed. Empirical researchers reexamined limited-effects assumptions about audiences and argued that people were not as passive as these effects theories implied. At the same time, cultural studies researchers were conducting their own audience research and discovering that the power of elites to manipulate audiences was not as great as had been assumed by the Frankfurt School theorists (Chapter 8).

Of course, the possibility of responsible audience activity was never totally ignored in early media research, but much of it gave audiences insufficient credit for selection, interpretation, and use of media content. We will see that early development of audience-centered theory was hampered by confusion about the ideas of "functions" and "functionalism" and by methodological and theoretical disputes.

We will discuss what it means to be an active audience member and examine in detail several audience-centered approaches.

The theories introduced in the early part of this chapter are important because they were among the first to make a priority of studying audience activity, viewing it in a more or less positive way. As we shall see, this doesn't mean they ignored the possibility of long-term negative consequences. Active audiences can still be misled by poorly constructed or inaccurate media presentations. We will explain how the development of audience-centered theories challenged the limited-effects perspective. In doing so, we revisit functional analysis and discuss how it formed the basis of much audience-centered theory. We describe the uses-and-gratifications approach, both as initially conceived and as it matured and developed. We explore some of its central notions—for example, the meaning of an active audience, how activity is measured, and the use of the approach to understand effects. We will also consider another audience-centered theory, reception studies, developed by cultural studies researchers in Britain. It also assumes that audiences are active, but it uses a different strategy for studying them and reaches different conclusions.

In the second section of this chapter, we look at three examples of theories grounded in and guided by postpositivist studies of media effects. They are a continuation of the inquiry that produced limited-effects conclusions in the 1950s and 1960s. Contemporary effects research is finding evidence of stronger effects than the earlier work, but these effects are still quite modest compared to those we consider in Chapter 11. The label *moderate-effects theory* can be applied to some of the theories we consider. They still identify many important barriers to media effects, but they have located many factors that increase the ability of media to have influence.

We conclude the chapter with a discussion of the future of audience theories. New technologies are transforming how media are used, and this has led some scholars to argue that the concept of *audiences* is outmoded. Are there *audiences* when only a few people use the same medium at the same time? Do the millions of people who log onto Facebook every day constitute an audience when they share content with each other, or are they an audience only when they use the various forms of media content supplied via Facebook? In the days of network television there were nationwide audiences, all watching a few channels at the same time. Audience members numbered in the tens of millions, and each individual member was exposed to exactly the same content at the same time. But today, the highest-rated programs would not rank in the top twenty-five from 1975. Should we be using the term *audience* to refer to *users* of Internet websites? Of interactive websites? Who's the audience and who's the source? Is a new concept needed? Might it be "networked publics," as suggested by the MacArthur Foundation's *Living and Learning with New Media Report*: "The growing availability of digital media-production tools and infrastructure, combined with the traffic in media across social connections and networks, is creating convergence between mass media and online communication…. Rather than conceptualize everyday media engagement as 'consumption' by 'audiences,' the term *networked publics* foregrounds the active participation of a distributed social network in the production and circulation of culture and knowledge" (Ito et al., 2009, p. xv).

AUDIENCE THEORIES: FROM SOURCE-DOMINATED TO ACTIVE-AUDIENCE PERSPECTIVES

Propaganda theories are concerned with audiences. As we saw in Chapter 4, the power of propaganda resides in its ability to quickly reach vast audiences and expose them to the same simple but subversive messages. In these theories, the propagandist dominates the audience and controls the messages that reach it. The focus is on how propagandists are able to manipulate audiences using messages that affect them as the propagandist intends. Most are source-dominated theories. They center their attention primarily on message sources and content, not on the audiences the sources want to influence. As media theories have developed, this focus has gradually shifted. As early as the 1940s, the work of people like Herta Herzog, Paul Lazarsfeld, and Frank Stanton reflected at least the implicit concern for studying an active, gratifications-seeking audience. Lazarsfeld and Stanton (1942) produced a series of books and studies throughout the 1940s that paid significant attention to how audiences used media to organize their lives and experiences. For example, they studied the value of early-morning radio reports to farmers. As part of the Lazarsfeld and Stanton series, Bernard Berelson (1949) published a classic media-use study of the disruption experienced by readers during a newspaper strike. He reported convincing evidence that newspapers formed an important part of many people's daily routine.

uses-and-gratifications approach
Approach to media study focusing on the uses to which people put media and the gratifications they seek from those uses

Herta Herzog is often credited as the originator of the **uses-and-gratifications approach**, although she most likely did not give it its label. Interested in how and why people listened to the radio, she studied fans of a popular quiz show (1940) and soap opera listeners (1944). This latter work, entitled "Motivations and Gratifications of Daily Serial Listeners," provides an in-depth examination of media gratifications. She interviewed one hundred radio soap opera fans and identified "three major types of gratification." First, listening was "merely a means of emotional release"; "a second and commonly recognized form of enjoyment concerns the opportunities for wishful thinking"; and the "third and commonly unsuspected form of gratification concerns the advice obtained from listening to daytime serials." Herzog wanted to understand why so many housewives were attracted to radio soap operas. In contrast with the typical effects research conducted in Lazarsfeld's shop, her work didn't try to measure the influence that soap operas had on women. She was satisfied with assessing their reasons and experiences—their uses and gratifications.

fraction of selection
Schramm's graphic description of how individuals make media and content choices based on expectation of reward and effort required

One of the first college mass communication textbooks, *The Process and Effects of Mass Communication,* offered an early active-audience conceptualization. Author Wilbur Schramm (1954) asked this question, "What determines which offerings of mass communication will be selected by a given individual?" (p. 19). The answer was the **fraction of selection**:

$$\frac{\text{Expectation of Reward}}{\text{Effort Required}}$$

His point was that people weigh the level of reward (gratification) they expect from a given medium or message against how much effort they must make to secure that reward. Review your own news consumption, for example. Of course, it's easier to watch the network television news or flip on CNN than it is to get your news online. Television news is presented attractively and dramatically. The images are usually arresting, and the narration and anchorperson's report are typically crisp and to the point. You never have to leave your chair to watch, once you settle on a specific news broadcast you don't have to touch the remote again, and when the show you're watching ends, you're already in place for *American Idol*. This concerns only the denominator (effort required), and there is little effort required to consume a televised news program.

But you might instead choose to get your news from the Internet because the reward you expect from your online news (news anytime you want it, ability to select just the stories you are interested in, more detail, greater depth, more variety of approach, more sophisticated reports, alternative perspectives, useful links) makes the additional effort (waiting for the server to connect you to your search engine, identifying the sites you're interested in, selecting specific reports, reading them, searching for alternative stories, accessing related links) worthwhile. You can develop your own fractions for your own media use of all kinds, but the essence of Schramm's argument remains: we all make decisions about which content we choose based on our expectations of having some need met, even if that decision is to not make a choice—say between two early evening situation comedies, for example, because we can't find the remote control and it's too much trouble to get up and change the channel—because all we really want is some background noise while we sit and daydream.

LIMITATIONS OF EARLY AUDIENCE-CENTERED RESEARCH

If this is all so seemingly logical and straightforward, why didn't early mass communication researchers create theories focused on active audiences? Why didn't such theories emerge as strong alternatives to limited-effects theories? Why were source-dominated theories so powerful and why did their influence persist so long? There are many possible answers. We have seen how mass society theory exaggerated the influence of media and centered widespread public concern on negative media effects. Since the 1930s, government agencies, private foundations, and the media industry all have been willing to provide funding to study a broad range of positive and negative effects, but little money was provided to study audience activity. Researchers also thought that it was possible to study effects more objectively than media uses could be studied. For example, behavioral or attitudinal effects might be observed in a laboratory following exposure to media content. On the other hand, studying gratifications meant asking people to report on their subjective experience of content. Herzog (1940) recommended using qualitative research to study media gratifications. During the 1940s and 1950s, postpositivist researchers were determined to avoid approaches that were unparsimonious and didn't meet what they regarded as scientific standards. They chose to focus their efforts on developing what they thought would be definitive, powerful explanations for the consequences of media use. They didn't see as much purpose or value in describing and cataloging people's subjective reasons for using media.

Additionally, these researchers could see little reason why studying people's subjective explanations would serve any purpose other than satisfying curiosity about why so many people wasted so much time using mass media. As far as they were concerned, the only thing they needed to know about an audience was its size and demographics (the social attributes of audience members like age, gender, income, education). Early media researchers devoted considerable effort and expense to developing scientific methods for measuring audience size and composition. These were things that advertisers wanted to know so they could better target their ads and gauge their effectiveness. But advertisers had little practical interest in why people sought out radio programs or read newspapers.

Early media researchers also had good reason to believe that the study of media gratifications would be difficult using available scientific methods. Most attitude researchers had strong behaviorist biases that led them to be suspicious of taking people's thoughts and experiences at face value. Did people really have any useful insight into why they use media? As we saw in Chapter 4, behaviorists believed that conscious thought only serves to provide rationalizations for actions people have been conditioned to make. To understand what really motivates people to act as they do, social scientists must observe how they have been conditioned through exposure to stimuli in past situations. But this would be very difficult and costly.

Postpositive researchers criticized active-audience research as too descriptive—it did little more than group people's reasons for using media into sets of arbitrarily chosen categories. Why one set of categories rather than another? Moreover, the categorization process itself was dismissed as arbitrary and subjective. For example, Herzog placed her listeners' reasons into three categories—why not five? Where did her categories come from, and how could we be certain she wasn't arbitrarily putting reasons into these categories? In contrast, experimental attitude-change research used what most researchers regarded as a scientifically sound set of procedures. This type of research produced causal explanations rather than simple descriptions of subjective perceptions. As long as this effects research (even that based on the limited-effects model) offered the hope of producing significant new insight into the causal power of media, researchers had little motivation to test alternate approaches.

CONFUSION OF MEDIA FUNCTIONS AND MEDIA USES

In Chapter 7, we described functional analysis and its use by early media researchers. By the 1960s, notions of an active and gratification-seeking audience had been absorbed into and confused with functional analysis. Failure to adequately differentiate media *uses* from media *functions* impeded the design and interpretation of audience-centered research. Charles Wright explicitly linked the active audience to functionalism in his 1959 textbook. This linkage to functions had a detrimental influence on the development of active-audience theories. Although Wright cautioned his readers to distinguish "between the consequences (functions) of a social activity and the aims or purposes behind the activity" (p. 16), functions were assumed by most communication theorists to be equivalent to (synonymous with) the aims or goals of the media industries themselves. To some extent this confusion over audience uses and societal functions also involves confusion about levels of analysis. As an audience member you may have certain purposes for reading a newspaper, and this activity will gratify some of these purposes. But you are only one of many people who will read that newspaper on a given day. Other people have other purposes that may be very different from your own. They will experience different gratifications. Functionalism is not concerned with individuals; it's concerned with overall functions for society that are served by mass media.

As explained in Chapter 7, functionalism often serves to legitimize the status quo. It tends to assume that if the social order is stable, things are in balance—bad functions are offset by good functions. To the extent that active-audience notions were conceptually confused with functionalism, they were seen by critics as merely another way to rationalize the way things are.

Let's use the classic four functions as an example. *Surveillance of the environment* refers to the media's collection and distribution of information. We know who was elected governor of Illinois because it was in the newspaper, and we know whether to wear a sweater to class because the radio weather forecaster said that it would be chilly today. *Correlation of parts of society* refers to the media's interpretive or analytical activities. We know that the failure of the highway bond proposition means that gasoline taxes will rise to cover necessary road repair because of the editorial in the Sunday paper. *Transmission of the social heritage* relates to the media's ability to communicate values, norms, and styles across time and between groups. What were typical attitudes toward women in the 1930s? What did an American home look like in the 1950s? Any of two hundred old movies can answer the former question, and *Leave It to Beaver* answers the latter. What's happening in French fashion today? Pick up a copy of *Paris Match*. Finally, *entertainment* means media's ability to entertain or amuse.

These seem like perfectly reasonable aims of the media, but there is a problem. These might be aims of given media organizations, but they might not necessarily be the purposes they serve for the people who consume those media, and these functions can be different from the intended uses of audience members. For example, you might intentionally watch an old black-and-white gangster movie to be entertained, and you might even learn (unintentionally) a bit about how people at the time viewed lawlessness. But in the course of watching you might also inadvertently learn how to use a pistol. The filmmaker's aim was to entertain, but the use (the purpose) to which you ultimately put the content was much different. Transmission of the cultural heritage occurred (although that was not the filmmaker's aim), as did some learning of potentially dangerous behavior (although that, too, was no one's aim). In other words, the source's aim is not always the ultimate function. If we confine our research to an investigation of functions intended by media practitioners (their aims), we are likely to ignore many negative effects. Because much early functional analysis was restricted to intended functions (again, aims), critics have charged that it is too apologetic to the media industries.

Wright, realizing how his conceptualization of media functions was misinterpreted, later wrote:

> Our working quartet of communications—surveillance, correlation, cultural transmission, and entertainment—was intended to refer to common kinds of activities that might or might not be carried out as mass communications or as private, personal communications. These activities were not synonymous for functions, which ... refer to the consequences of routinely carrying out such communication activities through the institutionalized processes of mass communications. (1974, p. 205)

The surveillance activity, its functions in our society, and the effects of those functions offer a good example of how Wright intended functionalism to be applied to media studies. Newspapers and television news devote significant energy and effort to covering political campaigns and delivering the product of that effort to their audiences. If readers and viewers ignore (i.e., fail to use) the reports, no communication happens and the intended functions fail to occur. But if readers and viewers do consume the reports, then the intended function we've been calling surveillance of the environment should take place. If so, then there should be certain effects—readers and viewers should learn specific information from the news. Thus media cannot serve their intended function unless people make certain uses of their content. For surveillance to occur, routine transmission of news information about key events must be accompanied by active audience use that results in widespread learning about those events. Thus news media can achieve this societal-level function only if enough audience members are willing and able to make certain uses of content and do so frequently and routinely.

As was implied in Chapter 5's discussion of Libertarianism, one historically important and widely intended function of public communication is the creation and maintenance of an enlightened and knowledgeable electorate, one capable of governing itself. But many of us might argue that most current-day news media transmit "infotainment" that actually serves a negative function (a dysfunction) in that it produces ill-educated citizens or citizens who actually become less involved in the political process because they substitute pseudo-involvement in overdramatized media depictions of campaign spectacles for actual involvement in real campaign activities (Edelman, 1988).

What we've done in this example, though, has been to confuse intended functions with unintended effects, just as Wright warned us against. The intended function of the reporting of those events and our intended use of the reports might be consistent with a normative theory (Libertarianism) underlying our political and media system. The overall consequences of that activity, however, might well be something completely different. As political campaigns cater more and more to the time, economic, and aesthetic demands of the broadcast media (less complexity, more staging of campaign spectacles, less talk about complex and controversial issues, more reliance on negative ads, and so on), voters might become cynical about politics, which might undermine support for government and inadvertently increase the influence of well-organized special interest groups. Voters' use of media might gradually change so instead of seeking information that isn't there, they turn to media for the mesmerizing spectacles that are available. In this example, the intended function of media hasn't changed, but its practical consequences have. These gaps between intended functions and observed societal consequences have impressed media critics, leading them to be suspicious of both functional analysis and theories that presume an active audience.

REVIVAL OF THE USES-AND-GRATIFICATIONS APPROACH

Interest in studying the audience's uses of the media and the gratifications the audience receives from the media had two revivals. The first occurred during the 1970s, partly as a response to the inconsequential and overqualified findings of run-of-the-mill effects research. As we discussed earlier, by the 1960s most of the important tenets of the limited-effects perspective had been worked out and demonstrated in study after study. In all this research, media's role was found to be marginal in comparison with other social factors. But how could this be true when media audiences were so vast and so many people spent so much time consuming media? Why were advertisers spending billions to purchase advertising time if their messages had no effect? Why were network television audiences continuing to grow? Didn't any of this media use have important consequences for the people who were engaging in it? If so, why didn't effects research document this influence? Was it overlooking something—and if so, what?

The limited-effects perspective had become so dominant in the United States that it was hard to ask questions about media that weren't stated in terms of measurable effects. There just didn't seem to be anything else worth studying. But if researchers restricted their inquiry to the study of effects, all they could obtain would be predictable, modest, highly qualified results. Though they were frustrated by this situation, few could see any practical alternative.

This first revival of interest in the uses-and-gratifications approach can be traced to three developments—one methodological and two theoretical:

1. **New survey research methods and data analysis techniques allowed the development of important new strategies for studying and interpreting audience uses and gratifications.** Researchers developed innovative questionnaires that allowed people's reasons for using media to be measured more systematically and objectively. At the same time, new data analysis techniques provided more objective procedures for developing categories and for assigning reasons to them. Also, a large new generation of media researchers entered the academy in the 1970s. They were trained in the use of survey methods. As the decade advanced, the computer resources necessary to apply these methods were increasingly available. These developments overcame some of the most serious methodological barriers to active-audience research.

2. **During the 1970s, some media researchers developed increasing awareness that people's active use of media might be an important mediating factor making effects more or less likely.** They argued that a member of an active audience can decide whether certain media effects are desirable and set out to achieve those effects. For example, you might have decided to read this book to learn about media theories. You intend the book to have this effect on you, and you work to induce the effect. If you lack this intent and read the book for entertainment, use of the book is less likely to result in learning. Does the book cause you to learn? Or do you make it serve this purpose for you? If you hold the latter view, then you share the perspective of active-audience theorists.

3. **Some researchers began expressing growing concern that effects research was focusing too much on unintended negative effects of media while intended positive uses of media were being ignored.** By 1975, we knew a lot about the influence of television violence on small segments of the audience (most notably preadolescent boys) but much less about how most people were seeking to make media do things that they wanted.

The second and more recent revival of interest in uses and gratifications, as you might have guessed from this chapter's opening, is the product of the ongoing development and diffusion of new Internet applications, most specifically because of the interactivity they encourage. Arguing that "uses-and-gratifications has always provided a cutting-edge theoretical approach in the initial stages of each new mass communications medium," Thomas Ruggiero (2000, p. 3) identified three characteristics of computer-mediated mass communication that "offer a vast continuum of communication behaviors" for uses-and-gratifications researchers to examine:

- *Interactivity* "significantly strengthens the core [uses-and-gratifications] notion of active user" (Ruggiero, 2000, p. 15) because interactivity in mass communication has long been considered "the degree to which participants in the communication process have control over, and can change roles in their mutual discourse" (Williams, Rice, and Rogers, 1988, p. 10).
- *Demassification* is "the ability of the media user to select from a wide menu.... Unlike traditional mass media, new media like the Internet provide selectivity characteristics that allow individuals to tailor messages to their needs" (Ruggiero, 2000, p. 16).
- *Asynchroneity* means that mediated messages "may be staggered in time. Senders and receivers of electronic messages can read mail at different times and still interact at their convenience. It also means the ability of an individual to send, receive, save, or retrieve messages at her or his convenience. In the case of television, asynchroneity meant the ability of VCR users to record a program for later viewing. With electronic mail [e-mail] and the Internet, an individual has the potential to store, duplicate, or print graphics and text, or transfer them to an online Web page or the e-mail of another individual. Once messages are digitized, manipulation of media becomes infinite, allowing the individual much more control than traditional means" (Ruggiero, 2000, p. 16).

In fact, people examining new technology have found uses-and-gratifications research to be quite helpful in studying a wide range of new media, especially e-mail. Boneva, Kraut, and Frohlich (2001) report that women find e-mail more useful than do men in maintaining social relationships. They demonstrated increasing use of e-mail by women to keep in touch with family and friends. John Dimmick and his colleagues at Ohio State University conduct ongoing studies tracing the uses and gratifications of the telephone, e-mail, and the Internet (Dimmick, Sikand, and Patterson, 1994; Stafford, Kline, and Dimmick, 1999). Uses-and-gratifications theory may prove to be essential in assessing how and why various computer-based or wireless communication services are used to supplement and in some cases replace older media.

THE ACTIVE AUDIENCE REVISITED

Whether they are engaged in new or traditional media use, the question remains: How active are media audiences? And what forms does this activity take? Critics of uses-and-gratifications research have long charged that the theory exaggerates the amount of active use. They contend that most media use is so passive and habitual that it makes no sense to ask people about it. Mark Levy and Sven Windahl (1985) attempted to put the issue in perspective:

> As commonly understood by gratifications researchers, the term "audience activity" postulates a voluntaristic and selective orientation by audiences toward the communication process. In brief, it suggests that media use is motivated by needs and goals that are defined by audience members themselves, and that active participation in the communication process may facilitate, limit, or otherwise influence the gratifications and effects associated with exposure. Current thinking also suggests that audience activity is best conceptualized as a variable construct, with audiences exhibiting varying kinds and degrees of activity. (p. 110)

Jay G. Blumler (1979) claimed that one problem in the development of a strong uses-and-gratifications tradition is the "extraordinary range of meanings" given to the concept of *activity*. He identified several meanings for the term, including the following:

- **Utility:** Media have uses for people, and people can put media to those uses.
- **Intentionality:** Consumption of media content can be directed by people's prior motivations.
- **Selectivity:** People's use of media might reflect their existing interests and preferences.
- **Imperviousness to influence:** Audience members are often obstinate; they might not want to be controlled by anyone or anything, even mass media. Audience members actively avoid certain types of media influence.

Blumler's list summarized the forms of audience activity that the early uses-and-gratifications researchers studied. They related to overall choices of content and media-use patterns. These types of audience activity did not, however, consider what people actually did with media content once they had chosen it. Recent research has begun to focus on this type of audience activity—the manner in which people actively impose meaning on content and construct new meaning that serves their purposes better than any meaning that might have been intended by the message producer or distributor.

A good example is the many meanings fans and critics made from the all-time movie box office hit *Avatar*. Conservatives said the film encouraged viewers "to root for the defeat of American soldiers at the hands of an insurgency" and fed "hatred of the military and American institutions." The movie offered "an incredibly disturbing anti-human, anti-military, anti-Western world view." It "maligned capitalism, promoted animism over monotheism and overdramatized the possibility of environmental catastrophe on earth" while "flirting with modern doctrines that promote the worship of nature as a substitute for religion" (all quotes from Leonard, 2010). Liberal critics condemned its obvious imperialist/racist theme of the beautiful but flawed colored people saved by the white man. When conservative critics used *Avatar* to bolster their contention that Hollywood is liberal, liberals used it to argue that its pro-environment and anti-war themes resonated with the public: the fact that *Avatar* is history's most successful movie means that people find gratification in those liberal themes; in other words, the market has decided. Or perhaps *Avatar* is something else, a special-effects laden, explosion-rich, holiday blockbuster designed to amass billions of dollars for its creators and investors while providing a pleasurable few hours of diversion for those willing to pay the price of a ticket.

Two ways to clarify the issue are to distinguish between "activity" and "activeness" and to see the "active audience" as a relative concept. "Activity" and "activeness" are related, but the former refers more to what the audience does (e.g., chooses to read the newspaper rather than to watch television news), and the latter is more what the uses-and-gratifications people had in mind—that is, the audience's freedom and autonomy in the mass communication situation, as illustrated in the *Avatar* example. This activeness, no doubt, varies from one person to the next. Some audience members are more active, and some are more passive. This is obvious; we all know too many couch potatoes, people who live their lives through the movies, or people addicted to their BlackBerries. But we also know many people who fit none of these descriptions. And an inactive user can become active. Our level of activity might vary by time of day and by type of content. We might be active users of the World Wide Web by day and passive consumers of late-night movies. What the uses-and-gratifications approach really does, then, is provide a framework for understanding when and how different media consumers become more or less active and what the consequences of that increased or decreased involvement might be.

The classic articulation of this framework is the one offered by Elihu Katz, Jay Blumler, and Michael Gurevitch (1974). They described five elements, or basic assumptions, of the uses-and-gratifications model:

1. **The audience is active and its media use is goal-oriented.** We've seen some confusion about exactly what is meant by *active,* but clearly various audience members bring various levels of activity to their consumption (if nothing else, at least in choice of preferred medium in given situations or preferred content within a given medium).

2. **The initiative in linking need gratification to a specific media choice rests with the audience member.** Bradley Cooper and Ed Helms, even teamed with Mike Tyson, cannot make you see *The Hangover.* Katie Couric and Wolf Blitzer cannot compel you to be a news junkie.

3. **The media compete with other sources of need satisfaction.** This is what Joseph Klapper meant when he said that media function "through a nexus of mediating factors and influences" (Chapter 6). Simply put, the media and their audiences do not exist in a vacuum. They are part of the larger society, and the relationship between media and audiences is influenced by events in that environment. If all your needs for information and entertainment are being satisfied by conversations with your friends, then you are much less likely to turn on a television set or go online for news. When students enter college, some forms of media use tend to sharply decline because these media don't compete as well for their time and attention. In the current media environment, old media (television, radio, newspapers) increasingly compete for our attention with a growing range of new media that serve similar needs more cheaply, easily, or efficiently.

4. **People are aware enough of their own media use, interests, and motives to be able to provide researchers with an accurate picture of that use.** This, as

we've seen earlier, is a debated methodological issue. As research methods are refined, however, researchers should be able to offer better evidence of people's awareness of media use. Evidence suggests that as media choices grow with the continued diffusion of technologies like DVD, cable and satellite, and the Internet, people are being forced to become more conscious of their media use. You can blunder into watching television shows by flipping to a channel and leaving the set tuned there all night. You can fall into certain viewing habits if everyone around you is regularly watching certain shows. But if you pay to download a movie, you are more likely to make an active choice. You don't pick the first title in the video-on-demand menu. You scan the options, weigh their merits, read the provided descriptions, maybe watch the offered trailers, and then settle on a movie. Your choice is much more likely to reflect your interests than when you "zone out" viewing one channel or watch whatever is on the screen in a lounge in the student center.

5. **Value judgments regarding the audience's linking its needs to specific media or content should be suspended.** For example, the "harmful effects" of consumer product advertising on our culture's values might only be harmful in the researcher's eyes. If audience members want those ads to help them decide what's "cool," that's their decision. This is perhaps the most problematic of Katz, Blumler, and Gurevitch's assertions. Their point is that people can use the same content in very different ways, and therefore the same content could have very different consequences. Viewing movies that show violent treatment of minorities could reinforce some people's negative attitudes and yet lead others to be more supportive of minority rights. We each construct our own meaning of content, and that meaning ultimately influences what we think and do. Defenders of new media advocate the merits of using social networking websites, e-mail, and text messaging to maintain contact with a wide range of distant friends. But what if people never develop new friendships because they are satisfied with keeping superficial contact with old friends? When you started college, did you stay in touch with high school friends using e-mail or social networking websites? Did this affect your desire to make new friends? Or did you use new media to seek out and establish new relationships in college?

This synopsis of the uses-and-gratifications perspective's basic assumptions raises several questions. What factors affect audience members' level of activeness or their awareness of media use? What other things in the environment influence the creation or maintenance of the audience members' needs and their judgments of which media use will best meet those needs? Katz, Blumler, and Gurevitch (1974, p. 27) argued that the "social situations" that people find themselves in can be "involved in the generation of media-related needs" in any of the following ways:

1. **Social situations can produce tensions and conflicts, leading to pressure for their easement through media consumption.** You're worried about your body image and think you have a weight problem, so you read magazines that give advice about dieting or you watch movies or sitcoms in which characters struggle with similar problems. Or you decide to watch some of YouTube's anorexia-themed videos.

2. **Social situations can create an awareness of problems that demand attention, information about which might be sought in the media.** You're out with friends and you notice that the most popular people in that circle are those who are the most socially outgoing; you also see that they get invitations that you do not. You increase your consumption of style and fashion magazines to better understand the social scene, or you go online, knowing that the Google search engine can help you find in-depth information about most social problems.

3. **Social situations can impoverish real-life opportunities to satisfy certain needs, and the media can serve as substitutes or supplements.** Your student budget does not allow you to buy the "in" clothes or to pay the cover charge at the dance club, so the Style Network's *How Do I Look?* keeps you company. When you come to college, you might use social networking websites to stay in contact with old friends as a substitute until you make new ones. Talk shows on radio and television provide an endless stream of chatter to fill up spaces in our lives and create a sense of being involved with other people.

4. **Social situations often elicit specific values, and their affirmation and reinforcement can be facilitated by the consumption of related media materials.** The fact that you are a single young adult in college often means that you are part of a group that values going to parties. To check this out, do some research on Facebook or MySpace and see the attention people your age give to their social lives. This media content not only promotes the party scene, it reinforces your attitudes toward it.

5. **Social situations can provide realms of expectations of familiarity with media, which must be met to sustain membership in specific social groups.** What? You don't watch *The Hills*? You don't know how Courtney Love became famous? You didn't know that Queen Latifah was a rap artist before she became a movie star? You haven't seen the latest dating flick? Or what about sports? Who won the World Series? Can LeBron replace Michael? How about those Patriots, those Bears, those Vikings?

Of course, if you see media as important sources of effects, you might ask whether the mass media themselves might have been instrumental in creating certain social situations (such as those in our example); and for making the satisfaction of those situations' attendant needs so crucial; and for making themselves, the media, the most convenient and effective means of gratifying those needs. Would we worry so much about body image if the media didn't present us with an endless parade of slender, attractive people? Would we care as much about sports if they weren't constantly being promoted by media? But that is typically not of concern in traditional uses-and-gratifications thinking because the members of the audience personally and actively determine what gratifications of what needs will and will not occur from their own exposure to media messages.

USES-AND-GRATIFICATIONS RESEARCH AND EFFECTS

This tendency to ignore the possibility of effects has led many researchers to dismiss uses-and-gratifications research as interesting but ultimately of little value. As a result, some contemporary proponents of the approach have taken on the challenge of linking gratifications and effects.

INSTANT ACCESS

Uses-and-Gratifications Theory

Strengths

1. Focuses attention on individuals in the mass communication process
2. Respects intellect and ability of media consumers
3. Provides insightful analyses of how people experience media content
4. Differentiates active uses of media from more passive uses
5. Studies the use of media as a part of everyday social interaction
6. Provides useful insight into adoption of new media

Weaknesses

1. Relies on functional analysis, which can create a bias toward the status quo
2. Cannot easily address the presence or absence of effects
3. Many of its key concepts are criticized as unmeasurable
4. Is too oriented toward the micro-level

Windahl (1981) argued that a merger of uses-and-gratifications research and the effects traditions was overdue and proposed what he called a "uses and effects" model that viewed the product of the use of media content as "conseffects." In a similar vein, Palmgreen, Wenner, and Rosengren (1985) wrote, "Studies have shown that a variety of audience gratifications (again, both sought and obtained) are related to a wide spectrum of media effects, including knowledge, dependency, attitudes, perceptions of social reality, agenda-setting, discussion, and various political effects variables" (p. 31).

Blumler also presented his ideas on how the uses-and-gratifications and effects approaches could be harmonized. You'll notice that his perspective still centers responsibility for the control of effects with the consumer rather than the media. He wrote:

> How might propositions about media effects be generated from … gratifications? First, we may postulate that cognitive motivation will facilitate information gain…. Second, media consumption for purposes of diversion and escape will favour audience acceptance of perceptions of social situations in line with portrayals frequently found in entertainment materials…. Third, involvement in media materials for personal identity reasons is likely to promote reinforcement effects. (1979, pp. 18–19)

Renewed interest in uses-and-gratifications developed when there was greater interest in effects perspectives, so it is no surprise that theorists are now focusing more on what unites rather than separates the two schools of thought. Alan Rubin writes that "the primary difference between the two traditions" is that effects researchers most often examine the mass communication process from the source's perspective, while uses and gratifications people begin with the audience member. But both "seek to explain the outcomes or consequences of communication such as attitude or perception formation (e.g., cultivation, third-person effects), behavioral changes (e.g., dependency), and societal effects (knowledge gaps). Uses and gratifications does so, however, recognizing the greater potential for audience initiative, choice, and activity" (2009, p. 172).

DEVELOPMENT OF RECEPTION STUDIES: DECODING AND SENSEMAKING

At the same time that audience-centered theory was attracting the attention of American empirical social scientists, British cultural studies researchers were developing a different but compatible perspective on audience activity. As we've seen, the uses-and-gratifications researchers challenged the limited-effects perspective, at the time the dominant view in U.S. mass communication research. In Britain, innovative cultural studies researchers were challenging a very different dominant perspective.

Chapter 8 introduced the Birmingham University Centre for Contemporary Cultural Studies and the work of Stuart Hall, its most prominent scholar. Initially, Hall (1973) produced a mimeographed report that proved important in developing and focusing the work of his center. It was later published as a book chapter (Hall, 1980a), arguing that researchers should direct their attention toward (1) analysis of the social and political context in which content is produced (encoding), and (2) the consumption of media content (decoding). Researchers shouldn't make unwarranted assumptions about either encoding or decoding, but instead should conduct research permitting them to carefully assess the social and political context in which media content is produced and the everyday life context in which it is consumed.

According to Shaun Moores (1993), Hall developed his approach in part as a reaction against a tradition of Marxist film criticism found in the film journal *Screen,* which viewed mainstream popular films as inherently deceptive and supportive of an elite-dominated status quo—a view pioneered by the Frankfurt School. *Screen's* writers favored avant-garde films in which there was no pretense about depicting a "real" social world. Hall objected to the cultural elitism inherent in this perspective. He thought it wrong to assume that popular films necessarily served to deceive and subvert working-class audiences. There might well be cases in which these films actually made moviegoers less supportive of the status quo. In fact, the message movies and British New Wave films mentioned at the start of Chapter 8 offered explicit and strong challenges to a United States and Great Britain committed to business as usual after World War II. In addition, Hall did not think that it was reasonable to expect that working-class audiences should embrace avant-garde films as providing a better way of understanding the social world.

In laying out his views about decoding, Hall proposed an approach to audience research known as **reception studies,** or reception analysis. One of its central features is its focus on how various types of audience members make sense of specific forms of content. Hall drew on French semiotic theory to argue that any media content can be regarded as a *text* made up of *signs.* These signs are structured; that is, they are related to one another in specific ways. To make sense of a text—to *read* a text—you must be able to interpret the signs and their structure. For example, when you read a sentence you must not only decode the individual words but also interpret its overall structure to make sense of it as a whole. Some texts are fundamentally ambiguous and can be legitimately interpreted in several different ways; they are **polysemic.** To return to an earlier example, Rebecca

reception studies Audience-centered theory that focuses on how various types of audience members make sense of specific forms of content (sometimes referred to as reception analysis)

polysemic The characteristic of media texts as fundamentally ambiguous and legitimately interpretable in different ways

INSTANT ACCESS

Reception Theory

Strengths

1. Focuses attention on individuals in the mass communication process
2. Respects intellect and ability of media consumers
3. Acknowledges range of meaning in media texts
4. Seeks an in-depth understanding of how people interpret media content
5. Can provide an insightful analysis of the way media are used in everyday social contexts

Weaknesses

1. Is usually based on subjective interpretation of audience reports
2. Cannot address presence or absence of effects
3. Uses qualitative research methods, which preclude causal explanations
4. Has been too oriented toward the micro-level (but is attempting to become more macroscopic)

---

preferred (or dominant) reading In reception studies the producer-intended meaning of a piece of content; assumed to reinforce the status quo (sometimes referred to as the dominant reading)

negotiated meaning In reception studies when an audience member creates a personally meaningful interpretation of content that differs from the preferred reading in important ways

oppositional decoding In reception studies when an audience member develops interpretations of content that are in direct opposition to a dominant reading

Keegan, James Cameron's biographer, said of the director's *Avatar*, "Some of the ways people are reading it are significant of Cameron's intent, and some are just by-products of what people are thinking about. It's really become this Rorschach test for your personal interests and anxieties." The film's producer, Jon Landau, added, "Movies that work are movies that have themes that are bigger than their genre. The theme is what you leave with, and you leave the plot at the theater" (both in Itzkoff, 2010, p. A1).

Hall argued that although most texts are polysemic, the producers of a message generally intend a **preferred, or dominant, reading** when they create a message. As a critical theorist, Hall assumed that most popular media content has a preferred reading reinforcing the status quo. But in addition to this dominant reading, it is possible for audience members to make alternate interpretations. They might disagree with or misinterpret some aspects of a message and come up with an alternative or **negotiated meaning** differing from the preferred reading in important ways. In some cases, audiences might develop interpretations in direct opposition to a dominant reading. In that case, they are said to engage in **oppositional decoding**. As explained by Jesus Martin-Barbero (1993), although people are susceptible to domination by communication technologies, "they are able to exploit contradictions that enable them to resist, recycle, and redesign those technologies, ... and people are capable of decoding and appropriating received messages and are not necessarily duped by them" (p. 225).

A student and colleague of Hall, David Morley, published one of the first detailed studies applying Hall's insights (Morley, 1980). It served as a model for subsequent reception analysis. Morley brought together twenty-nine groups of people drawn from various levels of British society. They ranged from business managers to trade unionists and apprentices. These groups were asked to view an episode from *Nationwide*, a British television news magazine show, assessing the economic consequences for three families of the government's annual budget. Once the program ended, the groups discussed what they had watched and offered their interpretations. *Nationwide* was chosen because an earlier analysis had identified it as a program that routinely offered status quo explanations for social issues

(Brunsdon and Morley, 1978). Moreover, it was produced in a way designed to appeal to lower- and middle-class audiences. Thus the researchers expected that the program would be able to communicate status quo perspectives to those audiences.

Morley tape-recorded the group discussions and analyzed them, placing them into one of three categories: (1) dominant, (2) negotiated, or (3) oppositional decoding. He found that although an upper-class group of business managers dismissed the program as mere entertainment, they had no complaints about the views it offered. Morley labeled their decoding as a dominant reading. At the other extreme, a group of union shop stewards liked the format of the program but objected to its message. They saw it as too sympathetic to middle management and failing to address fundamental economic issues. Morley labeled their decoding as oppositional. In the negotiated decoding category were groups of teacher trainees and liberal arts students. Very few groups articulated only a dominant reading of the program. Aside from managers, only a group of apprentices was found to merely repeat the views offered by the program. Most offered a negotiated reading, and several provided oppositional readings.

As the reception studies approach has developed in cultural studies, researchers have been careful to differentiate their empirical audience research from that conducted by postpositive researchers. They stress their effort to combine macroscopic encoding research with microscopic decoding studies. They also point to their reliance on qualitative rather than quantitative research methods. Reception studies are often conducted with focus groups. For example, people who frequently use certain types of content (fans) are sometimes brought together to discuss how they make sense of the content. In other cases, groups of people who belong to certain racial or ethnic groups are chosen so that the researcher can assess how these groups are routinely interpreting media content. In some cases, researchers undertake in-depth interviews to probe how individuals engage in "meaning making." In others, the researcher tries to assess how a focus group reaches a consensus concerning the meaning of content.

Sociologist Pertti Alasuutari (1999) has argued that reception research has entered a third stage. The first stage was centered on Hall's encoding-and-decoding approach. The second stage was dominated by Morley's pioneering audience ethnography work. Alasuutari wrote:

> The third generation entails a broadened frame within which one conceives of the media and media use. One does not necessarily abandon ethnographic case studies of audiences or analyses of individual programmes, but the main focus is not restricted to finding out about the reception or "reading" of a programme by a particular audience. Rather the objective is to get a grasp of our contemporary "media culture," particularly as it can be seen in the role of the media in everyday life, both as a topic and as an activity structured by and structuring the discourses within which it is discussed.... The big picture that one wants to shed light on, or the big question to pursue, is the cultural place of the media in the contemporary world. It may entail questions about the meaning and use of particular programmes to particular groups of people, but it also includes questions about the frames within which we conceive of the media and their contents as reality and as representations—or distortions—of reality.... The big research programme also includes questioning the role of media research itself. (pp. 6–7)

Thus, this third generation of reception studies attempts to return to some of the more macroscopic concerns that initially motivated critical theorists. It represents an effort to integrate these critical theory concerns with reception analysis to establish a challenging research agenda. This trend parallels developments in other areas of media theory we discuss in Chapter 11. You can read about what some critical theorists are calling reception studies' latest incarnation in the box entitled "Semiotic Disobedience."

FEMINIST RECEPTION STUDIES

Janice Radway (1984) was one of the first American cultural studies researchers to exemplify the shift away from an exclusive focus on textual analysis and toward an increased reliance on reception studies. Her work provided an influential model for American scholars and is frequently cited as one of the best examples of feminist cultural studies research. Radway initially analyzed the content of popular romance novels. She argued that romance characters and plots are derived from patriarchal myths in which a male-dominated social order is assumed to be both natural and just. Men are routinely presented as strong, aggressive, and heroic, whereas women are weak, passive, and dependent. Women must gain their identity through their association with a male character.

THINKING *about* THEORY   SEMIOTIC DISOBEDIENCE

British cultural theorist John Fiske (see Chapter 2) coined the phrase *semiotic democracy* to refer to audience members' ability to make their own meaning from television content. In his words, viewers possessed the skill—and the right—to produce personal "meanings and pleasures" when interacting with media texts (Fiske, 1987, p. 236). In "meanings" you can see evidence of reception studies, and in "pleasures" you can see hints of entertainment theory and uses-and-gratifications theory. But a new generation of active-audience writers and thinkers takes a more critical theory approach to the concept of an active audience. They argue that semiotic democracy, quite naturally, is evolving into **semiotic disobedience**, individuals' ability to reinvent or subvert media content, not to impose a personally meaningful reading, but to oppositionally redefine that content for themselves and others.

Examples abound. In San Francisco, the Billboard Liberation Front "improves" billboard advertising so the new "preferred" reading is in direct opposition to the one intended by the original advertiser. The

Media Foundation, best known for its Buy Nothing Day, Digital Detox Week, and its magazine *Adbusters,* produces a series of magazine ads featuring a smoking, cancerous Joe Chemo bearing a remarkable likeness to the cigarette icon Joe Camel. Its American flag, with fifty brand logos rather than fifty stars, has filled a full page of the *New York Times. Disaffected!* is an online videogame designed to "introduce" people to the copy company Kinko's. Developer Ian Bogost, who wants to show that "games can bite back" at "colonization" by advertisers, promotes the game on his company's website this way: "Feel the indifference of these purple-shirted malcontents first-hand and consider the possible reasons behind their malaise—is it mere incompetence? Managerial affliction? Unseen but serious labor issues?" (Walker, 2006, p. 18).

Hamburger giant McDonald's has also had its name and logo oppositionally subverted and redefined in online games. In *McDonald's Videogame* players decide how much rain forest to clear in order to raise more cows for slaughter. Thirty-thousand people submitted YouTube entries when automaker Chevrolet invited people to create commercials for its Tahoe sports utility vehicle in 2006. But it was those ads linking the big SUV to global warming and sexual inadequacy that received worldwide media attention (Manly, 2007). And *shopdropping* is the act of taking items from store shelves, for example canned goods or CDs, replacing their labels (or in the case of CDs, the music tracks themselves), and returning the items to their original spot in the store—to be seen or purchased by others.

These forms of protest have arisen, according to semiotic disobedience advocates such as technologist David Bollier, because in our contemporary hyper-commercialized, corporate-dominated media "we are being told that culture is a creature of the market, not a democratic birthright. It is privately owned and controlled, and our role is to be obedient consumers. Only prescribed forms of interactivity are permitted. Our role, essentially, is to be paying visitors at a cultural estate owned by major 'content providers'" (2005, p. 3). The new digital communication technologies, with their portability, ubiquity, and ease of use make possible this subversion of the preferred readings.

What do you think? Do you find value in the subversion of a content provider's intended reading? Do you think these activities serve any meaningful function? Do you see semiotic disobedience as the next logical cultural step for people in the Internet Age? After all, we are able to impose our own oppositional readings on various texts; now we have a ready technology permitting us to create our own preferred readings in opposition to some elite's idea of what is "preferred." But because we can, should we?

semiotic disobedience Individuals' ability to reinvent or subvert media content to oppositionally redefine that content for themselves and others.

After completing her content analysis of romance novels, Radway (1986) interviewed women who read them and met regularly in groups to discuss them. She was surprised to find that many readers used these books as part of a silent rebellion against male domination. They read them as an escape from housework or child rearing. Many of them rejected key assumptions of the patriarchal myths. They expressed strong preferences for male characters who combined traditionally masculine and feminine traits, for example, physical strength combined with gentleness. Similarly, readers preferred strong female characters who controlled their own lives but retained traditional feminine attributes. Thus romance reading could be interpreted as a form of passive resistance against male-dominated culture. Romance readers rejected the preferred reading and instead engaged in negotiated or oppositional decoding. British research on viewers of soap operas offered similar interpretations of their decoding of program content (Brunsdon and Morley, 1981; Hobson, 1982; Lovell, 1981).

Another feminist cultural studies researcher offers evidence that women routinely engage in oppositional decoding of popular media content. Linda Steiner (1988) examined ten years of the "No Comment" feature of *Ms.* magazine in which readers submit examples of subtle and not-so-subtle male domination. She argued that *Ms.* readers routinely engage in oppositional decoding and form a community acting together to construct these readings. Magazine examples can teach women how to identify these texts and help them develop interpretations serving their own interests rather than those of a patriarchal elite. Angela McRobbie (1984) came to a similar conclusion in her study of teenage girls' negotiated readings of the movies *Flashdance* and *Fame*. She concluded that young girls' "passion" for these films "had far more to do with their own desire for physical autonomy than with any simple notion of acculturation to a patriarchal definition of feminine desirability" (p. 47).

NEW DIRECTIONS IN AUDIENCE EFFECTS RESEARCH: THE RISE OF MODERATE-EFFECTS THEORIES

moderate-effects theories

Mass communication theories that conceptualize media as capable of inducing important effects under certain conditions

The remaining theories covered in this chapter and in the next two chapters continue the tradition of audience effects research that initially led to the development of the limited-effects perspective. Each of these theories moves beyond understandings of effects common in the 1960s and 1970s. As in the 1950s, most are to some extent grounded in psychological concepts and notions about psychological processes. In discussing each we have indicated how it builds on—and moves beyond—earlier effects notions. All are middle-range theories—they integrate many findings from previous research. They are referred to as **moderate-effects theories** because they conceptualize media as capable of inducing important effects under certain conditions. For example, if certain routine media uses persist over a long period of time, there could be cumulative effects—effects could keep building up until they become fairly strong.

Most of these theories do take into account audience activity, but they often don't assign a central role to it. Some of these theories view audience activity as mostly routinized and habitual rather than consciously planned. Activity is conceptualized as one of many audience attributes mediating between exposure to media content and the effects resulting from this exposure. These theories recognize that conscious use of media can enable people to moderate or control media effects. But there are many other things that could be even more important in moderating or limiting effects. In general, these theories retain some of the early behaviorist skepticism concerning people's ability to consciously control their behavior to achieve or avoid specific media effects. Our discussion of current audience effects research is not exhaustive. Numerous books (Bryant and Oliver, 2009; Harris, 2009; Perloff, 2010, Sparks, 2006; Preiss, 2007) provide in-depth discussions of this literature. Our intent here is to provide examples of some of the most interesting and best-developed theories created by postpositive effects researchers.

information-processing theory

Theory that uses mechanistic analogies to describe and interpret how people deal with all the stimuli they receive

Effects research has long been categorized by whether it involves one of the three major types of effects: cognitive, affective, and behavioral. Each of the theories we have chosen to look at focus on one of these types of effects. *Cognitive* effects involve knowledge or information—do people know more after being exposed to media? *Affective* effects involve feelings—are people's feelings influenced by media? *Behavioral* effects involve actions—do people act differently after exposure to media? We will begin by looking at a theory focusing on cognitive effects—**information-processing theory**. We put it first because it effectively illustrates the basic strengths and limitations of the effects theories currently developed by postpositivists. Information-processing theory is a middle-range theory integrating a myriad of empirical findings. It explains why most of the information provided by media is screened out. It also explains why certain bits and pieces of this information are plucked out and integrated into the cognitive maps we use to negotiate the social world.

elaboration likelihood model

Model of information processing that seeks to explain the level of elaboration, or effort, brought to evaluating messages

After information-processing theory, we look at the **elaboration likelihood model** (ELM), a way of understanding how individual aspects such as personal interest and relevance can lead to more or less information-processing effort, and eventually to behavior. ELM is one of the best contemporary recastings of the traditional limited-effects persuasion research and it offers meaningful insight to mass communication theory (Petty, Briñol, and Priester, 2009).

Then we look at **entertainment theory**. It seeks to understand what entertaining media content does *to* us—often without our awareness. Unlike uses-and-gratifications theory, it is much less concerned with what we think we're doing with that content. Entertainment theorists assume that most of us don't think enough about this content to have very useful insights about it. We're just doing what feels good—after all, it's only entertainment.

INFORMATION-PROCESSING THEORY

entertainment theory
Theory that conceptualizes and explicates key psychological mechanisms underlying audience use and enjoyment of entertainment-oriented media content

For more than three decades, cognitive psychologists have been developing a perspective on the way individuals routinely cope with sensory information: information-processing theory. It is actually a large set of diverse and disparate ideas about cognitive processes and provides yet another way to study media audience activity. Researchers work to understand how people take in, process, store, and then use various forms of information provided by media.

Drawing on the same metaphors as systems theory (Chapter 7), information-processing theory uses mechanistic analogies to describe and interpret how each of us takes in and makes sense of the flood of information our senses encounter every moment of each day. It assumes that individuals operate like complex biocomputers, with certain built-in information-handling capacities and strategies. Each day we are exposed to vast quantities of sensory information. We filter this information so only a small portion of it ever reaches our conscious mind. Only a tiny fraction of this information is singled out for attention and processing, and we finally store a tiny amount of this in long-term memory. We are not so much information *handlers* as information *avoiders*—we have developed sophisticated mechanisms for screening out irrelevant or useless information. Our capacity to cope with sensory information is easily overwhelmed so that we make mistakes by failing to take in and process critical information.

Cognitive psychologists make an important distinction between cognitive (or information) processes and consciousness. Much of what takes place in our brain never reaches our consciousness. Although this activity often affects our conscious thoughts, it does so only very indirectly through its influence on other cognitive processes. Our consciousness acts as a supreme overseer of this cognitive activity but has very limited and typically quite indirect control over it. This perspective on cognition is contrary to what most of us would like to assume about our ability to control what goes on in our minds. It contradicts our personal experience, which is largely based on what conscious reflection is able to reveal to us. When we watch a televised news report, we have the sense that we are getting every bit of useful information from it that is there. But recent research finds that only a fraction of the original information reaches us, even when we pay close attention. We get distracted by compelling pictures and waste precious cognitive resources processing them while important auditory information is missed.

How can we have so little control over these important processes supplying us with such critical information? If we are making mistakes and missing important information, maybe all we need to do is concentrate harder; but have you ever tried to force yourself to remember something on an exam? Did it work? If cognitive theorists are right, we need to be much more distrustful of the experiences our consciousness weaves together for us based on the very limited and attenuated flow of information that reaches it. Research is beginning to reveal just how easily and often consciousness fails to provide accurate or even useful representations of the social world.

Some cognitive psychologists argue that many of the processing mechanisms we use to screen in and screen out information must have developed when early human beings were struggling to adapt to and survive in a hostile physical environment (Wood and McBride, 1997). In that environment, it was critical that potential predators and prey be quickly identified so swift action could be taken. There was no time for conscious processing of such information and no need for conscious reflection before action. If you sensed a predator nearby, you ran away. If you sensed nearby prey, you attacked. Those who didn't either died at the hands of predators or died of starvation. Humans who developed the requisite cognitive skills survived.

These cognitive processing mechanisms became critical to adapting to and surviving in close social relationships with other human beings. For example, much of the cognitive processing capacity of the human brain is effectively devoted to taking in and unconsciously interpreting subtle body and facial movements enabling us to sense what others are feeling and anticipate how they are likely to act. We don't think about the information these cognitive processes produce. We experience this information as an intuition—we have a sense that others feel certain ways or will act certain ways. These processing mechanisms might have been more important to survival than processing information about prey and predators precisely because human beings are relatively weak and defenseless compared with many predators. Humans quickly die when food supplies fluctuate or temperatures vary. Human children require nurturing for much longer periods than do the young of other mammals. As a result, it is essential that humans form communities in which they can band together to survive. But living in communities requires cognitive skills far more sophisticated than those needed to sense predators and prey.

How relevant is this theory for understanding how we deal with sensory information? Think about it for a moment. As you sit reading this book, consider your surroundings. Unless you are seated in a white soundproof room with no other people present, there are many sensory stimuli around you. If you have been sitting for some time, your muscles might be getting stiff and your back might have a slight ache. Those around you might be laughing. A radio might be blaring. All this sensory information is potentially available, but if you are good at focusing your attention on reading, you are routinely screening out most of these external and internal stimuli in favor of the printed words on this page.

Now consider what you do when you watch a television program. Unless you have a VCR or a DVR player and can review scenes in slow motion, you can't pay attention to all the images and sounds. If you do watch them in slow motion, the experience is totally different from viewing them at normal speed. Viewing television is actually a rather complex task using very different information-processing skills than reading a textbook. You are exposed to rapidly changing images and sounds. You must sort these out and pay attention to those that will be most useful to you in achieving whatever purpose you have for your viewing. But if this task is so complex, why does television seem to be such an easy medium to use? Because the task of routinely making sense of television appears to be so similar to the task of routinely making sense of everyday experience. And making sense of that experience is easy, isn't it?

Information-processing theory offers fresh insight into our routine handling of information. It challenges some basic assumptions about the way we take in and use sensory data. For example, we assume that we would be better off if we could take in more information and remember it better. But more isn't always better. Consider what happens when you fill the hard drive of your computer with more and more content. It becomes increasingly difficult to find things quickly. A few important documents may be lost among thousands of useless items.

It's not surprising, then, that some people experience severe problems because they have trouble routinely screening out irrelevant environmental stimuli. They are overly sensitive to meaningless cues such as background noise or light shifts. Others remember too much information. You might envy someone with a photographic memory—especially when it comes to taking an exam on textbook material. But total recall of this type can pose problems as well. Recall of old information can intrude on the ability to experience and make sense of new information. A few cues from the present can trigger vivid recall of many different past experiences. If you've watched reruns of the same television show several times— *Scrubs* or *The Simpsons*, for example—you probably have found that as you watch one episode it triggers recall of bits and pieces of previous episodes. If you were asked to reconstruct a particular episode of either program, you would likely weave together pieces from several different shows. Everyday life is like that—if we remember too much, the past will constantly intrude into the present. Forgetting has advantages.

Another useful insight from information-processing theory is its recognition of the limitations of conscious awareness. Our culture places high value on conscious thought processes, and we tend to be skeptical or suspicious of the utility of mental processes only indirectly or not at all subject to conscious control. We associate consciousness with rationality—the ability to make wise decisions based on careful evaluation of all available relevant information. We associate unconscious mental processes with things like uncontrolled emotions, wild intuition, or even mental illness. We sometimes devalue the achievements of athletes because their greatest acts are typically performed without conscious thought. No wonder we are reluctant to acknowledge our great dependency on unconscious mental processes.

The overall task of coping with information is much too complex for conscious control to be either efficient or effective. We have to depend on routinized processing of information and must normally limit conscious efforts to instances when intervention is crucial. For example, when there are signs of a breakdown of some kind, when routine processing fails to serve our needs properly, then conscious effort might be required.

One advantage of the information-processing perspective is that it provides an objective perspective on learning. Most of us view learning subjectively. We blame ourselves if we fail to learn something we think we should have learned or that

limited cognitive resources
In information-processing theory, idea that as more resources are directed toward one task, another will suffer

appears to be easy to learn. We assume that with a little more conscious effort, we could have avoided failure. How often have you chided yourself by saying, "If only I'd paid closer attention"; "I should have given it more thought"; "I made simple mistakes that I could have avoided if only I'd been more careful"? But would a little more attention really have helped all that much? Information-processing theory says that we have **limited cognitive resources**. If more resources are directed toward one task, another task will be performed badly. A little more attention to one aspect of information processing often leads to a breakdown in some other aspect of processing. We typically deal with information in environments where it is coming at us from several different media at the same time. We're watching television, surfing the net, monitoring instant messages and talking on a cell phone—all at the same time. The current college generation is rightly labeled the "M" generation—both for its ubiquitous use of *media* and for its constant *multitasking*. No wonder our cognitive resources are pushed to the limit. No wonder we make mistakes and fail to learn what we intend.

For example, when we do something as simple as viewing television news, we are taking in visual and verbal information. We tend to place priority on processing visual information, so complex, powerful visual images will compel us to devote more cognitive resources to making sense of them. But if we do that, we miss the verbal information. Of course, sometimes additional conscious effort can do wonders. We can choose to ignore the compelling pictures and pay close attention to the verbal information. But what we might need is some overall revamping of our routine information-handling skills and strategies—a transformation of our information-processing system. This can take considerable time and effort—not just trying harder in one specific instance. Thus information-processing theory provides a means of developing a more objective assessment of the mistakes we make when processing information. These mistakes are routine outcomes from a particular cognitive process or set of processes—not personal errors caused by personal failings.

Information-processing theory doesn't blame audience members for making mistakes when they use media content. Instead it attempts to predict these mistakes based on challenges posed by the content and normal limitations in people's information-processing capacity. In some cases it links routine or common errors to breakdowns in information processing and suggests ways to avoid them. For example, research has repeatedly demonstrated that poorly structured news stories will routinely be misinterpreted even if journalists who write them are well intentioned and news consumers try hard to understand them (Gunter, 1987). Rather than retraining people to cope with badly structured stories, it is more efficient to change the structure of the stories so more people can use them without making mistakes.

PROCESSING TELEVISION NEWS

Information-processing theory has been used most extensively in mass communication research to guide and interpret research on how people decode and learn from television news broadcasts. Numerous studies have been conducted, and useful reviews of this literature are now available (Davis, 1990; Davis and Robinson,

INSTANT ACCESS

Information-Processing Theory

Strengths

1. Provides specificity for what is generally considered routine, unimportant behavior
2. Provides objective perspective on learning; mistakes are routine and natural
3. Permits exploration of a wide variety of media content
4. Produces consistent results across a wide range of communication situations and settings

Weaknesses

1. Is too oriented toward the micro-level
2. Overemphasizes routine media consumption
3. Focuses too much on cognition, ignoring such factors as emotion

1989; Graber, 1987; Gunter, 1987; Robinson and Davis, 1990; Robinson, Levy, and Davis, 1986). Remarkably similar findings have been gained from very different types of research, including mass audience surveys and small-scale laboratory experiments. A rather clear picture of what people do with television news is emerging.

Though most of us view television as an easy medium to understand and one that can make us eyewitnesses to important events, it is actually a difficult medium to use. Information is frequently presented in ways that inhibit rather than facilitate learning. Part of the problem rests with audience members. Most of us view television as primarily an entertainment medium. We have developed many information-processing skills and strategies for watching television that serve us well in making sense of entertainment content but that interfere with effective interpretation and recall of news. We approach televised news passively and typically are engaging in several different activities while viewing. Our attention is only rarely focused on the screen. We depend on visual and auditory cues to draw our attention to particular stories. When stories do get our attention, we rely on routine activation of **schemas** (more or less highly structured sets of categories or patterns, sets of interrelated conceptual categories) to help us make sense of what we are seeing and put it into useful categories so we can remember it. We rarely engage in deep, reflective processing of news content that might allow us to assume more conscious control over this meaning-making. So most news story content is never adequately processed and is quickly forgotten. Even when we do make a more conscious effort to learn from news, we often lack the schemas necessary to make in-depth interpretations of content or to store these interpretations in long-term memory.

But although we have many failings as an audience, news broadcasters also bear part of the blame. The average newscast is often so difficult to make sense of that it might fairly be called "biased against understanding." The typical broadcast contains too many stories, each of which tries to condense too much information into too little time. Stories are individually packaged segments typically composed of complex combinations of visual and verbal content. All too often, the visual information is so powerful that it overwhelms the verbal. Viewers are left with striking mental images but little contextual

schemas
More or less highly structured sets of categories or patterns; sets of interrelated conceptual categories

information. Often pictures are used that are irrelevant to stories—they distract and don't inform.

Findings presented by Dennis Davis and John Robinson (1989) are typical of this body of research. They interviewed more than four hundred viewers to assess what they learned or failed to learn from three major network news broadcasts. They identified numerous story attributes that enhanced or inhibited learning. Stories with complex structure and terminology or powerful but irrelevant visual images were poorly understood. Human-interest stories with simple but dramatic storylines were well understood. Viewers frequently confused elements of stories and wove together information drawn from similar reports. Given the inaccuracy of much of this recall, it may be best that most of it is quickly forgotten.

Information-processing theory has great potential to permit exploration of a wide variety of media content. Researchers apply it to such diverse topics as advertising (Lang, 1990), televised political content, and children's programming (Young, 1990). This research is rapidly revealing how we tailor our innate cognitive skills to make sense of and use media content. Our ability to do this is most strikingly demonstrated by children as they learn to watch television. Within a few years, children move from being dazzled by shifting colors and sound on the screen to making complex differentiations (good/bad, strong/weak, male/female) about program characters and making accurate predictions about the way story lines will unfold. For example, children come to recognize that Disney stories will have happy endings despite the efforts of evil characters. But underlying these seemingly simple and routine acts of meaning-making are complex cognitive processes that have been adapted to the task of watching television.

ELABORATION LIKELIHOOD MODEL

peripheral route
In ELM, information processing that relies on cues unrelated to the issue at hand

central route
In ELM, information processing characterized by heightened scrutiny of information related to the issue at hand

Social psychologists Richard Petty and John Cacioppo (1981) developed a model of information processing they called the elaboration likelihood model (ELM), which rested on the assumption that for social reasons, people are motivated to hold "correct" attitudes. Not everyone, however, is willing or able to process information in a way that will get them to that correct attitude, at least not all the time. Sometimes they work through an argument or issue; sometimes they take an easier, more automatic route to their opinion. You can hear echoes of dissonance theory and social categories from our earlier discussion of attitude change (Chapter 6). This is because this **peripheral route** of information processing does not rely on elaboration (scrutiny) of the message as much as it does on cues unrelated to the information—for example, attractive sources, catchy jingles, or political party labels—exactly as dissonance theory and social categories suggest. However, when motivated by the relevance of the information, a need for cognition, or a sense of responsibility, people will use the **central route** of information processing in which they bring as much scrutiny to the information as possible. Attitudes that are the product of this more stringent elaboration tend to be more deeply held, more enduring, and more predictive of subsequent behavior. Attitudes developed through the peripheral route tend to be less deeply held, less enduring, and less predictive of behavior.

ELM has been tested in scores of research trials in scores of settings and has enjoyed widespread acceptance. So it is no surprise that mass communication researchers find it useful, especially because much media consumption, even of obvious persuasive messages such as commercials, occurs routinely (without much elaboration) and theorists have identified difficulties in information processing even when audience members do attempt to pay attention to (elaborate) messages. ELM's most frequent application to mass communication, then, is in the realm of information campaigns. Petty, Briñol, and Priester explain:

> If the goal of a mass media influence attempt is to produce long-lasting changes in attitudes with behavioral consequences, the central route to persuasion appears to be the preferred persuasion strategy. If the goal is immediate formation of a new attitude, even if it is relatively ephemeral (e.g., attitudes toward the charity sponsoring a telethon), the peripheral route could prove acceptable…. [Research] on mass media persuasion has come a long way from the early optimistic (and scary) notion that the mere presentation of information was sufficient to produce persuasion, and the subsequent pessimistic view that media influence attempts were typically ineffective. We now know that media influence, like other forms of influence, is a complex, though explicable process. (2009, pp. 153–154)

Lance Holbert, Kelly Garrett, and Laurel Gleason attempt to reduce that complexity in arguing that the new media make clear ELM's value to mass communication theory and research. Traditional media are *push media*; they push information toward audience members, who either take it or don't. But new media are *pull media*; audience members pull from them the information they seek. "When you have the user in control, pulling down political media content, what do you have from the standpoint of ELM?" they write. "You have *motivation*— audience members who want to consume politically persuasive media messages. In addition, audience members in a pull media environment are more likely to consume their chosen political media messages at desirable times, in preferred places/ contexts, and utilizing formats that best match their particular learning styles. Each of these characteristics of the media-use experience facilitates greater *ability* to process political information" (2010, p. 27).

INSTANT ACCESS

Elaboration Likelihood Model

Strengths

1. Focuses attention on individuals in the mass communication process
2. Respects intellect and ability of media consumers
3. Provides specificity in describing process of information processing
4. Provides exploration of a wide variety of media information
5. Provides consistent results across a wide range of communication situations and settings

Weaknesses

1. Too oriented toward micro-level
2. Dismisses possibility of simultaneous, parallel information processing
3. Sacrifices testable causal relationships in favor of multiple cues present in messages

ENTERTAINMENT THEORY

As we saw in Chapter 5, Harold Mendelsohn pioneered an attempt to apply psychological theories to assess what entertainment media do for us and to us. We now look at his functional analysis approach to entertainment as biased toward a status quo that was not literally in disarray. But his view of the need to understand how audiences actually do use entertainment resonates today in some important work.

Dolf Zillmann is credited with leading the way in the development of contemporary entertainment theory (Bryant, Roskos-Ewoldsen, and Cantor, 2003). Its proponents place it within the larger context of a psychology of entertainment (Bryant and Vorderer, 2006). It seeks to conceptualize and explicate key psychological mechanisms underlying entertainment and to differentiate entertainment processes from those that underlie information, education, or persuasion (Bryant and Vorderer, 2006, p. ix). Current theorists can draw on much more research than did Mendelsohn (Zillmann and Vorderer, 2000). What separates current entertainment theory from earlier notions is that it doesn't see entertainment as simply an affective consequence of exposure to certain forms of media content. According to Bryant and Vorderer (2006), it envisions an overall process in which entertainment activity is "influenced, triggered and maybe even shaped by the media product that is selected" (p. 4). Audience members do voluntarily control their selection of entertainment content, but as in information-processing theory, there are many underlying psychological processes they don't consciously control. It is these processes that provide a comprehensive explanation of how and why we use entertainment media, and they help explain the consequences of this use.

Entertainment theory integrates findings from research examining the effects of many different types of entertainment content. Dolph Zillman and Peter Vorderer (2000) summarize research on horror, comedy, conflict, suspense, sex, affect-talk, sports, music, and videogames. They assess gender and age differences and identify a range of effects resulting from exposure to these forms of content. Some

INSTANT ACCESS

Entertainment Theory

Strengths

1. Stresses media's pro-social influence
2. Assesses cognitive, affective, and behavioral effects
3. Provides cogent multivariate explanations for why people seek entertainment from media
4. Is grounded in an expanding body of media effects research
5. Provides a useful basis for conducting experiments

Weaknesses

1. Tends to accept status quo uses of entertainment media as a starting point for research
2. Has so far found effects that are mostly limited and minimal
3. Tends to ignore and doesn't provide a good basis for assessing cumulative effects
4. Tends to consider entertainment effects in isolation from other types of effects

effects are intended by users, but many are not. For example, research finds that there may be a health benefit when we laugh, so viewing situation comedies could make us healthier. Regular viewing of television programs featuring sexual content was linked to phenomena such as ambivalence toward marriage, perceived frequency of sexual activity by others, and attitudes toward homosexuality. It's not likely that most viewers would have intended these effects or been aware of them.

A recent edited collection (Bryant and Vorderer, 2006) has chapters devoted to a large number of psychological processes thought to be involved in or associated with entertainment, including selective exposure, motivation, attention, comprehension, information processing, attribution, disposition, empathy, identification with characters, involvement, mood management, social identity, and parasocial interaction ("interaction" between audience members and characters in media content; for example, talking to the television set). Each can be studied individually or several can be combined and used to study one or more forms of entertainment content. Some processes are more likely to be involved with certain forms of content. One way that research can advance in the future is to assess which processes are most centrally involved with which forms of entertainment.

As entertainment theory evolved, "subtheories" were created that focused on the various psychological processes listed here. One of the most interesting of these is mood management theory. We'll take a closer look at this idea because you might find it useful in analyzing your own use of media. It argues that a predominant motivation for using entertainment media is to moderate or control our moods. It articulates some of our commonsense notions about what we are doing when we seek out entertainment. If we're in a "bad mood," we turn on our iPod and listen to music. When we're "stressing out" from studying, we can take a break and surf the net or turn on a televised comedy. Silvia Knobloch-Westerwick (2006) provides a description of mood management theory: "The core prediction of mood management theory claims that individuals seek out media content that they expect to improve their mood. Mood optimization in this sense relates to levels of arousal—plausibly, individuals are likely to avoid unpleasant degrees of arousal, namely boredom and stress. By selecting media content, media users can regulate their own mood with regard to arousal levels" (p. 240).

According to Knobloch-Westerwick, there are four types of media content attributes relevant to mood management: excitatory potential, absorption potential, semantic affinity, and hedonic valence. *Excitatory potential* involves the ability of content to arouse or calm emotion—to get us excited or to reduce stress. *Absorption potential* involves the ability of content to direct our thoughts away from things that induce a negative mood and toward other things that induce positive feelings. *Semantic affinity* concerns the degree to which entertaining content involves things that are similar to (mean the same as) the things that are inducing a bad mood. *Hedonic valence* refers specifically to the potential that content has to induce positive feelings.

It should be possible for you to think about your recent use of entertainment content and assess the extent to which mood management theory can explain what you did and what happened to you. First, did use of the content change your mood in the way you desired? If your mood did change, why do you think this happened? Did the content get you excited? Did it divert your thoughts from things that were bothering you? Was the content unrelated to your personal problems and therefore able to direct your thoughts toward something that made you feel better? Was the content capable of inducing positive feelings—of making you feel good? Can you remember an instance when you went to a movie and expected to be entertained but the opposite happened? What went wrong? Was the movie boring? Did it fail to distract you from your problems, or worse, did it actually remind you of the problems? Did it fail to arouse positive feelings?

Mood management theory can help to explain why our efforts to manage our moods can fail or why media content can be entertaining even when it concerns seemingly unpleasant things—like chainsaw massacres or devastating earthquakes. We might assume that situation comedies should always make us feel better, but they could remind us of our problems or they might just be boring. Conversely, we might expect that a horror movie or a thriller will arouse bad feelings, but it could be quite diverting and exciting—it could have high excitation and absorption potential.

Mood management theorists argue that we don't have to be consciously aware of these content attributes. We don't need to use them to consciously select content. Instead, we can be guided by our feelings about content—our vague expectations about what will make us feel better as opposed to having a well-thought-out, rational strategy guiding our selection. We don't ponder the hedonic valence or the semantic affinity of the television shows we select. According to Knobloch-Westerwick, "Awareness of mood optimization needs does not have to be assumed [by the researcher] … mood management processes may go by-and-large unnoticed by those who act on them—at least very little cognitive elaboration usually takes place" (2006, p. 241).

This view of audience members can be contrasted with that of uses-and-gratifications theorists, who rely on audience members to report both uses and gratifications. Mood management theorists don't expect audience members to be able to report how they use content to manage moods. They don't ask people to fill out questionnaires rating the expected hedonic valence or the excitation potential of various types of entertainment content. They know people don't consciously make these types of assessments about content.

Since they can't conduct surveys to study mood moderation, they base their conclusions primarily on findings produced by experiments. In these experiments, audience members are exposed to media content that mood management theory predicts should influence them in certain ways. Subjects are exposed to content with high or low excitation potential or semantic affinity. But these experiments can be difficult to design. Researchers need to develop stimulus materials containing the proper amount of the attributes they are manipulating. But how do you take people's moods into account? Research ethics would make it difficult to deliberately induce bad moods prior to exposure to content.

Some audience members (maybe you) would reject the mood management explanation of what audience members are doing when they seek out entertainment content. You might argue that you're choosing content that is aesthetically pleasing or just mindless entertainment. Altering your mood may be the furthest thing from your mind. But is it? Might you be more concerned about managing your mood than your conscious mind is willing to acknowledge? Could you have been "conditioned" by past experiences with media content to know which forms of content will induce feelings that you unconsciously want to experience? Maybe you should take another look at what you're doing when you choose to zone out in front of your television for an evening.

Knobloch-Westerwick reminds us that it's also important to differentiate between moods that tend to endure over time and temporarily induced changes in feelings. Moods could often be due to long-term, enduring personal or situational factors. They may be altered only temporarily by media content. For example, if you recently broke up with a close friend, this could induce a long-term negative mood. Watching a situation comedy might make you feel better temporarily, but the negative mood will return. You'd be managing your mood, but it would be only a short-term fix. In seeking out media content, you would need to avoid content that shows good friends because it will have too much "semantic affinity." Maybe horror movies or thrillers would be preferable. They would be exciting and diverting but wouldn't dwell much on human relationships.

Like most theories related to entertainment theory, mood management theory accepts media as a benign force in society. What could be wrong with providing people with solace for everyday troubles? These contemporary theories for the most part imply that the status quo is acceptable—much as Mendelsohn did forty years ago. Mood management theory implies that media can help us cope with problems in our lives—problems that regularly induce bad moods. We don't have to develop a complex strategy to make media be helpful to us; we can rely on what we've learned from past experience with media, from what media have taught us to expect, and from the way we've been conditioned by exposure to a lifetime of entertainment programming.

Recently some theorists have begun to combine postpositivist research findings on media entertainment into theories that raise more serious questions. A good example is a perspective on the psychology of entertainment media provided by L. J. Shrum (2004). Shrum argues that current marketing practices have begun to blur the boundaries between persuasion and entertainment. He believes that in a liberal democracy, people should know when they are being targeted by an advertisement. Ads shouldn't be embedded so deeply in entertainment content that most viewers aren't aware of them. Yet this is exactly what happens when products are prominently featured in movies, television shows, and even popular music.

Could this product placement operate similarly to black propaganda? Could our identification with or good feelings about movie characters make us more inclined to use the products we see them using? If we are already relatively poor information processors, isn't this stealth advertising a bit unfair? When routinely watching a favorite television show, it's unlikely that we will be motivated to activate our central information-processing route. Are ads embedded in the routine flow of standard entertainment fare intended to ensure an uncritical, peripheral route evaluation? Shrum asks many troubling questions. In Chapter 11, we'll look at how culture-centered theories of media assess these strategies, and we'll consider the types of evidence and arguments they offer in support of their views.

SUMMARY

The audience has never been completely absent from mass communication theory, but the uses-and-gratifications approach brought it to a more central position in thinking about media. The assertion that audiences are active proved valuable in refining our understanding of the mass communication process.

Audience activity can be defined in several ways—utility, intentionality, selectivity, imperviousness to influence, and meaning construction, for example—but activity should be seen as a relative concept; that is, some people are more active media consumers than others are. Other audience-centered theories accept this fact. Reception studies focus on people's ability to make sense of specific forms of content, presumably for personally relevant ends. Readers of media texts often apply their own negotiated and oppositional meanings to the preferred readings intended by content producers.

Information-processing theory describes how individuals process and make sense of the overwhelming amounts of information present even in the simplest media message and has been successfully applied to situations such as how people read television news. Elaboration likelihood describes the conditions under which we bring more or less scrutiny to the information with which we are presented and the factors that might produce more cognitive and therefore behavioral change. These issues are particularly salient in an era of pull, rather than push, media. With entertainment theory, both question our ability to consciously control our use of media. All argue that our actions are governed by numerous psychological processes operating below the level of conscious awareness. They explain why we often fail when we make conscious efforts to use media to achieve certain objectives. Our efforts are frustrated by processes over which we have no control.

The audience perspectives described in the first half of this chapter were developed as a counter to both mass society notions and the dominant limited-effects perspective. Audience perspectives argue that the media do not do things to people; rather, people do things with media. The basic tenet is that audiences are active and make media do things to serve their purpose. The theories discussed in the last half of this chapter are extensions of the limited-effects perspective. As they have developed, they have been able to locate consistent, moderate media effects. They provide many practical insights into what media can do, but they leave many questions about media unanswered.

Still, of all the chapters in this book, this one may leave you the most unsatisfied. Social cognitive theory was easy: People learn from the mass media through a process called modeling. Attitude-change theory is simple: Cognitive dissonance helps people protect themselves from persuasive messages. But the various audience theories introduced in this chapter often raise as many questions about the role of media in our lives as they answer. They suggest that our use of media is actually much more complicated than we might like to assume. When you relax by clicking the remote and watching *The Hills* or *So You Think You Can Dance,* you might like to assume that you are only being amused by these shows. Theories arguing that you are attempting to moderate your mood, theories asserting that you are actually unconsciously and inexpertly processing enormous amounts of information, or theories claiming that this seemingly routine choice is the result of your seeking a particular set of gratifications from a quite specific use of media might seem to be making something out of nothing. But they aren't. Our use of media is an infinitely complex process and an extremely important one.

In the next two chapters, we'll move beyond the limited focus of the theories covered in this chapter, and we'll examine ideas that address larger questions concerning the role of media in the social order and in culture. Some of these theories move beyond simply seeking answers to questions about the role of media. They offer ways of addressing problems posed by media—of taking greater control over them. Proponents of media literacy, as we'll see in Chapter 11, offer ways to help us all become more skilled consumers and readers of media and their content. What media literacy proponents emphasize is that it's not enough for audiences simply to be active. Audience activity must be grounded on informed critical reflection. If we are going to rely on media to make sense of our social world, then we need to take more control over how we do this.

A second reason that audience theories leave many observers unsatisfied is the difficulty these theories have in explaining media effects. Several authors we've cited have argued that uses-and-gratifications theory developed as a "counter" to the effects research dominant at the time. Blumler, for example, wrote that it developed "at a time of widespread disappointment with the fruits of attempts to measure the short-term [media] effects on people" (Blumler, 1979, p. 10). Palmgreen, Wenner, and Rosengren (1985) wrote: "The dominance of the 'effects' focus in pre– and post–World War II communication research tended to overshadow … concern with individual differences" (p. 12). In a sense, proponents of audience theory could not allow themselves the luxury of demonstrating or even postulating effects because that would have been heresy to the then-dominant limited-effects perspective.

Critical cultural theorists like Stuart Hall had another reason for disregarding media effects. Hall was convinced that effects research was useless because it largely served the status quo. He regarded the American focus on postpositivist effects research with great suspicion, believing that it primarily served the interests of the media industries. When researchers found effects, as with advertising, their findings were exploited to manipulate audiences. When they demonstrated no effects or the effects they did find were "limited," their work was used to fend off the regulation of media industries. Hall thought this was nonsense. He believed that the dominant readings embedded in most media content were obviously propping up a status quo in which most people were exploited. But how could he demonstrate this in a way that would be convincing to someone other than a neo-Marxist? His answer was reception analysis—a qualitative research strategy permitting in-depth exploration of how groups "read" popular media content from television sitcoms to punk rock videos. But political economists criticize reception analysis as providing a different kind of apology for the media industries because most reception analysis suggests that people cope quite nicely with problematic media content. Individuals negotiate meaning or they engage in oppositional decoding. Is this so different from the limited-effects findings produced by postpositivist effects researchers?

Finally, these audience theories might not seem as "clean" or straightforward as some of the other ideas we've studied because they are best regarded not as highly coherent, systematic conceptual frameworks (true theories) but rather as loosely structured perspectives through which a number of ideas and theories about media choice, consumption, sense-making, and even impact can be viewed. As Blumler himself said,

> There is no such thing as a or the uses and gratification theory, although there are plenty of theories about uses and gratification phenomena, which may well differ with each other over many issues. Together, they will share a common field of concern, an elementary set of concepts indispensable for intelligibly carving up that terrain, and an identification of certain wider features of the mass communication process with which such core phenomena are presumed to be connected. (1979, pp. 11–12)

Similarly, there is no one theory of reception analysis, entertainment, ELM, or information processing. All are quite open-ended. Although all three began as microscopic theories with a focus on how and why people make sense of and learn from specific media content, all have recently moved somewhat beyond this narrow focus. All are capable of being applied in innovative ways to the study of newer forms of media, having potential to provide significant insights into the audiences for these new as well as old media. They don't reveal a mass audience mesmerized by powerful elites, nor do they reveal an increasingly informed citizenry benefiting from the flood of information available via mass media and the Internet. Instead they show a very complex interrelationship between media, media content, and audiences in which considerable mutual influence is possible and likely. Taken together, these theories offer exciting challenges to the next generation of media researchers.

So where do we go from here? How can we move beyond the narrow focus of audience theories and address larger questions concerning the role of media in society or in culture? We will provide our answers to these questions in Chapter 10 and Chapter 11. But we will leave you now with hints provided by Blumler, Gurevitch, and Katz, the creators of the original 1974 volume *The Uses of Mass Communication*. When asked to write the concluding comments for a book to celebrate the tenth anniversary of that work, they had this advice, which can be applied to any of the audience theories we have reviewed in this chapter:

> Philosophically, lingering traces of "vulgar gratificationism" should be purged from our outlook. This implies the following:
> (1) Rejection of audience imperialism. Our stress on audience activity should not be equated with a serene faith in the full or easy realization of audience autonomy....
> (2) Social roles constrain audience needs, opportunities, and choices.... The individual is part of a social structure, and his or her choices are less free and less random than a vulgar gratificationism would presume. (3) Texts are also to some extent constraining. In our zeal to deny a one-to-one relationship between media content and audience motivation, we have sometimes appeared to slip into the less warranted claim that almost any type of content may serve any type of function. (1985, pp. 259–260)

Critical Thinking Questions

1. Where does the greater amount of power reside in the media/audience relationship? That is, do media do things to people, or do people do things with media? Are there circumstances when the "balance of power" might shift? That is, are there circumstances when audience members have greater control over their reading than others? Have the new digital media shifted the balance of power, giving individual audience members more power? How much control do you exercise over your meaning making when using digital media like video games and the Web? Do you ever make meaning with your friends using these media's interactivity? Why or why not?

2. Choose a media consumption choice that you may often have to make, such as selecting a movie streamed to your home TV versus one at the multiplex, choosing an episode of your favorite situation comedy downloaded to your cell phone versus one on your big-screen television set, or scanning online headlines versus spending thirty minutes with the newspaper. Subject that decision to Schramm's fraction of selection. Which "wins"? Which elements in the numerator and denominator might you change to produce a different outcome? What does this tell you about your media uses and gratifications?

3. Why would you ever impose an oppositional reading of a piece of media content? After all, the producers went to great lengths to create a text that would bring you some satisfaction. Why not just enjoy it? There are always other texts that can provide you with the reading you prefer.

Key Terms

active-audience theories

uses-and-gratifications approach

fraction of selection

reception studies

polysemic

preferred, or dominant, reading

negotiated meaning

oppositional decoding

semiotic disobedience

moderate-effects theories

information-processing theory

elaboration likelihood model

entertainment theory

limited cognitive resources

schemas

peripheral route

central route

10 | MEDIA AND SOCIETY: THE ROLE OF MEDIA IN THE SOCIAL WORLD

How do we keep up on news about what is going on in our neighborhood, our city, our state, our nation or around the world? How do we find out about the latest fashions, movies, technology, and diets? We live at a time when a lot is happening everywhere and all at once. Information about products, peers, family, community, state, nation, and the world constantly comes at us from an ever-growing array of media. News is created and packaged by an impressive array of sources ranging from journalists to bloggers to YouTube enthusiasts. With our news we face an ever-growing amount of promotional information produced by advertisers, public relations agents, and others engaging in strategic communication. This information is often integrated with news so it's hard to tell what is news and what is advertising or PR.

The way we receive and use information is being radically transformed by new media technology, and that has created a very difficult situation for traditional news providers. Print newspapers are rapidly losing readers, especially young readers, and they are hemorrhaging advertisers. More than a few have shuttered their operations. Many have reduced the physical size of their pages to cut the cost of paper. Some are publishing fewer days per week. A few have decided to exist only on the Internet. Some are becoming nonprofit corporations to reduce taxes, enabling them to stay in business.

Yet news on the Internet has been quite successful, as traffic on many news-oriented sites rapidly and steadily increases. And although newspapers often offer free access to much of the content published in their print editions, income from Internet advertising doesn't approach making up for revenue lost by their print editions. Industry research indicates that although the online newspaper audience is at record highs, growing by more than 60 percent between 2005 and 2008, a print reader is worth $940 a year while a Web reader is worth only $46. In other words, a print reader is worth more than 20 times an online reader (Chittum 2009; Sass, 2009b). In addition, on the Internet those same newspapers are competing against each other for regional and national audiences. They also compete against many other news sources, such as blogs and sites maintained by other media organizations and specialty information interest groups. The outcome of this competition is uncertain, but as you saw in Chapter 5, it could have very important consequences for us and for society.

If the news business is troubled, strategic communicators appear to be thriving. Ad agencies are weathering the transition to new media. Promotional communicators generally see new media as offering them great potential for delivering their messages more effectively to more narrowly targeted audiences at lower cost. Facebook advertising is a good example. Facebook provides advertisers with detailed information about users, allowing them to target their messages directly at people who like certain things or regularly engage in certain activities. Frequent movie goers get regular updates on showings in their area, while those who like certain types of music are sent ads for bands and CDs.

How do you deal with the flood of information that threatens to inundate you? If you are typical, this is a question you rarely ask yourself. You don't need to ask because you've already answered the question without needing to give it any thought. You deal with information by filtering most of it out. Most of it never reaches you because you don't pay any attention to the media that could deliver it. When you do attend to information, some of it is hard to understand and you skip over it and forget it. This may be information that you know is important but it really doesn't seem relevant to your life. But there is some information that you do find relevant. This is information that you seek out, information that you share with others face-to-face or by text or Facebook. This is information that you care enough about to want to be constantly updated, information that makes a difference in your life and the lives of those you care about.

Though most of us don't think much about it, the information we routinely consume or routinely ignore does much to determine the kind of person we are or can be. If we routinely ignore news about politics or social issues, we can't talk intelligently about these things with friends and we won't be prepared to engage in responsible political action. If we routinely seek out information about celebrities or sports, we will be prepared to talk about them with friends and to enjoy media content that features them. We'll be prepared to select and buy the fashions celebrities would like or to engage in activities that we see them doing. If we routinely attend to sports, we'll have knowledge that makes watching games more interesting. We'll know the standing and record of our favorite teams and the statistics of our favorite players.

Our use of information does much to determine who we are, and the way most people use information does much to shape the society we live in. In the preceding chapter we looked at uses-and-gratifications theory and information-processing theory. These theories have important implications when they are applied to information. In addition to keeping us informed about events, news serves many other gratifications. News gives us something to talk about. It is part of the daily rituals we use to reassure ourselves that everything is right with the world and we can live our lives without worrying too much about things happening around us.

A key assertion of information-processing theory is that our cognitive resources are limited. We can't pay attention to everything. We can only learn a small fraction of the information that we encounter. Over time we develop schemas that reflect our interests and allow us to make sense of the information that fits these interests. These schemas develop early in life and provide an ongoing means of interpreting our experiences. If we routinely consume news about celebrities or sports, we will develop schemas that enable us to quickly take in and remember news about them. Interests shape schemas—and once developed, schemas serve these interests.

The theories explained in this chapter and some of those in the following chapter are theories about information and the role it plays for us and others. These theories offer varying perspectives on information. Some are cautiously optimistic while others are pessimistic. They provide different ways of understanding how and why information affects each of us individually. They also explain how news or advertising can shape the social world. We don't often think of news as something that can alter the social world. News is supposed to be a report about things that are happening; it's not supposed to influence what is happening. Journalists continue to tell us that they only provide objective news coverage. As Fox News insists, "We report, you decide." The theories in this chapter reject this simple assertion and challenge us to look differently at news—not as a mirror that simply reflects the social world, but as a force capable of shaping that world.

Even if we don't pay attention to politics, we will live in a world shaped by the way news reports politics. Even if we despise celebrity culture or sports, for example, our live will be affected by them because so many people around us are influenced by them. Many of us may not know the name Umar Farouk Abdul Mutallab; we might not even have paid attention to the news of his Christmas Day, 2009, attempt to bring down an airliner by exploding a bomb in his underwear, but whether we did or didn't follow this story, we still have to deal with long lines, full body scans, and heightened security at airports and election campaigns that turn on which political party makes the best promises about keeping us safe from the terrorists.

OVERVIEW

The media theorists we consider in this chapter argue that the failings of news and other media content raise important questions about the motives of media practitioners and their professional norms. Are they really doing everything they can and should to provide us with useful services, or are they part of the problem? To what extent do their professional norms actually lead them to be socially irresponsible? These questions about the ideal social role of media are much like those raised in Chapter 5's discussion of normative theories. Moreover, they imply that the dominant normative theory, social responsibility theory, should be radically changed or replaced.

The earliest mass communication theories arose out of a concern for the preservation of social order in the face of the threat posed by propaganda. Ever since the appearance of modern mass media in the middle of the nineteenth century, social theorists have speculated about the power of media to create community on the one hand and disrupt important social institutions on the other. They embraced technology as a panacea or they feared it as a corrupting force. In Chapters 3 and 4, we traced the rise of mass society theory and that of the mass media industries. At its height, mass society theory painted a dire picture of a totalitarian future in which a cynical elite bent on creating and maintaining absolute power manipulated media.

In this chapter, we consider theories addressing many of the same questions and issues that sparked the development of mass society theory. We live today in an era that is being transformed by powerful new media—by communications satellites encircling the globe while computer-based media invade not only our homes, but every corner and every minute of our days. These technologies give rise to unrealistic hopes and inspire inordinate fears. Like our ancestors at the end of the nineteenth century, we harbor doubts about our political system. Though we aren't threatened by totalitarian propaganda, we are regularly deluged by negative news and political advertising that feed our cynicism about politics. Finally, concerns about the media barons of the nineteenth century echo today in worry about modern media power brokers, best exemplified by Rupert Murdoch and his News Corporation.

The contemporary media theories we consider might seem familiar to you based on your reading of previous chapters. Most draw on older theories to offer cogent and insightful analyses of the role of media in society. For the most part the theories discussed in this chapter are grounded in empirical social research. Although this work is quite diverse, the theories it supports have many similarities. As you will see, the assessment these theories provide of contemporary media and their social role is mostly negative. Several argue that media routinely disrupt important social institutions such as politics or education.

It is important to keep in mind that despite their negative tone, none of these contemporary media theories should be confused with mass society theory. None argues that media will inevitably destroy high culture, bring an end to democracy, and plunge us into a dark age of totalitarianism. The view of the social order found in these theories is far more sophisticated than the mass society thinking central to many earlier theories. Their understanding of individuals is similar to the perspectives presented in Chapter 9. It's generally positive but mixed, based in part on active audience assumptions but tempered by the recognition that much human behavior is not consciously controlled. People don't always do what's reasonable or most useful when it comes to media. On the other hand, media don't easily manipulate passive individuals. Instead, media's power rests in their ability to provide communication services routinely used by individuals and central to the maintenance of our social order.

INFORMATION (INNOVATION) DIFFUSION THEORY

In 1962, Everett Rogers combined information-flow research findings with studies about the flow of information and personal influence in several fields, including anthropology, sociology, and rural agricultural extension work. He developed what he called diffusion theory. Rogers's effort at integrating information-flow research with diffusion theory was so successful that information-flow theory became

information/ innovation diffusion theory
Theory that explains how innovations are introduced and adopted by various communities

meta-analysis
Identifies important consistencies in previous research findings on a specific issue and systematically integrates them into a fuller understanding

early adopters
In information/ innovation diffusion theory, people who adopt an innovation early, even before receiving significant amounts of information

change agents
In information/ innovation diffusion theory, those who directly influence early adopters and opinion leaders

known as **information diffusion theory** (and when it is applied to the diffusion of something other than information—that is, technologies—it is called *innovation diffusion theory*). Rogers used both labels to title subsequent editions of his book.

Roger's work also illustrates the power of **meta-analysis** when it comes to developing a more useful middle range theory. A meta-analysis identifies important consistencies in previous research findings on a specific issue and systematically integrates them into a fuller understanding. If previous research has been grounded in several different but related low-level theories, these can be combined to create new, more macroscopic theories. Meta-analysis is gaining popularity among post-positivist media researchers. We consider this trend in Chapter 12.

Rogers assembled data from numerous empirical studies to show that when new technological innovations are introduced, they pass through a series of stages before being widely adopted. First, most people become aware of them, often through information from mass media. Second, the innovations will be adopted by a very small group of innovators, or **early adopters**. Third, opinion leaders learn from the early adopters then try the innovation themselves. Fourth, if opinion leaders find the innovation useful, they encourage their friends—the opinion followers. Finally, after most people have adopted the innovation, a group of laggards, or late adopters, makes the change. Rogers found that this process applied to most American agricultural innovations.

Information/innovation diffusion theory is an excellent example of the strength and the limitations of a middle-range theory. It successfully integrates a vast amount of empirical research. Rogers reviewed thousands of studies. Information/ innovation diffusion theory guided this research and facilitated its interpretation. Nevertheless, it has some serious limitations. Like information-flow theory and social marketing theory (discussed later in this chapter), information/innovation diffusion theory is a source-dominated theory that sees the communication process from the point of view of an elite who has decided to diffuse specific information or an innovation. Diffusion theory "improves" on information-flow theory by providing more and better strategies for overcoming barriers to diffusion.

Information/innovation diffusion theory assigns a limited role to mass media: they mainly create awareness of new innovations. But it does assign a very central role to different types of people critical to the diffusion process. Media *do* directly influence early adopters, but these people are generally well informed and careful media users. Early adopters try out innovations and then tell others about them. They directly influence opinion leaders, who in turn influence everyone else. **Change agents** are also key people involved with diffusion. Their job is to be highly informed about innovations and assist anyone who wants to make changes. Rogers recommended that change agents lead diffusion efforts; they could go into rural communities and directly influence early adopters and opinion leaders. In addition to drawing attention to innovations, media can also be used to provide a basis for group discussions led by change agents. This strategy for using media was patterned after the success of agricultural extension agents in the American Midwest.

Rogers's theory was enormously influential. The United States Agency for International Development (USAID) used its strategy to spread agricultural innovations in the Third World. Rogers was personally involved in implementing and studying a number of these diffusion efforts. During the Cold War of the 1950s and 1960s, the United States competed against the Soviet Union for influence in the developing nations. The hope was that by leading a Green Revolution and helping them better feed themselves, America would gain their favor. But to help them do this, the United States needed to convince peasants and rural villagers to adopt a large number of new agricultural innovations as quickly as possible. Rogers's information/innovation diffusion theory became a training manual for that effort. Change agents from around the world were brought to Michigan State University to learn from Rogers. Many of these people became academics in their home countries, and unlike many other U.S. theories, information/innovation diffusion theory spread through the universities of the developing nations while agricultural innovations were spreading in their fields. In many parts of the world, Rogers's theory became synonymous with communication theory.

Information/innovation diffusion theory represented an important advance over earlier limited-effects theories. Like other classic work of the early 1960s, it drew from existing empirical generalizations and synthesized them into a coherent, insightful perspective. Information/innovation diffusion theory was consistent with most findings from effects surveys and persuasion experiments, and above all, it was very practical. In addition to guiding Third World development, it laid the foundation for numerous promotional communication and marketing theories and the campaigns they support even today.

But the limitations of information/innovation diffusion theory were also serious. It had some unique drawbacks stemming from its application. For example, it facilitated the adoption of innovations that were sometimes not well understood or even desired by adopters. To illustrate, a campaign to get Georgia farm wives to can vegetables was initially judged a great success until researchers found that very few women were using the vegetables. They mounted the glass jars on the walls of their living rooms as status symbols. Most didn't know any recipes for cooking canned vegetables, and those who tried using canned vegetables found that family members didn't like the taste. This sort of experience was duplicated around the world; corn was grown in Mexico and rice was grown in Southeast Asia that no one wanted to eat; farmers in India destroyed their crops by using too much fertilizer; farmers adopted complex new machinery only to have it break down and stand idle after change agents left. Mere top-down diffusion of innovations didn't guarantee long-term success.

INSTANT ACCESS

Information/Innovation Diffusion Theory

Strengths

1. Integrates large amount of empirical findings into useful theory
2. Provides practical guide for information campaigns in United States and abroad

Weaknesses

1. Is linear and source-dominated
2. Underestimates power of media, especially contemporary media
3. Stimulates adoption by groups that don't understand or want the innovation

SOCIAL MARKETING THEORY

social marketing theory
Collection of middle-range theories concerning the promotion of socially valuable information

During the early 1970s, a new macroscopic theory of media and society began to take shape that shares important similarities with diffusion theory. It is known as **social marketing theory.** Unlike diffusion theory that was largely focused on farming innovations in Third World nations, social marketing theory focused on the United States. It is not a unified body of thought but rather a more or less integrated collection of middle-range theories dealing with the promotion of beliefs and actions elite sources deem to be socially valuable. Public health practitioners have been especially drawn to this theory and use it to promote or discourage many different behaviors. Rather than describing each of the theories that make up social marketing theory, we will look at the overarching theoretical framework and then discuss some of its important features. Readers interested in a more extended discussion of these theories and their application might consult other sources (Goldberg, Fishbein, and Middlestadt, 1997; Rice and Atkin, 1989; Grier and Bryant, 2004).

Like diffusion theory, social marketing is an administrative theory (Chapter 1) and essentially source-dominated. It assumes the existence of a benign information provider seeking to bring about useful, beneficial social change. It gives these providers a framework for designing, carrying out, and evaluating information campaigns. In its most recent forms, it pays increased attention to audience activity and the need to reach active audiences with information they are seeking. Target audiences are identified according to their information needs. Recommendations are made for stimulating audiences to seek information and for packaging and distributing information so that audiences will find it easy to get and use.

In addition to sharing many assumptions and concerns with diffusion theory, social marketing theory is also a logical extension of the persuasion theories outlined in Chapter 6. It represents an effort to increase the effectiveness of mass media–based information campaigns through greater understanding and manipulation of aspects of societal and psychological factors. Social marketing theory does this by identifying a variety of social system–level and psychological barriers to the flow of information and influence through the mass media. It anticipates these barriers and includes strategies for overcoming them. Some strategies are ingenious; others involve the brute force of saturation advertising. Social marketing theory has several key features:

1. **Methods for inducing audience awareness of campaign topics or candidates.**
    A key first step in promoting ideas or candidates is to make people aware of their existence. The easiest but most costly way to do this is with a saturation television advertising campaign. As social marketing theories have gained sophistication, other methods have been developed that are almost as effective but much less costly. These include using news coverage and new media channels to induce awareness. During the last four presidential campaigns, the candidates successfully experimented with many new channels for reaching voters, including radio and television talk shows like *Larry King Live,* the MTV cable channel, late-night variety shows like *The Daily Show with Jon Stewart,* and the Internet. These efforts permitted candidates to reach voter segments that are difficult to reach effectively through mainstream media.

Most young people, for example, no longer read newspapers and have learned to selectively screen out political news stories on television. Thus new media channels—especially the Internet and the World Wide Web—offer a means of overcoming barriers to the flow of information that arise over time.

2. **Methods for targeting messages at specific audience segments most receptive or susceptible to those messages.** Limited-effects research demonstrated how to identify audience segments most vulnerable to specific types of messages. Once identified, messages can be targeted at them. **Targeting** is one of several concepts borrowed from product marketing research and converted to the marketing of ideas or political candidates. By identifying the most vulnerable segments and then reaching them with the most efficient channel available, targeting strategies reduce promotional costs while increasing efficiency.

targeting
Identifying specific audience segments and reaching them through the most efficient available channel

3. **Methods for reinforcing messages within targeted segments and for encouraging these people to influence others through face-to-face communication.** Even vulnerable audience members are likely to forget or fail to act on messages unless those messages are reinforced by similar information coming from several channels. Various strategies have been developed to make certain that multiple messages are received from several channels. These strategies include visits by change agents, group discussions, messages placed simultaneously in several media, and door-to-door canvassing.

4. **Methods for cultivating images and impressions of people, products, or services.** These methods are most often used when it is difficult to arouse audience interest. If people aren't interested in a topic, it is unlikely that they will seek and learn information about it. Lack of interest forms a barrier against the flow of information. But it is still possible to transmit images. The most prominent method used to cultivate images is image advertising in which easily recognizable, visually compelling images are presented. Relationships are implied between these and the objects being promoted. For example, a soft drink is presented as it is consumed by very attractive people in an interesting setting. To what extent are your impressions of the U.S. Army or Pepsi shaped by ads that invited you to "Be Army Strong" or be a member of the "Pepsi Generation"?

5. **Methods for stimulating interest and inducing information seeking by audience members.** Information seeking occurs when a sufficient level of interest in ideas or candidates can be generated. Numerous techniques have been developed that stimulate interest and induce information seeking. During political campaigns, candidates stage dramatic events designed to call attention to and stimulate interest in their positions on issues (or the positions of their opponents). Politicians have replaced ribbon-cutting at supermarket openings with standing in the food line at homeless shelters to demonstrate their concern for the poor, or hiking to a pristine mountain lake to represent their commitment to the environment. Various methods have been developed to provide easy access to those forms of information serving the campaign planners' interests once the information seeking has been induced.

6. **Methods for inducing desired decision making or positioning.** Once people are aware and informed, or at least have formed strong images or impressions, they can be moved toward either a conscious decision or an unconscious

prioritization or positioning. Media messages can be transmitted through a variety of channels and used to highlight the value of choosing a specific option or prioritizing one product, service, or candidate relative to others. Change agents and opinion leaders can also be used, though these are more expensive. This is a critical stage in any communication campaign because it prepares people to take an action desired by campaign planners.

7. **Methods for activating audience segments, especially those who have been targeted by the campaign.** Ideally, these audiences will include people who are properly positioned and have decided to act but have not yet found an opportunity. In other cases, people will have prioritized a product, service, or candidate but must be confronted with a situation in which they are compelled to make a choice. Many communication campaigns fail because they lack a mechanism for stimulating action. People seem to be influenced by campaigns, but that influence isn't effectively translated into action. A variety of techniques can be used to activate people, including change agents, free merchandise, free and convenient transportation, free services, moderate fear appeals, and broadcast or telephone appeals from high-status sources.

hierarchy-of-effects model Practical theory calling for the differentiation of persuasion effects relative to the time and effort necessary for their accomplishment

One of the simplest yet most comprehensive social marketing theories is the **hierarchy-of-effects model** (Rice and Atkin, 1989), which states that it is important to differentiate a large number of persuasion effects—some easily induced and others taking more time and effort. This model permits development of a step-by-step persuasion strategy in which the effort begins with easily induced effects, such as awareness, and monitors them using survey research. Feedback from that research is used to decide when to transmit messages designed to produce more difficult effects, such as decision making or activation. Thus the effort begins by creating audience awareness, then cultivates images or induces interest and information seeking, reinforces learning of information or images, aids people in making the "right" decisions, and then activates those people. At each step, the effectiveness of the campaign to that point is monitored, and the messages are changed when the proper results aren't obtained.

INSTANT ACCESS

Social Marketing Theory

Strengths

1. Provides practical guide for information campaigns in United States and abroad
2. Can be applied to serve good ends
3. Builds on attitude change and diffusion theories
4. Is gaining acceptance among media campaign planners and researchers

Weaknesses

1. Is source-dominated
2. Doesn't consider ends of campaigns
3. Underestimates intellect of average people
4. Ignores constraints to reciprocal flow of information
5. Can be costly to implement
6. Has difficulty assessing cultural barriers to influence

The hierarchy-of-effects model was first developed by product marketers but is now widely applied to social marketing. Critics argue that its assumption that certain effects necessarily precede others in time is unwarranted. Some people, for example, can be moved to act without ever being informed or even making a decision about an issue or a candidate. Social marketers respond that although they can't hope to induce all the desired effects in every targeted person, they have evidence that a well-structured step-by-step campaign using survey data to provide feedback is much more successful than persuasion efforts based on simple linear effects models.

Critics of social marketing point to limitations very similar to those raised in our discussion of information-flow theory and of diffusion theory. Though social marketing theory squeezes some benefit out of the older source-dominated linear-effects models, it also suffers many of their limitations. In social marketing models, sources use feedback from target audiences to adjust their campaigns. This use is generally limited to changes in messages; however, long-term persuasion or information goals don't change. If audiences seem resistant, social marketers try new messages in an effort to break down resistance. They give little thought to whether the audience might be justified or correct in resisting information or influence. If the effort to get out information fails, they blame the audience for being apathetic or ignorant—people simply don't know what's good for them.

Thus the social marketing model is tailored to situations in which elite sources are able to dominate elements of the larger social system. These powerful sources can prevent counter-elites from distributing information or marshaling organized opposition. The theory doesn't allow for social conflict and thus can't be applied to situations in which conflict has escalated to even moderate levels. It applies best to routine forms of information and works best when politics is reduced to marketing of competing candidate images or the transmission of innocuous public health messages.

Brenda Dervin (1989) tried to develop an audience-centered social marketing theory that could serve some of its purposes while overcoming obvious limitations. She argued that campaign planners must conceive of communication as a *dialogue* between elite sources and various audience segments. There must be a genuine commitment to the upward flow of information and ideas from audiences even at early stages of campaigns. The purpose of campaigns should not be to induce audiences to do things that elite sources want them to do, but rather to help people learn to responsibly reconstruct their lives in ways useful to them. For example, public health campaigns shouldn't scare people into adopting better diets but should encourage people to fundamentally reorient their lives so better eating habits become one aspect of a larger lifestyle change.

Dervin's model includes many systems theory ideas introduced in Chapter 7. It assumes that mutual interaction between sources and audiences is more effective than a source-dominated communication process. Sources will become better informed about the everyday situations faced by audiences, and audiences will gradually learn useful information for restructuring their lives. Dervin argued that elite sources should learn to respect their audiences. These audiences will then be more likely to see the wisdom of some of the things that those sources want them to do.

Unfortunately, Dervin's model will work only if the many constraints inhibiting or preventing this mutual interaction between elite sources and various audiences—especially lower-status or minority group audiences—can be overcome. This will not be easy. Traditional mass media–based communication systems permit only indirect, usually delayed, often very crude forms of feedback from audiences. This feedback is suitable for redesigning promotional messages but not for gaining deep insight into the life situation and information needs of audience members. Although the situation is improving, even new, more interactive technologies such as digital cable and the Internet suffer from a **digital divide**—the chronic lack of access to these technologies by specific groups of people. For example, although more than 80 percent of Americans have home computers and 92 percent regularly access the Internet, those numbers lag for less educated, lower-income, rural, Hispanic, and African-American households and households in the East South Central region of the country: Alabama, Mississippi, Tennessee, and Kentucky (McGowan, 2009).

digital divide
The lack of access to communication technology among people of color, the poor, the disabled, and those in rural communities

The greater this gap between the life situation of elite sources and that of lower-status audiences, the less likely it is that the exchange will produce useful feedback. Typically, message sources must be able to pay for sophisticated audience research and then be willing and able to act on it. Dervin believes that the new communication technologies will indeed soon significantly reduce the cost of maintaining mutual interaction between sources and audiences. Those who advocate Dervin's more egalitarian social marketing theory see the Internet as so unlike more traditional media technologies that it might allow this greater interaction and exchange. As a result, they vigorously oppose the overregulation and overcommercialization of the net, fearing that these will render the Internet no different from television and other elite-dominated media. They point to phenomena such as Change.gov, established by the Obama administration, which allows citizens to communicate directly with federal officials. Among its features is an *Open for Questions* page built on a Google model of user ranking. People vote on which specific, user-generated questions they would like answered. Vote totals are visible, making it difficult for the President or other officials to avoid questions they would rather not answer. The March, 2009, first-ever "Internet Town Hall" attracted 104,000 questions on which 3.6 million citizens voted (Madden, 2009).

One interesting development in social marketing theory involves the degree to which social marketing is being pitted against product marketing. Some of the most intensive social marketing campaigns are being targeted at teens and are designed to offset problematic behaviors such as binge drinking and junk food addiction typically encouraged by advertising. One example is the Healthy Weight Commitment Foundation, a coalition of more than forty food and beverage advertisers, retailers, and health and educational organizations that have undertaken a national, long-term social marketing effort designed to help reduce childhood obesity (Anthony, 2010).

MEDIA SYSTEM DEPENDENCY THEORY

In its simplest terms, **media system dependency theory** asserts that the more a person depends on having his or her needs met by media use, the more important will be the role that media play in the person's life, and therefore the more influence

media system dependency theory
Idea that the more a person depends on having needs gratified by media use, the more important the media's role will be in the person's life and, therefore, the more influence those media will have

those media will have on that person. From a macroscopic societal perspective, if more and more people become dependent on media, media institutions will be reshaped to serve these dependencies, the overall influence of media will rise, and media's role in society will become more central. Thus there should be a direct relationship between the amount of overall dependency and the degree of media influence or centrality at any given point in time.

Melvin DeFleur and Sandra Ball-Rokeach (1975, pp. 261–263) have provided a fuller explanation in several assertions. First, the "basis of media influence lies in the relationship between the larger social system, the media's role in that system, and audience relationships to the media." Effects occur not because all-powerful media or omnipotent sources compel that occurrence, but because the media operate in a given way in a given social system to meet given audience wants and needs.

Second, "the degree of audience dependence on media information is the key variable in understanding when and why media messages alter audience beliefs, feelings, or behavior." The ultimate occurrence and shape of media effects rests with the audience members and is related to how necessary a given medium or message is to them. The uses people make of media determine media's influence. If we rely on many sources other than media for our information about events, then the role of media is less than if we rely exclusively on a few media sources.

Third, "in our industrial society, we are becoming increasingly dependent on the media (a) to understand the social world, (b) to act meaningfully and effectively in society, and (c) for fantasy and escape." As our world becomes more complex and as it changes more rapidly, we not only need the media to a greater degree to help us make sense, to help us understand what our best responses might be, and to help us relax and cope, but we also ultimately come to know that world largely through those media. Friends and family may not know much about what is going on in the larger social world except what they learn from media. Note the emphasis on meaning making (discussed more fully in Chapter 11) in this assertion. As we use media to make sense of the social world, we permit media to shape our expectations.

Finally, fourth, "the greater the need and consequently the stronger the dependency ... the greater the likelihood" that the media and their messages will have an effect. Not everyone will be equally influenced by media. Those who have greater needs and thus greater dependency on media will be most influenced.

Recalling our discussion of what constitutes an active audience (Chapter 9), we know that the best way to think of activity is to think of it as existing on a continuum, from completely inactive media consumers to very active ones. Because they tied audience activity to audience dependence, DeFleur and Ball-Rokeach described media dependency in just that way. Moreover, they explained that an individual's (or society's) level of dependency is a function of (1) "the number and centrality (importance) of the specific information-delivery functions served by a medium," and (2) the degree of change and conflict present in society.

These assertions can be illustrated with an example involving media use during a crisis. Think of your own media use the last time you found yourself in a natural crisis—in other words, in a time of change or conflict (earthquake, tornado, hurricane, or serious rainstorm or snowstorm). You probably spent more time watching television news than you did watching comedy shows. Now consider what happens when electricity fails during a crisis and cell phone networks are overwhelmed by callers trying to locate family and friends. Your portable radio would likely assume the greater "number and centrality of information delivery functions." Radio and radio news would become your medium and content of choice, respectively. And no doubt, if the crisis deepened, your dependence would increase. So might your attentiveness and willingness to respond as "directed" by that medium and its messages. The point of media system dependency theory is that we have developed a range of routine uses for various media, and we can easily adapt these uses to serve our needs. If one medium fails or is temporarily unavailable, we have no difficulty turning to others. What is important is how we come to depend upon the range of media available to us.

DeFleur and Ball-Rokeach refined and expanded their media system dependency theory a number of times (e.g., DeFleur and Ball-Rokeach, 1989) to account for such "system change," but their thesis never varied much beyond their initial assertion that media can and do have powerful effects. Media dependency has been measured by postpositivist researchers in a variety of ways, and each has its drawbacks. It has not yet been conclusively demonstrated that the experience of media dependency by average people is strongly related to a broad range of effects. Can we be dependent on media without *experiencing* dependency? Can we experience dependency when we are actually quite independent? If so, maybe we should gauge dependency with behavioral rather than attitudinal measures. Or maybe we need to conduct experiments rather than collect survey data. Is this theory better at explaining the consequences of short-term situationally induced dependency (i.e., reaction to a crisis) than long-term chronic dependency?

Ball-Rokeach (1998) provided an interesting analysis of how changing relations between media and government in the late 1960s led to altered coverage of the Vietnam War, which in turn precipitated widespread public questioning of that conflict. The public's skepticism resulted in more dependency on media for information about the war and therefore more discussion of the war with networks of friends and family. The situation Ball-Rokeach describes is not unlike what has happened to news coverage of Iraq as that conflict has lingered on (Massing, 2004).

Finally, the theory doesn't directly address the question of whether there is some ideal level of media dependency. Are Americans currently too dependent on media or too independent? Is the trend toward increased or decreased dependency? Will new media increase our dependency or make us more independent? How will new user-directed technologies like the Internet, personal digital assistants (PDAs), and five-hundred-channel direct broadcast satellites reshape dependence and independence? "You see these tethered souls everywhere: The father joining in an intense Twitter debate at his daughter's dance recital. The woman cracking wise on Facebook while strolling through the mall. The guy on a date reviewing his fish tacos on Yelp. Not to mention drivers staring down instead of through their windshields," says technology writer Michael Rosenwald, "The stereotype of the computer-addicted recluse in the basement has been blown away; smartphones make it possible to turn off the physical world while walking through it. A recent Pew Research Center study found that 'a significant proportion of people

INSTANT ACCESS

Media Systems Dependency Theory

Strengths

1. Is elegant and descriptive
2. Allows for systems orientation
3. Integrates microscopic and macroscopic theory
4. Explains role of media during crisis and social change

Weaknesses

1. Is difficult to verify empirically
2. Meaning and power of dependency are unclear
3. Lacks power in explaining long-term effects

who visit public and semipublic spaces are online while in those spaces.' Parks. Libraries. Restaurants. Houses of worship" (2010, p. A1). The Internet's "# 1 site for BlackBerry users (and abusers)" is called CrackBerry.com. What is implied about devotees of that particular mobile device by that curious name?

Ball-Rokeach and her colleagues (Matei and Ball-Rokeach, 2003; Ball-Rokeach, Kim, and Matei, 2001) have proposed an innovative theory addressing some of these questions that is central to a major research project, the Metamorphosis Project, that Ball-Rokeach directs at the University of Southern California Annenberg School for Communication. In some respects an update of media system dependency theory, it makes more explicit the interconnection between media systems and interpersonal systems. It argues that viable, strong urban communities need an evolving communication infrastructure (including both mediated and interpersonal communication) based around a storytelling system. Storytelling systems provide individuals with the narratives orienting them to each other and to the larger social world. Various forms of media can be integrated into this infrastructure and provide support for the storytelling system. In a neighborhood with an effective communication infrastructure, discussion "transforms people from occupants of a house to members of a neighborhood" (Ball-Rokeach, Kim, and Matei, 2001, p. 392).

Sorin Matei and Sandra Ball-Rokeach (2003) looked at the role of the Internet in several ethnic neighborhoods in Los Angeles. They attempted to measure how the communication infrastructure was related to residents' experience of neighborhood "belongingness." They found that the Internet was linked to "belonging" in English-speaking neighborhoods but not in Asian or Hispanic areas. In those places, Internet usage was similar to mass media usage and at best assisted ethnic assimilation.

THE KNOWLEDGE GAP

Over several decades, a team of researchers at the University of Minnesota (Donohue, Tichenor, and Olien 1986; Tichenor, Donohue, and Olien 1970, 1980) developed a theory of society in which mass media and the use of media messages play a central role. Their model focused on the role played by news media in cities and towns of various sizes. It viewed these areas as subsystems within larger state and regional social systems. The team began by empirically establishing that news media systematically inform some segments of the population, specifically persons in higher socioeconomic groups, better than others. Over time, the differences between the better-informed and the less-informed segments tend to grow—the **knowledge gap** between them gets larger and larger. This research team conducted numerous surveys for twenty-five years to develop and support its theory.

knowledge gap
Systematic differences in knowledge between better-informed and less-informed segments of a population

But just how should we interpret these knowledge gaps? Do they pose long-term problems or could knowledge gaps actually be functional in some way? If we rely on classical democratic Libertarian theory (Chapter 5) to answer these questions, knowledge gaps are troubling. We can be concerned that the people who are less informed will not be able to act as responsible citizens. If they act at all, they will do so based on ignorance. On the other hand, if we use elite pluralism theory (Chapter 6) to speculate about the consequences of knowledge gaps, we are less concerned. After all, there is a strong correlation between political ignorance and political apathy. If the less informed don't vote, they can't upset the system. As long as there is an active, informed minority of societal leaders, the overall system should function smoothly—problems will be resolved by this elite based on their superior knowledge.

Thomas Holbrook (2002) examined knowledge gap on a national level, finding that the gaps narrowed during the course of presidential campaigns. He analyzed data from the National Election Studies from 1976 to 1996 and found that specific events such as political debates were linked to decreases in knowledge gaps. Holbrook's findings are consistent with earlier findings linking reduction of gaps to increases in social conflict that spark widespread public discussion and information seeking.

Naturally, the Internet, with its presumed "democracy" and all-information-all-the-time orientation, has reignited interest in knowledge gap theory. Heinz Bonfadelli (2002) offered a pessimistic view of the Internet's potential role. In Switzerland, he found a digital divide between affluent, better-educated young adults who regularly use the Internet for information and their less-affluent, less-educated peers who either don't have access to the Internet or use it only for entertainment. Not surprisingly, this divide was linked to gaps in knowledge. As our earlier discussion of the digital divide would also suggest, this is the case in the United States as well. The Knight Commission on the Information Needs of Communities in a Democracy (2009) discovered that there are two Americas—one completely wired, one not very well—that produced not only a knowledge-gap, but also literacy and social participation gaps as well.

But even when people are wired, a social participation gap remains. A Pew Internet & American Life Project national study discovered that "contrary to the hopes of some advocates, the Internet is not changing the socio-economic character of civic engagement in America. Just as in offline civic life, the well-to-do and well-educated are more likely than those less well off to participate in online political activities such as emailing a government official, signing an online petition, or making a political contribution" (Smith et al., 2009). These two realities prompted the FCC to call for increased federal spending on a program of digital literacy, possibly

digital literacy corps

Digital ambassadors in local communities helping people get online

through the creation of a **digital literacy corps** (digital ambassadors in local communities helping people get online), to accompany President Obama's plan to bring universal broadband to the United States (Stelter and Wortham, 2010).

It is not only variable access to media technologies, however, that produce knowledge gaps. Individual differences such as information-processing ability and level of cognitive complexity (McLeod and Perse, 1994) and perceived value of being informed (Ettema and Kline, 1997) also widen gaps, as does the quality of the information presented by news organizations. In a comparative study of knowledge gaps in four nations—the United States, Britain, Denmark, and Finland—James Curran, Shanto Iyengar, Brink Lund, and Inka Salovaara-Moring discovered a significant knowledge gap between American television news viewers and viewers of news in those other lands. They attributed the gap to the public service orientation of television news in those latter three countries, which "devotes more attention to public affairs and international news ... gives greater prominence to news [broadcasting news several times an evening in what Americans would call prime-time] ... and encourages higher levels of news consumption" (2009, p. 5). These factors were strong enough to minimize the knowledge gap in those countries between the well educated and less educated and between those who were financially well off and those who weren't.

AGENDA-SETTING

What were the crucial issues in the 2008 presidential election? The United States was faced with an escalating federal budget deficit and a slowly recovering economy. The war in Iraq, now an occupation unpopular with both Americans and Iraqis, regularly dominated the headlines with news about a troublesome insurgency and abuse of Iraqi civilians and detainees. Billions of dollars were being spent to pursue the war and rebuild Iraq. Difficulties encountered in Iraq prompted debate over increasing the size of the military and even raised the question of reinstituting the draft. The culture war that divided the country into red and blue states continued—gay unions and the fitness of homosexuals for military duty were hotly debated. The "No Child Left Behind" legislation mandated widespread testing of educational achievement, and the results were problematic. Despite passage of campaign-financing legislation seeking to limit the influence of money in politics, the presidential candidates raised and spent more money than ever. What do you remember from the mass media as the important issues and images of that campaign? John McCain's age? Sarah Palin and "Thanks, but no thanks?" Barack Obama's middle name, pastor's politics, birthplace, lapel flag pin, or "blackness"? Of all the issues that should or could have been aired and examined, only a few became dominant. Only a few were viewed by many Americans as the most important issues facing the United States. This is **agenda-setting**.

agenda-setting

The idea that media don't tell people what to think, but what to think about

With or without the label, the idea of agenda-setting has been with us since the days of the penny press. Walter Lippmann, in *Public Opinion* (1922), argued that the people do not deal directly with their environments as much as they respond to "pictures" in their heads. "For the real environment is altogether too big, too complex, and too fleeting for direct acquaintance. We are not equipped to deal with so much subtlety, so much variety, so many permutations and combinations.

INSTANT ACCESS

The Knowledge Gap

Strengths

1. Identifies potentially troublesome gaps between groups
2. Provides ideas for overcoming gaps
3. Presumes reciprocity and audience activity in communication
4. Is grounded in systems theory

Weaknesses

1. Assumes gaps are always dysfunctional; not all researchers agree
2. Limits focus to gaps involving news and social conflicts
3. Can't address fundamental reasons for gaps (e.g., poor schools or limited access to information sources)

And although we have to act in that environment, we have to reconstruct it on a simpler model before we can manage with it" (p. 16). If you remember our discussion of Lippmann in Chapters 4 and 5, then you know that he concluded that average people just can't be trusted to make important political decisions based on these simplified pictures. Average people have to be protected, and the important decisions have to be made by technocrats who use better models to guide their actions. Thus modern agenda-setting notions derive more or less directly from a mass society perspective. Critics have noted this connection.

Although he did not specifically use the term, Bernard Cohen (1963) is generally credited with refining Lippmann's ideas into the theory of agenda-setting. "The press is significantly more than a purveyor of information and opinion," he wrote. "It may not be successful much of the time in telling people what to think, but it is stunningly successful in telling its readers what to think about. And it follows from this that the world looks different to different people, depending not only on their personal interests, but also on the map that is drawn for them by the writers, editors, and publishers of the papers they read" (p. 13). Parenthetically, it's hard to ignore the limited-effects bias in Cohen's thinking. He first argued that the press is rarely successful in telling people what to think, but then said that the world looks different to different people depending on what the press offers them. Another way of interpreting this is that Cohen took a mass society perspective and revised it to make it compatible with the limited-effects perspective.

Cohen's writing became the basis for what we now call the agenda-setting function of the mass media. This perspective might have lingered in obscurity had it not been empirically confirmed by research conducted by Maxwell E. McCombs and Donald Shaw (1972). They explained their interpretation of agenda-setting: "In choosing and displaying news, editors, newsroom staff, and broadcasters play an important part in shaping political reality. Readers learn not only about a given issue, but how much importance to attach to that issue from the amount of information in a news story and its position.... The mass media may well determine the important issues—that is, the media may set the 'agenda' of the campaign" (p. 176).

During September and October of the 1968 presidential election, these researchers interviewed one hundred registered voters who had not yet committed to either candidate (presumably these people would be more open to media messages). By asking each respondent "to outline the key issues as he [sic] saw them, regardless of what the candidates might be saying at the moment," they were able to identify and rank by importance just what these people thought were the crucial issues facing them. They then compared these results with a ranking of the time and space accorded to various issues produced by a content analysis of the television news, newspapers, newsmagazines, and editorial pages available to voters in the area where the study was conducted. The results? "The media appear to have exerted a considerable impact on voters' judgments of what they considered the major issues of the campaign.... The correlation between the major item emphasis on the main campaign issues carried by the media and voters' independent judgments of what were the important issues was +.967," they wrote. "In short, the data suggest a very strong relationship between the emphasis placed on different campaign issues by the media ... and the judgments of voters as to the salience and importance of various campaign topics" (McCombs and Shaw, 1972, pp. 180–181).

This important and straightforward study highlights both the strengths and limitations of agenda-setting as a theory of media effects. It clearly establishes that there is an important relationship between media reports and people's ranking of public issues. On the negative side, we can see that the logic of agenda-setting seems well suited for the question of news and campaigns, but what about other kinds of content and other kinds of effects? More important, though, is the question of the actual nature of the relationship between news and its audience. Maybe the public sets the media's agenda and then the media reinforce it. The McCombs and Shaw analysis, like most early agenda-setting research, implies a direction of influence from media to audience—that is, it implies causality. But the argument that the media are simply responding to their audiences can be easily made. Few journalists have not uttered at least once in their careers, "We only give the people what they want." McCombs (1981) himself acknowledged these limitations.

It is important not to judge the utility of the agenda-setting approach based on the earliest studies. Although these had many limitations, they have inspired other research that is providing intriguing if still controversial results. For example, Shanto Iyengar and Donald Kinder attempted to overcome some of the problems of earlier work in a series of experiments published in 1987. Because of the unanswered questions about causality, they lamented, "agenda-setting may be an apt metaphor, but it is no theory. The lack of a theory of media effects has significantly impeded our understanding of how democracy works" (Iyengar and Kinder, 1987, p. 3). To develop such a theory, they offered a testable "agenda-setting hypothesis: Those problems that receive prominent attention on the national news become the problems the viewing public regards as the nation's most important" (1987, p. 16). Their series of experiments examined agenda-setting, the vividness of news reports, the positioning of stories, and what they called **priming**.

priming
In agenda-setting, the idea that media draw attention to some aspects of political life at the expense of others

- **Agenda-setting:** Iyengar and Kinder demonstrated causality. They wrote: "Americans' view of their society and nation are powerfully shaped by the stories that appear on the evening news. We found that people who were shown network broadcasts edited to draw attention to a particular problem assigned greater importance to that problem—greater importance than they themselves did before the experiment began, and greater importance than did people assigned to control conditions that emphasized different problems. Our subjects regarded the target problem as more important for the country, cared more about it, believed that government should do more about it, reported stronger feelings about it, and were much more likely to identify it as one of the country's most important problems" (Iyengar and Kinder, 1987, p. 112).

- **Vividness of presentation:** Iyengar and Kinder found that dramatic news accounts undermined rather than increased television's agenda-setting power. Powerfully presented personal accounts (a staple of contemporary television news) might focus too much attention on the specific situation or individual rather than on the issue at hand.

- **Position of a story:** Lead stories had a greater agenda-setting effect. Iyengar and Kinder offered two possible reasons for this result. First, people paid more attention to the stories at the beginning of the news, and these were less likely to fall victim to the inevitable interruptions experienced when viewing at home. Second, people accepted the news program's implicit designation of a lead story as most newsworthy.

- **Priming:** This is the idea that even the most motivated citizens cannot consider all that they know when evaluating complex political issues. Instead, people consider the things that come easily to mind, or as the researchers said, "those bits and pieces of political memory that are accessible." You can hear echoes of information-processing theory here. Iyengar and Kinder's research (1987) strongly demonstrated that "through priming [drawing attention to some aspects of political life at the expense of others] television news [helps] to set the terms by which political judgments are reached and political choices made" (p. 114). Writing in a later study, Iyengar (1991) offered this distinction: "While agenda-setting reflects the impact of news coverage on the perceived importance of national issues, priming refers to the impact of news coverage on the weight assigned to specific issues in making political judgments" (p. 133).

agenda-building
A collective process in which media, government, and the citizenry reciprocally influence one another in areas of public policy

Agenda-setting, primarily a micro-level effects perspective, has another interesting contemporary articulation as a more macro-level theory: **agenda-building,** "the often complicated process by which some issues become important in policy making arenas" (Protess et al., 1991, p. 6). Kurt Lang and Gladys Lang (1983) defined "agenda-building—a more apt term than agenda-setting—[as] a collective process in which media, government, and the citizenry reciprocally influence one another" (pp. 58–59). The Langs provided a useful case study of agenda-building during the Watergate crisis.

Agenda-building presumes cognitive effects (increases in knowledge), an active audience (as seen in the Lang and Lang definition), and societal-level effects (as seen in both definitions). Its basic premise—that media can profoundly affect how a society (or nation or culture) determines what are its important concerns and therefore can mobilize its various institutions toward meeting them—has allowed this line of inquiry, in the words of David Protess and his colleagues (1991), to "flourish."

framing theory
Idea that people use sets of expectations to make sense of their social world and media contribute to those expectations

second-order agenda-setting
The idea that media set the public's agenda at a second level or order—the attribute level ("how to think about it"), where the first order was the object level ("what to think about")

frames
In framing theory, a specific set of expectations used to make sense of some aspect of the social world in a specific situation and time

Agenda-setting pioneer McCombs has undertaken an effort to expand and develop the theory by linking it to a broad range of other media theories—for example, **framing theory** (McCombs and Ghanem, 2001). We provide a detailed description of framing theory in Chapter 11. He calls his new theory **second-order agenda-setting**. McCombs argues that agenda-setting operates at two levels, or orders: the object level and the attribute level. Conventional agenda-setting research has focused at the object level and has assessed how media coverage could influence the priority assigned to objects (e.g., issues, candidates, events, and problems). In doing this, media told us "*what* to think about." But media can also tell us "*how* to think about" some objects. Media do this by influencing second-order "attribute agendas." They tell us which object attributes are important and which ones are not. Alan Rubin and Paul Haridakis (2001) offer a similar view.

McCombs argues that second-order agenda-setting and framing share common concerns for attribute agendas (**frames**), the dynamics of the agenda-setting process (framing process), and agenda-setting influence (framing effects). McCombs believes that the integration of agenda-setting theory with framing theory will help clarify some of the concepts in framing theory. He advocates "explication of a more general theoretical structure describing the frames and attributes that are important to the communication process" (McCombs and Ghanem, 2001, p. 79).

Dietram Scheufele provided an overview of agenda-setting, priming, and framing theories in which he argued that agenda-setting and priming are compatible theories but that framing is quite different because it involves activation of entire interpretive schemas—not merely prioritization of individual objects or attributes. He wrote:

Agenda-setting and priming rely on the notion of attitude accessibility. Mass media have the power to increase levels of importance assigned to issues by audience members. They increase the salience of issues or the ease with which these considerations can be retrieved from memory.... Framing, in contrast, is based on the concept of prospect theory; that is, on the assumption that subtle changes in the wording of the description of a situation might affect how audience members interpret this situation. In other words, that framing influences how audiences think about issues, not by making aspects of the issue more salient, but by invoking interpretive schemas that influence the interpretation of incoming information. (Scheufele, 2000, p. 309)

INSTANT ACCESS

Agenda-Setting

Strengths

1. Focuses attention on audience interaction with media
2. Empirically demonstrates links between media exposure, audience motivation to seek orientation, and audience perception of public issues
3. Integrates a number of similar ideas, including priming, story positioning, and story vividness

Weaknesses

1. Has roots in mass society theory
2. Is too situationally specific to news and political campaigns
3. Direction of agenda-setting effect is questioned by some

Kevin Carragee and Wim Roefs raise other questions about this effort to link framing and agenda-setting:

> Reducing frames to story topics also characterizes framing research inspired by the agenda-setting perspective. McCombs, Llamas, Lopez-Escobar, and Rey (1997) claimed that framing is the second level of agenda-setting. They contend that "both the selection of objects for attention and the selection of attributes for thinking about these objects are powerful agenda-setting roles" (p. 704). The definition of frames within this tradition, however, differs considerably from past, and, in our view, richer definitions of this concept. (Carragee and Roefs, 2004, p. 217)

In Chapter 11, we will return to this disagreement about the links between framing and agenda-setting. Both theories continue to be widely applied and often are used together as a way of developing a comprehensive strategy for examining the production, dissemination, and comprehension of news stories.

THE SPIRAL OF SILENCE

spiral of silence
Idea that people holding views contrary to those dominant in the media are moved to keep those views to themselves for fear of rejection

A somewhat more controversial theory of media and public opinion is the concept of the **spiral of silence**. This can be regarded as a form of agenda-setting but one focused on macro-level rather than micro-level consequences. In the words of its originator, Elisabeth Noelle-Neumann (1984), "Observations made in one context [the mass media] spread to another and encourage people either to proclaim their views or to swallow them and keep quiet until, in a spiraling process, the one view dominated the public scene and the other disappeared from public awareness as its adherents became mute. This is the process that can be called a 'spiral of silence'" (p. 5).

In other words, because of people's fear of isolation or separation from those around them, they tend to keep their attitudes to themselves when they think they are in the minority. The media, because of a variety of factors, tend to present one (or at most two) sides of an issue to the exclusion of others, which further encourages those people to keep quiet and makes it even tougher for the media to uncover and register that opposing viewpoint. Spiral-of-silence theory provides an excellent example of a theory that argues for cumulative effects of media. Once a spiral of silence is initiated, the magnitude of media influence will increase to higher and higher levels over time. Many of the media theories we have looked at so far assume that personal communication is more powerful than media, but spiral-of-silence theory argues that media can have a powerful influence on everyday talk. Media can literally silence public discourse on certain topics by declaring them to be settled in favor of one position or another.

Noelle-Neumann's focus is not on micro-level understandings of how average people come to perceive the public agenda; rather, she is concerned with the macro-level long-term consequences of these perceptions. If various viewpoints about agenda items are ignored, marginalized, or trivialized by media reports, people will be reluctant to talk about them. As time passes, those viewpoints will cease to be heard in public and therefore cannot affect political decision making.

Noelle-Neumann (1973) argued that her perspective involves a "return to the concept of powerful mass media." She believed that the limited-effects perspective erred in its assertion that selective perception limits media to reinforcement effects—that people interpret media messages based on preexisting attitudes and beliefs and therefore reinforcement of those attitudes and beliefs is the result. Incorrect, she wrote, because "as regards the connection between selective perception and the effect of the mass media, one can put forward the hypothesis that the more restricted the selection the less the reinforcement principle applies, in other words the greater the possibility of mass media changing attitudes" (1973, p. 78).

The way news is collected and disseminated, she continued, effectively restricts the breadth and depth of selection available to citizens. She identified three characteristics of the news media that produce this scarcity of perspective:

1. **Ubiquity:** The media are virtually everywhere as sources of information.
2. **Cumulation:** The various news media tend to repeat stories and perspectives across their different individual programs or editions, across the different media themselves, and across time.
3. **Consonance:** The congruence, or similarity, of values held by newspeople influences the content they produce.

This view of media effects suggests that two different social processes, one macro-level and one micro-level, simultaneously operate to produce effects. Audience members, because of their desire to be accepted, choose to remain silent when confronted with what they perceive to be prevailing counteropinion. Newspeople, because of the dynamics of their news-gathering function, present a restricted selection of news, further forcing into silence those in the audience who wish to avoid isolation.

In an essay critical of spiral-of-silence theory, Ehhu Katz (1983) summarized Noelle-Neumann's thinking this way:

> (1) Individuals have opinions; (2) Fearing isolation, individuals will not express their opinions if they perceive themselves unsupported by others; (3) A "quasi-statistical sense" is employed by individuals to scan the environment for signs of support; (4) Mass media constitute the major source of reference for information about the distribution of opinion and thus the climate of support/nonsupport; (5) So do other reference groups ... ; (6) The media tend to speak in one voice, almost monopolistically; (7) The media tend to distort the distribution of opinion in society, biased as they are by the ... views of journalists; (8) Perceiving themselves unsupported, groups of individuals—who may, at times, even constitute a majority—will lose confidence and withdraw from public debate, thus speeding the demise of their position through the self-fulfilling spiral of silence. They may not change their own minds, but they stop recruitment of others and abandon the fight; (9) Society is manipulated and impoverished thereby. (p. 89)

This understanding led Katz to conclude that these "more subtle, more sociological [macro-level] definitions of effect" (p. 96) would have us "consider the dark side of mass communication. Even in the democracies, media—like interpersonal communication—can impose acquiescence and silence in defiance of the free flow of information" (p. 91). This commentary is especially noteworthy because it is offered by someone who helped pioneer uses-and-gratifications research and who coauthored a classic limited-effects study based on the data collected in Decatur (Katz and Lazarsfeld, 1955). Katz clearly was reluctant to accept Noelle-Neumann's assertions and discredited them by arguing that they are an updated version of mass society theory.

The spiral-of-silence idea has encountered other criticisms as well. Charles Salmon and F. Gerald Kline (1985) wrote that the effects explained by the spiral of silence could just as easily be understood as the product of the bandwagon effect (everybody wants to join a winner) or of projection (people's natural tendency to use their own opinions to form perceptions of the general climate of opinion around them). In addition, these critics argued that individual factors, such as a person's degree of ego-involvement in an issue, should be considered (regardless of the climate of opinion surrounding you, if you feel very strongly about the issue, you might not want to remain silent, even if isolation is a threat). Salmon and Kline call, too, for further examination of individual demographic differences that Noelle-Neumann suggested would combine to produce people who are more likely to speak out—males, younger people, and members of the middle and upper classes, for example.

Drawing on the notion that pluralistic groups can mediate media effects, Carroll Glynn and Jack McLeod (1985) faulted the spiral of silence for underestimating the power of people's communities, organizations, and reference groups in mitigating media influence on the larger society. Regardless of the consonant view of racial equality presented in the news, they might say, a Ku Klux Klan member would probably feel no great threat of alienation for expressing views to teammates between innings of a Klan softball game. Glynn and McLeod also questioned the generalizability of Noelle-Neumann's research (conducted almost exclusively in what was then West Germany) to the American situation, and they raised the possibility of situations in which media can actually move people to speak up rather than remain silent.

Noelle-Neumann (1985) responded simply that the media, especially television, adopt a prevailing attitude in any controversy as a matter of course, and as a result, they present a "dominant tendency." Holders of the minority viewpoint are willing to speak out if they feel that they are supported by the media dominant tendency (as during the civil rights movement). Moreover, she offered an alternative perspective of the media's ability to increase speaking out in the face of rejection:

> It appears that the intensive articulation of a certain viewpoint in the media gives the followers of this viewpoint the advantage of being better equipped to express their point of view.... The resulting willingness to talk has nothing to do with fear of

INSTANT ACCESS

The Spiral of Silence

Strengths

1. Has macro-and micro-level explanatory power
2. Is dynamic
3. Accounts for shifts in public opinion, especially during campaigns
4. Raises important questions concerning the role and responsibility of news media

Weaknesses

1. Has overly pessimistic view of media influence and average people
2. Ignores other, simpler explanations of silencing
3. Ignores possible demographic and cultural differences in the silencing effect
4. Discounts power of community to counteract the silencing effect

isolation, it only makes talking easier. By using words and arguments taken from the media to discuss a topic, people cause the point of view to be heard in public and give it visibility, thus creating a situation in which the danger of isolation is reduced. (p. 80)

Noelle-Neumann's arguments can be easily related to the news media's role in the muted debate over the necessity for the invasion of Iraq in 2003. You can read more about this in the box entitled "The War in Iraq as Theories Lab."

THINKING *about* **THEORY** | THE WAR IN IRAQ AS THEORIES LAB: SPIRAL OF SILENCE, NEWS PRODUCTION RESEARCH, AND OBJECTIVITY RITUALS

The media's performance in the run-up to the 2003 invasion of Iraq and coverage once the shooting began provide a real-world laboratory for many of the theories we've studied in this text. As we've already seen (Chapter 5), the government's claims regarding weapons of mass destruction and the media's apparent unwillingness to challenge them tell us much about contemporary propaganda, normative, and social responsibility theories. But as the war dragged on, people from all sides of the war debate—academics, media professionals, legislators, ordinary citizens—began asking tough questions about the hows and whys of what many felt was a colossal failure of our mass media. To their credit, the editors of the *New York Times* addressed their own inadequacies in an editorial page apology (Editors, 2004). They asked forgiveness for "a number of instances of coverage that was not as rigorous as it should have been." They continued:

> In some cases, information that was controversial then, and seems questionable now, was insufficiently qualified or allowed to stand unchallenged. Looking back, we wish we had been more aggressive in re-examining the claims as new evidence emerged—or failed to emerge.... Editors at several levels who should have been challenging reporters and pressing for more skepticism were perhaps too intent on rushing scoops into the paper.

Their promise to "be more aggressive" in the future and "set the record straight" left many critics unsatisfied, but it did provide the focus for a nationwide conversation on the media, one that, whether folks knew it or not, was a discussion of several of the mass communication theories presented in this chapter, especially the spiral of silence, news production research, and objectivity rituals.

The administration made several assertions about the impending war: Iraq possessed weapons of mass destruction, al Qaeda and Iraq were collaborators in terrorism, U.S. soldiers would be welcomed as heroes by the Iraqi people, the war would pay for itself with the resumption of the flow of Iraqi oil. Did the media's uncritical repetition of these "slam-dunk facts" (in the words of former CIA chief George Tenet) spiral people's antiwar criticism into silence? Reporter John Nichols (2002) tells the story of the Greensboro (NC) Peace Coalition: "After some hesitation," the group decided to enter an antiwar contingent in the annual Fourth of July parade. Although "many expressed qualms about marching into the thick of their hometown's annual patriotic celebration" carrying posters of noted antiwar activists from history such as Mark Twain and the Reverend Martin Luther King, "fifty activists showed up on the Fourth and got the surprise of their political lives. Along the mile-and-a-half parade route through downtown, ... they were greeted mostly with applause, and, at the end of their march, they were honored by parade organizers for Best Interpretation of the Theme" (which was American Heroes). Said coalition chairman Ed Whitfield, "There's a real lesson in this. If you scratch the surface of the poll numbers about ... overwhelming support, you get down to a lot of people with a lot of questions. Some of them are afraid that they are alone in what they are thinking" (p. 24).

Journalist Frances Cerra Whittelsey (2003) explained the source of that fear:

> For the public, this lack of coverage [of significant antiwar sentiment and activity] reinforced the image of a nation united behind George W. Bush. By failing to notice this citizen activity, the media made itself complicit in public apathy,

(Continued)

sustaining and in effect promoting the view that ordinary Americans are powerless non-participants in the game of government. In this view, the press need cover only the professional politicians and bureaucrats. (p. 13)

She may have been describing an example of spiral of silence, but can you see hints of news production research in her explanation? That body of thought can help answer journalist Michael Massing's challenge to his colleagues: "Where were you all before the war … when it might have made a difference?" (2004, p. 1). How well does your recollection of media coverage of the war match these elements of news production research?

Normalized news: Content analysis of war coverage by Fairness and Accuracy in Reporting found that "U.S. television news coverage of the Iraq situation continues to be dominated by government and military officials" (Whiten, 2004, p. 3). Of the 414 reports on Iraq aired on the three broadcast networks from September 2002 to the start of the invasion in March 2003, "all but thirty-four originated in the White House, the Pentagon, and State Department" (Cunningham, 2003, p. 26).

Personalized news: The war was Bush versus Saddam ("He tried to kill my dad," said the president). Headlines such as "Bush-Taliban Stalemate Grows" and "Bush to Saddam: 'Good Riddance'" were common.

Dramatized news: This was a titanic struggle, the resolute War President versus the Butcher of Baghdad. "Reporters are biased toward conflict because it is more interesting than stories without conflict," said *San Jose Mercury News* reporter Eric Nalder. "We are biased toward existing narratives because they are safe and easy" (quoted in Cunningham, 2003, p. 30).

Fragmented news: How much did you read or see of our long-standing military and industrial support of Saddam in the years before the Iraq invasion of Kuwait? Did your local paper or network television news run the readily available (on the Internet and in the alternative press) photograph of Vice President Dick Cheney, then-CEO of Halliburton, sitting with Saddam in his palace, negotiating for oil pipeline construction contracts for his company?

Media critics argued that some historical content and perspective on "The Butcher of Baghdad" might have helped citizens better judge the government's calls for conflict. But why, with war in the balance, did the media so easily fall back on these routine ways of producing the news? The answer resides, charged critics, in objectivity rituals. *Columbia Journalism Review* managing editor Brent Cunningham explained:

> In his March 6 press conference, in which he laid out his reasons for the coming war, President Bush mentioned al Qaeda or the attacks of September 11 fourteen times in fifty-two minutes. No one challenged him on it, despite the fact that the CIA had questioned the Iraq-al Qaeda connection, and that there has never been solid evidence marshaled to support the idea that Iraq was involved in the attacks of 9/11. (2003, pp. 24–25)

Why? The media, continued Cunningham, "allowed the principle of objectivity to make us passive recipients of news, rather than aggressive analyzers and explainers of it." ABC's Sam Donaldson clarified, telling *USA Today* that it is difficult for the media, especially during war, "to press very hard when they know that a large segment of the population doesn't want to see a president whom they have anointed having to squirm." But, asked *Columbia Journalism Review*, "If we're about to go to war—especially one that is controversial—shouldn't the president squirm?" (Cunningham, 2003, p. 30).

Do you think these theories apply to media coverage of the war and its run-up? What about some of the other theories described in this chapter? Can you apply them to the news coverage of the war in Iraq? In the wake of the September 11 terrorist attacks, might Americans have been especially dependent on media sources for information about the Middle East and potential threats? Did people on the wrong side of the knowledge gap have limited access to a wide range of perspectives? Has Iraq news coverage intruded into party politics?

Might people have been more critical, if not skeptical, recipients of the news about the need for war in Iraq had they been aware of these theories and how they manifest themselves in the real world? Do you think they might have formed different opinions about the conflict and its necessity and propriety? Can (and should) theory help people make these kinds of judgments?

As with any theoretical proposition that challenges the prevailing view of the time—specifically, the limited-effects perspective—spiral of silence and agenda-setting both encountered intense criticism, and their adherents had to overcome a fear of isolation and rejection from others in the discipline, just as Noelle-Neumann might have predicted. Nonetheless, these assertions of sometimes powerful mass media helped move mass communication theory toward its more contemporary stance.

NEWS PRODUCTION RESEARCH

During the past four decades, several studies have been conducted on the production and consumption of news content (Crouse, 1973; Epstein, 1973; Fishman, 1980; Gans, 1979; Gitlin, 1980; Tuchman, 1978; Whiten, 2004). Most of the research we discuss in this section was undertaken by British and American sociologists during the 1970s and 1980s. Their purpose was to critically analyze how journalists routinely cover news. Most of this research supports theories about the intrusion of media into politics as well as cultural commodification theories (see Chapter 11).

news production research

The study of how the institutional routines of news production inevitably produce distorted or biased content

W. Lance Bennett (1988, 2005a) surveyed **news production research** literature and summarized four ways in which current news production practices distort or bias news content:

1. **Personalized news:** Most people relate better to individuals than to groups or institutions, so most news stories center around people. According to Bennett (1988), "The focus on individual actors[s] who are easy to identify with positively or negatively invites members of the news audience to project their own private feelings and fantasies directly onto public life" (p. 27). Thus personalization helps people relate to and find relevance in remote events. It does this, however, at a cost. "When television news reports about poverty focus on an individual's situation rather than on poverty more generally," wrote *New York Times Magazine* editor Alexander Star, "viewers look for someone (the poor person or someone else) who caused the hardship. But this ... is to avoid the whole complicated process that brought someone grief. Stories call our attention away from chance, the influence of institutions or social structures, or the incremental contributions that different factors typically make to any outcome. And they follow conventions that verge on melodrama: events are caused by individuals who act deliberately, and what those individuals do reflects their underlying character. This, to put it mildly, is not how most things happen (2008, p. 10). Reality becomes little more than a series of small, individual soap operas.

2. **Dramatized news:** Like all media commodities, news must be attractively packaged, and a primary means of doing this involves dramatization. Edward Jay Epstein (1973) provided the following quotation from a policy memorandum written by a network television news producer: "Every news story should, without any sacrifice of probity or responsibility, display the attributes of fiction, of drama. It should have structure and conflict, problem and denouement, rising action and falling action, a beginning, a middle, and an end. These are not only the essentials of drama; they are the essentials of narrative" (pp. 4–5).

Consider the long, contentious national debate over health care reform that has gripped the nation for the last several years. Although most Americans would agree that "something must be done" about spiraling costs, denial of coverage, terminated policies, and the uninsured, "the problem with healthcare is that it's so big and so complicated that the public is never really going to understand all the moving parts," said National Public Radio's Julie Rovner. "It's not a journalism-friendly story," added the *New York Times*'s John Harwood (both in Hart, 2009b, p. 7). MSNBC's Dylan Ratigan explained, "Health care is bad for ratings" (in Rich, 2009, p. WK8).

News production research explains that the way to solve the problem is to add a bit of drama; Congressman Earl Blumenauer from Oregon explains how that was accomplished: "All the national news organizations monitored any meetings they could find between lawmakers and constituents [about healthcare reform], looking for flare-ups, for YouTube moments. The meetings that involved thoughtful exchanges or even support for the proposals would never find their way on air; coverage was given only to the most outrageous behavior, furthering distorting the true picture" (2009, p. WK12).

Media critic Howard Kurtz (2009) identified an archetypal moment. At the height of the raucous, sometimes violent public forums of summer, 2009, President Obama met with a group of citizens in New Hampshire in a nationally televised talk. Partway through the "low-key" discussion, Fox News anchor Trace Gallagher explained to viewers that his network would be leaving the event, but would return. "Any contentious questions, anybody yelling, we'll bring it to you." Fox News, generally unsympathetic to healthcare reform, was not atypical. A reporter for one of the three commercial broadcast networks told Congressman David Price of North Carolina that his network assigned ten reporters to cover meetings across the country but that he was advised by news executives that "your meeting doesn't get covered unless it blows up" (Dionne, 2009, p. A19).

3. **Fragmented news:** The typical newspaper and news broadcast is made up of brief capsulized reports of events—snapshots of the social world. By constructing news in this way, journalists attempt to fulfill their norm of objectivity. Events are treated in isolation with little effort to interconnect them. Connection requires putting them into a broader context, and this would require making speculative, sometimes controversial linkages. Is there a link between three isolated plane crashes, or between three separate toxic waste spills? Should journalists remind readers of a candidate's three divorces when reporting on that politician's opposition to gay unions in the name of "preserving the sanctity of marriage"? By compartmentalizing events, news reports make it difficult for news consumers to make their own connections. Bennett argued that when journalists attempt to do analysis, they create a collage. They assemble evidence and viewpoints from conflicting sources and then juxtapose these pieces in a manner that defies interpretation, especially by news consumers who lack interest or background knowledge. These stories might meet the norm of being "balanced," but they don't assist the reader in making sense of things.

4. **Normalized news:** Stories about disasters or about social movements tend to "normalize" these potential threats to the status quo. Elite sources are allowed

to explain disasters and to challenge movement members. Elites are presented as authoritative, rational, knowledgeable people who are effectively coping with threats. They can be trusted to bring things back to normal. If there is a problem with aircraft technology, it will be repaired—the FAA has the flight recorder and will pinpoint the cause of the crash as soon as possible. If movements make legitimate demands, they will be satisfied—the governor has announced that he is forming a blue-ribbon commission to study the problem. Threat of terrorist attack? Don't worry, the government will protect you (just don't ask too many questions).

There are several reasons for this tendency. One is availability; reporters can easily find officials. Another is the need to maintain access to valued news sources (more on this later). A third reason for the normalization resides in the political economy of the news business (Chapter 8), and it is evident in reporter Evan Thomas's *Newsweek* 2009 cover story on why liberals were upset with President Obama's handling of the economic recovery. He wrote, "If you are of the establishment persuasion (and I am), reading [these criticisms] makes you uneasy.... By definition, establishments believe in propping up the existing order. Members of the ruling class have a vested interest in keeping things pretty much the way they are. Safeguarding the status quo, protecting traditional institutions, can be healthy and useful, stabilizing and reassuring" (p. 22).

Gaye Tuchman (1978) provides a good example of news production research. She studied how the values held by journalists influence news, even when they make considerable effort to guard against that influence. She observed journalists as they covered social movements and concluded that production practices were implicitly biased toward support of the status quo. She found that reporters engage in **objectivity rituals**—they have set procedures for producing unbiased news stories that actually introduce bias.

objectivity rituals In news production research, the term for professional practices designed to ensure objectivity that are implicitly biased toward support of the status quo

For example, when leaders of a controversial movement were interviewed, their statements were never allowed to stand alone. Journalists routinely attempted to "balance" these statements by reporting the views of authorities who opposed the movements. Reporters frequently selected the most unusual or controversial statements made by movement leaders and contrasted these with the more conventional views of mainstream group leaders. Reporters made little effort to understand the overall philosophy of the movement. Lacking understanding, they inevitably took statements out of context and misrepresented movement ideals. Thus, though reporters never explicitly expressed negative views about these groups, their lack of understanding, their casual methods for selecting quotes, and their use of elite sources led to stories harmful to the movements they covered. Tuchman's arguments have been corroborated by Mark Fishman (1980) and Todd Gitlin (1980).

Environmental news, especially coverage of climate change, offers another example of how these objectivity rituals routinely support the status quo. Whereas the world scientific community overwhelmingly believes in global warming and the greenhouse effect, with some estimates as high as 95 percent of all scientists working in climatology, astronomy, and meteorology accepting these phenomena as scientific fact, when they are covered in the popular press, the issue is presented as in scientific dispute. Reporters, in their efforts to be "fair" and "objective," seek out spokespeople from "both sides," often turning to groups like the Global Climate Coalition, a public relations creation of the world's leading chemical companies. *Science* magazine's executive editor-in-chief, Donald Kennedy, explained the process to science writer Chris Mooney. "There's a very small set of people who question the consensus," he said. "And there are a great many thoughtful reporters in the media who believe that in order to produce a balanced story, you've got to pick one commentator from side A and one commentator from side B. I call it the two-card Rolodex problem" (Mooney, 2004, p. 29).

In a thirty-second television news spot that presents two experts, the logical audience reading is that this issue is in some scientific dispute. "The trouble with this conception of journalism," argues media critic Marty Kaplan, "is that it inherently tilts the playing field in favor of liars, who are expert at gaming this system. It

---

THINKING about THEORY   THE STENOGRAPHERS?

You might find Todd Gitlin's charge that journalists are "stenographers with amnesia" a bit harsh, but he was not alone in his condemnation of reporters' performance as the nation debated whether to go to war. Today, with the advantage of several years' of hindsight, critics—in academia and in the press—typically point to Judith Miller as the poster child for this phenomenon. Her self-defense has become media legend: "My job isn't to assess the government's information and be an independent intelligence analyst myself. My job is to tell readers of the *New York Times* what the government thought of Iraq's arsenal" (Sherman, 2004, pp. 4–5). Two other well-known reporters, David Ignatius and Dan Rather, offered the following defenses of their work:

> In a sense, the media were victims of their own professionalism. Because there was little criticism of the war from prominent Democrats and foreign policy analysts, journalistic rules meant we shouldn't create a debate on our own.
>
> Source: —*Washington Post* columnist David Ignatius

> Look, when a president of the United States, any President, Republican or Democrat, says these are the facts, there is heavy prejudice, including my own, to give him the benefit of any doubt, and for that I do not apologize.
>
> Source: —former CBS anchor, Dan Rather
> (both in Rendall, 2004, p. 6)

What do you think? Was it the opposition party's place to raise questions about the administration's assertions, or should reporters have been more aggressive? What about the nearly 156 mostly Democratic senators and representatives who voted against going to war in 2003? Did they not offer at least the appearance of debate? Do you believe that journalists should give prominent politicians "the benefit of the doubt"? If so, when? In every circumstance? The very first tenet in the Society of Professional Journalists Code of Ethics, under the heading "Seek Truth and Report It," is "Test the accuracy of information from all sources." Just below that is "The public is entitled to as much information as possible on sources' credibility" (*www.spj.org*). Can you reconcile the Ignatius and Rather defenses with the society's professional expectations?

Here, then, is fake reporter Rob Corddry's response to fake news anchor Jon Stewart after Stewart challenged Corddry's assertion that "established, incontrovertible fact is *one* side of the story" on Comedy Central's satirical news program *The Daily Show*: "I'm a reporter, Jon, and my job is to spend half the time repeating what one side says, and half the time repeating the other. Little thing called 'objectivity'—might want to look it up some time" (in Alterman, 2006, p. 10).

Can you reconcile Corddry's tongue-in-cheek defense with the society's professional expectations? Do you accept or reject the faux-journalist's claim that "objectivity" means that truth is but one side of the story?

muzzles reporters, forbidding them from crying foul, and requiring them to treat deception with the same respect they give to truth. It equates fairness with even-handedness, as though journalism were incompatible with judgment. 'Straight news' isn't neutral. It's neutered—devoid of assessment, divorced from accountability, floating in a netherworld of pseudo-scientific objectivity that serves no one except the rascals it legitimizes" (2008).

News production research remains a significant focus for researchers. In *Framing Public Life: Perspectives on Media and Our Understanding of the Social World*, Steve Reese, Oscar Gandy, and August Grant (2001) have included research on news production with framing studies that look at media content and audience reception. Their book demonstrates the importance of news production research as part of any comprehensive effort to probe the way that public understanding of news events develops.

News production research did indeed play an important role in the analysis of the press's performance in the months before the 2003 invasion of Iraq. The post-invasion failure to find weapons of mass destruction and cooperation between Iraq and al Qaeda in terrorism raised many questions about the media's independence and role in the formation of public opinion. As a result, news production research informed the work of critical scholars such as Todd Gitlin, who attributed the failure of the U.S. media to more fully examine the case for war to "on-the-one-hand, on-the-other-hand blah-blah and other unreflective stenography that passes for 'coverage' of the most powerful government in the history of the world." Reporters, bound by the production codes of their profession, were reduced to the role of "stenographers with amnesia" (Gitlin, 2004b, p. 32). You can see notions of objectivity rituals and fragmented news in this evaluation, and you can read more on the charge of stenography in the box entitled "The Stenographers?"

MEDIA INTRUSION THEORY

Another body of recent research dealing with political communication has been labeled **media intrusion theory** (Davis, 1990). It is not a clearly articulated set of ideas but rather exists as a loosely connected set of assumptions underlying a

---

INSTANT ACCESS

News Production Research

Strengths	Weaknesses
1. Provides recommendations for potentially useful changes in news production practices	1. Focuses on news production practices but has not empirically demonstrated their effect
2. Raises important questions about routine news production practices	2. Has pessimistic view of journalists and their social role
3. Can be used to study production of many different types of news	3. Has been ignored and rejected as impractical by practicing journalists

media intrusion theory
Idea that media have intruded into and taken over politics to the degree that politics have become subverted

broad range of empirical research in political science and communication. This theory is a contemporary variant of elite pluralism, especially the work of political scientist V. O. Key (see Chapter 6). It assumes that the political system operates best when a responsible and informed political elite mediates between the public and its elected leaders. This elite, however, has a grassroots base. Leaders work their way into positions of power through their involvement in local, regional, and national social organizations—from local parent-teacher groups to the national Red Cross. Political parties serve as umbrella organizations in which leaders of various groups broker power. Most members of this elite don't hold political office but work behind the scenes serving the interests of the groups they lead. Researchers are concerned because there is growing evidence that this political system is breaking down.

social capital
The influence potential leaders develop as a result of membership and participation in social groups

One concern is that many social groups that develop these leaders are losing membership and influence. Theorists refer to this as declining **social capital**, and a growing body of research has documented this decline in most Western nations. Media intrusion theorists blame media for this because many people stay home to consume media content rather than participate in local groups. The rise of television as a popular medium directly parallels this decline in social capital, so there is at least a plausible, if possibly spurious, link (Putnam, 2000).

The decline in social capital is seen as having many detrimental consequences. When politicians can no longer rely on local groups to which they had or have a connection to rally grassroots support for them, they are forced to turn to political consultants who advise them on how to use media to appeal to voters. But the televised political advertising and dramatic news coverage required to rally apathetic supporters come with a high price. Elites must spend precious time raising money and then spend it on questionable forms of campaign communication. For example, in the 2006 midterm congressional elections, the two major political parties spent nearly thirty dollars for each vote cast ($2.35 billion for 83 million votes) for cable and broadcast television time alone. That was more than double what was spent per vote on television in the 2002 midterm elections and triple the cost-per-vote in the 2000 presidential election (Johnson, 2006). Television stations reap windfall profits from this advertising, but broadcast journalists express frustration about the way political consultants manipulate news coverage.

The decline in social capital also has a direct impact on political parties. Ideally, parties function as "grand coalitions" of a broad range of social interest groups. They serve as a means by which these groups are able to achieve their goals. But as social capital has eroded, grassroots political party activity has also declined. This falloff has been well documented, as has been the drop in political affiliation and voting (Entman, 1989). Again, these changes in political parties occurred at the same time that television became a dominant medium.

In addition to eroding social capital, media intrusion theorists typically argue that television has directly subverted political campaign politics by undermining party control over elections. Some even argue that television has replaced parties in the election process (Patterson, 1980). Candidates no longer need party support—some actively avoid it. Instead, candidates hire political consultants to guide their media use. Candidates very often avoid all mention of their political party. Campaigns promote candidates, not parties.

Media intrusion theorists frequently cite the findings of the news production researchers to support their positions. They claim that political reports are too personalized, too dramatized, and too fragmented. Politics is often reported as a game between opposing teams, with the major politicians viewed as star players. Stories focus on media-hyped spectacles—on big plays, on life-and-death struggles to score points. These reports don't help news consumers—in other words, citizens—develop useful understandings of politics. They don't systematically inform people about issues and how candidates would deal with issues. Rather, they encourage consumers to become political spectators, content to sit on the sidelines while the stars play the game (Strupp, 2004).

"The triumph of the trivial is not a trivial matter," wrote *New York Times* columnist Paul Krugman about one particular election. "The failure of TV news to inform the public about the policy proposals of this year's presidential candidates is, in its own way, as serious a journalistic betrayal as the failure to raise questions about the rush to invade Iraq" (in Schechter, 2004).

Some journalists reject the media intrusion argument, asserting that they have little control over elections. They don't intrude into politics. Instead, their reporting efforts are being disrupted by political consultants. They point out that the political parties chose to give up control over presidential nominations when they decided to permit primary elections to be held across the nation. As the power of political parties has declined and the influence of political consultants has grown, manipulation of media by politicians has increased. Political consultants have developed very effective strategies for obtaining favorable news coverage for their candidates (Davis, 1990). During campaigns, journalists rely on particular production practices for gathering and generating news stories. Consultants are very knowledgeable about these practices and skilled at supplying useful information and convenient events. These "anticipated" events make it very easy to cover the candidate as the consultant wants and hard for journalists to find material for alternate stories.

For example, one recent news management strategy is to limit what a candidate says each day. By repeating the same terse comment over and over, the candidate hopes to force broadcast reporters to pick up and use the "sound bite of the day." The candidate avoids talking candidly to reporters because statements could be used to construct alternate stories. Journalists pride themselves on covering—not making—news, so they find it hard to break out of the limitations imposed by shrewd consultants.

There are no easy answers to the questions posed by media intrusion theory. If erosion of social capital is at the heart of the problem, changes in news coverage or political party activity won't ameliorate it. Thomas Patterson (1994) summarized findings from his research over the previous twenty years, presenting a devastating analysis of the deterioration of presidential campaign communication. The best solution he can offer is to shorten the campaigns. This he believes would return some power to the political parties and reduce the likelihood that overdramatized news coverage of trivial campaign happenings will determine who gets elected.

Robert Entman (1989) argues that a solution can be reached only if politicians, journalists, and the public change their behavior. Politicians must stop relying on manipulative and expensive strategies; journalists must cover issues rather than spectacles; the public must give serious attention to issues, not campaign spectacles and personalities. But how likely is it that these solutions can actually be implemented? Politicians and journalists are reluctant to change patterns of behavior that serve their immediate purposes—getting elected to office and attracting audiences to campaign coverage. And after every election campaign in recent years, private foundations have sponsored major conferences at which politicians and journalists have pledged to improve the quality of campaign communication. But the same mistakes are repeated in campaign after campaign. An increasingly alienated public seems unlikely to suddenly develop an interest in issues, even if they become bored with political spectacles.

Journalism professor Jay Rosen, however, sees the Internet and its expansion of the range of legitimate public discourse as an antidote to media intrusion and its attendant *audience atomization.* "In the age of mass media," he wrote, "the press was able to define the sphere of legitimate debate with relative ease because people on the receiving end were atomized—connected 'up' to Big Media but not across to each other. And now that authority is eroding" (2009). Drawing on ideas from Daniel Hallin's 1986 book, *The Uncensored War,* Rosen argued that traditional, mainstream news production practices and objectivity rituals intrude on public discourse by limiting it to the *sphere of consensus* (for example, America is the land of opportunity) about which everyone agrees, so no need to question its veracity; and the *sphere of legitimate debate,* the outer regions of which are represented by the two major political parties, so turning to official spokespeople is journalism at its best. What is missing is the *sphere of deviance,* political people and views that journalists and the political elite deem unworthy of being heard; "journalists maintain order by either keeping the deviant out of the news entirely or identifying it within the news frame as unacceptable, radical, or just plain impossible." He explained elsewhere, "The 'Net fundamentally changes that, not just because it introduces more voices into the published arena. That's part of it. But really that, it connects us to other people who feel the same way when they're watching the news, who have said to themselves: 'Wait, that's not the range of debate. Oh, wait a minute, that doesn't sound such a deviant idea to me, I know you're portraying it that way'" (in Greenwald, 2009c). Using the Internet, people can identify and discuss ideas and actions that they decide are legitimate, expanding the realm of public discourse, and around which they can generate and expend social capital.

INSTANT ACCESS

Media Intrusion Theory

Strengths

1. Provides basis for social change
2. Raises important questions about operation of news media organizations

Weaknesses

1. Focuses on operation of news media but has not empirically demonstrated its effect
2. Has overly pessimistic view of news media and their social role
3. Focuses too much on intrusion into politics
4. Is based on elite pluralism assumptions

SUMMARY

The theories reviewed in this chapter are diverse but provide a surprisingly coherent and complementary vision of contemporary American society. Even though they are grounded in post-positivist research, they have produced research findings demonstrating that media have moderate effects. Yet the picture of the role of media these theories provide is troubling. What we know about public issues, the terms we use to define them, and the importance we assign to various issues all might be strongly influenced by media. Defenders of limited-effects notions have questioned this "return to a powerful effects perspective on media" (Noelle-Neumann, 1973). In their view, the theories in this chapter often go too far and make assertions unwarranted by research findings. The theorists, they say, are over-generalizing—they are speculating too much. These defenders point out that there still is no convincing evidence that media ever have the power to alter attitudes on a large scale, especially if these attitudes are well established and associated with strong emotions. Audiences are too "obstinate" to permit this manipulation. Despite the erosion of social capital, American society is still strong.

But if media can't cause instant conversion of vast audiences to new ideologies, then just how powerful can they be? In Chapter 11, we will provide an answer to this question by expanding and extending the mantra of agenda-setting theory to encompass a set of culture-centered theories. Agenda-setting theory states that media don't tell people what to think (i.e., media don't directly influence attitudes), but media do tell people what to think about— they can and do affect the importance we assign to various public issues.

If we take this a little further, we can argue (as McCombs does in his second-order agenda-setting theory) that media also tell people how to think about issues specifically and the social world generally. In Chapter 11, we'll look at how media frame issues for us and cultivate our perceptions of the social world so we are more likely to make sense of things in some ways rather than others. We'll also look at cultivation theory, which asserts that heavy television viewing can lead viewers to believe they live in a world where crime is a direct threat. If we expect to see a "mean world," we will find our expectations constantly confirmed by television violence and on televised news.

Media might also tell people what to talk about (spiral of silence) when they discuss issues with others. Finally, media can have a profound influence on the accessibility and quality of information we use as we try to think, talk, and act in our social world. If the only information we can easily access is the information provided in "infotainment" or political spectacle, or if it is limited to a small range of agreed-upon legitimate (and legitimized) issues and perspectives, there will be many important things we never learn about from the media. Moreover, our impressions of the things that we do learn about might be strongly affected by the "packaging" of the information.

So how do you answer the questions raised about media by the theories in this chapter? Are you optimistic or pessimistic concerning the role of media? Will the rise of new communication technology like the Internet lead to important changes in how electronic media influence our views of the social world? Should media strive to serve the purposes that Libertarian thinkers assigned to them? Should we be demanding that media provide a range of public services, or should we be satisfied with the service that a competitive market provides? Or were these purposes too idealistic in the first place, given the necessity for media to earn profits in an increasingly competitive marketplace? Is it a problem if media act as a powerful agent for the status quo? To what extent do media shape your own view of your world?

Critical Thinking Questions

1. Have your opinions about a controversial issue in the news ever been spiraled into silence? If so, what was the situation? If not, have you ever had to resist the temptation to remain silent in the face of opposing opinion? If so, what were the circumstances? Has the emergence of the Internet, with its distance and anonymity, altered your willingness to speak out or remain silent?

2. Do you vote? Why or why not? How important do you think your participation in the democratic process really is? That is, can one citizen make a difference? If you answer yes, do you find the theories presented in this chapter troubling? Why or why not? If you answer no, can you find an explanation for that response in the theories discussed here? Are there forms of participation that do not involve traditional activities like voting or political party activities that you do engage in? What are they? Why do you choose these over more traditional forms of activity?

3. When it comes to technology (e.g., a new Internet application, the latest recording equipment, or an innovative automotive device) are you a change agent, an early adopter, an opinion leader, or an opinion follower? What is it about you that determines where you stand in the process of the diffusion of innovation? Do you know any technological early adopters? What makes them like or different from you? Do you think there are gender differences—that is, are there some innovations in which one gender rather than the other might be more likely to take the lead? Why or why not?

Key Terms

information diffusion theory

meta-analysis

early adopters

change agents

social marketing theory

targeting

hierarchy-of-effects model

digital divide

media system dependency theory

knowledge gap

digital literacy corps

agenda-setting

priming

agenda-building

framing theory

second-order agenda-setting

frames

spiral of silence

news production research

objectivity rituals

media intrusion theory

social capital

MEDIA AND CULTURE THEORIES: MEANING-MAKING IN THE SOCIAL WORLD

How would you describe yourself? What are your ideal personal attributes? Whom would you want to be like? How do you relate to other people? What expectations do others have of you, and what do you expect of them? How do you deal with difficult social situations? Where do you turn for information about your friends, and where do they find out about you? These are the sorts of questions we face every day as we work to find our place in the social world and develop relationships with other people. For most of us, even though the answers to these questions constantly shift, we don't have too much trouble dealing with them. As we move through the many different situations that structure our everyday lives, our sense of ourselves undergoes continual change, as does our understanding of others. Still, most of us don't think much about these sometimes dramatic changes; rarely do we question who we are or our understanding of others. We have developed habits that help us ably cope with the social world.

We live in a social world structured by the everyday culture we share with others around us. This culture consists of the personal identities we use to understand ourselves and to present ourselves to others, as well as the expectations we have that structure our communication and relationships with others. Everyday culture also involves the commonsense stock of knowledge about the social world that we have learned to cope with everyday problems and situations. Increasingly, media have become important to the way we develop this everyday culture. Media use has become central to developing and maintaining relationships with others. Texting, social networking websites, and Twitter connect us with others in ways we find essential. But, argues Himanshu Tyagi, a psychiatrist at the West London Mental Heath Trust, these media may be changing our lives in ways we don't yet understand. Those born after 1990, he said, may be different from previous generations because "young people who have no experience of a world without online societies put less value on their real world identities and can therefore be at risk in their real lives, perhaps more vulnerable to impulsive behaviour [sic] or even suicide…. The new generation raised alongside the Internet is attaching an entirely different meaning to friendship and relations, something we are largely failing to notice" (Facebook Generation, 2008).

Other researchers are questioning the changes that new media are producing in how we understand others and ourselves. They worry that there could be very serious long-term consequences. Are they correct, or is this simply another panic induced by the introduction of new forms of media like those in Chapter 3's discussion of mass society theory? Or can we dismiss these concerns with a little bit of functionalism's yes-but strategy (Chapter 7)? For example, can we balance findings that "individuals who perceive themselves as lacking self-presentational skill would be especially likely to perceive online social interaction more favorable than [face-to-face] communication … [but] preference for online social interaction leads to compulsive Internet use that results in negative outcomes" (Caplan, 2005, p. 730) with findings demonstrating that instant messaging (IM) has "a positive longitudinal effect on the quality of adolescents' existing friendships" (Valkenburg and Peter, 2009, p. 79)?

One thing that is certain in these debates is that people born after 1990 do use media much more often than those born earlier. Media have become an integral part of their daily lives. As we saw in Chapter 7, the average eight- to eighteen-year-old uses media for seven and a half hours each day. Since some of this use involves multitasking, total media exposure amounts to ten and three quarter hours a day. Media exposure for Hispanic and African American youngsters is even higher—around thirteen hours per day. Speaking specifically of cell phones, researchers Rideout, Foehr, and Roberts wrote, "Cell phones are the last thing they touch before falling asleep and the first thing they reach for upon waking. They spend the day accessing media using a variety of technologies that follow them everywhere they go" (2010, p. 2). On their own, these are interesting data. But add the facts that cell phone ownership among six- to eleven-year-olds grew 68 percent between 2005 and 2010; that talking and texting over mobile devices account for the top two ways mothers communicate with their children; and that cell phone kids also are much more likely (84 percent) to say that their parents let them go anywhere they want online than do those without the devices (Kelly, 2010). To these numbers, add data indicating that 91 percent of cell phone users of all ages use the devices to socialize and that youngsters are more likely to use their phones for shopping (44 percent) than the average cell phone owner (35 percent; Loechner, 2010). Clearly all of us, maybe especially children, are interacting with the world in new ways.

In previous chapters we have pointed out that the introduction of new media technologies has always been accompanied by unrealistic hopes and fears. Is this shift in media technology different from those that have happened before? Should we be more concerned about high levels of media use? It is the sheer amount of time being spent with media that bothers some critics of the technology. How can a "normal" life be lived if more than half of it involves the use of media? If much of our interaction with others, even our mothers, is mediated? Critics argue that media use can't help but be intrusive and disruptive. Technology proponents (and most young media users) respond that life hasn't really changed; it's been enhanced. Life now has a soundtrack courtesy of an iPod. Web surfing, mobile video, and portable video games keep boredom at bay. Google holds the answers to life's many questions and it can deliver them in a flash. Friends are a text message or a phone call away. Media enable constant connection with others and help us deal with everyday situations.

OVERVIEW

In Chapter 8, we traced the rise of cultural theories of media, giving particular attention to early schools of critical theory and cultural studies. This chapter also looks at contemporary critical cultural studies theories as well as other theories focusing on culture. Cultural theory has a long and, as we've seen, controversial history in the field of mass communication. It predates the rise of postpositivist theories examining media effects on individuals. From the 1950s to the 1980s, cultural theories were marginalized by American mass communication scholars. Media theory textbooks written in the United States during this era often omitted any mention of them or gave them little attention. We consider George Gerbner's cultivation theory in this chapter. It did get attention from effects researchers in the 1970s, but as we'll see, much of it was critical.

In the 1980s, when cultural theories began to be taken seriously in the discipline, a furious debate broke out between adherents and postpositivist opponents. The field was declared to be in ferment. Advocates of media effects perspectives said their theories were more scientific because they were based on highly structured empirical observations and they were falsifiable—new findings could lead to their rejection. They attacked cultural theories as speculative and based on loosely structured qualitative research methods. These theories couldn't be disproved because there was no way to test their causal assertions. But since that time, cultural theories have gained acceptance, as have the qualitative methods on which most of them are based. There is growing respect between postpositivists and advocates for cultural theories. Textbooks, like this one, increasingly consider the strengths and limitations of both types of theories and the research methods on which they are based.

We will first consider micro-level cultural theories and then move to theories dealing with more macro-level concerns. The former examine the everyday use of media by individuals and communities; the latter look at media's role in the larger social order. We use two terms to refer to the theories in this chapter. We refer to them as *culture-centered* because they study culture as a primary means of understanding the social world and the role media play in it. They provide different perspectives on how media influence culture and what the consequences of that influence are for individuals and society. We also refer to them as *meaning-making* theories because they are focused on understanding the way media influence how we make sense of the social world and our place in it—how we make meaning. Despite their common focus on culture and meaning-making, these theories are quite diverse. Some were developed by American scholars, whereas others originated in Europe. Some are critical—they assess how media frustrate or enhance our efforts to pursue valued objectives. Others are satisfied to provide in-depth descriptions of what we do with media and how our lives are affected.

We end this chapter with a consideration of the media literacy movement, which asserts that we should learn to assume more control over media so we can avoid problems and make media serve our purposes. The movement draws on ideas from many different meaning-making theories as well as from media effects theories, and it provides a good illustration of a new trend in the discipline—translating theory and research into action. Increasingly, media scholars, even postpositivists, see the desirability of applying research findings so problems created by media can be addressed and the positive influences of media can be enhanced.

SYMBOLIC INTERACTIONISM

symbolic interactionism
Theory that people give meaning to symbols and that those meanings come to control those people

social behaviorism
View of learning that focuses on the mental processes and the social environment in which learning takes place

Symbolic interactionism was one of the first social science theories to address questions of how communication is involved with the way we learn culture and how culture structures our everyday experience. Symbolic interaction theory developed during the 1920s and 1930s as a reaction to and criticism of behaviorism (see Chapter 4), and it had a variety of labels until Herbert Blumer gave it its current name in 1969. One early name was **social behaviorism**. Unlike traditional behaviorists, social behaviorists rejected simplistic conceptualizations of stimulus-response conditioning. They were convinced that attention must be given to the cognitive processes mediating learning. They also believed that the social environment in which learning takes place must be considered. Traditional behaviorists tended to conduct laboratory experiments in which animals were exposed to certain stimuli and conditioned to behave in specific ways. Social behaviorists judged these experiments too simplistic. They argued that human existence was far too complex to be understood through conditioning of animal behavior.

George Herbert Mead (1934), a University of Chicago philosopher and social activist, provided a way of understanding social life that differed profoundly from behaviorist notions. Rather than observe rats running through mazes, he proposed a better way to understand how people learn to make sense of everyday life and structure their actions. He suggested we look at how people learn to play baseball (or any team sport). How do we learn to play these games? Surely not by reading textbooks titled *The Theory of Playing Second Base*. Not simply through stimulus-response conditioning as we get rewarded or punished for specific actions. Mead argued that what occurs on a playing field is a sophisticated form of mutual conditioning: the players teach each other how to play the game while they are playing it. Players must learn to structure their actions in very complex ways to cover their positions effectively. But each position must be played differently, so teammates can't simply mimic one another. According to Mead, each player learns a social role—the pitcher role, the catcher role, or the left fielder role. Each role is learned by observing and modeling good players and by interacting with other team members. As they play, team members receive encouragement and friendly criticism from teammates and fans. If they play well, they have the satisfaction of being accepted by others as a productive member of a social unit.

Mead saw a baseball team as a microcosm of society. Each of us learns many different social roles through interaction with others. Our actions are subtly "conditioned" by others, while at the same time we are affecting their actions. The goal is not to manipulate or dominate each other but to create and sustain a productive social unit—a community providing its members with certain rewards in return for their willingness to take on specific roles. As we grow up we try out various roles, and then ideally we are able to select those that best fit our interests and personal abilities. Social roles and many other aspects of culture are learned through interaction—through experiences in daily life situations. Over time, we internalize the rules inherent in various situations and structure our actions accordingly.

Only in rare cases do we consciously reflect on and analyze our actions. If asked to explain what we are doing and why we are doing it, we are puzzled—the question seems strange. Why don't you call your mother by her first name? Why do you ride an elevator facing forward and not backward? Why do you text rather than phone? Why post a status report on Facebook rather than send an email? We are doing something because it is common sense; it's the way everybody does it; it's the normal, the logical, the right way to do things. Once internalized, these roles provide us with a powerful means of controlling our actions. In time, our identity becomes bound up with them: we understand ourselves, both emotionally and mentally, in terms of the roles we play and the personal identities that are associated with these roles. We value ourselves to the extent that these roles are respected by others. And sometimes, like athletes whose physical skills inevitably fail, we experience identity crises because we can't play a role as we or others expect us to or because we aspire to a role that proves to be beyond our ability or resources.

Mead's analogy is insightful and powerful, but it has some important limitations common to microscopic theories. Mead assumes that baseball teams operate as a sort of miniature democracy. But where do the teams come from? How do they get established? Who defines the rules of baseball games? Who sells the tickets, pays expenses, and profits from the game? Yes, team members mutually influence each other, but often coaches and a few older or more experienced players will dominate the team. And what about the team as a whole? It has a manager and owner who hire and fire team members.

The baseball team analogy also isn't very helpful for understanding how mass media might affect socialization. Ball players directly interact with one another. What happens when communication occurs through media—when people use Facebook to relate to hundreds of friends? Unlike baseball players who confront each other physically on the field, Facebook users meet each other in cyberspace. They sit at their personal computers or netbooks or tap away at their cell phones to log on to exchange messages with friends. They post information about themselves (express their personal identity), but often this information provides a very fragmentary or even fictional description of who they are. They get constant updates of the activities of friends and they post descriptions of what they are doing. How is everyday culture being created and shared on Facebook? Certainly not the way teammates do it.

Mead offered another important insight into the socialization process. Unlike animals conditioned to respond to stimuli in predetermined ways, humans are socialized in ways that permit more or less conscious interpretation of stimuli and planned responses. What is the secret that enables us to do what animals cannot? Symbols.

symbols
In general, arbitrary, often abstract representations of unseen phenomena

Symbols, in general, are arbitrary, often quite abstract, representations of unseen phenomena. Think of the words you use—all are arbitrary vocalizations that are essentially meaningless except to others who know how to decode them. When we write, we cover pages with complicated markings. To read them, someone must be literate in our language. According to Mead, the use of symbols transforms the socialization process—freeing it from the bonds of both space and time. Using symbols, we can create vivid representations of the past, and we can anticipate the future. We can be transported anywhere on the globe or even into the far reaches of space.

In *Mind, Self, and Society,* Mead (1934) argues that we use symbols to create our experience of consciousness (mind), our understanding of ourselves (self), and our knowledge of the larger social order (society). In other words, symbols mediate and structure all our experience because they structure our ability to perceive and interpret what goes on around us. This argument is similar to the one made by information-processing theorists (see Chapter 9). In information-processing theory, sets of symbols called *schemas* that we have learned in the past enable us to routinely make sense of the new sensory information we take in. Mead believed that mind, self, and society are internalized as complex sets of symbols. They serve as filtering mechanisms for our experiences. For information-processing theorists, schemas perform a similar function.

This might seem to be an extreme argument. Most of us take for granted our ability to look at the world around us and see the things that are obviously there. We might assume that we were born with this ability. But think about it. Why do we notice certain things and not others? As we move through daily life we're constantly encountering ambiguous, complex situations. Unless we are unusually fastidious, for example, we will not notice small amounts of dust and dirt when we enter a room. We'll ignore most of the background sounds. According to Mead, human perceptual processes are extremely malleable and can be shaped by the sets of symbols we learn so that we will see only what our culture has determined is worth seeing. (Has your perception of Middle Eastern cultures changed since September 11, 2001? Are you more likely now to notice a woman wearing a head scarf? What mental images spring to mind when you hear the word *terrorist?* Twenty years ago the image might have been of an Irish Republican Army bomber or a Latin American drug criminal—now it's most likely a Middle Eastern male.) Mead's arguments anticipated cognitive psychology research, which is beginning to empirically demonstrate much of what he hypothesized.

Thus symbolic interactionism posits that our actions in response to symbols are mediated (or controlled) largely by those same symbols. Therefore, a person's understanding of and relation to physical or objective reality is mediated by the symbolic environment—the mind, self, and society we have internalized. Put another way, the meanings we give to symbols define us and the realities we experience. As we are socialized, culturally agreed-upon meanings assume control over our interactions with our environments.

Consider the meaning that you attach to the stitched red, white, and blue cloth that constitutes an American flag. A flag is, in reality (objectively), little more than a piece of colored cloth. That is, it is little more than a piece of cloth until someone attaches symbolic meaning to it. We have decided that a particular array and formulation of colors and shapes should become our flag. Each of us experiences the flag differently, yet there is shared meaning as well. To many who support the conflict in the Middle East that began in Iraq in 2003, the flag flying over the twenty-seven-building, $800 million U.S. embassy that opened in 2010 symbolizes America's strength and its quest for democracy for all people. But for many who oppose that conflict, that same flag symbolizes America's occupation and quest for empire. Regardless of the meaning we individually attach to our flag, however, we are not free from its power. When a color guard passes before us at a sporting event, how free are we to remain sitting? At a school function, how free are we to continue chatting with our friends during the Pledge of Allegiance to that tricolored piece of fabric?

PRAGMATISM AND THE CHICAGO SCHOOL

Mead developed symbolic interactionism by drawing on ideas from pragmatism, as you may remember from Chapter 4, a philosophical school of theory emphasizing the practical function of knowledge as an instrument for adapting to reality and controlling it. Pragmatism developed in America as a reaction against ideas gaining popularity at home and in Europe at the end of the nineteenth century—simplistic forms of materialism such as behaviorism and German idealism. Both behaviorism and idealism rejected the possibility of human *agency*: that individuals could consciously control their thoughts and actions in some meaningful and useful way (Chapter 1). Idealism argued that people are dominated by culture, and behaviorism argued that all human action is a conditioned response to external stimuli. From the preceding description of Mead's ideas, you can see how he tried to find a middle ground between these two perspectives—a place that would allow for some degree of human agency. If we consider Mead's arguments carefully, they allow for individuals to have some control over what they do, but he is really arguing that agency lies with the community (or in the baseball example, with the team). Communities create and propagate culture: the complex sets of symbols that guide and shape our experiences. When we act in communities, we are mutually conditioned so we learn culture and use it to structure experience. These pragmatist notions about culture and human agency are at the heart of many of the cultural theories developed in the United States. As a school of thought, pragmatism continues to attract interest in a number of disciplines. In philosophy, Richard Rorty (1991; Rorty, Schneewind, and Skinner, 1982) has popularized neo-pragmatism. In political science a number of scholars have advocated John Dewey's pragmatism as a way of moving that field in a useful direction (Farr, 1999). In communication, Chris Russill (2006) and Robert Craig (2007) discuss the ongoing relevance of pragmatism.

For pragmatists, the basic test of the power of culture is the extent to which it effectively structures experience within a community. When some aspect of culture loses its effectiveness, it ceases to structure experience and becomes a set of words and symbols having essentially no meaning. For example, we can still find certain words in a dictionary and we could use them to decode old media content, but they would have no force in our lives—no connection to our experience. What does "twenty-three skidoo" mean? Do you have "the skinny"? You might understand these as "let's split" and "the 411," respectively. Or maybe not, depending on your experience. Culture is constantly changing—new elements are developed and old elements are abandoned. This change doesn't typically happen because it's planned by an elite who manipulates culture to serve its interests. Rather, culture changes as situations in which communities act change.

Many of the most productive symbolic interactionists were, like Mead, located at the University of Chicago. They became known as the Chicago School. We discussed the Chicago School in Chapter 5 when we considered the argument they made concerning social responsibility of the press. These ideas, pragmatism and social interactionism, were at the heart of that normative theory.

Chicago School theorists in the 1920s saw the city that housed their campus as a gigantic social experiment—a place where many folk cultures were suddenly thrown together in situations where people were forced to understand and relate to others whose culture was very different from their own. They used the term *great community* to refer to Chicago. It's useful to contrast this term with another used quite a bit in this textbook: *mass society*. The difference highlights some key differences between pragmatism and mass society theory—between a theory that's optimistic about the future of large-scale social orders and one that's quite pessimistic. Mass society theorists worried that individuals would become "atomized" in large-scale social orders. The networks of social relationships holding people together would necessarily break down as people moved from rural communities to urban ghettos. High culture would give way to mass culture so people's existence would be degraded and dehumanized. Media would just make things worse by providing a more efficient mechanism for transmitting mass culture.

If mass societies are places where human existence is degraded, great communities are places where the potential for human existence is explored and new opportunities for developing culture are found. One of the most creative members of the Chicago School was Robert E. Park, a man who worked as a journalist, studied philosophy with John Dewey in Michigan and sociology with Georg Simmel in Germany, exposed colonialism in the Belgian Congo, and served as an aide to educator, author, and early African American civil rights leader Booker T. Washington (Goist, 1971). With his colleagues, Park developed a perspective on urban life that was essentially optimistic while at the same time acknowledging that there were many problems. Cities were places where new forms of culture could be created— where many new and dynamic communities could be formed. Cities were made up of thousands of more or less interconnected local communities. It is this interconnection that allows for or compels the creation of more innovative forms of culture.

Not surprisingly, Park saw newspapers as playing an essential role in interconnecting the communities making up great communities. The most important thing about the newspaper, he thought, was that it served as a means of transmitting "news." This was an example of a

non-spatially defined, yet community-oriented phenomenon which functioned to hold the larger society together. The news, as Park presented it, played the dual role— making communication within the local area possible, but also acting to integrate individuals and groups into the wider society. He illustrated his point by indicating the function of the immigrant press. The effect of city life is to destroy the provincialism of the immigrant, and the foreign-language newspaper is the chief means of replacing older ties with a wider national loyalty. The press also makes it possible for the immigrant group to participate in American life, thus providing a first step in Americanization.

Park understood the metropolitan press to serve essentially the same function. Public opinion rests on news, on people talking about present events, and that is what newspapers make possible. While news is primarily local in character, the real power of the press, and other means of mass communication as well, is in providing the basis for public opinion and political action. Compatible with both permanence of location and with mobility, the metropolitan newspaper is an important means of holding together a city organism made up of various distinct parts. (Goist, 1971, p. 57)

Although Park made abstract arguments concerning the function of the press in cities, the Chicago School didn't develop a theory clearly explaining how and why newspapers performed their role. As we saw in Chapter 5, members of the Hutchins Commission on Freedom of the Press argued for extensive local coverage that would permit people living in different communities to learn more about other communities. Unfortunately, Chicago newspapers didn't see much reader interest in this type of news. In the 1950s and 1960s, big urban papers earned increasing amounts of money from sales in the growing and more affluent suburbs. Other than to report bad news about crime and social unrest, they ignored inner-city ethnic neighborhoods, often neglecting to deliver there as their residents depressed the papers' suburb-enriched, advertiser-attractive up-scale demographics (Kirkhorn, 2000). It's doubtful that these newspapers played the role Park envisioned for them. But they undoubtedly contributed to (and disrupted) urban culture in other ways.

CURRENT APPLICATIONS OF SYMBOLIC INTERACTIONISM

Although Mead first articulated his ideas in the 1930s, it was not until the 1970s and 1980s that mass communication researchers gave serious attention to symbolic interaction. Given the great emphasis that Mead placed on interpersonal interaction and his disregard for media, it is not surprising that media theorists were slow to see the relevancy of his ideas. Michael Solomon (1983), a consumer researcher, provided a summary of Mead's work that is especially relevant for media research:

1. Cultural symbols are learned through interaction and then mediate that interaction.
2. The "overlap of shared meaning" by people in a culture means that individuals who learn a culture should be able to predict the behaviors of others in that culture.
3. Self-definition is social in nature; the self is defined largely through interaction with the environment.
4. The extent to which a person is committed to a social identity will determine the power of that identity to influence his or her behavior.

Among the most notable efforts by communication scholars to apply this symbolic interactionist thinking to our use of mass media was the book *Communication and Social Behavior: A Symbolic Interaction Perspective,* written by Don F. Faules and Dennis C. Alexander in 1978. Basing their analysis on their definition of communication as "symbolic behavior that results in various degrees of shared meaning and values between participants," they offered three fundamental propositions on symbolic interaction and communication:

1. **People's interpretation and perception of the environment depend on communication.** In other words, what we know of our world is largely a function of our prior communication experiences in that world. This conforms to Solomon's idea of interaction with cultural symbols. As Faules and Alexander wrote, "Communication allows for the reduction of uncertainty without direct sensory experience. The media are a prime source of indirect experience and for that reason have impact on the construction of social reality" (p. 23).

2. **Communication is guided by and guides the concepts of self, role, and situations, and these concepts generate expectations in and of the environment.** Put differently, our use of communication in different settings is related to our understanding of ourselves and others in those situations. This is analogous to Solomon's point about learning a culture and predicting the behavior of others.

3. **Communication consists of complex interactions "involving action, interdependence, mutual influence, meaning, relationship, and situational factors"** (p. 23). Here we can see not only a communication-oriented restatement of Solomon's precepts three and four but also a rearticulation of James Carey's ritual perspective (see Chapter 8). Faules and Alexander are clearly reminding us that our understanding of our world and our place in it are created by us in interaction and involvement with media symbols.

sign
In symbolic interaction, any element in the environment used to represent another element in the environment

natural signs
In symbolic interaction, things occurring in nature that represent something else in nature

artificial signs
In symbolic interaction, elements that have been constructed to represent something else in the social world

signals
In symbolic interaction, artificial signs that produce highly predictable responses

symbols
In symbolic interaction, artificial signs for which there is less certainty of response

Before we get any further into symbolic interactionism, however, we must mention some definitional differences between this perspective and its close relative, social construction of reality, discussed in the next section of this chapter. In symbolic interaction theory, a **sign** is any element in the environment used to represent another element in the environment. Signs can be classified in two ways. **Natural signs**, those things in nature (like the changing color of leaves) represent something else in nature (like the coming of autumn). **Artificial signs** have been constructed (like a handshake) to represent something else in the social world (like a friendly greeting). These artificial signs work only if the people using them agree on their meaning—that is, if they are "interactive"; two or more people must agree on their meaning and must further agree to respond to that sign in a relatively consistent fashion. Social construction of reality uses the concept of signs somewhat differently, as you'll soon see.

Another difference between symbolic interactionism and social constructionism is the distinction between signals and symbols. In symbolic interactionism **signals** are artificial signs that produce highly predictable responses, like traffic signals. **Symbols,** on the other hand, are artificial signs for which there is less certainty and more ambiguity of response, like the flag. As Faules and Alexander (1978) explained, "Signals are used to regulate normative behavior in a society, and symbols are used to facilitate communicative behavior in a society" (p. 36).

INSTANT ACCESS

Symbolic Interactionism

Strengths	Weaknesses
1. Rejects simple stimulus-response conceptualizations of human behavior	1. Gives too little recognition to power of social institutions
2. Considers the social environment in which learning takes place	2. In some contemporary articulations, grants too much power to media content
3. Recognizes the complexity of human existence	
4. Foregrounds individuals' and the community's role in agency	
5. Provides basis for many methodologies and approaches to inquiry	

SOCIAL CONSTRUCTIONISM

social constructionism School of social theory that argues that individuals' power to oppose or reconstruct important social institutions is limited

What almost all theories classified as culture-centered have in common is an underlying assumption that our experience of reality is an ongoing social construction in which we have some responsibility, not something that is only sent, delivered, or otherwise transmitted by some authority or elite. But although there is general agreement that human communities construct the social world, there is disagreement concerning the level of agency individual humans have in the processes by which this world is constructed and maintained. We've seen that symbolic interactionists are strong believers in the power of individuals to have a significant level of control over culture and their social world. If culture is forged on a daily basis in the millions of situations in which we all participate, there should be great potential for cultural innovation and change. If nothing else, people make mistakes, and that alone should lead to innovation.

Another school of social theory, **social constructionism**, questions the amount of control individuals have over culture. Social constructionism argues that once social institutions such as schools, churches, businesses, and military organizations are constructed, individuals' power to oppose or reconstruct these institutions is limited. Its proponents see these institutions dominating the practice of culture on a day-to-day basis.

social construction of reality Theory that assumes an ongoing correspondence of meaning because people share a common sense about its reality

This school of social theory is also known as the **social construction of reality**. According to social constructionists, social institutions wield enormous power over culture because they view the culture they propagate as having a reality beyond our control. Here's an example. Students are often told that when they graduate they will get jobs in the *real* world. Implicit in this assertion is the assumption that college life is somehow *unreal* whereas the world of work is *real*. But what does *reality* mean in this context? Your daily life at college is not a fantasy world. There are classes to attend and exams to take. But you do have quite a bit of control over how you play your role as a student. You have the autonomy to decide what you will do and when you will do it. You can skip classes without risk of being expelled. Your grades must be consistently very low over a number of semesters before you might be asked to leave. On the other hand, a primary reason why the world of work is *real* is that individuals have much less control over their actions and any consequences they might produce. Although the rules governing work are becoming more flexible, most jobs still require people to work certain hours of the day. Between those hours, employees are required to do whatever tasks are assigned. Many workplaces are still hierarchically structured, with a few people at the top dictating what everyone else does. Unlike the university, even occasional violations of the rules of the workplace can get you fired. *Real,* in this example, then, means that work is socially constructed with less input from us and therefore more beyond our personal control than college.

Social constructionism's view of the role of media contrasts sharply with both mass society theory and the limited-effects perspective. Mass society theory envisioned vast populations living in nightmare realities dominated by demagogues. Limited-effects research focused on the more or less effective transmission of ideas, attitudes, and information from dominant sources to passive receivers. When social constructionism is applied to mass communication, it makes assumptions similar to those of symbolic interactionism; it assumes that audiences are active. Audience members don't simply passively take in and store bits of information in mental filing cabinets; they actively process this information, reshape it, and store only what serves culturally defined needs. They are active even when this activity largely serves to reinforce what they already know—to make them more willing to trust and act on views of the social world communicated to them by media. Thus, media can serve as an important way for social institutions to transmit culture to us; they let us know what social roles and personal identities are appropriate.

Active audience members use the media's symbols to make sense of their environments and the things in it, but those definitions have little value unless others share them—that is, unless the symbols also define things for other people in the same way. A Lexus, for example, can be as expensive an automobile as a Porsche, and both are functionally the same thing: automobiles that transport people from here to there. Yet the "realities" that surround both cars (and the people who drive them) are quite different. Moreover, how these different drivers are treated by other people may also vary, not because of any true difference in them as humans, but because the "reality" attached to each car is used to define their drivers (Baran and Blasko, 1984). We'll discuss this more later. For now, it's worth noting that your power as an individual to control the "realities" surrounding these cars is limited.

Alfred Schutz (1967, 1970), a banker whose avocation was sociology, provided some early systematic discussions of ideas that have become central to social constructionism. Like many meaning-making theorists, he was fascinated by what he regarded as the mysteries of everyday existence. For example, as a banker, he was conscious of how dependent our economic system was on people's willingness to routinely accept that money—identically printed on standardized pieces of paper, differing only slightly, primarily on the numbers printed on their face and back—could have radically different value. But money is just one everyday mystery. Schutz sought a broader understanding of how we make sense of the world around us in order to structure and coordinate our daily actions. He asked, "How are we able to do this with such ease that we don't even realize we are doing it?"

When it comes to money, Americans continue to be mysterious. The U.S. Treasury has found that it's impossible to introduce a dollar coin. It recently made a third attempt; it too failed ("Dollar Coins," 2008), as did a move, favored by President Obama, to retire the penny (Mankiw, 2009). Must a dollar be printed on paper to be real? Why the penny? It costs more to produce than its face value. Can't Americans round up or down? If you've traveled to a foreign country, you probably thought the money used there looked like play money. You didn't really trust it until you made a few purchases with it.

phenomenology
Theory developed by European philosophers focusing on individual experience of the physical and social world

For answers to this riddle about the origin and maintenance of social order, Schutz turned to a body of social theory developed in Europe, **phenomenology**. Relying on phenomenological notions, he asked his students at the New School for Social Research in New York to bracket, or set aside, their commonsense taken-for-granted explanations for what they were doing and recognize that everyday life was actually much more complicated than they assumed. Schutz argued that we conduct our lives with little effort or thought because we have developed stocks of social knowledge that we use to quickly make sense of what goes on around us and then structure our actions using this knowledge. Our knowledge of how to use money, with our attitudes toward and feelings about money, are just one example of a small part of these stocks of social knowledge.

It's important to note that we usually don't have much conscious awareness of this knowledge. When we are questioned about how or why we are engaging in a wide range of everyday actions, we find the questions puzzling or absurd. There's no obvious answers to these questions, but why would anyone even bother to ask them?

typifications
"Mental images" that enable people to quickly classify objects and actions and then structure their own actions in response

Schutz labeled one of the most important forms of knowledge we possess **typifications**. They enable us to quickly classify objects and actions we observe and then quickly and routinely structure our own actions in response. But typifications operate to some extent like stereotypes—though they make it easy to interpret even ambiguous situations, they also distort and bias our experience of these situations. Typifications we've learned before can be applied over and over again as long as we have the sense that they enable us to see things as they "really" are. We're likely to go on applying typifications even when problems arise and our interpretations cause trouble.

The concept of typifications is similar to Mead's idea of symbols and the notion of schemas in information-processing theory. It differs from these in emphasizing that these elements of culture can be beyond our conscious control even when they are quite crucial in making sense of things and guiding our actions. Mead thought of symbols as created in face-to-face interaction. But are the roles on his hypothetical baseball team really that flexible? Maybe they might better be conceived of as made up of Schutz's typifications. A little league team might tolerate a lot of innovation, but on a "real" team, when the game is being played "for real," players' actions are expected to closely adhere to certain norms, including such seemingly minor things as how to warm up or chatter from the bench.

Typifications may get communicated in face-to-face interactions, but they are propagated by social institutions and serve to preserve the power and authority of those institutions. Consider what happened to people who joked about bombs or weapons while going through airport security checks after 9/11 because they found it hard to take the new security procedures seriously. They were lucky if they only missed their flights. If we don't apply typifications correctly, our actions may be punished. We could be kicked off the team or wind up being grilled as potential terrorists.

Social constructionism also calls attention to the problematic consequences of taking typifications too seriously. When we rely on typifications to routinely structure our experience, we can make serious mistakes. You can test the power of typifications for yourself when reading the box entitled "Typifications Shaping Reality? Not Mine!"

THINKING *about* THEORY — TYPIFICATIONS SHAPING REALITY? NOT MINE!

Typifications, Alfred Schutz tells us, are the commonsense stocks of social knowledge that help us quickly make sense of the world around us and shape our actions accordingly. Because they help us interpret our experiences, it is important that we build accurate, useful typifications for the significant events, people, and things in our worlds. But consider recent talk of "Blue America" and "Red America," two "realities" of our country so different that there seems to be little civil discourse, never mind consensus between them. The "great cultural divide" surrounding the ongoing war in the Middle East is one obvious example. But there are others. Where do you stand on issues such as the right of homosexuals to marry? The war on drugs? Sex education in schools? These are only three of the many difficult issues dividing us from one another. Our realities of these matters are composed of our experiences with them, but how "accurate" are the typifications defining those experiences (and therefore, our realities), and where do they come from?

Let's test ourselves by answering these five quiz items:

1. Which of these three states has the highest divorce rate: Arkansas, Oklahoma, or Massachusetts?
2. Which religious category has the highest divorce rate: Baptists, nondenominational Christians, or atheists and agnostics?
3. What percentage of all users of illegal drugs in this country are people of color: 72 percent, 61 percent, or 22 percent?

4. Among New Hampshire, Mississippi, and Texas, which two states have the higher rate of teenage pregnancy?
5. Put these three cities in order of their crime rates, highest to lowest: Atlanta, New York, Memphis.

Of course, you know that only liberals and atheists on the Atlantic and Pacific coasts favor gay marriage. They don't hold the institution as sacred as do those in the heartland. And of course, drugs are a problem of the inner city, so tougher criminal sentencing is necessary to make the point for those people. And speaking of the city, at least heartland people have better morals than those East Coast blue staters, especially someplace like that modern-day Gomorrah, New York City.

But the divorce rate is lowest in northeast, liberal Massachusetts (2.3 out of every 1,000 marriages), far lower than that of Arkansas (5.7/1,000) and Oklahoma (5.3/1,000; Blow, 2009). Atheists and agnostics divorce at a rate of 21 percent, well below that of Baptists (29 percent) and nondenominational Christians (34 percent; *The Week,* 2004). Drug users? Of all American users of illegal drugs, 78 percent are white; minorities account for only 22 percent of the total (Glasser, 2006). Teen-age pregnancy rates are highest in Mississippi (68 pregnancies for every 1,000 teen girls) and Texas (63/1,000). New Hampshire (19/1,000) has the lowest, joined by two other New England states, Vermont and Massachusetts (21/1,000) with teen pregnancy rates below the national average of 42 births per 1,000 teen women

(Continued)

(Dunham, 2009). New York City is the safest big city in America, with a per capita crime rate of 4.2 percent, compared to Memphis (18 percent) and Atlanta (16 percent; Ott, 2009).

What was your reality of different locales' and believers' commitment to marriage, the demographics of illegal drug users, rates of teen pregnancy, and the prevalence of crime? Does it surprise you to learn that Massachusetts, the first state to legally permit homosexuals to marry, has the lowest divorce rate in America? How well did your typifications match the statistical actuality of the "real world"? How much do your individual realities contribute to your stance on gay marriage, the "drug war," teen pregnancy, and crime? Where and how were your, and the larger culture's, realities of these issues constructed (a social-construction-of-reality question)? How open was the media forum for your examination of these matters (a British cultural studies question)? What do marriage or atheists or people from the northeast and "the heartland" symbolize for you (a symbolic interaction question)? How have media covered these social issues and the advocates of their varying positions (a framing question)? Now that you have more accurate data on these controversial issues, will you reassess your opinions about them? Why or why not? Can you cite other theories from this or earlier chapters to support your answer?

Schutz's ideas were elaborated in *The Social Construction of Reality* by sociologists Peter Berger and Thomas Luckmann. Published in 1966, the book made virtually no mention of mass communication, but with the explosion of interest in the media accompanying the dramatic social and cultural changes of that turbulent decade, mass communication theorists (not to mention scholars from numerous other disciplines) quickly found Berger and Luckmann's work and identified its value for developing media theory.

In explaining how reality is socially constructed, the two sociologists assumed first that "there is an ongoing correspondence between my meanings and their meanings in the world [and] that we share a common sense about [their] reality" (Berger and Luckmann, 1966, p. 23). Let's use a common household article as our example. Here are three symbols for that object:

1. Knife

2.

3.

In social construction of reality, a **symbol** is an object (in these instances, a collection of letters or drawings on paper) representing some other object—what we commonly refer to as a knife. Here are three other symbols for that same object:

1. Messer
2. Cuchillo
3.

symbol
In social construction of reality, an object that represents some other object

But unless you speak German or Spanish, respectively, or understand the third symbol to be a drawing of a butter knife these symbols have no meaning for you; there is no correspondence between our meaning and yours. We share no common sense about the reality of the object being symbolized.

But who says that *knife* means what we all know it to mean? And what's wrong with those people in Germany and Mexico? Don't they know that it's *knife*, not *messer* or *cuchillo*? In English-speaking countries, the culture has agreed that *knife* means that sharp thing we use to cut our food, among other things, just as the folks in German- and Spanish-speaking lands have agreed on something else. There is no inherent truth, value, or meaning in the ordered collection of the letters k-n-i-f-e giving it the reality that we all know it has. *We* have given it meaning, and because we share that meaning, we can function as a people (at least when the issue is household implements).

signs
In social construction of reality, objects explicitly designed to serve as an index of subjective meaning

But Berger and Luckmann (1966, p. 35) recognized that there is another kind of meaning we attach to the things in our environments, one that is subjective rather than objective. They call these **signs**, objects explicitly designed "to serve as an index of subjective meaning"; this is analogous to symbolic interaction's concept of symbols. If you were to wake up tomorrow morning, head on your pillow, to find a knife stuck into the headboard inches above your nose, you'd be fairly certain that this was some sort of sign. In other words, people can produce representations of objects that have very specific, very subjective agreed-upon meanings. What does the knife in the headboard signify? Says who? What does a Lexus signify? Says who? What do several pieces of cloth—some red, some white, some blue—sewn together in a rectangle in such a way to produce thirteen alternating red and white stripes and a number of stars against a blue field in the upper-left-hand corner signify? Freedom? Democracy? Empire? The largest car dealer on the strip? A place to buy breakfast? Says who?

Remember that symbolic interaction defines signs and symbols in precisely the opposite way than does social construction of reality theory. This small problem aside, how do people use these signs and symbols to construct a reality that allows social order to be preserved? Berger and Luckmann (1966) developed Schutz's notion of typifications into what they refer to as **typification schemes**, collections of meanings we assign to some phenomenon that come from our stock of social knowledge to pattern our interaction with our environments and the things and people in it. A bit more simply, we as a people, through interaction with our environment, construct a "natural backdrop" for the development of "typification schemes required for the major routines of everyday life, not only the typification of others ... but typifications of all sorts of events and experiences, both social and natural" (p. 43).

typification schemes
In social construction of reality, collections of meanings assigned to some phenomenon, which come from a social stock of knowledge to pattern interaction with the environment and things and people in it

Of course, media theorists and practitioners, especially advertisers and marketing professionals, understand that whoever has the greatest influence over a culture's definitions of its symbols and signs has the greatest influence over the construction of the typification schemes individuals use to pattern their interactions with their various social worlds. In other words, social institutions have the most influence in or control over the social world because they often are able to dominate how typification schemes get created and used. Why, for example, is one beer more "sophisticated" than another? Are we less likely to serve an inexpensive local beer to our houseguests than we are to serve Michelob or Heineken? Why? What makes brand-name products or clothes with designer labels better than generic alternatives?

Alternately, consider the example of airport security checks. We as individuals don't have much control over what we're able to do during these checks. If we travel frequently, we've probably worked out strategies to enable ourselves to move efficiently through the security checks. We go to the airport early, expecting that there could be a long wait. As we wait, we remove all metal objects from our pockets to our luggage. We wear shoes that slip off easily. We place our photo ID and ticket where we can easily access them. But even after all this preparation, an alarm may go off as we go through the metal detector. We know to stop immediately and allow ourselves to be scanned with an intrusive hand wand. If we happen to travel on a day when security is especially tight, our carry-on luggage may be opened and searched. We may be asked to turn on our electronic equipment to make certain it is operational. In many other situations we would consider this kind of treatment demeaning and humiliating. But now it's just part of flying. We have learned a typification scheme enabling us to cope.

So who's right about the amount of agency exercised by individuals in the social world? Are symbolic interactionists correct when they argue that important ways of interpreting things (symbols) get created through everyday interaction? Or are social constructionists correct when they argue that typifications are handed down to us primarily by institutions that dominate the social world? Could both of these perspectives provide useful insights into different aspects of the social world?

We'll look next at framing theory as developed by Erving Goffman. Goffman based his ideas on notions derived from both symbolic interactionism and social constructionism. As we'll see, his theory is an interesting combination of these ideas. It allows for a certain amount of individual agency, but it also grants a fair amount of power to institutions. As we'll also see, Goffman asserted that social

INSTANT ACCESS

Social Constructionism

Strengths	Weaknesses
1. Rejects simple stimulus-response conceptualizations of human behavior	1. Gives too little recognition to power of individuals and communities
2. Considers the social environment in which learning takes place	2. In some contemporary articulations, grants too much power to media content
3. Recognizes the complexity of human existence	
4. Foregrounds social institutions' role in agency	
5. Provides basis for many methodologies and approaches to inquiry	

institutions can dictate the rules of the game, but we still have the power to decide how or even whether we will play the game. If we opt out of the game, we may wind up categorized as screwballs or mentally ill, but from Goffman's perspective that might mean that we have more sanity than the people who take the game too seriously.

FRAMING AND FRAME ANALYSIS

While critical cultural researchers were developing reception analysis during the 1980s, a new approach to audience research was taking shape in the United States. It had its roots in symbolic interaction and social constructionism. As we've seen, both argue that the expectations we form about ourselves, other people, and our social world are central to social life. You have probably encountered many terms in this and other textbooks that refer to such expectations—stereotypes, attitudes, typification schemes, and racial or ethnic bias. All these concepts assume that our expectations are socially constructed:

1. Expectations are based on previous experience of some kind, whether derived from a media message or direct personal experience (in other words, we aren't born with them).
2. Expectations can be quite resistant to change, even when they are contradicted by readily available factual information.
3. Expectations are often associated with and can arouse strong emotions such as hate, fear, or love.
4. Expectations often get applied by us without our conscious awareness, especially when strong emotions are aroused that interfere with our ability to consciously interpret new information available in the situation.

Developing and using expectations is a normal and routine part of everyday life. As human beings, we have cognitive skills allowing us to continually scan our environment, make sense of it, and then act on these interpretations. We do this with little or no conscious awareness. Our actions are routinized and habitual. Our inability to adequately understand these skills in no way prevents them from operating, but it does impede our ability to make sense of our own meaning-making. We inevitably make an interpretation of the world around us. Sometimes we will understand what we are doing, but more often we won't—typically it doesn't matter whether we do or not. But if we would like to or want to assume more responsibility for our actions, then we should be concerned.

frame analysis
Goffman's idea about how people use expectations to make sense of everyday life

Based in part on Ludwig Wittgenstein's linguistic philosophy—particularly his notion of language games, sociologist Erving Goffman (1974) developed **frame analysis** to provide a systematic account of how we use expectations to make sense of everyday life situations and the people in them (the theory is graphically represented in the box entitled "The Framing Process"). Goffman was fascinated by the mistakes we make as we go through daily life—including the mistakes we never notice, such as when one person mistakes another's courtesy for flirting, or when someone's effort to move quickly through an airport is seen as suspicious. Goffman was especially intrigued by the way con artists are able to trick people. Why are people often so gullible? Why have Nigerians been able to scam Americans out of millions of dollars using what appear to most people to be outrageous email scams? Like Alfred Schutz, Goffman was convinced that daily life is much more complicated than it appears (Ytreberg, 2002) and we have ways of dealing with these complications.

Although Goffman agreed with social constructionist arguments concerning typification schemes, he found them too simple. He argued that we constantly and often radically change the way we define or typify situations, actions, and other people as we move through time and space. We are able to adjust the schemes to fit specific circumstances and other individuals. We don't have only one typification scheme—we have whole sets of schemes ranging along various dimensions. But we usually won't have any conscious awareness of when we are making these changes. In other words, our experience of the world can be constantly shifting, sometimes in major ways, yet we may not notice these shifts. We can step from one realm of experience to another without recognizing that a boundary has been crossed. We don't operate with a limited or fixed set of expectations about social roles, objects, or situations. Thus, we don't have a simple stock of institutionally controlled knowledge as most social constructionists contend. Rather, we have enormous flexibility in creating and using expectations. Goffman argued that our experience of reality is bound up with our ability to move effortlessly through daily life making sense of situations and the people in them.

Let's consider the example of airport security checks again. We may be traveling with a group of friends. It's a nice day and we've been having fun. We find it hard to take the security check seriously or it slips our mind that we need to be careful. We forget some of the things we normally do when we're taking a security check seriously. But then the alarm goes off. Suddenly things get serious. We have to make fast readjustments but we do it fairly easily. Our smile vanishes. We stand up straight and pay close attention to the security agents. It's likely that we blame ourselves for making stupid mistakes; we forgot to take off our shoes or to remove our keys from our pockets. According to Goffman, we've gone from framing the situation playfully to imposing a serious frame.

If the symbolic interactionists are right and our meaning-making ability is so great, so innovative, and so flexible, why is there any pattern or order to daily existence? How are we able to coordinate our actions with others and experience daily existence as having order and meaning—how can we routinely adjust ourselves to life within the boundaries set by social institutions, as social constructionists believe we do? Life, Goffman argued, operates much like a staged dramatic performance. We step from one social realm or sphere to another in much the same way that actors move between scenes. Scenes shift, and as they shift we are able to radically alter how we make sense of them. As the scenes shift, we locate and apply new sets of expectations. Sometimes, as in the example of the problematic security check, we don't make the proper shift and then we're forced to do so.

social cues
In frame analysis, information in the environment that signals a shift or change of action

But just how do we and the people around us know when to make shifts? How do we know when one scene is ending and another beginning and act jointly so a shift can be made so seamlessly that we don't even notice that it has happened? According to Goffman, we are always monitoring the social environment for **social cues** that signal when we are to make a change, and we ourselves are often quite skilled at using these cues. For example, when we view a play in a theater, we rely on many conventional cues to determine when a shift in scenes takes place. One of the oldest and most obvious cues involves the curtain—it rises when a scene begins and falls when a scene ends. Other cues are more subtle—shifts in lighting and music tempo often signal changes. As lights dim and music becomes ominous, we know danger threatens. Movies employ many similar conventions. Goffman believed we use the same cognitive skills to make sense of daily life as we do to make sense of plays or movies. His theory implies that we learn social cues through everyday interaction and from observing how they are used in media content.

Back to the airport. What if security agents dressed in street clothes or in beachwear? What if they casually stood around and ignored scanner alarms? What if they were joking with each other instead of carefully monitoring equipment? Would we take them seriously? Would we frame the situation playfully? Social cues can make a big difference in how we decide to structure our actions.

frame
In frame analysis, a specific set of expectations used to make sense of a social situation at a given point in time

Goffman used the term **frame** to refer to a specific set of expectations used to make sense of a social situation at a given point in time. Frames are like Berger and Luckmann's typification schemes, but they differ in certain important respects. According to Goffman, individual frames are like notes on a musical scale—they spread along a continuum from those structuring our most serious and socially significant actions to those structuring playful, trivial actions. Like the notes on a musical scale, each is different, even though there is underlying structural continuity. For social action, the continuity is such that we can learn how to frame serious actions by first learning frames for playful actions. We can learn from playing little league baseball and then apply it when we play a more serious game—a real game of life in which there's more at stake. Using the musical scale analogy, we first learn to play simple tunes using a narrow range of the scale in preparation for playing complex musical scores. Likewise, many of our games and sports provide useful preparation for more serious forms of action. If we can perform well under the pressures of a big game, we may handle the demands of other life situations better. Goffman argued that we are like animal cubs that first play at stalking frogs and butterflies and then are able to transfer these skills to related but more serious situations.

downshift and upshift
In frame analysis, to move back and forth between serious and less serious frames

When we move from one set of frames to another, we **downshift or upshift**. We reframe situations so we experience them as more or less serious. Remember when you pretended to fight with a friend as a child, but someone got hurt and the fight turned serious? Suddenly, you no longer pulled punches but tried to make them inflict as much pain as possible; you downshifted. You used many of the fighting skills learned during play but with a different frame—now you were trying to hurt your friend. Perhaps, as you both got tired, one of you told a joke and cued the other that you wanted to upshift and go back to a more playful frame. In the airport security example, an alarm going off is likely to bring about a quick downshift in our framing.

According to Goffman, daily life involves countless shifts in frames, and these shifts are negotiated using social cues. Some cues are conventional and universal, like the curtain on a stage or the security alarm; others are very subtle and used by small groups. For example, couples often develop a very complex set of cues to signal when to upshift or downshift their interaction. During the course of a conversation, many upshifts and downshifts can occur based on subtle changes in

THINKING *about* **THEORY**   THE FRAMING PROCESS

In a different book (Davis and Baran, 1981), we developed this version of Goffman's theory of framing. Can you explain how it allows for upshifting and downshifting? Can you speculate on how errors in framing can occur?

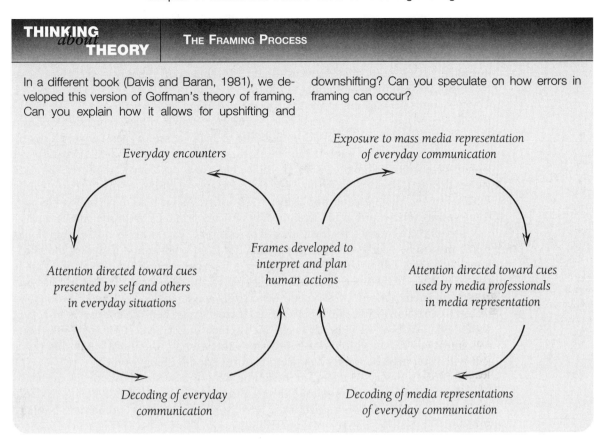

Everyday encounters

Exposure to mass media representation of everyday communication

Frames developed to interpret and plan human actions

Attention directed toward cues presented by self and others in everyday situations

Attention directed toward cues used by media professionals in media representation

Decoding of everyday communication

Decoding of media representations of everyday communication

voice tone or body movement. Upshifting and downshifting add a dimension of complexity to everyday interaction that Goffman argued should not be ignored. In general, social institutions dominate framing of serious action in the settings they control, but much of daily life is performed in less serious settings. After you clear airport security, you are free to upshift, to be as playful as you want browsing through airport shops.

So how do media come into this theory? Goffman made several heuristic explorations of the way media might influence our development and use of frames, including an essay entitled "Radio Talk" appearing in his book *Forms of Talk* (1981) and in another book, *Gender Advertisements* (1979). In the latter work he presented an insightful argument concerning the influence advertising could have on our perception of members of the opposite sex. According to Goffman, ads are **hyperritualized representations** of social action (Ytreberg, 2002). They are edited to highlight only the most meaningful actions. Advertising using the sex appeal of women to attract the attention of men could inadvertently teach or reinforce social cues that could have inadvertent but serious consequences. Goffman showed how women in many ads are presented as less serious and more playful than men. They smile, place their bodies in nonserious positions, wear playful clothing, and in various ways signal deference and a willingness to take direction from men.

hyperritualized representations Media content constructed to highlight only the most meaningful actions

Not only are they vulnerable to sexual advances, they signal their desire for them. No wonder these ads attract the attention of men. No wonder they are useful in positioning products. But could these representations of women be teaching or reinforcing social cues that have difficult consequences? Feminist theorists have made similar arguments (Walters, 1995).

We might be learning more than product definitions from these ads. We could be learning a vast array of social cues, some blatant but others quite subtle. Once learned, these cues could be used in daily life to make sense of members of the same or opposite sex and to impose frames on them, their actions, and the situations in which we encounter them. Or it's possible that these ads simply reinforce the cues we've already learned in daily life. But the constant repetition of the cues in the ads leads us to give them greater importance or priority. As we'll see later in this chapter, some researchers would argue that media cues can prime us to frame subsequent situations one way rather than another. For example, exposure to advertising could prime men to be overly sensitive to playful cues from women and increases the likelihood that they will upshift. Men learn such a vast repertoire of these cues that it might be hard for women to avoid displaying them. Men could routinely misinterpret inadvertent actions by women. Advertising might make it hard for women to maintain a serious frame for their actions. If they smile, bend their elbows in a particular way, or bow their heads even briefly, men might perceive a cue when none was intended. The more physically attractive the woman, the more likely this problem will arise, because most advertising features good-looking women.

Goffman's theory provides an intriguing way of assessing how media can elaborate and reinforce a dominant public culture. Advertisers didn't create sex-role stereotypes, but, Goffman argued, they have homogenized how women are publicly depicted. This is the danger of hyperritualization. Goffman contrasted the variety of ways that women are represented in private photos with their standardized (hyperritualized) depiction in advertising. Marketers routinely use powerful visual imagery to associate products with women who explicitly and implicitly signal their willingness to be playful sexual partners. There are many subtle and not-so-subtle messages in these ads. "Consume the product and get the girl" is one dominant message. Another is that physically attractive women are sexually active and fun-loving. Ads both teach and reinforce cues. They regularly prime us to frame situations one way rather than another. The specific messages each of us gets from the ads may be very different, but their long-term consequences may be similar—dominant myths about women are retold and reinforced.

primary, or dominant, reality
In frame analysis, the real world in which people and events obey certain conventional and widely accepted rules (sometimes referred to as the dominant reality)

Compared with the other theories we have examined in this chapter, Goffman's is the most open-ended and flexible. He was convinced that social life is a constantly evolving and changing phenomenon, and yet we experience it as having great continuity. Though we have the capacity to constantly reframe our experience from moment to moment, most of us can maintain the impression that our experiences are quite consistent and routine. According to Goffman, we do this by firmly committing ourselves to live in what we experience as the **primary, or dominant, reality**—a real world in which people and events obey certain conventional and widely accepted rules. We find this world so compelling and desirable that we are constantly reworking our experience and patching up flaws in it, and we don't notice when rule violations occur.

INSTANT ACCESS

Frame Analysis

Strengths

1. Focuses attention on individuals in the mass communication process
2. Micro-level theory but is easily applicable to macro-level effects issues
3. Is highly flexible and open-ended
4. Is consistent with recent findings in cognitive psychology

Weaknesses

1. Is highly flexible and open-ended (lacks specificity)
2. Is not able to address presence or absence of effects
3. Precludes causal explanations because of qualitative research methods
4. Assumes individuals make frequent framing errors; questions individuals' abilities

Goffman argued that we work so hard maintaining our sense of continuity in our experience that we inevitably make many framing mistakes. We literally see and hear things that aren't—but should—be there according to the rules we have internalized. For example, most college campuses in America today face the problem of date rape. And ultimately, what is the basic issue in most of these occurrences? Goffman might answer that the issue involves upshifting and downshifting problems between men and women as they attempt to frame the situations (dating) they find themselves in. Alcohol consumption is often associated with date rape, increasing the likelihood that social cues will be misread or ignored. Or consider the even more common problem on campuses of binge drinking. Most students have a hard time taking drinking seriously. They've learned to frame drinking as an essentially playful activity. Advertising continually reinforces this frame along with its related social cues. The unwanted consequences of drinking too much don't appear in advertising. When these consequences are portrayed in the anti–binge-drinking advertising, students have a hard time taking these ads seriously.

From Goffman's viewpoint, primary reality is the touchstone of our existence—the real world in every sense of that term. We do permit ourselves constant and socially acceptable escapes into clearly demarcated alternative realities we experience as recreational or fantasy worlds. These are worlds where we can escape the pressures of being center stage in an unfolding drama we know can have long-term consequences. Not many students would expect to earn a high grade on an important essay exam by writing jokes about the instructor, but as the date rape example suggests, when we make framing mistakes in a playful reality, the results can be devastating to our real world.

RECENT THEORIES OF FRAMES AND FRAMING

Frame analysis theory as developed by Goffman is a micro-level theory focusing on how individuals learn to routinely make sense of their social world. After Goffman's work in the 1960s and 1970s, framing theory continued to gain interest and acceptance. Other scholars took Goffman's ideas and extended them to create a conceptual framework that considers (1) the social and political context in which framing takes place, and (2) the long-term social and political consequences of media-learned frames. Most of this framing research has focused on journalism and on the way news influences our experience of the social world. Early examples of framing research applied to journalism can be found in the scholarship of two sociologists whom you met in the last chapter, Todd Gitlin (1980) and Gaye Tuchman (1978). Their work is frequently cited and played an important role in extending Goffman's ideas. Gitlin focused on news coverage of politically radical groups during the late 1960s. He argued that they were systematically presented in ways that demeaned their activities and ignored their ideas. These representations made it impossible for them to achieve their objectives. Tuchman focused on routine news production work and the serious limitations inherent in specific strategies for coverage of events. Although the intent of these practices is to provide objective news coverage, the result is news stories in which events are routinely framed in ways that eliminate much of their ambiguity and instead reinforce socially accepted and expected ways of seeing the social world.

One of the most productive and creative contemporary framing researchers is William Gamson (1989; Gamson et al., 1992). He authored and coauthored a series of books, book chapters, and articles that have helped shape current perspectives on framing theory and its explanation of how news has influence in the social world. Gamson argues that framing of many societal issues and events is highly contested. Increasingly, frames used in public discourse are developed and promoted by individuals and groups having an interest in advancing certain ways of seeing the social world rather than others. He has traced the success and failure of social movements in promoting frames consistent with their ideological interests, specifically in the realm of nuclear power and global warming (Gamson and Modigliani, 1989).

Gamson's interest is in the ability of activist movements to bring about social change. He shares the social constructionist view that social institutions and the elites who lead them are able to dominate the social world by propagating frames serving their interests. But he believes that movements have the ability to generate and promote alternate frames that can bring about important change in the social order. But for this to happen, movements need to develop cogent frames expressing their views, and they need to persuade journalists to produce news stories that present these frames effectively and sympathetically. Only then will such frames be disseminated to a larger audience so that more people begin to view the social world the way that movement members do. If enough people change their views, public pressure may build so that leaders of social institutions make changes.

FRAMING AND OBJECTIVITY

Framing theory challenges a long accepted and cherished tenet of journalism—the notion that news stories can or should be objective. Instead, it implies that journalism's role should be to provide a forum in which ideas about the social world are routinely presented and debated. As it is now, this forum is dominated by social institutions having the power to influence frames routinely used to structure news coverage of the social world. These institutions are able to promote frames that serve to reinforce or consolidate an existing social order and to marginalize frames that raise questions about or challenge the way things are.

Some framing research examines the strategies used by political and social elites to manipulate how journalists frame events. This practice was startlingly evident in internal marine memos that surfaced during the 2007 murder and dereliction-of-duty trials of men involved in the 2005 killing of twenty-four Iraqi men, women, and children in Haditha. In response to a series of questions posed by *Time* reporter Tim McGirk as he worked to confirm the official account that the deaths "occurred during combat and were justified, if regrettable," the commanding officers of the unit involved met and developed "talking points" designed to shape McGirk's account. They wrote: "One common tactic used by reporters is to spin a story in such a way that it is easily recognized and remembered by the general population through its association with an event that the general population is familiar with or can relate to. For example, McGirk's story will sell if it can be spun as 'Iraq's My Lai massacre.' Since there was not an officer involved, this attempt will not go very far. We must be on guard, though, of the reporter's attempt to spin the story to sound like incidents from well-known war movies, like *Platoon*" (von Zielbauer, 2007, p. K5).

Obviously, like the authors of this Marine memo, other elites have extensive knowledge of how news is produced. They are also quite cognizant of how committed reporters are to their news production practices. This allows them to stage events likely to be framed as they choose and to effectively suggest to journalists how events should be framed. The conflict in Iraq—with its accounts of weapons of mass destruction, the mushroom cloud as smoking gun, the heroic private Jessica Lynch, the toppling of Saddam's statue, the Mission Accomplished aircraft carrier landing, President Bush's Thanksgiving visit, and the gallant death of football star–turned-army ranger Pat Tillman—provided numerous examples of journalists framing events exactly as elites wished them to (Baran, 2011, pp. 310–311). They represent what W. Lance Bennett (2005b) calls **news reality frames**, because in each case, an interested elite "involves journalists in constructing news drama that blurs underlying contextual realities, ranging from passive reporting of routine pseudo events (such as the campaign stop), to more active co-production on the part of the press (such as the carrier landing), to a growing stream of journalistically-driven rumor, spin, and speculation-based stories" (p. 174). The rise of public relations as an increasingly important profession has served to institutionalize this control over framing. All major social institutions, most notably corporations and government, employ public relations staff to promote frames that enable them to maintain or extend their control over the social world (Entman, 2004; Entman and Rojecki, 1993; Martin and Oshagen, 1997). The Pentagon alone, for example, employs more than seven thousand public relations specialists (Seitel, 2004).

Goffman (1979) observed that most news is about *frame violations*; that's what makes news newsworthy. Newscasts report deviations from normality: "Dog Bites Man" is not news; "Man Bites Dog" is. When journalists report frame violations, they are implicitly serving as protectors of the status quo. Some of the most important frame violations involve events that severely disrupt the status quo. These news stories provide detailed coverage of the disruption, but more

news reality frames

News accounts in which interested elites involve journalists in the construction of news drama that blurs underlying contextual realities

important, they almost always document how elites go about restoring order (Gans, 1979). Bennett (1988, 2005a), as you saw in the last chapter, refers to this coverage as "normalizing" news—news framing the social world so social issues and problems are smoothed over and made to appear as though they are routinely (and effectively) dealt with by those in power.

Disorder comes in many forms. It arises when storms cause widespread damage. It happens when technologies fail—when airliners crash or power supplies are cut off. It happens when disease epidemics strike or when the environment is polluted. And it happens when social movements stage protest events challenging those in power and advocating social change. Herbert Gans (1979) concluded that news coverage of social unrest was overwhelmingly dominated by official sources, which framed events from a status quo point of view. He argued that journalists tend to most effectively present the perspective of the upper-middle-class professional strata and defend this class against those above and below it. Recall *Newsweek's* Evan Thomas from the last chapter explaining that in his work as a journalist, "Safeguarding the status quo, protecting traditional institutions, can be healthy and useful, stabilizing and reassuring" (2009, p. 22).

News audiences also may have a particular interest in and desire for normalizing news. James Carey (1989) argued that one of the most important things news does for average readers or viewers is to offer them ritualized messages providing reassurance that the world will go on as it always has. Framing research implies that there is a symbiotic relationship between journalists who use frames supporting the status quo and news consumers who typically want to be reassured that the status quo will endure and problems are only temporary. This relationship between journalists and consumers is likely to be especially strong during times when the status quo is severely challenged. At such times, it can be especially difficult for journalists to offer frames that contradict the status quo and raise questions about governing elites. Even if these frames are used to structure news, news consumers might well choose to ignore them or react against them.

EFFECTS OF FRAMES ON NEWS AUDIENCES

Over the past fifteen years, researchers have documented the influence frames can have on news audiences. The most common finding is that exposure to news coverage results in learning that is consistent with the frames that structure the coverage. If the coverage is dominated by a single frame, especially one originating from an elite source, learning will tend to be guided by this frame (Ryan, Carragee, and Meinhofer, 2001; Valkenburg and Semetko, 1999). What this research has also shown is that news coverage can strongly influence the way news readers or viewers make sense of news events and their major actors. This is especially true of news involving an ongoing series of highly publicized and relevant events, such as social movements (McLeod and Detenber, 1999; Nelson and Clawson, 1997; Terkildsen and Schnell, 1997). Typically, news coverage is framed to support the status quo, resulting in unfavorable views of movements. The credibility and motives of movement leaders are frequently undermined by frames that depict them as overly emotional, disorganized, or childish. Demonstrations organized by social movements are depicted as potentially violent so that police action is justifiable. Revisit Martin Luther King's lament over the coverage of his peaceful civil rights activities in Chapter 5, and in Chapter 8, revisit Paul Krugman's "confusion" over the difference between protesters in Communist China's Tiananmen Square ("heroes of democracy") and those in America's antiwar demonstrations ("the usual protesters" and "serial protesters" whose "rallies delight Iraq").

REFORMING JOURNALISM BASED ON FRAMING THEORY

participatory news
News that reports how citizens routinely engage in actions that have importance for their communities

Some framing theorists have begun to advocate changes in journalism that might overcome these limitations. Gans (2003) advocates what he calls **participatory news**. This is news that reports how citizens routinely engage in actions that have importance for their communities. He points out that this type of coverage has vanished even from local newspapers, but it could be a vital part of encouraging more people to become politically engaged. Participatory news could range from covering conversations in coffee shops to reports on involvement in social groups. Reports on social movements could be "reframed" so they feature positive aspects rather than threats posed to the status quo. He argues that coverage of participation is the best way for journalists to effectively promote it.

explanatory journalism
News that answers "why" questions

Gans also calls for **explanatory journalism**, which "seeks first and foremost to answer 'why' questions: to report why events and statements described by conventional journalism took place." Explanatory journalism involves offering frames for major events. It might mean presenting contrasting frames and providing news consumers a basis for choosing among them. Gans points out that "why stories" are vital "when visible, unusual changes take place in public life as well as private institutions, and people want to understand the effects of these changes on them" (2003, p. 99). If frames for these events aren't provided, people will make them up and circulate them as rumors.

Gans provides a historical analysis of news coverage of several major public policy issues in the United States: a steel industry shutdown, the Arab-Israeli conflict, affirmative action, abortion, and nuclear power. He demonstrates that in only one of these cases, abortion, was there ongoing coverage of social movements. All the other issues involved some coverage of movements at certain stages, but in almost every case that coverage was curtailed when powerful elites moved to force policy in a particular direction. The major exception to this was nuclear power news, in which coverage of movement activities continued despite the existence of powerful elites favoring nuclear power. Elites were most effective in ending movement coverage in affirmative action news stories. What do you think? Would you find more coverage of social movements useful or would it simply make news coverage more complicated and boring?

collective action frames
News frames highlighting positive aspects of social movements and the need for and desirability of action

Gamson (2001), too, has offered similar recommendations for news coverage to promote citizen engagement in politics. His advice centers on the use of what he calls **collective action frames**. These frames highlight positive aspects of social movements and would "offer ways of understanding that imply the need for and desirability of some form of action" (2001, p. 58). To be effective, these frames should offer three components: injustice, identity, and agency. They need to reveal an existing harm or wrong (injustice), identify specifically who is doing the harm and who is being harmed (identity), and finally, explain the possibility of collective action to address the injustice (agency). Gamson stresses the necessity of including agency in news frames. He argues that most Americans are discouraged about their ability to take collective action against injustice. Public policy is dominated by "centralized, hierarchical, national corporations and a national state" (p. 59). American political culture operates to produce quiescence and passivity. Injustice is often committed by government or corporations, institutions that most people find unassailable.

CULTIVATION ANALYSIS

cultivation analysis
Theory that television "cultivates" or creates a worldview that, although possibly inaccurate, becomes the reality because people believe it to be so

Cultivation analysis, a theory developed by George Gerbner during the 1970s and 1980s, addresses macro-level questions about the media's role in society, although it represents a hybrid combining aspects of both macroscopic and microscopic cultural theories. Some researchers regard it as a possible prototype for future research, whereas others consider it a poor example of how to do research. In our view, this controversy was a pivotal one in the development of mass communication theory. It came when the limited-effects perspective was strong but beginning to show signs of waning and cultural theories were receiving more serious attention from media scholars. The controversy reveals a great deal about various opposing perspectives, some of which are still widely held. As you'll see from our review of this theory, it has undergone and continues to undergo important changes. The cultivation theory employed by most researchers today is very different from the theory formulated by Gerbner. As the theory has been reformulated, it has attracted growing interest from post-positivist researchers. Somewhat ironically, a theory that was rejected by many post-positivists two decades ago is now widely accepted as a useful way to understand and explain media effects.

You can begin your own evaluation of cultivation analysis by answering three questions:

1. In any given week, what are the chances that you will be involved in some kind of violence: about 1 in 10 or about 1 in 100? In the actual world, about 0.41 violent crimes occur per 100 Americans, or less than 1 in 200. In the world of prime-time television, though, more than 64 percent of all characters are involved in violence. Was your answer closer to the actual or to the television world?

2. What percentage of all working males in the United States toil in law enforcement and crime detection: 1 percent or 5 percent? The U.S. Census says 1 percent; television says 12 percent. What did you say?

3. Of all the crimes that occur in the United States in any year, what proportion is violent crime, like murder, rape, robbery, and assault? Would you guess 15 or 25 percent? If you hold the television view, you chose the higher number. On television, 77 percent of all major characters who commit crimes commit the violent kind. The *Statistical Abstract of the United States* reports that in actuality only 10 percent of all crime in the country is violent crime.

These questions come from Gerbner and his colleagues, but their point was much more complex than simply stating that those who watch more television give answers more similar to the "TV answer" than to those provided by official data. Their central argument is that television is a "message system" that "cultivates" or creates a worldview that, although possibly inaccurate, becomes the reality simply because we, as a people, believe it to be the reality and base our judgments about our own everyday worlds on that "reality."

You'll remember from Chapter 7 that during the 1960s and early 1970s interest in television as a social force, especially the medium's relationship to increasing individual and societal violence, reached its zenith. Two very important national examinations of the media, again especially television, were undertaken. The first was the National Commission on the Causes and Prevention of Violence, held in 1967 and 1968, and the second was the 1972 Surgeon General's Scientific Advisory Committee on Television and Social Behavior. One scientist involved in both efforts was Gerbner.

Gerber's initial task was apparently simple enough: to produce an annual content analysis of a sample week of network television prime-time fare that would demonstrate, from season to season, how much violence was actually present in that programming—known as the **Violence Index**. The index, however, was not without critics, and serious controversy developed around it. *TV Guide* magazine even called it the "million-dollar mistake."

Debate raged about the definition of *violence*. How was "television violence" defined? Was verbal aggression really violence? Were two teenagers playfully scuffling violence? Was cartoon violence a problem? Critics raised other issues. Why examine only network prime-time? After school, early evening, and weekends are particularly heavy viewing times for most children. Why count only violence? Why not racism and sexism? Nonetheless, Gerbner and his associates attempted to meet the demands of their critics and each year refined their definitional and reporting schemes.

Regardless of the attacks on the researchers' work, one thing did not change: Year in, year out, violence still appeared on prime-time television to a degree unmatched in the "real world," and it was violence of a nature unlike that found in that "real world." If television was truly a mirror of society, or if that medium did simply reinforce the status quo, this video mirror, the Violence Index seemed to say, was more like one found in a fun house than in a home. In their 1982 analysis of television violence, for example, Gerbner and his colleagues discovered that "crime in prime time is at least ten times as rampant as in the real world [and] an average of five to six acts of overt physical violence per hour involves over half of all major characters" (Gerbner et al., 1982, p. 106).

Although the Violence Index identified similar disparities between real-world and televised violence from its very start, the single most important criticism of that annual measure—"So what?"—was addressed in 1973. To demonstrate a causal link between the fluctuating levels of annual televised mayhem and viewers' aggressive behavior, the Gerbner team moved beyond the Violence Index, redefining its work as the **Cultural Indicators Project**. In it the researchers conducted regular periodic examinations of television programming and the "conceptions of social reality that viewing cultivates in child and adult audiences" (Gerbner and Gross, 1976, p. 174). And now that they were addressing the "so what" question, they extended their research to issues well beyond violence.

Violence Index
Annual content analysis of a sample week of network television prime-time fare demonstrating how much violence is present

Cultural Indicators Project
In cultivation analysis, periodic examinations of television programming and the conceptions of social reality cultivated by viewing

The cultural indicators research made five assumptions strongly challenged by postpositivists in the early 1970s. These were first, *television is essentially and fundamentally different from other forms of mass media.* Television is in more than 98 percent of all American homes. It does not require literacy, as do newspapers, magazines, and books. Unlike the movies, it's free (if you don't count the cost of advertising added to the products we buy). It combines pictures and sound, unlike radio. It requires no mobility, as do churches, movies, and theaters. Television is the only medium in history with which people can interact at the earliest and latest years of life, not to mention all those years in between.

Because of television's accessibility and availability to everyone, the second assumption of the Cultural Indicators Project is *the medium is the "central cultural arm" of American society;* it is, as Gerbner and his colleagues argued, "the chief creator of synthetic cultural patterns (entertainment and information) for the most heterogeneous mass publics in history, including large groups that have never shared in any common public message systems" (1978, p. 178).

The third assumption flows logically from this shared reality: *"The substance of the consciousness cultivated by TV is not so much specific attitudes and opinions as more basic assumptions about the 'facts' of life and standards of judgment on which conclusions are based"* (Gerbner and Gross, 1976, p. 175).

Because most television stations and networks are commercially supported (and therefore entrenched in the status quo) and target more or less the same audiences, and because they depend on relatively generic, formulaic, cyclical, repetitive forms of programs and stories, the fourth cultural indicators assumption is the idea that *television's major cultural function is to stabilize social patterns, to cultivate resistance to change;* it is a medium of socialization and enculturation. Again, Gerbner and his cohorts said it well:

> The repetitive pattern of television's mass-produced messages and images forms the mainstream of the common symbolic environment that cultivates the most widely shared conceptions of reality. We live in terms of the stories we tell—stories about what things exist, stories about how things work, and stories about what to do—and television tells them all through news, drama, and advertising to almost everybody most of the time. (Gerbner et al., 1978, p. 178)

If you're reading closely, you can hear not only the echoes of social constructionism and symbolic interactionism, but also Carey's call to understand television as a ritual rather than transmissional medium.

In adopting this more ritualistic view, however, the cultural indicators researchers' fifth assumption—*the observable, measurable, independent contributions of television to the culture are relatively small*—caused additional controversy. In explaining this position, Gerbner used his **ice-age analogy:** "But just as an average temperature shift of a few degrees can lead to an ice age or the outcomes of elections can be determined by slight margins, so too can a relatively small but pervasive influence make a crucial difference. The 'size' of an 'effect' is far less critical than the direction of its steady contribution" (Gerbner et al., 1980, p. 14). The argument was not that television's impact was inconsequential, but rather that although television's measurable, observable, independent effect on the culture at any point in time might be small, that impact was, nonetheless, present and significant. Put somewhat

ice-age analogy
In cultivation analysis, idea that the degree of television's influence is less critical than the direction of its steady contribution

differently, television's impact on our collective sense of reality is real and important, even though that effect might be beyond clear-cut scientific measurement, might defy easy observation, and might be inextricably bound to other factors in the culture. As we saw in Chapter 10, contemporary effects researchers have begun to address these types of effects. They refer to them as cumulative effects.

THE CONTROVERSY

Throughout this text, we have introduced various controversies, schools of theory, and antagonistic perspectives. The debate (as well as its intensity) surrounding cultivation analysis, then, should come as no surprise, especially because, if nothing else, the Gerbner work attempted to use traditional postpositivist empirical research methods to address essential humanistic questions. In other words, Gerbner and his colleagues used tools of inquiry most often identified with the limited-effects perspective to examine questions most often identified with cultural studies.

Horace Newcomb, for example, wrote: "More than any other research effort in the area of television studies the work of Gerbner and Gross and their associates sits squarely at the juncture of the social sciences and the humanities" (Gerbner et al., 1978, p. 265). This, more than anything, is what fueled so much debate. By asserting effects beyond the apparent control of most audience members, the Cultural Indicators Project offended those humanists engaged in cultural studies who felt that their turf had been improperly appropriated and misinterpreted. In asserting significant but possibly unmeasurable, unobservable effects, the project challenged the work, if not the belief system, of the many postpositivists who adhered to the limited-effects perspective.

In a rather fundamental way, the Gerbner group dismissed virtually all existing attitude-change research, all television violence research conducted in laboratories, all television research accepting change as the only measure of the medium's effect, and all research employing an individual program or one particular type of program; in essence, almost all extant television effects research was deemed of small value. Yet Newcomb, one of the first and most influential cultivation critics, wrote of the Gerbner group:

> Their foresight to collect data on a systematic, long-term basis, to move out of the laboratory and away from the closed experimental model, will enable other researchers to avoid costly mistakes. Their material holds a wealth of information. The violence topic provides only one of many symbol clusters to be examined. As they move into new areas, and hopefully retrieve more, and more complex information from audiences, we should see whole new sets of questions and answers emerging to aid us in explaining television's role in our culture. (1978, p. 281)

What exactly were the conclusions drawn initially by the Violence Index, then ultimately by the Cultural Indicators Project, that generated so much disagreement, that so inflamed what we generally think of as scientific objectivity?

THE PRODUCTS OF CULTIVATION ANALYSIS

To scientifically demonstrate their view of television as a culturally influential medium, cultivation researchers depended on a four-step process. The first they called

message system analysis
In cultivation analysis, detailed content analyses of television programming to assess recurring and consistent presentations of images, themes, values, and portrayals

message system analysis, detailed content analyses of television programming to assess its most recurring and consistent presentations of images, themes, values, and portrayals. The second step is the formulation of questions about viewers' social realities. Remember the earlier questions about crime? Those were drawn from a cultivation study. The third step is to survey the audience, posing the questions from step two to its members and asking them about their amount of television consumption. Finally, step four entails comparing the social realities of light and heavy viewers. The product, as described by Michael Morgan and Nancy Signorielli, should not be surprising: "The questions posed to respondents do not mention television, and the respondents' awareness of the source of their information is seen as irrelevant. The resulting relationships ... between amount of viewing and the tendency to respond to these questions in the terms of the dominant and repetitive facts, values, and ideologies of the world of television ... illuminate television's contribution to viewers' conceptions of social reality" (2003, p. 99).

cultivation
In cultivation analysis, television's contribution to the creation of a culture's frameworks or knowledge and underlying general concepts

What is television's contribution? Cultivation theorists argue that its major contribution is **cultivation**, a cultural process relating "to coherent frameworks or knowledge and to underlying general concepts ... cultivated by exposure to the total and organically related world of television rather than exposure to individual programs and selections" (Gerbner, 1990, p. 255).

mainstreaming
In cultivation analysis, the process, especially for heavier viewers, by which television's symbols monopolize and dominate other sources of information and ideas about the world

This cultivation occurs in two ways. The first is **mainstreaming**, where, especially for heavier viewers, television's symbols monopolize and dominate other sources of information and ideas about the world. People's internalized social realities eventually move toward the mainstream, not a mainstream in any political sense, but a culturally dominant reality more closely aligned with television's reality than with any objective reality. Is the criminal justice system failing us? It is if we think it is.

The second way cultivation manifests itself is through **resonance**, when viewers see things on television that are most congruent with their own everyday realities. In essence, these people get a "double dose" of cultivation because what they see on the screen resonates with their actual lives. Some city dwellers, for example, might see the violent world of television resonated in their deteriorating neighborhoods.

THE MEAN WORLD INDEX

resonance
In cultivation analysis, when viewers see things on television that are congruent with their own everyday realities

Referring specifically to mainstreaming and resonance, cultivation pioneer Michael Morgan and his colleagues wrote, "But cultivation analysis is not limited to cases when television 'facts' vary from real-world ... statistics. The repetitive 'lessons' we learn from television, beginning with infancy, can become the basis for a broader world view, making television a significant source of general values, ideologies, and perspectives as well as specific beliefs. Some of the most interesting and important issues for cultivation analysis involve the symbolic transformation of message system data into more general issues and assumptions" (Morgan, Shanahan, and Signorielli, 2009, p. 39). As an example, cultivation researchers present the **Mean World Index**, a series of three questions:

1. Do you believe that most people are just looking out for themselves?
2. Do you think that you can't be too careful in dealing with people?

3. Do you think that most people would take advantage of you if they got the chance?

The Gerbner group argued that the answer provided by television to each of these questions is a resounding "YES." But would a survey of light and heavy viewers find that they gave different responses to these questions? Would the amount of television consumed erase individual distinctions like income and education? Gerbner and his colleagues (1980) reported survey findings supporting their theory. Heavy viewers were much more likely to see the world as a mean place than were light viewers. Better-educated, financially better-off viewers in general saw the world as less mean than did those with less education and income, but heavy viewers from the better-educated, better-off groups saw the world as every bit as dangerous as did low-income and less-educated people. In other words, heavy viewers held a "mainstreamed" perception of the world as a mean place even when they lived in a middle-class social world much less threatened by actual crime.

A FINAL NOTE ON CULTIVATION

Researchers have employed cultivation analysis to investigate the impact of television content on issues beyond violence and crime. It has been used in examinations of people's perceptions of affluence, divorce, and working women (Potter, 1991); acceptance of sexual stereotypes (Ward and Friedman, 2006); materialism (Reimer and Rosengren, 1990); values (Potter, 1990); mental health (Diefenbach and West, 2007); political participation (Besley, 2006); feelings of alienation (Signorielli, 1990); environmental concern (Shanahan, Morgan, and Stenbjerre, 1997); work (Signorielli and Kahlenberg, 2001); perceptions of welfare (Sotirovic, 2001); and marital expectations (Segrin and Nabi, 2002). The assumptions of cultivation are supported throughout, though the strength of findings and the quality of the

INSTANT ACCESS

Cultivation Analysis

Strengths

1. Combines macro- and micro-level theories
2. Provides detailed explanation of television's unique role
3. Applies empirical study to widely held humanistic assumptions
4. Redefines *effect* as more than observable behavior change
5. Applies to wide variety of effects issues
6. Provides basis for social change

Weaknesses

1. Is methodologically troubling to many
2. Assumes homogeneity of television content
3. Focuses on heavy users of television
4. Is difficult to apply to media used less heavily than television

3 Bs of television
In cultivation analysis, the idea that television blurs, blends, and bends reality

research vary greatly. These consistent results led the theory's creator, Gerbner, to identify what he called the **3 Bs of television:**

1. Television *blurs* traditional distinctions of people's views of their world.
2. Television *blends* their realities into television's cultural mainstream.
3. Television *bends* that mainstream to the institutional interests of television and its sponsors.

Gerbner's assessment of the way in which television dominates our social world is reminiscent of arguments about popular culture made by Max Horkheimer and Theodor Adorno more than half a century ago (Chapter 8):

> The historical circumstances in which we find ourselves have taken the magic of human life—living in a universe erected by culture—out of the hands of families and small communities. What has been a richly diverse hand-crafted process has become—for better or worse, or both—a complex manufacturing and mass-distribution enterprise. This has abolished much of the provincialism and parochialism, as well as some of the elitism, of the pretelevision era. It has enriched parochial cultural horizons. It also gave increasingly massive industrial conglomerates the right to conjure up much of what we think about, know, and do in common. (Gerbner, 1990, p. 261)

Clearly, Gerbner does not seem to think that this is a particularly fair trade-off, and as such, he places cultivation analysis in the realm of critical theory. Others do the same. James Shanahan and Vicki Jones, for example, state the following:

> Cultivation is sometimes taken as a return to a strong "powerful effects" view of mass media. This view isn't completely incorrect, but it misses the point that cultivation was originally conceived as a critical theory, which happens to address media issues precisely and only because the mass media (especially television) serve the function of storytelling.... Television is the dominant medium for distributing messages from cultural, social and economic elites.... Cultivation is more than just an analysis of effects from a specific medium; it is an analysis of the institution of television and its social role. (1999, p. 32)

Throughout the development of cultivation theory and the growing body of research based on it, Gerbner was able to retain control over essential elements of the theory despite ongoing arguments in favor of various changes. One of the most controversial elements of the theory is the focus on heavy users of television, with no regard for the specific programs that individuals were viewing. Cultivation, critics claimed, ignored the need to identify heavy users of specific types of programs—news users, sitcom users, soap opera users, and so on. James Potter (1993), for example, argued that cultivation's conceptualization of exposure to television is too global. Other researchers argue that cultivation theory will never have broad application unless it is revised to accommodate more specific measures of exposure (Kahlor, Gorham, and Gilhgan, 1999), and there is current research based on cultivation theory to support this contention (Sotirovic, 2001; Segrin and Nabi, 2002). But if cultivation theory is changed in this way, will it still be cultivation theory? If attention is turned away from the overall power of the "message system" to influence culture and instead is focused on the way different categories of television programming influence our cognitions and feelings—are we doing cultivation research or just postpositivist-style cumulative-effects research?

Since Gerbner's death in 2005, research using cultivation theory has steadily moved in the direction of attributing effects to large amounts of exposure to specific forms of media content. This content can be delivered by a variety of different media, including new media. One way of looking at new media is that to some extent they give each of us the power to shape the message system that cultivates our understanding of the social world. We're no longer at the mercy of three TV networks, but that doesn't mean that media have ceased to cultivate our understanding of ourselves and the people around us. "There is little evidence," write Michael Morgan, James Shanahan, and Nancy Signorielli, "that proliferation of channels has led to any substantially greater diversity of content. Indeed, the mere availability of more channels does not fundamentally change the socio-economic dynamics that drive the production and distribution of programs. On the contrary, that dynamic is intensified by increased concentration of ownership and control.... Even when new digital delivery systems threaten dominant interests, they are quickly swallowed up within the existing institutional structure. The much bally-hooed rise of user-generated video services such as YouTube have [*sic*] been absorbed by dominant players (Google) and are already being exploited for their benefits to advertisers" (2009, pp. 45–46).

MEDIA AS CULTURE INDUSTRIES: THE COMMODIFICATION OF CULTURE

commodification of culture

The study of what happens when culture is mass-produced and distributed in direct competition with locally based cultures

One of the most intriguing and challenging perspectives to emerge from critical cultural studies is the **commodification of culture**, the study of what happens when culture is mass-produced and distributed in direct competition with locally based cultures (Enzensberger, 1974; Hay, 1989; Jhally, 1987). According to this viewpoint, media are industries specializing in the production and distribution of cultural commodities. As with other modern industries, they have grown at the expense of small local producers, and the consequences of this displacement have been and continue to be disruptive to people's lives.

In earlier social orders, such as medieval kingdoms, the culture of everyday life was created and controlled by geographically and socially isolated communities. Though kings and lords might dominate an overall social order and have their own culture, it was often totally separate from and had relatively little influence over the folk cultures structuring the everyday experience of average people. Only in modern social orders have elites begun to develop subversive forms of mass culture capable of intruding into and disrupting the culture of everyday life, argue commodification-of-culture theorists. These new forms function as very subtle but effective ways of thinking, leading people to misinterpret their experiences and act against their own self-interests.

Elites are able to disrupt everyday cultures by using a rather insidious and ingenious strategy. They take bits and pieces of folk culture, weave them together to create attractive mass culture content, and then market the result as a substitute for everyday forms of folk culture (Tunstall, 1977). Thus, elites not only subvert legitimate local cultures, but also earn profits doing so. People actually subsidize the subversion of their everyday culture. If you've ever debated hip-hop and rap artists "selling out," you've been part of a discussion of the commodification of culture. How did rap evolve from its roots in urban verbal warfare into a billion-dollar recording genre and vehicle for paid product placements (Kaufman, 2003)?

Commodification-of-culture theorists argue that this strategy has been especially successful in the United States, where media entrepreneurs have remained relatively independent from political institutions. Mass culture gained steadily in popularity, spawning huge industries that successfully competed for the attention and interest of most Americans. As a result, compared to what occurred in Europe, criticism of mass culture in the United States was muted. Most Americans accepted the cultural commodities emerging from New York and Hollywood as somehow their own. But these same commodities aroused considerable controversy when U.S. media entrepreneurs exported them to other nations. The power of these commodities to reshape daily life was more obvious in most Third World nations, and even more disruptive.

In *The Media Are American* (1977), Jeremy Tunstall provided a cogent description of how American media entrepreneurs developed their strategy for creating universally attractive cultural commodities. He also traced how they succeeded internationally against strong competition from formerly dominant world powers France and Britain. In the late nineteenth and early twentieth centuries, American entrepreneurs had access to powerful new communications technology but no clear notion of how it could be used to make profits. Most big industrialists regarded media as no more than minor and highly speculative enterprises. Few were willing to invest the money necessary to create viable industries. How could messages broadcast through the air or crude black-and-white moving images on a movie screen be used to earn profits? Would people really pay to see or hear these things? How should industries be organized to manufacture and market cultural products? Most early attempts to answer these questions failed, but through trial and effort, wily entrepreneurs eventually developed a successful strategy.

According to Tunstall, Tin Pan Alley in New York City provided a model later emulated by other U.S. media industries. The authors of popular music specialized in taking melodies from folk music and transforming them into short, attractive songs. These were easily marketed to mass audiences who didn't have the time or the aesthetic training to appreciate longer, more sophisticated forms of music. In its early days, Tin Pan Alley was a musical sweatshop in which songwriters were poorly paid and overworked, while sheet music and recording company entrepreneurs reaped huge profits. By keeping production and distribution costs low, rapid expansion was possible and profits grew accordingly. Inevitably, expansion carried the entrepreneurs beyond the United States. Because many were first-generation European immigrants, they knew how to return to and gain a foothold in Europe. The Second World War provided an ideal opportunity to further subvert European culture. The American military demanded and received permission to import massive quantities of U.S.–style popular culture into Europe, where it proved popular. American Armed Forces Radio was especially influential in its broadcasts of popular music and entertainment shows.

What are the consequences of lifting bits of the culture of everyday life out of their context, repackaging them, and then marketing them back to people?

Commodification-of-culture theorists provide many intriguing answers to this question:

1. **When elements of everyday culture are selected for repackaging, only a very limited range is chosen, and important elements are overlooked or consciously ignored.** For example, elements of culture important for structuring the experience of small minority groups are likely to be ignored, whereas culture practiced by large segments of the population will be emphasized. For a good illustration of this, watch situation comedies from the 1960s like *Father Knows Best* and *Leave It to Beaver*. During this era, these programs provided a very homogeneous and idealized picture of American family life. They might make you wonder whether there were any poor people, working women, or ethnic groups living in the United States in the nineteen sixties.

2. **The repackaging process involves dramatization of those elements of culture that have been selected.** Certain forms of action are highlighted, their importance is exaggerated, and others are ignored. Such dramatization makes the final commodity attractive to as large an audience as possible. Potentially boring, controversial, or offensive elements are removed. Features are added that are known to appeal to large audience segments. Thus, attention-getting and emotion-arousing actions—for example, sex and violence—are routinely featured. This is a major reason that car chases, gunfights, and verbal conflict dominate prime-time television and Hollywood movies, but casual conversations between friends are rare (unless they include a joke every fifteen seconds—then we have comedy).

3. **The marketing of cultural commodities is undertaken in a way that maximizes the likelihood that they will intrude into and ultimately disrupt everyday life.** The success of the media industries depends on marketing as much content as possible to as many people as possible with no consideration for how this content will actually be used or what its long-term consequences will be. An analogy can be made to pollution of the physical environment caused by food packaging. The packaging adds nothing to the nutritional value of the food but is merely a marketing device—it moves the product off the shelf. Pollution results when we carelessly dispose of this packaging or when there is so much of it that there is no place to put it. Unlike trash, media commodities are less tangible and their packaging is completely integrated into the cultural content. There are no recycling bins for cultural packaging. When we consume the product, we consume the packaging. It intrudes and disrupts.

4. **The elites who operate the cultural industries generally are ignorant of the consequences of their work.** This ignorance is based partly on their alienation from the people who consume their products. They live in Hollywood or New York City, not in typical neighborhoods. They maintain ignorance partly through strategic avoidance of or denial of evidence about consequences in much the same way the tobacco industry has concealed and lied about research documenting the negative effects of smoking. Media industries have developed formal mechanisms for rationalizing their impact and explaining away consequences. One involves supporting empirical social research and the limited-effects findings it produces. Another involves professionalization.

INSTANT ACCESS

The Commodification of Culture

Strengths

1. Provides basis for social change
2. Identifies problems created by repackaging of cultural content

Weaknesses

1. Argues for, but does not empirically demonstrate, effects
2. Has overly pessimistic view of media influence and average people

Although this can have positive benefits (see Chapter 5), media practitioners can also use it to justify routine production practices while they reject potentially useful innovations.

5. **Disruption of everyday life takes many forms—some disruptions are obviously linked to consumption of especially deleterious content, but other forms are very subtle and occur over long periods.** Disruption ranges from propagation of misconceptions about the social world—like those cultivation analysis has examined—to disruption of social institutions. Consequences can be both microscopic and macroscopic and may take many different forms. For example, Joshua Meyrowitz (1985) argued that media deprive us of a sense of place. Neil Postman (1985) believes that media focus too much on entertainment, with serious long-term consequences. He has also examined media disruption in books entitled *The Disappearance of Childhood* (1994) and *The End of Education* (1996). Disruption of childhood, as you saw in Chapter 7, is also the focus of Susan Linn's *Consuming Kids* (2004), Benjamin Barber's *Consumed: How Markets Corrupt Children, Infantilize Adults, and Swallow Citizens Whole* (2007), and Shirley Steinberg and Joe Kincheloe's *Kinderculture: The Corporate Construction of Childhood* (1997). Kathleen Jamieson (1988) lamented the decline of political speech making brought about by electronic media and, with Karlyn Campbell (1997), media's corruption of the meaning of citizen action. Michael Parenti (1992), in *Make-Believe Media: The Politics of Entertainment*, also explores this theme.

ADVERTISING: THE ULTIMATE CULTURAL COMMODITY

Not surprisingly, critical cultural studies researchers direct some of their most devastating criticism toward advertising. They view it as the ultimate cultural commodity (Hay, 1989; Jhally, 1987). Advertising packages promotional messages so they will be attended to and acted on by people who often have little interest in and often no real need for most of the advertised products or services. Marketers routinely portray consumption of specific products as the best way to construct a worthwhile personal identity, have fun, make friends and influence people, or solve problems (often ones we never knew we had). You deserve a break today. Just do it. DewMocracy!

Compared to other forms of mass media content, advertising comes closest to fitting older Marxist notions of ideology. It is intended to encourage consumption that serves the interest of product manufacturers but may not be in the interest of individual consumers. Advertising is clearly designed to intrude into and disrupt routine buying habits and purchasing decisions. It attempts to stimulate and reinforce consumption, even if consumption might be detrimental to individuals' long-term health. For some products, such as cigarettes, alcohol, and even fast food, successful advertising campaigns move people to engage in self-destructive actions. In other cases, we are simply encouraged to consume things serving little real purpose for us or serving only the purposes that advertising itself creates. One obvious example is when we buy specific brands of clothing because their advertising has promoted them as status symbols. Clothing does indeed provide basic protection for our bodies, but used clothing from a thrift store provides the same protection as do the most well-known brands.

THE MEDIA LITERACY MOVEMENT

Implicitly or explicitly, communication scholars are responding to the many theories and research findings discussed in this and preceding chapters. There is a growing sense that the role of media for individuals and for society is problematic—but not beyond people's control. Many scholars feel that our current understanding of the role of media for individuals and society is sufficiently developed that action can and should be taken. This view is no longer restricted to critical theorists—it is generally expressed by leading postpositivist as well as critical cultural researchers. One way scholars are taking action is that they are helping to lead the drive to improve **media literacy**.

media literacy
The ability to access, analyze, evaluate, and communicate messages

The media literacy movement is based on insights derived from many different sources. We list some of the most important here:

- Audience members are indeed active, but they are not necessarily very aware of what they do with media (uses and gratifications).
- The audience's needs, opportunities, and choices are constrained by access to media and media content (critical cultural studies).
- Media content can implicitly and explicitly provide a guide for action (social cognitive theory, social semiotic theory, symbolic interaction, social construction of reality, cultivation, framing).
- People must realistically assess how their interaction with media texts can determine the purposes that interaction can serve for them in their environments (cultural theory).
- People have differing levels of cognitive processing ability, and this can radically affect how they use media and what they are able to get from media (information-processing theory).

From a postpositivist perspective, the best way to ensure functional (rather than dysfunctional) use of media is to improve individuals' media-use skills. From a cultural studies perspective, we all need to develop our ability to critically reflect on the purposes media and media content serve for us. We need to be able to decide which media to avoid and which to use in ways that best serve our purposes. From the perspective of normative theory, we as citizens of a democracy must make good and effective use of our free press. This is media literacy.

Anthropologists, sociologists, linguists, historians, communication scientists—researchers from virtually all disciplines that study how people and groups communicate to survive and prosper—have long understood that as humans moved from preliterate, or oral, culture to literate culture, they assumed greater control over their environments and lives. With writing came the ability to communicate across time and space. People no longer had to be in the presence of those with whom they wished to communicate (Eisenstein 1979; Inglis, 1990; Innis, 1951).

The invention of the movable-type printing press in the mid-1400s infinitely expanded the importance and reach of the written word, and power began to shift from those who were born into it to those who could make the best use of communication. If literacy—traditionally understood to mean the ability to read and write—increases people's control over their environments and lives, it logically follows that an expanded literacy—one necessitated by a world in which so much "reading" and "writing" occurs in the mass media—should do the same. Critical theorist Stuart Ewen writes:

> Historically, links between literacy and democracy are inseparable from the notion of an informed populace, conversant with the issues that touch upon their lives, enabled with tools that allow them to participate actively in public deliberation and social change. Nineteenth-century struggles for literacy and education were never limited to the ability to read. They were also about learning to write and thus about expanding the number and variety of voices heard in published interchanges and debates. Literacy was about crossing the lines that had historically separated men of ideas from ordinary people, about the social enfranchisement of those who had been excluded from the compensation of citizenship. (2000, p. 448)

As such, he argues elsewhere:

> In a society where instrumental images are employed to petition our affections at every turn—often without a word—educational curricula must … encourage the development of tools for critically analyzing images. For democracy to prevail, image making as a communicative activity must be undertaken by ordinary citizens as well. The aesthetic realm—and the enigmatic ties linking aesthetic, social, economic, political, and ethical values—must be brought down to earth as a subject of study. (1996, p. 413)

Alan Rubin (1998) offered three definitions of media literacy: (1) from the National Leadership Conference on Media Literacy—the ability to access, analyze, evaluate, and communicate messages; (2) from media scholar Paul Messaris—knowledge about how media function in society; and (3) from mass communication researchers Justin Lewis and Sut Jhally—understanding cultural, economic, political, and technological constraints on the creation, production, and transmission of messages. Rubin added: "All definitions emphasize specific knowledge, awareness, and rationality, that is, cognitive processing of information. Most focus on critical evaluations of messages, whereas some include the communication of messages. Media literacy, then, is about understanding the sources and technologies of communication, the codes that are used, the messages that are produced, and the selection, interpretation, and impact of those messages" (Rubin, 1998, p. 3).

Communication scholars William Christ and W. James Potter offer an additional overview of media literacy: "Most conceptualizations [of media literacy] include the following elements: Media are constructed and construct reality; media have commercial implications; media have ideological and political implications; form and content are related in each medium, each of which has a unique aesthetic, codes, and conventions; and receivers negotiate meaning in media" (1998, pp. 7–8).

A careful reader can easily find evidence in these two summations of all the audience- and culture-centered theories we've discussed in this book.

TWO VIEWS OF MEDIA LITERACY

Mass communication scholar Art Silverblatt provided one of the first systematic efforts to place media literacy in audience- and culture-centered theory and frame it as a skill that must and can be improved. His core argument parallels a point made earlier: "The traditional definition of *literacy* applies only to print: 'having a knowledge of letters; instructed; learned.' However, the principal channels of media now include print, photography, film, radio, and television. In light of the emergence of these other channels of mass communications, this definition of literacy must be expanded" (1995, pp. 1–2). As such, he identified five elements of media literacy (1995, pp. 2–3):

1. An awareness of the impact of the media on the individual and society
2. An understanding of the process of mass communication
3. The development of strategies with which to analyze and discuss media messages
4. An awareness of media content as a "text" that provides insight into our contemporary culture and ourselves
5. The cultivation of an enhanced enjoyment, understanding, and appreciation of media content

Potter (1998) takes a slightly different approach, describing several foundational or bedrock ideas supporting media literacy:

1. **Media literacy is a continuum, not a category.** "Media literacy is not a categorical condition like being a high school graduate or being an American.... Media literacy is best regarded as a continuum in which there are degrees.... There is always room for improvement" (p. 6).
2. **Media literacy needs to be developed.** "As we reach higher levels of maturation intellectually, emotionally, and morally we are able to perceive more in media messages.... Maturation raises our potential, but we must actively develop our skills and knowledge structures in order to deliver on that potential" (pp. 6–7).
3. **Media literacy is multidimensional.** Potter identifies four dimensions of media literacy. Each operates on a continuum. In other words, we interact with media messages in four ways, and we do so with varying levels of awareness and skill:
   a. The cognitive domain refers to mental processes and thinking.
   b. The emotional domain is the dimension of feeling.

    c. The aesthetic domain refers to the ability to enjoy, understand, and appreciate media content from an artistic point of view.

    d. The moral domain refers to the ability to infer the values underlying the messages (p. 8).

4. **The purpose of media literacy is to give us more control over interpretations.** "All media messages are interpretations.... A key to media literacy is not to engage in the impossible quest for truthful or objective messages. They don't exist" (p. 9).

Every state in the United States calls for a media literacy component in its primary and secondary school curricula (Tugend, 2003). The Federal Communications Commission (2009) announced that it was undertaking hearings to determine if democracy requires a minimum necessary level of media literacy and to ensure that all citizens had access to media literacy resources. The *Journal of Communication* devoted a special issue to the subject (Media Literacy Symposium, 1998). The *American Behavioral Scientist* devoted two entire issues to media literacy, entitled "'Disillusioning' Ourselves and Our Media: Media Literacy in the 21st Century" (Galician, 2004a, 2004b). Scores of sites on the World Wide Web are expressly devoted to helping individuals improve their media literacy skills. And although many observers see the media literacy movement as the natural product of mass communication theory's long journey to its present state, others see it as another factor that, if ever fully realized, will cause even more ferment because new theories will have to be developed to account for its impact on the audience/media relationship.

SUMMARY

This chapter has examined contemporary cultural and critical cultural theories. Some are primarily microscopic, examining individuals' and communities' everyday use of media, and others are more macroscopic, assessing media's role in the larger social order. But as you read, you saw that when dealing with cultural and critical cultural theory, the microscopic perspective has much to say about the macroscopic. The theories in this chapter are "culture-centered" because they focus on culture as a primary means of understanding the social world and media's role in it. They are also meaning-making theories because they examine the manner in which media influence how we make sense of the social world and our place in it.

One such theory is symbolic interaction, which assumes that our experience of reality is a social construction—as we learn to assign meaning to symbols, we give them power over our experience. Early symbolic interactionism was an outgrowth of pragmatism, which emphasized individual agency as essential and influential in people's ability to adapt to and control reality. Another theory, social construction of reality, also assumes that people have a correspondence of meaning when they use symbols (an object that represents some other object) and signs (objects explicitly designed to serve as indexes of subjective meaning). These signs and symbols combine into collections of meanings, or typification schemes, that form the social stock of knowledge that patterns people's interactions with their environments.

Closely related to these is frame analysis, which assumes that people use their expectations of situations to make sense of them and to determine their actions in them. Individuals use the cues inherent in these situations to determine how to frame, or understand, the situation and whether they should downshift or upshift: that is, the level of seriousness they should bring to their actions. Media's contribution to this framing is in influencing people's expectations, or readings, of those cues. Frame analysis has been applied with some success to journalists' production of news accounts, elites' power to shape the frames that journalists employ, and the meaning people make from those frames.

As media frame issues for us, they cultivate our perceptions of the social world so that we are more likely to make sense of things in some ways rather than others. If we expect to see a "mean world," for example, we will find our expectations constantly confirmed by television violence and televised news. Another way of summarizing the arguments of these theories—drawn from cultivation analysis but expanded beyond that theory's initial focus on television—is through the following five assumptions:

1. Electronic media are fundamentally different from the print media that preceded them.
2. Electronic media constitute a culture industry that has become central to the formation, transmission, and maintenance of culture in American society.
3. Electronic media cultivate a general consciousness, or worldview, on which many people's conclusions, judgments, and actions are based.

4. Electronic media's major cultural influence is to stabilize social patterns, preserve the status quo, and allow power to be increasingly centralized.
5. The measurable, identifiable contributions of electronic media to the culture at any one time are relatively small. But the overall long-term influence is all-pervasive.

As such, media can have a profound influence on the *accessibility and quality of information* we use as we try to think, talk, and act in our social world. As our culture becomes increasingly commodified, the information we access is primarily that provided in infotainment or political spectacle. Because this content necessarily serves the interests of those who produce it, there may be many important things we never learn about from the media. Moreover, our impressions of the things that we *do* learn about might be strongly affected by the "packaging" of that information.

Naturally, if we are to be meaningful actors in the drama that is our own lives, we must improve our control over our use of the media and the meaning we make from their content. This is media literacy, a skill that can be improved and one that exists on a continuum—we are not equally media literate in all situations, all the time, and with all media.

Critical Thinking Questions

1. How attached are you to your cell phone? Consider that you can keep only one—television, refrigerator, newspaper, radio, or cell phone. Which one would you retain? Why? Have you ever lost your cell phone? How connected (or disconnected) from your environment did you feel? Why? How quickly did you replace it?
2. Politicians were among the first professionals to understand the power of framing. What routinized or habitual meanings come to mind when you encounter frames like *pro-life, pro-choice, death tax, tax relief, tax*

and spend, welfare queen, death panel, socialized medicine, Medicare for All? All are terms specifically designed to frame the meaning of the discussion that surrounds each. What meaning does each frame? What fuller or deeper meaning might be obscured? What is the intent of those who would employ these expressions? Is it consistent with honest democratic discourse? Why or why not?
3. Advertisers, through product positioning, make extensive use of symbolic interaction. Can you look around your life and find

products (symbols) that you have intentionally acquired specifically to "position" yourself in others' meaning-making of you? For example, what car do you drive and why? Do you favor a specific scent or brand of clothes? What reality are you trying to create with your product choices?

Key Terms

symbolic interactionism

social behaviorism

symbols

sign

natural signs

artificial signs

signals

symbol

social constructionism

social construction of reality

phenomenology

typifications

symbols

signs

typification schemes

frame analysis

social cues

frame

downshift or upshift

hyperritualized representations

primary, or dominant, reality

news reality frames

participatory news

explanatory journalism

collective action frames

cultivation analysis

Violence Index

Cultural Indicators Project

ice-age analogy

message system analysis

cultivation

mainstreaming

resonance

Mean World Index

3 Bs of television

commodification of culture

media literacy

AFTERWORD: THE FUTURE OF MEDIA THEORY AND RESEARCH

As you read these words, two thousand communications satellites are circling the globe. They provide instantaneous worldwide telephone service, direct home and car reception of audio and video, and incredibly fast and expanded access to the Internet and the World Wide Web. Back on earth, turn-of-the-twenty-first-century media consumers are increasingly signing on for direct satellite or fiber optic–delivered television, rushing to buy large-screen plasma HDTV sets, setting up elaborate home theater systems, and growing more dependent on the services offered via an expanding array of appliances accessing the Internet.

Considering only home media use, in 1980 Americans received seven hours of information a day. Today they receive 11.8 hours, or more precisely, "3.6 zettabytes [a zettabyte is a billion trillion bytes]. Imagine a stack of paperback novels stacked seven feet high over the entire United States, including Alaska" (Young, 2009). Considering only video, by 2013, 90 percent of all the traffic carried on the Internet will be video, and "the surface area of the world's digital screens will be nearly 11 billion square feet, or the equivalent of 2 billion large-screen TVs. Together, this amount would be more than 15 times the surface area of Manhattan. If laid end-to-end, these screens would circle the globe more than 48 times" (Cisco, 2009). America's 205 million Internet users are exceeded by China's 359 million, but top Japan's 93 million, India's 60 million, and Germany's 50 million (Penetration, 2010). Social networking site Facebook has 500 million members socializing in 40 languages across the globe; its 124 million monthly visitors account for 44 percent of all Internet sharing of links, photos, and videos, five billion pieces of content a week (Schonfeld, 2010).

Several government agencies, including the Federal Communications Commission and the Department of Commerce's National Telecommunications and Information Administration, are busy working out rules and regulations to keep pace with and control this telecommunications revolution domestically, and other international agencies are attempting to regulate it worldwide. As all this unfolds, the population of the United States is becoming more multicultural and pluralistic, with demographers predicting that within a generation there will be no one majority race or nationality in the United States.

Internationally there are trends toward development of worldwide networks of social service organizations and greater integration of nation-states (the ever-expanding European Union is a prime example), while at the same time there is resurgence in the reestablishment of historically important local or indigenous cultures. Communications technology serves both these trends. It allows groups of nation-states to communicate with great ease and flexibility across their linguistic, cultural, and physical boundaries. Nongovernmental organizations (NGOs) use this technology to link their global operations to serve a broad range of societal needs, from providing medical care and nutrition to monitoring human rights and environment conservation. This same technology allows advocates for local cultures to produce and distribute sophisticated and attractive media content that is readily accessible to anyone interested in identifying with a culture and adopting its practices. In many parts of the world, from Wales to New Zealand, television channels have been established to serve ethnic groups and carry broadcasts in their languages.

Additionally, one of the most important forces operating in the post–Cold War world is international capitalism. Multinational corporations now reach into nearly every corner of the world, where they organize and manage a broad range of business enterprises, from telecommunications and product manufacturing to food production and a wide range of social services. These corporations also rely on telecommunications technology for cross-border data flows essential to transnational business management. Privatization of government enterprises has been under way worldwide for more than two decades. Multinational corporation ownership frequently replaces state ownership. This trend has led to the dismantling of a variety of sometimes unwieldy and inefficient state-run enterprises and has allowed multinational companies to restructure them as part of their global operations.

These privatization trends have had enormous worldwide consequences for telecommunications generally, and mass media systems specifically. Multinational telecommunications companies based in the United States have aggressively expanded their operations. In many parts of the world, the role of public service media has been disrupted and marginalized. In Europe, where the model for public service media was first developed and where the British Broadcasting Corporation (BBC) still serves as a leading enterprise, most countries permit private media to operate in direct and relatively uncontrolled competition with public service media. The latter have not fared especially well in this competition.

The Internet has emerged as an essential worldwide medium. English speakers account for 27.6 percent of all net users, and this proportion will drop while the proportion of Chinese speakers—currently 22.1 percent—will rise (Internet World Stats, 2009). The net's future is impossible to predict, since it has such flexibility to develop in so many different ways. It operates as a hub for the development of a variety of services easily shared within or across ethnic, national, linguistic, and cultural boundaries. Its influence is increasingly reinforced by a growing range of new software and hardware allowing Internet-based content to be more easily created, accessed, stored, and shared by individuals and groups located anywhere in the world.

Politically, the end of the Cold War did not bring to a close political, religious, and ethnic conflict. Despite fear of nuclear attack during the Cold War, and although the United States and the USSR sponsored small-scale wars in the Middle East, Latin America, Africa, and Asia, Americans had little to fear from domestic terrorism. Now the United States finds itself struggling to understand and decide how to deal with foreign conflicts threatening it at home. Hope for a New World Order that would minimize armed conflict has faded. Technologies like the Internet and cell phones, seemingly beneficial to us all, are used effectively by terrorist groups to organize their opposition to the United States both inside and outside its borders. As terrorism expert David Kilcullen explains, "If bin Laden didn't have access to global media, satellite communications, and the Internet, he'd just be a cranky guy in a cave" (in Packer, 2006a, p. 61).

Throughout this text we have considered how societal upheaval was related to the development of differing theories about the role of media. Rapid industrialization was linked to the development of mass society theory; the rise of totalitarian political systems occasioned the development of propaganda theories; World War II concerns for harnessing the power of mass communication for democracy while minimizing harmful media impact led to the development of the limited-effects perspective; the social unrest of the 1960s spurred renewed interest in theories like cultivation, the spiral of silence, and agenda-setting that could explain how media play important roles for individuals and for society. At each turn in mass communication theory, the *introduction of new technologies, interest in and efforts at controlling them,* and *a concern that their use not conflict with democratic and pluralistic ideals* have initiated and shaped emerging ideas about the role of media in the lives of individuals and in the cultures and societies they occupy. Contemporary media theory must evolve—and is evolving—to accommodate these rapidly moving and powerful alterations in the relationship between people and media.

Although it is possible to outline the many forces at work in the world today, it is difficult to say which will shape future media theory. Will the escalating conflict between the United States and Islamic fundamentalists be influential? Though conceptualization of the role of the Internet seems central to future theory, what this theory might look like is as unclear as the technology it tries to define and understand. Multinational corporations rely heavily on older media theories as they seek out new markets for their products and services. Will new theories allow greater perspective on the global role of these corporations and their consequences for nation-states and ethnic cultures? What about the trends toward greater cultural and ethnic diversity, toward the resurgence of long-suppressed minorities? It is becoming increasingly important to understand how media can support rather than subvert cultural identity.

Earlier in this book we argued that one key to understanding the future of media theory is to look at the way scholarly researchers define themselves and their research. We differentiated four types of theory:

1. postpositivism (traditional social science inquiry)
2. interpretive theory (hermeneutics)
3. critical cultural theory
4. normative theory

We argued that historic disputes and misunderstandings between proponents of these theories were fading and that there was growing likelihood that they could develop complementary rather than competing or contradictory bodies of research. We continue to see evidence that this trend is occurring in the United States. Postpositivist, interpretive, and critical cultural researchers have all used framing theory and cultivation theory to ground important lines of research. W. James Potter, a leading postpositivist researcher, has recently published *Arguing for a General Framework for Mass Media Scholarship* (2009) that, as the name suggests, makes the case for a general framework for mass media scholarship that integrates many of the approaches to theory and research discussed in this book.

But it is also increasingly important to take into account what is happening worldwide. Here, too, there is some evidence of cooperation and reduced competition. Although critical cultural and interpretive approaches remain dominant overseas, the influence of postpositivism is expanding in Europe, with growing programs at a number of universities and important institutions located at the University of Amsterdam, the University of Munich, and the University of Munster. Postpositivism has also gained wider acceptance in Asia and in some universities in Australia, Africa, and Latin America, especially in programs focused on preparing students for jobs in media-related industries. Critical cultural, hermeneutic, and—as traditional media norms and practices are increasingly strained by economic and technological upheaval—normative studies have continued to gain ground in the United States, where their scholars enjoy growing influence within major academic associations, including the National Communication Association, the International Communication Association, and the Association for Education in Journalism and Mass Communication.

We have reached a point in time where once disparate media researchers are beginning to function as a global research community. This community increasingly shares a common body of theories and research methods. European researchers are very active in the U.S.-based International Communication Association, and American participation is welcomed in the European-based International Association for Mass Communication Research. Participation by scholars from other parts of the world is also growing in both these associations. The Internet provides global access to a common set of journals, and these journals publish articles written by scholars located around the world. Cross-national and international research projects are increasingly common.

CHALLENGES

One challenge facing the global media research community is the ongoing revolution in communications technology. It is producing technologies and applications filling every niche on the communication spectrum, ranging from the intrapersonal and interpersonal communication we carry on with ourselves and with others to powerful forms of mass communication capable of simultaneously sending messages to every person on earth. Each of these new media can play different roles in society and in our personal lives. Most will quickly disappear, but a handful will succeed—often for unexpected reasons. Some older media will persist, but their roles will be greatly altered or diminished. This is what happened to radio and movies after the rise of television in the 1950s and 1960s. Others will disappear entirely, as did weekly mass circulation magazines in the 1950s, the vinyl records that served us so well for 130 years, and the much-ridiculed eight-track cartridge player of the Sixties and Seventies. We will almost certainly witness the demise of the CD and DVD as content becomes easier and less expensive to download.

Media researchers will struggle to keep pace with and make sense of this rapidly changing media landscape and the questions it raises for the quality of personal life and of society. Will instant messaging and e-mail replace personal conversations as a way of staying in touch with friends? If they do, will that alter the quality of our relationships, or will we simply be able to more easily connect with distant friends? American teens are already more likely to stay in touch with high school friends because they can use e-mail to maintain these relationships. Will this affect the number and types of friendships formed after high school? What about the high level of media use found for Generation M? Will this lead to totally new ways to develop and sustain communities as suggested by research on networked publics? Or will this use prove to be problematic?

The sudden end to the Cold War in the 1990s upended a world order that had endured for half a century. That structure has yet to be replaced. This is the second challenge to developing new media theory. The United States has emerged as the world's only superpower, but ongoing wars in the Middle East and the world economic crisis revealed the limits of its power. The European Union has created an enviable level of social stability for twenty-seven nations across the European continent, but its influence outside that region is limited. Multinational corporations are working to make the world safe for business but are challenged by a variety of local, regional, and global opponents.

Other forces for change are at work. A wide variety of alliances is developing between nation-states to facilitate a broad range of useful contacts. One of the most prominent and powerful of these is the G8, an alliance of major industrial nations that has been holding annual summit conferences since 1975. In recent years, it has been the target of antiglobalization demonstrations. Many different NGOs have been created to address significant issues and deliver important services. One way that people have tried to describe this situation is with the word *globalization*. But this term is quite ambiguous. For some, it is synonymous solely with the growing power and order imposed by multinational corporations; for others it involves the global order created by multinational alliances like the G8 and NGOs (Smith, 1991). Given its ambiguity, it's not surprising that some people regard globalization with great suspicion while others hail it as the force that will gradually create a new, beneficial world order.

Powerful communications technologies, such as satellites and the Internet, enable influence to be exercised and order imposed over space and time. As the global order expands, that of individual nation-states tends to contract. There is growing hope that NGOs could play an especially important role in development of civil society in emerging democracies around the world. Research is needed to assess this possibility and exploit whatever potential exists for them to serve as buffers between national governments, multinational alliances, and multinational corporations.

The third challenge involves rapidly expanding scientific insight into the powers and limitations of the human organism. Psychologists, medical researchers, and biologists are pursuing lines of research that continually alter our knowledge and understanding of human beings. This research will necessitate constant reformulation of media theories—already it is transforming and guiding communication experiments, as we saw in information-processing and entertainment theories. In a variety of fields ranging from the biological sciences to cognitive psychology, research is likely to produce powerful insight into the ways we deal with and act on information from both the physical and social environment. Ironically, the more we come to understand the power of computers to emulate and simulate human communication abilities, the more we come to understand our own cognitive capacities and their limitations.

THE END OF MASS COMMUNICATION THEORY: THE RISE OF MEDIA THEORY

In 1999, a few days before his untimely death, Steven Chaffee (a prolific researcher and thinker you met in Chapter 1) lectured on the subject of "the end of mass communication." That talk became the basis of an article coauthored with Miriam Metzger (2001). In it, they explore this topic at length. Their essential argument is that new media are bringing an end to mass communication and are fundamentally altering how media will be structured, used, and conceptualized in the twenty-first century. As such, *mass communication theory* is best understood today as *media theory*. Here are some of their observations:

> One of the assumptions of empirical studies of media content has been that the media are limited [in number], identifiable, and therefore, knowable through quantitative research. This is changing. . . . The amount of material available from the new media is vast, which makes studies of media content more difficult than ever before. In fact, Internet content is literally unbounded. . . . To exacerbate this problem, each individual user's experience with content may differ in the new media environment, as interactive technologies allow for users to select a subset of the available content on, for example, an entire Web site.
>
> Studies of media audiences may suffer the same fate as audiences become harder to identify and monitor in the new media environment. . . . Media effects studies, too, may be more difficult with audiences that are not as well assembled or accessible to researchers as they once were. In addition, mass communication law and policy will have to change dramatically.
>
> *Mass communication* is typified by television, whereas videogames and Web sites may be considered the archetypes of *media communication.* User motivation also changes as communication moves from *mass* to *media.* (Chaffee and Metzger, 2001, pp. 371–373; italics added)

Chaffee and Metzger offered a few examples of this transformation from *mass communication* to *media* theory. They point out that theories such as agenda-setting and cultivation are based on the assumption that audiences regularly and routinely use a finite number of media for news and entertainment. If cultivation theory is limited to heavy viewing of television, as Gerbner argued, its future is tied to whether people continue watching television as much as they did when the theory was developed. Gerbner focused on television because he considered it to be our culture's dominant message system. But television has evolved from three national networks when he began his original Violence Index into a system with hundreds of cable channels. These channels supplement their broadcasts with Internet websites and specialized magazines. Is cultivation theory still applicable to this expanding message system? Critical theory and cultural studies may need less alteration, because they tend to be concerned with media systems rather than specific media or with the way media content from a specific form of media affects culture. With the emergence of major new media companies like Google (itself owning YouTube) and Yahoo, old worries about media concentration have continued relevance in the new media environment. Concerns about access to media will remain important as we confront the "digital divide" between those with easy access to new media and those without.

We have seen over the short life (in scientific terms) of mass communication theory that media scholars have always had the resources necessary to address the challenges they faced in their times and circumstances. There is every reason to believe that contemporary thinkers and researchers are equally up to the task. Future theories—whether we call them mass communication or media theories—will need to address the full spectrum of mediated communication, from cell phones to the Internet. These theories must assess how mediation takes place, the social context and social implications of using various media, the cognitive processes and skills necessary to encode and decode various types of messages from different types of media, and how individuals can take more control of the media they use to send and receive messages. Theories also need to critically assess the role media play in culture and society.

Despite the challenges facing media (or mass communication) theory, this is likely to be an exciting and productive era, one in which the conceptual and methodological tools developed over the past century will be used to understand the rise of entirely new media systems. We hope that this book has encouraged at least some of you to pursue careers as communication scholars, and we hope that all of you have gained an understanding of media that is useful to you.

REFERENCES

Adbusters. (2002). "The Rev. Jerry Falwell." *Adbusters*, January/February, no page number.

Adorno, T., and M. Horkheimer. (1972). *Dialectic of Enlightenment*. New York: Herder and Herder.

Alasuutari, P. (1999). "Introduction: Three Phases of Reception Studies." In P. Alasuutari, ed., *Rethinking the Media Audience*. Thousand Oaks, CA: Sage.

"All Survive Jet Plunge into Hudson." (2009). *Providence Journal*, January 16: A1, A4.

Allport, G. W. (1967). "Attitudes." In M. Fishbein, ed., *Readings in Attitude Theory and Measurement*. New York: Wiley.

Allport, G. W., and L. J. Postman. (1945). "The Basic Psychology of Rumor." *Transactions of the New York Academy of Sciences*, 8: 61–81.

Alterman, E. (2009a). "David Broder: Eyes Wide Shut." *The Nation*, May 25: 10.

Alterman, E. (2009b). "Is Jon Stewart Our Ed Murrow? Maybe …" *The Nation*, April 3: 10.

Alterman, E. (2006). "Truth Is for 'Liberals.'" *The Nation*, June 26: 10.

Alterman, E. (2003). "What Liberal Media?" *The Nation*, December 14: 10.

Alterman, E. (2008). "The News from Quinn-Broderville." *The Nation*, February 24: 11–14.

Altschull, J. H. (1990). *From Milton to McLuhan: The Ideas behind American Journalism*. New York: Longman.

Anderson, C. A., L. Berkowitz, E. Donnerstein, L. R. Huesmann, J. D. Johnson, D. Linz, N. M. Malamuth, and E. Wartella. (2003). "The Influence of Media Violence on Youth." *Psychological Science in the Public Interest*, 4: 81–110.

Anderson, C. A., and B. J. Bushman (2001). "Effects of Violent Video Games on Aggressive Behavior, Aggressive Cognition, Aggressive Affect, Physiological Arousal, and Prosocial Behavior: A Meta-Analytical Review of the Scientific Literature." *Psychological Science*, 12: 353–359.

Anderson, C. A., and K. E. Dill. (2000). "Video Games and Aggressive Thoughts, Feelings, and Behavior in the Laboratory and in Life." *Journal of Personality and Social Psychology*, 78: 772–790.

Anderson, C. A., A. Shibuya, N. Ihori, E. L. Swing, B. J. Bushman, A. Sakamoto, H. R. Rothstein, and M. Saleem. (2010). "Violent Video Game Effects on Aggression, Empathy, and Prosocial Behavior in Eastern and Western Countries: A Meta-Analytic Review." *Psychological Review*, 136: 151–173.

Anderson, D. R., and E. P. Lorch. (1983). "Looking at Television: Action or Reaction?" In J. Bryant and D. R. Anderson, eds., *Children's Understanding of Television: Research on Attention and Comprehension*. New York: Academic.

Andison, F. S. (1977). "TV Violence and Viewer Aggression: A Culmination of Study Results, 1956–1976." *Public Opinion Quarterly*, 41: 314–331.

Andrews, R., M. Biggs, and M. Seidel. (1996). *The Columbia World of Quotations*. New York: Columbia University Press.

Anthony, R. (2010). "Food Industry Launches Initiative to Help Reduce Obesity." (*www.healthyweight commit.org/news/Food-Industry-Launches-Initiative*).

Arango, T., and B. Stelter. (2009). "For Press, Rumors of Straying but No Hard Evidence." *New York Times*, June 25: A14.

Arato, A., and E. Gebhardt, eds. (1978). *The Essential Frankfurt School Reader*. New York: Urizen.

Auletta, K. (2010). "Non-Stop News." *New Yorker*, January 25: 38–47.

Bagdikian, B. H. (2004). "Print Will Survive." *Editor & Publisher*, March: 70.

Bagdikian, B. H. (2000). *The Media Monopoly*, 6th ed. Boston: Beacon.

Bagdikian, B. H. (1992). *The Media Monopoly*, 4th ed. Boston: Beacon.

Bailey, K. D. (1982). *Methods of Social Research*. New York: Free Press.

Baker, W. F. (2009). "How to Save the News." *The Nation*, October 12: 21–23.

Baker, R. K., and S. J. Ball. (1969). *Violence and the Media: A Staff Report to the National Commission on the Causes and Prevention of Violence*, vol. 9A. Washington, DC: U.S. Government.

Ball-Rokeach, S. J. (2001). "The Politics of Studying Media Violence: Reflections 30 Years after the Violence Commission." *Mass Communication and Society*, 4: 3–18.

Ball-Rokeach, S. J. (1998). "A Theory of Media Power and a Theory of Media Use: Different Stories, Questions, and Ways of Thinking." *Mass Communication and Society*, 1: 5–40.

Ball-Rokeach, S. J., Y. C. Kim, and S. Matei. (2001). "Storytelling Neighborhood: Paths to Belonging in Diverse Urban Environments." *Communication Research*, 28: 392–428.

Bamford, J. (2004). *A Pretext for War*. New York: Doubleday.

Bandura, A. (2009). "Social Cognitive Theory of Mass Communication." In J. Bryant and M. B. Oliver, eds., *Media Effects: Advances in Theory and Research*. New York: Routledge.

Bandura, A. (2008). "The Reconstrual of 'Free Will' from the Agentic Perspective of Social Cognitive Theory." In J. Baer, J. C. Kaufman, and R. F. Baumeister, eds., *Are We Free? Psychology and Free Will*. Oxford: Oxford University Press.

Bandura, A. (1994). "Social Cognitive Theory of Mass Communication." In J. Bryant and D. Zillman, eds., *Media Effects: Advances in Theory and Research*. Hillsdale, NJ: Erlbaum.

Bandura, A. (1971). *Psychological Modeling: Conflicting Theories*. Chicago: Aldine Atherton.

Bandura, A. (1965). "Influence of Models' Reinforcement Contingencies on the Acquisition of Imitative Responses." *Journal of Personality and Social Psychology*, 1: 589–595.

Bandura, A., D. Ross, and S. A. Ross. (1963). "Imitation of Film-Mediated Aggressive Models." *Journal of Abnormal Social Psychology*, 66: 3–11.

Baran, S. J. (2011). *Introduction to Mass Communication: Media Literacy and Culture*. New York: McGraw-Hill.

Baran, S. J., and V. J. Blasko. (1984). "Social Perceptions and the Byproducts of Advertising." *Journal of Communication*, 34: 12–20.

Baran, S. J., and T. P. Meyer. (1974). "Imitation and Identification: Two Compatible Approaches to Social Learning from the Electronic Media." *AV Communication Review*, 22: 167–179.

Barber, B. R. (2007). *Consumed: How Markets Corrupt Children, Infantilize Adults, and Swallow Citizens Whole*. New York: W. W. Norton.

Barker, C. (2004). *Cultural Studies: Theory and Practice*. Thousand Oaks, CA: Sage.

Barmann, T. C. (2004). "Jack's Industry." *Providence Journal*, May 14: E1, E8.

Barnouw, E. (1966). *A History of Broadcasting in the United States: A Tower in Babel*, vol. 1. New York: Oxford University Press.

Barrow, J. D. (1998). *Impossibility: The Limits of Science and the Science of Limits*. New York: Oxford University Press.

Bates, S. (2001). "Realigning Journalism with Democracy: The Hutchins Commission, Its Times, and Ours." (*www.annenberg.nwu.edu*).

Bauer, R. A., and A. H. Bauer. (1960). "America, Mass Society, and Mass Media." *Journal of Social Issues*, 10: 3–66.

Becker, H. (1949). "The Nature and Consequences of Black Propaganda." *American Sociological Review*, 14: 221–235.

Belkin, L. (2000). "The Making of an 8-Year-Old Woman." *New York Times Magazine*, December 24: 38–43.

Bennett, W. L. (2005a). *News: The Politics of Illusion*, 6th ed. New York: Longman.

Bennett, W. L. (2005b). "News as Reality TV: Election Coverage and the Democratization of Truth." *Critical Studies in Media Communication*, 22: 171–177.

Bennett, W. L. (1988). *News: The Politics of Illusion*, 2nd ed. New York: Longman.

Bennett, W. L., and M. Edelman. (1985). "Toward a New Political Narrative." *Journal of Communication*, 35: 128–138.

Bennett, W. L., and S. Iyengar. (2008). "A New Era of Minimal Effects? The Changing Foundations of Political Communication." *Journal of Communication*, 58: 707–731.

Benoit, W. L., and R. L. Holbert. (2008). "Empirical Intersections in Communication Research: Replication, Multiple Quantitative Methods, and Bridging the Quantitative-Qualitative Divide." *Journal of Communication*, 58: 615–628.

Berelson, B. (1959). "The State of Communication Research." *Public Opinion Quarterly*, 23: 1–6.

Berelson, B. (1949). "What 'Missing the Newspaper' Means." In P. F. Lazarsfeld and F. N. Stanton, eds., *Communications Research, 1948–1949*. New York: Harper.

Berelson, B., P. F. Lazarsfeld, and W. N. McPhee. (1954). *Voting: A Study of Opinion Formation in a Presidential Campaign*. Chicago: University of Chicago Press.

Berger, C. R. (2005). "Interpersonal Communication: Theoretical Perspectives, Future Prospects." *Journal of Communication*, 55: 415–447.

Berger, P. L., and T. Luckmann. (1966). *The Social Construction of Reality: A Treatise in the Sociology of Knowledge*. Garden City, NY: Doubleday.

Berkowitz, L. (1965). "Some Aspects of Observed Aggression." *Journal of Personality and Social Psychology*, 2: 359–369.

Berkowitz, L., and R. G. Geen. (1966). "Film Violence and the Cue Properties of Available Targets." *Journal of Personality and Social Psychology*, 3: 525–530.

Bernays, E. L. (1928). *Propaganda*. New York: Liveright.

Besley, J. (2006). "The Role of Entertainment Television and Its Interactions with Individual Values in Explaining Political Participation." *Press/Politics*, 11: 41–63.

"Bill Moyers on Journalism and Democracy." (2007). *Christian*

Century, April 17. (*www.truthout. org/docs_2006/prmter_042507H. shtml*).

Black, E. (2003). "After Iraq, It's a War of Words, Evidence; Was Arms Threat Exaggerated?" *Minneapolis Star-Tribune*, June 8: 1A.

Bloom, A. D. (1987). *The Closing of the American Mind: How Higher Education Has Failed Democracy and Impoverished the Souls of Today's Students*. New York: Simon & Schuster.

Blow, C. M. (2009). "The Purient Trap." *New York Times*, June 27: A19.

Blumenauer, E. (2009). "My Near Death Panel Experience." *New York Times*, November 15: WK12.

Blumer, H. (1969). *Symbolic Interactionism*. Englewood Cliffs, NJ: Prentice Hall.

Blumer, H., and Hauser, P. (1933). *Movies, Delinquency, and Crime*. New York: Macmillan.

Blumler, J. G. (1979). "The Role of Theory in Uses and Gratifications Studies." *Communication Research*, 6: 9–36.

Blumler, J. G., M. Gurevitch, and E. Katz. (1985). "Reaching Out: A Future for Gratifications Research." In K. E. Rosengren, L. A. Wenner, and P. Palmgreen, eds., *Media Gratifications Research: Current Perspectives*. Beverly Hills, CA: Sage.

Blumler, J. G., and E. Katz, eds. (1974). *The Uses of Mass Communication: Current Perspectives on Gratifications Research*. Beverly Hills, CA: Sage.

Bollier, D. (2005). *Brand Name Bullies*. New York: Wiley.

Boneva, B., R. Kraut, and D. Frohlich. (2001). "Using E-mail for Personal Relationships: The Difference Gender Makes." *American Behavioral Scientist*, 45: 530–550.

Bonfadelli, H. (2002). "The Internet and Knowledge Gaps: A Theoretical and Empirical Investigation." *European Journal of Communication*, 17: 65–85.

Bowers, J. W., and J. A. Courtright. (1984). *Communication Research Methods*. Glenview, IL: Scott Foresman.

Bradshaw, K. A. (2003). "Persuasive Communication/Collective Behavior and Public Opinion: Rapid Shifts in Opinion and Communication/The Dynamics of Persuasion: Communication and Attitudes in the 21st Century." *Journalism and Mass Communication Quarterly*, 80: 754.

Braiker, B. (2007). "Poll: What Americans (Don't) Know." *Newsweek*, June 23. (*www.msnbc. msn.com/id/19390791/site/ newsweek*).

Brantlinger, P. (1983). *Bread and Circuses: Theories of Mass Culture as Social Decay*. Ithaca, NY: Cornell University Press.

Bronfenbrenner, U. (1970). *Two Worlds of Childhood: U.S. and U.S.S.R.* New York: Sage.

Brooks, D. (2002). "Looking Back on Tomorrow." *Atlantic Monthly*, April: 20–22.

Brownell, B. A. (1983). "Interpretations of Twentieth-Century Urban Progressive Reform." In D. R. Colburn and G. E. Pozzetta, eds., *Reform and Reformers in the Progressive Era*. Westport, CT: Greenwood.

Brunsdon, C, and D. Morley. (1981). "'Crossroads' Notes on Soap Opera." *Screen*, 22: 327.

Brunsdon, C, and D. Morley. (1978). *Everyday Television: 'Nationwide'*. London: British Film Institute.

Bryant, J., and D. R. Anderson. (1983). *Children's Understanding of Television: Research on Attention and Comprehension*. New York: Academic.

Bryant, J., and D. Miron. (2004). "Theory and Research in Mass Communication." *Journal of Communication*, 54: 662–704.

Bryant, J., D. R. Roskos-Ewoldsen, and J. Cantor, eds. (2003). *Communication and Emotion: Essays in Honor of Dolf Zillmann*. Mahwah, NJ: Erlbaum.

Bryant, J., and R. L. Street. (1988). "From Reactivity to Activity and Action: An Evolving Concept and *Weltanschauung* in Mass and Interpersonal Communication." In R. P. Hawkins, J. M. Wiemann, and S. Pingree, eds., *Advancing Communication Science: Merging Mass and Interpersonal Processes*. Newbury Park, CA: Sage.

Bryant, J., and P. Vorderer. (2006). *Psychology of Entertainment*. Mahwah, NJ: Erlbaum.

Bryant, J., and D. Zillmann. (2002). *Media Effects: Advances in Theory and Research*. Mahwah, NJ: Erlbaum.

Bryner, J. (2009). "TV Causes Learning Lag in Infants." *Live Science*, June 1. (*www.livescience.com/culture/ 090601–infants-television.html*).

Bryson, L. (1954). *The Drive Toward Reason: In the Service of a Free People*. New York: Harper.

Burr, T. (2005). "'Good Night' Delivers Realism and Relevance." *Boston Globe*, October 7: E1, E13.

Burrell, G., and G. Morgan. (1979). *Sociological Paradigms and Organisation Analysis*. London: Heinemann.

Campbell, A., P. W. Converse, W. E. Miller, and D. E. Stokes. (1960). *The American Voter*. New York: Wiley.

Campbell, W. J. (2010). *Getting It Wrong: Ten of the Greatest Misreported Stories in American Journalism*. Berkeley: University of California Press.

Cantril, H., H. Gaudet, and H. Herzog. (1940). *Invasion from Mars*. Princeton, NJ: Princeton University Press.

Caplan, S. E. (2005). "A Social Skill Account of Problematic Internet Use." *Journal of Communication*, 55: 721–736.

Carey, J. (1989). *Communication as Culture: Essays on Media and Society*. Winchester, MA: Unwin Hyman.

Carey, J. (1977). "Mass Communication Research and Cultural Studies: An American View." In J. Curran, M. Gurevitch, J. Woollacott, J. Marriott, and C. Roberts, eds., *Mass Communication and Society*. London: Open University Press.

Carey, J. (1975a). "Culture and Communications." *Communication Research*, 2: 173–191.

Carey, J. (1975b). *Sociology and Public Affairs: The Chicago School*. Beverly Hills, CA: Sage.

Carey, J. W. (1996). "The Chigaco School and Mass Communication Research." In E. E. Dennis and E. Wartella, eds., *American Communication Research: The Remembered History*. New York: Routledge.

Carr, N. (2008a). "Who Killed the Blogosphere?" *Rough Type*,

November 7. (*www.roughtype.com/archives/2008/11/who_killed_the.php*).

Carr, N. (2008b). "Is Google Making Us Stupid?" *Atlantic Monthly*, July/August: 56–63.

Carragee, K. M., and W. Roefs. (2004). "The Neglect of Power in Recent Framing Research." *Journal of Communication*, 54: 214–233.

Carter, G. (2004). "Neoconned: The Path to War." *Vanity Fair*, May: 58–62.

Cellular Telecommunications and Internet Association (CTIA). (2004). "Wireless Communications: It's More Than Just Talk." *Time* (Special Advertising Section), March 22: 75–78.

Chaffee, S. (2001). "Studying the New Communication of Politics." *Political Communication*, 18: 237–245.

Chaffee, S. H., and C. R. Berger. (1987). "What Communication Scientists Do." In C. R. Berger and S. H. Chaffee, eds., *Handbook of Communication Science*. Newbury Park, CA: Sage.

Chaffee, S. H., and M. J. Metzger. (2001). "The End of Mass Communication?" *Mass Communication and Society*, 4: 365–379.

Chandra, A., S. C. Martino, R. L. Collins, M. N. Elliott, S. H. Berry, D. E. Kanouse, and A. Miu. (2008). "Does Watching Sex on Television Predict Teen Pregnancy? Findings from a National Longitudinal Survey of Youth." *Pediatrics*, 122: 1047–1054.

Chiang, O. J. (2010). "Apps and Videogames to Keep You Healthy." *Forbes*, January 20. (*www.forbes.com/2010/01/20/iphone-apps-videogames-technology-breakthroughs-health.html?boxes=Homepagechannels*).

Chittum, R. (2009). "The Chasm Between the Value of Print and Web Readers." *Columbia Journalism Review*, August 21. (*http://www.cjr.org/the_audit/post_11.php*).

Chomsky, N. (1991). *Deterring Democracy*. New York: Verso.

Chomsky, N. (1969). *American Power and the New Mandarins*. New York: Pantheon.

Christ, W. G., and W. J. Potter. (1998). "Media Literacy, Media Education, and the Academy." *Journal of Communication*, 48: 5–15.

Christians, C. G., J. P. Ferre, and P. M. Fackler. (1993). *Good News: Social Ethics and the Press*. New York: Oxford University Press.

Cisco Systems. (2009). "New Cisco Visual Networking Index Forecasts Global IP traffic to Increase Fivefold by 2013." June 9. (*http://newsroom.cisco.com/dlls/2009/prod_060909.html*).

Clark, L., and M. Tiggemann. (2007). "Sociocultural Influences and Body Image in 9- to 12-Year-Old Girls: The Role of Appearance Schemas." *Journal of Clinical Child and Adolescent Psychology*, 36: 76–86.

Clark, M. (2005). "'Good Night': Great Movie." *USA Today*, October 7: 4E.

Clarke, R. A. (2004). *Against All Enemies: Inside America's War on Terror*. New York: Free Press.

Cohen, B. C. (1963). *The Press and Foreign Policy*. Princeton, NJ: Princeton University Press.

Cohen, J. (2008). "McClellan and His Media Collaborators." *Truthout*, May 30. (*www.truthout.org/article/mcclellan-and-his-media-collaborators?print*).

Cohen, J., and G. Weimann. (2000). "Cultivation Revisited: Some Genres Have Some Effects on Some Viewers." *Communication Reports*, 13: 99–115.

Committee on Communications. (2006). "Children, Adolescents, and Advertising." *Pediatrics*, 118: 2562–2569.

Comstock, G. (1991). *Television and the American Child*. San Diego: Academic.

Conway, M., M. E. Grabe, and K. Grieves. (2007). "Villains, Victims and Virtuous in Bill O'Reilly's 'No Spin Zone': Revisiting World War I Propaganda Techniques." *Journalism Studies*, 8: 197–224.

Cooper, A. (2008). "The Bigger Tent." *Columbia Journalism Review*, September/October: 45–47.

Cooper, C. (2004). "Gates: Convergence Is for Real." CIVET *News.com*. (*http://news.cnet.com/Gates-Convergence-is-for-real/2008-7353_3-5137118.html*).

Coulter, A. (2006). *Godless: The Church Of Liberalism*. New York: Crown.

Coulter, A. (2002). *Slander: Liberal Lies about the American Right*. New York: Crown.

Craig, R. T. (2007). "Pragmatism in the Field of Communication Theory." *Communication Theory*, 17: 125–145.

Crouse, T. (1973). *The Boys on the Bus*. New York: Random House.

Crowley, D. J., and P. Heyer. (1991). *Communication in History: Technology, Culture, Society*. New York: Longman.

Crowther, H. (2004). "With Trembling Fingers." *The Progressive Populist*, June 1: 12–13.

Cunningham, B. (2009). "Take a Stand." *Columbia Journalism Review*, September/October: 32–39.

Cunningham, B. (2003). "Re-thinking Objectivity." *Columbia Journalism Review*, July/August: 24–32.

Cunningham, S. (2000). "Responding to Propaganda: An Ethical Enterprise." Paper presented at Colloquium 2000 in Applied Media Ethics.

Curran, J. (1991). "Mass Media and Democracy: A Reappraisal." In J. Curran and M. Gurevitch, eds., *Mass Media and Society*. London: Edward Arnold.

Curran, J., S. Iyengar, B. Lund, and I. Salovaara-Moring. (2009). "Media System, Public Knowledge and Democracy: A Comparative Study." *European Journal of Communication*, 25: 5–26.

Daly, J. A. (2000). "Colloquy: Getting Older and Getting Better: Challenges for Communication Research." *Human Communication Research*, 26: 331–338.

Davis, D. K. (1990). "News and Politics." In D. L. Swanson and D. Nimmo, eds., *New Directions in Political Communication*. Newbury Park, CA: Sage.

Davis, D. K., and S. J. Baran. (1981). *Mass Communication and Everyday Life: A Perspective on Theory and Effects*. Belmont, CA: Wadsworth.

Davis, D. K., and J. P. Robinson. (1989). "Newsflow and Democratic Society in an Age of Electronic Media." In G. Comstock, ed., *Public Communication and Behavior*, vol. 3. New York: Academic.

Davis, R. E. (1976). *Response to Innovation: A Study of Popular*

Argument about New Mass Media. New York: Arno.

DeFleur, M. L. (1970). *Theories of Mass Communication.* New York: David McKay.

DeFleur, M. L., and S. Ball-Rokeach. (1989). *Theories of Mass Communication,* 5th ed. New York: David McKay.

DeFleur, M. L., and S. Ball-Rokeach. (1975). *Theories of Mass Communication,* 3rd ed. New York: David McKay.

DeFleur, M. L., and O. N. Larsen. (1958). *The Flow of Information.* New York: Harper.

Delia, J. (1987). "Communication Research: A History." In C. Berger and S. Chaffee, eds., *Handbook of Communication Science.* Beverly Hills, CA: Sage.

Denby, D. (2005). "Getting the Story." *New Yorker,* October 10: 94–95.

Dervin, B. (1989). "Changing Conceptions of the Audience." In R. E. Rice and C. Atkin, eds., *Public Communication Campaigns,* 2nd ed. Beverly Hills, CA: Sage.

Deutschmann, P. J., and W. A. Danielson. (1960). "Diffusion of Knowledge of the Major News Story." *Journalism Quarterly,* 37: 345–355.

Dewey, J. (1927). *The Public and Its Problems.* New York: Holt.

Dickinson, T. (2009). "Shift + Control." *Mother Jones,* January/February: 15–19.

Diefenbach, D., and M. West. (2007). "Television and Attitudes Toward Mental Health Issues: Cultivation Analysis and Third Person Effect." *Journal of Community Psychology,* 35: 181–195.

Dimmick, J., S. Patterson, and J. Sikand. (1996). "Personal Telephone Networks: A Typology and Two Empirical Studies." *Journal of Broadcasting and Electronic Media,* 40: 45–59.

Dimmick, J. W., J. Sikand, and S. J. Patterson. (1994). "Gratifications of the Household Telephone: Sociability, Instrumentality, and Reassurance." *Communication Research,* 21: 643–663.

Dionne, E. J. (2009). "The Real Town Hall Story." *Washington Post,* September 3: A19.

Dollar Coins: Retire the Paper. (2008). *Seattle Post-Intelligencer,* January 2. (*www.seattlepi.com/opinion/ 345527_dollard.html*).

Donohue, G. A., P. J. Tichenor, and C. N. Ohen. (1986). "Metro Daily Pullback and Knowledge Gaps, within and between Communities." *Communication Research,* 13: 453–71.

Drum, K. (2009). "Torture for Thee, But Not for Me." *Mother Jones,* July 8. (*www.motherjones.com/ kevin-drum/2009/07/torture-thee- not-me*).

Dumenco, S. (2009). "Citizen Journalism? Um, How About Crowdsourcing Journalism With Actual Journalists?" *Mother Jones,* October 22. (*http://adage.com/ mediaworks/article? article_id=139842*).

Dunham, W. (2009). "Mississippi Has Highest Teen Birth Rate." *Reuters,* January 7. (*www.reuters.com/ article/idUSTRE50679220090107*).

Dunstan, D. W., E. L. M. Barr, G. N. Healy, J. Salmon, J. E. Shaw, B. Balkau, D. J. Magliano, A. J. Cameron, P. Z. Zimmet, and N. Owen. (2010). "Television Viewing Time and Mortality. The Australian Diabetes, Obesity and Lifestyle Study." *Circulation,* Jan 2010; doi: 10.1161/CIRCULATION- AHA.109.894824.

Durkheim, E. (1951). *Suicide: Etude de Sociologie.* New York: Free Press.

Durose, M. R., and P. A. Langan. (2001). *Bureau of Justice Statistics, State Court Sentencing of Convicted Felons, 1998 Statistical Tables.* Washington, DC: U.S. Department of Justice.

Edelman, M. (1988). *Constructing the Political Spectacle,* 3rd ed. Chicago: University of Chicago Press.

Editors. (2004). "*The Times* and Iraq." *New York Times,* May 26: A2.

Edwards, J. (2009). "Campbell's Gay Soup Ad Causes Storm in a Bread Bowl. *BNET,* January 6. (*http:// industry.bnet.com/advertising/ 1000485/campbells-gay-soup-ad- causes-storm-in-a-bread-bowl/*).

Eggerton, J. (2004). "Brownback: Stern Is Indecent." *Broadcasting and Cable,* March 31. (*www. broadcastingcable.com/index.asp? layoutarticlePrint&articleIDCA40 7176*).

Ehrenreich, B. (2009). "Too Poor to Make the News." *New York Times,* June 14: WK 10.

Eisenstein, E. L. (1979). *The Printing Press as an Agent of Change: Communications and Cultural Transformations in Early-Modern Europe.* Cambridge, UK: Cambridge University Press.

Elms, A. C. (1972). *Social Psychology and Social Relevance.* Boston: Little, Brown.

Engelberg, E., and L. Sjöberg. (2004). "Internet Use, Social Skills, and Adjustment." *CyberPsychology & Behavior,* 7: 41–47.

Entman, R. M. (2004). *Projections of Power: Framing News, Public Opinion, and U.S. Foreign Policy.* Chicago: University of Chicago Press.

Entman, R. M. (1989). *Democracy without Citizens: Media and the Decay of American Politics.* New York: Oxford University Press.

Entman, R. M., and A. Rojecki. (1993). "Freezing Out the Public: Elite and Media Framing of the U.S. Anti- Nuclear Movement." *Political Communication,* 10: 155–173.

Enzensberger, H. M. (1974). *The Consciousness Industry.* New York: Seabury.

Epps, G. (2008). "The FCC-Word." *Nation,* June 16: 6–8.

Epstein, E. J. (1973). *News from Nowhere: Television and the News.* New York: Random House.

Ettema, J. S., and F. G. Kline. (1977). "Deficits, Differences, and Ceilings: Contingent Conditions for Understanding the Knowledge Gap." *Communication Research,* 4: 179–202.

Eveland, W. P. (2003). "A 'Mix of Attributes' Approach to the Study of Media Effects and New Communication Technologies." *Journal of Communication,* 53: 395–410.

Ewen, S. (2000). "Memoirs of a Commodity Fetishist." *Mass Communication and Society,* 3: 439–452.

Ewen, S. (1996). *PR! A Social History of Spin.* New York: Basic Books.

Facebook Generation Faces Identity Crisis. (2008). *Medical News Today,* July 4. (*www. medicalnewstoday.com/articles/ 113878.php*).

FAIR. (2005). "Media Shrug Off Mass Movement Against War." September 27. (*http://www.fair.org/*

index.php?page=2677&printer_friendly=1).

Famed Author John Updike Dies of Cancer at 76. (2009). *CNN.com*, January 27. (*www.cnn.com/2009/SHOWBIZ/books/01/27/obit.updike/index.html*).

Farr, J. (1999). "John Dewey and American Political Science." *American Journal of Political Science*, 43: 520–541.

Farsetta, D. (2006). "Accuracy of Report on Video News Releases Affirmed: CMD Issues Full Rebuttal of RTNDA Claims." *Center for Media and Democracy*, October 9. (*www.prwatch.org/node/5283/print*).

Faules, D. F., and D. C. Alexander. (1978). *Communication and Social Behavior: A Symbolic Interaction Perspective*. Reading, MA: Addison-Wesley.

"Fear Factor." (2001). *Broadcasting and Cable*, July 9: 54.

Federal Communications Commission. (2009). "FCC 09–94." *Notice of Inquiry*, October 22.

Fengler, S. (2003). "Holding the News Media Accountable: A Study of Media Reporters and Media Critics in the United States." *Journalism and Mass Communication Quarterly*, 80: 818–833.

"Ferment in the Field." (1983). *Journal of Communication* (Special Issue): 33.

Feshbach, S. (1961). "The Stimulating versus Cathartic Effects of a Vicarious Aggressive Activity." *Journal of Abnormal and Social Psychology*, 63: 381–385.

Feshbach, S., and R. D. Singer. (1971). *Television and Aggression: An Experimental Field Study*. San Francisco: Jossey-Bass.

Festinger, L. (1962). "Cognitive Dissonance." *Scientific American*, 207: 93.

Festinger, L. (1957). A *Theory of Cognitive Dissonance*. Stanford, CA: Stanford University Press.

"The Final Word is Hooray!" (2006). *Fair.org*, March 15. (*www.fair.org/index.php?page=2842*).

Fine, J. (2009). "Newspapers: Less Liked than Airlines?" *BusinessWeek*, May 19. (*www.businessweek.com/innovate/FineOnMedia/archives/2009/05/newspapers_less.html*).

Fishman, M. (1980). *Manufacturing the News*. Austin: University of Texas Press.

Fiske, J. (1987). *Television Culture*. London: Routledge.

Flavell, J. H. (1992). "Cognitive Development: Past, Present, and Future." *Developmental Psychology*, 28: 998–1005.

Framm, A., and T. Tompson. (2007). " U.S. Optimism Sinks to Record Lows." *TheLedger.com*, May 21. (*www.theledger.com/apps/pbcs.dll/article?AID=/20070521/NEWS/705210376/1039*).

Freedman, L. Z. (1961). "Daydream in a Vacuum Tube: A Psychiatrist's Comment on the Effects of Television." In W. Schramm, J. Lyle, and E. B. Parker, eds., *Television in the Lives of Our Children*. Stanford, CA: Stanford University Press.

Friedrich, C. J. (1943). "Principles of Informational Strategy." *Public Opinion Quarterly*, 7: 77–89.

Frost, R., and J. Stauffer. (1987). "The Effects of Social Class, Gender, and Personality on Psychological Responses to Filmed Violence." *Journal of Communication*, 37: 29–45.

Fukuyama, F. (1999). "The Great Disruption: Human Nature and the Reconstruction of Social Order." *Atlantic Monthly*, May: 55–80.

Funkhouser, G., and M. McCombs. (1971). "The Rise and Fall of News Diffusion." *Public Opinion Quarterly*, 50: 107–113.

Gadamer, H. (1995). *Truth and Method*. Translation by J. Weinsheimer and D. G. Marshall. New York: Continuum.

Galician, Mary-Lou, ed. (2004a). "'Disillusioning' Ourselves and Our Media: Media Literacy in the 21st Century, Part I: Strategies for Schools." *American Behavioral Scientist*, 48: 1–136.

Galician, Mary-Lou, ed. (2004b). "'Disillusioning' Ourselves and Our Media: Media Literacy in the 21st Century, Part II: Strategies for the General Public." *American Behavioral Scientist*, 48: 143–272.

Gamson, W. A. (2001). "How Storytelling Can Be Empowering." In K. A. Cerulo, ed., *Culture in Mind: Toward a Sociology of Culture and Cognition*. New York: Routledge.

Gamson, W. A. (1989). "News as Framing." *American Behavioral Scientist*, 33: 157–161.

Gamson, W. A., D. Croteau, W. Hoynes, and T. Sasson. (1992). "Media Images and the Social Construction of Reality." *Annual Review of Sociology*, 18: 373–393.

Gamson, W. A., and A. Modigliani. (1989). "Media Discourse and Public Opinion on Nuclear Power: A Constructionist Approach." *American Journal of Sociology*, 95: 1–37.

Gans, H. (2003). *Democracy and the News*. New York: Oxford University Press.

Gans, H. (1979). *Deciding What's News: A Study of CBS Evening News, NBC Nightly News, Newsweek and Time*. New York: Pantheon Books.

Garnham, N. (1995). "Political Economy and Cultural Studies: Reconciliation or Divorce?" *Critical Studies in Mass Communication*, 12: 95–100.

Gary, B. (1996). "Communication Research, the Rockefeller Foundation, and Mobilization for the War on Words, 1938–1944." *Journal of Communication*, 46: 124–147.

Gentile, D. A., P. J. Lynch, J. R. Linder, and D. A. Walsh. (2004). "The Effects of Violent Video Games Habits on Adolescent Hostility, Aggressive Behavior, and School Performance." *Journal of Adolescence*, 27: 5–22.

Gerbner, G. (2001). "The Cultural Arm of the Corporate Establishment: Reflections on the Work of Herb Schiller." *Journal of Broadcasting and Electronic Media*, 45: 186–190.

Gerbner, G. (1990). "Epilogue: Advancing on the Path of Righteousness (Maybe)." In N. Signorielli and M. Morgan, eds., *Cultivation Analysis: New Directions in Media Effects Research*. Newbury Park, CA: Sage.

Gerbner, G., and L. Gross. (1979). "Editorial Response: A Reply to Newcomb's 'Humanistic Critique.'" *Communication Research*, 6: 223–230.

Gerbner, G., and L. Gross. (1976). "Living with Television: The Violence Profile." *Journal of Communication*, 26: 173–199.

Gerbner, G., L. Gross, M. Jackson-Beeck, S. Jeffries-Fox, and N. Signorielli. (1978). "Cultural Indicators: Violence Profile No. 9." *Journal of Communication*, 28: 176–206.

Gerbner, G., L. Gross, M. Morgan, and N. Signorielli. (1982). "Charting the Mainstream: Television's Contributions to Political Orientations." *Journal of Communication*, 32: 100–127.

Gerbner, G., L. Gross, M. Morgan, and N. Signorielli. (1980). "The 'Mainstreaming' of America: Violence Profile No. 11." *Journal of Communication*, 30: 10–29.

Giddens, A. (1991). *Modernity and Self-Identity: Self and Society in the Late Modern Age*. Stanford, CA: Stanford University Press.

Gilmor, D. (2004). *We the Media— Grassroots Journalism by the People, for the People*. Sebastopol, CA: O'Reilly. (*www.authorama. com/book/we-the-media.html*).

Gillmor, D. M., and J. A. Barron. (1974). *Mass Communication Law. Cases and Comments*. St. Paul, MN: West.

Gitlin, T. (2007). The Murderer and the Media. *Huffington Post*, April 22. (*www.huffingtonpost.com/todd-gitlin/the-murdered-and-the-medi_b_46529.html*).

Gitlin, T. (2004a). "The Great Media Breakdown." *Mother Jones*, November/December: 56–59.

Gitlin, T. (2004b). "It Was a Very Bad Year." *The American Prospect*, July: 31–34.

Gitlin, T. (1991). "Bites and Blips: Chunk News, Savvy Talk, and the Bifurcation of American Politics." In P. Dahlgren and C. Sparks, eds., *Communication and Citizenship: Journalism and the Public Sphere in the New Media Age*. London: Routledge.

Gitlin, T. (1980). *The Whole World Is Watching: Mass Media in the Making and Unmaking of the New Left*. Berkeley: University of California Press.

Gizbert, R. (2007). "London Calling: NBC, the Cho Tapes and Responsibility." *Huffington Post*, April 23. (*www.huffington-post. com/richard-gizbert/london-calling-nbc-the-_b_46568.html*).

Glander, T. (2000). *Origins of Mass Communication Research During the American Cold War: Educational Effects and Contemporary Implications*. Mahwah, NJ: Erlbaum.

Glasgow University Media Group, eds. (1980). *More Bad News*. London: Routledge and Kegan Paul.

Glasgow University Media Group, eds. (1976). *Bad News*. London: Routledge and Kegan Paul.

Glasser, I. (2006). "Drug Busts = Jim Crow." *The Nation*, July 10: 24–26.

Gleick, J. (1987). *Chaos: Making a New Science*. New York: Viking.

Glenn, D. (2007). "Bohemian Rhapsodies." *Columbia Journalism Review*, July/August: 46–50.

Glynn, C. J., and J. M. McLeod. (1985). "Implications of the Spiral of Silence Theory for Communication and Public Opinion Research." In K. R. Sanders, L. L. Kaid, and D. D. Nimmo, eds., *Political Communication Yearbook*, 1984. Carbondale, IL: Southern Illinois University Press.

Goetz, T. (2006). "75 Million Americans May Have Something Called Metabolic Syndrome. How Big Pharma Turned Obesity into a Disease—Then Invented Drugs to Cure It." *Wired*, October: 152–157.

Goffman, E. (1981). *Forms of Talk*. Philadelphia: University of Pennsylvania Press.

Goffman, E. (1979). *Gender Advertisements*. New York: Harper Colophon.

Goffman, E. (1974). *Frame Analysis: An Essay on the Organization of Experience*. New York: Harper & Row.

Goist, P. D. (1971). "City and 'Community': The Urban Theory of Robert Park." *American Quarterly*, 23: 46–59.

Goldberg, B. (2009). *A Slobbering Love Affair: The True (And Pathetic) Story of the Torrid Romance Between Barack Obama and the Mainstream Media*. Washington, DC: Regnery.

Goldberg, B. (2003). *Arrogance: Rescuing America from the Media Elite*. New York: Warner Books.

Goldberg, B. (2002). *Bias: A CBS Insider Exposes How the Media Distort the News*. Washington, DC: Regnery.

Goldberg, M. E., M. Fishbein, and S. E. Middlestadt, eds. (1997). *Social Marketing: Theoretical and Practical Perspectives*. Hillsdale, NJ: Erlbaum.

Goodman, A. (2004). *The Exception to the Rulers: Exposing Oily Politicians, War Profiteers, and the Media That Love Them*. New York: Hyperion.

Goodman, M. (2001). "The Radio Act of 1927 as a Product of Progressivism." (*www.scripps. ohiou.edu/mediahistory/ mhmjour2-2.htm*).

Gould, J. (1972). "TV Violence Held Unharmful to Youth." *New York Times*, January 11: 27.

Gould, S. J. (2000). *The Lying Stones of Marrakech: Penultimate Reflections in Natural History*. New York: Harmony Books.

Graber, D. (1987). *Processing the News*, 2nd ed. New York: Longman.

Greenberg, B., and E. Parker, eds. (1965). *The Kennedy Assassination and the American Public*. Stanford, CA: Stanford University Press.

Greenwald, G. (2009a). "Meet the Press's Idea of a Debate." *Salon*, September 7. (*www.salon.com/ opinion/greenwald/2009/09/07/ mtp/*).

Greenwald, G. (2009b). "What Every American Should Be Made to Learn about the IG Torture Report." *Salon*, August 24. (*www.salon.com/ opinion/greenwald/2009/08/24/ ig_report/index.html*).

Greenwald, G. (2009c). "Jay Rosen on the Media's Control of Political Debates." *Salon*, January 16. (*www.salon.com/opinion/ greenwald/radio/2009/01/16/ rosen/*).

Greenwald, G. (2008). "CNN/MSNBC Reporter: Corporate Executives Forced Pro-Bush, Pro-War Narrative." *Salon*, May 29. (*www. salon.com/opinion/greenwald/2008/ 05/29/yellinprint.html*).

Grier, S., and A. Brumbaugh. (2007). "Compared to Whom? The Impact of Status on Third Person Effects in Advertising in a South African Context." *Journal of Consumer Behaviour*, 6: 5–18.

Grier, S., and C. A. Bryant. (2004). "Social Marketing in Public Health." *Annual Review of Public Health*, 26: 319–339.

Griffin, E. A. (1994). *A First Look at Communication Theory*. New York: McGraw-Hill.

Grossberg, L. (1989). "The Circulation of Cultural Studies." *Critical Studies in Mass Communication*, 6: 413–421.

Gross, D. (2010). "You're Rich. Get Over It." *Newsweek*, February 3. (http://www.newsweek.com/id/232964).

Grossberg, L. (1983). "Cultural Studies Revisited and Revised." In M. S. Mander, ed., *Communications in Transition*. New York: Praeger.

Grossberg, L., and C. Nelson. (1988). "Introduction: The Territory of Marxism." In C. Nelson and L. Grossberg, eds., *Marxism and the Interpretation of Culture*. Urbana, IL: University of Illinois Press.

Grossberg, L., C. Nelson, and P. Treichler, eds. (1992). *Cultural Studies*. London: Routledge.

Grossman, B. (2007). "The Gathering Storm of Coverage." *Broadcasting & Cable*, April 23: 14–15.

Grosswiler, P. (1997). *Method in the Message: Rethinking McLuhan through Critical Theory*. Montreal: Black Rose Books.

Gumpert, G. (2007). "Looking Past Disciplines." *Critical Studies in Media Communication*, 24: 170–171.

Gunter, B. (1987). *Poor Reception: Misunderstanding and Forgetting Broadcast News*. Hillsdale, NJ: Erlbaum.

Habermas, J. (1989). *The Structural Transformation of the Public Sphere*. Cambridge, MA: MIT Press.

Habermas, J. (1971). *Knowledge and Human Interest*. Boston: Beacon.

Hachten, W. A. (1992). *The World News Prism*. Ames, IA: Iowa State University Press.

Hafner, K., and M. Lyon. (1996). *Where Wizards Stay Up Late: The Origins of the Internet*. New York: Simon & Schuster.

Hall, E. (2006). "Brit Ban on Junk-Food Ads to Cost TV Titans $75 Mil." *Advertising Age*, November 27: 18.

Hall, S. (1982). "The Rediscovery of 'Ideology': Return of the Repressed in Media Studies." In M. Gurevitch, T. Bennett, J. Curran, and J. Woollacott, eds., *Culture, Society, and the Media*. New York: Methuen.

Hall, S. (1981a). "Notes on Deconstructing 'The Popular.'" In R. Samuel, ed., *People's History and Socialist Theory*. London: Routledge.

Hall, S. (1981b). "The Whites of Their Eyes: Racist Ideologies and the Media." In G. Bridges and R. Brundt, eds., *Silver Linings*. London: Lawrence and Wishart.

Hall, S. (1980a). "Encoding and Decoding in the Television Discourse." In S. Hall, ed., *Culture, Media, Language*. London: Hutchinson.

Hall, S. (1980b). "Cultural Studies: Two Paradigms." *Media, Culture and Society*, 2: 57–72.

Hall, S. (1973). *Encoding and Decoding in the Television Discourse*. CCCS Stencilled Paper 7, University of Birmingham.

Hall, S., D. Hobson, A. Lowe, and P. Willis, eds. (1982). *Culture, Media, Language*. London: Hutchinson.

Halloran, J. D. (1964/1965). "Television and Violence." *The Twentieth Century*, Winter: 61–72.

Hamelink, C. J. (2001). "Considering Communication Issues and Problems around the Globe." *ICA News*, November: 8–9.

Hampton, K., L. Sessions, E. J. Her, and L. Rainie. (2009). "Social Isolation and New Technology." *Pew Internet & American Life Project*, November 4. (www.pewinternet.org/Reports/2009/18--Social-Isolation-and-New-Technology.aspx).

Hardt, H. (1999). "Shifting Paradigms: Decentering the Discourse of Mass Communication Research." *Mass Communication and Society*, 2: 175–183.

Harkinson, J. (2009). "Facebook's Privacy Faceoff." *Mother Jones*, February 17. (www.motherjones.com/print/21333).

Harmon, M. (2001). "Laboring to Be Fair: U.S. Network TV Strike Coverage." *Electronic News: A Journal of Applied Research & Ideas*, 1: 13–22, 39–40.

Harris, R. J. (2009). *A Cognitive Psychology of Mass Communication*, 5th ed. New York: Routledge.

Hart, P. (2009a). "Hard Times for the Overclass." *Extra!* November: 5–6.

Hart, P. (2009b). "Healthcare Reform Minus the Public Option—or the Public." *Extra!* October: 7–8.

Hart, P. (2005). "Why Is Labor Off TV?" *Extra! Update*, August: 3.

Hart, P., and S. Ackerman. (2002). "Patriotism and Censorship." *Extra!* November/December: 6–9.

Hawkins, E. T. (2003). "Bridging Latin America's Digital Divide: Government Policies and Internet Access." *Journalism and Mass Communication Quarterly*, 80: 646.

Hay, J. (1989). "Advertising as a Cultural Text (Rethinking Message Analysis in a Recombinant Culture)." In B. Dervin, L. Grossberg, B. J. O'Keefe, and E. Wartella, eds., *Rethinking Communication, Vol. 2: Paradigm Exemplars*. Newbury Park, CA: Sage.

Heath, I. (2006). "Combating Disease Mongering: Daunting but Nonetheless Essential." *Public Library of Science Medicine*. 3: e146.

Heath, T. (2010). "U.S. Cellphone Users Donate $22 Million to Haiti Earthquake Relief via Text." *Washington Post*, January 19. (www.washingtonpost.com/wp-dyn/content/article/2010/01/18/AR2010011803792.html?wpisrc=nl_tech).

Hedges, C. (2008). "Bad Days for Newsrooms—and Democracy." *Truthdig.com*, July 21. (www.truthdig.com/report/item/20080721_so_goes_the_newsroom_the_empire_and_the_world).

Hellmich, N. (2004). "Obesity on Track as No. 1 Killer." *USA Today*, March 10: 1A.

Hendriks, A. (2002). "Examining the Effects of Hegemonic Depictions of Female Bodies on Television: A Call for Theory and Programmatic Research." *Critical Studies in Media Communication*, 19: 106–124.

Herman, E. S. (1996). "The Propaganda Model Revisited." *Monthly Review*, July–August: 115–128.

Herman, E. S., and N. Chomsky. (1988). *Manufacturing Consent*. New York: Pantheon.

Herzog, B. (2000). *States of Mind*. Winston-Salem, NC: John F. Blair.

Herzog, H. (1944). "Motivations and Gratifications of Daily Serial Listeners." In P. F. Lazarsfeld and F. N. Stanton, eds., *Radio Research*,

1942–1943. New York: Duell, Sloan and Pearce.

Herzog, H. (1940). "Professor Quiz: A Gratification Study." In P. F. Lazarsfeld, ed., *Radio and the Printed Page*. New York: Duell, Sloan, and Pearce.

Herzstein, R. E. (1978). *The War That Hitler Won*. New York: Putnam.

Hightower, J. (2007). "Left-Wing Penguins and Devilish Tofu." *Progressive Populist*, February 1: 3.

Hitler, A. (1933). *Mein Kampf: Zwe Bande in Enemband*. Miinchen: F. Eher.

Hobson, D. (1982). *Crossroads: The Drama of a Soap Opera*. London: Methuen.

Holbert, R. L., R. K. Garrett, and L. S. Gleason. (2010). "A New Era of Minimal Effects? A Response to Bennett and Iyengar." *Journal of Communication*, 60: 15–34.

Holbrook, T. M. (2002). "Presidential Campaigns and the Knowledge Gap." *Political Communication*, 19: 437–465.

"Home Internet Access: Continuing to Grow, But Big Differences Among Demographics." (2009). *Nielsen News*, March 6. (*http://blog.nielsen. com/nielsenwire/online_mobile/ home-internet-access-continuing-to- grow-but-big-differences-among- demographics/*).

Hopkinson, N. (2003). "Youngsters Awash in High-Tech Media." *Providence Journal*, October 29: A3.

Hovland, C. I., I. L. Jams, and H. H. Kelley. (1953). *Communication and Persuasion*. New Haven, CT: Yale University Press.

Hovland, C. I., A. A. Lumsdaine, and F. D. Sheffield. (1949). *Experiments on Mass Communication*. Princeton, NJ: Princeton University Press.

Howe, J. (2007). "Your Web, Your Way." *Time*, December 25–January 1: 60–61.

Huang, C. (2003). "Transitional Media vs. Normative Theories: Schramm, Altschull, and China." *Journal of Communication*, 53: 444–459.

Hughes, C. (2002). *Key Concepts in Feminist Theory and Research*. Newbury Park, CA: Sage.

Human Rights Watch. (2009). "US: Drug Arrests Skewed by Race." March 2. (*www.hrw.org/en/news/ 2009/03/02/us-drug-arrests- skewed-race*).

Human Rights Watch. (2000). "Key Recommendations from Punishment and Prejudice: Racial Disparities in the War on Drugs." June. (*www.hrw.org/campaigns/ drugs/war/key-reco.htm*).

Huston, A. C, E. Donnerstein, H. Fairchild, N. D. Feshbach, P. A. Katz, J. P. Murray, E. A. Rubenstein, B. L. Wilcox, and D. Zuckerman. (1992). *Big World, Small Screen*. Lincoln, NE: University of Nebraska Press.

Inglis, F. (1990). *Media Theory: An Introduction*. Oxford: Basil Blackwell.

Innis, H. A. (1951). *The Bias of Communication*. Toronto: University of Toronto Press.

Innis, H. A. (1950). *Empire and Communication*. Toronto: University of Toronto Press.

Institute of Medicine. (2006). *Food Marketing to Children and Youth: Threat or Opportunity?* Washington, DC: National Academies Press.

Internet World Stats. (2009). "Top Ten Languages Used in the Web." (*www.internetworldstats.com/ stats7.htm*).

Ito, M., H. A. Hors, M. Bittanti, D. Boyd, B. Herr-Stephenson, P. C. Lange, C. J. Pascoe, and L. Robinson. (2009). *Living and Learning with New Media*. Cambridge, MA: MIT Press.

Itzkoff, D. (2010). "You Saw What in 'Avatar'? Pass Those Glasses!" *New York Times*, January 20: A1.

Iyengar, S. (1991). *Is Anyone Responsible? How Television Frames Political Issues*. Chicago: University of Chicago Press.

Iyengar, S., and D. R. Kinder. (1987). *News That Matters: Television and American Opinion*. Chicago: University of Chicago Press.

Iyengar, S., and D. R. Kinder. (1986). "More Than Meets the Eye: TV News, Priming, and Public Evaluations of the President." In G. Comstock, ed., *Public Communication and Behavior*, vol. 1. New York: Academic.

Jamieson, K. H. (1988). *Eloquence in an Electronic Age: The Transformation of Political Speechmaking*. New York: Oxford University Press.

Jamieson, K. H., and K. K. Campbell. (1997). *The Interplay of Influence: News, Advertising, Politics, and the Mass Media*. Belmont, CA: Wadsworth.

Jamieson, K. H., and M. E. P. Seligman. (2001). "Six Rules for Government and Press on Terrorism: Undercutting Fear Itself." Unpublished report, Philadelphia, November.

Jamieson, K. H., and P. Waldman. (2003). *The Press Effect*. New York: Oxford University Press.

Jeffery, C. (2009). "Cost of the *NYT Magazine* NOLA Story Broken Down." *Mother Jones*: August 28. (*www.motherjones.com/mojo/ 2009/08/cost-nyt-magazine-nola- story-broken-down*).

Jensen, K. B. (1995). *The Social Semiotics of Mass Communication*. Thousand Oaks, CA: Sage.

Jensen, K. B. (1990). "Television Futures: A Social Action Methodology for Studying Interpretive Communities." *Critical Studies in Mass Communication*, 7: 129–146.

Jhally, S., ed. (1987). *The Codes of Advertising: Fetishism and the Political Economy of Meaning in the Consumer Society*. New York: St. Martin's.

Jo, E., and L. Berkowitz. (1994). "A Priming Effect Analysis of Media Influences: An Update." In J. Bryant and D. Zillman, eds., *Media Effects: Advances in Theory and Research*. Hillsdale, NJ: Erlbaum.

Johnson, A. (2009). "New Role for Web in Iranian Politics." *Campaign.com*, June 11. (*http://abcnews.go.com/ International/wireStory? id=7817251*).

Johnson, B. (2006). "The Cost of Democracy." *Advertising Age*, November 20: 3.

Johnson, J. D., L. A. Jackson, and L. Gatto. (1995). "Violent Attitudes and Deferred Academic Aspirations: Deleterious Effects of Exposure to Rap Music." *Basic and Applied Social Psychology*, 16: 27–11.

Kahlor, L., B. W. Gorham, and E. Gilligan. (1999). "A Reconceptualization of Cultivation as a 'Good Theory' with Help from the 'Thin Ideal.'" Paper presented to the Annual Conference of the Association for Education in

Journalism and Mass Communication, New Orleans.

Kaiser Family Foundation. (2007). *Food for Thought: Television Advertising to Children in the United States.* Washington, DC: Kaiser Family Foundation.

Kamiya, G. (2009). "The Death of News." *Salon*, February 17. (*www.salon.com/opinion/kamiya/ 2009/02/17/newspapers/print. html*).

Kang, C. (2010). "Facebook to Hit 500 Million Users, But Meteoric Rise Has Come With Growing Pains." *Washington Post*, July 19. (*http:// voices.washingtonpost.com/ posttech/2010/07/facebook_ hits_500_million_user.html*).

Kang, C. (2009). "Cable Giants to Put Shows Online." *Washington Post*, December 3: A30.

Kaplan, M. (2008). "All the News That's Fit to Neuter." *Huffington Post*, December 2. (*www. huffingtonpost.com/marty-kaplan/ all-the-news-thats-fit-to_b_147703. html*).

Kapur, S. (2009). "Jeremy Scahill Slams NBC's Chuck Todd on Real Time with Bill Maher." *Alternet*, August 24. (*www.alternet.org/blogs/peek/ 142155/jeremy_scahill_slams _nbc's_chuck_todd_on_% 22real_time_with_bill_ maher%22/*)

Katz, E. (1983). "Publicity and Pluralistic Ignorance: Notes on 'The Spiral of Silence.'" In E. Wartella and D. C. Whitney, eds., *Mass Communication Review Yearbook 4*. Beverly Hills, CA: Sage.

Katz, E., J. G. Blumler, and M. Gurevitch. (1974). "Utilization of Mass Communication by the Individual." In J. G. Blumler and E. Katz, eds., *The Uses of Mass Communication: Current Perspectives on Gratifications Research*. Beverly Hills, CA: Sage.

Katz, E., and P. F. Lazarsfeld. (1955). *Personal Influence: The Part Played by People in the Flow of Communications*. New York: Free Press.

Kaufman, G. (2003). "Push the Courvoisier: Are Rappers Getting Paid for Product Placement?" *VH1.com*, June 6. (*http://www.mtv. com/news/articles/1472393/ 20030606/puff_daddy.jhtml*).

Keane, J. (1991). *The Media and Democracy*. Cambridge: Polity Press.

Kellner, D. (1997). "Overcoming the Divide: Cultural Studies and Political Economy." In M. Ferguson and P. Golding, eds., *Cultural Studies in Question*. Thousand Oaks, CA: Sage.

Kelly, A. M. (2010). "The Kids Are All Right: They Have Cell Phones." *MediaChannel News*, January 14. (*www.medicalnewstoday.com/ articles/113878.php*).

Kenny, C. (2009). "Revolution in a Box." *Foreign Policy*, November/ December: 68–74.

Kerlinger, F. N. (1986). *Foundations of Behavioral Research*. New York: Holt, Rinehart, & Winston.

Key, V. O. (1961). *Public Opinion and American Democracy*. New York: Knopf.

Kirkhorn, M. J. (2000). "Media Increasingly Ignore Poor." *San Jose Mercury News*, February 20: 3C.

Klapper, J. T. (1960). *The Effects of Mass Communication*. New York: Free Press.

Klapper, J. T. (1949). *The Effects of Mass Media*. New York: Columbia University Bureau of Applied Social Research.

Knight Commission on the Information Needs of Communities in a Democracy. (2009). *Informing Communities: Sustaining Democracy in the Digital Age*. Washington, DC: Knight Foundation.

Knobloch-Westerwick, S. (2006) "Mood Management: Theory, Evidence, and Advancements." In D. Zillmann and P. Vorderer, eds., *Media Entertainment: The Psychology of Its Appeal*. Mahwah, NJ: Erlbaum.

Kornhauser, A., and P. F. Lazarsfeld. (1935). "The Technique of Market Research from the Standpoint of a Psychologist." *Institute of Management*, 16: 3–15, 19–21.

Kornhauser, W. (1959). *The Politics of Mass Society*. New York: Free Press.

Kreiling, A. (1984). "Television in American Ideological Hopes and Fears." In W. D. Rowland Jr. and B. Watkins, eds., *Interpreting Television: Current Research Perspectives*. Beverly Hills, CA: Sage.

Krippendorf, K. (1986). *Information Theory: Structural Models for Qualitative Data*. Newbury Park, CA: Sage.

Krugman, P. (2003). *The Great Unraveling: Losing Our Way in the New Century*. New York: Norton.

Kuhn, T. (1970). *The Structure of Scientific Revolutions*, 2nd ed. Chicago: University of Chicago Press.

Kunkel, D., B. L. Wilcox, J. Cantor, E. Palmer, S. Linn, and P. Dominick. (2004). *Report of the APA Task Force on Advertising and Children*. Washington, DC: American Psychological Association.

Kurtz, H. (2009). "Death Panels Smite Journalism." *Washington Post*, August 24. (*www.washingtonpost. com/wp-dyn/content/article/2009/ 08/24/AR2009082400996.html*).

Kurtz, H. (2005). "The Judy Chronicles." *Washington Post*, October 17. (*http:// www.washingtonpost.com/wp-dyn/ content/blog/2005/10/17/ BL2005101700259.html*).

Laitinen, R. E., and R. F. Rakos. (1997). "Corporate Control of Media and Propaganda: A Behavior Analysis." In P. A. Lamal, ed., *Cultural Contingencies: Behavior Analytic Perspectives on Cultural Practices*. Westport, CT: Praeger.

Lang, A. (1990). "Involuntary Attention and Physiological Arousal Evoked by Structural Features and Mild Emotion in TV Commercials." *Communication Research*, 17: 275–299.

Lang, K., and G. E. Lang. (1983). *The Battle for Public Opinion: The President, the Press, and the Polls during Watergate*. New York: Columbia University Press.

Langewiesche, W. (2009). *The Geese, the Glide, the Miracle on the Hudson*. New York: Farrar, Straus & Giroux.

Lasswell, H. D. (1949). "The Structure and Function of Communication in Society." In W. S. Schramm, ed., *Mass Communication*. Urbana, IL: University of Illinois Press.

Lasswell, H. D. (1948). "The Structure and Function of Communication in Society." In L. Bryson, ed., *The Communication of Ideas*. New York: Harper.

Lasswell, H. D. (1934). *World Politics and Personal Insecurity*. Chicago: University of Chicago Press.

Lasswell, H. D. (1927a). *Propaganda Technique in the World War*. New York: Knopf.

Lasswell, H. D. (1927b). "The Theory of Political Propaganda." *American Political Science Review*, 21: 627–631.

Lavey, W. G. (1993). "Inconsistencies in Applications of Economics at the Federal Communications Commission." *Federal Communications Law Journal*, 45: 437–490.

Lazarsfeld, P. F. (1969). "An Episode in the History of Social Research: A Memoir." In D. Fleming and B. Bailyn, eds., *The Intellectual Migration: Europe and America, 1930–1960*. Cambridge, MA: Belknap Press of Harvard University.

Lazarsfeld, P. F. (1941). "Remarks on Administrative and Critical Communication Research." *Studies in Philosophy and Social Science*, 9: 2–16.

Lazarsfeld, P. F., B. Berelson, and H. Gaudet. (1944). *The People's Choice: How the Voter Makes Up His Mind in a Presidential Campaign*. New York: Duell, Sloan & Pearce.

Lazarsfeld, P. F., and R. H. Franzen. (1945). "Prediction of Political Behavior in America." *American Sociological Review*, 10: 261–273.

Lazarsfeld, P. F., and R. K. Merton. (1948). "Mass Communication, Popular Taste and Organized Social Action." *The Communication of Ideas*. New York: Institute for Religious and Social Studies.

Lazarsfeld, P., and F. N. Stanton, eds. (1942). *Radio Research, 1941*. New York: Duell, Sloan & Pearce.

Lee, A. M., and Lee, E. B. (1939). *The Fine Art of Propaganda*. New York: Harcourt Brace.

Lee, E., J. Lee, and D. W. Schumann. (2002). "The Influence of Communication Source and Mode on Consumer Adoption of Technological Innovations." *Journal of Consumer Affairs*, 36: 1–28.

Leedy, P. D. (1997). *Practical Research: Planning and Design*. New York: Macmillan.

Lenhart, A. (2009). "Adults and Social Network Websites." *Pew Internet and American Life Project*, January 14. (*www.pewinternet.org/Reports/ 2009/Adults-and-Social-Network-Websites.aspx*).

Leonard, A. (2010). "The Conservative Backlash Against 'Avatar.'" *Salon*, January 5. (*www.salon.com/ entertainment/movies/avatar/index. html?story=/tech/htww/2010/01/05/ the_conservative_backlash_ against_avatar*).

Levy, A. (2009). "Lift and Separate." *New Yorker*, November 16: 78–80.

Levy, M., and S. Windahl. (1985). "The Concept of Audience Activity." In K. E. Rosengren, L. A. Wenner, and P. Palmgreen, eds., *Media Gratifications Research: Current Perspectives*. Beverly Hills, CA: Sage.

Lewis, C. (2009). "Great Expectations." *Columbia Journalism Review*, September/ October: 17–18.

Licklider, J.C.R., (1960). "Man-Computer Symbiosis." *IRE Transactions on Human Factors in Electronics*, vol. HFE-1: 4-11.

Liebert, R. M., and J. N. Sprafkin. (1988). *The Early Window: Effects of Television on Children and Youth*. New York: Pergamon.

Lind, R. A., and N. Rockier. (2001). "Competing Ethos: Reliance on Profit versus Social Responsibility by Laypeople Planning a Television Newscast." *Journal of Broadcasting and Electronic Media*, 45: 118–134.

Linn, S. (2004). *Consuming Kids*. New York: The New Press.

Lippmann, W. (1922). *Public Opinion*. New York: Macmillan.

Littlejohn, S. W., and K. A. Foss. (2008). *Theories of Human Communication*. Belmont, CA: Wadsworth.

Littleton, C. (2008). "TV's Class Struggle." *Variety*, September 22–28: 1, 81.

Loechner, J. (2010). "Mobile Phones Organize Lives." *Rudder-Finn*, February 23. (*www.ruderfinn.co. uk/blogs/dotcom/2010/02/intent-index-mobile-edition/*).

Long, E. (1989). "Feminism and Cultural Studies." *Critical Studies in Mass Communication*, 6: 427–435.

Lovell, T. (1981). "Ideology and 'Coronation Street.'" In R. Dyer, C. Geraghty, M. Jordan, T. Lovell, R. Paterson, and J. Stewart, eds., *Coronation Street*. London: British Film Institute.

Lowery, S. A., and M. L. DeFleur. (1995). *Milestones in Mass Communication Research*, 3rd ed. White Plains, NY: Longman.

Luo, M. (2007). "God '08: Whose, and How Much, Will Voters Accept?" *New York Times*, July 22: WK4.

Madden, M. (2009). "Obama Goes Back to the Grass Roots." *Salon*, March 27. (*www.salon.com/news/ feature/2009/03/27/ obama_town_hall/*).

Madland, D. (2008). *Journalists Give Workers the Business. Center for American Progress*. (*www. americanprogress.org/issues/2008/ 06/pdf/world_without_workers. pdf*).

Maloney, C. (2009). "Newspapers for a New Age." *Huffington Post*, September 24. (*www. huffingtonpost.com/rep-carolyn-maloney/newspapers-for-a-new-age_b_298261.html*).

Mankiw, G. (2009). "A Penny Anti Protest." *Greg Mankiw's Blog*, January 19. (*http://gregmankiw. blogspot.com/2009/01/penny-anti-protest.html*).

Manly, L. (2007). "Brew Tube." *New York Times Magazine*, February 4: 51–55.

Marcuse, H. (1978). *An Essay on Liberation*. Boston: Beacon.

Marcuse, H. (1969). *The Aesthetic Dimension*. Boston: Beacon.

Marcuse, H. (1941). "Some Social Implications of Modern Technology." In A. Arato and E. Gebhardt, eds., (1978). *The Essential Frankfurt School Reader*. New York: Urizen.

Martin, C. (2004). *Framed! Labor and the Corporate Media*. Ithaca, NY: Cornell University Press.

Martin, C, and H. Oshagen. (1997). "Disciplining the Workforce: The News Media Frame a General Motors Plant Closing." *Communication Research*, 24: 669–697.

Martin-Barbero, J. (1993). *Communication, Culture, and Hegemony: From the Media to Mediations*. Translation by E. Fox and R. A. White. Newbury Park, CA: Sage.

Martindale, D. (1960). *The Nature and Types of Sociological Theory*. Boston: Houghton-Mifflin.

Massing, M. (2004). "Now They Tell Us." *New York Review of Books*,

February 26. (*www.nybooks.com/articles/16922*).

Mast, G., and B. F. Kawin. (1996). *A Short History of the Movies*. Boston: Allyn & Bacon.

Matei, S., and S.J. Ball-Rokeach. (2003). "The Internet in the Communication Infrastructure of Urban Residential Communities: Macro- or Mesolinkage?" *Journal of Communication*, 53: 642–658.

Matson, F. M. (1964). *The Broken Image: Man, Science, and Society*. New York: Braziller.

Mattelart, A. (2003). *The Information Society*. Thousand Oaks, CA: Sage.

Mawhinney, H. B. (2001). "Theoretical Approaches to Understanding Interest Groups." *Educational Policy*, 15: 187–215.

Mayer, J. (2009). "The Secret History." *New Yorker*, June 22: 50–59.

McChesney, R. W. (2004). *The Problem of the Media: U.S. Communication Politics in the 21st Century*. New York: Monthly Review Press.

McChesney, R. W. (1997). *Corporate Media and the Threat to Democracy*. New York: Seven Stories.

McCombs, M. E. (1981). "The Agenda-Setting Approach." In D. D. Nimmo and K. R. Sanders, eds., *Handbook of Political Communication*. Beverly Hills, CA: Sage.

McCombs, M., and S. I. Ghanem. (2001). "The Convergence of Agenda Setting and Framing." In S. D. Reese, O. H. Gandy, and A. E. Grant, eds., *Framing Public Life: Perspectives on Media and Our Understanding of the Social World*. Mahwah, NJ: Erlbaum.

McCombs, M., J. Llamas, E. Lopez-Escobar, and F. Rey. (1997). "Candidate Images in Spanish Elections: Second-Level Agenda-Setting Effects." *Journalism and Mass Communication Quarterly*, 74: 703–717.

McCombs, M. E., and D. L. Shaw. (1972). "The Agenda-Setting Function of Mass Media." *Public Opinion Quarterly*, 36: 176–187.

McCoy, M., and O. Hargie. (2003). "Implications of Mass Communication Theory for Asymmetric Public Relations Evaluation." *Journal of Communication Management*, 7: 304–317.

McGowan, S. (2009). "Home Internet Access: Continuing to Grow, But Big Differences Among Demographics." *NielsenWire*, March 6. (*http://blog.nielsen.com/nielsenwire/online_mobile/home-internet-access-continuing-to-grow-but-big-differences-among-demographics/*).

McIntyre, J. S. (1987). "Repositioning a Landmark: The Hutchins Commission and Freedom of the Press." *Critical Studies in Mass Communication*, 4: 95–135.

McIntyre, J. S. (1975). "The Structure of Communication in an Emerging Frontier Community." *Journal of Communication Inquiry*, 1: 71–78.

McLeary, P. (2007). "How TalkingPointsMemo Beat the Big Boys on the U.S. Attorney Story." *Columbia Journalism Review*, March 15. (*www.cjr.org/behind_the_news/how_talkingpointsmemo_beat_the.php*).

McLeod, D. M., and B. H. Detenber. (1999). "Framing Effects of Television News Coverage of Social Protest." *Journal of Communication*, 49: 3–23.

McLeod, J. M., and E. M. Perse. (1994). "Direct and Indirect Effects of Socioeconomic Status on Public Affairs Knowledge." *Journalism Quarterly*, 71: 433–442.

McLuhan, M. (1964). *Understanding Media: The Extensions of Man*. New York: McGraw-Hill.

McLuhan, M. (1962). *The Gutenberg Galaxy: The Making of Typographic Man*. Toronto: University of Toronto Press.

McLuhan, M. (1951). *The Mechanical Bride*. New York: Vanguard.

McLuhan, M., and G. E. Stern. (1967). "A Dialogue: Q & A." In M. McLuhan and G. E. Stern, eds., *McLuhan: Hot and Cool: A Primer for the Understanding of McLuhan and a Critical Symposium with a Rebuttal by McLuhan*. New York: Dial Press.

McMichael, W. H. (2009). "DoD, AP Battle Over Photo of Dying Marine." *Army Times*, September 5. (*www.armytimes.com/news/2009/09/military_ap_photo_gates_bernard_090409w/*).

McQuail, D. (1994). *Mass Communication Theory: An*

Introduction, 4th ed. Beverly Hills, CA: Sage.

McQuail, D. (1987). *Mass Communication Theory: An Introduction*, 2nd ed. Beverly Hills, CA: Sage.

McRobbie, A. (1984). "Settling Accounts with Subcultures: A Feminist Critique." *Screen Education*, 34: 37–49.

Mead, G. H. (1934). *Mind, Self, and Society*. Chicago: University of Chicago Press.

Media Literacy Symposium. (1998). *Journal of Communication*, 48.

Medved, M. (1992). *Hollywood vs. America: Popular Culture and the War on Traditional Values*. New York: HarperCollins.

Medved, M., and D. Medved. (1998). *Saving Childhood: Protecting Our Children from the National Assault on Innocence*. New York: HarperCollins.

Meehan, E. R., V. Mosco, and J. Wasco. (1994). "Rethinking Political Economy: Change and Continuity." In M. Levy and M. Gurevitch, eds., *Defining Media Studies: Reflections on the Future of the Field*. New York: Oxford University Press.

Mendelsohn, H. (1966). *Mass Entertainment*. New Haven, CT: College and University Press.

Merton, R. K. (1967). *On Theoretical Sociology*. New York: Free Press.

Merton, R. K. (1949). *Social Theory and Social Structure*. Glencoe, IL: Free Press.

Meyers, M. (2004). "African American Women and Violence: Gender, Race, and Class in the News." *Critical Studies in Media Communication*, 21: 95–118.

Meyrowitz, J. (2008). "Power, Pleasure, Patterns: Intersecting Narratives of Media Influence." *Journal of Communication*, 58: 641–663.

Meyrowitz, J. (1985). *No Sense of Place: The Impact of Electronic Media on Social Behavior*. New York: Oxford University Press.

Miller, C. R. (1941). "Some Comments on Propaganda Analysis and the Science of Democracy." *Public Opinion Quarterly*, 5: 657–665.

Miller, G. R., and M. Burgoon. (1978). "Persuasion Research: Review and Commentary." In B. D. Ruben, ed., *Communication Yearbook 2*. New Brunswick, NJ: Transaction.

Miller, K. (2005). *Communication Theories: Perspectives, Processes, and Contexts.* New York: McGraw-Hill.

Miller, N. E., and J. Dollard. (1941). *Social Learning and Imitation.* New Haven, CT: Yale University Press.

Mills, C. W. (1959). *The Sociological Imagination.* New York: Oxford University Press.

Mills, C. W. (1957). *The Power Elite.* New York: Oxford University Press.

Mindlin, A. (2009). "Web Passes Papers as a News Source Web Passes Papers as a News Source." *New York Times,* January 5: B3.

Mitchell, G. (2009). "Watchdogs Failed to Bark on Economy." *Editor & Publisher,* April: 16.

Moerman, M. (1992). "Life After C. A.: An Ethnographer's Autobiography." In G. Watson and R. M. Seller, eds., *Text in Context: Contributions to Ethnomethodology.* Newbury Park, CA: Sage.

Mooney, C. (2004). "Blinded by Science." *Columbia Journalism Review,* November/December: 25–35.

Moores, S. (1993). *Interpreting Audiences: The Ethnography of Media Consumption.* Thousand Oaks, CA: Sage.

Morgan, M., J. Shanahan, and N. Signorielli. (2009). "Growing Up With Television: Cultivation Processes." In J. Bryant and M. B. Oliver, eds., *Media Effects: Advances in Theory and Research.* New York: Routledge.

Morgan, M., and N. Signorielli. (1990). "Cultivation Analysis: Concept-ualization and Methodology." In N. Signorielli and M. Morgan, eds., *Cultivation Analysis: New Directions in Media Effects Research.* Newbury Park, CA: Sage.

"More Than Half the Homes in U.S. Have Three or More TVs." (2009). *Nielsenwire,* July 20. (*http://blog. nielsen.com/nielsenwire/media_ entertainment/more-than-half- the-homes-in-us-have-three-or- more-tvs/*).

Morley, D. (1980). *The "Nationwide" Audience: Structure and Decoding.* London: British Film Institute.

Morris, D., and E. McGann. (2008). *Fleeced.* New York: Harper.

Mosco, V., and A. Herman. (1981). "Critical Theory and Electronic Media." *Theory and Society,* 10: 869–896.

Mott, F. L. (1941). *American Journalism.* New York: Macmillan.

Moyers, B. (2001). "Journalism and Democracy: On the Importance of Being a 'Public Nuisance.'" *The Nation,* May 7: 11–17.

Mucha, T. (2009). "Fake News Gets Real." *Truthout.* July 1. (*www. truthout.org/070209U*).

Murdock, G. (1989a). "Critical Activity and Audience Activity." In B. Dervin, L. Grossberg, B. J. O'Keefe, and E. Wartella, eds., *Rethinking Communication, vol. 2: Paradigm Exemplars.* Newbury Park, CA: Sage.

Murdock, G. (1989b). "Critical Studies: Missing Links." *Critical Studies in Mass Communication,* 6: 436–40.

Muwakkil, S. (2003). "Racial Bias Still Haunts Media." *In These Times.* (www.inthesetimes.com/article/ 478/).

Napoli, P. M. (1999). "The Marketplace of Ideas Metaphor in Communications Regulation." *Journal of Communication,* 49: 151–169.

Naureckas, J. (2009). "Before We 'Save' Journalism." *Extra!* July: 5.

Naureckas, J. (2002). "Patriotism vs. Jingoism." *Extra!* January/ February: 2.

"NBC President Says Decision to Air Cho Video Was 'Good Journalism.'" (2007). *International Herald Tribune,* April 24. (*www. iht. com/bin/print.php ? id=5421762*).

NBC President Says Decision to Air Cho Video Was "Good Journalism." (2007). *WHDH.com,* April 25. (http://www1.whdh.com/news/ articles/entertainment/BO50193/).

Negt, O. (1978). "Mass Media: Tools of Domination or Instruments of Liberation? Aspects of the Frankfurt School's Com-munications Analysis." *New German Critique,* 14: 61–80.

Nelson, C, and L. Grossberg, eds. (1988). *Marxism and the Interpretation of Culture.* Urbana, IL: University of Illinois Press.

Nelson, T. E., and R. A. Clawson. (1997). "Media Framing of a Civil Liberties Conflict and Its Effect on Tolerance." *American Political Science Review,* 91: 567–583.

Newcomb, H., ed. (2007). *Television: The Critical View,* 7th ed. New York: Oxford University Press.

Newcomb, H., ed. (1994). *Television: The Critical View,* 5th ed. New York: Oxford University Press.

Newcomb, H., ed. (1978). "Assessing the Violence Profile Studies of Gerbner and Gross: A Humanistic Critique and Suggestion." *Communication Research,* 5: 264–283.

Newcomb, H., ed. (1974). *TV: The Most Popular Art.* New York: Oxford University Press.

Newcomb, H., and P. M. Hirsch. (1983). "Television as a Cultural Forum: Implications for Research." *Quarterly Review of Film,* 8: 45–55.

Nichols, J. (2002). "Standing Up for Dissent." *The Nation,* September 23: 24.

Nichols, J., and R. W. McChesney. (2010). "How to Save Journalism." *The Nation,* January 25: 11–16.

"Nielsen: Newspapers Getting More Web Visits." (2009). *TVNewscheck,* January 29. (*www. tvnewscheck.com/articles/2009/01/ 29/daily.3/*).

Noelle-Neumann, E. (1985). "The Spiral of Silence: A Response." In K. R. Sanders, L. L. Kaid, and D. D. Nimmo, eds., *Political Com-munication Yearbook, 1984.* Carbondale: Southern Illinois University Press.

Noelle-Neumann, E. (1984). *The Spiral of Silence: Our Social Skin.* Chicago: University of Chicago Press.

Noelle-Neumann, E. (1973). "Return to the Concept of the Powerful Mass Media." *Studies of Broadcasting,* 9: 68–105.

Nordenson, B. (2008). "Overload!" *Columbia Journalism Review,* November/December: 30–40.

O'Brien, C. (2010). "Facebook Changes Spark Anger." *Providence Journal,* May 23: E4.

O'Brien, M. (2009). "Obama Open to Newspaper Bailout Bill." *The Hill,* September 20. (*http://thehill.com/ blogs/blog-briefing-room/news/ 59523–obama-open-to-newspaper- bailout-bill*).

O'Brien, S., and I. Szeman. (2004). *Popular Culture.* Scarborough, Ontario: Nelson.

O'Connor, A. (1989). "The Problem of American Cultural Studies." *Critical Studies in Mass Communication*, 6: 405–413.

Okrent, D. (2004). "The Public Editor: Weapons of Mass Destruction? Or Mass Distraction?" *New York Times*, May 30: sect. 4, p. 2.

Olbermann, K. (2005). "Pineapple Under the Sea." *MSNBC.COM.* January 25. (*www.msnbc.msn.com/id/6844293*).

Orenstein, P. (2009). "Growing Up on Facebook." *New York Times Magazine*, March 15: 11–12.

Oreskovic, A. (2009). "Facebook Makes Money, Tops 300 million Users." *Reuters*, September 16. (*www.reuters.com/article/technologyNews/idUSTRE58E7ZK20090916*).

Orwell, G. (1960). 1984. New York: Signet Books. (Reprint of Harcourt Brace Jovanovich, 1949).

Ott, B. (2009). "America's Safest Cities." *Real Clear Politics*, June 5. (*www.realclearpolitics.com/articles/2009/06/05/americas_safest_cities_96815.html*).

Packer, G. (2006a). "Knowing the Enemy." *New Yorker*, December 18: 61–69.

Packer, G. (2006b). "Keep Out." *New Yorker*, October 16: 59–60.

Palmgreen, P., L. A. Wenner, and K. E. Rosengren. (1985). "Uses and Gratifications Research: The Past Ten Years." In K. E. Rosengren, L. A. Wenner, and P. Palmgreen, eds., *Media Gratifications Research: Current Perspectives.* Beverly Hills, CA: Sage.

Parenti, M. (1992). *Make-Believe Media: The Politics of Entertainment.* New York: St. Martin's.

Park, D. W., and J. Pooley. (2008). *The History of Media and Communication Research: Contested Memories.* New York: Peter Lang.

Patterson, K. (2004). "Violence in Media Linked to Aggression in Youths." *Providence Journal*, April 19: A1, A4.

Patterson, T. E. (1994). *Out of Order.* New York: Vintage.

Patterson, T. E. (1980). *The Mass Media Election: How Americans Choose Their President.* New York: Praeger.

Peirce, C. (1955). "Essentials of Pragmatism." In J. Buchler, ed., *Philosophical Writings of Pierce.* New York: Dover.

Penetration. (2010). "Digital Market Facts 2010." *Advertising Age*, February 22. Insert.

Pérez-Peña, R. (2010). "New Study Traces History of Government Subsidies for the Media." *New York Times*, January 28. (*http://mediadecoder.blogs.nytimes.com/2010/01/28/new-study-traces-history-of-government-subsidies-for-the-media/*).

Perloff, R. M. (2010). *The Dynamics of Persuasion: Communication and Attitudes in the 21st Century*, 4th ed. New York: Routledge.

Perse, E. M. (2001). *Media Effects and Society.* Mahwah, NJ: Erlbaum.

Peterson, D. L., and K. S. Pfost. (1989). "Influence of Rock Videos on Attitudes of Violence against Women." *Psychological Reports*, 64: 319–322.

Petty, R. E., P. Briñol, and J. R. Priester. (2009). "Mass Media Attitude Change: Applications of the Elaboration Likelihood Model of Persuasion." In J. Bryant and M. B. Oliver, eds., *Media Effects: Advances in Theory and Research.* New York: Routledge.

Petty R. E., and J. T. Cacioppo. (1981). *Attitudes and Persuasion: Classic and Contemporary Approaches.* Dubuque, IA: Brown.

Pew Research Center for the People and the Press. (2007). "What Americans Know: 1989–2007." (*http://people-press.org/reports/print.php3?PageID=1137*).

Pickler, N. (2009). "Judge to Review Cheney Interview in CIA Leak Case." *ABC News.* June 18. (*http://aconstantineblacklist.blogspot.com/2009/06/judge-to-review-cheney-interview-in-cia.html*).

Pingree, S., J. M. Wiemann, and R. P. Hawkins. (1988). "Editors' Introduction: Toward Conceptual Synthesis." In R. P. Hawkins, J. M. Wiemann, and S. Pingree, eds., *Advancing Communication Science: Merging Mass and Interpersonal Processes.* Newbury Park, CA: Sage.

Pippa, N. (1996). "Did Television Erode Social Capital? A Reply to Putnam." *PS: Political Science and Politics*, XXIX: 474–480.

Pooley, J. (2008). "The New History of Mass Communication Research." In D. W. Park and J. Pooley, eds., *The History of Media and Communication Research: Contested Memories.* New York: Peter Lang.

Pooley, J. (2006). "Fifteen Pages that Shook the Field: Personal Influence, Edward Shils, and the Remembered History of Mass Communication Research." *The ANNALS of the American Academy of Political and Social Science*, November, 608: 130–156.

Postman, N. (1996). *The End of Education.* New York: Vintage.

Postman, N. (1994). *The Disappearance of Childhood.* New York: Vintage.

Postman, N. (1985). *Amusing Ourselves to Death: Public Discourse in the Age of Show Business.* New York: Penguin.

Potter, D. (2001). "News for Sale." *American Journalism Review*, September: 68.

Potter, W. J. (2009). *Arguing for a General Framework for Mass Media Scholarship.* Thousand Oaks, CA: Sage.

Potter, W. J. (1998). *Media Literacy.* Thousand Oaks, CA: Sage.

Potter, W. J. (1997). "The Problem of Indexing Risk of Viewing Television Aggression." *Critical Studies in Mass Communication*, 14: 228–248.

Potter, W. J. (1993). "Cultivation Theory and Research: A Conceptual Critique." *Human Communication Research*, 19: 564–601.

Potter, W. J. (1991). "The Relationships between First and Second Order Measures of Cultivation." *Human Communication Research*, 18: 92–113.

Potter, W. J. (1990). "Adolescents' Perceptions of the Primary Values of Television Programming." *Journalism and Mass Communication Quarterly*, 67: 843–851.

Powers, T. (2003). "The Vanishing Case for War." *New York Review of Books*, December 4: 12.

Pratkanis, A. R., and E. Aronson. (1992). *Age of Propaganda: The Everyday Use and Abuse of Persuasion.* New York: W. H. Freeman.

Preiss, R. W. (2007). *Mass Media Effects Research: Advances Through Meta-Analysis*. Mahwah, NJ: Erlbaum Associates.

Prevention and Men's Health Magazines. (2003). "Consumer Reaction to DTC Advertising of Prescription Medicines, 1997–2002." New York: Rodale.

Protess, D. L., F. L. Cook, J. C. Doppelt, J. S. Ettema, M. T. Gordon, D. R. Leff, and P. Miller. (1991). *The Journalism of Outrage*. New York: Guilford.

Putnam, R. (2000). *Bowling Alone: The Collapse and Revival of American Community*. New York: Simon & Schuster.

Radio-Television News Directors Association. (2000). "Code of Ethics and Professional Conduct." (*http://www.rtdna.org/pages/media_items/code-of-ethics-and-professional-conduct48.php*).

Radway, J. (1986). "Identifying Ideological Seams: Mass Culture, Analytical Method, and Political Practice." *Communication*, 9: 93–123.

Radway, J. (1984). *Reading the Romance: Women, Patriarchy, and Popular Literature*. Chapel Hill, NC: University of North Carolina Press.

Rasmussen, S. (2009). "37% Support Government Subsidies to Keep Newspapers Going." *Rasmussen Reports*, April 1. (*www.rasmussenreports.com/public_content/business/general_business/april_2009/37_support_government_subsidies_to_keep_newspapers_going*).

Reese, S. D., O. H. Gandy, and A. E. Grant, eds. (2001). *Framing Public Life: Perspectives on Media and Our Understanding of the Social World*. Mahwah, NJ: Erlbaum.

Reimer, B., and K. E. Rosengren. (1990). "Cultivated Viewers and Readers: A Life-Style Perspective." In N. Signorielli and M. Morgan, eds., *Cultivation Analysis: New Directions in Media Effects Research*. Newbury Park, CA: Sage.

Rendall, S. (2004). "Meet the Stenographers." *Extra!* November/December: 6–8.

Rice, R. E., and C. Atkin. (1989). *Public Communication Campaigns*, 2nd ed. Beverly Hills, CA: Sage.

Rich, F. (2009). "Small Beer, Big Hangover." *New York Times*, August 2: WK8.

Rich, F. (2004). "A Perfect Storm of Mind-Bending Pictures from Iraq." *Providence Journal*, May 9: 12.

Rich, M. (2008). "Literacy Debate: Online, R U Really Reading? *New York Times*, July 27: 1, 14–15.

Richardson, L., and V. Luchsinger. (2005). "Direct-to-Consumer Advertising of Pharmaceutical Products: Issue Analysis and Direct-to-Consumer Promotion." *Journal of American Academy of Business*, 7: 100–105.

Rideout, V. J., U. G. Foehr, and D. F. Roberts. (2010). *Generation M2: Media in the Lives of 8- to 18-Year-Olds*. Menlo Park, CA: Kaiser Family Foundation.

Ritchie, A. (2009). "Blair Iraq War Admission Sparks Fresh Outrage." *Yahoo News*, December 13. (*http://www.google.com/hostednews/afp/article/ALeqM5jTebENCJbPdSLM1qftov5P0JhsvQ*).

Ritzer, G. (1983). *Sociological Theory*. New York: Knopf.

Robinson, J. P., and D. K. Davis. (1990). "Television News and the Informed Public: Not the Main Source." *Journal of Communication*, 40: 106–119.

Robinson, J. P., and M. Levy, with D. K. Davis, eds. (1986). *The Main Source: Learning from Television News*. Newbury Park, CA: Sage.

Rogers, E. M. (2000). "The Extensions of Men: The Correspondence of Marshall McLuhan and Edward T. Hall." *Mass Communication and Society*, 3: 117–135.

Rogers, E. M. (1986). "History of Communication Science." In E. M. Rogers, ed., *Communication Technology: The New Media in Society*. New York: Free Press.

Rogers, E. M. (1983). *Diffusion of Innovations*, 3rd ed. New York: Free Press.

Rogers, E. M. (1962). *Diffusion of Innovations*. New York: Free Press.

Rogers, E. M., J. W. Dearing, and D. Bergman. (1993). "The Anatomy of Agenda-Setting Research." *Journal of Communication*, 43: 68–84.

Romer, D., K. H. Jamieson, and S. Aday. (2003). "Television News and the Cultivation of Fear of Crime." *Journal of Communication*, 53: 88–105.

Rorty, R. (1991). *Objectivity, Relativism, and Truth: Political Papers I*. Cambridge, UK: Cambridge University Press.

Rorty, R., J. B. Schneewind, and Q. Skinner. (1982). *Consequences of Pragmatism*. Minneapolis, MN: University of Minnesota Press.

Rosen, C. (2008). "People of the Screen." *The New Atlantis*, Fall: 20–32.

Rosen, J. (2009). "Audience Atomization Overcome: Why the Internet Weakens the Authority of the Press." *Pressthink*, January 12. (*http://journalism.nyu.edu/pubzone/weblogs/pressthink/2009/01/12/atomization.html*).

Rosenwald, M. S. (2010). "Obsessed with Smartphones, Oblivious to the Here and Now." *Washington Post*, February 22: A01.

Rosnow, R. L., and E. J. Robinson. (1967). *Experiments in Persuasion*. New York: Academic.

Rubin, A. M. (1998). "Editor's Note: Media Literacy." *Journal of Communication*, 48: 3–4.

Rubin, A. M. (1994). "Media Uses and Effects: A Uses-and-Gratifications Perspective." In J. Bryant and D. Zillman, eds., *Media Effects: Advances in Theory and Research*. Hillsdale, NJ: Erlbaum.

Rubin, A. M. (2009). "Uses-and-Gratifications Perspective on Media Effects." In J. Bryant and M. B. Oliver, eds., *Media Effects: Advances in Theory and Research*. New York: Routledge.

Rubin, A. M., and P. M. Haridakis. (2001). "Mass Communication Research at the Dawn of the 21st Century." In W. B. Gudykunst, ed., *Communication Yearbook 24*. Thousand Oaks, CA: Sage.

Rubin, L. C. (2004). "Merchandising Madness: Pills, Promises, and Better Living Through Chemistry." *Journal of Popular Culture*, 38: 369–383.

Ruggiero, T. E. (2000). "Uses and Gratifications Theory in the 21st Century." *Mass Communication and Society*, 3: 3–37.

Russill, C. (2006). "For a Pragmatist Perspective on Publics: Advancing Carey's Cultural Studies through John Dewey … and Michel Foucault?!" In J. Packer and

C. Robertson, eds., *Thinking with James Carey: Essays on Communications, Transportation, History*. New York: Peter Lang.

Ryan, C., K. M. Carragee, and W. Meinhofer. (2001). "Framing, the News Media, and Collective Action." *Journal of Broadcasting and Electronic Media*, Winter: 175–182.

Salmon, C. T., and F. G. Kline. (1985). "The Spiral of Silence Ten Years Later: An Examination and Evaluation." In K. R. Sanders, L. L. Kaid, and D. D. Nimmo, eds., *Political Communication Yearbook, 1984*. Carbondale, IL: Southern Illinois University Press.

Sass, E. (2009a). "NAA: Newspaper Sites Enjoy Higher Traffic." *Mediapost*, August 5. (*www. mediapost.com/publications/? fa=Articles. showArticle&art_aid=111166*).

Sass, E. (2009b). "Newspaper Web Audience Grows, Revs Decline." *MediaPost*, January 30. (*www. mediapost.com/publications/? fa=Articles. showArticle&art_aid=99455*).

Savage, D. G. (2009). "Court Sides with FCC on Expletives." *Providence Journal*, April 29: A4.

Schechter, D. (2004). "It's Like Iraq, All Over Again." *Alternet*, September 9. (*www.alternet.org/story/19838*).

Scheufele, D. A. (2000). "Agenda Setting, Priming, and Framing Revisited: Another Look at Cognitive Effects of Political Communication." *Mass Communication and Society*, 3: 297–316.

Schiller, H. I. (2000). *Living in the Number One Country: Reflections from a Critic of American Empire*. New York: Seven Stories Press.

Schiller, H. I. (1989). *Culture, Inc.: The Corporate Takeover of Public Expression*. New York: Oxford University Press.

Schiller, H. I. (1973). *The Mind Managers*. Boston: Beacon.

Schonfeld, E. (2010). "Facebook Drives 44 Percent of Social Sharing on the Web." *TechCrunch*, February 16. (*http://techcrunch. com/2010/02/16/facebook-44- percent-social-sharing/*).

Schorr, D. (1992). "True Confessions of a Lifetime TV Journalist." *San Jose Mercury News*, May 17: 1C, 5C.

Schramm, W. (1960). *Mass Communication*, 2nd ed. Urbana, IL: University of Illinois Press.

Schramm, W. (1954). *The Process and Effects of Mass Communication*. Urbana, IL: University of Illinois Press.

Schramm, W., J. Lyle, and E. Parker, eds. (1961). *Television in the Lives of Our Children*. Stanford, CA: Stanford University Press.

Schutt, R. K. (2009). *Investigating the Social World*, 6th ed. Thousand Oaks, CA: Sage.

Schutz, A. (1970). *On Phenomenology and Social Relations*. Chicago: University of Chicago Press.

Schutz, A. (1967). *The Phenomenology of the Social World*. Evanston, IL: Northwestern University Press.

Scruton, R. (2000). *An Intelligent Person's Guide to Modern Culture*. South Bend, IN: St. Augustine's Press.

Secor, L. (2009). "The Iran Show." *New Yorker*, August 31: 25–26.

Segrin, C., and R. L. Nabi. (2002). "Does Television Viewing Cultivate Unrealistic Expectations about Marriage?" *Journal of Communication*, 52: 247–263.

Seitel, F. P. (2004). *The Practice of Public Relations*. Upper Saddle River, NJ: Pearson.

Shade L. R., N. Porter, and W. Sanchez. (2005). "You Can See Everything on the Internet, You Can Do Anything on the Internet! Young Canadians Talk about the Internet." *Canadian Journal of Communication*, 30: 503–526.

Shanahan, J., and V. Jones. (1999). "Cultivation and Social Control." In D. Demers and K. Viswanath, eds., *Mass Media, Social Control, and Social Change*. Ames, IA: Iowa State University Press.

Shanahan, J., M. Morgan, and M. Stenbjerre. (1997). "Green or Brown? Television and the Cultivation of Environmental Concern." *Journal of Broadcasting and Electronic Media*, 45: 118–134.

Sherman, S. (2004). "Floating with the Tide." *The Nation*, March 15: 4–5.

Shields, T. (2009). "U.S. Will Consider Single Rating System for TV, Phones, Games." *Bloomberg.com*, August 26. (*www.bloomberg.com/ apps/news?pid=20601204&sid= aP9DO.D35St0*).

Shirky, C. (2009). "Newspapers and Thinking the Unthinkable." *Shirky.com*, March 13. (*www. shirky.com/weblog/2009/03/ newspapers-and-thinking-the- unthinkable/*).

Shrum, L. J. (2009). "Media Consumption and Perceptions of Social Reality." In J. Bryant and M. B. Oliver, eds., *Media Effects: Advances in Theory and Research*. New York: Routledge.

Shrum, L. J. (2004). *The Psychology of Entertainment Media: Blurring the Lines between Entertainment and Persuasion*. Mahwah, NJ: Erlbaum.

Siebert, F. S., T. Peterson, and W. Schramm. (1956). *Four Theories of the Press*. Urbana, IL: University of Illinois Press.

Signorielli, N. (1990). "Television's Mean and Dangerous World: A Continuation of the Cultural Indicators Perspective." In N. Signorielli and M. Morgan, eds., *Cultivation Analysis: New Directions in Media Effects Research*. Newbury Park, CA: Sage.

Signorielli, N., and S. Kahlenberg. (2001). "Television's World of Work in the Nineties." *Journal of Broadcasting and Electronic Media*, 41: 305–323.

Signorielli, N., and M. Morgan, eds. (1990). *Cultivation Analysis: New Directions in Media Effects Research*. Newbury Park, CA: Sage.

Silverblatt, A. (1995). *Media Literacy: Keys to Interpreting Media Messages*. Westport, CT: Praeger.

Simon, H. A. (1981). *The Sciences of the Artificial*. Cambridge, MA: MIT Press.

Simon, T., T. Atwater, and R. Alexander. (1988). "FCC Broadcast Content Regulation: Policymaking in a Vacuum." Paper presented at the annual meeting of the Association for Education in Journalism and Mass Communication, Portland, OR, August.

Singer, J. L., and D. G. Singer. (1983). "Implications of Childhood Television Viewing for Cognition, Imagination, and Emotion." In J. Bryant and D. R. Anderson, eds., *Children's Understanding of Television: Research on Attention and Comprehension*. New York: Academic.

Smillie, D. (2009). "Pew Piles on the Press." *Forbes*, September 14. (*www.forbes.com/2009/09/14/pew-news-polling-business-media-pew.html*).

Smith, A. (1991). *The Age of Behemoths: The Globalization of Mass Media Firms*. New York: Priority.

Smith, A., K. L. Schlozman, S. Verba, and H. Brady. (2009). "The Internet and Civic Engagement." *Pew Internet & American Life Project*, September. (*www.pewinternet.org/Reports/2009/15—The-Internet-and-Civic-Engagement.aspx*).

Smith, B. L. (1941). "Propaganda Analysis and the Science of Democracy." *Public Opinion Quarterly*, 5: 250–259.

Smith, J. F. (2009). "News of Iran, Edited in Newton." *Boston Globe*, June 20. (*www.boston.com/news/world/middleeast/articles/2009/06/20/news_of_iran_edited_in_newton/*).

Snowball, D. (1999). "Propaganda and Its Discontents." *Journal of Communication*, 49: 165–172.

Solomon, M. R. (1983). "The Role of Products as Social Stimuli: A Symbolic Interactionism Perspective." *Journal of Consumer Research*, 10: 319–329.

Solomon, N. (2009). "Media Absence of Class War." *Progressive Populist*, October 15: 16.

Solomon, N. (2006). "Media New Year's Resolutions for 2006." *Truthout*, January, 3. (*www.truthout.org/docs_2006/printer_010306M.shtml*).

Sotirovic, M. (2001). "Media Use and Perceptions of Welfare." *Journal of Communication*, 51: 750–774.

Soundbites. (2010). "The Quarter-Million-Dollar Middle." *Extra!* March: 3.

Soutar, G. N., and J. C. Sweeney, (2003). "Are There Cognitive Dissonance Segments?" *Australian Journal of Management*, 28: 227–250.

Sparks, G. G. (2006). *Media Effects Research: A Basic Overview*. Belmont, CA: Thomson/Wadsworth.

Sproule, J. M. (1997). *Propaganda and Democracy: The American Experience of Media and Mass Persuasion*. New York: Cambridge University Press.

Sproule, J. M. (1994). *Channels of Propaganda*. Bloomington, IN: EDINFO.

Stafford, L., S. L. Kline, and J. Dimmick. (1999). "Home E-mail: Relational Maintenance and Gratification Opportunities." *Journal of Broadcasting and Electronic Media*, 43: 659–669.

Stafford, T. F., M. R. Stafford, and L. L. Schkade. (2004). "Determining Uses and Gratifications for the Internet." *Decision Sciences*, 35: 259–289.

Star, A. (2008). "Judgment Call." *New York Times Book Review*, August 17: 10–11.

Starkman, D. (2009). "Power Problem." *Columbia Journalism Review*, May/June: 24–30.

"State of the Blogosphere/2008." *Technorati*. (*http://technorati.com/blogging/feature/state-of-the-blogosphere-2008/*).

Steinberg, S. R., and J. L. Kincheloe, (1997). "Introduction: No More Secrets—Kinderculture, Information Saturation, and the Postmodern Childhood." In S. R. Steinberg and J. L. Kincheloe, eds., *Kinderculture: The Corporate Construction of Childhood*. Boulder, CO: Westview Press.

Steiner, L. (1988). "Oppositional Decoding as an Act of Resistance." *Critical Studies in Mass Communication*, 5: 1–15.

Stepp, C. S. (2006). "The Blog Revolution." *American Journalism Review*, February/March: 62.

Stelter, B., and J. Wortham. (2010). "F. C. C. Plan to Widen Internet Access in U. S. Sets Off Battle." *New York Times*, March 13: 1.

Stevenson, R. L. (1994). *Global Communication in the Twenty-first Century*. New York: Longman.

Stouffer, S. A., E. A. Suchman, L. C. DeVinney, S. A. Star, and R. M. Williams. (1949). *The American Soldier: Adjustment During Army Life*, vol. 1. Princeton, NJ: Princeton University Press.

Strupp, J. (2009). "A 'Secret' Controversy." *Editor & Publisher*, August: 5–7.

Strupp, J. (2004). "On the Can-Pain Trail." *Editor & Publisher*, June: 34–42.

Sullivan, A. (2009). "The Evidence Mounts Still Further." *Atlantic*, August 25. (*http://andrewsullivan. theatlantic.com/the_daily_dish/2009/08/the-evidence-mounts-still-further.html*).

Sullivan, A. (2008). "Why I Blog." *Atlantic Monthly*, November: 106–112.

Summers, J. H. (2006). "The Deciders." *New York Times Book Review*, May 14: 39.

Summers, J. H. (2006). "Perpetual Revelations: C. Wright Mills and Paul Lazarsfeld." *The ANNALS of the American Academy of Political and Social Science*, November, 608: 25–40.

Sumser, J. (1996). *Morality and Social Order in Television Crime Dramas*. Jefferson, NC: McFarland & Company.

Suskind, R. (2004). *The Price of Loyalty: George W. Bush, the White House, and the Education of Paul O'Neill*. New York: Simon & Schuster.

Swanson, D. (2005). "Labor Media, or the Lack Thereof." *Truthout*, April 25. (*www.truthout.org/is-sues_05/printer_042605LA.shtml*).

Terkildsen, N., and F. Schnell. (1997). "How Media Frames Move Public Opinion: An Analysis of the Women's Movement." *Political Research Quarterly*, 50: 879–900.

Thomas, E. (2009). "Obama's Nobel Headache." *Newsweek*, April 6: 20–25.

Thomaselli, R. (2003). "DTC Ads Influence Majority of Consumers, Say Doctors." *Advertising Age*, January 20: 6–8.

Thomson, O. (1977). *Mass Persuasion in History*. Edinburgh, UK: Paul Harris.

Tichenor, P. J., G. A. Donohue, and C. N. Olien. (1980). *Community Conflict and the Press*. Beverly Hills, CA: Sage.

Tichenor, P. J., G. A. Donohue, and C. N. Olien. (1970). "Mass Media Flow and Differential Growth of Knowledge." *Public Opinion Quarterly*, 34: 159–170.

Time/CNN. (2004). "Crossroads for Bush?" *Time*, May 24: 34.

Trench, M. (1990). *Cyberpunk*. Mystic Fire Videos. New York: Intercon.

Tuchman, G. (1978). *Making News: A Study in the Construction of Reality*. New York: Free Press.

Tugend, A. (2003). "Reading between the Lines." *American Journalism Review*, March: 46–51.

Tunstall, J. (1983). "The Trouble with U.S. Communication Research." *Journal of Communication*, 33: 2–95.

Tunstall, J. (1977). *The Media Are American: Anglo-American Media in the World*. New York: Columbia University Press.

Turner, J. H. (1998). *The Structure of Sociological Theory*, 6th ed. Belmont, CA: Wadsworth.

U.S. Congress Senate Subcommittee on Communications. (1972). *Surgeon General's Report by the Scientific Advisory Committee on Television and Social Behavior*. 92nd Cong., 2nd sess., March 21–24.

U.S. Election Project. (2009). "2008 General Election Turnout Rates." April 26. (*http://elections.gmu.edu/ Turnout_2008G.html*).

Valkenburg, P. M., and J. Peter. (2009). "The Effects of Instant Messaging on the Quality of Adolescents' Existing Friendships: A Longitudinal Study." *Journal of Communication*, 59: 79–97.

Valkenburg, P. M., and H. A. Semetko. (1999). "The Effects of News Frames on Readers' Thoughts and Recall." *Communication Research*, 26: 550–569.

Vander Neut, T. (1999). "Do Violent Images Cause Violent Behavior?" *Risk and Insurance*, November: 38–40.

von Zielbauer, P. (2007). "A Marine Tutorial on Media 'Spin.'" *New York Times*, June 24: K5.

Walker, R. (2006). "Gaming the System." *New York Times Magazine*, September 3: 18.

Walters, S. D. (1995). *Material Girls: Making Sense of Feminist Cultural Theory*. Berkeley, CA: University of California Press.

Ward, L., and K. Friedman. (2006). "Using TV as a Guide: Associations Between Television Viewing and Adolescents' Sexual Attitudes and Behavior." *Journal of Research on Adolescence*, 16: 133–156.

Wartella, E. (1997). *The Context of Television Violence*. Boston: Allyn & Bacon.

Wartella, E. (1979). "The Developmental Perspective." In E. Wartella, ed., *Children Communicating: Media and Development of Thought, Speech, and Understanding*. Beverly Hills, CA: Sage.

Wartella, E., and B. Reeves. (1985). "Historical Trends in Research on Children and the Media, 1900–1960." *Journal of Communication*, 35: 118–133.

Wasserman, E. (2009). "The *Washington Post's* Sleazy Confab Plan." *Providence Journal*, July 25: B7.

The Week. (2004). "Marriage: The Solution to Urban Poverty?" January 30: 19.

Westley, B. H., and M. MacLean. (1957). "A Conceptual Model for Mass Communication Research." *Journalism Quarterly*, 34: 31–38.

Wheeler, M. (2009). "This Miracle Brought to You by America's Unions." *Firedoglake.com*, January 16. (*http://emptywheel.firedoglake. com/2009/01/16/this-miracle-brought-to-you-by-americas-unions/*).

White, R. W. (1972). *The Enterprise of Living: Growth and Organization in Personality*. New York: Holt, Rinehart & Winston.

Whiten, J. (2004). "Bad News from Iraq? Blame the Source—U. S. Officials." *Extra! Update*, February: 3.

Whittelsey, F. C. (2003). "Dead Letter Office." *Extra!* January/February: 13–16.

Wicker, T. (2004). "Pressing Problems." *Editor and Publisher*, July: 62.

Wiener, N. (1961). *Cybernetics*, 2nd ed. Cambridge, MA: MIT Press.

Wiener, N. (1954). *The Human Use of Human Beings: Cybernetics and Society*. Garden City, NY: Doubleday Anchor.

Williams, A. (2007). "MySpace.com Networking Site May Help Elect Next President." *Providence Journal*, March 21: E1.

Williams, B. (2009). "Jon Stewart." *Newsweek*, November 21. (*http:// 2010.newsweek.com/top-10/new-thought-leaders/jon-stewart.html*).

Williams, F., R. E. Rice, and E. M. Rogers. (1988). *Research Methods and the New Media*. New York: Free Press.

Williams, R. (1974). *Television: Technology and Cultural Form*. London: Fontana.

Williams, R. (1967). *Communications*. New York: Barnes and Noble.

Windahl, S. (1981). "Uses and Gratifications at the Crossroads." In G. C. Wilhoit and H. De Bock, eds., *Mass Communication Review Yearbook*. Beverly Hills, CA: Sage.

Winship, M. (2009). "What's So Funny About Washington?" *Truthout*, June 3. (*www.truthout.org/ 051709Z?*).

Winstead, L. (2009). "Big Think: "*Daily Show*" Creator Lizz Winstead on News and Comedy." *Salon*, July 6. (*http://www.salon.com/ entertainment/video_dog/big_think/ 2009/07/06/bt_winstead/index.html*).

Wolf, G. (1996). "The Wisdom of Saint Marshall, the Holy Fool." *Wired*, January: 122–125, 182–187.

Wood, G., and T. McBride. (1997). "Origins of Orienting and Defensive Responses: An Evolutionary Perspective." In P. J. Lang, R. F. Simons, and M. Balaban, eds., *Attention and Orienting: Sensory and Motivational Processes*. Hillsdale, NJ: Erlbaum.

World War II, The Propaganda Battle, Walk through the 20th Century. (1982). New York: PBS Video.

Wright, C. R. (1986). *Mass Communication: A Sociological Perspective*, 3rd ed. New York: Random House.

Wright, C. R. (1974). "Functional Analysis and Mass Communication Revisited." In J. G. Blumler and E. Katz, eds., *The Uses of Mass Communication: Current Perspectives on Gratifications Research*. Beverly Hills, CA: Sage.

Wright, C. R. (1959). *Mass Communication: A Sociological Perspective*. New York: Random House.

Yan, Z. (2009). "Limited Knowledge and Limited Resources: Children's and Adolescents' Understanding of the Internet." *Journal of Applied Developmental Psychology*, 30: 103–115.

Ybarra, M. L., M. Diener-West, D. Markow, P. J. Leaf, M. Hamburger, and P. Boxer. (2008). "Linkages Between Internet and Other Media Violence with Seriously Violent Behavior by Youth." *Pediatrics*, 122: 929–937.

Young, B. (2009). "Human Capacity for Information is Massive but Finite." *TechNewsWorld*, December 10. (*www. technewsworld.com/perl/search.pl?*)

query=Human+capacity+for+ information+is+massive+ but+finite).

Young, B. (1990). *Television Advertising to Children*. Oxford, UK: Clarendon Press.

Ytreberg, E. (2002). "Erving Goffman as a Theorist of the Mass Media." *Critical Studies in Media Communication*, 19: 481–498.

Zillmann, D., and P. Vorderer. (2000). *Media Entertainment: The Psychology of Its Appeal*. Mahwah, NJ: Erlbaum.

Zimbardo, P. G., and A. L. Weber. (1997). *Psychology*. New York: Longman.

INDEX

383